Lecture Notes in Computer Science 7762

Commenced Publication in 1973
Founding and Former Series Editors:
Gerhard Goos, Juris Hartmanis, and Jan van Leeuwen

Erzsébet Csuhaj-Varjú
Marian Gheorghe   Grzegorz Rozenberg
Arto Salomaa   György Vaszil (Eds.)

Membrane Computing

13th International Conference, CMC 2012
Budapest, Hungary, August 28-31, 2012
Revised Selected Papers

 Springer

Volume Editors

Erzsébet Csuhaj-Varjú
Eötvös Loránd University
1117 Budapest, Hungary
E-mail: csuhaj@inf.elte.hu

Marian Gheorghe
University of Sheffield
Sheffield S1 4DP, UK
E-mail: m.gheorghe@sheffield.ac.uk

Grzegorz Rozenberg
Leiden University
2333 CA Leiden, The Netherlands
E-mail: rozenber@liacs.nl

Arto Salomaa
Turku Centre for Computer Science (TUCS)
20520 Turku, Finland
E-mail: asalomaa@cs.utu.fi

György Vaszil
University of Debrecen
4028 Debrecen, Hungary
E-mail: vaszil.gyorgy@inf.unideb.hu

ISSN 0302-9743   e-ISSN 1611-3349
ISBN 978-3-642-36750-2   e-ISBN 978-3-642-36751-9
DOI 10.1007/978-3-642-36751-9
Springer Heidelberg Dordrecht London New York

Library of Congress Control Number: 2013931552

CR Subject Classification (1998): F.1.1-2, F.2.1-2, D.2.2, K.2

LNCS Sublibrary: SL 1 – Theoretical Computer Science and General Issues

Typesetting: Camera-ready by author, data conversion by Scientific Publishing Services, Chennai, India

Printed on acid-free paper

Springer is part of Springer Science+Business Media (www.springer.com)

Preface

This volume contains a selection of papers presented at CMC13, the 13th International Conference on Membrane Computing, held in Budapest, Hungary, during August 28–31, 2012 (*http://www.sztaki.hu/tcs/cmc13/*).

The CMC series was initiated by Gheorghe Păun as the Workshop on Multiset Processing in the year 2000. Then two workshops on Membrane Computing were organized in Curtea de Argeş, Romania, in 2001 and 2002. A selection of papers from these three meetings were published as volume 2235 of the *Lecture Notes in Computer Science* series, as a special issue of *Fundamenta Informaticae* (volume 49, numbers 1–3, 2002), and as volume 2597 of *Lecture Notes in Computer Science*, respectively. The next six workshops were organized in Tarragona, Spain (in July 2003), Milan, Italy (in June 2004), Vienna, Austria (in July 2005), Leiden, The Netherlands (in July 2006), Thessaloniki, Greece (in June 2007), and Edinburgh, UK (in July 2008), with the proceedings published in *Lecture Notes in Computer Science* as volumes 2933, 3365, 3850, 4361, 4860, and 5391, respectively. The 10th workshop returned to Curtea de Argeş in August 2009 (LNCS volume 5957).

From 2010, the series of meetings on membrane computing continued as the Conference on Membrane Computing with the 2010 and 2011 editions held in Jena, Germany (LNCS volume 6501) and in Fontainebleau, France (LNCS volume 7184). Today the Steering Committee oversees the continuation of the CMC series, which is organized under the auspices of the European Molecular Computing Consortium (EMCC). In October 2012, also a regional version of CMC, the Asian Conference on Membrane Computing, ACMC, took place in Wuhan, China.

CMC13 was organized by MTA SZTAKI, the Computer and Automation Research Institute of the Hungarian Academy of Sciences, in cooperation with the PhD School of Computer Science of the Faculty of Informatics at the Eötvös Loránd University in Budapest, the Department of Algorithms and Their Applications of the Faculty of Informatics at the Eötvös Loránd University, and the Department of Computer Science of the Faculty of Informatics at the University of Debrecen.

The Program Committee of CMC13 invited lectures from Rudolf Freund (Vienna, Austria), Vincenzo Manca (Verona, Italy), Solomon Marcus (Bucharest, Romania), and Yurii Rogozhin (Chişinău, Moldova). In addition to the regular program, a special session, chaired by Gabriel Ciobanu (Iaşi, Romania), was devoted to "Process Calculi, Petri Nets, and Their Relationships with Membrane Computing." As part of the celebrations of the Turing Centenary, a special session was also dedicated to "Turing Computability and Membrane Computing as an Unconventional Computing Paradigm" with invited speakers Jozef Kelemen (Bratislava, Slovakia / Opava, Czech Republic), and Mike Stannett (Sheffield,

UK). Based on the votes of the CMC13 participants, the Best Paper Award of this year's CMC conference was given to Petr Sosík for his paper "Limits of the Power of Tissue P Systems with Cell Division."

In addition to the texts of the invited talks, this volume contains 21 papers out of 25 presented at the conference. Each paper was subject to at least two referee reports for the conference and of an additional one for this volume.

The editors warmly thank the Program Committee, the invited speakers, the authors of the papers, the reviewers, and all the participants for their contributions to the success of CMC13.

December 2012

Erzsébet Csuhaj-Varjú
Marian Gheorghe
Grzegorz Rozenberg
Arto Salomaa
György Vaszil

Organization

Program Committee

Artiom Alhazov	Chişinău, Moldova and Milan, Italy
Gabriel Ciobanu	Iaşi, Romania
Erzsébet Csuhaj-Varjú	Budapest, Hungary (Co-chair)
Giuditta Franco	Verona, Italy
Rudolf Freund	Vienna, Austria
Pierluigi Frisco	Edinburgh, UK
Marian Gheorghe	Sheffield, UK (Co-chair)
Oscar H. Ibarra	Santa Barbara, USA
Florentin Ipate	Piteşti, Romania
Shankara Narayanan Krishna	Mumbai, India
Alberto Leporati	Milan, Italy
Vincenzo Manca	Verona, Italy
Maurice Margenstern	Metz, France
Giancarlo Mauri	Milan, Italy
Linqiang Pan	Wuhan, China
Andrei Păun	Ruston, USA and Bucharest, Romania
Gheorghe Păun	Bucharest, Romania and Seville, Spain
Mario J. Pérez-Jiménez	Seville, Spain
Francisco J. Romero-Campero	Seville, Spain
Dragoş Sburlan	Constanţa, Romania
György Vaszil	Debrecen, Hungary (Co-chair)
Sergey Verlan	Paris, France
Claudio Zandron	Milan, Italy

Steering Committee

Gabriel Ciobanu	Iaşi, Romania
Erzsébet Csuhaj-Varjú	Budapest, Hungary
Rudolf Freund	Vienna, Austria
Pierluigi Frisco	Edinburgh, UK
Marian Gheorghe	Sheffield, UK (Chair)
Oscar H. Ibarra	Santa Barbara, USA
Vincenzo Manca	Verona, Italy
Maurice Margenstern	Metz, France
Giancarlo Mauri	Milan, Italy
Gheorghe Păun	Bucharest, Romania and Seville, Spain
Mario J. Pérez-Jiménez	Seville, Spain

Organizing Committee

Erzsébet Csuhaj-Varjú	Eötvös Loránd University, Budapest
Anikó Győri	Kult-Turist-ITH, Budapest
Zsolt Németh	Computer and Automation Research Institute of the Hungarian Academy of Sciences, Budapest
György Vaszil	University of Debrecen

Table of Contents

Invited Papers

Regular Papers

(Tissue) P Systems with Decaying Objects

Rudolf Freund

Faculty of Informatics, Vienna University of Technology
Favoritenstr. 9, 1040 Vienna, Austria
rudi@emcc.at

Abstract. Objects generated in P systems usually are assumed to survive as long as the computation goes on. In this paper, decaying objects are considered, i.e., objects only surviving a bounded number of computation steps. Variants of (tissue) P systems with decaying objects working in transition modes where the number of rules applied in each computation step is bounded, are shown to be very restricted in their generative power, i.e., if the results are collected in a specified output cell/membrane, then only finite sets of multisets can be generated, and if the results are specified by the objects sent out into the environment, we obtain the regular sets. Only if the decaying objects are regenerated within a certain period of computation steps, i.e., if we allow an unbounded number of rules to be applied, then computational completeness can be obtained, yet eventually more ingredients are needed for the rules than in the case of non-decaying objects, e.g., permitting and/or forbidden contexts. As special variants of P systems, catalytic P systems, P systems using cooperative rules, and spiking neural P systems are investigated.

1 Introduction

Cells in a living creature usually are not surviving the whole life time of this creature, e.g., the erythrocytes in the blood of humans have a life cycle of around four months. Hence, objects in systems modeling the functioning of structures of living cells – as for example, P systems – may be considered to have bounded time to survive, too. Formally, these objects will be called *decaying objects*, as their remaining time to survive without being involved in a rule is decreasing with each computation step.

In the area of P systems, decaying objects have already been considered in the case of spiking neural P systems: in [8] it was shown that with spiking neural P systems with decaying objects, which in this case are just the spikes stored in the neurons, only finite sets can be obtained, if the result is taken as the number of spikes contained in the output cell at the end of a computation; if the result is defined as the distance of the first two spikes sent to the environment from the output cell, then the linear sets of natural numbers can be characterized.

The idea of decaying objects also appears in the area of reaction systems, there being called the *assumption of no permanency*: an entity from a current configuration vanishes unless it is (re)produced by the application of a rule

E. Csuhaj-Varjú et al. (Eds.): CMC 2012, LNCS 7762, pp. 1–25, 2013.

(see [3]). In contrast to P systems, reaction systems work with sets of objects, i.e., multiplicities of objects are not taken into account, all ingredients are assumed to be available in a sufficient amount.

In the area of splicing systems, the effect of killing all strings not undergoing a splicing operation, turned out to be a powerful tool to control the evolution of splicing systems, in the end allowing for an optimal computational completeness result (see [14]) for time-varying distributed H systems using only one test tube (cell), to be compared with using splicing rules in P systems with only one membrane.

In this paper, the idea of decaying objects is extended to many other variants of (tissue) P systems. The combination of decaying objects and bounding the number of rules applicable in each computation step, drastically restricts the generative power of such systems usually known to be computationally complete with non-decaying objects: as in the case of spiking neural P systems, only finite sets can be generated if the output is taken as the number of (terminal) objects in an output cell/membrane, whereas a characterization of the regular sets is obtained if the output is defined as the collection or sequence of objects sent out to the environment. For catalytic P systems and for P systems using cooperative rules, computational completeness can be shown for several combinations of maximally parallel transition modes and halting conditions, yet in contrast to the computational completeness results for non-decaying objects, now for catalytic P systems permitting and forbidden context conditions are needed for the rules.

The rest of this paper is organized as follows: In the second section, we recall well-known definitions and notions. Then we define a general class of multiset rewriting systems containing, in particular, many variants of P systems and tissue P systems as well as even (extended) spiking neural P systems without delays, and formalize the idea of *decaying objects* in these systems. Moreover, we give formal definitions of the most important well-known *transition modes* (maximally parallel, minimally parallel, asynchronous, sequential) as well as the k-restricted minimally/maximally parallel transition modes and the parallel transition mode using the maximal number of objects; finally, we define variants of *halting*: the normal halting condition when no rules are applicable anymore (total halting), partial halting, adult halting, and halting with final states. In the third section, we first give some examples for P systems with decaying objects and discuss the restriction of the generative power of such systems in combination with transition modes only allowing for a bounded number of rules to be applied in parallel in each transition step in the general case. As a specific variant, first systems working in the sequential mode are considered; then, we investigate the effect of decaying objects in P systems working in the 1-restricted minimally parallel transition mode, i.e., spiking neural P systems without delays (in every neuron where a rule is applicable exactly one rule has to be applied) and purely catalytic P systems; finally, we investigate the k-restricted maximally parallel transition mode. In the fourth section, computational completeness results are established, especially for variants of catalytic P systems and of P systems using cooperative rules. An outlook to future research topics for (tissue) P systems with decaying objects concludes the paper.

2   Definitions

In this section, we recall some well-known notions and define the basic model of networks of cells we use for describing different variants of (tissue) P Systems.

2.1   Preliminaries

The set of integers is denoted by $\mathbb{Z}$, the set of non-negative integers by $\mathbb{N}$. The interval $\{n \in \mathbb{N} \mid k \leq n \leq m\}$ is abbreviated by $[k..m]$. An *alphabet* V is a finite non-empty set of abstract *symbols*. Given V, the free monoid generated by V under the operation of concatenation is denoted by V^*; the elements of V^* are called strings, and the *empty string* is denoted by λ; $V^* \setminus \{\lambda\}$ is denoted by V^+. Let $\{a_1, \cdots, a_n\}$ be an arbitrary alphabet; the number of occurrences of a symbol a_i in a string x is denoted by $|x|_{a_i}$; the *Parikh vector* associated with x with respect to $a_1, \cdots, a_n$ is $\left(|x|_{a_1}, \cdots, |x|_{a_n}\right)$. The *Parikh image* of a language L over $\{a_1, \cdots, a_n\}$ is the set of all Parikh vectors of strings in L, and we denote it by $Ps(L)$. For a family of languages FL, the family of Parikh images of languages in FL is denoted by $PsFL$.

A (finite) multiset over the (finite) alphabet V, $V = \{a_1, \cdots, a_n\}$, is a mapping $f : V \longrightarrow \mathbb{N}$ and represented by $\langle f(a_1), a_1 \rangle \cdots \langle f(a_n), a_n \rangle$ or by any string x the Parikh vector of which with respect to $a_1, \cdots, a_n$ is $(f(a_1), \cdots, f(a_n))$. In the following we will not distinguish between a vector $(m_1, \cdots, m_n)$, its representation by a multiset $\langle m_1, a_1 \rangle \cdots \langle m_n, a_n \rangle$ or its representation by a string x having the Parikh vector $\left(|x|_{a_1}, \cdots, |x|_{a_n}\right) = (m_1, \cdots, m_n)$. Fixing the sequence of symbols $a_1, \cdots, a_n$ in the alphabet V in advance, the representation of the multiset $\langle m_1, a_1 \rangle \cdots \langle m_n, a_n \rangle$ by the string $a_1^{m_1} \cdots a_n^{m_n}$ is unique. The set of all finite multisets over an alphabet V is denoted by V°. For two multisets f_1 and f_2 from V° we write $f_1 \sqsubseteq f_2$ if and only if $f_1(a_i) \leq f_2(a_i)$ for all $1 \leq i \leq n$, and we say that f_1 is a submultiset of f_2.

A *context-free string grammar* is a construct $G = (N, T, P, S)$ where N is the alphabet of nonterminal symbols, T is the alphabet of terminal symbols, P is a set of context-free rules of the form $A \to w$ with $A \in N$, $w \in (N \cup T)^*$, and S is the start symbol. If all rules in P are of the forms $A \to bC$ with $A, C \in N$ and $b \in T^*$ or $A \to \lambda$ with $A \in N$, then G is called *regular*. A string v is derivable from a string u, $u, v \in (N \cup T)^*$, if $u = xAy$ and $v = xwy$ for some $x, y \in (N \cup T)^*$ and there exists a rule $A \to w$ in P; we write $u \Longrightarrow_G v$. The reflexive and transitive closure of the derivation relation $\Longrightarrow_G$ is denoted by $\Longrightarrow_G^*$. The string language generated by G is denoted by $L(G)$ and defined as the set of terminal strings derivable from the start symbol, i.e., $L(G) = \{w \mid w \in T^* \text{ and } S \Longrightarrow_G^* w\}$.

The family of regular, context-free, and recursively enumerable string languages is denoted by REG, CF, and RE, respectively. The family of finite languages is denoted by FIN, its complement, i.e., the family of co-finite languages, by *co-FIN*. Two languages of strings or multisets L and L' are considered to be equal if and only if $L \setminus \{\lambda\} = L' \setminus \{\lambda\}$.

For more details of formal language theory the reader is referred to the monographs and handbooks in this area such as [5] and [19]. Basic results in multiset rewriting can be found in [13]. Moreover, we assume the reader to be familiar with the main topics of membrane computing as described in the books [17] and [18]. For the actual state of the art in membrane computing, we refer the reader to the P Systems Webpage [20].

2.2 Register Machines

For our main results establishing computational completeness for specific variants of (tissue) P systems working in different transition modes, we will need to simulate register machines. A *register machine* is a tuple $M = (m, B, l_0, l_h, P)$, where m is the number of registers, P is the set of instructions bijectively labeled by elements of B, $l_0 \in B$ is the initial label, and $l_h \in B$ is the final label. The instructions of M can be of the following forms:

- $l_1 : (ADD(j), l_2, l_3)$, with $l_1 \in B \setminus \{l_h\}$, $l_2, l_3 \in B$, $1 \leq j \leq m$
  Increase the value of register j by one, and non-deterministically jump to instruction l_2 or l_3. This instruction is usually called *increment*.
- $l_1 : (SUB(j), l_2, l_3)$, with $l_1 \in B \setminus \{l_h\}$, $l_2, l_3 \in B$, $1 \leq j \leq m$
  If the value of register j is zero then jump to instruction l_3, otherwise decrease the value of register j by one and jump to instruction l_2. The two cases of this instruction are usually called *zero-test* and *decrement*, respectively.
- $l_h : HALT$. Stop the execution of the register machine.

A *configuration* of a register machine is described by the contents of each register and by the value of the program counter, which indicates the next instruction to be executed. Computations start by executing the first instruction of P (labeled with l_0), and terminate with reaching a $HALT$-instruction. Without loss of generality, we assume the $HALT$-instruction to be the only instruction where the register machine halts.

Register machines provide a simple universal computational model [15]. In the generative case as we need it later, we start with empty registers, use the first two registers for the necessary computations and take as results the contents of the $m - 2$ registers 3 to m in all possible halting computations; during a computation of M, only the registers 1 and 2 can be decremented, and when M halts in l_h, these two registers are empty. In the following, we shall call a specific model of P systems *computationally complete* if and only if for any such register machine M we can effectively construct an equivalent P system Π of that type simulating each step of M in a bounded number of steps and yielding the same results.

2.3 Networks of Cells

In [10], a formal framework for (tissue) P systems capturing the formal features of various transition modes was developed, based on a general model of membrane systems as a collection of interacting cells containing multisets of objects, which can be compared with the models of networks of cells as discussed in [2] and networks of language processors as considered in [4]. Continuing the formal approach started in [10], k-restricted variants of the minimally and the maximally parallel transition modes were considered in [11], i.e., we considered a partitioning of the whole set of rules and allowed only multisets of rules to be applied in parallel which could not be extended by adding a rule from a partition from which no rule had already been taken into this multiset of rules, but only at most k rules could be taken from each partition. Most of the following definitions are taken from [7] and [11].

Definition 1. *A network of cells with checking sets of degree $n \geq 1$ is a construct $\Pi = (n, V, T, w, R, i_0)$ where*

1. n *is the number of cells;*
2. V *is a finite alphabet;*
3. $T \subseteq V$ *is the terminal alphabet;*
4. $w = (w_1, \ldots, w_n)$ *where $w_i \in V^\circ$, for each i with $1 \leq i \leq n$, is the multiset initially associated to cell i;*
5. R *is a finite set of rules of the form $(E : X \to Y)$ where E is a recursive condition for configurations of Π (see definition below), while $X = (x_1, \ldots, x_n)$, $Y = (y_1, \ldots, y_n)$, with $x_i, y_i \in V^\circ$, $1 \leq i \leq n$, are vectors of multisets over V; we will also use the notation*

$$(E : (x_1, 1) \ldots (x_n, n) \to (y_1, 1) \ldots (y_n, n))$$

for a rule $(E : X \to Y)$; moreover, the multisets x_i and y_i may be split into several parts or be omitted in case they equal the empty multiset;
6. i_0 *is the output cell.*

A network of cells (in the following also simply called *P system*) consists of n cells, numbered from 1 to n and containing multisets of objects over V; initially cell i contains w_i. A *configuration* C of Π is an n-tuple $(u_1, \ldots, u_n)$ of multisets over V; the *initial configuration* of Π, C_0, is described by w, i.e., $C_0 = w = (w_1, \ldots, w_n)$. Cells can interact with each other by means of the rules in R. A rule $(E : (x_1, 1) \ldots (x_n, n) \to (y_1, 1) \ldots (y_n, n))$ is applicable to a configuration C with $C = (w_1, 1) \ldots (w_n, n)$ if and only if C fulfills condition E and $x_i \sqsubseteq w_i$, $1 \leq i \leq n$; its application means rewriting objects x_i from cells i into objects y_j in cells j, $1 \leq i, j \leq n$. In this paper, only regular conditions are considered, i.e., $E = (E_1, \ldots, E_n)$, where the E_i, $1 \leq i \leq n$, are regular sets; if $(w_1, 1) \ldots (w_n, n)$ describes the current configuration C, then C fulfills condition E if and only if $w_i \in E_i$, $1 \leq i \leq n$.

As specific conditions we will use *random contexts*, specified as sets of n-tuples of pairs $((P_1, Q_1), \ldots, (P_n, Q_n))$ where the P_i are the *permitting* and the Q_i are the *forbidden* contexts and are finite sets of multisets over V. An n-tuple $((P_1, Q_1), \ldots, (P_n, Q_n))$ allows for the application of the rule $(x_1, 1) \ldots (x_n, n) \to (y_1, 1) \ldots (y_n, n)$ to the configuration $(w_1, 1) \ldots (w_n, n)$ if, besides $x_i \sqsubseteq w_i$, $1 \leq i \leq n$, for all $u \in P_i$, $u \sqsubseteq w_i$ and for no $v \in Q_i$, $v \sqsubseteq w_i$.

The set of all multisets of rules *applicable* to C is denoted by $Appl\,(\Pi, C)$; a procedural algorithm how to obtain $Appl\,(\Pi, C)$ was described in [10].

For the specific *transition modes* to be defined in the following, the selection of multisets of rules applicable to a configuration C has to be a specific subset of $Appl\,(\Pi, C)$; for the transition mode ϑ, the selection of multisets of rules applicable to a configuration C is denoted by $Appl\,(\Pi, C, \vartheta)$.

Definition 2. *For the* asynchronous *transition mode (asyn),*

$$Appl\,(\Pi, C, asyn) = Appl\,(\Pi, C),$$

i.e., there are no particular restrictions on the multisets of rules applicable to C.

Definition 3. *For the* sequential *transition mode (sequ),*

$$Appl\,(\Pi, C, sequ) = \{R' \mid R' \in Appl\,(\Pi, C) \ \ and \ |R'| = 1\},$$

i.e., any multiset of rules $R' \in Appl\,(\Pi, C, sequ)$ has size 1.

The most important transition mode considered in the area of P systems is the *maximally parallel* transition mode where we only select multisets of rules R' that are not extensible, i.e., there is no other multiset of rules $R'' \supsetneq R'$ applicable to C.

Definition 4. *For the* maximally parallel *transition mode (max),*

$$Appl\,(\Pi, C, max) = \{R' \mid R' \in Appl\,(\Pi, C) \ \ and \ there \ is \\ no \ R'' \in Appl\,(\Pi, C) \ \ with \ R'' \supsetneq R'\}.$$

For the *minimally parallel* transition mode, we need an additional feature for the set of rules R, i.e., we consider a partitioning Θ of R into disjoint subsets R_1 to R_p. Usually, this partition of R may coincide with a specific assignment of the rules to the cells. For any set of rules $R' \subseteq R$, let $\|R'\|$ denote the number of sets of rules R_j, $1 \le j \le p$, with $R_j \cap R' \ne \emptyset$.

In an informal way, the minimally parallel transition mode can be described as applying multisets such that from every set R_j, $1 \le j \le p$, at least one rule – if possible – has to be used. For the basic variant as defined in the following, in each transition step we choose a multiset of rules R' from $Appl\,(\Pi, C, asyn)$ that cannot be extended to $R'' \in Appl\,(\Pi, C, asyn)$ with $R'' \supsetneq R'$ and such that $(R'' - R') \cap R_j \ne \emptyset$ and $R' \cap R_j = \emptyset$ for some j, $1 \le j \le p$, i.e., extended by a rule from a set of rules R_j from which no rule has been taken into R'.

Definition 5. *For the* minimally parallel *transition mode with partitioning Θ (min(Θ)),*

$$Appl\,(\Pi, C, min(\Theta)) = \{R' \mid R' \in Appl\,(\Pi, C, asyn) \ \ and \\ there \ is \ no \ R'' \in Appl\,(\Pi, C, asyn) \\ with \ R'' \supsetneq R', \ (R'' \setminus R') \cap R_j \ne \emptyset \\ and \ R' \cap R_j = \emptyset \ for \ some \ j, \ 1 \le j \le p\}.$$

In the k-restricted minimally parallel transition mode, a multiset of rules from $Appl\,(\Pi, C, min(\Theta))$ can only be applied if it contains at most k rules from each partition R_j, $1 \leq j \leq p$.

Definition 6. *For the k-restricted minimally parallel transition mode with partitioning Θ ($min_k(\Theta)$),*

$$Appl\,(\Pi, C, min_k(\Theta)) = \{R' \mid R' \in Appl\,(\Pi, C, min(\Theta))\ and$$
$$|R' \cap R_j| \leq k\ for\ all\ j,\ 1 \leq j \leq p\}.$$

Each multiset of rules obtained by min_1 can be seen as a kind of basic maximally parallel vector; this interpretation also allows for capturing the understanding of the minimally parallel transition mode as introduced by Gheorghe Păun:

Definition 7. *For the base vector minimally parallel transition mode with partitioning Θ ($min_{GP}(\Theta)$),*

$$Appl\,(\Pi, C, min_{GP}(\Theta)) = \{R' \mid R' \in Appl\,(\Pi, C, min(\Theta))\ and\ R' \supseteq R''$$
$$for\ some\ R'' \in Appl\,(\Pi, C, min_1(\Theta))\}.$$

In the k-restricted maximally parallel transition mode, a multiset of rules can only be applied if it is maximal but only contains at most k rules from each partition R_j, $1 \leq j \leq p$.

Definition 8. *For the k-restricted maximally parallel transition mode with partitioning Θ ($max_k(\Theta)$),*

$$Appl\,(\Pi, C, max_k(\Theta)) = \{R' \mid R' \in Appl\,(\Pi, C, max)\ and$$
$$|R' \cap R_j| \leq k\ for\ all\ j,\ 1 \leq j \leq p\}.$$

Definition 9. *For the the k-restricted maximally parallel transition mode with only one partition, $max_k(\{R\})$, we also use the notion k-restricted maximally parallel transition mode (max_k), i.e., we get*

$$Appl\,(\Pi, C, max_k) = \{R' \mid R' \in Appl\,(\Pi, C, max)\ and\ |R'| \leq k\}.$$

Example 1. Consider the P system

$$\Pi = (1, \{a, b\}, \{b\}, aa, \{a \to b\}, 1).$$

Then the rule $a \to b$ (this notation represents the rule $(I : (a, 1) \to (b, 1))$ where I is the condition which is always fulfilled) must be applied twice in the maximally parallel transition mode, whereas in the minimally parallel mode it can be applied twice or only once. In the transition mode $min_1(\{R\})$, the rule is applied once, whereas in the mode max_1 no multiset of rules is applicable, because in the maximally parallel way the rule should be applied twice.

A variant of maximal parallelism requires the maximal number of objects to be affected by the application of a multiset of rules:

Definition 10. *For the transition mode requiring a* maximal number of objects to be affected *(maxobj),*

$$Appl\,(\Pi, C, maxobj) = \{R' \mid R' \in Appl\,(\Pi, C, asyn)\ and$$
$$there\ is\ no\ R'' \in Appl\,(\Pi, C, asyn)$$
$$with\ |Bound\,(R'')| > |Bound\,(R')|\}\,,$$

where $Bound\,(R')$ for any $R' \in Appl\,(\Pi, C, asyn)$ denotes the multiset of symbols from C affected by R'.

For all the transition modes defined above, we now can define how to obtain a next configuration from a given one by applying an applicable multiset of rules according to the constraints of the underlying transition mode:

Definition 11. *Given a configuration C of Π and a transition mode ϑ, we may choose a multiset of rules $R' \in Appl\,(\Pi, C, \vartheta)$ in a non-deterministic way and apply it to C. The result of this transition step (or computation step) from the configuration C with applying R' is the configuration $Apply\,(\Pi, C, R')$, and we also write $C \Longrightarrow_{(\Pi,\vartheta)} C'$. The reflexive and transitive closure of the transition relation $\Longrightarrow_{(\Pi,\vartheta)}$ is denoted by $\Longrightarrow^*_{(\Pi,\vartheta)}$.*

Definition 12. *A computation in a P system Π, $\Pi = (n, V, T, w, R, i_0)$, starts with the initial configuration $C_0 = w$ and continues with transition steps according to the chosen transition mode ϑ; it is called* successful *if we reach a halting configuration C with respect to the halting condition γ.*

We now define several variants of halting conditions (e.g., see [7]): The usual way of considering a computation in a P system to be successful is to require that no rule can be applied anymore in the whole system, i.e., $Appl\,(\Pi, C, \vartheta) = \emptyset$ (we shall also use the notion *total halting* in the following, abbreviated by H). Taking a partitioning of the rule set (as for the minimally parallel mode), we may require that there exists an applicable multiset of rules containing one rule from each partition. A biological motivation for this variant of halting (*partial halting*, abbreviated by h) comes from the idea that a system may only survive as long as there are enough resources to give all subsystems the chance to continue their evolution. Computations also may be considered to be successful if at some moment a specific pattern appears (*halting with final states*, abbreviated by F). If the computation runs into an infinite loop with a specific configuration never changing again, we speak of *adult halting*, abbreviated by A.

$N(\Pi, \vartheta, \gamma, \rho)$ denotes the set of natural numbers computed by halting (with respect to the halting condition γ) computations of Π in the transition mode ϑ, with the numbers extracted from the output cell i_0 with respect to specific constraints specified by ρ, i.e., we either take the whole contents or only take the terminal symbols or else subtract a given constant l from the resulting numbers of objects in i_0. Moreover, we also consider an additional variant of obtaining the results by allowing the rules to send out multisets of objects into the environment, where we assume them to be collected as non-decaying objects; the environment is considered as an additional cell labelled by 0, the rules therefore being of the form

$$(E : (x_1, 1) \ldots (x_n, n) \to (y_0, 0)(y_1, 1) \ldots (y_n, n)).$$

We use the notation

$$NO_m C_n (\vartheta, \gamma, \rho) \, [\text{parameters for rules}]$$

to denote the family of sets of natural numbers generated by networks of cells $\Pi = (n, V, T, w, R, i_0)$ with $m = |V|$; γ specifies the way of halting, i.e., $\gamma \in \{H, h, A, F\}$; ϑ indicates one of the transition modes $asyn$, $sequ$, max, and max_k for $k \in \mathbb{N}$ as well as $min(p)$, $min_k(p)$, and $max_k(p)$ for $k \in \mathbb{N}$ with p denoting the number of partitions in the partitioning Θ; $\rho \in \{E, N, T\} \cup \{-l \mid l \in \mathbb{N}\}$ specifies how the results are taken from the number of objects in the specified output cell i_0 (if we take the whole contents, we use N; we take T if the results are taken modulo the terminal alphabet or else $-l$ when subtracting the constant l from the resulting numbers of objects in i_0) or else sent out to the environment (specified by E); the *parameters for rules* describe the specific features of the rules in R. If any of the parameters m and n is unbounded, we replace it by $*$. If we are not only interested in the total number of objects obtained in the output cell, but want to distinguish the different terminal symbols, in all the definitions given above we replace the prefix N by Ps indicating that then we get sets of vectors of natural numbers, corresponding with sets of Parikh vectors. In that case, the parameter $-l$ for ρ means that (at most) l nonterminal symbols may appear in the output cell, whereas N indicates that the number of additional nonterminal symbols is added to the first component of the result vector.

2.4 P Systems with Decaying Objects

In all the variants of P systems as defined above, we now may introduce the concept of decaying objects, i.e., for each object in the initial configuration and for each object generated by the application of a rule, we specify its decay d, i.e., the number of computation steps it may survive without having been affected by a rule. A decay of one means that the object b will die if it is not affected by a rule, which in some sense could be interpreted as the additional application of a rule $b \to \lambda$. We use the notation $b^{[k]}$ to specify that this object b may still survive k computation steps before having to be affected by the application of a rule. Assigning an additional value to each symbol b here is used to specify the remaining life time of this object in the system; another interpretation could be the concept of assigning a specific amount of energy; in this respect, there are similar approaches to be found in the literature, e.g., see the conformon P systems as introduced by Pierluigi Frisco ([18], chapter 10).

The contents of each membrane/cell of a P system has to be described by multisets of objects $b^{[k]}$, i.e., for each object b we also have to specify the remaining life time k. If $b^{[k]}$ occurring in a configuration C in cell j is not affected by a rule in the multiset of rules R' chosen from $Appl(\Pi, C, \vartheta)$, then this symbol appears as $b^{[k-1]}$ in the next configuration C' derived from C by applying R', where formally we interpret $b^{[0]}$ as λ; in fact, applying R' in total can be interpreted as having applied a multiset of rules $R'^{[d]}$ obtained from R' by

a) interpreting each object b on the left-hand side as an object $b^{[k]}$ for some k with $1 \leq k \leq d$ and introducing each object c on the right-hand side as $c^{[d]}$;
b) adding a rule $(b^{[k]}, j) \to (b^{[k-1]}, j)$ for each object $b^{[k]}$ not affected by a rule from R' following the strategy in a).

In fact, in order to correctly specify these informal descriptions in the formal framework, we have to extend the definition of how the P system Π works with decaying objects of decay d as follows:

Definition 13. *For any (finite) alphabet V and any $d \in \mathbb{N}$,*

$$V^{\langle d \rangle} = \left\{ b^{[k]} \mid 1 \leq k \leq d \right\}.$$

The projection $h_d : \left(V^{\langle d \rangle} \right)^* \to V^*$ is defined by $h_d \left(b^{[k]} \right) = b$ for all $b \in V$ and $1 \leq k \leq d$. Given any additional finite set M, h_d can be extended to a projection $h_{d,M} : \left(V^{\langle d \rangle} \cup M \right)^* \to (V \cup M)^*$ by $h_{d,M} \left(b^{[k]} \right) = b$ for all $b \in V$ and $1 \leq k \leq d$ and $h_{d,M} (x) = x$ for all $x \in M$. If M is obvious from the context, we may write h_d instead of $h_{d,M}$ for short.

Given a P system Π and a decay d, we now are able to define the associated P system $\Pi^{[d]}$:

Definition 14. *For a P system $\Pi = (n, V, T, w, R, i_0)$ and a decay d, we define*

$$\Pi^{[d]} = \left(n, V^{\langle d \rangle}, T^{\langle d \rangle}, w^{[d]}, R^{[d]} \cup R_0^{[d]}, i_0 \right)$$

and the rules in $R^{[d]}$ are obtained from the rules in R as follows:
For each rule

$$r = (E : (x_1, 1) \ldots (x_n, n) \to (y_0, 0) (y_1, 1) \ldots (y_n, n))$$

from R we take every rule

$$(x_1', 1) \ldots (x_n', n) \to (y_0, 0) \left(y_1^{[d]}, 1 \right) \ldots \left(y_n^{[d]}, n \right)$$

with $h_d (x_i') = x_i$, $1 \leq i \leq n$, into $R^{[d]}$, i.e., the right-hand sides are all equal, whereas the left-hand sides could be interpreted as the elements of

$$\left(h_{d, \{(,)\} \cup \{,\} \cup [1..n]} \right)^{-1} ((x_1, 1) \ldots (x_n, n)),$$

and we denote this set of rules obtained from r by $\hat{h}_d (r)$. Each newly generated object staying in the system gets the initial decay d; in the case objects are sent out into the environment, these are assumed to have no decay there, hence, we *just take the original multiset y_0 instead of $y_0^{[d]}$. A multiset of rules $\hat{R}'$ from $R^{[d]}$ is called an* instance *of the rule set R' from R if and only if there exists a bijection $g : R' \to \hat{R}'$ such that $g(r) \in \hat{h}_d(r)$ for all $r \in R'$.*

Finally, we define

$$R_0^{[d]} = \left\{ \left(b^{[k]}, i\right) \to \left(b^{[k-1]}, i\right) \mid b \in V, 1 \leq k \leq d, 1 \leq i \leq n\right\},$$

i.e., the set of rules needed for reducing the remaining life time of objects not involved in a rule from $R^{[d]}$; $b^{[0]}$ formerly is to be interpreted as λ.

The P system Π and the associated P system $\Pi^{[d]}$ have to be considered in parallel to describe the computations in the P system Π with decaying objects of decay d:

Definition 15. *Given a P system $\Pi = (n, V, T, w, R, i_0)$ with decaying objects of decay d and a configuration C of $\Pi^{[d]}$ together with a transition mode ϑ, we may choose a multiset of rules $R' \in Appl(\Pi, h_d(C), \vartheta)$ in a non-deterministic way; then we have to find an instance $\hat{R}'$ of R' and a set $R'' \in R_0^{[d]}$ such that $\hat{R}' \cup R'' \in Appl\left(\Pi^{[d]}, C, maxobj\right)$ and apply $\hat{R}' \cup R''$ to C. The result of this transition step (or computation step) from the configuration C with applying $\hat{R}' \cup R''$ is the configuration $Apply^{[d]}(\Pi, C, R')$, and we also write $C \Longrightarrow_{(\Pi^{[d]}, \vartheta)} C'$. The reflexive and transitive closure of the transition relation $\Longrightarrow_{(\Pi^{[d]}, \vartheta)}$ is denoted by $\Longrightarrow^*_{(\Pi^{[d]}, \vartheta)}$.*

A computation *in the P system Π with decaying objects of decay d starts with the initial configuration represented by $w^{[d]}$ as a configuration in $\Pi^{[d]}$ and continues with transition steps according to the chosen transition mode ϑ as described above; it is called* successful *if we reach a configuration C such that $h_d(C)$ is a halting configuration of Π with respect to the halting condition γ; the results of this successful computation are taken from $h_d(C)$.*

Whereas the choice of the rule set to be applied only depends on the conditions given by the rules in R and the transition mode ϑ for Π (this justifies to not take into account the conditions E of rules $(E : X \to Y)$ from R in the corresponding rules of $R^{[d]}$), the total effect to the current configuration C represented as a configuration of $\Pi^{[d]}$ always affects all objects in C due to the mode $maxobj$ used in $\Pi^{[d]}$. Although in the associated system $\Pi^{[d]}$ we always use the mode $maxobj$, no matter which transition mode is specified for Π itself, the results we obtain mostly will depend on the original transition mode specified for Π. Moreover, we emphasize that the condition of halting also only depends on the halting condition given for Π.

Remark 1. In order to make the condition for adult halting only depending on the halting condition given for Π, in this paper we assume a configuration C obtained by a computation in the P system Π with decaying objects of decay d to be a final one with respect to *adult halting* if and only if the set of multisets of rules applicable to $h_d(C)$ in Π is not empty, but the application of any of these multisets of rules to $h_d(C)$ in Π yields $h_d(C)$ again. On the other hand, we might also assume a configuration C to be a final one with respect to adult halting if and only if there exists an infinite computation from C in the P system Π with decaying objects of decay d such that every configuration reachable along this computation is C; we might even require every possible computation starting from C to be infinite and never yielding another configuration than C. Although the arguments in the succeeding examples and proofs are given having in mind the first definition it is worth mentioning that the results hold true in each of the interpretations mentioned above.

It is easy to see that the use of decaying objects causes side-effects; for example, in the sequential mode *one* instance of a rule from R is applied, but in parallel *all* other remaining symbols are affected, too, by the decaying rules $\left(b^{[k]}, j\right) \to \left(b^{[k-1]}, j\right)$ applied in the associated system $\Pi^{[d]}$. The main problem with the application of these additional rules is that they allow symbols b to stay alive for a bounded period only without having been consumed by the application of another rule than these decaying rules. Another side-effect is the increase of non-determinism, as in the rules $(E : X \to Y)$ we specify the life time (decay) of the objects we generate in Y, but we do not specify which remaining life time the objects we take in X still should have; for example, the application of the rule $a \to b$ to the configuration $\left(a^{[2]}a^{[1]}, 1\right)$, in the sequential mode, yields the result $\left(b^{[2]}, 1\right)$ (assuming that a newly generated object starts with decay 2) if we consume the object $a^{[2]}$ by the application of the rule, whereas we obtain $\left(a^{[1]}b^{[2]}, 1\right)$ if we consume the object $a^{[1]}$ instead.

$N^{[d]}(\Pi, \vartheta, \gamma, \rho)$ $(Ps^{[d]}(\Pi, \vartheta, \gamma, \rho))$ denotes the set of (vectors of) natural numbers computed by halting (with respect to the halting condition γ) computations of Π with decaying objects of decay d in the transition mode ϑ, with the numbers extracted from the output cell i_0 with respect to the specific constraints specified by ρ. For the sets of (vectors of) natural numbers generated by P systems with decaying objects of decay $1 \le k \le d$ we now use the notation

$$YO_m^{[d]}C_n(\vartheta, \gamma, \rho) \text{ [parameters for rules]}$$

with $Y \in \{N, Ps\}$, i.e., we add the superscript $[d]$ to specify the maximal life time of the objects.

3 P Systems with Decaying Objects and Transition Modes Bounding the Number of Rules in Applicable Multisets of Rules

In this section, we consider P systems having a constant K such that in each computation step the number of rules in an applicable multiset of rules is bounded by K.

3.1 Examples for P Systems with Decaying Objects

In this subsection, a few simple examples are exhibited to illustrate the effect of decays. For P systems with only one membrane/cell, we omit the indication of the cell number, i.e., instead of writing $(w, 1)$ we simply write w and instead of writing $(E : (x_1, 1) \to (y_1, 1))$ we may write $E : x_1 \to y_1$; moreover, if E is a condition which is always fulfilled, we may only write $x_1 \to y_1$.

Example 2. Consider the P systems

$$\Pi(d) = (1, \{s, a\}, \{a\}, s, \{s \to as, s \to \lambda\}, 1)$$

for $d > 1$. Then the only computations consist of applying n times the rule $s \to as$ and finally ending up with applying the rule $s \to \lambda$. For $n = 0$, we get $s^{[d]} \Longrightarrow_{(\Pi(d)^{[d]}, \vartheta)} \lambda$, for $1 \leq n \leq d$, we obtain the sequence of configurations

$$s^{[d]} \Longrightarrow_{(\Pi(d)^{[d]}, \vartheta)}^{n} a^{[d-n+1]} \dots a^{[d]} s^{[d]} \Longrightarrow_{(\Pi(d)^{[d]}, \vartheta)} a^{[d-n]} \dots a^{[d-1]},$$

whereas for $n > d$ we get

$$s^{[d]} \Longrightarrow_{(\Pi(d)^{[d]}, \vartheta)}^{d+1} a^{[1]} a^{[2]} \dots a^{[d]} s^{[d]}$$
$$\Longrightarrow_{(\Pi(d)^{[d]}, \vartheta)}^{*} a^{[1]} a^{[2]} \dots a^{[d]} s^{[d]} \Longrightarrow_{(\Pi(d)^{[d]}, \vartheta)} a^{[1]} \dots a^{[d-1]}.$$

Hence, in sum we obtain

$$N^{[d]}(\Pi(d), \vartheta, \gamma, \rho) = \{n \mid 0 \leq n < d\},$$

for $\rho \in \{N, T\} \cup \{-l \mid l \in \mathbb{N}\}$ and any of the transition modes ϑ as defined in the preceding section as well as with γ denoting total halting, partial halting (the whole rule set forms the only partition), or halting with final states (defined by the regular set of multisets $\{a\}^\circ$, which in fact means the same as taking $\rho = T$). Therefore, the family of P systems $\Pi(d)$ with $d \in \mathbb{N}$ forms a very simple infinite hierarchy with respect to the decay d in any of these cases.

Example 3. Let M be a finite subset of T°. Consider the P system

$$\Pi(M) = (1, \{s\} \cup T, T, s, \{s \to w \mid w \in M\}, 1).$$

Obviously, $Ps^{[d]}(\Pi(M), \vartheta, \gamma, \rho) = M$ for $\rho \in \{N, T\} \cup \{-l \mid l \in \mathbb{N}\}$ and any of the transition modes ϑ as defined in the preceding section as well as with $\gamma \in \{H, h, F\}$; hence, for all $n, d \geq 1$,

$$PsO_*^{[d]} C_n(\vartheta, \gamma, \rho)[ncoo] \supseteq PsFIN,$$

where ncoo indicates (the use of) noncooperative rules (in general, a *noncooperative rule* is of the form $(I : (a, i) \to (y_1, 1) \dots (y_n, n))$ where a is a single symbol and I denotes the condition that is always fulfilled).

In the case of adult halting, we restrict ourselves to the transition modes $\vartheta \in \{max, maxobj\}$: If we add the rules $a \to a$ for all $a \in T$, then we obtain a P system $\Pi'(M)$ with $Ps^{[d]}(\Pi'(M), \vartheta, A, \rho) = M$ with respect to our convention to consider two multisets L and L' to be equal if and only if $L \setminus \{\lambda\} = L' \setminus \{\lambda\}$. In that sense, we have

$$Ps O_*^{[d]} C_n (\vartheta, A, \rho) [\text{ncoo}] \supseteq PsFIN.$$

Example 4. Let $G = (N, T, P, S)$ be a regular grammar (without loss of generality, we assume G to be reduced, i.e., every nonterminal symbol can be reached from the start symbol S and from every nonterminal symbol a terminal string can be derived). Consider the P system

$$\Pi(G) = (1, N \cup T, T, S, R, 1)$$

with

$$R = \{(I : (A, 1) \to (b, 0)(C, 1)) \mid A \to bC \in P\}$$
$$\cup \{(I : (A, 1) \to (\lambda, 1)) \mid A \to \lambda \in P\}.$$

Obviously, $Ps^{[d]}(\Pi(M), \vartheta, \gamma, E) = Ps(L(G))$ for any of the transition modes ϑ as defined in the preceding section as well as with $\gamma \in \{H, h, F\}$; hence, for all $n, d \geq 1$,

$$Ps O_*^{[d]} C_n (\vartheta, \gamma, E) [\text{ncoo}] \supseteq PsREG.$$

In fact, the objects for the results of successful computations are collected in the environment, and all successful computations halt with empty cell 1.

Using the P system with decaying objects

$$\Pi'(G) = (1, N \cup T \cup \{F\}, T, S, R', 1)$$

with

$$R' = \{(I : (A, 1) \to (b, 0)(C, 1)) \mid A \to bC \in P\}$$
$$\cup \{(I : (A, 1) \to (F, 1)) \mid A \to \lambda \in P\} \cup \{(I : (F, 1) \to (F, 1))\}$$

we obtain $Ps^{[d]}(\Pi'(M), \vartheta, A, E) = Ps(L(G))$ for any of the transition modes ϑ as defined in the preceding section; all successful computations end up with looping in the final configuration F; hence, for all $n, d \geq 1$,

$$Ps O_*^{[d]} C_n (\vartheta, A, E) [\text{ncoo}] \supseteq PsREG.$$

3.2 A General Lemma

The following result holds in general for all possible variants of rules as well as with all transition modes and halting conditions defined in the preceding section:

Lemma 1. *For all $d \geq 1$ and each $Y \in \{N, Ps\}$ as well as for ϑ being any transition mode guaranteeing that in each computation step only a bounded number of rules can be applied, we have that*

a)   *for any halting condition $\gamma \in \{H, h, F\}$ and for any $\rho \in \{N, T\} \cup \{-l \mid l \in \mathbb{N}\}$,*

$$YO_*^{[d]}C_* (\vartheta, \gamma, \rho) \, [parameters \ for \ rules] \subseteq YFIN$$

as well as,
b)   *for any halting condition $\gamma \in \{H, h, A, F\}$,*

$$YO_*^{[d]}C_* (\vartheta, \gamma, E) \, [parameters \ for \ rules] \subseteq YREG.$$

Proof (sketch). Let Π be an arbitrary P system with decaying objects of decays at most d, and let Z be the maximal number of objects generated by a rule from Π. Moreover, let K be the maximal number of rules applicable in a computation step in Π according to the transition mode ϑ. Then, no matter how many objects have been in the initial configuration, after d steps at most KdZ objects can be distributed over the cells of Π, as all the initial objects have either be used in the application of a rule or else have faded away due to their decay $\leq d$. Therefore, in any configuration computed in more than d steps, at most KdZ objects can be distributed over the cells of Π. No matter how these objects are distributed and how big is their actual decay, in sum only a finite number of different configurations may evolve from the initial configuration. Hence, also the number of results of successful computations in Π must be finite, which proves a).

For proving b), we construct a regular grammar $G = (N, T, P, S)$ as follows: All the different configurations that eventually may be computed from the initial configuration constitute the set of nonterminal symbols N; as shown before, their number is finite. The initial configuration is represented by the start symbol S. For each transition step from a configuration represented by the nonterminal A to a configuration represented by the nonterminal C thereby sending out the multiset w to the environment, we take the rule $A \to wC$ into P. If A represents a final configuration according to the halting condition γ, we take the rule $A \to \lambda$ into P. According to this construction it is easy to see that $Ps(L(G)) = Ps^{[d]}(\Pi, \vartheta, \gamma, E)$, which observation completes the proof.   □

In combination with the Examples 3 and 4 we immediately infer the following characterizations of $YFIN$ and $YREG$, $Y \in \{N, Ps\}$:

Theorem 1. *For all $d \geq 1$ and each $Y \in \{N, Ps\}$ as well as for ϑ being any of the transition modes sequ, max_k for $k \in \mathbb{N}$, $min_k(p)$, or $max_k(p)$ for $k \in \mathbb{N}$ (with p denoting the number of partitions in the partitioning Θ),*

a)   *for any halting condition $\gamma \in \{H, h, F\}$ and for any $\rho \in \{N, T\} \cup \{-l \mid l \in \mathbb{N}\}$,*

$$YO_*^{[d]}C_* (\vartheta, \gamma, \rho) \, [ncoo] = YFIN$$

as well as,
b)   *for any halting condition $\gamma \in \{H, h, A, F\}$,*

$$YO_*^{[d]}C_* (\vartheta, \gamma, E) \, [ncoo] = YREG.$$

Proof (sketch). We only have to show that the given transition modes fulfill the condition needed for the application of Lemma 1. The maximal number K of rules applicable in Π according to the transition modes ϑ can be given as follows:

- for $\vartheta = sequ$, $K = 1$;
- for $\vartheta = max_k$, $k \in \mathbb{N}$, $K = k$;
- for $min_k(p)$ and $max_k(p)$, $k, p \in \mathbb{N}$, $K = kp$.

In all cases, the condition of Lemma 1 is fulfilled, which yields the inclusions $\subseteq$; the opposite inclusions follow by taking the P systems elaborated in Examples 3 and 4. $\qquad\square$

In the remaining subsections of this section, we compare these results for specific variants of P systems with decaying objects from Theorem 1 with the computational completeness results obtained in [11] for the corresponding variants of P systems with non-decaying symbols.

3.3   Models for the 1-Restricted Minimally Parallel Transition Mode

In this subsection, as already described in [11], we use the ability of the 1-restricted minimally parallel transition mode to capture characteristic features of well-known models of P systems to compare the generative power of extended spiking neural P systems as well as of purely catalytic P systems with decaying and with non-decaying objects.

Extended Spiking Neural P Systems. We first consider extended spiking neural P systems (without delays), see [1], where the rules are applied in a sequential way in each neuron, but on the level of the whole system, the maximally parallel transition mode is applied – every neuron which may use a spiking rule has to spike, i.e., to apply a rule (see the original paper [12]). When partitioning the rule set according to the set of neurons, the application of the 1-restricted minimally parallel transition mode exactly models the original transition mode defined for spiking neural P systems.

An *extended spiking neural P system* (of degree $m \geq 1$) (in the following we shall simply speak of an *ESNP system*) is a construct $\Pi = (m, S, R, i_0)$ where

- m is the number of *neurons*; the neurons are uniquely identified by a number between 1 and m;
- S describes the *initial configuration* by assigning an initial value (of spikes) to each neuron;
- R is a finite set of *rules* of the form $\left(i, E/a^k \to P\right)$ such that $i \in [1..m]$ (specifying that this rule is assigned to neuron i), $E \subseteq REG\left(\{a\}\right)$ is the *checking set* (the current number of spikes in the neuron has to be from E if this rule shall be executed), $k \in \mathbb{N}$ is the "number of spikes" (the energy) consumed by this rule, and P is a (possibly empty) set of *productions* of the

form (l, a^w) where $l \in [1..m]$ (thus specifying the target neuron), $w \in \mathbb{N}$ is the *weight* of the energy sent along the axon from neuron i to neuron l.
- i_0 is the *output neuron*.

A *configuration* of the ESNP system is described by specifying the actual number of spikes in every neuron. A *transition* from one configuration to another one is executed as follows: for each neuron i, we non-deterministically choose a rule $(i, E/a^k \to P)$ that can be applied, i.e., if the current value of spikes in neuron i is in E, neuron i "spikes", i.e., for every production (l, w) occurring in the set P we send w spikes along the axon from neuron i to neuron l. A *computation* is a sequence of configurations starting with the initial configuration given by S. An ESNP system can be used to generate sets from NRE (we do not distinguish between NRE and $RE(\{a\})$) as follows: a computation is called *successful* if it halts, i.e., if for no neuron, a rule can be activated; we then consider the contents, i.e., the number of spikes, of the *output neuron* i_0 in halting computations.

We now consider the ESNP system $\Pi = (m, S, R, i_0)$ as a network of cells $\Pi' = (m, \{a\}, \{a\}, S, R', i_0)$ working in the 1-restricted minimally parallel transition mode, with

$$R' = \left\{ \left(E : \left(a^k, i\right) \to \left(a^{w_1}, l_1\right) \ldots \left(a^{w_n}, l_n\right)\right) \mid \\ \left(i, E/a^k \to (l_1, a^{w_1}) \ldots (l_n, a^{w_n})\right) \in R\right\}$$

and the partitioning R'_i, $1 \le i \le m$, of the rule set R' according to the set of neurons, i.e.,

$$R'_i = \left\{ \left(E : \left(a^k, i\right) \to \left(a^{w_1}, l_1\right) \ldots \left(a^{w_n}, l_n\right)\right) \mid \\ \left(E : \left(a^k, i\right) \to \left(a^{w_1}, l_1\right) \ldots \left(a^{w_n}, l_n\right)\right) \in R'\right\}.$$

The 1-restricted minimally parallel transition mode chooses one rule – if possible – from every set R_i and then applies such a multiset of rules in parallel, which directly corresponds to applying one spiking rule in every neuron where a rule can be applied. Hence, it is easy to see that Π' and Π generate the same set from $RE\{a\}$ if in both systems we take the same cell/neuron for extracting the output. Due to the results valid for ESNP systems, see [1], we obtain:

Theorem 2. *For all* $n \ge 3$,

$$NRE = NO_1C_n\left(min_1(n), H, N\right)[ESNP].$$

In [8] the following results are shown for ESNP systems with decaying objects:

Theorem 3. *For all* $n \ge 2$ *and* $d \ge 1$,

a) $NFIN = NO_1^{[d]}C_n\left(min_1(n), H, N\right)[ESNP]$ *and*
b) $NREG = NO_1^{[d]}C_n\left(min_1(n), H, E\right)[ESNP]$.

Purely Catalytic P Systems. Already in the original papers by Gheorghe Păun (see [16] and also [6]), membrane systems with catalytic rules were defined, but computational completeness was only shown with using a priority relation on the rules. In [9] it was shown that only three catalysts are sufficient in one membrane, using only catalytic rules with the maximally parallel transition mode, in order to generate any recursively enumerable set of natural numbers. Hence, by showing that P systems with purely catalytic rules working in the maximally parallel transition mode can be considered as P systems working with the corresponding noncooperative rules in the 1-restricted minimally parallel transition mode when partitioning the rule sets for each membrane with respect to the catalysts, we obtain the astonishing result that in this case we get a characterization of the recursively enumerable sets of natural numbers by using only noncooperative rules.

A *noncooperative rule* is of the form $(I : (a, i) \to (y_1, 1) \ldots (y_n, n))$ where a is a single symbol and I denotes the condition that is always fulfilled. A *catalytic rule* is of the form $(I : (c, i)(a, i) \to (c, i)(y_1, 1) \ldots (y_n, n))$ where c is from a distinguished subset $C \subset V$ such that in all rules (noncooperative evolution rules, catalytic rules) of the whole system the y_i are from $(V \setminus C)^*$ and the symbols a are from $(V \setminus C)$. Imposing the restriction that the noncooperative rules and the catalytic rules in a network of cells allow for finding a hierarchical tree structure of membranes such that symbols either stay in their membrane region or are sent out to the surrounding membrane region or sent into an inner membrane, then we get the classical catalytic P systems without priorities. Allowing regular sets checking for the non-appearance of specific symbols instead of I, we even get the original P systems with priorities.

Catalytic P systems using only catalytic rules are called *purely catalytic P systems*. As we know from [9], only two (three) catalysts in one membrane are needed to obtain NRE with (purely) catalytic P systems without priorities working in the maximally parallel transition mode, i.e., we can write these results as follows (*cat* indicates that noncooperative and catalytic rules are allowed, whereas *pcat* indicates that only catalytic rules are allowed):

Theorem 4. *([9]) For all $n \in \mathbb{N}$ and $k \geq 2$, as well as $\gamma \in \{H, h, F\}$*

$$NRE = NO_*C_n\,(max, \gamma, -k)\,[cat_k] = NO_*C_n\,(max, \gamma, -(k+1))\,[pcat_{k+1}]\,.$$

As the results can be collected in a second membrane without catalysts, we even have

$$NRE = NO_*C_{n+1}\,(max, \gamma, N)\,[cat_k] = NO_*C_{n+1}\,(max, \gamma, N)\,[pcat_{k+1}]\,.$$

If we now partition the rule set in a purely catalytic P system according to the catalysts present in each membrane, this partitioning replaces the use of the catalysts when working in the 1-restricted minimally parallel transition mode, because by definition from each of these sets then – if possible – exactly one rule (as with the use of the corresponding catalyst) is chosen: from the set of purely catalytic rules R we obtain the corresponding set of noncooperative rules R' as

$$R' = \{(I : (a, i) \to (y_1, 1) \dots (y_n, n)) \mid$$
$$(I : (c, i)\,(a, i) \to (c, i)\,(y_1, 1) \dots (y_n, n)) \in R\}$$

as well as the corresponding partitioning of R' as

$$R'_{i,c} = \{(I : (a, i) \to (y_1, 1) \dots (y_n, n)) \mid$$
$$(I : (c, i)\,(a, i) \to (c, i)\,(y_1, 1) \dots (y_n, n)) \in R\}\,.$$

Considering purely catalytic P systems in one membrane, we immediately infer that when using the 1-restricted minimally parallel transition mode for a suitable partitioning of rules we only need noncooperative rules:

Corollary 1. *For all $n \in \mathbb{N}$ and $k \geq 3$ as well as $\gamma \in \{H, F\}$,*

$$NRE = NO_*C_n\,(min_1(k), \gamma, N)\,[ncoo]\,.$$

On the other hand, when using the asynchronous, the sequential or even the maximally parallel transition mode, we only obtain regular sets (see [11]):

Theorem 5. *For each $Y \in \{N, Ps\}$, for any $\vartheta \in \{asyn, sequ, max\}$, any $\gamma \in \{H, h, A, F\}$, and any $\rho \in \{N, T\} \cup \{-l \mid l \in \mathbb{N}\}$,*

$$YREG = YO_*C_*\,(\vartheta, \gamma, \rho)\,[ncoo]\,.$$

Combining the results of Theorem 5 with those from Theorem 1, we immediately obtain the following corollary for the sequential transition mode:

Corollary 2. *For any halting condition $\gamma \in \{H, h, A, F\}$, any $\rho \in \{N, T\} \cup \{-l \mid l \in \mathbb{N}\}$, and each $Y \in \{N, Ps\}$,*

$$YREG = YO_*^{[d]}C_*\,(sequ, \gamma, E)\,[ncoo] = YO_*C_*\,(sequ, \gamma, \rho)\,[ncoo]\,,$$

for all $d \geq 1$.

For purely catalytic P systems with decaying objects, even in the maximally parallel transition modes max and $maxobj$ the conditions of Lemma 1 are fulfilled, hence, we get the following results:

Theorem 6. *For all $n, d, k \geq 1$, each $Y \in \{N, Ps\}$, for any $\vartheta \in \{max, maxobj\}$, as well as for any halting condition $\gamma \in \{H, h, A, F\}$,*

$$YREG = YO_*^{[d]}C_n\,(\vartheta, \gamma, E)\,[pcat_k]\,.$$

Theorem 7. *For all $n, d, k \geq 1$, each $Y \in \{N, Ps\}$, for any $\vartheta \in \{max, maxobj\}$, as well as for any halting condition $\gamma \in \{H, h, F\}$, and for any $\rho \in \{N, T\} \cup \{-l \mid l \in \mathbb{N}\}$,*

$$YFIN = YO_*^{[d]}C_n\,(\vartheta, \gamma, -k)\,[pcat_k] = \cup_{k \geq 1}YO_*^{[d]}C_n\,(\vartheta, A, -k)\,[pcat_k]$$
$$= YO_*^{[d]}C_{n+1}\,(\vartheta, \gamma, \rho)\,[pcat_k] = \cup_{k \geq 1}YO_*^{[d]}C_{n+1}\,(\vartheta, A, \rho)\,[pcat_k]\,.$$

In all these systems with decaying objects, the catalysts are assumed to only have life time d, too.

3.4   The k-Restricted Maximally Parallel Transition Mode

In this subsection, we investigate the k-restricted maximally parallel transition mode. With this transition mode and cooperative rules, we again obtain computational completeness, a result which immediately follows from the results proved in the preceding section, i.e., from Theorem 4 and Corollary 1 (see [11]):

Corollary 3. *For all $n \geq 1$ and $k \geq 3$, as well as for any halting condition $\gamma \in \{H, h, F\}$,*

$$NRE = NO_*C_n\,(max_k, \gamma, -k)\,[coo] = NO_*C_n\,(max_k, \gamma, -k)\,[pcat_k]\,.$$

Yet in contrast to the results proved in the preceding section for the 1-restricted minimally transition mode, now with noncooperative rules we only obtain semilinear sets when using the k-restricted maximally parallel transition mode:

Theorem 8. *For all $n, k \geq 1$, each $Y \in \{N, Ps\}$, for every $k \in \mathbb{N}$ as well as any possible partitioning Θ of the rule sets in the P systems, i.e., for all $p \in \mathbb{N}$, for any halting condition $\gamma \in \{H, h, A, F\}$ and for any $\rho \in \{N, T\} \cup \{-l \mid l \in \mathbb{N}\}$,*

$$YREG = YO_*C_n\,(max_k(p), \gamma, \rho)\,[ncoo]\,.$$

Again, with decaying objects, the conditions of Lemma 1 are fulfilled, hence, we get the following results:

Theorem 9. *For all $n, d, k, p \geq 1$, each $Y \in \{N, Ps\}$, as well as for any halting condition $\gamma \in \{H, h, A, F\}$,*

$$YREG = YO_*^{[d]}C_n\,(max_k\,(p), \gamma, E)\,[coo]\,.$$

Theorem 10. *For all $n, d, k, p \geq 1$, each $Y \in \{N, Ps\}$, as well as for any halting condition $\gamma \in \{H, h, F\}$, and for any $\rho \in \{N, T\} \cup \{-l \mid l \in \mathbb{N}\}$,*

$$YFIN = YO_*^{[d]}C_n\,(max_k\,(p), \gamma, \rho)\,[coo] = \cup_{k \geq 1}YO_*^{[d]}C_n\,(max_k\,(p), A, \rho)\,[coo]\,.$$

4   Computational Completeness Results for P Systems with Decaying Objects

In this section we prove computational completeness for catalytic P systems as well as for P systems using cooperative rules with decaying objects. Moreover, we only consider P systems with one membrane/cell.

Catalytic P systems can be seen as a specific variant of P systems using cooperative rules, hence, we first establish the computational completeness result for P systems using cooperative rules; when using arbitrary cooperative rules, additional ingredients such as context conditions can be avoided, yet only when using the transition mode $maxobj$ instead of max as well as with adult halting or halting with final state:

Theorem 11. *For all $n \geq 1$ and all $d \geq 2$ as well as any $\gamma \in \{A, F\}$, any $\rho \in \{N, T\} \cup \{-l \mid l \in \mathbb{N}\}$, and each $Y \in \{N, Ps\}$,*

$$YRE = YO_*^{[d]}C_n\,(maxobj, \gamma, \rho)\,[coo].$$

Proof (sketch). We only show $PsRE \subseteq PsO_*^{[2]}C_1\,(maxobj, \gamma, \rho)\,[coo]$. The instructions of a register machine $M = (m, B, l_0, l_h, P)$ can be simulated by a P system $\Pi = (1, V, T, l_0, R, 1)$ with decaying objects of decay $d = 2$ using cooperative rules in the transition mode $maxobj$. As usual, the contents of a register j is represented by the corresponding number of copies of the symbol a_j; T consists of the symbols a_j, $3 \leq j \leq m$. For keeping the objects a_j, $1 \leq j \leq m$, alive, we use the rules $a_j \to a_j$.

- $l_1 : (ADD\,(j), l_2, l_3)$, with $l_1 \in B \setminus \{l_h\}$, $l_2, l_3 \in B$, $1 \leq j \leq m$, is simulated by the rules $l_1 \to l_2 a_j$ and $l_1 \to l_3 a_j$ in R.
- $l_1 : (SUB\,(j), l_2, l_3)$, with $l_1 \in B \setminus \{l_h\}$, $l_2, l_3 \in B$, $1 \leq j \leq 2$, is simulated in three steps:
  in the first step, the rule $l_1 \to l_1' h_j$ is used;
  in the second step, $l_1' \to \bar{l}_1$ is used, eventually in parallel with the rule $h_j a_j \to \bar{h}_j$ which is the crucial step of the simulation where we need the features of the transition mode $maxobj$ – it guarantees that for exactly one object a_j the rule $h_j a_j \to \bar{h}_j$ has priority over the rule $a_j \to a_j$ which involves less objects than the other one;
  finally, depending on the availability of an object a_j in the second step for the application of the rule $h_j a_j \to \bar{h}_j$, in the third step either $\bar{h}_j$ is present and the rule $\bar{l}_1 \bar{h}_j \to l_2$ is applied, or else h_j is still present so that the rule $\bar{l}_1 h_j \to l_3$ is used.
- $l_h : HALT$ is simulated by the rule $l_h \to \lambda$.

Collecting all objects used in the rules defined above, we get

$$V = B \cup \{l', \bar{l} \mid l \in B \setminus \{l_h\}\} \cup \{h_1, \bar{h}_1, h_2, \bar{h}_2\}$$
$$\cup\, \{a_j \mid 1 \leq j \leq m\}.$$

At the end of a successful computation, only the objects a_j, $3 \leq j \leq m$, representing the result are present and kept in an infinite loop by the rules $a_j \to a_j$, hence, the condition for adult halting is fulfilled; in sum we have shown that $L\,(M) = Ps^{[2]}\,(\Pi, maxobj, A, \rho)$.

For halting with final states, we can use the condition that only the objects a_j, $3 \leq j \leq m$, may be present. It seems to be impossible to stop the application of the rules $a_j \to a_j$ without using context conditions (or priorities on the rules), hence, we have to restrict ourselves to the halting conditions A and F. $\square$

The idea for simulating the SUB-instruction elaborated in the preceding proof does not work with the transition mode max as the application of the rule $h_j a_j \to \bar{h}_j$ cannot be enforced without giving it priority over the rule $a_j \to a_j$; on the other hand, when adding only these two priorities

$$h_j a_j \to \bar{h}_j > a_j \to a_j,\ 1 \le j \le 2,$$

(priorities were already used in the original paper [6]), then the rest of the proof of Theorem 11 also works with the transition mode *max*.

We now return to catalytic P systems and establish the computational completeness result for catalytic P systems with decaying objects using the standard transition mode *max* (and the standard total halting):

Theorem 12. *For all* $n \ge 1$, $k \ge 2$, *and all* $d \ge 2$ *as well as any* $\gamma \in \{H, h, A, F\}$, *any* $\rho \in \{T\} \cup \{-l \mid l \ge 0\}$, *and each* $Y \in \{N, Ps\}$,

$$YRE = YO_*^{[d]}C_n\,(max, \gamma, \rho)\,[cat_k].$$

Proof (sketch). We only show $PsRE \subseteq PsO_*^{[2]}C_1\,(max, \gamma, -0)\,[cat_2]$. The instructions of a register machine $M = (m, B, l_0, l_h, P)$ can be simulated by a P system $\Pi = (1, V, T, l_0 c_1 c_2, R, 1)$ with decaying objects of decay $d = 2$ using noncooperative and catalytic rules in the transition mode *max*. The contents of a register j is represented by the corresponding number of copies of the symbol a_j; T consists of the symbols a_j, $3 \le j \le m$. For keeping the objects a_j, $1 \le j \le m$, alive, we now use the rules with context conditions

$$\{(\{l'\}, \emptyset) \mid l \in B\} : a_j \to a_j.$$

- $l_1 : (ADD\,(j), l_2, l_3)$, with $l_1 \in B \setminus \{l_h\}$, $l_2, l_3 \in B$, $1 \le j \le m$, is simulated in two steps by the rules
  $c_1 l_1 \to c_1 l_1'$ as well as $c_2 l_1' \to c_2 l_2 a_j$ and $c_2 l_1' \to c_2 l_3 a_j$ in R.
- $l_1 : (SUB\,(j), l_2, l_3)$, with $l_1 \in B \setminus \{l_h\}$, $l_2, l_3 \in B$, $1 \le j \le 2$, is simulated in two steps, too:
  in the first step, the rule $c_1 l_1 \to c_1 l_1'$ and eventually the rule with context conditions

$$\{(\{l_1\}, \emptyset) \mid l_1 : (SUB\,(j), l_2, l_3) \in R\} : c_2 a_j \to c_2 a_j'$$

  is used;
  in the second step, if a_j' is present, then the rules $c_1 a_j' \to c_1$ and $c_2 l_1' \to c_2 l_2$ are used in parallel; otherwise, only the rule with context conditions

$$\{(\emptyset, \{a_j'\})\} : c_2 l_1' \to c_2 l_3$$

  is used.
- $l_h : HALT$ is simulated by the sequence of rules $l_h \to l_h'$, $l_h' \to \lambda$.

Collecting all objects used in the rules defined above, we get

$$V = B \cup \{l' \mid l \in B\} \cup \{c_1, c_2\}$$
$$\cup\ \{a_j \mid 1 \le j \le m\} \cup \{a_1', a_2'\}.$$

At the end of a successful computation, only the objects a_j, $3 \leq j \leq m$, representing the result are present and kept alive three steps when l_h appears, whereas the catalysts die after two steps and the computation successfully halts with no rule being applicable anymore; in sum we have shown that $L(M) = Ps^{[2]}(\Pi, max, H, -0)$. Partial halting with the trivial partitioning $\{R\}$ successfully stops as total halting. For halting with final states, we can use the condition that only the objects a_j, $3 \leq j \leq m$, may be present. Using again the rules $a_j \rightarrow a_j$ instead of the corresponding ones with context conditions, the condition for adult halting can be fulfilled. $\qquad\square$

5 Summary and Future Research

The main purpose of this paper has been to investigate the effect of using decaying objects in contrast to the non-decaying objects used in most cases so far in the area of P systems. Many variants of P systems known to be computationally complete with non-decaying objects can be shown to only characterize the finite or the regular sets of multisets in combination with transition modes only allowing for the application of a bounded number of rules in each computation step. On the other hand, in combination with the maximally parallel mode, computational completeness can be obtained for catalytic and P systems using cooperative rules, respectively, yet only with also using permitting and forbidden contexts. As an interesting special result, computational completeness can be obtained for P systems using cooperative rules with the mode using the maximal number of objects, yet without needing context conditions.

With respect to the maximally parallel mode and the mode using the maximal number of objects, a lot of technical details remain for future research, especially concerning the need of using context conditions, not only in connection with catalytic P systems and P systems using cooperative rules, but also with many other variants of (static) P systems.

The effect of using decaying objects in combination with the asynchronous transition mode has been left open in this paper. With non-decaying objects, the asynchronous mode usually yields the same results as the sequential mode. Yet in connection with using decaying objects, the situation becomes more difficult, and although the generative power seems to become rather degenerate, precise characterizations might be challenging problems for future research.

In this paper, only generative P systems with decaying objects are investigated. Obviously, decaying objects can also be considered for accepting P systems as well as for P systems computing functions. In order to obtain high computational power, it again is necessary to keep objects alive for an arbitray long period of computation steps. Yet we may expect slightly different results compared with those obtained in the generative case, e.g., with transition modes only allowing for the application of a bounded number of rules in each computation step, specific variants of such P systems allow for at least accepting $FIN \cup co\text{-}FIN$.

The idea of decaying objects can be extended from static (tissue) P systems to dynamic P systems, where membranes (cells) may be newly generated and/or deleted. In addition, the idea of decaying entities can be extended to membranes, too, i.e., we may consider membranes (cells) only surviving for a certain number of computation steps. Moreover, in nature different types of cells have different life cycles; hence, it is quite natural to allow different objects to have different decays or even to allow to introduce different decays for the same object in different rules.

Another challenging problem is to find non-trivial infinite hierarchies with respect to the decay of objects for specific kinds of P systems with decaying objects; Example 2 shows a very simple example of such an infinite hierarchy with respect to the decay of the objects.

When going from multisets to sets of objects, another wide field of future research may be opened; in this case, reaction systems can be seen as very specific variants of such a kind of P systems.

Acknowledgements. The author gratefully acknowledges the useful suggestions and remarks from Erzsébet Csuhaj-Varjú, Marion Oswald, and Sergey Verlan during the preparation of this paper; special thanks go to Marion and Sergey, as many definitions and results presented in this paper came up from long discussions with them and were taken over from joint papers.

References

1. Alhazov, A., Freund, R., Oswald, M., Slavkovik, M.: Extended Spiking Neural P Systems. In: Hoogeboom, H.J., Păun, G., Rozenberg, G., Salomaa, A. (eds.) WMC 2006. LNCS, vol. 4361, pp. 123–134. Springer, Heidelberg (2006)
2. Bernardini, F., Gheorghe, M., Margenstern, M., Verlan, S.: Networks of cells and Petri nets. In: Gutiérrez-Naranjo, M.A., Păun, G., Romero-Jiménez, A., Riscos-Núñez, A. (eds.) Proc. Fifth Brainstorming Week on Membrane Computing, Sevilla, pp. 33–62 (2007)
3. Brijder, R., Ehrenfeucht, A., Main, M.G., Rozenberg, G.: A tour of reaction systems. Int. J. Found. Comput. Sci. 22(7), 1499–1517 (2011)
4. Csuhaj-Varjú, E.: Networks of language processors, pp. 771–790 (2001)
5. Dassow, J., Păun, G.: Regulated Rewriting in Formal Language Theory. Springer (1989)
6. Dassow, J., Păun, G.: On the power of membrane computing. Journal of Universal Computer Science 5(2), 33–49 (1999)
7. Freund, R.: Transition and Halting Modes in (Tissue) P Systems. In: Păun, G., Pérez-Jiménez, M.J., Riscos-Núñez, A., Rozenberg, G., Salomaa, A. (eds.) WMC 2009. LNCS, vol. 5957, pp. 18–29. Springer, Heidelberg (2010)
8. Freund, R., Ionescu, M., Oswald, M.: Extended spiking neural P systems with decaying spikes and/or total spiking. Int. J. Found. Comput. Sci. 19(5), 1223–1234 (2008)
9. Freund, R., Kari, L., Oswald, M., Sosík, P.: Computationally universal P systems without priorities: two catalysts are sufficient. Theoretical Computer Science 330, 251–266 (2005)

10. Freund, R., Verlan, S.: A Formal Framework for Static (Tissue) P Systems. In: Eleftherakis, G., Kefalas, P., Păun, G., Rozenberg, G., Salomaa, A. (eds.) WMC 2007. LNCS, vol. 4860, pp. 271–284. Springer, Heidelberg (2007)

11. Freund, R., Verlan, S.: (Tissue) P systems working in the k-restricted minimally or maximally parallel transition mode. Natural Computing 10(2), 821–833 (2011)

12. Ionescu, M., Păun, G., Yokomori, T.: Spiking neural P systems. Fundamenta Informaticae 71(2-3), 279–308 (2006)

13. Kudlek, M., Martín-Vide, C., Păun, G.: Toward a Formal Macroset Theory. In: Calude, C.S., Pun, G., Rozenberg, G., Salomaa, A. (eds.) Multiset Processing. LNCS, vol. 2235, pp. 123–134. Springer, Heidelberg (2001)

14. Margenstern, M., Rogozhin, Y., Verlan, S.: Time-varying Distributed H Systems with Parallel Computations: the Problem is Solved. In: Chen, J., Reif, J.H. (eds.) DNA9. LNCS, vol. 2943, pp. 48–53. Springer, Heidelberg (2004)

15. Minsky, M.L.: Computation: Finite and Infinite Machines. Prentice Hall, Englewood Cliffs (1967)

16. Păun, G.: Computing with membranes. J. of Computer and System Sciences 61(1), 108–143 (1998); and TUCS Research Report 208 (1998), http://www.tucs.fi

17. Păun, G.: Membrane Computing. An Introduction. Springer, Berlin (2002)

18. Păun, G., Rozenberg, G., Salomaa, A.: The Oxford Handbook of Membrane Computing. Oxford University Press (2010)

19. Rozenberg, G., Salomaa, A.: Handbook of Formal Languages, vol. 3. Springer, Heidelberg (1997)

20. The P Systems Web Page, http://ppage.psystems.eu

Alan Turing and John von Neumann - Their Brains and Their Computers

Sorin Istrail[1] and Solomon Marcus[2]

[1] Brown University, Department of Computer Science
Box 1910, Providence, RI 02912, USA
[2] Stoilow Institute of Mathematics, Romanian Academy
P.O. Box 1-764014700 Bucharest, Romania

"There exists today a very elaborate system of formal logic, and specifically, of logic as applied to mathematics. This is a discipline with many good sides, but also with certain serious weaknesses. ... Everybody who has worked in formal logic will confirm that it is one of the technically most refractory parts of mathematics. The reason for this is that it deals with rigid, all-or-none concepts, and has very little contact with the continuous concept of the real or of complex number, that is, with mathematical analysis. Yet analysis is the technically most successful and best-elaborated part of mathematics. Thus formal logic is, by the nature of its approach, cut off from the best cultivated portions of mathematics, and forced onto the most difficult part of mathematical terrain, into combinatorics."

- John von Neumann

1 The Duo

Were it not for two decades of the intertwined intellectual lives of Alan Turing and John von Neumann, the disciplines of mathematics and computer science would not be what they are today.

Their shared intellectual path began in 1933, when college student Turing wrote to his mother, Sarah, that his prize book was von Neumann's Mathematical Foundations of Quantum Mechanics, which he described as being "very interesting, and not at all difficult reading, although the applied mathematicians seem to find it rather strong."

Shortly after, in 1935, von Neumann finds his way into the first line of the first sentence in Turing's first paper: "In his [1934] paper Almost periodic functions in a group, J. v. Neumann has used independently the ideas of left and right periodicity. I shall now show that these are equivalent." Such a demonstration of Turing's power of proof surely must have caught von Neumann's attention, for in 1937, he wrote a letter in support of a Princeton fellowship for Turing, and in 1938 offered Turing a position as his assistant which, although it paid $1,500 a year, Turing declined as the shadows of war lengthened in Europe.

The admiration was mutual. In a letter written home from Princeton, von Neumann's is the first name on a list of Princeton luminaries that included "Weyl, Courant, Hardy, Einstein, Lefschetz, as well as hosts of smaller fry."

E. Csuhaj-Varjú et al. (Eds.): CMC 2012, LNCS 7762, pp. 26–35, 2013.

Though Turing returned to his native England, the two continued to correspond and collaborate for the rest of their all-too-short lives. In 1939, after hearing of a continuous group problem from von Neumann, Turing proved the general negative solution and sent it to von Neumann for Annals of Mathematics (see von Neumann letter to Turing and Stan Ulam letter). A 1949 letter from von Neumann to Turing acknowledged receipt of Turing's submission of a paper for Annals of Mathematics for which von Neumann served as an editor. "Exceedingly glad to get your paper" and "agree with your assessment of the paper character ... our machine-project is moving along quite satisfactory but we are not at the point you are" [16]. (It may be interesting to note that von Neumann would be assigning Turing's famous paper on computable numbers as required reading for his collaborators in the EDVAC project of constructing his computers.)

Even in critical discourse, Turing and von Neumann are intertwined. "The fathers of the field had been pretty confusing," E. W. Dijkstra wrote. "John von Neumann speculated about computers and the human brain in analogies sufficiently wild to be worthy of a medieval thinker and Alan M. Turing thought about criteria to settle the question of whether Machines Can Think, which we now know is about as relevant as the question of whether Submarines Can Swim."

Although Turing was 10 years younger than von Neumann, they acknowledged one another's intellectual seniority, with von Neumann serving as an elder in mathematics to Turing and Turing the elder in computer science to von Neumann. Turing papers on almost periodicity, Lie groups, numerical matrix analysis and word problem for compact groups follow from two relatively deep theorems - one due to Tarski and the other to von Neumann. In a letter to Max Newman, Turing talks about Gödel and von Neumann: "Gödel's paper has reached me at last. I am very suspicious of it now but will have to swot up the Zermelo-v. Neumann system a bit before I can put objections down in black and white. The present report gives a fairly complete account of the proposed calculator. It is recommended however that it be read in conjunction with J. von Neumann's 'Report on the EDVAC' [Proposal for the Development of an Automatic Computing Engine]. Most of the most hopeful scheme, for economy combined with speed, seems to be the 'storage tube' or 'iconoscope' (in J. v. Neumann's terminology)."

Their age difference is irrelevant in another respect: We could consider Turing the grandfather of computer science and von Neumann its father, because the Turing machine was invented in the 1930s, while von Neumann's basic work in the field belongs to the 1940s and 1950s.

We find similarities on many fronts: Turing and von Neumann were essentially involved in the creative intellectual effort required by their governments during the Second World War against Nazism and Fascism, and each was considered a war hero by his country, with von Neumann receiving the Presidential Medal of Freedom and Turing the OBE; both showed interest for biology (although von Neumann's interest in this respect was much longer and deeper); they both were struck by Gödel's incompleteness theorem and both contributed to a better understanding of its meaning and significance; they both were strongly related in some periods of their lives to Princeton University; they both were attracted by game aspects of computing and of life; and they both left some important unpublished manuscripts. Did they meet? No sign exists in this respect in the available writings. Both lived lives that were too short: Just 41 when he died, Turing lived two years longer than Bernard Riemann; von Neumann died at 53, four years younger than Henri Poincaré was at the time of his death.

Von Neumann was a high achiever from a young age. At 15, he began to study advanced calculus. At 19, he published two major mathematical papers, the second of which gave the modern definition of ordinal numbers. He was 21 when he published *An axiomatization of set theory*, 22 when he began his work on *Mathematical Foundations of Quantum Mechanics* (finished when he was 25) and 24 when he published his minimax theorem. By 26, he was one of the first four people (among them Einstein and Gödel) Princeton University selected for the faculty of its Institute for Advanced Study. He was the first to capture the meaning and significance of Gödel's incompleteness theorem, realizing that "if a system of mathematics does not lead into contradiction, then this fact cannot be demonstrated with the procedures of that system" [12].

In examining the totality of von Neumann's work, it is difficult to find names equal in class. If we refer to those historically near to him, maybe Poincaré and David Hilbert before him and A.N. Kolmogorov, after him. But even with respect to these great names, it is important to observe that von Neumann's impact spans the whole landscape of sciences, be they more or less exact, natural sciences or social sciences, science or engineering (like in his work related to nuclear weapons). From axiomatic foundations of set theory to the foundation of continuous geometry, from measure theory to ergodic theory, from operator theory to its use to build the foundations of quantum mechanics, from probability theory to lattice theory, from quantum logic to game theory, from mathematical economics to linear programming, mathematical statistics and nuclear weapons, computer science, fluid dynamics, weather systems, politics and social affairs, everywhere he shined new light upon the very essential roots of the respective problems. Mediocrity was not his neighbor.

Turing's achievements as a young man are no less remarkable than von Neumann's. On the strength of his fellowship dissertation, *On the Gaussian Error Function*, completed and submitted in November 1934, the 22-year-old Turing was elected a Fellow of King's College four months later, on March 16, 1935. Economist John Maynard Keynes was among the committee members electing him. The paper contained a proof of the Central Limit Theorem, one of the most fundamental in probability theory. In 1937 at age 25 he published his seminal paper *On Computable Numbers, with an Application to the Entscheidungsproblem*, solving one of the most famous problems in mathematics proposed by Hilbert. This paper, with negative and positive results of greatest depth, defining the Turing machine, and inspiring the designers of electronic computers in England and United States – von Neumann, in particular, in such a decisive way – is without question the most important and influential paper in computer science, one offering proof positive that the new field had emerged.

2 From Leibniz, Boole, Bohr and Turing to Shannon, McCullogh-Pitts and von Neumann - The Emergence of the Information Paradigm

The middle of the past century has been very hot, characterized by the appearance of the new fields defining the move from the domination of the energy paradigm, characterizing the second half of the 19th century and the first half of the 20th century, to the domination of the information-communication-computation paradigms, appearing at the crossroad of the first and the second halves of the 20th century. So, John von Neumann's reflection, by which he became a pioneer of the new era, developed in the context of concomitant emergence in the fifth and the sixth decades of the 20th century of theory of algorithms (A.A. Markov), simply typed lambda calculus (Alonzo Church), game theory (von Neumann and Oskar Morgenstern), computer science (Turing and von Neumann), cybernetics (Norbert Wiener), information theory (Claude Shannon), molecular genetics (Francis Crick, James Watson, Maurice Wilkins, among others), coding theory (R. W. Hamming), system theory (L. von Bertalanffy), control theory, complexity theory, and generative grammars (Noam Chomsky). Many of these lines of development were no longer available to von Neumann and we are in the situation to question the consequences of this fact.

Von Neumann was impressed by Warren McCullogh and Walter Pitts's result connecting logic, language and neural networks, [10]. In von Neumann's formulation, this result shows "that anything that can be exhaustively and unambiguously described, anything that can be completely and unambiguously put into words, is ipso facto realizable by a suitable finite neural network. Three things deserve to be brought into attention in this respect: a) In the 19th century, George Boole's project to unify logic, language, thought and algebra (continuing Leibniz's dream in this respect) was only partially realized (An investigation in the laws of thought, on which are founded the mathematical theories of logic and probabilities, 1854) and it prepared the way for similar projects in the 20th century; b) Claude Shannon, in his master's thesis (A symbolic analysis of relay and switching circuits) submitted in 1937, only one year after Turing published his famous Non-computable..., proved the isomorphism between logic and electrical circuits; c) Niels Bohr, in his philosophical writings, developed the idea according to which the sphere of competence of the human language is limited to the macroscopic universe; see, in this respect, [5]. Putting together all these facts, we get an image of the strong limitations that our sensations, our intuitions, our logic and our language have to obey. We can put all these things in a more complete statement: The following restrictions are mutually equivalent: to be macroscopic; to be Euclidean (i.e. to adopt the parallel axiom in the way we represent space and spatial relations); to be Galileo-Newtonian in the way we represent motion, time and energy; to capture the surrounding and to act according to our sensorial-intuitive perception of reality; to use and to represent language, in both its natural and artificial variants (moreover, to use human semiosis in all its manifestations).

So a natural sequence emerges, having Leibniz, Boole, Bohr, Turing, Shannon, McCullogh-Pitts and von Neumann as successive steps. It tells us the idea of the unity of human knowledge, the unifying trend bringing in the same framework logic, language, thought and algebra. But we have here only the discrete aspects, while von Neumann wanted much more.

3   John von Neumann's Brain - von Neumann's Unification: Formal Logic + Mathematical Analysis + Thermodynamic Error

It was only too fitting for von Neumann to study the most inspiring automaton of all: the brain. "Our thoughts ... mostly focused on the subject of neurology, and more specifically on the human nervous system, and there primarily on the central nervous system. Thus in trying to understand the function of the automata and the general principles governing them, we selected for prompt action the most complicated object under the sun - literally."

His theory of building reliable organs from unreliable components and the associated probabilistic logics was focused on modeling system errors in biological cells, central nervous systems cells in particular. His research program aimed boldly at the unification of the "most refractory" and "rigid" formal logic (discrete math) with the "best cultivated" mathematical analysis (continuous math) proposals via a concept of thermodynamic error. "It is the author's conviction, voiced over many years, that error should be treated by thermodynamical methods, and be the subject of a thermodynamical theory, as information has been, by the work of L. Szilard and C. E. Shannon." Turing also uses thermodynamics arguments in dealing with errors in computing machines. For von Neumann this was at the core of a theory of information processing for the biological cell, the nervous system and the brain. The error model was given the latitude to approximate and therefore was not an explicit model of "the more complicated aspects of neuron functioning: threshold, temporal summation, relative inhibition, changes of the threshold by aftereffects of stimulation beyond synaptic delay, etc." He proposed two models of error. One, concrete - ala Weiner and Shannon "error is noise" where in every operation the organ will fail to function correctly in a statistically independent way with respect with the state of the network, i.e. with "the (precise) probability epsilon" and another one, more realistic assuming an unspecified dependence of the errors on the network and among them. For detailing the dependence to the general state of the network, more needed to be known about the biological "microscopic" mechanism, about which von Neumann was growing increasingly frustrated since technology had not yet advanced to the point necessary. Indeed, it is here where molecular biology developments since von Neumann's time could bring the next well-defined concepts of errors that would satisfy his axioms. He managed in the paper to prove a constructive version of biological channel "capacity" that Shannon could only prove nonconstructively.

In a 1946 letter to Norbert Wiener, von Neumann expresses his unhappiness with the results of "Turing-cum-Pitts-and-McCulloch:"

"What seems worth emphasizing to me is, however, that after the great positive contribution of Turing-cum-Pitts-and-McCulloch is assimilated, the situation is rather worse than before. Indeed, these authors have demonstrated in absolute and hopeless generality that anything and everything Browerian can be done by an appropriate mechanism, and specifically by a neural mechanism - and that even one, definite mechanism can be 'universal.' Inverting the argument: Nothing that we may know or learn about the functioning of the organism can give, without 'microscopic,' cytological work any clues regarding the further details of neural mechanism ... I think you will feel with me the type of frustration that I am trying to express."

He expresses skepticism that neurological methods would help in understanding the brain as much as experimenting with a fire hose on a computing machine. "Besides the system is not even purely digital (i.e. neural): It is intimately connected to a very complex analogy (i.e. humoral or hormonal) system, and almost every feedback loop goes through both sectors, if not through the 'outside' world (i.e. the world outside the epidermis or within the digestive system) as well. And it contains, even in its digital part, a million times more units than the ENIAC."

Another basic idea in von Neumann's writings is related to the analog-digital distinction and to the fact that the noise level is strongly inferior in digital machines than in the analog ones. However, in living organisms both analog and digital aspects are essential, and von Neumann indicates the contrast between the digital nature of the central nervous system and the analog aspect of the humoral system. To capture the novelty of these considerations, we have to point out several aspects. The analog-digital distinction is a particular form of the more general distinction between discreteness and continuity. In mathematics, the use of expressions such as discrete mathematics and continuous mathematics became frequent only in the second half of the 20th century, in contrast with other fields, such as biology, psychology and linguistics, where the discrete-continuous distinction appeared earlier. The famous mind-body problem considered by Leibniz is just the expression of the dual discrete-continuous nature of the human being. Leibniz is announcing both the computing era, by his digital codification, and the theory of dynamical systems as a framework of the mathematical model of the human body.

4 "You Would Certainly Say That Watson and Crick Depended on von Neumann"

Nobel laureate Sydney Brenner talks about von Neumann as one of his heroes in his memoir, [2]. Brenner was a close collaborator with Francis Crick. These reflections and story are possibly the greatest mathematical insight of all times for biology. That qualifies von Neumann as a prophet.

Freeman Dyson noted that what today's high school students learn about DNA is what von Neumann discovered purely by mathematics.

Brenner recalls a symposium titled "The Hixton Symposium on Cerebral Mechanism in Behaviour," held in Pasadena, California, in 1948. "The symposium was published in 1951, and in this book was a very famous paper by John von Neumann, which few people have read. The brilliant part of his paper in the Hixton Symposium is his description of what it takes to make a self-reproducing machine. Von Neumann shows that you have to have a mechanism for not only copying the machine, but copying the information that specifies the machine. So he divided - the automaton as he called it - into three components: the functional part of the automaton; a decoding section which actually takes a tape, reads the instructions and builds the automaton; and a device that takes a copy of this tape and inserts it into the new automaton.

"Now this was published in 1951, and I read it a year later in 1952. But we know from later work that these ideas were first put forward by him in the late 1940s. ... It is one of the ironies of the entire field that were you to write a history of ideas of the whole DNA, simply from the documented information as it exists in the literature - that is, a kind of Hegelian history of ideas - you would certainly say that Watson and Crick depended on von Neumann, because von Neumann essentially tells you how it's done. But of course no one knew anything about the other. It's a great paradox to me that in fact this connection was not seen."

He claims that von Neumann made him see "what I have come to call this 'Schrödinger's fundamental error' in his famous book *What is Life?* When asked who are his scientific heroes he lists three names. 'There are many people whom I admire, both people I've known and whom I've read about. Von Neumann is a great hero to me, because he seemed to have something special. Of course it may be envy rather than admiration, but it's good to envy someone like von Neumann.' " The other two names in his heroes list: Francis Crick and Leo Szilard.

5   Turing's Brain and the Most Important Paper in Computer Science

"The exactness of mathematics is well illustrated by proofs of impossibility. When asserting that doubling the cube ... is impossible, the statement does not merely refer to a temporary limitation of human ability to perform this feat. It goes far beyond this, for it proclaims that never, no matter what, will anybody ever be able to [double the cube]. No other science, or for that matter no other discipline of human endeavor, can even contemplate anything of such finality."

- Mark Kac and Stan Ulam, 1968

Turing's seminal paper solved Hilbert's Entscheidungsproblem (decision problem) in the negative. After Gödel's first hit to Hilbert's program to find a mechanical process for deciding whether a theorem is true or false in a given axiomatic system, Turing provided the second hit, effectively terminating Hilbert's program.

Papers with negative results as such Turing's are the most impressive and deep in mathematics. To understand the magnitude of Turing's challenge to prove mathematically "such finality," one has to rule out "everything," and this needed a definition of what a most general "mechanical process" is, i.e., a machine that could compute "everything" that is computable. In turn, the Turing machine was one of the most positive and powerful results in mathematics. The computer era, with Turing and von Neumann as founding fathers, had this paper with negative-and-positive results of greatest depth possible as its foundation. For both von Neumann and Turing, mathematical proof was a philosophy of how truth is won. In discovering it, they possessed a power almost unequaled by mathematicians of any era.

6   From Universal Turing Machine to Universal Grammar

Universality is an important concept in mathematics, in computer science, in linguistics, in philosophy. There are universal sets in set theory and topology, universal functions in mathematical analysis, universal recursive functions in logic, universal grammars in linguistics.

According to a long tradition that originated with Roger Bacon and endures still, awareness of an idea of a universal grammar came from multiple directions – Joseph Greenberg [6] and Noam Chomsky [4] sought universals of natural languages; Richard Montague [11] for universals of all human languages, be they natural or artificial. In the theory of formal languages and grammars, results outline in what conditions universality is possible in the field of context free languages, of context sensitive languages, of recursively enumerable languages (Takumi Kasai [8], Sheila Greibach [7], Grzegorz Rozenberg [15]).

Each of these types of universal grammars can be used to obtain a specific cognitive model of the brain activity; it concerns not only language, but any learning process. The potential connection between universal Turing machines and the nervous system is approached just towards the end of CB, at the moment when von Neumann had to stop his work, defeated by his cancer. We are pushed to imagine possible continuations, but we cannot help but consider ideas, results, theories which did no yet exist at the moment of his death. A joint paper with Cristian Calude and Gheorghe Păun [3] adopted the assumption according to which any type of human or social competence is based on our linguistic generative competence. This assumption was motivated in a previous paper, see [9] The generative linguistic nature of most human competences may be interpreted as a hypothesis about the way our brain works. But it is more than this, because nature and society seem to be based on similar generative devices.

It seems to be more realistic to look for a metaphorical brain (see [1]), giving an a posteriori explanation of various creative processes. But, for Arbib, the metaphorical brain is just the computer. Other authors speak of artificial brains; see [14].

Our aim is to explain how so many human competences, i.e. so many grammars, find a place in our brain, how we successfully identify the grammar we need and, after this, how we return it to its previous place for use again when necessary. An adequate alternation of actualizations and potentialisations needs a hyper-grammar. For instance, if we know several languages, at each moment only one of them does, it is actualized, all the other are only, they remain only in a potential stage. We are looking for a hyper-competence, i.e. a universal competence, a competence of the second order, whose role is just to manage, to activate at each moment the right individual competence. This is *the universal grammar as a hypothetical brain*, appearing in the title of our joint paper.

Behind this strategy is the philosophy according to which any human action is the result of the activity of a generative machine, defining a specific human competence, while the particular result of this process is the corresponding performance. Chomsky used the slogan "linguistics is a branch of cognitive psychology." Learning processes are the result of the interaction among the innate and the acquired factors, in contrast with the traditional view, seeing these processes only as the interaction among stimuli and responses to them. The historical debate organized in 1979 between Chomsky and Piaget aimed just to make the point in this respect (see [13]). With respect to the claim formulated by von Neumann on page 82 in his final book - "The logics and mathematics in the central nervous system, when viewed as languages, must structurally be essentially different from those languages to which our common experience refers" – it seems that the prevalent view today, at least in the field of linguistics, is to replace the strong requirement asking for the grammar of the brain by the weak requirement asking for a grammar whose result is similar to that of the brain. In the first case, the form of the generative rules should be iconic images of the operations taking place in the brain; in the second case, this strong requirement, for which there is little evidence in the existing experiments, is replaced with the less demanding requirement that the result of the grammar is similar to the result of the brain activity. Chomsky never claimed that the regular, the context free and the context sensitive rules have their correspondent in the brain's activity, despite the fact that he imagined the architecture of his grammars having as term of reference the grammatical needs of natural languages. No such claims were formulated with respect to other generative devices used in logic or in computer science.

An idea emerging frequently in his writings is clearly expressed in GLTA (p. 526-527): "Natural organisms are, as a rule, much more complicated and subtle, and therefore much less understood in detail, than artificial automata." The highest complexity is realized by the human central nervous system. We can approach it by decomposing it in various parts and by analyzing each part (component) on its own. Physics, chemistry and, in a near future, quantum mechanics are involved here, believed von Neumann. But for the mathematician and the logician, the data of the first step can be organized in a system of axioms, adopting for each component the representation as a black-box metaphor used in Norbert Wiener's cybernetics. Then, in a second step, we try to understand how these different components interact as a whole and how the functioning of the whole is obtained by the right interaction of the components. While the first step is just here, logic and mathematics are at home.

References

1. Arbib, M.: The Metaphorical Brain: An Introduction to Cybernetics as Artificial Intelligence and Brain Theory. Wiley-Interscience, New York (1972)
2. Brenner, S.: My Life in Science. BioMed Central Limited, London (2001)
3. Calude, C., Marcus, S., Păun, G.: The Universal Grammar as a Hypothetical Brain. Revue Roumaine de Linguistique 24, 479–489 (1979)
4. Chomsky, N.: Aspects of the Theory of Syntax. MIT Press (1965)
5. Favrholdt, D.: Niels Bohr's Views Concerning Language. Semiotica 94, 5–34 (1993)
6. Greenberg, J.: Language Universals. The Hague, Mouton (1966)
7. Greibach, S.A.: Comments on Universal and Left Universal Grammars, Context-Sensitive Languages, and Context-Free Grammar Forms. Information and Control 39, 135–142 (1978)
8. Kasai, T.: A Universal Context-Free Grammar. Information and Control 28, 30–34 (1975)
9. Marcus, S.: Linguistics as a Pilot Science. In: Sebeok, T.A. (ed.) Current Trends in Linguistics, vol. XII, pp. 2871–2887. The Hague-Paris, Mouton (1974)
10. McCullogh, W., Pitts, W.: A Logical Calculus of the Ideas Imminent in Nervous Activity. Bull. Math. Biophysics 5, 115–133 (1943)
11. Montague, R.: Formal Philosophy (1974)
12. von Neumann, J.: The Mathematician. In: Heywood, R.R. (ed.) The Works of the Mind, pp. 180–196. University of Chicago Press (1947)
13. Piatelli-Palmarini, M. (ed.): Language and Learning. The Debate between Jean Piaget and Noam Chomsky. Harvard University Press, Cambridge (1980)
14. Ramacher, U., von der Malsburg, C. (eds.): On the Construction of Artificial Brains. Springer, Heidelberg (2010)
15. Rozenberg, G.: A Note on Universal Grammars. Information and Control 34, 172–175 (1977)
16. Turing digital archive, http://www.turingarchive.org/browse.php/D/5

Turing's Three Pioneering Initiatives and Their Interplays

Jozef Kelemen

Institute of Computer Science, and IT4I Institute
Silesian University, Opava, Czech Republic
and School of Management, Bratislava, Slovak Republic
kelemen@fpf.slu.cz

Abstract. The purpose of this article is to recall three fundamental contributions by A. M. Turing to three important fields of contemporary science and engineering (theory of computation, artificial intelligence, and biocomputing), and to emphasize the connections between them. The article recalls and formulates resp., also three hypotheses related to the three initiatives and discusses in short their mutual interrelatedness.

1   Introduction

The dramatic increase of the use of machines which did physical work begun during the 19th century. The industrial revolution of the 19th century accelerated during the 20th century owing to the machines intended for information processing. From a larger perspective, considering human-machine relationship, we can nominate the emergence of cybernetics as a turning point dividing the history of this relationship to before- and after- cybernetic period. In the before-cybernetic period, technology was generally understood in terms of mechanics and power interchange. Cybernetics and few years later in parallel with it the field of computers and a little later the field of computer science, technology, and engineering brought significant alteration into human attitudes and feelings toward machines. Human-machine relationship is since the turning option of cybernetics understood as a kind of research of communication, interaction, and information representation, acquisition, and sharing. This technical developmental step encouraged by the few years earlier activities in the field of mathematics brings about dramatic scientific as well as social and cultural changes, and considerably influenced also the self-image of the western mankind. One among the men who started with mathematical study of computability already before the construction of the first computers (in the meaning of the 20th century understanding) was Alan M. Turing.

The purpose of this article is to remind Turing's three fundamental contributions to three important fields of contemporary science and engineering - to the theory of computation, to the field of artificial intelligence, and to first approaches to set up formal models of the biological reality. All these contributions are vivid up to now in science. However, because the listed fields are mutually

E. Csuhaj-Varjú et al. (Eds.): CMC 2012, LNCS 7762, pp. 36–46, 2013.

relatively distant, the interplays between the contributions made by Turing to them remain often out of discussions. As its central goal this article tries to make these connections more distinct.

The first Turing's fundamental contribution is the proposal of the first abstract formal model of a computing machine, called the a-machine in Turing's original article [13], and renamed later by Alonzo Church - who has also inspired in his research, similarly as Turing, by the so called Entscheidungsproblem formulated by David Hilbert in 1900, and solved by Yuri Matiyasevich in 1970, presented during a conference in Bucharest, 1971, and published in [8] - to the generally accepted *Turing machine* of the present times.

The second fundamental contribution is the Turing's proposal to use the so called imitation game as a base for testing the level of intelligence of the computers through comparison with the human level intelligence [15] known in the literature on Artificial Intelligence of our times as the *Turing test*.

The third Turing's initiatives we will deal with in the present contribution is his attempt to construct a precise mathematical model of the biochemical process of *morphogenesis* [16] treated as an important problem up to now.

We will try to show that there is possible to find some perhaps interesting interplay between the three above mentioned Turing's initiatives, and will give some arguments for supporting that proposition. We remind also three hypotheses related to the three initiatives, and discuss in short their mutual interrelatedness.

2 The Machine and Turing's 1st Hypothesis

As it was mentioned above, the machinery called now as the Turing machine and forming the headstone of the present days theory of computation, and in certain sense of the all theoretical computer science has been introduced in [13] under the name *a-machine* (staying for the *abstract machine*) and particularized in the corrections of the previously mentioned publication in [14]. The original definition of the a-machine is rather different from the present days definitions, but its basic idea remains unchanged. This actual definition of the Turing machine can be found practically in all of the present days textbooks or monographs related to theory of computation. The basic idea is in an acceptable form but sketched relatively informally also in the Wikipedia from where we recall the definition of the Turing machine[1]:

"A Turing machine consists of:

A *tape* which is divided into cells, one next to the other. Each cell contains a symbol from some finite alphabet. The alphabet contains a special *blank* symbol (here written as 'B') and one or more other symbols. The tape is assumed to be arbitrarily extendable to the left and to the right, i.e., the Turing machine is always supplied with as much tape as it needs for its computation. Cells that have not been written are assumed to be filled with the blank symbol. In some

---

[1] See http://en.wikipedia.org/wiki/Turing_machine (January 22, 2012). For a more precise and slightly understandable definition see e.g. [11] or the old but gold [6].

models the tape has a left end marked with a special symbol; the tape extends or is indefinitely extensible to the right.

A *head* that can read and write symbols on the tape and move the tape left and right one (and only one) cell at a time. In some models the head moves and the tape is stationary.

A finite *table* (occasionally called an *action table* or *transition function*) of instructions (usually quintuples [5-tuples] : $q_i a_j \leftarrow q_{i1} a_{j1} d_k$, but sometimes 4-tuples) that, given the state(q_i) the machine is currently in *and* the *symbol*(a_j) it is reading on the tape (symbol currently under the head) tells the machine to do the following in sequence (for the 5-tuple models):

Either erase or write a symbol (instead of a_j, write a_{j1}), and then move the head (which is described by d_k and can have values: 'L' for one step left or 'R' for one step right or 'N' for staying in the same place), and then assume the same or a new state as prescribed (go to state q_{i1}).

In the 4-tuple models, erase or write a symbol (a_{j1}) and move the head left or right (d_k) are specified as separate instructions. Specifically, the table tells the machine to (ia) erase or write a symbol *or* (ib) move the head left or right, *and then* (ii) assume the same or a new state as prescribed, but not both actions (ia) and (ib) in the same instruction. In some models, if there is no entry in the table for the current combination of symbol and state then the machine will halt; other models require all entries to be filled.

A *state register* that stores the state of the Turing machine, one of finitely many. There is one special *start state* with which the state register is initialized. These states, writes Turing, replace the "state of mind" a person performing computations would ordinarily be in.

Note that every part of the machine-its state and symbol-collections-and its actions-printing, erasing and tape motion-is *finite*, *discrete* and *distinguishable*; it is the potentially unlimited amount of tape that gives it an unbounded amount of storage space."

Let us mention that the original definition of the a-machine has been invented in order to make mathematically as precise as possible the notion of computability, especially in connection with the computability of real numbers, and making possible to answer the question on deciding whether all of the real numbers are computable in certain constructive way as results of some algorithm or not. The Turing's effort to define mathematically precisely the meaning of the algorithm led him top the concept of the abstract computing machine. The Turing's own explanation concerning that from the early beginning of [13] is the following:

"The 'computable' numbers may be described briefly as the real numbers whose expressions as a decimal are calculable by finite means. Although the subject of this paper is ostensibly the computable *numbers*, it is almost equally easy to define and investigate computable functions of an integral variable or a real or computable variable, computable predicates, and so forth. The fundamental problems involved are, however, the same in each case, and I have chosen the computable numbers for explicit treatment as involving the least cumbrous technique. I hope shortly to give an account of the relations of the computable

numbers, functions, and so forth to one another. This will include a development
of the theory of functions of a real variable expressed in terms of computable
numbers. According to my definition, a number is computable if its decimal can
be written down by a machine."

In [13] a very important statement is proved, too: It is possible to invent
(in a constructive way) a single a-machine which can be used to compute any
computable numbers (more generally, any sequence of symbols). If this machine,
say I, is supplied with a tape on the beginning of which is written the so called
standard description of some computing machine, say M, then the machine I
will compute the same sequence as M, outlined Turing the idea in [13].

However from our perspective with respect to the next section contents will
have a key importance the observations, made in [13] concerning the generalization of the meaning of computability of numbers to other mathematical objects,
too. Although his subject is ostensibly the computable numbers, it is, citing from
[13] "... almost equally easy to define and investigate computable functions of an
integral variables or a real or computable variable, computable predicates, and
so forth." In this way the approach is general in the sense that it makes possible
to divide all mathematically definable functions into two classes with respect to
their computability by appropriate Turing machines or, more generally, by the
mentioned above universal Turing machine.

Shortly after the proposal of the formal model of the universal digital computer - the Turing machine - Alonzo Church who was deeply interested in the
theory of computability, too, formulated a hypothesis called today as the *Church-
Turing hypothesis* or simply the *Turing hypothesis*. In the core of it stays the
question 'Whether or not are all imaginable computations transformable into the
form of computations executable by Turing machines?' The hypothesized answer
is: "Whatever can be calculated by a machine (working on finite data in accordance with a finite program of instructions) is Turing-machine-computable". One
among the informal definitions of the thesis has been formulated personally by
Turing: "The idea behind digital computers may be explained by saying that
these machines are intended to carry out any operations which could be done
by a human computer" [15][2].

3   A Small Comment to the 1st Turing Hypothesis

In the cases of above mentioned model, and more generally, in all the cases when
our formal models are built on the conceptual base of rule governed symbol ma-
nipulating conceptual devices like formal grammars and languages, for instance,
the rules governing the dynamics of the behavior of agent-like entities are described in the form of rewriting rules. This formulation defines, in fact (trivially
simple, but it is not a disadvantage!) agents: Each rule has its own sensor capacity (to sense the appearance of its left-hand side string), and an action capacity
to make a change in its environment (to rewrite the sensed pattern to the string

---

[2] More about the thesis see e.g. in
http://plato.stanford.edu/entries/church-turing/.

defined by the rule's right-hand side). The ways of rules interactions are specified by different derivation modes and rewriting regulations.

This is, at least from the methodological point of view, a fundamental advantage. We know very well, that some specific multi-agent systems (formal grammars) define very well-specified behaviors (formal languages) with very interesting relation to different models of computation (to different types of automata) which have very important relations to real engineered (computing) machines. What we do not know, it is the answer to the question of the universality of the approach accepted for describing languages (behaviors). What kind of behaviors are we able to describe using the just described framework behind the Turing-computable ones?

In this Section we will - following argumentations from [7] - sketch a our formal model of a system based on formal grammars with functional components producing a rule-governed Turing-computable behaviors each, but producing - as a whole - a behavior which does not be generated traditionally by any Turing-equivalent generative device, so which requires the generative power of hyper-computation. So, we will consider the so-called eco-grammar systems. First, we introduce in a few words this model, presented originally in [4].

According [4], an *eco-grammar system* Σ consists, roughly speaking, of

- a finite alphabet V,
- a fixed number (say n) of components evolving according sets of rules P_1, $P_2, \ldots, P_n$ applied in a parallel way as it is usual in L-systems [10], and of
- an environment of the form of a finite string over V (the states of the environment are described by strings of symbols w_E, the initial one by w_0).
- the functions φ and ψ which define the influence of the environment and the influence of other components, respectively, to the components (these functions will be supposed in the following as playing no roles, and will not be considered in the model of eco-grammar systems as treated in this article).

The rules of components depend, in general, on the state (on the just existing form of the string) of the environment. The particular components act in the commonly shared environment by sets of sequential rewriting rules R_1, R_2, $\ldots$, R_n. The environment itself evolves according a set P_E of rewriting rules applied in parallel as in L systems[3].

The evolution rules of the environment are independent on components' states and of the state of the environment itself. The components' actions have priority over the evolution rules of the environment. In a given time unit, exactly those symbols of the environment that are not affected by the action of any agent are rewritten.

In the EG-systems we assume the existence of the so-called *universal clock* that marks time units, the same for all components and for the environment, and according to which the evolution of the components and of the environment is considered.

---

[3] So, the triplet (V, P_E, w_E) is (and works as) a Lindenmayer-system.

In [17] a variant of EG-systems without internal states of components is proposed and studied. The fixed number of components of the so called teams of components in EG systems originally proposed in [5] is replaced by a dynamically changing number of components in teams. As the mechanism of reconfiguration, a function, say f, is defined on the set N of integers with values in the set $\{0, 1, 2, \ldots, n\}$ (where n is the number of components in the corresponding EG-system) in order to define the number of components in teams. For the i-th step of the work of the given EG-system, the function f relates a number $f(i) \in \{0, 1, 2, \ldots, n\}$. The subset of the set of all components of thus EG-system of the cardinality $f(i)$ is then selected for executing the next derivation step of the EG system working with Wätjen-type teams. So, Wtjen, roughly speaking, proved that there exist EG-systems such that if f is (in the traditional sense) non-recursive function, then the corresponding EG-system generates a non-recursive (in fact a super-recursive) language.

The *emergent nature* of the behavior (language) generated by the above described EG system is - applying the above mentioned test of emergence - rather clear: The components of a given EG system generate *recursive languages* each, the local interactions of the components are given only and, *surprisingly*, the whole system generates a non-recursive language (behavior).

4   The Turing Test and the 2nd Hypothesis

"I propose to consider the question, 'Can machines think?' This should begin with definitions of the meaning of the terms 'machine' and 'think'. The definitions might be framed so as to reflect so far as possible the normal use of the words, but this attitude is dangerous. If the meaning of the words 'machine' and 'think 'are to be found by examining how they are commonly used it is difficult to escape the conclusion that the meaning and the answer to the question, 'Can machines think?' is to be sought in a statistical survey such as a Gallup poll. But this is absurd. Instead of attempting such a definition I shall replace the question by another, which is closely related to it and is expressed in relatively unambiguous words".

This is the first paragraph of Turing's fundamental paper originated after his participation at the Manchester University discussion on the mind and computing machines of the philosophy seminar chaired by Dorothy Emmet in October 27, 1949. Turing has been dissatisfied by his own argumentation against the arguments of colleagues like Michael Polanyi, neurophysiologist J. Z. Young, and mathematician Max H. A. Newman, for instance. Turing early after the discussion started to write an article devoted to the topic and published it as [15]. The question 'Can machines think' he replaced by the new question described in terms of a game he called them the 'imitation game' as follows:

The game "... is played with three people, a man (A), a woman (B), and an interrogator (C) who may be of either sex. The interrogator stays in a room apart from the other two. The object of the game for the interrogator is to determine which of the other two is the man and which is the woman. He knows them by labels X and Y, and at the end of the game he says either 'X is A and Y is B' or 'X is B and Y is A'. The interrogator is allowed to put questions to A and B thus:

C: Will X please tell me the length of his or her hair?

Now suppose X is actually A, then A must answer. It is A's object in the game to try and cause C to make the wrong identification. His answer might therefore be

'My hair is shingled, and the longest strands, are about nine inches long.'

In order that tones of voice may not help the interrogator the answers should be written, or better still, typewritten. The ideal arrangement is to have a teleprinter communicating between the two rooms. Alternatively the question and answers can be repeated by an intermediary. The object of the game for the third player (B) is to help the interrogator. The best strategy for her is probably to give truthful answers. She can add such things as 'I am the woman, don't listen to him!' to her answers, but it will avail nothing as the man can make similar remarks.

We now ask the question, 'What will happen when a machine takes the part of A in this game?' Will the interrogator decide wrongly as often when the game is played like this as he does when the game is played between a man and a woman? These questions replace our original, 'Can machines think?' Then the article in Section 3 co continues with determining the meaning of the computer. Turing refers to the circumstances concerning the computer he has in his mind. Turing writes:

"It is natural that we should wish to permit every kind of engineering technique to be used in our machines. We also wish to allow the possibility than an engineer or team of engineers may construct a machine which works, but whose manner of operation cannot be satisfactorily described by its constructors because they have applied a method which is largely experimental. Finally, we wish to exclude from the machines men born in the usual manner". Following the previous suggestions he concludes that only digital computers are permitted to take part in his imitation game. In connection to the digital computers he refers as to the historically first machines of such type to Charles Babbage, who, according the Turing remark at the end of the Chapter 4 of [15] has planned (but never constructed) such a machine - the so called *analytical engine*.

Concerning digital computers he emphasizes that the idea behind them may be explained by saying that this type of machines are intended to carry out any operations which could be done by a human computer who is supposed to be following fixed rules as "supplied in a book" and he (the *human* computer, sic!) has no authority to deviate from them in any detail. With respect to digital computers he emphasizes that they are regarded as consisting of three basic architectural components: *the store* (the memory in today's terminology), *the executive unit* (the processor in the today's terminology), and *the control* (the program in the today's wording).

In Section 5 of [15] the universality of the digital computer is discussed with only small references to the formal model proposed in [13], and without any reference to the formalized notion of the universal a-machine. However, he mentioned, informally and without referring to the formally precise definition or the corresponding proof to the universality of the digital computers. But this remark evokes more the idea of a really existing hardware rather than of an abstract, formalized device. After that Turing reformulates his original question 'Can machines think?' into the equivalent form of 'Are there imaginable digital computers which would do well in the imitation game?'.

Let us turn off the Turing's original flow of argumentation in this moment, and focus to the formalized meaning of the universal Turing machine and to its capacity to compute any Turing-computable functions in the sense sketched in the previous Section of the present article. The last formulated question then looks like follows: "Are there imaginable a system of Turing-computable functions (a mutually interconnected system of such functions of this property, so a composed function) which would do well in the imitation game?" But having in the mind of the universality property of digital computer, we have the question in the form from the end of the Chapter 5 if [15]: "Let us fix our attention on one particular digital computer C. Is it true that by modifying this computer to have an adequate storage, suitably increasing its speed of action, and providing it with an appropriate program, C can be made to play satisfactorily the part of A in the imitation game, the part of B being taken by a man?"

We can conclude that the Turing machine and the Turing test are strongly connected in this point which emphasized the deep strong connection not only between computer programming and the field of Artificial Intelligence, but also the similar connection between the theory of abstract computing devices and the research in the field of artificial intelligence. The above formulated original questions might be reformulated into a more general form of *'Be the human intelligence transformable to the form of any Turing-computable (interconnected system of) functions?'* Let us call this question as the core of the 2nd Turing hypothesis.

5   Morphogenesis and Turing's 3rd Hypothesis

The purpose of [16] is to discuss a possible mechanism by which the genes of a zygote may determine the anatomical structure of the resulting organism. The theory, according Turing's words, does not make any new hypotheses. It merely suggests only that certain well-known physical laws are sufficient to account for many of the facts. Continuing in the station of the abstract of [16] we read that 'it is suggested that a system of chemical substances, called morphogens, reacting together and diffusing through a tissue, is adequate to account for the main phenomena of morphogenesis' and that 'A system of reactions and diffusion on a sphere is also considered.' This first look to the abstract is sufficient for strengthen our conviction that the article contains some pioneering steps in the field developed today e.g. in the frame of so called membrane computing or molecular computing. So let us focus our attention to [16] form the position of bio-inspired computation, ore specifically form the standpoint of membrane computing.

'The theory which has been developed here', resumes Turing the [16] 'depends essentially on the assumption that the reaction rates are linear functions of the concentrations, an assumption which is justifiable in the case of a system just beginning to leave a homogeneous condition. Such systems certainly have a special interest as giving the first appearance of a pattern, but they are, he point out, the exception rather than the rule. Most of an organism, most of the time, is developing from one pattern into another, rather than from homogeneity into a pattern. One would like to be able to follow this more general process mathematically also. The difficulties are, however, such that one cannot hope to have any very embracing *theory* of such processes, beyond the statement of the equations. It might be possible, however, to treat a few particular cases in detail with the aid of a digital computer.'

Turing recognizes two basic possibilities of how the digital computer might make useful for the research of some biochemical phenomena: First, he suppose that computer simulations might allow simplifying assumptions required if we decide to use another approaches to the formal study. Second, he recognizes the approaches which use computer simulations make possible to take the "mechanical" aspects of the modeled reality into account during the study. Moreover, he add a very short but from today perspective important comment to the previously mentioned advantages writing: 'Even with the (. . .) problem, considered in this paper, for which a reasonably complete mathematical analysis was possible, the computational treatment of a particular case was most illuminating' [16].

The proposal to be interested in computational aspects of chemical and biological structures and processes, and becomes into the focus of many of present days research activities. As an example from the large spectrum of approaches we mention as an example the so called *membrane computing paradigm* presented in [9]. Păun characterizes the membrane systems - the basic computing machinery of the membrane computing) as a ". . . distributed parallel computing devices, processing multisets of objects, synchronously, in the compartments delimited by a membrane structure. The objects, which correspond to chemicals evolving in the compartments of a cell, can also pass through membranes. The membranes form a hierarchical structure - they can be dissolved, divided, created, and their permeability can be modified. A sequence of transitions between configurations of a system forms a computation." The monograph [9] form the Preface of which we cited the previous lines contains tens of theorems concerning the computational power of different variations of the membrane systems in comparison with the different computing models (more often formal grammars) but also with the (universal) Turing Machine. The result proves the existence of certain variations of membrane systems which are equivalent with the Turing Machine with respect their computational power.

In the consequence of that and from the perspective followed in this contribution we can conclude the third version of the Turing hypothesis, the 3rd *Turing*

Hypothesis and formulate it in the following form, for instance: Biochemical systems are able - at list in principle - perform all computations performable by the universal Turing Machine.

This hypothesis competes in certain sense our speculations providing a possibility for us to mention the surprising conclusions: The computation as defined by the universal Turing Machine, the human ability to perform intellectual tasks, and the nature of biochemical (living) systems are in their certain their capacities (almost) identical. The computation, mind, and life are in certain sense the same phenomena... Can it be true? In what sense?

6   A Short End-Note

This contribution proposed a sketch of an integrative view of the three basic initiatives made by Alan M. Turing to the development of the 20th Century origin of the theoretical computer science in mathematics, and to the development of computationally influenced researches during the past decades. The integrative power lies in the formulation of the so called Church-Turing Thesis on the generality of the Turing machines end their supervalence or equivalence with other computing devices proposed up to now, and in the showed possibility to formulate other two hypotheses which make a bridge between theoretical study of computation, and fields like artificial intelligence - in which the classical Turing test can be formulated as a variation of the Church-Turing Thesis - and artificial life (natural computing), where the third proposed variation guides to the hypothesis that computational models of the processes and phenomena taking place in the living organisms require also nothing more general than the Turing Machine can provide for modeling them formally.

Acknowledgment. This contribution has been partially supported by the project IT4Innovations Centre of Excellence, reg. no. CZ.1.05/1.1.00/02.0070, and sponsored by the Research and Development for Innovations Operational Program from the Structural Funds of the European Union, and from the state budget of the Czech Republic. The author thanks for the continuous support also to the Gratex International, Slovakia.

References

1. Burgin, M., Klinger, A.: Three aspects of super-recursive algorithms and hypercomputation or finding black swans. Theoretical Computer Science 317, 1–11 (2004)
2. Church, A.: A note on the Entscheidungsproblem. Journal of Symbolic Logic 1, 40–41 (1930)
3. Church, A.: An unsolvable problem of elementary number theory. American Journal of Mathematics 58, 345–363 (1936)
4. Csuhaj-Varjú, E., et al.: Grammar Systems. Gordon and Breach, Yverdon (1994)

5. Csuhaj-Varjú, E., Kelemenová, A.: Team behavior in eco-grammar systems. Theoretical Computer Science 209, 213–224 (1998)
6. Hopcroft, J.E., Ullman, J.D.: Formal Languages and their Relation to Automata. Addison-Wesley, Reading (1969)
7. Kelemen, J.: May Embodiment Cause Hyper-Computation? In: Capcarrère, M.S., Freitas, A.A., Bentley, P.J., Johnson, C.G., Timmis, J. (eds.) ECAL 2005. LNCS (LNAI), vol. 3630, pp. 31–36. Springer, Heidelberg (2005)
8. Matiyasevich, Y.: On recursive unsolvability of Hilbert's tenth problem. In: Proc. 4th International Congress on Logic, Methodology and Philosophy of Science, pp. 89–110. North-Holland, Amsterdam (1973)
9. Păun, G.: Membrane computing: An introduction. Springer, Berlin (2002)
10. Rozenberg, G., Salomaa, A.: The Mathematical Theory of L Systems. Academic Press, New York (1980)
11. Singh, A.: Elements of Computation Theory. Springer, London (2009)
12. Stannett, M.: Hypercomputational models. In: Teuscher, C. (ed.) Alan Turing - Life and Legacy of a Great Thinker, pp. 135–157. Springer (2004)
13. Turing, A.M.: On computable numbers, with an application to the Entscheidungsproblem. Proc. of the London Mathematical Society, series 2 42, 230–265 (1936)
14. Turing, A.M.: On computable numbers, with an application to the Entscheidungsproblem, a correction. Proc. of the London Mathematical Society, series 2 43, 544–546 (1937)
15. Turing, A.M.: Computing machinery and intelligence. Mind 59, 433–460 (1950)
16. Turing, A.M.: The chemical basis of morphogenesis. Philosophical Transactions of the Royal Society B 237, 37–72 (1952)
17. Wätjen, D.: Function-dependent teams in eco-grammar systems. Theoretical Computer Science 306, 39–53 (2003)

An Outline of MP Modeling Framework

Vincenzo Manca

University of Verona

Abstract. MP systems concepts will be revisited, in more general terms, by stressing their special role in solving dynamical inverse problems. Then, a main application of MP systems to Systems Biology will be outlined, which concerns gene expression in breast cancer (in cooperation with Karmanos Cancer Institute, Wayne State University, Detroit MI, USA). From recent experimental results developed at KCI, it follows that MP systems can provide "good" models of pathological phenomena, where good, in this case, means useful to oncologists. In fact, the MP systems methodology has identified previously unknown intermediaries in a breast cancer cell-specific signaling circuit. This could provide a significant contribution to the task of mapping complete oncogenic signaling networks to improve cancer treatments.

1 Introduction

The theory of MP systems (Metabolic P systems) started about fifteen years ago [22,40,2,3,4] as a discrete mathematical method for describing biological dynamics, inspired from P systems [46,47,48,9,49]. Algorithms, theorems, and software were developed for the analysis and simulation of many biological phenomena [31,6,23,24,25,26]. MP systems are easily described by MP graphs [29] (see Fig. 2) and in many aspects are resembling other discrete formalisms well developed and widely investigated (for example, Petri nets [50,51,8]). However, in MP systems the emphasis of their dynamics is focused on the transformation fluxes of reactions, seen as multiset rewriting rules. This dynamical perspective is related to ODE (Ordinary Differential Equation), which remains the mathematical framework of many approach in Systems biology [52], even in the stochastic and rule-based discrete methods [14,11]. In MP systems the fluxes of MP reactions replace derivatives of ODE models [12]. However, a peculiarity of MP systems is that they constitute a natural setting for expressing and systematically solving inverse dynamical problems, even when the mechanisms of observed phenomena are hard to be known [33,35,34,37,38,5]. This possibility was confirmed by many complex models that where developed within the MP theory, and compared with models already developed in literature [15,16,13,45,41,34,39,45,43,42].

Dynamical inverse problems were at the origin of differential models for planetary orbits. Their discrete formulations and solutions are crucial in many biological situations. A dynamical system is given by a set of real variables changing in time and a set of invariants, that is, conditions (constraints) which are satisfied by the variables during their change. Let us observe the variables of a (discrete) dynamical system along a number of (equally spaced) time points (steps). The sequences of these values constitute a set of time series representing the behavior of the observed system that we may know

E. Csuhaj-Varjú et al. (Eds.): CMC 2012, LNCS 7762, pp. 47–55, 2013.

in a very partial way (for example, only the stoichiometry of their reactions can be determined). We pose the following kind of **MP inverse dynamical problem**: "Can we determine an MP system with a dynamics reproducing the time series of the variables of a given system?" If this reconstruction is possible (even with some approximation), then we are able to infer an internal logic that is responsible of what we observe. Therefore, we can deduce a mechanism ruling the observed phenomenon, by passing from an "explicit" manifestation of the system to an "implicit" causation law. Here we remark that the solution of a dynamical inverse problem, as previously formulated, corresponds to a passage from an observed behavior appearing along time, to a framework of internal rules that obey a state logic. In conclusion, an MP reconstruction is the discovery of an MP grammar "inside" the system. Its determination may give, for example, hints about what to do for changing what is "wrong" in a given process.

A (generalized) MP grammar extends the previous definition given (with small differences) in [22-42]. It is defined by a set of MP rules over a set of variables plus some initial values of these variables. An MP rule consists of a reaction with an associated function, called regulator. A reaction such as $X \rightarrow Y$ transforms the variable X (metabolite, gene expression level, etc.) according to a flux, that is a quantity computed by its regulator which is subtracted to X and added to Y (for example, a number of molecules X are eliminated and the same number of molecules Y are introduced). In general, a reaction is constituted by left variables (decreasing) and right variables (increasing), separated by symbol $\rightarrow$, and each variable has a corresponding multiplicity. The regulator provides the flux of the reaction, in dependence of the values of some variables (called tuners of the rule). The flux of a rule, at any state of the system, defines the decrease of every (occurrence of) a left variable and, at same time, the increase of every (occurrence of) a right variable (in the case that a variable occurs with multiplicity k_1 on the left and k_2 on the right, then its increase/decrease is $k_2 - k_1$ times the value of the flux of the rule). Given an MP grammar, when we start from an initial state, by applying all the rules of the grammar, we obtain the next state, and so on, for all the subsequent steps. This notion of MP grammar suggests a new reading of MP letters, as initials of **Minus-Plus**, which clearly express the way MP rules work.

An MP grammar becomes an MP system when some numerical values are fixed for the physical interpretation of the time series: the time interval between two consecutive applications of rules, and other values related to the quantity units (depending on the physical nature of the variables). Variables which do not occur in reactions, but occur in regulators are called parameters. Therefore, given the time series of parameters (if they are present), an MP grammar is a discrete dynamical system that deterministically generates a time series for each variable (different from a parameter). The following definition is a generalization of the notion of MP grammar, previously developed for formalizing metabolic processes. In this general sense, its wide applicability provides the basis of an important methodology for solving many kinds of dynamical inverse problems in systems biology.

Definition 1 (Generalized MP Grammar). *A (generalized) MP grammar is a structure:*

$$(X, Y, R, X[0])$$

where ($\mathbb{N}, \mathbb{R}$ are the sets of natural and real numbers, respectively):

- X is a set of real **variables**;
- Y is a (possibly empty) subset of variables, called **parameters**. The elements of X/Y are also called **proper variables**;
- R is a set of MP **rules**, that is, pairs of type (**reaction, regulator**):

$$\alpha_r \to \beta_r \quad ; \quad \varphi_r.$$

For any $r \in R$, a reaction $\alpha_r \to \beta_r$ is a pair of multisets over the set X/Y of proper variables, and a regulator φ_r is a function from X-states to $\mathbb{R}$ (an X-state is a function from X to $\mathbb{R}$). Variables that are arguments of φ_r are the **tuners** of φ_r;

- $X[0] = (x[0] \mid x \in X)$ is an **initial state**, constituted by the values of variables at an initial time 0.

For any X-state s, and for any proper variable $x \in X/Y$, the rules determine a decrease-increase $\Delta_x(s)$ of x, according to the following formula (each reaction decreases any left occurrence of x and increases any right occurrence of x):

$$\Delta_x(s) = \sum_{r \in R} (\beta_r(x) - \alpha_r(x))\varphi_r(s). \tag{1}$$

($\alpha_r(x) = \beta_r(x) = 0$ if x does not occur in the reaction of r). Let us set, for every $i \in \mathbb{N}$:

$$X[i] = (x[i] \mid x \in X)$$

then, the (proper) variable variation (column) vector $\Delta[i]$ is given by (superscript T denotes matrix transposition):

$$\Delta[i] = (\Delta_x[i] \mid x \in X/Y)^T$$

therefore, if $\mathbb{A}$ is the **stoichiometric reaction matrix** (with proper variables as row indexes, and rules as column indexes):

$$\mathbb{A} = ((\beta_r(x) - \alpha_r(x)) \mid x \in X/Y, r \in R)$$

and the **flux** (column) **vector** is given by:

$$U[i] = (\varphi_r(X[i]) \mid r \in R)^T \tag{2}$$

then, assuming to know at every step $i > 0$ the values of parameters, Eq. (1) can be expressed in vector form by ($\times$ is matrix product):

$$\Delta[i] = \mathbb{A} \times U[i] \tag{3}$$

that is, the finite difference recurrence equation EMA (Equational Metabolic Algorithm) of [22-42].

The MP grammar of Table 1 defines the system Sirius, widely investigated in the theory of MP grammars [23]. It provides a regular shape of oscillatory phenomenon (the quantities of A, B, C are periodical functions). It was initially discovered by using a

Table 1. The MP grammar of Sirius oscillator. Its dynamics with initial values $A[0] = 100$, $B[0] = 100$, $C[0] = 0.02$, is given in Fig. 1.

$$
\begin{aligned}
r_1 &: \emptyset \to A \ ; & \varphi_1 &= 0.047 + 0.087A \\
r_2 &: A \to B \ ; & \varphi_2 &= 0.002A + 0.0002AC \\
r_3 &: A \to C \ ; & \varphi_3 &= 0.002A + 0.0002AB \\
r_4 &: B \to \emptyset \ ; & \varphi_4 &= 0.4B \\
r_5 &: C \to \emptyset \ ; & \varphi_5 &= 0.4C
\end{aligned}
$$

different notion of MP grammar (that is, MP grammars with reaction maps, see [23], in order to answer a qualitative dynamical inverse problem: "Is there an oscillating MP grammar?".

An important mathematical aspect of MP grammars is their representation in linear algebra notation (by means of vectors and matrices). This makes very efficient the computation of the dynamics generated by an MP grammar, which provides a particular kind of finite difference recurrent vector equation. Moreover, an algorithm was discovered, called LGSS (Log Gain Stoichiometric Stepwise algorithm, see [32-35]) that solves the inverse dynamical problem in terms of MP grammars. The initial idea underlying the LGSS algorithm is very simple. Let us assume we know the kind of reactions of an MP grammar, and we are searching for the right regulators to associate to these reactions in order to obtain an observed behavior. Let us fix a set of primitive functions that we call *regressors* (polynomials, rational functions, etc.). Our search for regulators can be transformed into the search for the right linear combination of regressors to assign to each regulator. In this way, any regulator is represented with a linear combination of regressors, and the initial problem becomes the identification of the coefficients of these linear combinations. If $\varphi_1, \varphi_2, \ldots, \varphi_m$ are the regulators, $g_1, g_2, \ldots, g_d$ are the regressors, and $s_1, s_2, \ldots, s_t$ the states of the system in t time points, we have, for $1 \le i \le t$:

$$
\begin{aligned}
\varphi_1(s_i) &= c_{1,1}g_1(s_i) + c_{1,2}g_2(s_i) + \ldots + c_{1,d}g_d(s_i) \qquad (4)\\
\varphi_2(s_i) &= c_{2,1}g_1(s_i) + c_{2,2}g_2(s_i) + \ldots + c_{2,d}g_d(s_i) \\
\ldots &= \ldots \ldots \ldots \ldots \\
\varphi_m(s_i) &= c_{m,1}g_1(s_i) + c_{m,2}g_2(s_i) + \ldots + c_{m,d}g_d(s_i).
\end{aligned}
$$

Equation (4) can be written, in matrix notation, in the following way, where $U[i]$ is the column vector of regulators evaluated at state s_i, $\mathbb{G}[i]$ the column vector of regressors evaluated at the same state, and $\mathbb{C}$ is the matrix $m \times d$ of the unknown coefficients of regressors:

$$
U[i] = \mathbb{C} \times \mathbb{G}[i]. \qquad (5)
$$

Let us consider the EMA equation (3) (where $\mathbb{A}$ is the stoichiometric matrix and $\Delta[i]$ is the column vector of variable differences between steps s_{i+1} and s_i):

$$
\mathbb{A} \times U[i] = \Delta[i] \qquad (6)
$$

substituting the right member of Eq. (5) in Eq. (6), we obtain the following system of equations:

$$\mathbb{A} \times \mathbb{C} \times \mathbb{G}[i] = \Delta[i]. \tag{7}$$

Now, if we consider t systems of type (7), for $1 \leq i \leq t$, and if n is the number of variables, we obtain nt equations with md unknown coefficients of $\mathbb{C}$. If $nt > md$ and the system has maximum rank, then we can apply a Least Square Evaluation which provides the coefficients that minimize the errors between left and right sides of the equations. These coefficients provide the regulator representations that we are searching for.

The LGSS algorithm is obtained by integrating a suitable algebraic formulation of a Least Square Evaluation problem with a stepwise statistical regression method [10,1,18,19], which provides, among a given fixed set of possible primitive functions, the right subset has to be considered for expressing regulators as their linear combinations. When regressors are found, the following theorem gives a compact representation for the regressor coefficients [38].

Theorem 1. *Let* $\mathbb{A}, \mathbb{C}, \mathbb{G}[i], \Delta[i]$ *be the matrices and vectors defined above,* $\mathbb{D}$ *the matrix having* $\Delta[i]$ *as rows, and* $\mathbb{G}$ *the matrix having* $\mathbb{G}[i]$ *as columns. The coefficients of regressors providing the best approximation to the dynamical inverse problem (relative to* $\mathbb{D}$*) are given by the following equation:*

$$vec(\mathbb{C}^T) = \left((\mathbb{A} \otimes \mathbb{G})^T \times (\mathbb{A} \otimes \mathbb{G})\right)^{-1} \times (\mathbb{A} \otimes \mathbb{G})^T \times vec(\mathbb{D}). \tag{8}$$

where:

- *the exponent* T *denotes matrix transposition.*
- $\otimes$ *is the matrix tensor product (Kroeneker product) [21],*
- *vec is the matrix operation transforming a matrix in a vector where all the column vectors are concatenated in a unique vector.*

Fig. 1 shows the dynamics of MP grammar of Sirius. This grammar was deduced by means of the LGSS algorithm from three time series that were sampled from curves of variables A, B, C previously defined. The curves generated by the grammar yield a very good approximation with the target curves that it was required to approximate, and, most important, the regulators discovered by LGSS agree completely with the rules used for generating the target curves of variables A, B, C (see [37] for further details).

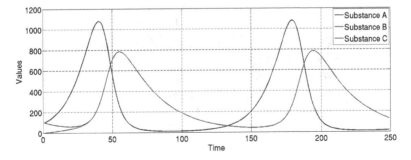

Fig. 1. The Sirius dynamics discovered by means of the LGSS algorithm

2   MP Analysis of Gene Expression

We will briefly describe a specific application of MP grammars to breast cancer gene expression, developed in cooperation with Karmanos Cancer Institute, Wayne State University, Detroit MI, USA (the research is in progress, therefore detailed data are not available for publication) .

   We started from the time series of gene expressions of a cancer cell under an effect E that inhibits the cancer growth factor HER2. After standard procedures of error filtering and data normalization [44,20], we selected the expression time that have shown a behavior clearly correlated to the inhibitory effect E. This means that genes having time series that are constant in time, or with a chaotic shape, were considered to be scarcely related to E. Only about one thousand genes with "regular shapes" were selected. Then we clustered these genes in eight types C1, C2, C3, C4, C5, C6, C7, C8, depending on the kind of time behavior: *linear-quick-up, linear-slow-up, linear-quick-down, linear-slow-down, parabolic-up, parabolic-down, cubic-up-down, cubic-down-up.* An average curve was associated to each cluster. These clusters, with their curves, constituted the variables of a dynamical system under investigation. The LGSS algorithm was applied to the eight curves, each one sampled in sixteen time points. The LGSS provided several MP grammars able to reconstruct the observed dynamics with a good approximation. In the application of the LGSS algorithm regressors were chosen among simple monomials over the variables C1, C2, C3, C4, C5, C6, C7, C8.. One of these MP grammars had the most reasonable set of regulation maps (all linear maps), according to the literature about gene regulatory networks (this evaluation was motivated by the oncologists).

   The main question posed at beginning of our investigation was the following: *We know that the cancer cell presents a resistance to the inhibition of the HER2 factor. Can MP grammars tell us something about this resistance phenomenon?*

   A deduction, coming from the obtained MP grammar, concerned with clusters with cubic behavior C7, C8. In fact, from the MP grammar we obtained, after a very easy translation [42], the regulation networks among gene clusters. In this network it appears clearly that the HER2 factor promotes C7, while inhibits C8. However, their curves behave in the opposite way, because, under the effect of HER2, C7 increases and C8

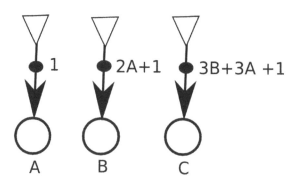

Fig. 2. An MP grammar with linear regulators generating non-linear functions (variables B, C)

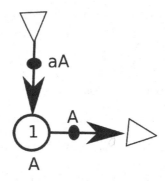

Fig. 3. An MP grammar with auto-regulation that provides an exponential function (initial value 1)

decreases. We interpreted this phenomenon as a clue of resistance. What happens is a systemic effect influencing C7 and C8, which show cubic behaviors, even if all the regulators are linear.

The phenomenon of non-linear effect in a network of mutual linear influences can easily be explained in terms of MP grammars (see Fig.2, triangles denote external values, that is, increase without a corresponding decrease, or decrease without a corresponding increase). In fact, the MP graph here described has only linear regulators, but starting with the values $A = B = C = 0$, after n steps, the values $A[n] = n, B[n] = n^2, C[n] = n^3$ are obtained, respectively. This is due to the fact that, for any natural number n (and any real value x), the difference $(x + 1)^n - x^n$ is a polynomial having degree $n-1$ (a discrete version of the derivation rule for powers). This means that, by induction, we can construct any kind of polynomial function in terms of connected linear regulations. This simple, but very important, effect of non-linearity, happens also for exponential functions, which can be defined by a sort of auto-regulation (see Fig. 3).

In the case of the gene-expression MP grammar, the non-linear systemic effect on variable C7 and C8 causes the conflict with the direct effect that HER2 has on the two variables. A deep biological investigation of genes included of the clusters regulating C7 and C8 provided the discovery of genes with an unknown crucial effect in this regulatory mechanism. Namely, when they are inhibited the resistance disappears, with a dramatic effect on the possibility of contrasting this cancer pathology.

References

1. Aczel, A.D., Sounderpandian, J.: Complete Business Statistics, International Edition. Mc Graw Hill (2006)
2. Bernardini, F., Manca, V.: Dynamical aspects of P systems. Biosystems 70(2), 85–93 (2003)
3. Bianco, L.: Membrane models of biological systems. PhD Thesis. University of Verona (2007)
4. Bianco, L., Fontana, F., Franco, G., Manca, V.: P systems for biological dynamics. In: [9] (2005)
5. Castellini, A., Zucchelli, M., Busato, M., Manca, V.: From time series to biological network regulations. Molecular Biosystems (2012), doi:10.1039/C2MB25191D

6. Bianco, L., Manca, V., Marchetti, M., Petterlini, M.: Psim: a simulator for biochemical dynamics based on P systems. In: CEC 2007 - IEEE Congress on Evolutionary Computation, Singapore, September 25-28 (2007)
7. Castellini, A.: Algorithms and software for biological MP modeling by statistical optimization techniques. PhD Thesis. University of Verona (2010)
8. Castellini, A., Franco, G., Manca, V.: Hybrid Functional Petri Nets as MP systems. Natural Computing 9, 61–81 (2010)
9. Ciobanu, G., Păun, G., Perez-Jimenez, M.J.: Applications of Membrane Computing. Springer (2005)
10. Draper, N., Smith, H.: Applied Regression Analysis, 2nd edn. John Wiley & Sons, New York (1981)
11. Gheorghe, M., Manca, V., Romero-Campero, F.J.: Deterministic and stochastic P systems for modelling cellular processes. Natural Computing 9, 457–473 (2010)
12. Fontana, F., Manca, V.: Discrete solutions to differential equations by metabolic P systems. Theoretical Computer Science 372, 165–182 (2007)
13. Fontana, F., Manca, V.: Predator-prey dynamics in P systems ruled by metabolic algorithm. BioSystems 91, 545–557 (2008)
14. Goldbeter, A.: A minimal cascade model for the mitotic oscillator involving cyclin and cdc2 kinase. PNAS 88(20)
15. Gillespie, D.T.: A general method for numerically simulating the stochastic time evolution of coupled chemical reactions. J. Comp. Phys. 22, 403–434 (1976)
16. Goldbeter, A.: Biochemical Oscillations and Cellular Rhythms: The molecular bases of periodic and chaotic behaviour. Cambridge University Press (1996)
17. Goldbeter, A.: Computational approaches to cellular rhythms. Nature 420, 238–245 (2002)
18. Hocking, R.R.: The Analysis and Selection of Variables in Linear Regression. Biometrics 32 (1976)
19. Hoerl, A.E., Kennard, R.W.: Biased Estimation of Nonorthogonal Problems. Thechnometrics 42(1), Special 40th Anniversary Issue, 80–86 (2000)
20. Johnson, S.C.: Hierarchical Clustering Schemes. Psychometrika 2, 241–254 (1967)
21. Jain, A.K.: Fundamentals of Digital Image Processing. Prentice Hall (1989)
22. Manca, V.: String rewriting and metabolism. A logical perspective. In: [46], pp. 36–60 (1998)
23. Manca, V.: The metabolic algorithm: principles and applications. Theoretical Computer Science 404, 142–157 (2008)
24. Manca, V.: Log-Gain Principles for Metabolic P Systems. In: Condon, A., Harel, D., Kok, J.N., Salomaa, A., Winfree, E. (eds.) Algorithmic Bioprocesses. Natural Computing Series, pp. 585–605. Springer, Heidelberg (2009)
25. Manca, V.: Fundamentals of Metabolic P Systems. In: [49], ch. 19 (2010)
26. Manca, V.: Metabolic P Dynamics. In: [49], ch. 20 (2010)
27. Manca, V.: From P to MP Systems. In: Păun, G., Pérez-Jiménez, M.J., Riscos-Núñez, A., Rozenberg, G., Salomaa, A. (eds.) WMC 2009. LNCS, vol. 5957, pp. 74–94. Springer, Heidelberg (2010)
28. Manca, V.: Metabolic P systems. Scholarpedia 5(3), 9273 (2010)
29. Manca, V., Bianco, L.: Biological networks in metabolic P systems. BioSystems 91, 489–498 (2008)
30. Manca, V., Bianco, L., Fontana, F.: Evolution and Oscillation in P Systems: Applications to Biological Phenomena. In: Mauri, G., Păun, G., Jesús Pérez-Jímenez, M., Rozenberg, G., Salomaa, A. (eds.) WMC 2004. LNCS, vol. 3365, pp. 63–84. Springer, Heidelberg (2005)
31. Manca, V., Franco, G., Scollo, G.: State transition dynamics: basic concepts and molecular computing perspectives. In: Gheorghe, G. (ed.) Molecular Computational Models: Unconventional Approaches, ch. 2, pp. 32–55 (2005)

32. Manca, V., Lombardo, R.: Computing with Multi-membranes. In: Gheorghe, M., Păun, G., Rozenberg, G., Salomaa, A., Verlan, S. (eds.) CMC 2011. LNCS, vol. 7184, pp. 282–299. Springer, Heidelberg (2012)

33. Manca, V., Marchetti, L.: Metabolic approximation of real periodical functions. The Journal of Logic and Algebraic Programming 79, 363–373 (2010)

34. Manca, V., Marchetti, L.: Goldbeter's Mitotic Oscillator Entirely Modeled by MP Systems. In: Gheorghe, M., Hinze, T., Păun, G., Rozenberg, G., Salomaa, A. (eds.) CMC 2010. LNCS, vol. 6501, pp. 273–284. Springer, Heidelberg (2010)

35. Manca, V., Marchetti, L.: Log-Gain Stoichiometic Stepwise regression for MP systems. Int. J. of Foundations of Computer Science 22(1), 97–106 (2011)

36. Marchetti, L., Manca, V.: A Methodology Based on MP Theory for Gene Expression Analysis. In: Gheorghe, M., Păun, G., Rozenberg, G., Salomaa, A., Verlan, S. (eds.) CMC 2011. LNCS, vol. 7184, pp. 300–313. Springer, Heidelberg (2012)

37. Manca, V., Marchetti, L.: Solving inverse dynamics problems by means of MP systems. BioSystems 109, 78–86 (2012)

38. Manca, V., Marchetti, L.: An algebraic formulation of inverse problems in MP dynamics. International Journal of Computer Mathematics (2012), doi:10.1080/00207160.2012.735362

39. Manca, V., Marchetti, L., Pagliarini, R.: MP modelling of glucose-insulin interactions in the Intravenous Glucose Tolerance Test. International Journal of Natural Computing Research 2(3), 13–24 (2011)

40. Manca, V., Martino, M.D.: From String Rewriting to Logical Metabolic Systems. In: Păun, G., Salomaa, A. (eds.) Grammatical Models of Multiagent Systems, pp. 297–315. Gordon and Breach (1999)

41. Manca, V., Pagliarini, R., Zorzan, S.: A photosynthetic process modelled by a metabolic P system. Natural Computing 8, 847–864 (2009)

42. Marchetti, L., Manca, V.: A Methodology Based on MP Theory for Gene Expression Analysis. In: Gheorghe, M., Păun, G., Rozenberg, G., Salomaa, A., Verlan, S. (eds.) CMC 2011. LNCS, vol. 7184, pp. 300–313. Springer, Heidelberg (2012)

43. Marchetti, L.: MP representations of biological structures and dynamics. PhD Thesis. University of Verona (2012)

44. Marquardt, D.W., Snee, R.D.: Ridge Regression in Practice. The American Statistician 29(1), 3–20 (1975)

45. Pagliarini, R.: Modeling and reverse engineering of biological phenomena by means of metabolic P systems. PhD Thesis. University of Verona (2011)

46. Păun, G. (ed.): Computing with biomolecules. Theory and Experiments, pp. 36–60. Springer, Singapore (1998)

47. Păun, G.: Computing with Membranes. Journal of Computer and Systems Science 61(1), 108–143 (2000)

48. Păun, G.: Membrane Computing. An Introduction. Springer (2002)

49. Păun, G., Rozenberg, G., Salomaa, A.: Oxford Handbook of Membrane Computing. Oxford University Press (2010)

50. Reising, W., Rozenberg, G. (eds.): Lectures on Petri Nets. Springer (1998)

51. Szallasi, Z., Stelling, J., Periwal, V. (eds.): System Modeling in Cellular Biology Lectures on Petri Nets. The MIT Press (2006)

52. Voit, E.O.: Computational Analysis of Biochemical Systems. Cambridge University Press (2000)

Turing Computability and Membrane Computing

Yurii Rogozhin and Artiom Alhazov

Institute of Mathematics and Computer Science
Academy of Sciences of Moldova
Academiei 5, Chişinău MD-2028 Moldova
{rogozhin,artiom}@math.md

Abstract. Alan Turing began a new area in science; he discovered that there are universal computers, which in principal are very simple. Up to now this is the basis of a modern computing theory and practice. In the paper one considers Turing computability in the frame of P (membrane) systems and other distributive systems. An overview of the recent results about small universal P and DNA systems and some open problems and possible directions of investigation are presented.

1 Introduction

In the paper several very small universal computing devices inspired by molecular biology are presented. Alan Turing [43] discovered that there are universal computing devices, which in principal are very simple. Claude Shannon [42] suggested to find universal Turing machine of smallest size (he considered a descriptional complexity of universal programs). Current state of the art in solving Shannon's task is presented in [30]. In the paper one applies the Shannon's task to other computing models, especially to modern computing models inspired by molecular biology, namely for Membrane computing, DNA computing and some others computing models. Before proceeding, we outline selected small universal systems.

1.1 Selected Small Universal Systems

Turing Machines

We should mention references A. Turing [43]; C. Shannon [42]; M. Minsky [28]; R. Robinson [38]; M. Margenstern [21,22]; L. Pavlotskaya [31]; M. Margenstern and L. Pavlotskaya [23]; Yu. Rogozhin [39]; T. Neary and D. Woods [30]. The best known results are Turing machines with 24 rules, simulating Tag systems or cyclic Tag systems.

Circular Post Machines and Tag Systems

We should mention references E. Post [36]; J. Cocke and M. Minsky [9]; A. Alhazov, M. Kudlek and Yu. Rogozhin [5]; L. De Mol [29]; T. Neary and D.

E. Csuhaj-Varjú et al. (Eds.): CMC 2012, LNCS 7762, pp. 56–77, 2013.

Woods [30]; A. Alhazov, A. Krassovitskiy and Yu. Rogozhin [3]. Circular Post machines are a one-way variant of Turing machines that can insert and delete cells. Tag systems are a restricted model of Post normal systems, i.e., systems rewriting strings by removing a prefix and appending a suffix.

Besides being a tool for Turing machines, Tag systems have been used to obtain small universal devices in a number of splicing-based models, presented in this paper.

Circular Post machines have been used to obtain small universal Tag P systems and also small universal obligatory hybrid networks of evolutionary processors.

Cellular Automata

The most famous cellular automaton is the Conway's Game of Life. In two dimensions, cellular automata are known to be universal with two states, even with the von Neumann neighborhood (the center cell and 4 neighbours). In one dimension, there exists an intrinsically universal cellular automaton with 4 states. We are not discussing the elementary cellular automata in this paper, since the details of the universality notion already become a separate topic.

With more states, universal cellular automata have been obtained having radius-1/2 neighborhood (the center cell and only 1 neighbour), or having additional properties, such as number conservation, reversibility or symmetries.

Register Machines and Counter Automata

The smallest known universal register machines are constructed by I. Korec in 1996. The main result is a machine with 32 instructions (or 22 if the decrement and zero-test are counted as one instruction) and 8 registers. Its flowchart has 13 branchings.

This result has been used to obtain small universal spiking neural P systems and small universal P colonies, as well as a small universal antiport P system, presented in this paper. The latter is equivalent to maximally parallel multiset rewriting.

1.2 Computing Models Based on Splicing or Multiset Rewriting

Head splicing systems (H systems) [17] were one of the first theoretical models of biomolecular computing (DNA-computing). The molecules from biology are replaced by words over a finite alphabet and the chemical reactions are replaced by the *splicing* operation. An H system specifies a set of rules used to perform a splicing and a set of initial words or axioms. The computation is done by applying iteratively the rules to the set of words until no more new words can be generated. This corresponds to a bio-chemical experiment where one has enzymes (splicing rules) and initial molecules (axioms) which are put together in a tube and one waits until the reaction stops.

From the formal language theory point of view, the computational power of the obtained model is rather limited, only regular languages can be generated. Various additional control mechanisms were proposed in order to "overcome" this obstacle and to generate all recursively enumerable languages. An overview of such mechanisms can be found in [34].

One of the goals of this work is to present several of small size universal systems based on splicing. Like in [40,6] we consider the number of rules as a measure of the size of the system. This approach is coherent with investigations related to small universal Turing machines, e.g. [39].

One of the first ideas to increase the computational power of splicing systems is to consider them in a distributed framework. Such a framework introduces test tubes, corresponding to H systems, which are arranged in a communicating network. The computation is then performed as a repeated sequence of two steps: computation and communication. During the computational step, each test tube evolves as an ordinary H system in an independent manner. During the communication step, the words at each test tube are redistributed among other tubes according to some communication protocol.

Test tube systems based on splicing, introduced in [10], communicate through redistribution of the contents of the test tubes via filters that are simply sets of letters (in a similar way to the *separate* operation of Lipton-Adleman [20,1]). These systems, with finite initial contents of the tubes and finite sets of splicing rules associated to each component, are computationally complete, they characterize the family of recursively enumerable languages. The existence of universal splicing test tube distributed systems was obtained on this basis, hence the theoretical proof of the possibility to design universal programmable computers with the structure of such a system. After a series of results, the number of tubes sufficient to achieve this result was established to be 3 [37]. The computational power of splicing test tube systems with two tubes is still an open question. The descriptional complexity for such kind of systems was investigated in [4] where it was shown that there exist universal splicing test tube systems with 10 rules. The best known result shows that there exist universal splicing test tube system with 8 rules [7] and this result is presented in this paper.

A simple possibility to turn splicing-based systems into computationally complete devices are time-varying distributed H systems (TVDH systems). Such systems work like H systems, but on each computational step the set of active rules is changed in a cycle. These sets are called *components*. It was shown [34] that 7 components are enough for the computational completeness; further this number was reduced to 1 [24,26]. This last result shows a fine difference between the definitions of a computational step in H systems. If one iterates the splicing operation while keeping all generated strings, then such systems are regular. If only the result of each splicing step is kept, then the resulting systems are computationally complete. An overview of results on TVDH systems may be found in [27]. Recently one constructed very small universal TVDH systems with two components and 15 rules and with one component and 17 rules [4]. These results also are presented in the paper.

Another extension of H systems was done using the framework of P systems [32], see also [16] and [35]. In a formal way, splicing P systems can be considered like a graph, whose nodes contain sets of strings and sets of splicing rules. Every rule permits to perform a splicing and to send the result to some other node. Since splicing P systems generate any recursively enumerable language, it is clear that there are universal splicing P systems. Like for small universal Turing machines, we are interested in such universal systems that have a small number of rules. A first result was obtained in [40] where a universal splicing P system with 8 rules was shown. Recently a new construction was presented in [6] for a universal splicing P system with 6 rules. The best known result [7] shows that there exists a universal splicing P system with 5 rules and this result is presented in this paper. Notice, that this result (5 rules) is the best known for "classical" approach to construct small universal devices. Similar investigations for P systems with symbol-objects were done in [11,8] and the latter article constructs a universal antiport P system with 23 rules. This result also is presented in the paper.

We also consider a class of H systems which can be viewed as a counterpart of the matrix grammars in the regulated rewriting area. These systems are called double splicing extended H systems [34]. In [7] one obtains an unexpected result: 5 rules are enough for such kind of H systems in order to be universal.

The following series of results claim existence of universal devices of very small size is presented in the paper. We only present the constructions with some important explanations. Thus, there exist the following universal devices:

- A double splicing extended H system with 5 rules [7],
- An extended splicing test tube system with 3 tubes with 8 rules [7],
- A TVDH system with two components and 15 rules [4],
- A TVDH system with one component and 17 rules [4],
- A splicing P system with 5 rules [7],
- An antiport P system with 23 rules [8].

2 Definitions

In this section, we recall some very basic notions and notations we use throughout the paper. We assume the reader to be familiar with the basics of formal language theory. For more details, we refer to [41].

We denote the empty word by λ and finite alphabets by V and U. A morphism is a mapping $h : V \to U^*$, extended to $h : V^* \to U^*$ by $h(\lambda) = \{\lambda\}$ and $h(xy) = h(x)h(y)$, $x, y \in V^*$. An inverse morphism, denoted as h^{-1} is defined as $h^{-1}(y) = \{x \mid h(x) = y\}$. A weak coding is a morphism $\xi : V \to U \cup \{\lambda\}$, *i.e.*, it can only rename or erase.

Register Machines

A deterministic *register machine* is the following construction:

$$M = (Q, R, q_0, q_f, P),$$

where Q is a set of states, $R = \{R_1, \ldots, R_k\}$ is the set of registers, $q_0 \in Q$ is the initial state, $q_f \in Q$ is the final state and P is a set of instructions (called also rules) of the following form:

1. $(p, [R_k P], q) \in P$, $p, q \in Q, p \neq q, R_k \in R$ (being in state p, increase register R_k and go to state q).
2. $(p, [R_k M], q) \in P$, $p, q \in Q, p \neq q, R_k \in R$ (being in state p, decrease register R_k and go to state q).
3. $(p, \langle R_k \rangle, q, s) \in P$, $p, q, s \in Q, R_k \in R$ (being in state p, go to q if register R_k is not zero or to s otherwise).
4. $(p, \langle R_k ZM \rangle, q, s) \in P$, $p, q, s \in Q, R_k \in R$ (being in state p, decrease register R_k and go to q if successful or to s otherwise).
5. $(q_f, STOP)$ (may be associated only to the final state q_f).

We note that for each state p there is only one instruction of the types above.

A configuration of a register machine is given by the $(k+1)$-tuple $(q, n_1, \cdots, n_k)$, where $q \in Q$ and $n_i \in \mathbb{N}, 1 \leq i \leq k$, describing the current state of the machine as well as the contents of all registers. A transition of the register machine consists in updating/checking the value of a register according to an instruction of one of types above and by changing the current state to another one. We say that the machine stops if it reaches the state q_f. We say that M computes a value $y \in \mathbb{N}$ on the *input* $x \in \mathbb{N}$ if, starting from the initial configuration $(q_0, x, 0, \cdots, 0)$, it reaches the final configuration $(q_f, y, 0, \cdots, 0)$.

It is well-known that register machines compute all partial recursive functions and only them, [28]. For every $n \in \mathbb{N}$, with every register machine M having n registers, an n-ary partial recursive function Φ_M^n is associated. Let $\Phi_0, \Phi_1, \Phi_2, \cdots$, be a fixed admissible enumeration of the set of unary partial recursive functions. Then, a register machine M is said to be *strongly universal* if there exists a recursive function g such that $\Phi_x(y) = \Phi_M^2(g(x), y)$ holds for all $x, y \in \mathbb{N}$.

We also note that the power and the efficiency of a register machine M depends on the set of instructions that are used. In [19] several sets of instructions are investigated. In particular, it is shown that there are strongly universal register machines with 22 instructions of form $[RiP]$ and $\langle RiZM \rangle$. Moreover, these machines can be effectively constructed.

Figure 1 shows this special universal register machine (more precisely in [19] only a machine with 32 instructions of type $[R_k P]$, $[R_k M]$ and $\langle R_k \rangle$ is constructed, and the machine below may be simply obtained from that one).

Here is the list of rules of this machine.

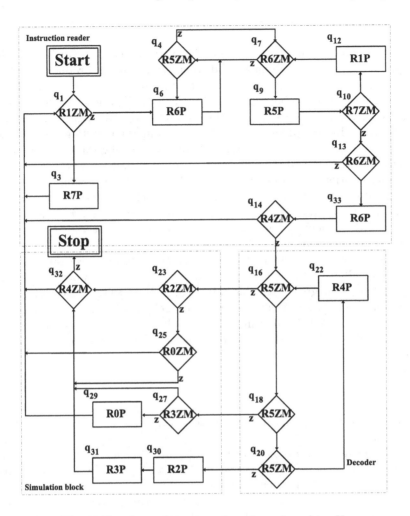

Fig. 1. Flowchart of the strongly universal machine U_{22}

$(q_1, \langle R_1 Z M \rangle, q_3, q_6)$ $(q_3, [R_7 P], q_1)$ $(q_4, \langle R_5 Z M \rangle, q_6, q_7)$

$(q_6, [R_6 P], q_4)$ $(q_7, \langle R_6 Z M \rangle, q_9, q_4)$ $(q_9, [R_5 P], q_{10})$

$(q_{10}, \langle R_7 Z M \rangle, q_{12}, q_{13})$ $(q_{12}, [R_1 P], q_7)$ $(q_{13}, \langle R_6 Z M \rangle, q_{33}, q_1)$

$(q_{33}, [R_6 P], q_{14})$ $(q_{14}, \langle R_4 Z M \rangle, q_1, q_{16})$ $(q_{16}, \langle R_5 Z M \rangle, q_{18}, q_{23})$

$(q_{18}, \langle R_5 Z M \rangle, q_{20}, q_{27})$ $(q_{20}, \langle R_5 Z M \rangle, q_{22}, q_{30})$ $(q_{22}, [R_4 P], q_{16})$

$(q_{23}, \langle R_2 Z M \rangle, q_{32}, q_{25})$ $(q_{25}, \langle R_0 Z M \rangle, q_1, q_{32})$ $(q_{27}, \langle R_3 Z M \rangle, q_{32}, q_1)$

$(q_{29}, [R_0 P], q_1)$ $(q_{30}, [R_2 P], q_{31})$ $(q_{31}, [R_3 P], q_{32})$

$(q_{32}, \langle R_4 Z M \rangle, q_1, q_f)$

Tag Systems

A *tag system* of degree $m > 0$, see [9] and [28], is the triplet $T = (m, V, P)$, where $V = \{a_1, \ldots, a_{n+1}\}$ is an alphabet and where P is a set of productions of the form $a_i \to P_i, 1 \le i \le n, P_i \in V^*$. For every a_i, $1 \le i \le n$, there is exactly one production in P. The symbol a_{n+1} is called the halting symbol. A configuration of the system T is a word $w \in V^*$. If $|w| < m$ or $w = a_{n+1}a_{i_2} \ldots a_{i_m}w'$, with $w' \in V^*$, then w is a halting configuration. We pass from a non-halting configuration $w = a_{i_1}a_{i_2} \ldots a_{i_m}w'$ to the next configuration z by erasing the first m symbols of w and by adding P_{i_1} to the end of the word: $w \Rightarrow z$, if $z = w'P_{i_1}$.

The computation of T over the word $x \in V^*$ is a (finite or infinite) sequence of configurations $x = x_0 \Rightarrow x_1 \Rightarrow \cdots \Rightarrow x_r \Rightarrow \ldots$ such that for each $j \ge 0$, x_{j+1} is the next configuration of x_j. In the case of a finite sequence $x = x_0 \Rightarrow x_1 \Rightarrow \cdots \Rightarrow x_r$, with x_r being a halting configuration we say that x_r is the result of the computation of T over x.

We say that T recognizes the language L if there exists a recursive coding ϕ such that for all $x \in L$, T halts on $\phi(x)$, and T halts only on words from $\phi(L)$.

Tag systems of degree 2 are able to recognize the family of recursively enumerable languages [9,28]. Moreover, the construction in [9] has non-empty productions and halts only by reaching the symbol a_{n+1} in the first position.

In what follows, for convenience, we consider that the halting symbol is a_1 and $P = \{a_i \to P_i \mid 2 \le i \le n\}$.

H Systems

Now we briefly recall the basic notions concerning the splicing operation and related constructs [18,34].

A *splicing rule* (over an alphabet V) is a 4-tuple (u_1, u_2, u_3, u_4) where $u_1, u_2, u_3, u_4 \in V^*$ and it is frequently written as $u_1\#u_2\$u_3\#u_4$, $\{\$, \#\} \not\subseteq V$. Strings u_1u_2 and u_3u_4 are called splicing *sites*.

We say that a word x *matches* rule r if x contains an occurrence of one of the two sites of r. We also say that x and y are *complementary* with respect to a rule r if x contains one site of r and y contains the other one. In this case we also say that x or y may *enter* rule r. When x and y can enter a rule $r = u_1\#u_2\$u_3\#u_4$, i.e., $x = x_1u_1u_2x_2$ and $y = y_1u_3u_4y_2$, it is possible to define the application of r to the couple x, y. The result of this application are w and z, where $w = x_1u_1u_4y_2$ and $z = y_1u_3u_2x_2$. We also say that x and y are spliced and w and z are the result of this splicing. We write this as follows: $(x, y) \vdash_r (w, z)$ or

$(x_1u_1|u_2x_2, y_1u_3|u_4y_2) \vdash_r (x_1u_1u_4y_2, y_1u_3u_2x_2)$.

The pair $h = (V, R)$, where V is an alphabet and R is a set of splicing rules, is called a *splicing scheme* or an *H scheme*. For a splicing scheme $h = (V, R)$ and for a language $L \subseteq V^*$ we define

$$\sigma_h(L) \stackrel{\text{def}}{=} \{w, z \in V^* \mid \exists x, y \in L, \exists r \in R : (x, y) \vdash_r (w, z)\}.$$

Now we can introduce the iteration of the splicing operation.

$$\sigma_h^0(L) = L,$$
$$\sigma_h^{i+1}(L) = \sigma_h^i(L) \cup \sigma(\sigma^i(L)), \ i \geq 0,$$
$$\sigma_h^*(L) = \cup_{i \geq 0} \sigma_h^i(L).$$

It is known that the iterated splicing preserves the regularity of a language [34].

A *Head-splicing-system* [17,18], or *H system*, is a construct $H = (h, A) = ((V, R), A)$, which consists of an alphabet V, a set $A \subseteq V^*$ of initial words over V, the *axioms*, and a set $R \subseteq V^* \times V^* \times V^* \times V^*$ of splicing rules. System H is called finite if A and R are finite sets.

The language generated by an H system H is defined as $L(H) \overset{\text{def}}{=} \sigma_h^*(A)$.

An *extended* H system is the quadruple $H = (V, T, A, R)$, where $H' = ((V, R), A)$ is an H system and $T \subseteq V$ is a terminal alphabet. The language generated by the extended H system H is defined as $L(H) = L(H') \cap T^*$.

We now consider a class of H systems which can be viewed as a counterpart of the matrix grammars in the regulated rewriting area. They require that the work of an H system proceeds in a couple of steps: the two strings obtained after a splicing immediately enter a second splicing. The rules used in the two steps are not prescribed or dependent in any way on each other.

Consider an extended H system $\Gamma = (V, T, A, R)$. For $x, y, w, z, u, v \in V^*$ and $r_1, r_2 \in R$ we write

$$(x, y) \vdash_{r_1, r_2} (w, z) \text{ iff } (x, y) \vdash_{r_1} (u, v) \text{ and } (u, v) \vdash_{r_2} (w, z) \text{ or } (v, u) \vdash_{r_2} (w, z).$$

For a language $L \subseteq V^*$ we define

$$\sigma_d(L) = \{w, z \mid (x, y) \vdash_{r_1, r_2} (w, z) \text{ for } x, y \in L, r_1, r_2 \in R\},$$
$$\sigma_d^*(L) = \bigcup_{i \geq 0} \sigma_d^i(L), \text{ where}$$
$$\sigma_d^0(L) = L,$$
$$\sigma_d^{i+1}(L) = \sigma_d^i(L) \cup \sigma_d(\sigma_d^i(L)), \ i \geq 0.$$

Then, we associate with Γ the language

$$L_d(\Gamma) = \sigma_d^*(A) \cap T^*.$$

We say that $L_d(\Gamma)$ is the language generated by the *double splicing extended H system* Γ.

By $EH_2(FIN)$ we denote the family of languages $L_d(\Gamma)$ generated as above by double splicing extended H systems. It is known that $RE = EH_2(FIN)$ [34].

We say that $\Gamma = (V, T, A, R)$ *computes* $L \subseteq V^*$ on input w if $L = L_d(\Gamma')$, where $\Gamma' = (V, T, A \cup \{w\}, R)$ and we denote this as $L_d(\Gamma, w)$.

Splicing Test Tube Systems

There are several variants of splicing test tube systems, called also *communicating distributed H systems*. We consider the (historically) first variant introduced in [10] and also described in [34].

A *splicing test tube* T is a couple $T = (H, F)$ consisting of an H system $H = (h, A) = ((V, R), A)$ and an alphabet $F \subseteq V$, called the *filter* for T.

A *splicing test tube system* with n test tubes is a tuple $\Delta = (V, T_1, \cdots, T_n)$, where V is an alphabet and $T_i = (H_i, F_i) = (((V, \mathcal{R}_i), A_i), F_i)$, $1 \leq i \leq n$, are n splicing test tubes.

The *computation* in Δ is a sequence of two subsequent steps, a computation step and a communication step, which are repeated iteratively and change the configuration of the system. By a *configuration* of Δ, above, we mean an n-tuple $(\mathcal{L}_1, \ldots, \mathcal{L}_n)$, where $\mathcal{L}_i \in V^*$, $1 \leq i \leq n$. The initial configuration of Δ is $(A_1, \ldots, A_n)$.

The *computation* step consists in an iterative application of $\mathcal{R}_i$, $\sigma_{\mathcal{R}_i}^*$, at each node i of G to strings found there. We say that configuration $C' = (\mathcal{L}'_1, \ldots, \mathcal{L}'_n)$ is obtained from configuration $C = (\mathcal{L}_1, \ldots, \mathcal{L}_n)$ by a computation step in Δ, denoted by $(\mathcal{L}_1, \ldots, \mathcal{L}_n) \vdash_{comp} (\mathcal{L}'_1, \ldots, \mathcal{L}'_n)$, if $\mathcal{L}'_i = \sigma_{\mathcal{R}_i}^*(\mathcal{L}_i)$ holds for $1 \leq i \leq n$.

During the *communication* step, the actual contents of the test tubes are redistributed to all other tubes. More formally, we say that configuration $(\mathcal{L}'_1, \ldots, \mathcal{L}'_n)$ is obtained from configuration $(\mathcal{L}_1, \ldots, \mathcal{L}_n)$ by a communication step in Δ, denoted by $(\mathcal{L}_1, \ldots, \mathcal{L}_n) \vdash_{comm} (\mathcal{L}'_1, \ldots, \mathcal{L}'_n)$, if $\mathcal{L}'_i$ consists of all words $w \in V^*$ which satisfy one of the following conditions:

- $w \in \mathcal{L}_j$, for some j, $1 \leq j \leq n$, and $w \in F_i^*$,
- $w \in \mathcal{L}_i$ and there is no such j, $1 \leq j \leq n$, such that $w \in F_j^*$.

For two configurations C and C' we denote by $C \vdash C'$ the sequence $C \vdash_{comp} C'' \vdash_{comm} C'$, where C'' is an intermediate configuration. By $\vdash^*$ we denote the reflexive and transitive closure of $\vdash$.

We can define the *communication graph* of the system which is the graph where a node corresponds to a test tube and an edge from node i to j corresponds to a possibility to send a word from tube i to tube j. It is clear that in the case of the standard definition the communication graph is complete and also contains self-loops. Variants where the communication graph has other forms are known under the name of *splicing P systems*, see [32,33].

The *result* of the computation of Δ is the contents of the first test tube. More formally, $L(\Delta) = \{L_1 \subseteq V^* \mid \exists L_2, \cdots, L_n \subseteq V^* : (A_1, \cdots, A_n) \vdash^* (L_1, \cdots, L_n)\}$.

An *extended splicing test tube system* Γ is a pair $\Gamma = (\Delta, \mathcal{T})$, where Δ is a splicing test tube system defined as above and $\mathcal{T} \subseteq V$ is an alphabet. The computation of such system is similar to splicing test tube system, the only difference is the result of the computation which is defined as follows: $L(\Gamma) = L(\Delta) \cap \mathcal{T}^*$.

It is known that splicing test tube systems with one tube are isomorphic to H systems, hence they generate the family of regular languages and extended splicing test tube systems with 3 tubes are computationally complete [37]. If two tubes are used, the computational power of such systems is not known, however non-regular languages can be generated, as shown in [34].

If a different definition of the filter is considered, then two tubes are enough for the computational completeness, see [14,15,45,46].

In this article we consider extended splicing test tube systems that have an input. A computation of an extended splicing test tube system Γ on an input w is performed by adding w to some A_i, $1 \leq i \leq n$, and after that evolving Γ as usual. The resulting language is denoted $L(\Gamma, w)$.

Time-Varying Distributed H Systems

A *time-varying distributed H system* (of degree n, $n \geq 1$), (TVDH system) is a construct:

$$D = (V, T, A, R_1, R_2, \ldots, R_n),$$

where V is *an alphabet*, $T \subseteq V$ is *a terminal alphabet*, $A \subseteq V^*$ is a finite set of *axioms*, and *components* R_i are finite sets of splicing rules over V, $1 \leq i \leq n$.

At each moment $k = n \cdot j + i$, for $j \geq 0$, $1 \leq i \leq n$, only component R_i is used for splicing the currently available strings. Specifically, we define

$$L_1 = A, \qquad L_{k+1} = \sigma_{h_i}(L_k), \text{ for } i \equiv k(mod\ n),\ k \geq 1, 1 \leq i \leq n,\ h_i = (V, R_i).$$

Therefore, from a step k to the next step, $k + 1$, one passes only the result of splicing the strings in L_k according to the rules in R_i for $i \equiv k(mod\ n)$; the strings in L_k that cannot enter a splicing rule are removed.

The language generated by D is, by definition:

$$L(D) \overset{\text{def}}{=} (\cup_{k \geq 1} L_k) \cap T^*.$$

In this article we consider TVDH systems that have an input. A computation of a TVDH system D on an input w is performed by adding w to A and after that evolving D as usual. The resulting language is denoted $L(D, w)$.

Splicing (Tissue) P Systems

A *splicing tissue P system* of degree $m \geq 1$ is a construct

$$\Pi = (V, T, G, A_1, \ldots, A_m, R_1, \ldots, R_m),$$

where V is an alphabet, $T \subseteq V$ is the terminal alphabet and G is the underlying directed labeled graph of the system. The graph G has m nodes (cells) numbered from 1 to m. Each node i contains a set of strings (a language) A_i over V. Symbols R_i, $1 \leq i \leq m$, are finite sets of rules (associated to nodes) of the form

$(r; tar_1, tar_2)$, where r is a splicing rule: $r = u_1 \# u_2 \$ u_3 \# u_4$ and $tar_1, tar_2 \in \{here, out\} \cup \{go_j \mid 1 \le j \le m\}$, are target indicators. The communication graph G can be deduced from the sets of rules. More precisely, G contains an edge (i, j), iff there is a rule $(r; tar_1, tar_2) \in R_i$ with $tar_k = go_j$, $k \in \{1, 2\}$. If one of tar_k is equal to $here$, then G contains the loop (i, i).

A *configuration* of Π is the m-tuple $(N_1, \ldots, N_m)$, where $N_i \subseteq V^*$. A *transition* between two configurations $(N_1, \ldots, N_m) \Rightarrow (N_1', \ldots, N_m')$ is defined as follows. In order to pass from one configuration to another, splicing rules of each node are applied in parallel to all possible words that belong to that node. After that, the result of each splicing is distributed according to target indicators. More exactly, if there are x, y in N_i and $r = (u_1 \# u_2 \$ u_3 \# u_4; tar_1, tar_2)$ in R_i, such that $(x, y) \vdash_r (w, z)$, then words w and z are sent to the nodes indicated by tar_1, respectively tar_2. We write this as follows $(x, y) \vdash_r (w, z)(tar_1, tar_2)$. If $tar_k = here$, $k = 1, 2$, then the word remains in node i (is added to N_i'); if $tar_k = go_j$, then the word is sent to node j (is added to N_j'); if $tar_k = out$, the word is sent outside of the system.

Since the words are present in an arbitrarily many number of copies, after the application of rule r in node i, words x and y are still present in the same node.

A *computation* in a splicing tissue P system Π is a sequence of transitions between configurations of Π which starts from the initial configuration $(A_1, \ldots, A_m)$. The result of the computation consists of all words over terminal alphabet T which are sent outside the system at some moment of the computation. The equivalent definition of the result is to define the output node i_{out} (in this case we define splicing tissue P system of degree $m \ge 1$ as follows $\Pi = (V, T, G, A_1, \ldots, A_m, R_1, \ldots, R_m, i_{out})$, $1 \le i_{out} \le m$) and consider as result of all words over terminal alphabet that will appear in this output node i_{out}. We denote by $L(\Pi)$ the language generated by system Π.

We also define the notion of an *input* for the system above. An input word for a system Π is simply a word w over the non-terminal alphabet of Π. The computation of Π on input w is obtained by adding w to the axioms of A_1 and after that by evolving Π as usual. We denote by $L(\Pi, w)$ the result of the computation of Π on w.

We consider the following restricted variant of splicing tissue P systems. A *restricted splicing tissue P system* is a subclass of splicing tissue P systems which has the property that for any rule $(r; tar_1, tar_2)$ either $tar_1 = tar_2 = go_j$, or $tar_1 = tar_2 = out$ or $tar_1 = tar_2 = here$. This means that both resulting strings are moved over the same connection. In this case, we may associate splicing rules to corresponding edges.

3 Small Universal Splicing (Tissue) P system

In this section we consider a small universal splicing (tissue) P system from [7]. Here and in sections below we use the unary codings $c : V \to \{\alpha, \beta\}^*$ and $\bar{c} : V \to \{\alpha, \beta\}^*$ defined as $c(a_i) = \alpha^i \beta$, $\bar{c}(a_i) = \beta \alpha^i$ where $V = \{a_1, \ldots, a_n\}$.

Theorem 1. *Let $TS = (2, V, P)$ be a tag system. Then, there is a morphism h, a weak coding ξ and a restricted splicing tissue P system $\Pi = (V', T, G, A_1, A_2, A_3, R_1, R_2, R_3, 3)$ with 5 rules which simulates TS as follows:*

1. *for any word $w \in V^*$ on which TS halts producing the result v, the application of $h^{-1} \circ \xi$ to the result of the computation of Π on the input $X\beta\beta c(w)\beta Y$ gives v, i.e., $\xi(h^{-1}(L(\Pi, X\beta\beta c(w)\beta Y))) = \{v\}$.*
2. *for any word $w \in V^*$ on which TS does not halt, the system Π generates the empty set given the input $X\beta\beta c(w)\beta Y$, i.e., $L(\Pi, X\beta\beta c(w)\beta Y) = \emptyset$.*

We construct a restricted splicing P system $\Pi = (V', T, G, A_1, A_2, A_3, R_1, R_2, R_3, 3)$ as follows. Let $|V| = n$, $n \geq 2$. We put $V' = \{\alpha, \beta, X, Y, Y', Z, Z'\}$, and $T = \{X, Y', \alpha, \beta\}$.

The initial languages A_j, $j \in \{1, 2, 3\}$ are given as follows.

$$A_1 = \{Z'c(P_i)\bar{c}(a_i)Y \mid a_i \to P_i \in P\} \cup \{X\beta Z, ZY, Z'Y'\},$$
$$A_2 = \{XZ\},$$
$$A_3 = \{XZ\}.$$

The set of rules R_j, $j \in \{1, 2, 3\}$ are given as follows.

$$R_1 = \{1.1 : (\lambda\#\beta Y\$Z'\#\lambda; go_3, go_3); \ 1.2 : (\lambda\#\alpha Y\$Z\#Y; go_2, go_2);$$
$$1.3 : (X\beta\alpha\#\lambda\$X\beta\#Z; here, here)\};$$
$$R_2 = \{2.1 : (X\alpha\#\lambda\$X\#Z; go_1, go_1)\};$$
$$R_3 = \{3.1 : (X\beta\beta\#\alpha\alpha\$X\#Z; go_1, go_1)\}.$$

The graph G can be deduced from the rules above and it is represented in Figure 2.

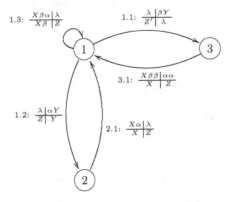

Fig. 2. The communication graph G associated to the construction of Π

The simulation of TS is performed as follows. For every step of the derivation in TS there is a sequence of several derivation steps in Π. The current configuration w of TS is encoded by a string $X\beta\beta c(w)\beta Y$ present in node 1 of Π (the initial configuration of Π satisfies this property). The simulation of a production $a_i \to P_i$, $2 \le i \le n$ is performed using the rotate-and-simulate method used for many proofs in this area. We use this method works as follows. First, suffixes $c(P_j)\bar{c}(a_j)$, $2 \le j \le n$ are attached to the string producing $X\alpha^i\beta c(a_k w')c(P_j)\beta\alpha^j Y$. After that the number of symbols α at both ends is decreased simultaneously. Hence, only the string for which $j = i$ will remain at the end, producing $X\beta c(a_k w')\beta Y$. After that the symbol a_k is removed (by removing corresponding α's) and a new round begins. The simulation stops when the first symbol is a_1.

Consider also the morphism h and the weak coding ξ defined as follows:

$$h(a) = \begin{cases} \alpha^i\beta & \text{if } a = a_i \in V, \\ X\beta\beta\alpha\beta & \text{if } a = \bar{X}, \\ Y' & \text{if } a = \bar{Y}. \end{cases} \qquad \xi(a) = \begin{cases} a & \text{if } a \in V, \\ a_1 & \text{if } a = \bar{X}, \\ \lambda & \text{if } a = \bar{Y}. \end{cases}$$

From the definition of h and from the form of words that can be in node 3 in Π it is clear that $h^{-1}(w)$ is not empty iff w contains both $X\beta\beta\alpha\beta$ and Y'. However such a word corresponds to the resulting word from Π'. Hence using h^{-1} it is possible to filter out the words that do not correspond to the final result. At the same time h^{-1} decodes the remaining part of the string. Finally, the weak coding ξ removes the markers for the beginning and for the end of the word ($\bar{X}$ and $\bar{Y}$).

The universality of the corresponding system follows from the existence of universal tag systems.

Theorem 2. *There exists a universal splicing (tissue) P system with 5 rules.*

4   Small Universal Double Splicing Extended H System

In this section we consider a small universal double splicing extended H system from [7].

Theorem 3. *Let $TS = (2, V, P)$ be a tag system. Then, there is a double splicing extended H system $\Gamma_1 = (V', T, A, R)$ with 5 rules that simulates TS as follows:*

1. *for any word $w \in V^*$ on which TS halts producing the result v, the system Γ_1 produces a unique result $X'c(v)Y'$, i.e. $L_d(\Gamma_1, X\beta\alpha\beta c(w)\beta Y) = \{X'c(v)Y'\}$,*
2. *for any word $w \in V^*$ on which TS does not halt, the system Γ_1 computes infinitely without producing a result, i.e. $L_d(\Gamma_1, X\beta\alpha\beta c(w)\beta Y) = \emptyset$.*

We construct the system Γ_1 as follows.

Let $|V| = n$, $n \ge 2$ and $1 \le j \le n$. The terminal and non-terminal alphabets of Γ_1 are the following:

$V' = \{\alpha, \beta, X, Y, X', Y', Z_1, Z_2, Z_3, Z_4\}$, $T = \{X', Y', \alpha, \beta\}$.

The axioms A and rules R are given as follows.

$A = \{XZ_1c(P_i)\bar{c}(a_i)Y \mid a_i \to P_i \in P\} \cup \{XZ_2Y, X\beta Z_3Z_1\beta Y, X'Z_4Z_1Y'\}$.

$$R = \{1 : \beta\#\beta Y\$Z_1\#\lambda, \qquad\qquad 2 : X\beta\alpha\beta\#\alpha\alpha\$X\#Z_1,$$
$$3 : \lambda\#\alpha Y\$Z_2\#Y, \qquad\qquad 4 : X\alpha\#\lambda\$X\#Z_2,$$
$$5 : X\beta\alpha\#\lambda\$X\beta\#Z_3\}.$$

Now one uses the following morphism h and the weak coding ξ to get resulting strings:

$$h(a) = \begin{cases} \alpha^i\beta & \text{if } a = a_i \in V, \\ X\beta\alpha\beta\alpha\beta & \text{if } a = \bar{X}, \\ Y' & \text{if } a = \bar{Y}. \end{cases} \qquad \xi(a) = \begin{cases} a & \text{if } a \in V, \\ a_1 & \text{if } a = \bar{X}, \\ \lambda & \text{if } a = \bar{Y}. \end{cases}$$

The universality of the corresponding system follows from the existence of universal tag systems.

Theorem 4. *There exists a universal double splicing extended H system with 5 rules.*

5 Small Universal Extended Splicing Test Tube System

In this section we present a small universal splicing test tube system from [7].

Theorem 5. *[7] Let $TS = (2, \Sigma, P)$ be a tag system. Then, there is an extended splicing test tube system with 3 tubes $\Gamma_2 = ((V, T_1, T_2, T_3), \mathcal{T})$ and 8 rules, which simulates TS as follows:*

1. *for any word $w \in \Sigma^*$ on which TS halts producing the result v, the system Γ_2 produces a unique result $X_0c(v)Y$, i.e., $L(\Gamma_2, Xc(w)\beta Y) = \{X_0c(v)Y\}$.*
2. *for any word $w \in \Sigma^*$ on which TS does not halt, the system Γ_2 computes infinitely without producing a result, i.e., $L(\Gamma_2, Xc(w)\beta Y) = \emptyset$.*

We construct the system Γ_2 as follows.

$V = \{\alpha, \beta, X, X', X_0, Y, Y', Y'', Z\}$, $\mathcal{T} = \{X_0, Y, \alpha, \beta\}$.

$T_1 = (((V, R_1), A_1), F_1)$ with $F_1 = \{\alpha, \beta, X, X_0, Y, Y'\}$ and $A_1 = \{Zc(P_i)\bar{c}(a_i)Y'' \mid a_i \to P_i \in P\} \cup \{X'Z, ZY''\}$. R_1 consists of the following splicing rules:

$$1.1 : \beta\#\beta Y\$Z\#\alpha \; ; \qquad 1.2 : X\#\lambda\$X'\#Z \; ; \qquad 1.3 : \lambda\#Y'\$Z\#Y''.$$

$T_2 = (((V, R_2), A_2), F_2)$ with $F_2 = \{\alpha, \beta, X', Y''\}$ and $A_2 = \{XZ, ZY'\}$. R_2 consists of the following splicing rules:

$$2.1 : X'\alpha\#\lambda\$X\#Z \; ; \qquad\qquad 2.2 : \lambda\#\alpha Y''\$Z\#Y'.$$

$T_3 = (((V, R_3), A_3), F_3)$ with $F_3 = \{\alpha, \beta, X', Y''\}$ and $A_3 = \{X'\beta Z, XZ,$ $X_0 Z, Z\beta Y\}$. R_3 consists of the following splicing rules:

$$3.1 : X'\beta\alpha\#\lambda\$X'\beta\#Z \; ; \qquad 3.2 : \quad X'\beta\beta\#\lambda\$X\#Z \; ; \qquad 3.3 : \lambda\#\beta Y''\$Z\#\beta Y.$$

Now one uses the following morphism h and the weak coding ξ to get resulting strings:

$$h(a) = \begin{cases} \alpha^i\beta & \text{if } a = a_i \in V, \\ X\beta\beta\alpha\beta & \text{if } a = \bar{X}, \\ \beta Y & \text{if } a = \bar{Y}. \end{cases} \qquad \xi(a) = \begin{cases} a & \text{if } a \in V, \\ a_1 & \text{if } a = \bar{X}, \\ \lambda & \text{if } a = \bar{Y}. \end{cases}$$

The universality of the corresponding system follows from the existence of universal tag systems.

Theorem 6. *There exists a universal extended splicing test tube system with 3 test tubes and 8 rules.*

6   Small Universal TVDH Systems

In this section we present two small universal TVDH systems from [4].

Theorem 7. *Let $G = (2, \Sigma, P)$ be a tag system and $w \in \Sigma^*$. Then, there is a TVDH system of degree 2, $D_1 = (V, T, A, R_1, R_2)$, with 15 rules, which given the word $Xc(w)Y_0 \in V^*$ as input simulates G on input w, i.e. such that:*

1. *for any word w on which TS halts producing the result z, the system D_1 produces a unique result $c(z)Y_0$, i.e., $L(D_1, w) = \{c(z)Y_0\}$.*
2. *for any word w on which TS does not halt, the system D_1 computes infinitely without producing a result, i.e., $L(D_1, w) = \emptyset$.*

We construct the system D_1 as follows.
$V = \{\alpha, \beta, X, X', X'', Y, Y', Y'', Y_0, Z, Z_1, Z_2, \mathcal{Z}_1, \mathcal{Z}_2\}$, $T = \{Y_0, \alpha, \beta\}$.
The axioms are given as follows.
$A = \{\mathcal{Z}_1 c(P_i)\bar{c}(a_i)Y \mid a_i \to P_i \in P\} \cup \{XZ_1Y_0, XZ_2Y_0, XZ_1Y, XZ_2Y,$ $X'Z_1Y', X'Z_2Y', X''Z_1Y'', X''Z_2Y'', \mathcal{Z}_2Z\}$.
The rules are given as follows (the first number indicates the component to which the rule belongs).

$1.1 : \alpha\beta\#Y_0\$\mathcal{Z}_1\#\alpha$;	$1.2 : \varepsilon\#\alpha Y\$Z_1\#Y$;	$1.3 : X\beta\#\varepsilon\$X'\#Z_1$;
$1.4 : X''\#\varepsilon\$X'\#Z_1$;	$1.5 : X'\beta\#\alpha\alpha\$X\#Z_1$;	$1.6 : X'\beta\#\alpha\beta\$\varepsilon\#\mathcal{Z}_2Z$;
$1.7 : Z_1\#\varepsilon\$Z_2\#\varepsilon$;	$1.8 : \mathcal{Z}_1\#\alpha\$\mathcal{Z}_2\#Z$	$2.1 : X\alpha\#\varepsilon\$X\#Z_2$;
$2.2 : \beta\#\beta Y\$Z_2\#Y'$;	$2.3 : X'\alpha\#\varepsilon\$X''\#Z_2$;	$2.4 : \beta\#Y'\$Z_2\#Y''$
$2.5 : \beta\#Y''\$Z_2\#Y_0$;	$2.6 : Z_1\#\varepsilon\$Z_2\#\varepsilon$;	$2.7 : \mathcal{Z}_1\#Z\$\mathcal{Z}_2\#\alpha$;

The construction follows the idea from [40,25]. The simulation of TS is performed as follows. For every step of the derivation in TS there is a sequence of several derivation steps in D_1. The current configuration $w = a_i a_k w'$, $i \neq 1$ of TS is encoded by a string $Xc(w)Y_0$ present in component 1 of D_1 (the initial configuration of D_1 satisfies this property). The simulation of a production $a_i \to P_i$, $2 \leq i \leq n$ is performed using the rotate-and-simulate method used for many proofs in this area. We use this method as follows. First, by rule 1.1, suffixes $c(P_j)\bar{c}(a_j)$, $2 \leq j \leq n$ are attached to the string producing words $X\alpha^i\beta c(a_k w')c(P_j)\beta\alpha^j Y$. After that symbols α is removed at both ends simultaneously by rules 1.2 and 2.1. The strings having $j \neq i$ will be eliminated, corresponding checks are done by rules 1.3 and 2.2. Hence, only the string for which $j = i$ will remain at the end, producing $X'c(a_k w')Y'$. After that the symbol a_k is removed (by removing corresponding α's) by rules 2.3 and 1.4 and after applying rules 2.4, 1.5 and 2.5 string $Xc(w')Y_0$ will appear at component 1 and a new round begins. The simulation stops when the first symbol is the halting symbol a_1. In this case rule 1.6 is used producing $c(z)Y_0$.

The universality of the corresponding system follows from the existence of universal tag systems.

Theorem 8. *There exists a universal TVDH system of degree 2 with 15 rules.*

Theorem 9. *Let $G = (2, \Sigma, P)$ be a tag system and $w \in \Sigma^*$. Then, there is a TVDH system of degree 1, $D_2 = (V, T, A, R_1)$, with 17 rules, which given the word $Xc(w)Y_0 \in V^*$ as input simulates G on input w, i.e. such that:*

1. *for any word w on which TS halts producing the result w', the system D_1 produces a unique result $X_0 c(w')Y_0$, i.e., $L(D_2, w) = \{X_0 c(w')Y_0\}$.*
2. *for any word w on which TS does not halt, the system D_1 computes infinitely without producing a result, i.e., $L(D_2, w) = \emptyset$.*

We construct the system D_2 as follows.

$V = \{\alpha, \beta, X, X', X'', Y, Y', Y'', X_0, Y_0, Z, Z_1, Z_2, K\}$, $T = \{X_0, Y_0, \alpha, \beta\}$.

The axioms are given as follows.

$A = \{ZZ_1Kc(P_i)\bar{c}(a_i)Y \mid a_i \to P_i \in P\} \cup \{ZZ_1Y, X'Z_1Z, XZ_1Z, X_1Z_1Z,$
$X_0Z_1Z, XZ_2Z', Z'Z_2Y', Z'Z_2Z_2Y'', X''Z_2Z', Z'Z_2Y_0, Z'Z_2Y_1\}$.

1.1 :$\alpha\beta\#Y_0\$ZZ_1K\#\alpha$;	1.2 :$\varepsilon\#\alpha Y\$ZZ_1\#Y$;	1.3 :$X\beta\#\alpha\$X_1\#Z_1Z$;
1.4 :$X_1\alpha\#\varepsilon\$X'\#Z_1Z$;	1.5 :$X''\#\varepsilon\$X'\#Z_1Z$;	1.6 :$X'\beta\#\alpha\alpha\$X\#Z_1Z$;
1.7 :$X'\beta\#\alpha\beta\$X_0\#Z_1Z$;	1.8 :$X\alpha\#\varepsilon\$X\#Z_2$;	1.9 :$\beta\#\beta Y\$ZZ_2\#Y_1$;
1.10 :$\beta\#Y_1\$ZZ_2\#Y'$;	1.11 :$X'\alpha\#\varepsilon\$X''\#Z_2Z$	1.12 :$\beta\#Y'\$ZZ_2Z_2\#Y''$;
1.13 :$\beta\#Y''\$ZZ_2\#Y_0$;	1.14 :$Z\#Z_1\$Z'\#Z_2$;	1.15 :$Z\#Z_2\$Z'\#Z_1$;
1.16 :$Z_1\#Z\$Z_2\#Z'$;	1.17 :$Z_2\#Z\$Z_1\#Z'$.	

The universality of the corresponding system follows from the existence of universal tag systems.

Theorem 10. *There exists a universal TVDH system of degree 1 with 17 rules.*

7   Small Universal Antiport P System

In this section we present a small universal antiport P system from [8], constructed by simulating the universal register machine U_{22} from [19], see Figure 1 in Section 2.

Theorem 11. *There exists a universal antiport P system with 23 rules.*

The proof has been presented in terms of maximally parallel multiset rewriting systems. Indeed, a multiset rewriting system directly correponds to a one-membrane symport/antiport system with environment containing an unbounded supply of all objects, and rule $u \to v$ corresponds to rule $(u, out; v, in)$.

We now present the formal description of the system; the flowchart representing its finite state transition graph is illustrated by Figure 4:

$$\gamma = (O, R, \{R_1\}, \mathcal{I}, \mathcal{P}), \text{ where}$$
$$O = R \cup \{C_3, C_5', C_6'\} \cup \{q_{16}, q_{27}\} \cup \{T, I, J, K, L, M, N, O, P, Q, T, X\},$$
$$R = \{R_i \mid 0 \le i \le 7\},$$
$$\mathcal{I} = LQLQJJNXXXR_0^{i_0} \cdots R_7^{i_7}.$$

Here $i_0, \cdots, i_7$ is the contents of registers 0 to 7 of U_{22} and $LQLQJJNXX$ is the encoding of the initial state $q_1 C_1 S$. The table below gives the set $\mathcal{P}$ of rules.

$phase : XX \to XT$	$a : LQLQJJNTT \to JJLOR_6XX$
$D0 : IJKPQR_0 \to LQLQJJM$	$b : LC_5'TT \to JJLOR_6XX$
$D1 : LQLQJJNR_1 \to LPLPJJMR_7$	$c : OC_6'TT \to IILQLQNR_5XX$
$D2 : IIKPQR_2 \to JJKPQ$	$d : QLQNC_6'TT \to JJKQQR_6XX$
$D3 : q_{27}C_3R_3 \to JJKPQ$	$e : q_{27}C_3TT \to LQLQJJNR_0XX$
$D4 : JJKR_4 \to JJLLM$	$f : q_{16}JJOC_5'C_5'TT \to LQLQJJNR_2R_3XX$
$D5 : JJOR_5 \to C_5'$	$g : q_{16}C_5'C_5'C_5'TT \to q_{16}JJOJJOJJOXX$
$D6 : IJLR_6 \to C_6'$	$1 : JJLOTT \to IJLOXX$
$D7 : IILQLQNR_7 \to IJLOR_1$	$5 : JJKQQTT \to q_{16}JJOJJOJJOXX$
$A : ITT \to JXX$	$8 : q_{16}JJOJJOJJOTT \to IIKPQMXX$
$B : JJMTT \to JJNXX$	$12 : q_{16}JJOJJOC_5'TT \to q_{27}C_3XX$
$C : LP \to LQ$	

In fact, by simulation all objects except $R_0, \cdots, R_7$ appear inside the system in bounded quantities, so the constructed system is explained by projections of configurations onto $O' = O \setminus \{R_0, \cdots, R_7\}$, yielding a finite transition graph. We refer to its nodes as *finite states*. The possibility of some transitions, however, depends on the availability of objects R_j, $0 \le j \le 7$. In [8] one thus speaks about *finite-state maximally parallel multiset rewriting systems* (FsMPMRSs).

Machine U_{22} may be simulated in a *straightforward* way, by rule $q \to R_i q_1$ for each instruction $(q, [R_k P], q_1)$ and by rules

$$q \to q' C_q, \ q' \to q'', \ C_q R_{i_q} \to C_q', \ q'' C_q \to q_1, \ q'' C_q' \to q_2$$

for each instruction $(q, \langle R_{i_q} ZM \rangle, q_1, q_2)$. This yields a universal P system with 73 symport/antiport rules, reported already in [11] (together with some optimizations). The number of rules is then decreased at the expense of their weight. The overall behaviour eventually gets quite complicated, so flowcharts are used to describe it. A square represents a finite state (see the previous paragraph), and a circle attached to it represents a (possibly partial) application of rules; multiple circles may be drawn as one for simplicity.

Multiple techniques are used to decrease the number of rules. First, if one rule (e.g., increment) is always applied after another one, then they can be merged, *eliminating an intermediate state*. A state then typically contains a *checker* (object C with an index, possibly primed), verifying whether a specific register is present in the system (is non-zero); addition instructions and renaming rules are no longer present as separate rules. This increases the weight of rules to 5.

A very important optimization is *gluing*: the representation of the configurations is changed such that the effect of multiple rules is obtained by one rule. A general scheme is the following: suppose we have rules $r_1 : c_1 \rightarrow c_2$ and $r_2 : d_1 \rightarrow d_2$. They both can be replaced by a rule $r : X \rightarrow Y$ if we transform the representation as follows: $c_1 = cX$, $c_2 = cY$, $d_1 = dX$, $d_2 = dY$. It is, however, needed that no state is a submultiset of another state.

We now proceed with two simple special cases of gluing. The first case is *phases*. Representing states q and q' by qS and qS' lets us glue all rules $q \rightarrow q'$ (waiting while the checker gets a chance to decrement a register) yielding a single rule $S \rightarrow S'$. Later, *three phases* help to further optimize the other rules, but the transitions $S \rightarrow S'$ and $S' \rightarrow S''$ are also glued by substitution $S = XXX$,

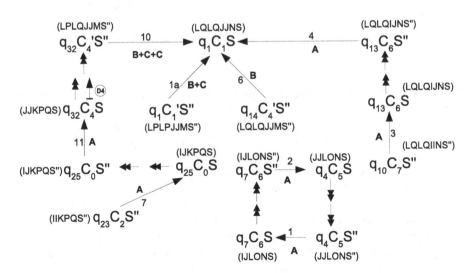

Fig. 3. Part of the multiset rewriting flowchart of U_{22} showing only glued rules and the corresponding encoding

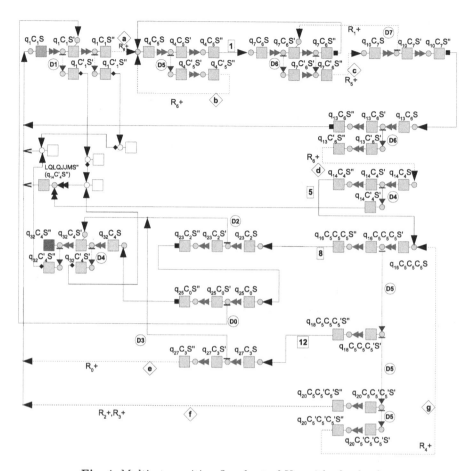

Fig. 4. Multiset rewriting flowchart of U_{22} with glued rules

$S' = XXT$, $S'' = XTT$ yielding a single rule $XX \to XT$. This phase rule is represented on flowcharts by a double-headed arrow.

The second simple special case of gluing is *unifying the checkers* that decrement the same register. Now the state typically contains a phase, a checker, and the rest of the state is currently a symbol q with an index, derived from U_{22}. We now proceed to the structural optimizations.

The first structural optimization is reducing the decoder block of U_{22}, responsible for dividing value of R_5 by three. Instead of three conditional decrement instructions, a loop decrementing three is replaced by one rule, and three other rules implement exits from this loop, depending on the remainder. One further rule acts on the register by the checker; it may be used up to 3 times in parallel.

The second structural optimization exploits the fact that registers 0, 1, 2, 3, 7 are only decremented by one instruction. The corresponding rules may be merged with the rules that follow them. However, rule $S \to S'$ is performed independently; this is solved by introducing the third phase (re-glued as described above; the phases on flowcharts are still represented by S, S' and S'' only for compactness), the move to the next state changes phase 3 into phase 1. For register 1, the rule cannot be combined with the next one, but the duty of incrementing of register 7 is moved into it from the next rule.

We present the final *encoding optimization*: 3 rules $A : ITT \rightarrow JXX$, $B : JJMTT \rightarrow JJNXX$ and $C : LP \rightarrow LQ$ perform the effect of 9 rules, see Figure 3. This yields the system γ defined above; its flowchart is illustrated by Figure 4.

As described above, γ corresponds to a universal antiport system with 23 rules. It is still quite incredible that 23 rules are sufficient for such a simple computational model.

8 Conclusions

In this article we present several very small universal systems, i.e., universal systems having a small number of rules (5 for universal splicing P system, 5 for universal double splicing H system, 8 for universal splicing test tube system with 3 tubes, 15 for TVDH system of degree 2, 17 for TVDH system of degree one, and 23 for antiport P system).

We do not know whether the results from this paper are optimal. Since the smallest known universal system based on splicing has 5 rules it is possible that some of results presented in the paper can be improved.

Another possibility for further research is to investigate other computational devices based on splicing like ETVDH systems [44], modified splicing test tube systems [46], and length-separating splicing test tube systems [12].

References

1. Adleman, L.: Molecular Computation of Solutions to Combinatorial Problems. Science 226, 1021–1024 (1994)
2. Alhazov, A., Freund, R., Rogozhin, Y.: Computational Power of Symport/Antiport: History, Advances, and Open Problems. In: Freund, R., Păun, G., Rozenberg, G., Salomaa, A. (eds.) WMC 2005. LNCS, vol. 3850, pp. 1–30. Springer, Heidelberg (2006)
3. Alhazov, A., Krassovitskiy, A., Rogozhin, Y.: Circular Post Machines and P Systems with Exo-insertion and Deletion. In: Gheorghe, M., Păun, G., Rozenberg, G., Salomaa, A., Verlan, S. (eds.) CMC 2011. LNCS, vol. 7184, pp. 73–86. Springer, Heidelberg (2012)
4. Alhazov, A., Kogler, M., Margenstern, M., Rogozhin, Y., Verlan, S.: Small Universal TVDH and Test Tube Systems. International Journal of Foundations of Computer Science 22(1), 143–154 (2011)
5. Alhazov, A., Kudlek, M., Rogozhin, Y.: Nine Universal Circular Post Machines. Computer Science Journal of Moldova 10, 3(30), 247–262 (2002)
6. Alhazov, A., Rogozhin, Y., Verlan, S.: A Small Universal Splicing P System. In: Gheorghe, M., Hinze, T., Păun, G., Rozenberg, G., Salomaa, A. (eds.) CMC 2010. LNCS, vol. 6501, pp. 95–102. Springer, Heidelberg (2010)

7. Alhazov, A., Rogozhin, Y., Verlan, S.: On Small Universal Splicing Systems. Fundamenta Informaticae (in press)
8. Alhazov, A., Verlan, S.: Minimization Strategies for Maximally Parallel Multiset Rewriting Systems. TUCS Report No. 862 (2008), and arXiv:1009.2706v1 [cs.FL], and Theoretical Computer Science 412, 1581–1591 (2011)
9. Cocke, J., Minsky, M.: Universality of Tag Systems with P = 2. Journal of the Association for Computing Machinery 11(1), 15–20 (1964)
10. Csuhaj-Varjú, E., Kari, L., Păun, G.: Test Tube Distributed Systems Based on Splicing. Computers and Artificial Intelligence 15(2–3), 211–232 (1996)
11. Csuhaj-Varjú, E., Margenstern, M., Vaszil, G., Verlan, S.: Small Computationally Complete Symport/Antiport P systems. Theoretical Computer Science 372(2-3), 152–164 (2007)
12. Csuhaj-Varjú, E., Verlan, S.: On Length-Separating Test Tube Systems. Natural Computing 7(2), 167–181 (2008)
13. Freund, R., Alhazov, A., Rogozhin, Y., Verlan, S.: Communication P Systems. In: Păun, G., Rozenberg, G., Salomaa, A. (eds.) The Oxford Handbook of Membrane Computing, ch. 5, pp. 118–143 (2010)
14. Freund, F., Freund, R.: Test Tube Systems: When Two Tubes are Enough. In: Rozenberg, G., Thomas, W. (eds.) Developments in Language Theory, Foundations, Applications and Perspectives, pp. 338–350. World Scientific Publishing Co., Singapore (2000)
15. Frisco, P., Zandron, C.: On Variants of Communicating Distributed H Systems. Fundamenta Informaticae 48(1), 9–20 (2001)
16. Frisco, P.: Computing with Cells: Advances in Membrane Computing. Oxford University Press (2009)
17. Head, T.: Formal Language Theory and DNA: An Analysis of the Generative Capacity of Recombinant Behaviors. Bulletin of Mathematical Biology 49, 737–759 (1987)
18. Head, T., Păun, G., Pixton, D.: Language Theory and Molecular Genetics. Generative Mechanisms Suggested by DNA Recombination. In: [41], ch. 7, vol. 2
19. Korec, I.: Small Universal Register Machines. Theoretical Computer Science 168, 267–301 (1996)
20. Lipton, R.J.: DNA Solution of Hard Computational Problems. Science 268, 542–545 (1995)
21. Margenstern, M.: Frontier Between Decidability and Undecidability: A Survey. Theoretical Computer Science 231(2), 217–251 (2000)
22. Margenstern, M.: Surprising Areas in the Quest for Small Universal Devices. Electronic Notes in Theoretical Computer Science 225, 201–220 (2009)
23. Margenstern, M., Pavlotskaya, L.: On the Optimal Number of Instructions for Universality of Turing Machines Connected with a Finite Automaton. International Journal of Algebra and Computation 13(2), 133–202 (2003)
24. Margenstern, M., Rogozhin, Y.: A universal time-varying distributed H system of degree 1. In: Jonoska, N., Seeman, N.C. (eds.) DNA 2001. LNCS, vol. 2340, pp. 371–380. Springer, Heidelberg (2002)
25. Margenstern, M., Rogozhin, Y., Verlan, S.: Time-Varying Distributed H Systems of Degree 2 Can Carry Out Parallel Computations. In: Hagiya, M., Ohuchi, A. (eds.) DNA 2002. LNCS, vol. 2568, pp. 326–336. Springer, Heidelberg (2003)
26. Chen, J., Reif, J.H. (eds.): DNA 2003. LNCS, vol. 2943, pp. 48–53. Springer, Heidelberg (2004)
27. Margenstern, M., Verlan, S., Rogozhin, Y.: Time-varying distributed H systems: an overview. Fundamenta Informaticae 64, 291–306 (2005)

28. Minsky, M.: Computation, Finite and Infinite Machines. Prentice-Hall, Englewood Cliffs (1967)
29. De Mol, L.: Tag Systems and Collatz-like Functions. Theoretical Computer Science 390, 92–101 (2008)
30. Neary, T., Woods, D.: The Complexity of Small Universal Turing Machines: A Survey. In: Bielíková, M., Friedrich, G., Gottlob, G., Katzenbeisser, S., Turán, G. (eds.) SOFSEM 2012. LNCS, vol. 7147, pp. 385–405. Springer, Heidelberg (2012)
31. Pavlotskaya, L.: Solvability of the Halting Problem for Certain Classes of Turing Machines. Mathematical Notes 13(6), 537–541 (1973); Translated from Matematicheskie Zametki 13(6), 899–909 (1973)
32. Păun, G.: Computing with Membranes. Journal of Computer and System Sciences 1(61), 108–143 (2000); Also TUCS Report No. 208 (1998)
33. Păun, G., Yokomori, T.: Membrane Computing Based on Splicing. In: Winfree, E., Gifford, D.K. (eds.) DNA Based Computers V. DIMACS Series in Discrete Mathematics and Theoretical Computer Science, vol. 54, pp. 217–232. American Mathematical Society (1999)
34. Păun, G., Rozenberg, G., Salomaa, A.: DNA Computing: New Computing Paradigms. Springer, Heidelberg (1998)
35. Păun, G., Rozenberg, G., Salomaa, A. (eds.): The Oxford Handbook of Membrane Computing. Oxford University Press (2010)
36. Post, E.L.: Formal Reductions of the General Combinatorial Decision Problem. American Journal of Mathematics 65(2), 197–215 (1943)
37. Priese, L., Rogozhin, Y., Margenstern, M.: Finite H-systems with 3 Test Tubes are not Predictable. In: Altman, R., Dunker, A., Hanter, L., Klein, T. (eds.) Proceedings of Pacific Simposium on Biocomputing, pp. 545–556. World Sci.Publ., Singapore (1998)
38. Robinson, R.M.: Minsky's Small Universal Turing Machine. International Journal of Mathematics 2(5), 551–562 (1991)
39. Rogozhin, Y.: Small Universal Turing Machines. Theoretical Computer Science 168(2), 215–240 (1996)
40. Rogozhin, Y., Verlan, S.: On the Rule Complexity of Universal Tissue P Systems. In: Freund, R., Păun, G., Rozenberg, G., Salomaa, A. (eds.) WMC 2005. LNCS, vol. 3850, pp. 356–362. Springer, Heidelberg (2006)
41. Rozenberg, G., Salomaa, A.: Handbook of Formal Languages, vol. 3. Springer, Heidelberg (1997)
42. Shannon, C.E.: A Universal Turing Machines with Two Internal States. Automata Studies, Ann. of Math. Stud. 34, 157–165 (1956)
43. Turing, A.M.: On Computable Real Numbers, with an Application to the Entscheidungsproblem. Proc. London Math. Soc. Ser. 2 42, 230–265 (1936)
44. Verlan, S.: A Boundary Result on Enhanced Time-Varying Distributed H Systems with Parallel Computations. Theoretical Computer Science 344(2-3), 226–242 (2005)
45. Verlan, S.: Communicating Distributed H Systems with Alternating Filters. In: Jonoska, N., Păun, G., Rozenberg, G. (eds.) Aspects of Molecular Computing. LNCS, vol. 2950, pp. 367–384. Springer, Heidelberg (2003)
46. Verlan, S.: Head Systems and Application to Bio-Informatics. PhD thesis, LITA, Université de Metz, Metz, France (2004)

Membrane Systems and Hypercomputation

Mike Stannett[*]

Department of Computer Science, University of Sheffield
Regent Court, 211 Portobello, Sheffield S1 4DP, United Kingdom

Abstract. We present a brief analysis of hypercomputation and its relationship to membrane systems theory, including a re-evaluation of Turing's analysis of computation and the importance of timing structure,
and suggest a 'cosmological' variant of tissue P systems that is capable
of super-Turing behaviour. No prior technical background in hypercomputation theory is assumed.

1 Re-evaluating Turing's Analysis

In his seminal paper [21], Turing gave a careful and powerfully intuitive analysis
of what it means for a human being to compute something, and described how the
processes involved could be captured mechanistically via the machine model that
now bears his name. By analysing the behaviour of his model, Turing was then
able to show that certain problems could not be solved computationally. Against
this, hypercomputation theorists, myself included, claim that certain physical
forms of computation may in fact be more powerful than Turing envisaged. It
is incumbent on us, therefore, to explain why and where Turing's analysis is
incomplete, and why computation might indeed be capable of solving problems
that appear on first analysis to be formally undecidable.

1.1 The Halting Problem Revisited

Let us begin by recalling the reasons underpinning the insolubility of the Halting
Problem (essentially a recasting of Richard's Paradox [17], see also [12, pp. 142–
144]). Our goal in doing so is to not to re-establish the standard underlying
paradox, but to investigate its possible sources. For ease of argument, we will
express things in terms of modern computers and programming languages. Our
focus is the set of programs that accept a single natural number as input.

Preliminaries
A standard (Western) computer keyboard allows users to express roughly 105
distinct characters. Think of the characters on the keyboard as distinct digits in

---

[*] The author is partially supported under the Royal Society International Exchanges
Scheme (ref. IE110369). This work was partially undertaken whilst the author was
a visiting fellow at the Isaac Newton Institute for the Mathematical Sciences in the
programme *Semantics & Syntax: A Legacy of Alan Turing.*

E. Csuhaj-Varjú et al. (Eds.): CMC 2012, LNCS 7762, pp. 78–87, 2013.

this base. Since computer programs can be expressed as finite strings typed on such a keyboard, each program can be regarded as a natural number (written in base 105). We can therefore arrange the set of all programs, acting on a single natural number input, in some definite order: $P_0, P_1, P_2, \ldots$.

Step 1. Suppose **HP** can be built

We would like someone to build us a labour saving tool (**HP**). Given two natural numbers m and n, **HP** should output *yes* if $P_m(n)$ eventually halts, and *no* if it doesn't. Let us assume that **HP** can indeed be built.

Step 2. Use **HP** to build **Diag**

The clerk can use **HP** to build a program, **Diag**, that halts if $P_n(n)$ runs forever, and loops forever if $P_n(n)$ will eventually halt (Fig. 1(a)).

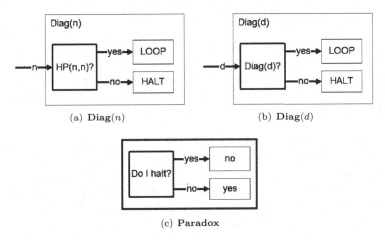

(a) **Diag**(n)   (b) **Diag**(d)

(c) **Paradox**

Fig. 1. Behaviour of **Diag**(n), **Diag**(d) and **Paradox**

Step 3. Apply **Diag** to its own code

Because **Diag** takes a single natural number input, it must occur somewhere in the list $P_0, P_1, P_2, \ldots$. Suppose then that **Diag** is P_d, and consider what happens when we compute **Diag**(d). Because P_d is just **Diag**, the subroutine **HP**(d, d) resolves the question "Does **Diag**(d) halt?", indicated "**Diag**(d)?" in Fig. 1(b).

Step 4. Establish a paradox

The value d is simply a fixed natural number. We can therefore consider it to be 'hard-wired' as **Diag**(d)'s input, and re-interpret **Diag**(d) as a program, **Paradox**, taking no inputs. In informal terms, **Paradox** asks itself the question '*Do I halt?*', and behaves paradoxically in the sense that it apparently halts if and only if it runs forever (Fig. 1(c)).

Step 5. Resolve the contradiction

Since a paradox appears to have been generated, one of our assumptions must be wrong. However, the only assumption we seem to have made is that **HP** can be built, since the other steps presumably follow automatically. Therefore, **HP** cannot in fact be built.

2   Towards Hypercomputation

Given the paradoxical behaviour established in Step 4, Turing's argument relies on the judgment (Step 5) that the only questionable assumption is that **HP** can be built (Step 1). However, there are at least three other key assumptions built into this argument, any of which can also be used to provide an alternative resolution of the paradox:

– Can **HP** be implemented via a physical system (an *oracle* [22, 3]) that is not itself computational?

– Is the ability to use tools as components in the construction of larger systems reflected only in those systems' structure, or does it also affect *what* can be computed? If so, it need not be **HP**'s existence that should be called into question, but the way in which it has been used as a component in the larger system, **Diag**.

– The argument tacitly assumes that computational systems can be built that behave deterministically, since we are using our definite knowledge of what **Diag**'s output *ought to be* in order to derive the paradox. While the uncertainties of quantum theory obviously throw this assumption into question, we will see below that mechanistic determinism cannot be achieved even in the setting of classical Newtonian dynamics.

The first of these caveats needs careful analysis. The existence of a physical **HP** solver would not prevent the construction of **Diag**, and one can still envisage a situation where **Diag** must be one of the programs $P_0, P_1, P_2, \ldots$, because there is nothing to stop us using a language whose commands include statements of the form *"Feed the values into the black box on the table, and use its subsequent output in what follows"*. It is important to remember, however, that the problem **HP** depends on the computational system under analysis. If we add the ability to use **HP** as a basic instruction type, Turing's proof then shows that the halting problem for this *extended* system cannot be solved by a (Turing+**HP**)-machine. In other words, we may well be able to find a physical oracle that solves **HP** in the context of standard digital computing, but there will always be other problems that remain undecidable no matter how powerful the components we allow. The existence of a physical **HP** solver cannot be answered definitively given our present knowledge of physics, but the evidence (reviewed below) is encouraging; it appears, in particular, that relativistic phenomena could be exploited to solve problems like **HP** that are insoluble via Turing machine.

Addressing the third issue leads to somewhat more surprising results. Underpinning all our discussions of computation so far is the notion that the physics of computation is essentially deterministic. We are used to the idea that quantum theory introduces inherent uncertainties, but as we now explain, even such classical systems as Newtonian dynamics *must* be non-deterministic. This is quite surprising, since the Newtonian model has traditionally been seen as an archetype of deterministic physics: as Laplace puts it [14, p. 4]

> An intellect [*Laplace's demon*] which at a certain moment would know all forces that set nature in motion, and all positions of all items of which nature is composed, if this intellect were also vast enough to submit these data to analysis, it would embrace in a single formula the movements of the greatest bodies of the universe and those of the tiniest atom; for such an intellect nothing would be uncertain and the future just like the past would be present before its eyes.

The failure of this claim follows from a remarkable result of Zhihong Xia, published some 20 years ago [24], demonstrating that the Newtonian n-body problem possesses 'non-collision singularities.' That is, we can have a system of objects interacting gravitationally, one or more of which are propelled to infinity in finite time. The key point here is that the laws of Newtonian physics are unaffected if we mentally reverse the direction of time. If we do so in the context of Xia's result, this tells us that objects can appear *from* infinity in finite time, and indeed there is no limit to how quickly they can do so. Consequently, even if Laplace's demon were equipped with complete knowledge of the current state of the universe, it would *not* be able to determine the subsequent state even one second later, because the spontaneous arrival of new material during the intervening period would inevitably introduce gravitational forces, or even collisions, that could not have been forecast in advance.

2.1   The Significance of Interaction

In Step 2 the clerk uses **HP** as a component in the construction of **Diag**. For the sake of argument we will assume that **HP** is implemented as a separate agent (i.e., on a separate machine) with which the clerk and **Diag** can interact; furthermore, to avoid circular reasoning, we will assume throughout that the agent is essentially just a digital computer, with no hypercomputational capabilities of its own. Using agents in this way is permitted under Turing's analysis, as he explains in another of his landmark papers [23, emphasis added]:

> The human computer is supposed to be following fixed rules; he has no authority to deviate from them in any detail. We may suppose that these rules are supplied in a book, which is altered whenever he is put on to a new job. He has also an unlimited supply of paper on which he does his calculations. *He may also do his multiplications and additions on a "desk machine," but this is not important.*

As we shall see, the problem with this analysis lies not in the description of the human computer's (i.e., the clerk's) behaviour, but in the 'throw-away' claim that allowing the clerk to interact with another agent – in this case a desk machine – is "not important." We stress again that we are not assuming that the agent itself has 'super-Turing' capabilities of any kind; indeed, the agent in question might simply be another clerk. The important feature of agent-assisted computation is, rather, the physical separation between clerk and agent, since this implies that they can be in motion relative to one another, subject to different forces and accelerations – and as Einstein has taught us, this means that their perceptions of space and time need not agree with one another [8].

2.2 Accelerating Machines

Suppose the agent is based high above the Earth's surface, while the clerk operates at sea level. The difference in gravitational potential between the two locations will ensure that time for the agent appears to run faster than for the clerk.[1] While there are limits to the speed-up that can be achieved in this way, the scenario naturally raises the question whether *accelerating machines* can be implemented. In its simplest form, an accelerating machine is one in which each instruction takes half as long to execute as its predecessor, so that if the first instruction takes 1 sec, even a non-terminating computation will have run to completion after 2 sec – for example, if we placed the agent on board a rocket so that it moves ever further away from us and with ever increasing acceleration, this could result in each instruction taking less time to run (from our point of view) than its predecessor. Such a simple scheme is fraught with physical and logical difficulties [20], but it is nonetheless instructive to consider how it might be used to solve **HP**, and what the difficulties would be in doing so. We will then be in a position to relate our findings to the (arguably more realistic) hypercomputational potential of, e.g., tissue P systems [4].

Accelerating machines have been discussed in the context of P systems by Calude and Păun [5], based on the observation that reactions tend to run faster in smaller volumes (assuming that concentration increases accordingly). By recursively constructing ever smaller subregions and having them compute subroutines ever faster, one can achieve exactly the speed-up required to solve **HP** and its kindred problems. More recently, Gheorghe and Stannett [10] have extended this principle to solve problems at all levels of the *arithmetical hierarchy* (and beyond) [2]. Taking $\mathcal{P}_0$ to be the class of 'standard' P systems, we can define a hierarchy of systems $\mathcal{P}_1, \mathcal{P}_2, \mathcal{P}_3, \ldots$, where a $\mathcal{P}_{n+1}$ system is a Calude-Păun accelerating P system in which the systems replicated at each stage are $\mathcal{P}_n$ systems. For example, the original Calude-Păun accelerating P system model generates a $\mathcal{P}_1$ system under this scheme, since the replicated components are all standard $\mathcal{P}_0$ systems. As shown in [10], each $\mathcal{P}_n$ is strictly more powerful than its predecessor, and together they exhaust the entire hierarchy.

---

[1] See, e.g., [6] for experimental confirmation of this long-standing claim.

How might an accelerating machine be implemented physically? Notice first that neither the agent nor the clerk can solve **HP** on their own, because their separate behaviours are still susceptible to the limitations identified by Turing's analysis; solving **HP** requires the agent and clerk to *cooperate* with one another. Provided they agree to do so, deciding whether or not some computation $P_m(n)$ eventually terminates is simple.

1. The clerk transmits the values m and n to the accelerating agent.
2. The accelerating agent executes $P_m(n)$, and has agreed that in the event of the computation halting, a message will be sent back to the clerk saying so.
3. The clerk waits two seconds to allow the agent sufficient time to run the program, adds a further delay corresponding to the maximum transit time of the potential signals involved, and then checks to see whether a message has been received from the agent. If so, the computation halted, and the clerk reports *yes*. If not, the clerk reports *no*.

Let us analyse the timing structure of this system in more detail, since it is the same for *any* system in which (a) the clerk uses an agent to execute $P_m(n)$; and (b) the clerk has to determine in finite time whether or not the agent's execution of $P_m(n)$ terminated.

- The clerk (A) and the agent (B) communicate at the start of the procedure;
- The agent may need to run the program forever, but even in this case the clerk has to perceive the computation as requiring only finite time relative to her own clock.
- There must come a point later in the clerk's life where the termination or otherwise of the agent's program execution can be identified.

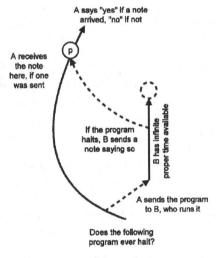

Fig. 2. The underlying timing structure involved in the cooperative solution of **HP** is that of Malament-Hogarth spacetime

In relativistic language, we are saying (Fig. 2) that

1. the agent's worldline should allow the agent *infinite proper time*;
2. there is a point, p, on the clerk's worldline such that: at any point x on the agent's worldline it is possible for the agent (eventually) to send an agreed signal s from x to the clerk, so that s is received by the clerk earlier than p.

Cosmological spacetimes that include timing structures of this nature are called *Malament-Hogarth* (MH) spacetimes [7], and schemes have been proposed showing that the existence of stable MH-spacetimes is sufficient to allow *cosmological hypercomputation* to be implemented [9]. The analysis above suggests that the use of MH timing structures is also *necessary* if problems like **HP** are to be solved cooperatively by standard computational systems.

While MH structures seem exotic at first sight, they are associated with large slowly-rotating (*slow Kerr*) blackholes of the kind thought to exist at the centre of many galaxies (including our own [11]), and this makes them usable by the clerk for computational purposes. It might be argued, of course, that using the Galactic centre in this way is of only technical interest but has no practical relevance due to the vast distances involved. However, this neglects another important aspect of Turing's analysis. In proposing his model of human computation, Turing placed no limitations on how long a task might take to complete; and indeed complexity theory has shown that even fairly simple tasks may take longer than the current age of the Universe to run to completion on a standard PC. In contrast, a rocket travelling at 11 km s^{-1} (escape velocity at the Earth's surface) towards the Galactic centre (roughly 28,000 light years away [11, 15]) would require only around 763 million years to arrive there. While this is certainly a long time, it nonetheless compares well with the expected runtime of certain computations; it is therefore hard to see why the use of the Galactic centre should be considered any less reasonable than the use of arbitrarily long-lived Turing machines when determining what can and can't be computed.

The use of slowly rotating massive blackholes for hypercomputational purposes[2] is discussed in detail by Etesi and Németi [9]. As one falls into the blackhole one is inexorably drawn through a region linking an outer to an inner event horizon, but thereafter things return to 'normal' in the sense that one can move freely, and in particular one can avoid hitting the singularity. In their scenario the clerk chooses to fall into the blackhole, leaving the agent orbiting outside. Due to time dilation effects the agent's time appears to run ever faster the nearer the clerk gets to the horizon, thereby implementing the required MH timing structure. After crossing the horizon, the clerk knows whether or not a signal has been received from the agent, and then continues into the inner 'safe zone' where she makes use of the information. This scheme is not without its problems, however, since there are clear indications that the blackholes in question may exhibit inherent instabilities [16, 13]. An important open question, therefore, is whether other cosmological examples of MH timing structures can be identified for which these instabilities are provably absent.

2.3 Cosmological P Systems

One can easily adapt the MH-spacetime model of (hyper)computation to produce a new hypercomputational tissue-based model, which we will refer to as a *cosmological P system*. Looking again at Fig. 2, we begin by envisaging a contiguous population of membrane systems ("cells") which begins as a small population based where A and B first diverge. This population replicates, spreading at the

---

[2] Other cosmological approaches also exist e.g., the exploitation of closed timelike curves (CTCs) and wormholes [1, 19].

same, constant, average speed in all directions. It is not the cells which generate the hypercomputational speed-up, but the geometry of the spacetime in which they are replicating, for by the time a new cell has been created at p, it will 'perceive' infinitely many cells to have been generated along B. From the viewpoint of any cell on B, however, there is nothing unusual happening locally – the regeneration time remains unchanged from its own point of view.

To see how the computation proceeds, we observe that the original model involves three distinct entities: the clerk, the agent, and the spacetime through which signals are propagated. Accordingly, we need the cells that form along A and B to differentiate themselves both from each other and from those which fill the rest of space at any given moment. We therefore assume that the cell strain is initially *spacetime* – this cell type simply propagates signals in straight lines (in other words, it includes rewrite rules of the form "*if* signal *is present in the cell, place a copy of* signal *in all neighbouring cells*", thereby ensuring recursive re-transmission of incoming signals). In contrast, we assume that as the clerk and agent move along their respective trajectories, they emit promoters into the cells' environment which trigger the conversion of *spacetime* cells into A-type or B-type cells, respectively. This ensures the generation of two filaments within the general population, one composed of A-type cells, the other of B-types (Fig. 3).

The behaviour of A- and B-type cells is essentially straightforward.

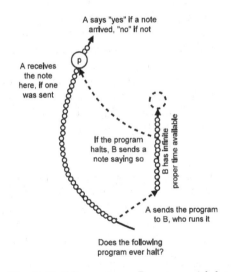

- A-type cells respond to the presence of a *signal* compound by converting it into a *yes*, which is then replicated in all descendants. At all times, an A-type cell responds to the clerk's chemical promoter by extending the filament along A's trajectory, while replicating standard *spacetime* cells in all other directions. If at any point a *signal* or a *yes* is present in the cell, it includes *yes* in the 'genome' of its immediate descendants.

- B-type cells perform the actual computation of $P_m(n)$. We encode the program counter and registers as chemical species in the cell,

Fig. 3. Building a tissue P system with hypercomputational power

along with the program itself. Each cell simulates the execution of one instruction, and then generates the next cell along the B-trajectory so that it contains a full copy of the program, together with the coded versions of the updated program counter and registers. If at any point the cell determines that the program counter and registers remain unchanged (i.e., the program halts), the cell emits a *signal* in all directions.

In this way, $P_m(n)$ is executed by the growing B-filament, and a *signal* is received at p if and only if the program eventually terminates – thereby solving **HP**. This is, of course, unsurprising, since neither the clerk nor the agent need be entities with continuous existence. All that matters is the information they carry with them as they travel along their respective trajectories. By replicating these information flows, we automatically replicate the associated computational power.

3   Summary and Further Research

In this paper we have revisited Turing's analysis of computation, and considered how it can be subverted by taking into account the physical separation between cooperative agents. This in turn leads to analysis of cosmological models of hypercomputation based on Malament-Hogarth spacetimes, and their simulation via tissue P systems. This suggests a number of avenues for further research, for example:

– The behaviour of a 'cosmological' P system can clearly be replicated instead using a cellular automaton. The advantage of the P system approach lies in the system's self-generation – instead of presupposing a pre-existing infinite population of communicating automata, the cells of the tissue simply replicate as time goes by, filling spacetime as they do so. However, the model relies on interactions between the three component cell strains and two 'external' entities (the clerk and the agent) which move through the underlying spacetime scattering promoter molecules. Can these be modelled directly within the P system paradigm, or is their autonomous nature necessary for the model to work?

– We have only discussed one approach to hypercomputation, namely the use of slow-Kerr black holes. However, the wider literature discusses numerous computational models of super-Turing computation (analogue recursive neural networks, trial-and-error machines, and the like [18]). To what extent can each of these models be extended or re-interpreted in the context of membrane systems?

– Can the models in question be formalised, and their properties verified mechanistically via a theorem prover or proof assistant? Providing concrete formal analyses can be expected to add support to our claims that hypercomputation in the context of P systems is physically meaningful. My colleagues and I have recently started investigating this area, but much work remains to be done.

References

[1] Andréka, H., Németi, I., Székely, G.: Closed Timelike Curves in Relativistic Computation (2012), arXiv:1105.0047 [gr-qc]

[2] Ash, C.J., Knight, J.F.: Computable Structures and the Hyperarithmetical Hierarchy. Elsevier, Amsterdam (2000)

[3] Beggs, E.J., Costa, J.F., Loff, B., Tucker, J.V.: Computational complexity with experiments as oracles. Proc. Royal Society, Series A 464, 2777–2801 (2008)

[4] Bernardini, F., Gheorghe, M.: Tissue and Population P Systems. In: Păun, G., Rozenberg, G., Salomaa, A. (eds.) The Oxford Handbook of Membrane Computing, pp. 227–250. OUP, Oxford (2010)

[5] Calude, C.S., Păun, G.: Bio-steps beyond turing. BioSystems 77, 175–194 (2004)

[6] Chou, C.W., Hume, D.B., Rosenband, T., Wineland, D.J.: Optical Clocks and Relativity. Science, 1630–1633 (September 24, 2010)

[7] Earman, J., Norton, J.: Forever is a Day: Supertasks in Pitowsky and Malament-Hogarth Spacetimes. Philosophy of Science 5, 22–42 (1993)

[8] Einstein, A.: Relativity: The Special and General Theory. Henry Holt, New York (1920)

[9] Etesi, G., Németi, I.: Non-Turing computations via Malament-Hogarth spacetimes. Int. J. Theoretical Physics 41, 341–370 (2002), arXiv:gr-qc/0104023v2

[10] Gheorghe, M., Stannett, M.: Membrane system models for super-Turing paradigms. Natural Computing 11, 253–259 (2012)

[11] Gillessen, S., Eisenhauer, F., Trippe, S., Alexander, T., Genzel, R., Martins, F., Ott, T.: Monitoring stellar orbits around the Massive Black Hole in the Galactic Center. The Astrophysical Journal 692, 1075–1109 (2009)

[12] van Heijenoort, J. (ed.): From Frege to Gödel: A Source Book in Mathematical Logic, pp. 1879–1931. Harvard University Press, Cambridge (1977)

[13] Hod, S.: On the instability regime of the rotating Kerr spacetime to massive scalar perturbations (2012), arXiv:1205.1872v1 [gr-qc]

[14] Laplace, P.S.: A Philosophical Essay on Probabilities. Dover Publications, New York (1951); translated into English from the original French 6th ed. by F. W. Truscott and F. L. Emory

[15] Majaess, D.: Concerning the Distance to the Center of the Milky Way and its Structure. Acta Astronomica 60(1), 55–74 (2010)

[16] Penrose, R.: Structure of spacetime. In: DeWitt, C.M., Wheeler, J.A. (eds.) Battelle rencontres, pp. 121–235. W.A. Benjamin, New York (1968)

[17] Richard, J.: Les Principes des Mathématiques et le Problème des Ensembles. Revue Générale des Sciences Pures et Appliquées (June 30, 1905)

[18] Stannett, M.: The case for hypercomputation. Applied Mathematics and Computation 178, 8–24 (2006)

[19] Stannett, M.: Computation and Spacetime Structure. Int. J. Unconventional Computing (in press, 2013), special Issue on New Worlds of Computation 2011

[20] Thomson, J.F.: Tasks and Super-Tasks. Analysis 15(1), 1–13 (1954)

[21] Turing, A.M.: On computable numbers, with an application to the Entscheidungsproblem. Proc. London Math. Soc., Series 2 42, 230–265 (submitted May 1936) (1937)

[22] Turing, A.M.: Systems of Logic Based on Ordinals. Proc. London Math. Soc., Series 2 45, 161–228 (1939)

[23] Turing, A.M.: Computing machinery and intelligence. Mind 59, 433–460 (1950)

[24] Xia, Z.: The existence of noncollision singularies in Newtonian systems. Annals of Mathematics 135, 411–468 (1992)

A Case-Study on the Influence
of Noise to Log-Gain Principles
for Flux Dynamic Discovery

Tanvir Ahmed[1], Garrett DeLancy[1], and Andrei Păun[1,2]

[1] Department of Computer Science, Louisiana Tech University, Ruston
PO Box 10348, Louisiana, LA-71272 USA
{tah025,rgd006,apaun}@latech.edu
[2] Bioinformatics Department, National Institute of Research and Development for
Biological Sciences, Splaiul Independenţei, Nr. 296, Sector 6, Bucharest, Romania
apaun@fmi.unibuc.ro

Abstract. In this paper we show problems associated with the log-gain procedure [13] for determining flux-dynamics from time series by means of applying noise to the data sets. We illustrate this by first creating a set of flux functions and using these flux functions to derive a time series which we then apply Gaussian noise to [7]. This perturbed time series is then used in the log-gain procedure to determine flux-dynamics. The error from the two sets of flux functions is found to be extremely large for signal-to-noise ratios of less than about 25. To further illustrate the disparity in the results, we use these derived flux functions to discover new time series. We show that the log-gain procedure is very susceptible to noise, and that for it to be of practical use with data collect in vivo it must be made much more robust.

1 Introduction

One of many goals in the field of bioinformatics is the creation of tools [2] used to interpret raw biological data and generate models based on this data. A problem that may be encountered is that the amount of data these accurate models require sometimes far exceeds the amount of data we can feasibly collect from the biological source. One method that some have used in an attempt to bypass this problem is the extrapolation of predicted data from the gathered data. Care must be taken in this process as it becomes increasingly easy to create an accurate model that can only make predictions based on extrapolated data, perfect data gathered under ideal conditions, or data that contains no noise. Such a model obviously has little use, and as our techniques for gathering biological data evolve and become more efficient and refined, we will find ourselves needing to create filler data less and less often.

The word noise is commonly used to refer to unwanted sound; however, in many scientific areas the term is extended to cover any unwanted signal or data that interferes with the collection of wanted data. This is very much like sound

E. Csuhaj-Varjú et al. (Eds.): CMC 2012, LNCS 7762, pp. 88–100, 2013.

noise interfering with one's ability to listen to a conversation, and as such the term fits. The vast majority of data gathered from scientific experiments in almost all of the sciences contains at least a small amount of noise; biology is no exception. Noise is actually extremely prevalent in data gathered from the area of molecular biology; many of the tools we use to gather in vivo biological data are capable of (and often do) also inadvertently gather data produced by other biological functions. Because of this, overcoming the noise problem is one of the many challenges in that field.

P systems [20], [18] are computational models that preform computations based upon an abstraction in the way that chemicals interact with and move across various cellular membranes. [18], [19], [20], [14] Metabolic P systems (MP systems) can be defined as deterministic P systems proposed to compute the dynamics of various biological processes (like metabolism) in cells.

Key to our research are two very important tools: Matlab and MetaPlab. For the uninformed, Matlab is a programming environment with a wide range of uses including but not limited to algorithm development and data analysis. For the purposes of of our research we made use of Matlab to apply generated noise to noiseless data. MetaPlab is a modeling tool used by researchers to better understand and predict the internal mechanisms of biological systems [5], [6] and their responses to external stimuli, environmental conditions, and structural changes. The MetaPlab framework is based on a core module which enables the design and management of biological models and an extensive set of plugins. [16] MetaPlab is used extensively in our research for both model creation and data collection. Without MetaPlab much of the work done here would have been much more difficult.

The log-gain principle states that we can compute future behavior of a given system within an acceptable approximation. Furthermore, it is believed that in some situations we can determine an MP system that is a good model of a few discovered metabolic dynamics. Using current methods it is difficult to measure a reaction's fluxes. This is due to the microscopic nature of chemical elements, the complex interactions among these elements and the sheer number of elements. Log-gain principles allow us to calculate the approximate values of fluxes if we know the time series of the system. With an appropriate model, this would allow us to quickly and easily retrieve the reaction fluxes for every instant. The process is believed to be such that a ratio should hold between change of substances and related change of flux units. [13]

Here we hope to show the effects that noise may have on MP systems and explore the underlying mechanisms of flux-dynamics discovery in log-gain principles. As such, the addition of noise to the data used in the log-gain procedure will act as a sort of stress test to determine how well the whole process can handle noisy data. The importance of such an experiment is almost self-relevant. By showing how well the log-gain procedure can handle noise we will hopefully be able to determine how well the procedure could handle data gathered completely from an in vivo source.

2   Motivation

Because of the prevalence of noise and the fact that it is considered a nuisance, it is important that the models we design be equipped to tolerate a degree of noise relative to the amount commonly encountered in their relative fields of study. Biological data is often said to be quite noisy, and usually has a signal-to-noise ratio (SNR) which is considered to be quite low; due to the nature of the calculation, the lower the SNR, the greater the percentage of noise present in the data. As such, observing some amount of noise in biological data is considered to be inevitable. Randomness in constantly occurring biochemical processes will by it's very nature always be affecting other processes, and these interactions will be detected; this is biological noise. It is extremely unlikely that we will ever be able to completely remove these influences from the biological data we collect, and we must be prepared to deal with the reality that the conclusions and inferences we make based on noisy data may be quite wrong if the models and tools we use to make these conclusions and inferences are ill-equipped to deal with an appropriate degree of noise. For instance, if we assume that a model that cannot correctly handle noise is correct in all cases, then we may be led to believe that our model is correct when it is in fact wrong. This could potentially have dire consequences depending on the model and circumstances. Therefore, we can plainly see that the study of the effects of noise on our models and other tools is of great importance, and that all care should be taken when designing models designed to work with typically noisy data.

3   Experimental Setup

Our experimental setup consists of a few basic steps followed by a comparison of results generated. [16] First, we assume some substances and associated flux functions and initial values. Using the various tools in MetaPlab we compute the time series data for these substances. This time series data acts as a sort of pseudo-experimental data set, as it is currently not feasible to gather time series data from biological sources. To better represent what would be collected from biological sources Gaussian noise is applied to this time series data. The next step is to apply log-gain principles to our noisy time series data to test the log-gain procedure. To apply these principles to our data we will once again be making use of MetaPlab. The application of log-gain principles to our noisy time series will result in a set of flux functions. These flux functions can then be compared to the flux functions we assumed and error between the two sets can be quantified. Furthermore, we then use these new flux functions to show the noiseless time series that would have resulted in their creation via log-gain principles. By comparing these time series to the ones actually used we can see a representation of the error inherent in the process.

The table 1 shows the initial concentrations and molar weights for three arbitrary substances: A, B, and C. Using this data we could use log-gain theory to compute the flux-dynamics of each of these substances. However, for the purpose

Table 1. Description of substances of our MP-model for case study

Substance	Initial Concentration	Molar Weight(gram)
A	100	1
B	100	1
C	0.02	1

Table 2. Reactions and Flux regulation functions for our model to case study

Reactions	Flux regulation maps
R_0: A→ 2A	F_0: 0.000002 * A * B * C
R_1: A→ B	F_1: 0.00003 * B * C
R_2: A→ C	F_2: 0.00004 * C * A
R_3: B→ λ	F_3: 0.0005 * B
R_4: C→ λ	F_4: 0.007 * C

of this study we will instead assume some flux functions and use the MetaPlab tool, Simulation Plugin 2, in an effort to derive the flux-dynamics without needing to resort to a microscopic analysis of the MP systems.

Table 2 shows the assumed reactions and corresponding flux regulation maps. These functions are then used along with the initial concentrations and molar weights in MetaPlab to construct a model to be used to help us fill out any other missing relevant information to be derived from what we know about our substances that we will need to successfully run Simulation Plugin 2. Worth noting is that the mappings show the inputs and outputs in moles. Reactions R3 and R4 have inputs of substances B and C respectively, but neither produce any outputs that are used in the model. This explains both their lack of a known output (it is irrelevant to our research) and their positions on the model.

A model was constructed using MetaPlab where R0, R1, R2, R3, and R4 were designated as our reactions; A, B, and C, our substances; and F0, F1, F2, F3, and F4 our flux regulation maps. For the construction of this model we have no data about the time series, but do know that we can use MetaPlab to generate a time series based on the flux functions we have assumed. The mappings to and from the various nodes on the model represent the functions that regulate moving from one node to another. For instance, we can see from the table 2 above that F0 is dependent on the values from substances A, B, and C and as such there are mappings from A, B, and C to F0. Likewise, we can tell that R2 takes one mole of substance A and converts it into one mole of substance C. The I/O gates show where a reaction's products leave the model.

With the data we constructed about the flux functions, our model, initial concentrations, molar weights, and the appropriate multiplicity of each edge we were able to run Simulation Plugin 2 for MetaPlab and obtain the time series for each substance. Next, we took this data and used MathLab to plot the time series for each substance (shown below). These are the time series that we expect the log-gain theory to yield for perfect, noiseless data.

Simulation Plugin 2 is a plugin that simply runs the computations for the given inputs of a given model. Using this plugin we can quickly and easily determine the time series for various substances in a model, given that we know sufficient data (initial values and regulation functions) of the substances. Since this data is assumed for our experiment, we already have it.

As such, our next step is to add noise to the data. To this end we made use of the genSignalForSNR function of Matlab, which allows us to specify a particular value for the SNR to be applied to a time series of our choosing. Through the use of this function we can approximate what in vivo biological data may look like by applying noise to the time series we have generated.

Worth noting is that genSignalForSNR will be adding Gaussian noise to our data set. Gaussian noise is a statical noise that is normally distributed. The choice to add Gaussian noise was made in an attempt to have an ideal mix of data with noise. The uniform distribution of Gaussian was believed to aid in this area.

We use genSignalForSNR with various inputs for our three time series with an SNR parameter of 20. An SNR of 20 implies that the signal strength will be 20 times greater than the strength of the noise. In our original research we considered all SNR values less than or equal to 80 in increments of 5; for the purposes of this paper, we will only consider SNR values of 40, 25, and 10. The purpose for this choice will become apparent later.

This genSignalForSNR function must be run for every substance at every SNR value we wish to test. The substance inputs take the form of three .txt files (A.txt, B.txt, and C.txt) which contain the time series of the three substances as shown above. The raw time series data used to create these .txt files was obtained by exporting the time series data for each of the three substances.

We use the genSignalForSNR function in Matlab to simulate the noise. The genSignalForSNR function generates Gaussian noise, scales the input signal according to the given SNR, calculates the signal power and noise power, calculates the SNR for the scaled signal and generated noise, and finally applies the generated noise to the input signal. For the purpose of this research, the signal used in this function was our time series data.

The genSignalForSNR gives us the modified time series data values that we would see if the data collection process had contained noise. We can now take this noisy data that we have generated using genSignalForSNR and use Matlab to plot these new noisy time series.

Using the log-gain theory requires that we know the initial values of all fluxes and at least 1,000 steps of each time-series. [16] With data collected from the noisy time series we constructed, we are easily able to supply this information. For our study, we used both the initial values of the fluxes and 10,000 steps of our noisy time series data for the log-gain MetaPlab plugin.

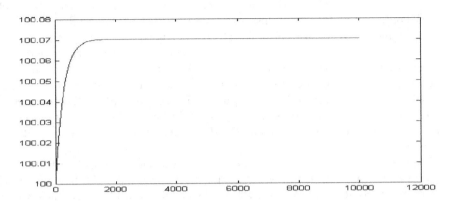

Fig. 1. Time Series of A without noise

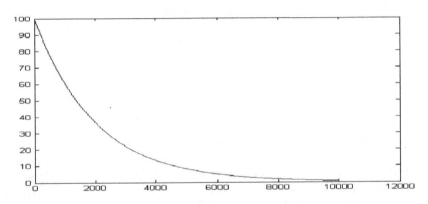

Fig. 2. Time Series of B without noise

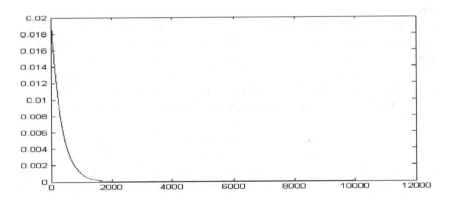

Fig. 3. Time Series of C without noise

Our next step was to take the noisy time series data and import it into a model which contained no flux functions. The above model has had it's flux functions removed and the relevant data replaced with our noisy time series data. Such a model is what would typically be used with the log-gain theory, as the log-gain process should generate flux-dynamics by utilizing the time series data gathered from experimentation and without making use of known flux functions. This model is a prime candidate for being used with the MetaPlab log-gain plugin. With noiseless data this process would be quickly verified; however, for our noisy data additional tests will be required. After importing all noisy data and the initial values for the flux functions, we were ready to begin the log-gain process.

We made use of the following set of tuners in using our model with the log-gain process. Tuner selection was a simple task as we knew the flux functions before hand (recall that we simply assumed some flux functions). As such, tuner selection was a simple process of determining which reactions were governed by which substances.

$$R_0 = A, B, C$$
$$R_1 = B, C$$
$$R_2 = C, A$$
$$R_3 = B$$
$$R_4 = C$$

As mentioned above, we made use of the MetaPlab log-gain plugin to apply log-gain theory to our model. This plugin requires the initial values of all fluxes and at least 1,000 steps of each time-series. The time series data used is the 10,000 step noisy data we generated. The reaction set was input into the plugin with a good Covering Offset Log Gain Property [4], and a polynomial was then generated through the plugin by selecting an appropriate substance. Descriptions for the polynomials were given at the time of generation. The reactions were set up in the following manner: R0 covered substance A, R3 covered substance B, and R2 covered substance C. After all tuners and coverings were input into MetaPlab, we ran the plugin. We also used a linear regression plugin to apply curve fitting to the clean noise effect and retrieve the flux functions. This only required that we make use of the flux functions and the initial values of the various time series. The time series can either be imported from external files by the log-gain plugin or computed by using the dynamic computation plugin.

The log-gain plugin applied log-gain theory to the noisy time series data, but to better understand our results, we took one last step. We noticed that our generated flux functions [9], [10] did not match the flux functions we assumed to create time series data. Using these flux functions, we once again preformed some calculations to determine the time series that these new flux functions would yield. The results are presented below, adjacent to the most relevant data for comparison.

4 Results

The following is the presentation of all of the collected results found from applying the noisy time series data to log-gain theory as well as a plot of the input time series. Further explanation of the results follows.

Table 3. SNR 40 Results

Original Functions	Flux Functions when SNR = 40
F_0: 0.000002 * A * B * C	4.71E-5 + 2.09E-6*A*B*C
F_1: 0.00003 * B * C	4.70E-5 + 3.91E-5*B*C
F_2: 0.00004 * C * A	6.52E-8 + 3.91E-5*C*A
F_3: 0.0005 * B	-1.90E-16 + 5.00E-4*B
F_4: 0.007 * C	5.46E-20 + 0.007*C

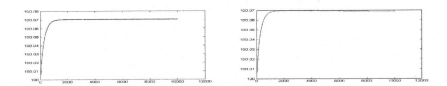

Fig. 4. Left: noisy time series of A when SNR = 40, right: time series of A calculated from the flux dynamics given by log-gain theory

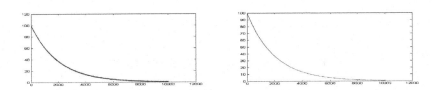

Fig. 5. Left: noisy time series of B when SNR = 40, right: time series of B calculated from the flux dynamics given by log-gain theory

Table 4. Error Calculation for an SNR of 40

A	B	C	Average
0.0012	2.5066	38281867303	12760622435

Table 5. SNR 25 Results

Original Functions	Flux Functions when SNR = 25
F_0: 0.000002 * A * B * C	0.0012 - 1.7117E-4*A*B*C
F_1: 0.00003 * B * C	0.0013 - 0.0173*B*C
F_2: 0.00004 * C * A	2.16306E-6 + 7.1273E-6*C*A
F_3: 0.0005 * B	4.0050E-17 + 5.0352E-4*B
F_4: 0.007 * C	4.7763E-21 + 0.0069*C

Table 6. Error Calculation for an SNR of 25

A	B	C	Average
0.026050201	64.57143304	6.32E+011	2.11E+011

Table 7. SNR 10 Results

Original Functions	Flux Functions when SNR = 10
F_0: 0.000002 * A * B * C	0.0374 - 0.0067*A*B*C
F_1: 0.00003 * B * C	0.0373 - 0.6660*B*C
F_2: 0.00004 * C * A	5.9732E-5 - 8.6151E-4*C*A
F_3: 0.0005 * B	1.3867E-14 + 4.9587E-4*B
F_4: 0.007 * C	-5.3717E-19 + 0.0070*C

Table 8. Error Calculation for an SNR of 10

A	B	C	Average
0.0165	1109.0357	1.16E+012	3.87E+011

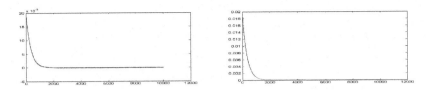

Fig. 6. Left: noisy time series of C when SNR = 40, right: time series of C calculated from the flux dynamics given by log-gain theory

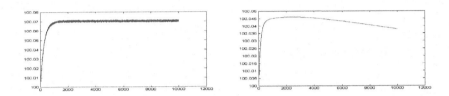

Fig. 7. Left: noisy time series of A when SNR = 25, right: time series of A calculated from the flux dynamics given by log-gain theory

As seen above, we calculated percentage of error in all substances and found the average error. The error shown here between the log-gain generated dynamics and what we know the true flux-dynamics to be is caused by introducing noise into the time series.

As shown by the above results, log-gain theory fails to generate accurate flux dynamics for our substances when the data becomes sufficiently noisy. This was expected; using enough noise will break even the most robust models. What was not expected was just how quickly the model began to fall apart. Biological data is said to have relatively low SNR values due in part to the sensitivity of the equipment required to record the data and the randomness inherent in all biological processes. Our experimentation finds that there is sufficient noise present in SNR values of 40 and below to break the process.

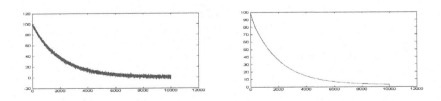

Fig. 8. Left: noisy time series of B when SNR = 25, right: time series of B calculated from the flux dynamics given by log-gain theory

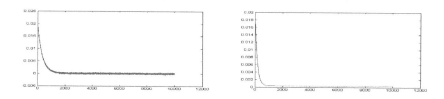

Fig. 9. Left: noisy time series of C when SNR = 25, right: time series of C calculated from the flux dynamics given by log-gain theory

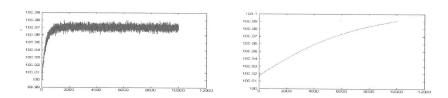

Fig. 10. Left: noisy time series of A when SNR = 10, right: time series of A calculated from the flux dynamics given by log-gain theory

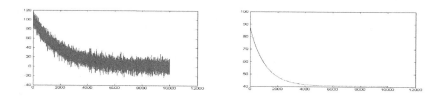

Fig. 11. Left: noisy time series of B when SNR = 10, right: time series of B calculated from the flux dynamics given by log-gain theory

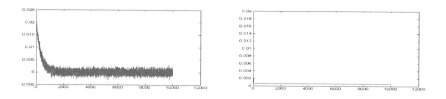

Fig. 12. Left: noisy time series of C when SNR = 10, right: time series of C calculated from the flux dynamics given by log-gain theory

Also shown are the flux functions derived from the log-gain theory. These functions are shown to deviate further from their actual values as SNR decreases. Like the flux dynamics and error, this is expected as noise is interfering with our data set. Once again these results are disproportionately disturbed for the amount of noise present in the data at many steps.

5 Conclusion

Based on the data derived from these tests we have determined that the log-gain procedure fails to account for noise and begins to break down at when the SNR drops below 40. This corresponds to the signal being 40 times stronger than the noise, or 2.5 percent observed noise in the recorded data. Since biological processes are often considered to have low SNR values (and are therefore fairly noisy), we must conclude that further work must be done to modify these log-gain algorithms before they can be applied to data gathered completely from living cells.

There may, however, be some error present in how we applied noise to the data. We have very little basis for the decision to use Gaussian noise, and noise that more closely resembles data that would be collected in vivo would be much preferable, and may not break the process quite so easily. That said, the choice to use Gaussian noise was done so that our noisy data would more closely resemble the noiseless test data the log-gain theory has been shown to work on. As such, we find it unlikely that using a more random or disruptive noise would produce more favorable results from the log-gain process. Thus, we must once again conclude that the log-gain process be further refined before usage in analyzing data from living cells.

Acknowledgements. The authors acknowledge support in part from NSF CCF–1116707, BIODIV–105 and UEFISCDI – PNII–TE 92/2010.

References

1. Bertalanffy, L.: General system theory. 9. Braziller, New York (1984)
2. Castellini, A.: Algorithm and Software for Biological MP Modeling by Statistical and Optimization Techniques. Universit'a degli Studi di Verona (2010)
3. Deane, C.M., Salwiaski, A., Xenarios, I., Eisenberg, D.: Protein interactions: two methods for assessment of the reliability of high throughput observations. Molecular & Cellular Proteomics: MCP 1, 349–356 (2002)
4. Franco, G., Manca, V., Pagliarini, R.: Regulation and Covering Problems in MP Systems. In: Păun, G., Pérez-Jiménez, M.J., Riscos-Núñez, A., Rozenberg, G., Salomaa, A. (eds.) WMC 2009. LNCS, vol. 5957, pp. 242–251. Springer, Heidelberg (2010)
5. Fontana, F., Manca, V.: Discrete solutions to differential equations by metabolic P systems. Theoretical Computer Science 372, 165–182 (2007)
6. Fontana, F., Manca, V.: Predator-prey dynamics in P systems ruled by metabolic algorithm. Bio Systems 91, 545–557 (2008)

7. Gillespie, D.T.: Exact stochastic simulation of coupled chemical reactions. The Journal of Physical Chemistry 81, 2340–2361 (1977)
8. Goldbeter, A.: A minimal cascade model for the mitotic oscillator involving cyclinand cdc2 kinase. Proceedings of the National Academy of Sciences 88, 9107–9111 (1991)
9. Hassani, H., Amiri, S., et al.: The efficiency of noise reduction for curve fitting in growth curve models. Umea: Centre of Biostochastics, Swedish University of Agricultural Sciences (2008)
10. Hong, S., Cui, X., Li, S., June, N.C.T., Kwack, K., Kim, H.: Noise removal for multi-echo MR images using global enhancement. In: 2010 IEEE International Conference on Systems Man and Cybernetics, SMC, pp. 3616–3621 (2010)
11. Jost, J.: Dynamical systems examples of complex behaviour. Springer, Berlin (2005)
12. Lestas, I., Vinnicombe, G., Paulsson, J.: Fundamental limits on the suppression of molecular fluctuations. Nature 467, 174–178 (2010)
13. Manca, V.: Log-gain Principles for Metabolic P Systems. In: Condon, A., Harel, D., Kok, J.N., Salomaa, A., Winfree, E. (eds.) Algorithmic Bioprocesses, pp. 585–605. Springer, Heidelberg (2009)
14. Manca, V.: Topics and problems in metabolic P systems. In: Gutierrez-Naranjo, M.A., Paun, G., Riscos-Nunez, A., Romero-Campero, F.J. (eds.) Proc. of the Fourth Brainstorming Week on Membrane Computing, BWMC4, Fenix Editora, pp. 173–183 (2006)
15. Manca, V., Bianco, L.: Biological networks in metabolic P systems. Bio Systems 91, 489–498 (2008)
16. Manca, V., Castellini, A., Giuditta, F., Marchetti, L., Pagliarini, R.: MetaPlab 1.2 User Guide (2010)
17. von Mering, C., et al.: Comparative assessment of large-scale data sets of protein-protein interactions. Nature 417, 399–403 (2002)
18. Păun, G.: Computing with Membranes. Journal of Computer and System Sciences 61, 108–143 (2000)
19. Păun, G.: A guide to membrane computing. Theoretical Computer Science 287, 73–100 (2002)
20. Păun, G.: Membrane computing: an introduction. Springer, Berlin (2002)
21. Segel, L.: Design principles for the immune system and other distributed autonomous systems. Oxford University Press, Oxford (2001)
22. Voit, E.: Computational analysis of biochemical systems: a practical guide for biochemists and molecular biologists. Cambridge University Press, New York (2000)

Asynchronous and Maximally Parallel Deterministic Controlled Non-cooperative P Systems Characterize $NFIN$ and $coNFIN$

Artiom Alhazov[1,2] and Rudolf Freund[3]

[1] Institute of Mathematics and Computer Science
Academy of Sciences of Moldova
Academiei 5, Chişinău MD-2028 Moldova
artiom@math.md

[2] Università degli Studi di Milano-Bicocca
Dipartimento di Informatica, Sistemistica e Comunicazione
Viale Sarca 336, 20126 Milano, Italy
artiom.alhazov@unimib.it

[3] Faculty of Informatics, Vienna University of Technology
Favoritenstr. 9, 1040 Vienna, Austria
rudi@emcc.at

Abstract. Membrane systems (with symbol objects) are distributed controlled multiset processing systems. Non-cooperative P systems with either promoters or inhibitors (of weight not restricted to one) are known to be computationally complete. In this paper we show that the power of the deterministic subclass of such systems is computationally complete in the sequential mode, but only subregular in the asynchronous mode and in the maximally parallel mode.

1 Introduction

The most famous membrane computing model where determinism is a criterion of universality versus decidability is the model of catalytic P systems, see [3] and [5].

It is also known that non-cooperative rewriting P systems with either promoters or inhibitors are computationally complete, [1]. Moreover, the proof satisfies some additional properties:

- Either promoters of weight 2 or inhibitors of weight 2 are enough.
- The system is non-deterministic, but it restores the previous configuration if the guess is wrong, which leads to correct simulations with probability 1.

The purpose of this paper is to formally prove that computational completeness cannot be achieved by deterministic systems when working in the asynchronous or in the maximally parallel mode.

E. Csuhaj-Varjú et al. (Eds.): CMC 2012, LNCS 7762, pp. 101–111, 2013.

2   Definitions

An *alphabet* is a finite non-empty set V of abstract *symbols*. The free monoid generated by V under the operation of concatenation is denoted by V^*; the *empty string* is denoted by λ, and $V^* \setminus \{\lambda\}$ is denoted by V^+. The set of non-negative integers is denoted by $\mathbb{N}$; a set S of non-negative integers is called *co-finite* if $\mathbb{N} \setminus S$ is finite. The family of all finite (co-finite) sets of non-negative integers is denoted by $NFIN$ ($coNFIN$, respectively). The family of all recursively enumerable sets of non-negative integers is denoted by NRE. For a finite set V, a (finite) multiset over V is a mapping from V into $\mathbb{N}$; we say that M' is a submultiset of M if $M'(a) \le M(a)$ for all $a \in V$. In the following, we will use $\subseteq$ both for the subset as well as the submultiset relation. We also write $|x|$ and $|M|$ to denote the length of a word $x \in V^*$ and the weight (i.e., sum of multiplicities $M(a)$ of all symbols $a \in V$) of a multiset M, respectively.

For more details of formal language theory the reader is referred to the monographs and handbooks in this area such as [2] and [10]. Basic results in multiset rewriting can be found in [6].

Although we are going to give all definitions necessary to understand the topics we are dealing with in this paper, we assume the reader to be familiar with the main topics of membrane computing as described in the books [8] and [9]. For the actual state of the art in membrane computing, we refer the reader to the P Systems Webpage [11].

Flattening the membrane structure is a well-known technique transforming a P system into a one-region P system, representing each object a in each region i by an object a_i in the single region of the new system. A configuration of a membrane system (with a fixed structure) is the tuple of multisets contained in each region. We say that a system is deterministic if at every step, there is (at most) one multiset of applicable rules. Since flattening the membrane structure of a membrane system preserves both determinism and the model, in the following we restrict ourselves to consider membrane systems as one-region multiset rewriting systems.

A *(one-region) membrane system (P system)* is a tuple $\Pi = (O, \Sigma, w, R')$ where O is a finite alphabet, $\Sigma \subseteq O$ is the input subalphabet, $w \in O^*$ is a string representing the initial multiset, and R' is a set of rules of the form $r : u \to v$, $u \in O^+$, $v \in O^*$.

A configuration of the system Π is represented by a multiset of objects from O contained in the region, the set of all configurations over O is denoted by $\mathbb{C}(O)$. A rule $r : u \to v$ is applicable if the current configuration contains the multiset specified by u. Furthermore, applicability may be controlled by *context conditions*, specified by pairs of sets of multisets.

Definition 1. *Let P_i, Q_i be (finite) sets of multisets over O, $1 \le i \le m$. A rule with context conditions $(r, (P_1, Q_1), \cdots, (P_m, Q_m))$ is applicable to a configuration C if r is applicable and there exists some $j \in \{1, \cdots, m\}$ for which*

- *there exists some $p \in P_j$ such that $p \subseteq C$ and*
- *$q \not\subseteq C$ for all $q \in Q_j$.*

In words, context conditions are satisfied if there exists a pair of sets of multisets (called *promoter set* and *inhibitor set*, respectively) such that at least one multiset in the promoter set is a submultiset of the current configuration, and no multiset in the inhibitor set is a submultiset of the current configuration.

Definition 2. *A* P system with context conditions and priorities on the rules *is a construct* $\Pi = (O, \Sigma, w, R', R, >)$ *where* (O, Σ, w, R') *is a (one-region) P system as defined above,* R *is a set of rules with context conditions and* $>$ *is a priority relation on the rules in* R; *if rule* r' *has priority over rule* r, *denoted by* $r' > r$, *then* r *cannot be applied if* r' *is applicable.*

Throughout the paper, we will use the word *control* to mean that at least one of these features is allowed (context conditions or promoters or inhibitors only and eventually priorities).

In the *sequential mode (sequ)*, a computation step consists of the non-deterministic application of one applicable rule r, replacing its left-hand side $(lhs\,(r))$ with its right-hand side $(rhs\,(r))$. In the *maximally parallel mode (maxpar)*, multiple applicable rules may be chosen non-deterministically to be applied in parallel to the underlying configuration to disjoint submultisets, possibly leaving some objects idle, under the condition that no further rule is simultaneously applicable to them (i.e., no supermultiset of the chosen multiset is applicable to the underlying configuration). Maximal parallelism is the most common computation mode in membrane computing, see also Definition 4.8 in [4]. In the *asynchronous mode (asyn)*, any positive number of applicable rules may be chosen non-deterministically to be applied in parallel to the underlying configuration to disjoint submultisets.

The computation step between two configurations C and C' is denoted by $C \Rightarrow C'$, thus yielding the binary relation $\Rightarrow: \mathbb{C}\,(O) \times \mathbb{C}\,(O)$. A computation halts when there are no rules applicable to the current configuration (*halting configuration*) in the corresponding mode.

The computation of a *generating* P system starts with w, and its result is $|x|$ if it halts, an *accepting* system starts with wx, $x \in \Sigma^*$, and we say that $|x|$ is its result – is accepted – if it halts. The set of numbers generated/accepted by a P system working in the mode α is the set of results of its computations for all $x \in \Sigma^*$ and denoted by $N_g^\alpha(\Pi)$ and $N_a^\alpha(\Pi)$, respectively. The family of sets of numbers generated/accepted by a family of (one-region) P systems with context conditions and priorities on the rules with rules of type β working in the mode α is denoted by $N_\delta OP_1^\alpha\left(\beta, (pro_{k,l}, inh_{k',l'})_d, pri\right)$ with $\delta = g$ for the generating and $\delta = a$ for the accepting case; d denotes the maximal number m in the rules with context conditions $(r, (P_1, Q_1), \cdots, (P_m, Q_m))$; k and k' denote the maximum numbers of promoters/inhibitors in the P_i and Q_i, respectively; l and l' indicate the maximum of weights of promotors and inhibitors, respectively. If any of these numbers k, k', l, l' is not bounded, we replace it by $*$.

As types of rules we here will distinguish between cooperative ($\beta = coo$) and non-cooperative (i.e., the left-hand side of each rule is a single object; $\beta = ncoo$) ones.

In the case of accepting systems, we also consider the idea of determinism, which means that in each step of any computation at most one (multiset of) rule(s) is applicable; in this case, we write *deta* for δ. It follows that, for any given input, the system has only one computation.

In the literature, we find a lot of restricted variants of P systems with context conditions and priorities on the rules, e.g., we may omit the priorities or the context conditions completely. If in a rule $(r, (P_1, Q_1), \cdots, (P_m, Q_m))$ we have $m = 1$, we say that $(r, (P_1, Q_1))$ is a rule with a *simple context condition*, and we omit the inner parentheses in the notation. Moreover, context conditions only using promoters are denoted by $r|_{p_1, \cdots, p_n}$, meaning $(r, \{p_1, \cdots, p_n\}, \emptyset)$, or, equivalently, $(r, (p_1, \emptyset), \cdots, (p_n, \emptyset))$; context conditions only using inhibitors are denoted by $r|_{\neg q_1, \cdots, \neg q_n}$, meaning $(r, \lambda, \{q_1, \cdots, q_n\})$, or $r|_{\neg\{q_1, \cdots, q_n\}}$. Likewise, a rule with both promoters and inhibitors can be specified as a rule with a simple context condition, i.e., $r|_{p_1, \cdots, p_n, \neg q_1, \cdots, \neg q_n}$ stands for $(r, \{p_1, \cdots, p_n\}, \{q_1, \cdots, q_n\})$. Finally, promoters and inhibitors of weight one are called *atomic*.

In what follows, when speaking about the effect of rules, we mean the behavior induced by them. Hence, two sets of rules have the same effect if substituting one of them by the other one does not change the computations of the system.

Remark 1. If we do not consider determinism, then (the effect of) the rule $(r, (P_1, Q_1), \cdots, (P_m, Q_m))$ is equivalent to (the effect of) the collection of rules $\{(r, P_j, Q_j) \mid 1 \le j \le m\}$, no matter in which mode the P system is working (obviously, the priority relation has to be adapted accordingly, too).

Remark 2. Let $(r, \{p_1, \cdots, p_n\}, Q)$ be a rule with a simple context condition; then we claim that (the effect of) this rule is equivalent to (the effect of) the collection of rules $\{(r, \{p_j\}, Q \cup \{p_k \mid 1 \le k < j\}) \mid 1 \le j \le m\}$ even in the the case of a deterministic P system: If the first promoter is chosen to make the rule r applicable, we do not care about the other promoters; if the second promoter is chosen to make the rule r applicable, we do not allow p_1 to appear in the configuration, but do not care about the other promoters p_3 to p_m; in general, when promoter p_j is chosen to make the rule r applicable, we do not allow p_1 to p_{j-1} to appear in the configuration, but do not care about the other promoters p_{j+1} to p_m; finally, we have the rule $\{(r, \{p_m\}, Q \cup \{p_k \mid 1 \le k < m\})\}$. If adding $\{p_k \mid 1 \le k < j\}$ to Q has the effect of prohibiting the promotor p_j from enabling the rule r to be applied, this makes no harm as in this case one of the promoters p_k, $1 \le k < j$, must have the possibility for enabling r to be applied. By construction, the domains of the new context conditions now are disjoint, so this transformation does not create (new) non-determinism. In a similar way, this transformation may be performed on context conditions which are not simple.

Therefore, without restricting generality, the set of promoters may be assumed to be a singleton. In this case, we may omit the braces of the multiset notation for the promoter multiset and write (r, p, Q).

Example 1. Let H be an arbitrary finite set of numbers and $K = \max(H) + 1$; then we construct the following deterministic accepting P system with promoters and inhibitors:

$$\Pi = (O, \{a\}, s_0 f_0 \cdots f_K, R', R),$$
$$O = \{a\} \cup \{s_i, f_i \mid 0 \leq i \leq K\},$$
$$R' = \{s_i \to s_{i+1} \mid 0 \leq i \leq K-1\} \cup \{f_i \to f_i \mid 0 \leq i \leq K\},$$
$$R = \{s_i \to s_{i+1}|_{a^{i+1}}, \mid 0 \leq i \leq K-1\}$$
$$\cup \{f_i \to f_i|_{s_i, \neg a^{i+1}}, \mid 0 \leq i < K, \ i \notin H\} \cup \{f_K \to f_K|_{s_K}\}.$$

The system step by step, by the application of the rule $s_i \to s_{i+1}|_{a^{i+1}}, 0 \leq i < K$, checks if (at least) $i + 1$ copies of the symbol a are present. If the computation stops after i steps, i.e., if the input has consisted of exactly i copies of a, then this input is accepted if and only if $i \in H$, as exactly in this case the system does not start an infinite loop with using $f_i \to f_i|_{s_i, \neg a^{i+1}}$. If the input has contained more than $\max(H)$ copies of a, then the system arrives in the state s_K and will loop forever with $f_K \to f_K|_{s_K}$. Therefore, exactly H is accepted.

To accept the complement of H instead, we simply change $i \notin H$ to $i \in H$ and as well omit the rule $f_K \to f_K|_{s_K}$. It is easy to see that for the maximally parallel mode, we can replace each rule $f_i \to f_i|_{s_i, \neg a^{i+1}}$ by the corresponding rule $f_i \to f_i|_{s_i}$; in this case, this rule may be applied with still some a being present while the system passes through the state s_i, but it will not get into an infinite loop in that case.

In sum, we have shown that

$$N_{deta}OP_1^{asyn}(ncoo, (pro_{1,*}, inh_{1,*})_1) \supseteq FIN \cup coNFIN \text{ and}$$
$$N_{deta}OP_1^{maxpar}(ncoo, pro_{1,*}) \supseteq FIN \cup coNFIN.$$

Example 2. For P systems working in the maximally parallel mode we can even construct a system with inhibitors only:

$$\Pi = (O, \{a\}, ts_K, R', R),$$
$$O = \{a, t\} \cup \{s_i \mid 0 \leq i \leq K\},$$
$$R' = \{s_i \to ts_{i-1}, s_i \to s_i \mid 1 \leq i \leq K\} \cup \{t \to \lambda, s_0 \to s_0\},$$
$$R = \{s_i \to ts_{i-1}|_{\neg a^i} \mid 1 \leq i \leq K\}$$
$$\cup \{t \to \lambda\} \cup \{s_i \to s_i|_{\neg t} \mid 0 \leq i \leq K, \ i \notin H\}.$$

This construction does not carry over to the case of the asynchronous mode, as the rule $t \to \lambda$ is applied in parallel to the rules $s_i \to ts_{i-1}|_{\neg a^i}$ until the input a^i is reached. In this case, the system cannot change the state s_i anymore, and then it starts to loop if and only if $i \notin H$. To accept the complement of H instead, change $i \in H$ to $i \notin H$, i.e., in sum, we have proved that

$$N_{deta}OP_1^{maxpar}(ncoo, inh_{1,*}) \supseteq FIN \cup coNFIN.$$

As we shall show later, all the inclusions stated in Example 1 and Example 2 are equalities.

2.1   Register Machines

In what follows we will need to simulate register machines; here we briefly recall their definition and some of their computational properties. A *register machine* is a tuple $M = (m, B, l_0, l_h, P)$ where m is the number of registers, P is the set of instructions bijectively labeled by elements of B, $l_0 \in B$ is the initial label, and $l_h \in B$ is the final label. The instructions of M can be of the following forms:

- $l_1 : (ADD\,(j), l_2, l_3)$, with $l_1 \in B \setminus \{l_h\}$, $l_2, l_3 \in B$, $1 \leq j \leq m$.
  Increase the value of register j by one, and non-deterministically jump to instruction l_2 or l_3. This instruction is usually called *increment*.
- $l_1 : (SUB\,(j), l_2, l_3)$, with $l_1 \in B \setminus \{l_h\}$, $l_2, l_3 \in B$, $1 \leq j \leq m$.
  If the value of register j is zero then jump to instruction l_3, otherwise decrease the value of register j by one and jump to instruction l_2. The two cases of this instruction are usually called *zero-test* and *decrement*, respectively.
- $l_h : HALT$. Stop the execution of the register machine.

A register machine is *deterministic* if $l_2 = l_3$ in all its ADD instructions. A *configuration* of a register machine is described by the contents of each register and by the value of the program counter, which indicates the next instruction to be executed. Computations start by executing the first instruction of P (labelled with l_0), and terminate with reaching a $HALT$-instruction.

Register machines provide a simple universal computational model [7]. We here consider register machines used as *accepting* or as *generating* devices. In accepting register machines, a vector of non-negative integers is accepted if and only if the register machine halts having it as input. Usually, without loss of generality, we may assume that the instruction $l_h : HALT$ always appears exactly once in P, with label l_h. In the generative case, we start with empty registers and take the results of all possible halting computations.

3   Results

In this section we mainly investigate deterministic accepting P systems with context conditions and priorities on the rules (*deterministic P systems* for short) using only non-cooperative rules and working in the sequential, the asynchronous, and the maximally parallel mode.

Remark 3. We first notice that maximal parallelism in systems with non-cooperative rules means the total parallelism for all symbols to which at least one rule is applicable, and determinism guarantees that "at least one" is "exactly one" for all reachable configurations and objects. Determinism in the sequential mode requires that at most one symbol has an associated applicable rule for all reachable configurations. Surprisingly enough, in the case of the asynchronous mode we face an even worse situation than in the case of maximal parallelism – if more than one copy of a specific symbol is present in the configuration, then no rule can be applicable to such a symbol in order not to violate the condition of determinism.

We now define the *bounding* operation over multisets, with a parameter $k \in \mathbb{N}$ as follows:

$$\text{for } u \in O^*, \, b_k(u) = v \text{ with } |v|_a = \min(|u|_a, k) \text{ for all } a \in O.$$

The mapping b_k "crops" the multisets by removing copies of every object a present in more than k copies until exactly k remain. For two multisets u, u', $b_k(u) = b_k(u')$ if for every $a \in O$, either $|u|_a = |u'|_a < k$, or $|u|_a \geq k$ and $|u'|_a \geq k$. Mapping b_k induces an equivalence relation, mapping O^* into $(k+1)^{|O|}$ equivalence classes. Each equivalence class corresponds to specifying, for each $a \in O^*$, whether no copy, one copy, or $\cdots k-1$ copies, or "k copies or more" are present. We denote the range of b_k by $\{0, \cdots, k\}^O$.

Lemma 1. *Context conditions are equivalent to predicates defined on boundings.*

Proof. We start by representing context conditions by predicates on boundings. Consider a rule with a simple context condition (r, p, Q), and let the current configuration be C. Then, it suffices to take $k \geq \max(|p|, \max\{|q| \mid q \in Q\})$ and $C' = b_k(C)$. The applicability condition for (r, p, Q) may be expressed as $p \subseteq C' \wedge \left(\bigwedge_{q \in Q} q \not\subseteq C' \right)$. Indeed, $x \subseteq C \longleftrightarrow x \subseteq C'$ for every multiset x with $|x| \leq k$, because for every $a \in O$, $|x|_a \leq |C|_a \longleftrightarrow |x|_a \leq \min(|C|_a, k)$ holds if $|x|_a \leq k$. Finally, we notice that context conditions which are not simple can be represented by a disjunction of the corresponding predicates.

Conversely, we show that any predicate $E \subseteq \{0, \cdots, k\}^O$ for the bounding mapping b_k for rule r can be represented by some context conditions. For each multiset $c \in E$, we construct a simple context condition to the effect of "contains c, but, for each a contained in c for less than k times, not more than $|c|_a$ symbols a":

$$\left\{ \left(r, c, \left\{ a^{|c|_a + 1} \mid |c|_a < k \right\} \right) \mid c \in E \right\}.$$

Joining multiple simple context conditions over the same rule into one rule with context conditions concludes the proof. $\square$

The following theorem is valid even when the rules are not restricted to non-cooperative ones, and when determinism is not required, in either derivation mode (also see [4]).

Theorem 1. *Priorities are subsumed by conditional contexts.*

Proof. A rule is prohibited from being applicable due to a priority relation if and only if at least one of the rules with higher priority might be applied. Let r be a rule of a P system $(O, \Sigma, w, R', R, >)$, and let $r_1 > r, \cdots, r_n > r$. Hence, the rule r is not blocked by the rules $r_1, \cdots, r_n$ if and only if the left-hand sides of the rules $r_1, \cdots, r_n$, i.e., $lhs(r_1), \cdots, lhs(r_n)$, are not present in the current configuration or the context conditions given in these rules are not fulfilled. According to Lemma 1, these context conditions can be formulated as predicates on the bounding b_k where k is the maximum of weights of all left-hand sides, promoters, and inhibitors in the rules with higher priority $r_1, \cdots, r_n$. Together with the context conditions from r itself, we finally get context conditions for a new rule r' simulating r, but also incorporating the conditions of the priority relation. Performing this transformation for all rules r concludes the proof. □

Remark 4. From [4] we already know that in the case of rules without context conditions, the context conditions in the new rules are only sets of atomic inhibitors, which also follows from the construction given above. A careful investigation of the construction given in the proof of Theorem 1 reveals the fact that the maximal weights for the promoters and inhibitors to be used in the new system are bounded by the number k in the bounding b_k.

Remark 5. As in a P system $(O, \Sigma, w, R', R, >)$ the set of rules R' can easily be deduced from the set of rules with context conditions R, in the following we omit R' in the description of the P system. Moreover, for systems having only rules with a simple context condition, we omit d in the description of the families of sets of numbers and simply write

$$N_\delta OP_1^\alpha \left(\beta, pro_{k,l}, inh_{k',l'}, pri \right).$$

Moreover, each control mechanism not used can be omitted, e.g., if no priorities and only promoters are used, we only write $N_\delta OP_1^\alpha \left(\beta, pro_{k,l} \right)$.

3.1 Sequential Systems

Although throughout the rest of the paper we are not dealing with sequential systems anymore, the proof of the following theorem gives us some intuition why, for deterministic non-cooperative systems, there are severe differences between the sequential mode and the asynchronous or the maximally parallel mode.

Theorem 2. $N_{deta}OP_1^{sequ} \left(ncoo, pro_{1,1}, inh_{1,1} \right) = NRE.$

Proof. Let $M = (m, B, l_0, l_h, P)$ be an arbitrary deterministic register machine. We simulate M by a deterministic P system $\Pi = (O, \{a_1\}, l_0, R)$ where

$$O = \{a_j \mid 1 \leq j \leq m\} \cup \{l, l_1, l_2 \mid l \in B\},$$
$$R = \{l \to a_j l' \mid (l : ADD(j), l') \in P\}$$
$$\cup \{l \to l_1|_{a_j}, \ a_j \to a_j'|_{l_1, \neg a_j'}, \ l_1 \to l_2|_{a_j'}, \ a_j' \to \lambda|_{l_2}, \ l_2 \to l'|_{\neg a_j'},$$
$$l \to l''|_{\neg a_j} \mid (l : SUB(j), l', l'') \in P\}.$$

We claim that Π is deterministic and non-cooperative, and it accepts the same set as M. □

As can be seen in the construction of the deterministic P system in the proof above, the rule $a_j \to a_j'|_{l_1, \neg a_j'}$ used in the sequential mode can be applied exactly once, priming exactly one symbol a_j to be deleted afterwards. Intuitively, in the asynchronous or the maximally parallel mode, it is impossible to choose only one symbol out of an unbounded number of copies to be deleted. The bounding operation defined above will allow us to put this intuition into a formal proof.

3.2 Asynchronous and Maximally Parallel Systems

Fix an arbitrary deterministic controlled non-cooperative P system. Take k as the maximum of size of all multisets in all context conditions. Then, the bounding does not influence applicability of rules, and $b_k(u)$ is halting if and only if u is halting. We proceed by showing that bounding induces equivalence classes preserved by any computation using the maximally parallel mode.

Lemma 2. *Assume* $u \Rightarrow x$ *and* $v \Rightarrow y$.
Then $b_k(u) = b_k(v)$ *implies* $b_k(x) = b_k(y)$.

Proof. Equality $b_k(u) = b_k(v)$ means that for every symbol $a \in O$, if $|u|_a \neq |v_a|$ then $|u|_a \geq k$ and $|v|_a \geq k$, and we have a few cases to be considered. If no rule is applicable to a, then the inequality of symbols a will be indistinguishable after bounding also in the next step (both with at least k copies of a). Otherwise, exactly one rule r is applicable to a (by determinism, and bounding does not affect applicability), then the difference of the multiplicities of the symbol a may only lead to differences of the multiplicities of symbols b for all $b \in rhs(r)$. However, either all copies of a are erased by the rule $a \to \lambda$ or else at least one copy of a symbol b will be generated from each copy of a by this rule alone, so $|x|_b \geq |u|_a \geq k$ and $|y|_b \geq |v|_a \geq k$; hence, all differences of multiplicities of an object b in u and v will be indistinguishable after bounding in this case, too. $\square$

Corollary 1. *If* $b_k(u) = b_k(v)$, *then* u *is accepted if and only if* v *is accepted.*

Proof. Let w be the fixed part of the initial configuration. Then we consider computations from uw and from vw. Clearly, $b_k(uw) = b_k(vw)$. Equality of boundings is preserved by one computation step, and hence, by any number of computation steps.

Assume the contrary of the claim: one of the computations halts after s steps, while the other one does not, i.e., let $uw \Rightarrow^s u'$ and $vw \Rightarrow^s v'$. By the previous paragraph, $b_k(u') = b_k(v')$. Since bounding does not affect applicability of rules, either both u' and v' are halting, or none of them. The contradiction proves the claim. $\square$

We should like to notice that the arguments in the proofs of Lemma 2 and Corollary 1 are given for the maximally parallel mode, but following the observation stated at the end of Remark 3, these two results can also be argued for the asynchronous mode.

Theorem 3. *For deterministic P systems working in the asynchronous or in the maximally parallel mode, we have the following characterization:*

$$
\begin{aligned}
NFIN \cup coNFIN &= N_{deta}OP_1^{asyn}\left(ncoo, pro_{1,*}, inh_{1,*}\right) \\
&= N_{deta}OP_1^{maxpar}\left(ncoo, pro_{1,*}\right) \\
&= N_{deta}OP_1^{maxpar}\left(ncoo, inh_{1,*}\right) \\
&= N_{deta}OP_1^{asyn}\left(ncoo, (pro_{*,*}, inh_{*,*})_*, pri\right) \\
&= N_{deta}OP_1^{maxpar}\left(ncoo, (pro_{*,*}, inh_{*,*})_*, pri\right).
\end{aligned}
$$

Proof. Each equivalence class induced by bounding is completely accepted or completely rejected. If no infinite equivalence class is accepted, then the accepted set is finite (containing numbers not exceeding $(k-1) \cdot |O|$). If at least one infinite equivalence class is accepted, then the rejected set is finite (containing numbers not exceeding $(k-1) \cdot |O|$). This proves the "at most $NFIN \cup coNFIN$" part.

In Examples 1 and 2 we have already shown that

$$N_{deta}OP_1^\alpha (ncoo, pro_{1,*}, inh_{1,*}) \supseteq FIN \cup coNFIN, \ \alpha \in \{asyn, maxpar\},$$
$$N_{deta}OP_1^{maxpar} (ncoo, \gamma_{1,*}) \supseteq FIN \cup coNFIN, \ \gamma \in \{pro, inh\}.$$

This observation concludes the proof.   □

There are several questions remaining open, for instance, whether only inhibitors in the rules or only priorities in the rules are sufficient to yield $FIN \cup coNFIN$ with the asynchronous mode, too.

4   Conclusions

We have shown that, like in case of catalytic P systems, for non-cooperative P systems with promoters and/or inhibitors (with or without priorities), determinism is a criterion drawing a borderline between universality and decidability. In fact, for non-cooperative P systems working in the maximally parallel or the asynchronous mode, we have computational completeness in the unrestricted case, and only all finite number sets and their complements in the deterministic case.

Acknowledgements. The first author gratefully acknowledges the project RetroNet by the Lombardy Region of Italy under the ASTIL Program (regional decree 6119, 20100618).

References

1. Alhazov, A., Sburlan, D.: Ultimately Confluent Rewriting Systems. Parallel Multiset–Rewriting with Permitting or Forbidding Contexts. In: Mauri, G., Păun, G., Pérez-Jímenez, M.J., Rozenberg, G., Salomaa, A. (eds.) WMC 2004. LNCS, vol. 3365, pp. 178–189. Springer, Heidelberg (2005)
2. Dassow, J., Păun, G.: Regulated Rewriting in Formal Language Theory. Springer (1989)
3. Freund, R., Kari, L., Oswald, M., Sosík, P.: Computationally universal P systems without priorities: two catalysts are sufficient. Theor. Comp. Sci. 330, 251–266 (2005)
4. Freund, R., Kogler, M., Oswald, M.: A General Framework for Regulated Rewriting Based on the Applicability of Rules. In: Kelemen, J., Kelemenová, A. (eds.) Computation, Cooperation, and Life. LNCS, vol. 6610, pp. 35–53. Springer, Heidelberg (2011)

5. Ibarra, O.H., Yen, H.-C.: Deterministic catalytic systems are not universal. Theor. Comp. Sci. 363, 149–161 (2006)
6. Kudlek, M., Martín-Vide, C., Păun, G.: Toward a Formal Macroset Theory. In: Calude, C.S., Pun, G., Rozenberg, G., Salomaa, A. (eds.) Multiset Processing. LNCS, vol. 2235, pp. 123–134. Springer, Heidelberg (2001)
7. Minsky, M.L.: Computation: Finite and Infinite Machines. Prentice Hall, Englewood Cliffs (1967)
8. Păun, G.: Membrane Computing. An Introduction. Springer (2002)
9. Păun, G., Rozenberg, G., Salomaa, A.: The Oxford Handbook of Membrane Computing. Oxford University Press (2010)
10. Rozenberg, G., Salomaa, A.: Handbook of Formal Languages, vol. 3. Springer (1997)
11. The P Systems Web Page, http://ppage.psystems.eu

Sequential P Systems with Regular Control

Artiom Alhazov[1,4], Rudolf Freund[2], Hilbert Heikenwälder[2], Marion Oswald[2],
Yurii Rogozhin[1], and Sergey Verlan[3]

[1] Institute of Mathematics and Computer Science
Academy of Sciences of Moldova
Str. Academiei 5, Chişinău, MD-2028, Moldova
{artiom,rogozhin}@math.md

[2] Faculty of Informatics, Vienna University of Technology
Favoritenstr. 9, 1040 Vienna, Austria
{rudi,hilbert,marion}@emcc.at

[3] LACL, Département Informatique, Université Paris Est
61, av. Général de Gaulle, 94010 Créteil, France
verlan@univ-paris12.fr

[4] Università degli Studi di Milano-Bicocca
Dipartimento di Informatica, Sistemistica e Comunicazione
Viale Sarca 336, 20126 Milano, Italy
artiom.alhazov@unimib.it

Abstract. In this article we introduce the regulating mechanism of control languages for the application of rules assigned to the membranes of a sequential P system and the variant of time-varying sets of rules available at different transition steps. Computational completeness can only be achieved when allowing the system to have no rules applicable for a bounded number of steps; in this case we only need one membrane and periodically available sets of non-cooperative rules, i.e., time-varying sequential P systems. On the other hand, even with an arbitrary number of membranes and regular control languages, only Parikh sets of matrix languages can be obtained if the terminal result has to be taken as soon as the system cannot apply any rule anymore.

1 Introduction

P systems are formal models derived from the functioning of living cells, closely related to multiset rewriting. We refer to [16], [17], and to the web page [21] for more details on P systems. In this article, we investigate the power of controlling the availability of the sets of rules assigned to the membranes of a (static) P system by a regular control language L, especially for languages L being of the form $\{w\}^*$, which leads to the notion of a *time-varying* P system where the set of rules available at each membrane varies periodically with time.

The notion of the time-varying controlled application of rules comes from the area of regulated rewriting; comprehensive overviews of this area can be found in [6], [8], and [9]. Periodically time-varying grammars were already mentioned in

E. Csuhaj-Varjú et al. (Eds.): CMC 2012, LNCS 7762, pp. 112–127, 2013.
© Springer-Verlag Berlin Heidelberg 2013

[20] following the work on time-varying automata [19]. This notion was also considered in the area of Lindenmayer systems, corresponding to controlled tabled Lindenmayer systems, with the tables being used periodically (see [14]). We can also interpret these systems as counterparts of cooperating distributed grammar systems ([2], [7]) with the order of enabling the components controlled by a graph having the shape of a ring. Subregular control mechanisms were already considered in [3] and [4], an overview is given in [5]. In the field of DNA computing several models using the variation in time of the set of available rules were considered. The first model in this area – time-varying distributed H systems – was introduced in [15] and using the splicing operation. A similar model having some differences in the operation application was considered in [12]. In [22] the time-varying mechanism was used in conjunction with splicing test tube systems; there no direct action on the splicing rules was considered, yet instead a time-varying dependency in the communication step.

2   Preliminaries

After some preliminaries from formal language theory, we define the main concept of P systems with control languages considered in this paper.

The set of integers is denoted by $\mathbb{Z}$, the set of non-negative integers by $\mathbb{N}$. An *alphabet* V is a finite non-empty set of abstract *symbols*. Given V, the free monoid generated by V under the operation of concatenation is denoted by V^*; the elements of V^* are called strings, and the *empty string* is denoted by λ; $V^* \setminus \{\lambda\}$ is denoted by V^+. Let $\{a_1, \cdots, a_n\}$ be an arbitrary alphabet; the number of occurrences of a symbol a_i in a string x is denoted by $|x|_{a_i}$; the *Parikh vector* associated with x with respect to $a_1, \cdots, a_n$ is $\left(|x|_{a_1}, \cdots, |x|_{a_n}\right)$. The *Parikh image* of a language L over $\{a_1, \cdots, a_n\}$ is the set of all Parikh vectors of strings in L, and we denote it by $Ps(L)$. For a family of languages FL, the family of Parikh images of languages in FL is denoted by $PsFL$.

A (finite) multiset over the (finite) alphabet V, $V = \{a_1, \cdots, a_n\}$, is a mapping $f : V \longrightarrow \mathbb{N}$ and represented by $\langle f(a_1), a_1 \rangle \cdots \langle f(a_n), a_n \rangle$ or by any string x the Parikh vector of which with respect to $a_1, \cdots, a_n$ is $(f(a_1), \cdots, f(a_n))$. In the following we will not distinguish between a vector $(m_1, \cdots, m_n)$, its representation by a multiset $\langle m_1, a_1 \rangle \cdots \langle m_n, a_n \rangle$ or its representation by a string x having the Parikh vector $\left(|x|_{a_1}, \cdots, |x|_{a_n}\right) = (m_1, \cdots, m_n)$. Fixing the sequence of symbols $a_1, \cdots, a_n$ in the alphabet V in advance, the representation of the multiset $\langle m_1, a_1 \rangle \cdots \langle m_n, a_n \rangle$ by the string $a_1^{m_1} \cdots a_n^{m_n}$ is unique. The set of all finite multisets over an alphabet V is denoted by V°.

The family of regular and recursively enumerable string languages is denoted by REG and RE, respectively. For more details of formal language theory the reader is referred to the monographs and handbooks in this area as [6] and [18].

2.1   Register Machines

For our main result establishing computational completeness for time-varying P systems, we will need to simulate register machines. A *register machine* is a tuple $M = (m, B, l_0, l_h, P)$, where m is the number of registers, P is the set of instructions bijectively labeled by elements of B, $l_0 \in B$ is the initial label, and $l_h \in B$ is the final label. The instructions of M can be of the following forms:

- $l_1 : (ADD(j), l_2, l_3)$, with $l_1 \in B \setminus \{l_h\}$, $l_2, l_3 \in B$, $1 \leq j \leq m$
  Increase the value of register j by one, and non-deterministically jump to instruction l_2 or l_3. This instruction is usually called *increment*.
- $l_1 : (SUB(j), l_2, l_3)$, with $l_1 \in B \setminus \{l_h\}$, $l_2, l_3 \in B$, $1 \leq j \leq m$
  If the value of register j is zero then jump to instruction l_3, otherwise decrease the value of register j by one and jump to instruction l_2. The two cases of this instruction are usually called *zero-test* and *decrement*, respectively.
- $l_h : HALT$. Stop the execution of the register machine.

A *configuration* of a register machine is described by the contents of each register and by the value of the current label, which indicates the next instruction to be executed. Computations start by executing the first instruction of P (labeled with l_0), and terminate with reaching the $HALT$-instruction.

Register machines provide a simple universal computational model [13]. In the generative case as we need it later, we start with empty registers, use the first two registers for the necessary computations and take as results the contents of the k registers 3 to $k + 2$ in all possible halting computations; during a computation of M, only the registers 1 and 2 can be decremented. In the following, we shall call a specific model of P systems *computationally complete* if and only if for any register machine M we can effectively construct an equivalent P system Π of that type simulating each step of M in a bounded number of steps and yielding the same results.

2.2   Sequential Grammars

A *grammar* G of type X is a construct $(O, O_T, A, P, \Longrightarrow_G)$ where O is a set of *objects*, $O_T \subseteq O$ is a set of *terminal objects*, $A \in O$ is the *axiom*, and P is a finite set of *rules* of type X. Each rule $p \in P$ induces a relation $\Longrightarrow_p \subseteq O \times O$; p is called *applicable* to an object $x \in O$ if and only if there exists at least one object $y \in O$ such that $(x, y) \in \Longrightarrow_p$; we also write $x \Longrightarrow_p y$. The derivation relation $\Longrightarrow_G$ is the union of all $\Longrightarrow_p$, i.e., $\Longrightarrow_G := \cup_{p \in P} \Longrightarrow_p$. The reflexive and transitive closure of $\Longrightarrow_G$ is denoted by $\overset{*}{\Longrightarrow}_G$.

The *language generated by* G is the set of all terminal objects derivable from the axiom, i.e., $L(G) = \left\{ v \in O_T \mid A \overset{*}{\Longrightarrow}_G v \right\}$. The family of languages generated by grammars of type X is denoted by $\mathcal{L}(X)$.

In this paper, we consider string grammars and multiset grammars:

String Grammars. In the general notion as defined above, a *string grammar* G_S is represented as

$$((N \cup T)^*, T^*, w, P, \Longrightarrow_{G_S})$$

where N is the alphabet of *non-terminal symbols*, T is the alphabet of *terminal symbols*, $N \cap T = \emptyset$, $w \in (N \cup T)^+$, P is a finite set of *rules* of the form $u \to v$ with $u \in V^+$ and $v \in V^*$, with $V := N \cup T$; the derivation relation for $u \to v \in P$ is defined by $xuy \Longrightarrow_{u \to v} xvy$ for all $x, y \in V^*$, thus yielding the well-known derivation relation $\Longrightarrow_{G_S}$ for the string grammar G_S. As special types of string grammars we consider string grammars with arbitrary rules, context-free rules of the form $A \to v$ with $A \in N$ and $v \in V^*$, and (right-)regular rules of the form $A \to v$ with $A \in N$ and $v \in TN \cup \{\lambda\}$. In the following, we shall also use the common notation $G_S = (N, T, w, P)$ instead, too. The corresponding types of grammars are denoted by ARB, CF, and REG, thus yielding the families of languages $\mathcal{L}(ARB)$, i.e., the family of recursively enumerable languages RE, as well as $\mathcal{L}(CF)$ and $\mathcal{L}(REG)$, i.e., the families of context-free and regular languages (also denoted by REG), respectively.

The subfamily of REG only consisting of 1-star languages of the form W^* for some finite set of strings W is denoted by REG^{1*}; to be more specific, we also consider $REG^{1*}(k, p)$ consisting of all 1-star languages of the form W^* with k being the maximum number of strings in W and p being the maximum lengths of the strings in W. If $W = \{w\}$ for a singleton w, we call the set $\{w\}^*$ *periodic* and $|w|$ its *period*; thus, $REG^{1*}(1, p)$ denotes the family of all periodic sets with period at most p. If any of the numbers k or p may be arbitrarily large, we replace it by $*$.

Multiset Grammars. A *multiset grammar [1,11]* G_m is of the form

$$\left((N \cup T)^\circ, T^\circ, w, P, \Longrightarrow_{G_m}\right)$$

where N is the alphabet of *non-terminal symbols*, T is the alphabet of *terminal symbols*, $N \cap T = \emptyset$, w is a non-empty multiset over V, $V := N \cup T$, and P is a (finite) set of multiset rules yielding a derivation relation $\Longrightarrow_{G_m}$ on the multisets over V; the application of the rule $u \to v$ to a multiset x has the effect of replacing the multiset u contained in x by the multiset v. For the multiset grammar G_m we also write $(N, T, w, P, \Longrightarrow_{G_m})$.

As special types of multiset grammars we consider multiset grammars with *arbitrary* rules, *context-free* rules of the form $A \to v$ with $A \in N$ and $v \in V^\circ$, and *regular* rules of the form $A \to v$ with $A \in N$ and $v \in T^\circ N \cup \{\lambda\}$; the corresponding types X of multiset grammars are denoted by $mARB$, mCF, and $mREG$, thus yielding the families of multiset languages $\mathcal{L}(X)$. Even with arbitrary multiset rules, it is not possible to get $Ps(\mathcal{L}(ARB))$ [11]:

$$Ps(\mathcal{L}(REG)) = \mathcal{L}(mREG) = \mathcal{L}(mCF) = Ps(\mathcal{L}(CF))$$
$$\subsetneqq \mathcal{L}(mARB) \subsetneqq Ps(\mathcal{L}(ARB)).$$

2.3   Graph-Controlled and Programmed Grammars

A *graph-controlled grammar* (with appearance checking) of type X is a construct

$$G_{GC} = (G, g, H_i, H_f, \Longrightarrow_{GC})$$

where $G = (O, O_T, w, P, \Longrightarrow_G)$ is a grammar of type X; $g = (H, E, K)$ is a labeled graph where H is the set of node labels identifying the nodes of the graph in a one-to-one manner, $E \subseteq H \times \{Y, N\} \times H$ is the set of edges labeled by Y or N, $K : H \to 2^P$ is a function assigning a subset of P to each node of g; $H_i \subseteq H$ is the set of *initial labels*, and $H_f \subseteq H$ is the set of *final labels*. The derivation relation $\Longrightarrow_{GC}$ is defined based on $\Longrightarrow_G$ and the control graph g as follows: For any $i, j \in H$ and any $u, v \in O$, $(u, i) \Longrightarrow_{GC} (v, j)$ if and only if either

- $u \Longrightarrow_p v$ by some rule $p \in K(i)$ and $(i, Y, j) \in E$ *(success case)*, or
- $u = v$, no $p \in K(i)$ is applicable to u, and $(i, N, j) \in E$ *(failure case)*.

The language generated by G_{GC} is defined by

$$L(G_{GC}) = \left\{ v \in O_T \mid (w, i) \Longrightarrow^*_{G_{GC}} (v, j), \ i \in H_i, j \in H_f \right\}.$$

If $H_i = H_f = H$, then G_{GC} is called a *programmed grammar*. The families of languages generated by graph-controlled and programmed grammars of type X are denoted by $\mathcal{L}(X\text{-}GC_{ac})$ and $\mathcal{L}(X\text{-}P_{ac})$, respectively. If the set E contains no edges of the form (i, N, j), then the graph-controlled grammar G_{GC} is said to be *without appearance checking*; the corresponding families of languages are denoted by $\mathcal{L}(X\text{-}GC)$ and $\mathcal{L}(X\text{-}P)$, respectively. If $(i, Y, j) \in E$ if and only if $(i, N, j) \in E$ for all $i, j \in H$, then G_{GC} is said to be a graph-controlled grammar or programmed grammar *with unconditional transfer*, the corresponding families of languages are denoted by $\mathcal{L}(X\text{-}GC_{ut})$ and $\mathcal{L}(X\text{-}P_{ut})$, respectively. In the case of string grammars, it is well-known (e.g., see [9]) that

$$RE = \mathcal{L}(CF\text{-}GC_{ac}) = \mathcal{L}(CF\text{-}P_{ac}) = \mathcal{L}(CF\text{-}GC_{ut}) = \mathcal{L}(CF\text{-}P_{ut})$$
$$\not\supseteq \mathcal{L}(CF\text{-}GC) = \mathcal{L}(CF\text{-}P).$$

2.4   Matrix Grammars

A *matrix grammar* (with appearance checking) of type X is a construct

$$G_M = (G, M, F, \Longrightarrow_{G_M})$$

where $G = (O, O_T, w, P, \Longrightarrow_G)$ is a grammar of type X, M is a finite set of sequences of the form $(p_1, \ldots, p_n)$, $n \geq 1$, of rules in P, and $F \subseteq P$. For $w, z \in O$ we write $w \Longrightarrow_{G_M} z$ if there are a matrix $(p_1, \ldots, p_n)$ in M and objects $w_i \in O$, $1 \leq i \leq n+1$, such that $w = w_1$, $z = w_{n+1}$, and, for all $1 \leq i \leq n$, either

- $w_i \Longrightarrow_G w_{i+1}$ or
- $w_i = w_{i+1}$, p_i is not applicable to w_i, and $p_i \in F$.

$L(G_M) = \{v \in O_T \mid w \Longrightarrow^*_{G_M} v\}$ is the language generated by G_M. The family of languages generated by matrix grammars of type X is denoted by $\mathcal{L}(X\text{-}MAT_{ac})$. If the set F is empty (or if $F = P$), then the grammar is said to be *without appearance checking (with unconditional transfer)*; the corresponding family of languages is denoted by $\mathcal{L}(X\text{-}MAT)$ ($\mathcal{L}(X\text{-}MAT_{ut})$).

2.5   Grammars with Regular Control and Time-Varying Grammars

Another possibility to capture the idea of controlling the derivation in a grammar as with a control graph is to consider the sequence of rules applied during a computation and to require this sequence to be an element of a regular language: A *grammar with regular control and appearance checking* is a construct

$$G_C = (G, H_C, L, F)$$

where $G = (O, O_T, w, P, \Longrightarrow_G)$ is a grammar of type X and L is a regular language over H_C, where H_C is the set of labels identifying the subsets of productions from P in a one-to-one manner (H_C is a bijective function on 2^P), and $F \subseteq H_C$. The language generated by G_C consists of all terminal objects z such that there exist a string $H_C(P_1) \cdots H_C(P_n) \in L$ as well as objects $w_i \in O$, $1 \leq i \leq n+1$, such that $w = w_1$, $z = w_{n+1}$, and, for all $1 \leq i \leq n$, either

- $w_i \Longrightarrow_G w_{i+1}$ by some production from P_i or
- $w_i = w_{i+1}$, no production from P_i is applicable to w_i, and $H_C(P_i) \in F$.

It is rather easy to see that the model of grammars with regular control is closely related with the model of graph-controlled grammars in the sense that the control graph corresponds to the deterministic finite automaton accepting L. Hence, we may also speak of a *grammar with regular control and without appearance checking* if $F = \emptyset$, and if $F = H_C$ then G_C is said to be a *grammar with regular control and unconditional transfer*. The corresponding families of languages are denoted by $\mathcal{L}(X\text{-}C(REG)_{ac})$, $\mathcal{L}(X\text{-}C(REG))$, and $\mathcal{L}(X\text{-}C(REG)_{ut})$.

Obviously, the control languages can also be taken from another family of languages Y, e.g., $\mathcal{L}(CF)$, thus yielding the families $\mathcal{L}(X\text{-}C(Y)_{ac})$, etc., but in this paper we shall restrict ourselves to the cases $Y = REG$ and $Y = REG^{1*}(k, p)$. For $Y = REG^{1*}(1, p)$, these grammars are also known as *(periodically) time-varying grammars*, as a control language $\{H_C(P_1) \cdots H_C(P_p)\}^*$ means that the set of productions available at a time t in a derivation is P_i if $t = kp + i$, $k \geq 0$; p is called the *period* of the time-varying system. The corresponding families of languages generated by time-varying grammars with appearance checking, without appearance checking, with unconditional transfer and with period p are denoted by $\mathcal{L}(X\text{-}TV_{ac}(p))$, $\mathcal{L}(X\text{-}TV(p))$, and $\mathcal{L}(X\text{-}TV_{ut}(p))$, respectively; if p may be arbitrarily large, p is replaced by $*$ in these notions.

In many cases it is not necessary to insist that the control string $H_C(P_1) \cdots H_C(P_n)$ of a derivation is in L, it usually also is sufficient that $H_C(P_1) \cdots H_C(P_n)$ is a prefix of some string in L. We call this control *weak* and replace C by wC and TV by wTV in the notions of the families of languages. We should like to mention that in the case of wTV the control words are just prefices of the ω-word $(H_C(P_1) \cdots H_C(P_p))^{\omega}$.

In the case of string grammars, from the results stated in [9], we obtain the following, for $\alpha \in \{\lambda, w\}$:

$$RE = \mathcal{L}(CF\text{-}GC_{ac}) = \mathcal{L}(CF\text{-}P_{ac}) = \mathcal{L}(CF\text{-}MAT_{ac})$$
$$= \mathcal{L}(CF\text{-}GC_{ut}) = \mathcal{L}(CF\text{-}P_{ut})$$
$$= \mathcal{L}(CF\text{-}\alpha C(REG)_{ac}) = \mathcal{L}(CF\text{-}\alpha C(REG)_{ut})$$
$$= \mathcal{L}(CF\text{-}\alpha TV_{ac}) = \mathcal{L}(CF\text{-}\alpha TV_{ut})$$
$$\not\supseteq \mathcal{L}(CF\text{-}GC) = \mathcal{L}(CF\text{-}P) = \mathcal{L}(CF\text{-}MAT).$$

Remark 1. We would like to point out that we have not forbidden $H_C(\emptyset)$ to appear in a control word. Whereas in the case of unconditional transfer or in the case of appearance checking, provided that $H_C(\emptyset) \in F$, this just means that this derivation step is done without making any changes on the underlying object, in the case of grammars with regular control and without appearance checking, reaching $H_C(\emptyset)$ means that the derivation has to have stopped with the preceding derivation step.

3   P Systems

In this section we consider several variants of P systems with control languages guiding the applicability of rules assigned to each membrane at a specific step of a computation.

A *(sequential) P system of type X* with n membranes is a construct

$$\Pi = (G, \mu, R, A, f)$$

where $G = (O, O_T, A', P, \Longrightarrow_G)$ is a grammar of type X and

- μ is the membrane (tree) structure of the system with n membranes (μ usually is represented by a string containing correctly nested marked parentheses); we assume the membranes, i.e., the nodes of the tree representing μ, being uniquely labeled by labels from a set H;
- R is a set of rules of the form (h, r, tar) where $h \in H$, $r \in P$, and tar, called the *target indicator*, is taken from the set $\{here, in, out\} \cup \{in_j \mid 1 \le j \le n\}$; the rules assigned to membrane h form the set $R_h = \{(r, tar) \mid (h, r, tar) \in R\}$, i.e., R can also be represented by the vector $(R_h)_{h \in H}$; for the systems considered in this paper, we do not consider communication with the environment, i.e., no objects may be sent out from the skin membrane (the outermost membrane) or taken into the skin membrane from the environment;
- A is the initial configuration specifying the objects from O assigned to each membrane at the beginning of a computation, i.e., $A = \{(h, A_h) \mid h \in H\}$;
- f is the final membrane where the terminal results are taken from at the end of a computation.

A configuration C of the P system Π can be represented as a set $\{(h, w_h) \mid h \in H\}$, where w_h is the current contents of objects contained in the membrane labeled by h. In the sequential transition mode, one rule from R is applied to the objects in the current configuration in order to obtain the next configuration in one *transition*. A sequence of transitions between configurations of

Π, starting from the initial configuration A, is called a *computation* of Π. A *halting computation* is a computation ending with a configuration $\{(h, w_h) \mid h \in H\}$ such that no rule from R can be applied to the objects w_h, $h \in H$, anymore, and the object w from (f, w) then is called the result of this halting computation if $w \in O_T$. $L(\Pi)$, the language generated by Π, consists of all terminal objects obtained as results of a halting computation in Π. By $\mathcal{L}(X\text{-}OP)$ $(\mathcal{L}(X\text{-}OP_n))$ we denote the family of languages generated by P systems (with at most n membranes) of type X.

In a similar way as for grammars themselves, we are able to consider various control mechanisms as defined in the previous section for P systems, too, e.g., using a control graph. In this paper, we are going to investigate the power of regular control.

A *(sequential) P system of type X with n membranes and regular control* is a construct $\Pi_C = (\Pi, H_C, L, F)$ where $\Pi = (G, \mu, R, A, f)$ is a (sequential) P system of type X, L is a regular language over H_C, where H_C is the set of labels identifying the subsets of productions from R in a one-to-one manner, and $F \subseteq H_C$. The language generated by Π_C consists of all terminal objects z obtained in membrane region f as results of a halting computation in Π. Observe that as in the case of normal grammars, the sequence of computation steps must correspond to a string $H_C(R_1) \cdots H_C(R_m) \in L$ with $R_1, \cdots, R_m$ being subsets of R. The corresponding families of languages generated by P systems with regular control Π_C (with at most n membranes) are denoted by $\mathcal{L}\left(X\text{-}\alpha C(REG)_\beta OP_n\right)$, $\alpha \in \{\lambda, w\}$, $\beta \in \{\lambda, ac, ut\}$.

Yet in contrast to the previous case, appearance checking and unconditional transfer have a special effect, as we cannot make a derivation step without applying a rule, but the derivation thus will halt immediately. In order to cope with this problem specific for P systems, we allow the system to be inactive for a bounded number of steps before it really "dies", i.e., halts. We call this specific way of terminating a computation *halting with delay d*, i.e., a computation halts if for a whole sequence of length d of production sets in a control word no rule has become applicable. In that way we obtain the language classes $\mathcal{L}\left(X\text{-}\alpha C(REG)_\beta OP_n, d\right)$, $\alpha \in \{\lambda, w\}$, $\beta \in \{\lambda, ac, ut\}$; if any of the numbers n or d may be arbitrarily large, we replace it by $*$. The case $k = 0$ describes the situation with normal halting, i.e., by definition

$$\mathcal{L}\left(X\text{-}\alpha C(REG)_\beta OP_n, 0\right) = \mathcal{L}\left(X\text{-}\alpha C(REG)_\beta OP_n\right).$$

In the P systems area we often deal with multisets, i.e., the underlying grammar is a multiset grammar. In the following, we first restrict ourselves to non-cooperative rules, the corresponding type is abbreviated by *ncoo*.

Theorem 1. *For all $\alpha \in \{\lambda, w\}$, $\beta \in \{\lambda, ac, ut\}$, and $n \geq 1$,*

$$\mathcal{L}\left(ncoo\text{-}\alpha C(REG)_\beta OP_n\right) \subseteq Ps\mathcal{L}(CF\text{-}MAT).$$

Proof. According to the arguments given above, we only have to consider the case of regular control languages without appearance checking, i.e., we only have to show that

$$\mathcal{L}\left(ncoo\text{-}\alpha C\left(REG\right)OP_n\right) \subseteq Ps\mathcal{L}\left(CF\text{-}MAT\right).$$

So let $\Pi_C = (\Pi_0, H_0, L_0)$ be a P system of degree n with regular control (and without appearance checking) where $\Pi_0 = (G_0, \mu, R_0, A_0, f)$ and $G_0 = (N_0, T_0, w_0, P_0, \Longrightarrow_{G_0})$ is a multiset grammar. As we are dealing with static P systems not communicating with the environment, it is clear that we can use the well-known flattening procedure reducing it to an equivalent system P system $\Pi_1 = (\Pi, H, L)$ where $\Pi = (G_m, [_1\ ]_1, R, A, 1)$, $G_m = (N, T, w, P_1, \Longrightarrow_{G_m})$ is a multiset grammar and L is a regular control set over H, i.e., H is the set of labels for the subsets of R; Π_1 uses non-cooperative rules in only one membrane region, i.e., we may consider this P system as a multiset rewriting device where a symbol b from membrane region i in the original P system Π_C is represented as $[i, b]$; it is easy to see that the control language L_0 can be changed accordingly to obtain the regular control set L for Π_1. We also observe that the terminal objects $b \in T_0$ in the output region f of the original system Π_C in Π_1 now are represented as objects $[f, b]$.

Let $M = (Q, H, \delta, q_0, Q_f)$ be the deterministic finite automaton accepting L where Q is the set of states, δ is the transition function, q_0 is the initial state, Q_f is the set of final states. The simulation then works in several steps:

- We first construct a matrix grammar with context-free rules

$$G_M = (G, M, \Longrightarrow_{G_M})$$

  where

$$G = \left(N \cup T \cup Q \cup \bar{Q}, N' \cup T' \cup Q', q_0 A, P, \Longrightarrow_G\right).$$

  For any non-cooperative rule $a \to u \in R$, we take the matrix $(p \to q, a \to u)$ into M if and only if $a \to u$ is in the set of rules R_p labeled by p and $(p, R_p, q) \in \delta$. At the end of a computation, arriving at some q, with $q \in F$ for $\alpha = \lambda$ or $q \in Q$ for $\alpha = w$, we may prime every remaining symbol to make it a terminal one by using the matrices $(q \to \bar{q})$ as well as $(\bar{q} \to \bar{q}, a \to a')$ for all $a \in N \cup T$ and finally ending up with the matrix $(\bar{q} \to q')$. In that way we can simulate the computations in Π_1, but

- it remains to check that we have arrived at a configuration to which no rule is applicable anymore. This can be achieved by intersecting the language $L(G_M)$ generated by G_M with a regular set L_r that cuts out all elements of $L(G_M)$ representing a configuration containing a primed version of a symbol which would allow for the application of a rule from the set of rules labeled by q represented by q' in a string in $L(G_M)$. In that way we get a language $L(G'_M)$ for a matrix grammar G'_M, as $\mathcal{L}(CF\text{-}MAT)$ is closed under intersection with regular languages.

– In order to filter out the desired terminal results of $L(\Pi_C)$ from $L(G'_M)$, we need a morphism h which maps any symbol $[f, b]'$ to the terminal symbol b for $b \in T$ and all other symbols to λ. As $\mathcal{L}(CF\text{-}MAT)$ is closed under morphisms, we can construct a matrix grammar G''_M with

$$L(G''_M) = h(L(G'_M)) = h(L(G_M) \cap L_r) = L(\Pi_C).$$

These observations conclude the proof.   □

It is somehow surprising that the proof technique elaborated in the proof of Theorem 1 also works for cooperative multiset rules, which type is abbreviated by *coo*.

Corollary 1. *For all* $\alpha \in \{\lambda, w\}$, $\beta \in \{\lambda, ac, ut\}$, *and* $n \geq 1$,

$$\mathcal{L}\left(coo\text{-}\alpha C\,(REG)_\beta\,OP_n\right) \subseteq Ps\mathcal{L}\,(CF\text{-}MAT).$$

Proof. We proceed exactly as in the proof of Theorem 1, except that for any cooperative rule $a_1 \cdots a_k \to u \in R$, we now take the matrix $(q \to p, a_1 \to \lambda, \cdots, a_{k-1} \to \lambda, a_k \to u)$ into M if and only if $a_1 \cdots a_k \to u$ is in the set of rules R_q labeled by q and $(q, R_q, p) \in \delta$. Moreover, the regular set L_r has to check for the (non-)appearance of a bounded number of symbols for each rule, yet the main parts of the proof remain valid as elaborated before.   □

As $Ps\mathcal{L}(CF\text{-}MAT) = \mathcal{L}(mCF\text{-}MAT)$, from Theorem 1 and Corollary 1 we finally obtain a characterization of $\mathcal{L}(mARB\text{-}MAT)$ via specific families of languages generated by P systems with regular control:

Theorem 2. *For all* $\alpha \in \{\lambda, w\}$, $\beta \in \{\lambda, ac, ut\}$, *and* $k, n, p \geq 1$,

$$
\begin{aligned}
\mathcal{L}(mARB\text{-}MAT) &= \mathcal{L}(mCF\text{-}MAT) \\
&= Ps\mathcal{L}(CF\text{-}MAT) \\
&= \mathcal{L}(mARB) \\
&= \mathcal{L}(coo\text{-}TV(p)\,OP_n) \\
&= \mathcal{L}\left(coo\text{-}\alpha C\,(REG)_\beta\,OP_n\right) \\
&= \mathcal{L}\left(ncoo\text{-}\alpha C\,(REG^{1*}\,(*, p+1))_\beta\,OP_n\right) \\
&= \mathcal{L}\left(ncoo\text{-}\alpha C\,(REG)_\beta\,OP_n\right).
\end{aligned}
$$

Proof. We first show that

$$\mathcal{L}(mCF\text{-}MAT) \subseteq \mathcal{L}\left(ncoo\text{-}C\,(REG^{1*}\,(*, 2))\,OP_1\right).$$

Let $G_{mM} = (G_m, M, \Longrightarrow_{G_{mM}})$ be a matrix grammar without appearance checking and $G_m = (N, T, w, P, \Longrightarrow_{G_m})$ the underlying multiset grammar. We now construct a P system with regular control $\Pi_C = (\Pi, H, L)$ with

$$\Pi = (G_m, [_1\ ]_1, P, \{(1, w)\}, 1)$$

generating $L(G_{mM})$ as follows: Let $M = \{m_i \mid 1 \leq i \leq k\}$ and $m_i = (m_{i,1}, \cdots, m_{i,k_i})$, $m_{i,j} \in P$, $1 \leq j \leq k_i$, $1 \leq i \leq k$. A matrix m_i can be simulated by Π_C by having the sequence of labels of singleton sets $H_C(\{m_{i,1}\}) \cdots H_C(\{m_{i,k_i}\})$ in L, i.e., we just take

$$L = \{H_C(\{m_{i,1}\}) \cdots H_C(\{m_{i,k_i}\}) \mid 1 \leq i \leq k\}^*.$$

This basic result with a one-star control language containing words of arbitrary length can be improved to a one-star control language containing words of length two only when starting with a matrix grammar in binary normal form, i.e., N is divided into two disjoint alphabets N_1 and N_2, the axiom w is of the form $X_0 S$ with $X_0 \in N_1$ and $S \in N_2$, and all the matrices are of the special (binary) form $(X \to Y, A \to w)$ with $X \in N_1$, $Y \in N_1 \cup \{\lambda\}$, $A \in N_2$, and $w \in (N_2 \cup T)^*$.

In the case of allowing cooperative rules, the two rules in the binary matrix $(X \to Y, A \to w)$ can be put together into the single rule $(XA \to Yw)$, i.e., for this new set of cooperative multiset rules

$$P' = \{XA \to Yw \mid (X \to Y, A \to w) \in M\}$$

and the corresponding labeling function H'_C we can take the control language

$$L' = \{H'_C(\{XA \to Yw\}) \mid (X \to Y, A \to w) \in M\}^*$$

and, equivalently,

$$L'' = \{H'_C(\{XA \to Yw \mid (X \to Y, A \to w) \in M\})\}^*,$$

which proves the assertion for time-varying P systems with cooperative rules, i.e.,

$$\mathcal{L}(mCF\text{-}MAT) \subseteq \mathcal{L}(coo\text{-}TV(1)OP_1).$$

In fact, we have proved even more, as the multiset grammar

$$G'_m = (N_1 \cup N_2, T, X_0 S, P', \Longrightarrow_{G'_m})$$

generates the same multiset language as the original matrix grammar G_{mM}, which shows that

$$\mathcal{L}(mCF\text{-}MAT) \subseteq \mathcal{L}(mARB).$$

As the binary normal form for matrix grammars is not restricted to context-free multiset rules, we immediately infer that we even have

$$\mathcal{L}(mARB\text{-}MAT) \subseteq \mathcal{L}(coo\text{-}TV(1)OP_1).$$

In sum, all the families of languages considered in the statement of the theorem coincide with $\mathcal{L}(mARB\text{-}MAT)$. □

We now turn our attention to the case of time-varying P systems with delay $d > 0$. Already allowing halting with delay two, in contrast to the preceding results, we obtain computational completeness, needing only time-varying P systems using non-cooperative rules in one membrane region even with unconditional transfer:

Theorem 3. *For all $\alpha \in \{\lambda, w\}$, $\beta \in \{ac, ut\}$, $n \geq 1$, $p \geq 12$, and $d \geq 2$,*

$$\mathcal{L}\left(ncoo\text{-}\alpha TV_\beta OP_n\left(p\right), d\right) = PsRE.$$

Proof. As appearance checking is at least as powerful as unconditional transfer, we only have to show that

$$PsRE \subseteq \mathcal{L}\left(ncoo\text{-}TV_{ut}OP_1\left(12\right), 2\right).$$

The proof is based on a construction used for purely catalytic P systems, see [10], having in mind that the rules being applied with the (three) catalysts in parallel there can be applied sequentially when periodically using different sets of rules. In fact, the first two catalysts were used to guide the simulation of the instructions applied to the first two registers of a register machine, whereas the third one was used for all the trapping rules only to be applied in case a non-deterministic choice for a rule assigned to the other two catalysts was taken in a wrong way. As the simulation of a SUB-instruction there took four steps with rules for the first two catalysts, we now need three sequential substeps for each of these four steps, i.e., in total a period of 12.

Now let us consider a language from $PsRE$, i.e., there exists a register machine $M = (m, B, 1, f, P)$ which uses its first two registers for the necessary computations; during a computation of M, only these registers 1 and 2 can be decremented. The remaining registers 3 to m are used to store the results of a computation. We now construct a time-varying P system $\Pi_C = (\Pi, H, L)$ where $\Pi = (G_m, [_1\ ]_1, R, A, 1)$, $G_m = (N, T, w, P, \Longrightarrow_{G_m})$ is a multiset grammar and L is a control language having periodicity 12; Π_C halts with bounded delay 2, i.e., the P system Π_C definitely halts if for more than two steps no rule can be applied anymore.

One basic principle for the construction of the P system Π_C is that we represent the contents of register i by the corresponding number of symbols o_i and variants of the labels of instructions to be simulated lead through the simulation steps. In the following we give a sketch of how the rule sets P_i, $1 \leq i \leq 12$, are to be constructed, which contain the rules to be applied periodically in the derivation steps $12k + i$, $k \geq 0$. We start with the axiom $A = p_1\tilde{p}_1$; in fact, when reaching P_1 again, only such a pair $p_j\tilde{p}_j$ for some label $j \in B \setminus \{f\}$ should be present besides the symbols o_i, $1 \leq i \leq m$; the numbers of copies of these symbols represent the numbers currently stored in the registers.

The following table shows which rules have to be taken into the rule sets P_i, $1 \leq i \leq 12$, to simulate a SUB-instruction $j : (SUB(a), k, l)$, with $j \in B \setminus \{l_h\}$, $k, l \in B$, $a \in \{1, 2\}$; in any case, the rule sets P_3, P_6, P_9, and P_{12} contain the rule $\# \to \#$, where $\#$ is a trap symbol which guarantees that as soon as this symbol is introduced the computation can never stop, as at least in every third step this rule is applicable, because due to the halting condition with delay 2 the system enters an infinite loop and never halts.

Simulation of SUB-instruction $j : (SUB\,(a)\,,k,l)$ in case the contents of

register a is non-empty

register a is empty

$$
\begin{array}{lll}
P_a : & p_j \to \hat{p}_j \hat{p}_j' & p_j \to \bar{p}_j \bar{p}_j' \bar{p}_j'' \\
P_{3-a} : & \tilde{p}_j \to \lambda & \tilde{p}_j \to \lambda \\
P_3 : & p_j \to \#,\ \tilde{p}_j \to \# & p_j \to \#,\ \tilde{p}_j \to \# \\
P_{3+a} : & o_a \to o_a',\ \hat{p}_j' \to \# & \bar{p}_j \to \lambda \\
P_{6-a} : & \hat{p}_j \to \lambda & \bar{p}_j'' \to p_j'' \\
P_6 : & \hat{p}_j \to \# & \bar{p}_j \to \#,\ \bar{p}_j'' \to \# \\
P_{6+a} : & o_a' \to o_a'' & o_a \to o_a' \\
P_{9-a} : & \hat{p}_j' \to \hat{p}_j'' & p_j'' \to p_j' \\
P_9 : & \hat{p}_j' \to \#,\ o_a' \to \# & p_j'' \to \#,\ o_a' \to \# \\
P_{9+a} : & \hat{p}_j'' \to p_k \tilde{p}_k & p_j' \to p_l \tilde{p}_l \\
P_{12-a} : & o_a'' \to \lambda & \bar{p}_j' \to \lambda \\
P_{12} : & o_a'' \to \#,\ \hat{p}_j'' \to \# & p_j' \to \#,\ \bar{p}_j' \to \#
\end{array}
$$

In case register a is assumed to be non-empty and the guess is wrong, $\hat{p}_j' \to \#$ has to be applied instead of $o_a \to o_a'$ from P_{3+a}, hence, the symbol $\hat{p}_j'$ cannot wait to be applied with the rule $\hat{p}_j' \to \hat{p}_j''$ in P_{9-a}. In the other case, when assuming register a to be empty, the rule $o_a \to o_a'$ should not be applicable from rule set P_{6+a}, as then $o_a' \to \#$ would become applicable from rule set P_9. Observe that these arguments only work because we interchange the rule sets for $a = 1$ and $a = 2$, e.g., $o_1 \to o_1'$ is in P_4 and $o_2 \to o_2'$ is in P_5.

For an ADD-instruction $j : (ADD\,(a)\,,k,l)$, with $j,k,l \in B \setminus \{l_h\}$, $1 \le a \le m$, it would be sufficient to just use the rules $\tilde{p}_j \to \lambda$ and $p_j \to o_a p_k \tilde{p}_k$ or $p_j \to o_a p_l \tilde{p}_l$ in a sequence of two steps, but we have to extend this to a sequence of total length 12 in order to have the same period as in the case of the simulation of a SUB-instruction. Hence, for each ADD-instruction $j : (ADD\,(a)\,,k,l)$, we take the following rules into the rule sets P_i, $1 \le i \le 12$; in this case, we need not interchange the rule sets for different registers a, $a \in \{1,2\}$:

Simulation of ADD-instruction $j : (ADD\,(a)\,,k,l)$

$$
\begin{array}{ll}
P_1 : & p_j \to p_j' \\
P_2 : & \tilde{p}_j \to \lambda \\
P_3 : & \tilde{p}_j \to \#,\ p_j \to \# \\
P_4 : & p_j' \to \bar{p}_j \\
P_5 : & \bar{p}_j \to \bar{p}_j' \\
P_6 : & p_j' \to \#,\ \bar{p}_j \to \# \\
P_7 : & \bar{p}_j' \to \hat{p}_j \\
P_8 : & \hat{p}_j \to \hat{p}_j' \\
P_9 : & \bar{p}_j' \to \#,\ \hat{p}_j \to \# \\
P_{10} : & \hat{p}_j' \to \hat{p}_j'' \\
P_{11} : & \hat{p}_j'' \to o_a p_k \tilde{p}_k,\ \hat{p}_j'' \to o_a p_l \tilde{p}_l \\
P_{12} : & \hat{p}_j' \to \#,\ \hat{p}_j'' \to \#
\end{array}
$$

The trap rules introduced in the rule sets P_3, P_6, P_9, and P_{12} guarantee that the rules in the rule sets P_1, P_2, P_4, P_5, P_7, P_8, P_{10}, and P_{11} have to be applied in a correct way to avoid the introduction of the trap symbol #.

Without loss of generality, we may assume that the last instruction applied in the register machine M is a SUB-instruction (labeled by j) being applied to the empty register 1; instead of taking the rule $p'_j \to p_f \tilde{p}_f$ we take the rule $p'_j \to \lambda$ into P_{10}. If until then the actions of the register machine have been simulated correctly in Π_C, only the terminal results consisting of specific numbers of copies of the symbols o_i, $3 \le i \le m$, remain in the membrane region. The P system therefore finally stops before entering a new cycle $P_1 \cdots P_{12}$; hence, in sum we have shown that the language generated by the register machine is also generated by the time-varying P system Π_C with delay 2, i.e.,

$$PsRE \subseteq \mathcal{L}\left(ncoo\text{-}TV_{ut}OP_1\left(12\right), 2\right).$$

As weak control is the less restrictive control variant, we immediately infer

$$PsRE \subseteq \mathcal{L}\left(ncoo\text{-}wTV_{ut}OP_1\left(12\right), 2\right).$$

too.   □

As a challenge for future research it remains to search for a proof which eventually allows to obtain computational completeness with delay one only. Another parameter to be improved is the period of the control language. Eventually there might also be a trade-off between these two parameters: It is easy to see that using p_j only instead of the pair $p_j \tilde{p}_j$ we could save the second rule set at the beginning of a simulation; then, in addition, we might even omit P_3 and P_{12}, but with these rather obvious changes we would increase the delay to 3.

The construction given in the preceding proof shows that any action in the time-varying P system can be seen as simple multiset rewriting, hence, we obviously get the following result:

Corollary 2. *For all $\alpha \in \{\lambda, w\}$, $\beta \in \{ac, ut\}$, and $p \ge 12$,*

$$\mathcal{L}\left(mCF\text{-}\alpha TV_\beta\left(p\right)\right) = PsRE.$$

4   Conclusion

In this paper we have considered (sequential) P systems where the applications of the rules assigned to each membrane are controlled by a regular language. We have shown that with usual halting we can only get $Ps\mathcal{L}\left(CF\text{-}MAT\right)$. On the other hand, with delayed halting, i.e., allowing the system to wait a bounded number d of computation steps to become active again, even with delay two and control languages of the form $\{w\}^*$, i.e., even time-varying P systems with only one membrane and delay 2 characterize $PsRE$.

The same proof ideas as used in Theorem 3 can be used to show a similar result for string languages, i.e., collecting terminal symbols sent out of the skin membrane during a computation of a time-varying P system into a string we can obtain any recursively enumerable string language. Moreover, a lot of variants deserve to be considered in the future, e.g.,

- other transition modes, especially the maximally parallel mode max, the minimally parallel mode min, the min_1-mode, etc.;
- other variants of halting, especially adult halting, halting with final state, and partial halting;
- variants of combinations of types of rules assigned to the membranes and types of control languages;
- dynamic P systems, i.e., control languages are assigned to labels of membranes and not to membranes themselves;
- etc.

We shall return to these questions and related ones in an extended version of this paper.

References

1. Cavaliere, M., Freund, R., Oswald, M., Sburlan, D.: Multiset random context grammars, checkers, and transducers. Theor. Comput. Sci. 372(2-3), 136–151 (2007)
2. Csuhaj-Varjú, E., Dassow, J., Kelemen, J., Păun, G.: Grammar Systems: A Grammatical Approach to Distribution and Cooperation. Gordon and Breach (1994)
3. Dassow, J.: Subregularly controlled derivations: the context-free case. Rostocker Mathematisches Kolloquium 34, 61–70 (1988)
4. Dassow, J.: Subregularly controlled derivations: restrictions by syntactic parameters. In: Where Mathematics, Computer Science, Linguistics and Biology Meet, pp. 51–61. Kluwer Academic Publishers (2001)
5. Dassow, J.: Subregular restrictions for some language generating devices. In: Freund, R., Holzer, M., Truthe, B., Ultes-Nitsche, U. (eds.) Fourth Workshop on Non-Classical Models for Automata and Applications, NCMA 2012, Fribourg, Switzerland, August 23-24, vol. 290, pp. 11–26 (2012), books@ocg.at
6. Dassow, J., Păun, G.: Regulated Rewriting in Formal Language Theory. Springer (1989)
7. Dassow, J., Păun, G., Rozenberg, G.: Grammar systems. In: [18], vol. 2, pp. 155–172 (1997)
8. Dassow, J., Păun, G., Salomaa, A.: Grammars with controlled derivations. In: [18], vol. 2, pp. 101–154 (1997)
9. Fernau, H.: Unconditional transfer in regulated rewriting. Acta Informatica 34(11), 837–857 (1997)
10. Freund, R., Kari, L., Oswald, M., Sosík, P.: Computationally universal P systems without priorities: two catalysts are sufficient. Theor. Comp. Sci. 330, 251–266 (2005)
11. Kudlek, M., Martín-Vide, C., Păun, G.: Toward a Formal Macroset Theory. In: Calude, C.S., Pun, G., Rozenberg, G., Salomaa, A. (eds.) Multiset Processing. LNCS, vol. 2235, pp. 123–134. Springer, Heidelberg (2001)
12. Margenstern, M., Rogozhin, Y.: About Time-Varying Distributed H Systems. In: Condon, A., Rozenberg, G. (eds.) DNA 2000. LNCS, vol. 2054, pp. 53–62. Springer, Heidelberg (2001)

13. Minsky, M.L.: Computation: Finite and Infinite Machines. Prentice Hall (1967)
14. Nielsen, M.: OL systems with control devices. Acta Informatica 4(4), 373–386 (1975)
15. Păun, G.: DNA computing: Distributed Splicing Systems. In: Mycielski, J., Rozenberg, G., Salomaa, A. (eds.) Structures in Logic and Computer Science. LNCS, vol. 1261, pp. 353–370. Springer, Heidelberg (1997)
16. Păun, G.: Membrane Computing. An Introduction. Springer (2002)
17. Păun, G., Rozenberg, G., Salomaa, A.: The Oxford Handbook of Membrane Computing. Oxford University Press (2010)
18. Rozenberg, G., Salomaa, A.: Handbook of Formal Languages, vol. 3. Springer (1997)
19. Salomaa, A.: On finite automata with a time-variant structure. Information and Control 13(2), 85–98 (1968)
20. Salomaa, A.: Periodically time-variant context-free grammars. Information and Control 17, 294–311 (1970)
21. The P Systems Web Page, http://ppage.psystems.eu
22. Verlan, S.: Communicating Distributed H Systems with Alternating Filters. In: Jonoska, N., Păun, G., Rozenberg, G. (eds.) Aspects of Molecular Computing. LNCS, vol. 2950, pp. 367–384. Springer, Heidelberg (2003)

Mobile Membranes with Objects on Surface as Colored Petri Nets

Bogdan Aman and Gabriel Ciobanu

Romanian Academy, Institute of Computer Science
Blvd. Carol I no.8, 700505 Iași, Romania
bogdan.aman@gmail.com, gabriel@info.uaic.ro

Abstract. Mobile membranes with objects on surface represent a rule-based formalism involving parallelism and mobility. We use this class of mobile membranes to model the low-density lipoprotein degradation. A translation of this formalism into colored Petri nets is provided in order to analyze, using CPN Tools, some important properties of mobile membranes: reachability, boundedness, liveness, fairness. In order to show how this translation works, we translate the model of the low-density lipoprotein degradation using mobile membranes into colored Petri nets.

1 Introduction

Formal models are used for many purposes, and each purpose influences the degree of abstraction and detail. If a greater detail is provided , the number of systems to which our model applies will decrease. A formal model should have three properties, and each of these trades off against the other two [12]: *generality*: the number of systems and situations to which the model correctly applies, *realism*: the degree to which the model mimics the real world, *power and precision*: collection of revealed properties, and the accuracy of the model predictions.

In this paper we use two formalisms: mobile membranes (realism, being inspired by cell biology) and colored Petri nets (power and precision provided by complex software tools). A relation can be established between these two formalisms by providing an encoding of mobile membranes into colored Petri nets. By considering the endocytic pathway for low-density lipoprotein degradation, we show how mobile membranes can be used to model such a biological phenomenon, while colored Petri nets can be used to analyze and verify automatically some behavioral properties of this pathway. The endocytic pathway for low-density lipoprotein (LDL) degradation has been modeled before using other formalisms (e.g., bioambients [15]). However, none of the previous descriptions of the pathway is not translated into a formalism having software tools able to check automatically some complex behavioral properties.

The first connections between membrane systems and Petri nets are presented in [6] and [16]. In [10], a direct structural relationship between these two formalisms is established by defining a new class of Petri nets called Petri nets with localities. This new class of Petri nets has been used to show how maximal

E. Csuhaj-Varjú et al. (Eds.): CMC 2012, LNCS 7762, pp. 128–144, 2013.

evolutions from membrane systems are faithfully reflected in the maximally concurrent step sequence semantics of their corresponding Petri nets with localities.

In this paper, contains the syntax and semantics of mobile membranes with objects on surface in Section 2, and in Section 3 this formalism is used to model the LDL pathway. In order to be able to use a complex software called CPN Tools, a translation of a system with a bounded number of mobile membranes into colored Petri nets (described briefly in Section 4) is provided in Section 5. The description of the LDL degradation obtained via the given translation is presented in Section 6. The CPN Tools are used to analyze automatically some behavioral properties. Conclusion and references end the paper.

2   Mobile Membranes with Objects on Surface

To be able to model nondeterministic, spatial, and dynamic biological processes, a rule-based model of computation called mobile membranes [2] is used. The first systems with mobile membranes were introduced in [11] as a particular class of membrane computing [14], while mobile membranes were studied in detail in [3]. A specific feature of this formalism is given by the parallel application of rules; this feature is inspired from biology, and it is not present in process calculi with mobility that use interleaving semantics [1]. The parallel application of rules depends on the available resources (i.e., elements of the left hand side of the rules). The mobile membranes systems are defined by two features:

1. A spatial structure consisting of a hierarchy of membranes (which are either disjoint or included) with multisets of objects on their surface; a membrane without any other membrane inside is called elementary, while a non-elementary membrane is called a composite membrane.
2. The biologically inspired rules describing the mobility of membranes inside the structure: pinocytosis (engulfing zero external membranes), phagocytosis (engulfing just one external membrane), and exocytosis (expelling the content of a membrane outside the membrane where it is placed). Pinocytosis and phagocytosis represent different types of endocytosis.

In terms of computation, membrane configurations are used. The set $\mathcal{M}$ of membrane configurations (ranged by $M, N, \dots$) is defined using the free monoid O^* (ranged over by $u, v, \dots$) generated by a finite alphabet O of objects (ranged over by $a, \bar{a}, b, \bar{b}, \dots$).

Definition 1. *The set $\mathcal{M}(\Pi)$ of membrane configurations in a system Π of mobile membranes with objects on their surfaces is defined inductively as follows:*

- *if w is a multiset over O, then $[\ ]_w \in \mathcal{M}(\Pi)$;*
  $[\ ]_w$ is called an elementary *membrane configuration;*
- *if $M_1, \dots, M_n \in \mathcal{M}(\Pi)$, $n \geq 1$, and w is a multiset of objects over O then $[M_1 \| \dots \| M_n]_w \in \mathcal{M}(\Pi)$; $[M_1 \| \dots \| M_n]_w$ is called a* composite membrane *and $M_1, \dots, M_n$ are called* adjacent *membrane configurations.*

The string representation of multisets of objects is used; thus, multisets of objects are represented by sequences w, meaning that every permutation of such a sequence is allowed (as an equivalent representation of the same multiset).

Inspired from the immune system [8], we define specific rules called pino, phago, and exo in which the membranes agree on their movement by using complementary objects a and $\bar{a}$. Biologically speaking, the objects a and their corresponding co-objects $\bar{a}$ fit properly.

If M and N are arbitrary membrane configurations, and u and v are arbitrary multisets of objects, the evolution from a configuration to another is provided by a set R of rules defined as follows:

- $[\,]_{a\,u\,\bar{a}\,v} \rightarrow [[\,]_c\,u]_{d\,v}$, for $a, \bar{a} \in O, c, d, u, v \in O^*$ pino

$$M_1 \left(M_2 \right)_{a u \bar{a} v} \longrightarrow M_1 \left(M_2 \bigcirc_{cu} \right)_{dv}$$

An object a together with its complementary object $\bar{a}$ indicate the creation of an empty membrane within the membrane on which a and $\bar{a}$ objects are attached. Imagine that this initial membrane buckles towards the inside, and pinches off by breaking the connection between a and $\bar{a}$. The multiset of objects u on the new created (empty) membrane is transferred from the initial membrane. The objects a and $\bar{a}$ can be modified during this step into the multisets c and d, respectively. On the surface of the membrane appearing in the left hand side of the rule there are some objects (others than $au\bar{a}v$) which are ignored; these objects are also not specified on the right hand side of the rule, being randomly distributed between the two resulting membranes. By M_1 and M_2 are denoted (possible empty) multisets of elementary and composite membranes.

- $[\,]_{a\,u}\|\,[\,]_{\bar{a}\,v} \rightarrow [[[\,]_c\,u]_d]_v$, for $a, \bar{a} \in O, c, d, u, v \in O^*$ phago

$$M_1 \bigcirc_{au} \left(M_2 \right)_{\bar{a}v} \longrightarrow M_1 \left(M_2 \bigcirc_{cu} \right)_{d}{}_{v}$$

An object a together with its complementary object $\bar{a}$ indicate a membrane (the one with $\bar{a}$ on its surface) "eating" an elementary membrane (the one with a on its surface). The membrane having $\bar{a}$ and v on its surface wraps around the membrane having a and u on its surface. An additional membrane is created around the eaten membrane; the objects a and $\bar{a}$ are modified during this evolution into the multisets c and d (the multiset c corresponds to a and remains on the eaten membrane, while the multiset d corresponds to $\bar{a}$ and is placed on the new created membrane). On the surface of the membranes appearing in the left hand side of the rule there are some objects (others than au and $\bar{a}v$) which are ignored; these objects are also not specified on the right hand side of the rule. The objects appearing on the membrane having initially the object a on surface remain unchanged, while the objects appearing on the membrane having initially the object $\bar{a}$ on surface are randomly distributed between the two resulting membranes (the ones with d

and v). By M_1 and M_2 are denoted (possible empty) multisets of elementary and composite membranes.

- $[\,[\,]_{a\,u}]_{\overline{a}\,v} \to [\,]_{c\,u\,d\,v}$, for $a, \overline{a} \in O, c, d, u, v \in O^*$ exo

$$M_1 \underbrace{\left[M_2 \boxed{M_3}_{au} \right]}_{\overline{a}v} \longrightarrow M_1 \underbrace{\left(\quad M_2 \quad \right)}_{cudv} M_3$$

An object a together with its complementary object $\overline{a}$ indicate the merging of a nested membrane with its surrounding membrane. Imagine that the connection between a and $\overline{a}$ represent the point where the membranes connect each other. In this merging process (which is a smooth and continuous process), the membrane having the multiset $a\,u$ on its surface is expelled to the outside, and all objects of the two membranes are united into a multiset on the membrane which initially contained v. The objects a and $\overline{a}$ can be modified during this evolution into the multisets c and d, respectively. If the membrane having on its surface the object a is composite, then its content is released near the newly merged membrane after applying the rule. On the surface of the membranes appearing in the left hand side of the rule there are some objects (others than au and $\overline{a}v$) which are ignored; these objects are also not specified on the right hand side of the rule, being moved on the resulting membrane. By M_1, M_2 and M_3 are denoted (possible empty) multisets of elementary and composite membranes.

Definition 2. *For a system Π of mobile membranes with objects on their surfaces, if M and N are two membrane configurations from $\mathcal{M}(\Pi)$, then*

- *M reduces to N (denoted by $M \to N$) if there exists a rule in R applicable to configuration M such that configuration N is obtained;*
- *a transition from M to N represents a number of reductions performed in one step using a maximal set of rules from R (such that no further rule can be added to the set); by $M \overset{R'}{\Rightarrow} M'$ we denote that M evolves to M' due to the parallel applications of the rules from a set $R' \subseteq R$;*
- *a sequence of transitions is a computation, and a computation is successful if it halts (it reaches a membrane configuration where no rule can be applied).*

3 LDL Degradation Pathway Using Mobile Membranes

LDL is one of several complexes carrying cholesterol through the bloodstream. An LDL particle is a lipoprotein complex that contains one thousand or more cholesterol molecules in the form of cholesteryl esters. A monolayer of phospholipid surrounds the cholesterol and contains a single molecule of a large protein apolipoprotein B (known as apoB). In a receptor-mediated endocytosis, a cell engulfs a particle of low-density lipoprotein from the outside. To do this, the cell uses receptors that specifically recognize and bind to the LDL particle. By this mechanism, cells acquire from the bloodstream the cholesterol required for the membrane synthesis that occurs during the cell growth.

The degradation of LDL particles is realized in five steps (see Figure 1):

1. Cell-surface LDL receptors bind to an apoB protein of an LDL particles forming an receptor-ligand complex.
2. Clathrin-coated pits containing receptor-LDL complexes are pinched off.
3. After the vesicle coat is shed, the uncoated endocytic vesicle (early endosome) fuses with the late endosome. The acidic pH in this compartment causes a conformational change in the LDL receptor that leads to freeing the bound LDL particle.
4. The late endosome fuses with the lysosome, and the proteins and lipids of the free LDL particle are broken down to their constituent parts by enzymes in the lysosome.
5. The LDL receptor recycles to the cell surface where, at the neutral pH of the exterior medium, the receptor undergoes a conformational change such that it can bind another LDL particle.

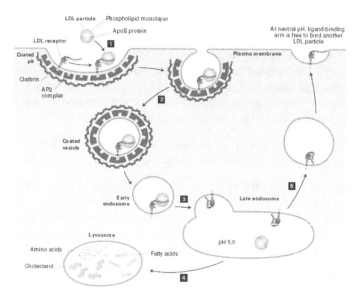

Fig. 1. Endocytic Pathway for Low-Density Lipoprotein [13]

We illustrate how the LDL degradation pathway can be described in terms of mobile membranes with objects on surface, and simulate all these steps. An LDL particle is described as $[\ ]_{apoB\ cho}$ representing the monolayer of phospholipid that contains a single $apoB$ protein, and cholesterol cho. A cell engulfing the LDL particle is described as $[[\ ]_{lyso} \parallel [\ ]_{late\ aux}]_{recep\ recep}$, where:

- $[\ ]_{recep\ recep}$ represents the cell containing on its surface two receptors $recep$ able to recognize an $apoB$ protein; clathrin and others receptors of the cell are not use since we are not interested in their evolution;
- $[\ ]_{lyso}$ represents the lysosome;
- $[\ ]_{late\ aux}$ represents the late endosome, and aux is an auxiliary object in creating new membranes by pino and phago rules.

The initial configuration of the systems is

$$M_1 = [\ ]_{apoB}\ cho\ ||\ [[\ ]_{lyso}\ aux\ ||\ [\ ]_{late}\ aux]_{recep}\ recep$$

The steps presented in Figure 1 are described by using the following rules:

1. $[\ ]_{apoB}\ ||\ [\ ]_{recep}\ recep \rightarrow [[[\ ]_{apoB}]_{recep}]_{recep}$ (phago) $(recep = \overline{apoB})$

2. $[\ ]_{recep}\ ||\ [\ ]_{late}\ aux \rightarrow [[[\ ]_{recep}]_{aux}]_{late}$ (phago) $(aux = \overline{recep})$

3. $[[\ ]_{recep}]_{aux} \rightarrow [\ ]_{recep1}\ aux$ (exo) $(aux = \overline{recep})$

4. $[[\ ]_{aux}]_{late} \rightarrow [\ ]_{aux4}\ late$ (exo) $(late = \overline{aux})$

5. $[\ ]_{lyso}\ aux\ ||\ [\ ]_{late} \rightarrow [[[\ ]_{late}]_{aux1}]_{lyso}$ (phago) $(aux = \overline{late})$

6. $[[\ ]_{recep1}]_{aux1} \rightarrow [\ ]_{recep2}\ aux2$ (exo) $(aux1 = \overline{recep1})$

7. $[\ ]_{late}\ recep2\ aux2\ aux4 \rightarrow [[\ ]_{late}\ recep3\ aux4]_{aux3}$ (pino) $(aux2 = \overline{recep2})$

8. $[[\ ]_{aux3}]_{lyso} \rightarrow [\ ]_{lyso}\ aux$ (exo) $(lyso = \overline{aux3})$

9. $[[\ ]_{apoB}]_{lyso} \rightarrow [\ ]_{lyso}\ apoB$ (exo) $(lyso = \overline{apoB})$

10. $[\ ]_{late}\ recep3\ aux4 \rightarrow [[\ ]_{recep4}\ aux4]_{late}$ (pino) $(late = \overline{recep3})$

11. $[\ ]_{aux4}\ recep4 \rightarrow [[\ ]_{recep5}]_{aux5}$ (pino) $(aux4 = \overline{recep4})$

12. $[[\ ]_{aux5}]_{late} \rightarrow [\ ]_{late}\ aux$ (exo) $(late = \overline{aux5})$

13. $[[\ ]_{recep5}]_{recep} \rightarrow [\ ]_{recep}\ recep$ (exo) $(recep = \overline{recep5})$

where $(recep = \overline{apoB})$ denotes an object $recep$ that is complementary to an object $apoB$.

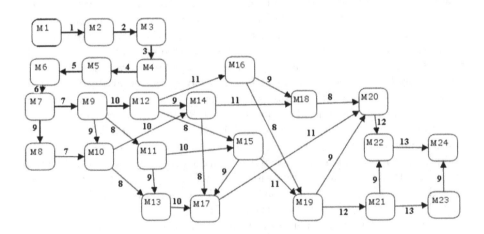

Fig. 2. Evolution of the LDL degradation

The evolution of the LDL degradation could be represented graphically as in Figure 2. By $M_1, \ldots, M_{24}$ are denoted the possible configurations of the system, and on each arrow from a M_i to a M_j is placed the number of the rule which is applied in order to evolve from M_i to M_j. To denote that an object $recep$ changes its position and interacts with different objects, different notations are used (namely, $recep, recep1, \ldots, recep5$) in the evolution of the system.

Remark 1. The number of the applied rules to reach the configuration M_{24} starting from the configuration M_1 is always 13.

4   Colored Petri Nets

Colored Petri nets (CPN) represent a graphical language used to describe systems in which communication, synchronization and resource sharing play an important role [9]. The CPN model contains places (drawn as ellipses or circles), transitions (drawn as rectangular boxes), a number of directed arcs connecting places and transitions, and finally some textual inscriptions located near the places, transitions and arcs.

The places are used to represent the state of the modeled system, and this state is given by the number of tokens of all the places. Such a state is called a marking of the CPN model. By convention, the names of the places are written inside the ellipses. The names have no formal meaning, but they have a practical importance for the readability of a CPN model, just like the use of mnemonic names in traditional programming.

The arc expressions on the input arcs of a transition determine when the transition is enabled, i.e., to be activated by a certain marking. A transition is enabled whenever it is possible to find a binding of the variables that appear in the surrounding arc expressions of the transition such that the arc expression of each input arc evaluates to a multiset of tokens that is present in the corresponding input place. When a transition occurs with a given binding, it removes from each input place the multiset of tokens to which the corresponding input arc expression evaluates. Analogously, it adds to each output place the multiset of tokens to which the corresponding output arc expression evaluates.

The colored Petri nets have also a mathematical representation with a well defined syntax and semantics. This formal representation is the framework for the study of different behavioral properties. $EXPR$ denotes the set of expressions provided by the inscription language (which is ML in the case of CPN Tools), and $Type[e]$ denotes the type of an expression $e \in EXPR$, i.e., the type of the values obtained when evaluating e. The set of free variables in an expression e is denoted $Var[e]$, and the type of a variable x is denoted $Type[x]$. The set of variables is denoted by X; the set of expressions $e \in EXPR$, for which $Var[e] \subseteq X$, is denoted by $EXPR_X$. S_{MS} denotes the set of all multisets over S.

The following definition differs from that presented in [9] just because simultaneous parallel arcs from the same place to the same transition are not allowed (i.e., it is enough to have only one arc).

Definition 3. *A* **non-hierarchical Colored Petri Net** *is a nine tuple*
$$CPN = (P, T, A, \Sigma, X, C, G, E, I), \text{ where}$$

1. *P is a finite set of* **places***;*
2. *T is a finite set of* **transitions** *such that* $P \cap T = \emptyset$*;*
3. $A \subseteq (P \times T) \cup (T \times P)$ *is a set of directed* **arcs***;*
4. Σ *is a finite set of non-empty* **color set***;*

5. X is a finite set of **typed variables** such that $Type[x] \in \Sigma$ for all $x \in X$;

6. $C : P \to \Sigma$ is a **color set function** that assigns a color set to each place;

7. $G : T \to EXPR_X$ is a **guard function** that assigns a guard to each transition t such that $Type[G(t)] = Bool$;

8. $E : A \to EXPR_X$ is an **arc expression function** that assigns a guard to each arc a such that $Type[E(a)] = C(p)_{MS}$, where p is the place connected to the arc a;

9. $I : P \to EXPR_\emptyset$ is an **initialization function** that assigns an initialization expression to each place p such that $Type[I(p)] = C(p)_{MS}$.

A distribution of tokens over the places of a net is called a marking. Given two markings m and m', the fact that m leads to m' by a set U of transitions, is denote by $m[U\rangle m'$.

5   Mobile Membranes as Colored Petri Nets

We denote by $\Pi = (M_0, R)$ a system of mobile membranes with a set R of rules having an initial membrane configuration $M_0 = (w_1^0, \ldots, w_n^0, \mu)$, where w_i^0 denotes the initial multisets of objects placed on membrane i, $1 \leq i \leq n$, and μ the initial membrane structure. We consider that a well-defined system has at any point of evolution at most $k > 2$ membranes. Given such a system of mobile membranes, the corresponding colored Petri net is denoted by $CPN_\Pi = (P, T, A, \Sigma, X, C, G, E, I)$, where the components are as follows:

- $P = \{1, \ldots, k\} \cup \{structure\}$, where $structure$ is a place that contains the structure of the corresponding membrane system, namely the pairs (i, j).

- $T = \bigcup_{1 \leq k \leq s} t_k$, where each t_k represents a distinct transition for a rule of R;

  since the rules of R contain no explicit label for membranes, it means that:

  - a *pino* rule can be instantiated at most k times in each step;

  - a *phago* rule can be instantiated at most $\dfrac{k!}{2!(k-2)!}$ times in each step;

  - an *exo* rule can be instantiated at most $\dfrac{k!}{2!(k-2)!}$ times in each step;

    2 represents the number of membranes from the left hand side of an *exo* rule, and $\dfrac{k!}{2!(k-2)!}$ all the possible combinations of membranes.

  Thus, $s = s_1 * k + s_2 * \dfrac{k!}{2!(k-2)!} + s_3 * \dfrac{k!}{2!(k-2)!}$, where s_1, s_2, and s_3 represent the numbers of pino, phago, and exo rules from R.

- A contains input arcs $(P \times T)$ and output arcs $(T \times P)$; for a rule r and its associated transition t, the arcs are built as follows:

  - the input arcs are both from the places that represent the membranes appearing in the left hand side of the evolution rule r and from the place *structure* to the transition t;

- the output arcs are from the transition t to both the places that represent the membranes appearing in the right hand side of the evolution rule r and to the place *structure*.

○ $\Sigma = U \cup L$, where U represents tokens (color) set containing all the objects from O, and $L = \{1, \ldots, k\} \times \{1, \ldots, k\}$ is a color set containing the membrane structure.

○ $X = \{x, y, z, \ldots\}$ is a set of variables used when modifying the content of place *structure*.

○ $C(p) = \begin{cases} U, & \text{if } p \in \{1, \ldots, k\} \\ L, & \text{if } p = structure. \end{cases}$

○ $G(t) = \begin{cases} [x = y], & \text{if } t \text{ is a transition corresponding to a } phago \text{ rule; it checks} \\ & \text{if both membranes from the left hand side of a phago rule} \\ & \text{have the same parent;} \\ true, & \text{otherwise.} \end{cases}$

○ For a rule r and its associated transition t, E is built as follows:
  - the multiset of objects u is placed on an input arc from a place that represents a membrane appearing in the left hand side of the evolution rule r (being marked with a multiset of objects u) to the transition t;
  - all the pairs (i, j), describing the membrane structure appearing in the left hand side rule r, are placed on the input arc from the place *structure* to the transition t;
  - the multiset of objects v is placed on an output arc from a transition t to a place that represents a membrane appearing in the right hand side of the evolution rule r (being marked with a multiset of objects v);
  - all the pairs (i, j), describing the membrane structure appearing in the right hand side rule r, are placed on the output arc from the transition t to the place *structure*.

○ $I(p) = \begin{cases} w_p^0, & \text{if } p \in \{1, \ldots, k\} \\ \{(i, j) \mid i, j \in \{1, \ldots, k\}, (i, j) \in \mu\}. \end{cases}$

The relationship between the dynamics of the mobile membrane Π and that of the corresponding colored Petri net CPN_Π is proven in what follows:

Theorem 1. *If M and M' are two membrane configurations of Π, then*
$$M \overset{R'}{\Rightarrow} M' \text{ if and only if } \phi(M) [\psi(R')\rangle \phi(M'),$$
where
$$\phi(M)(i) = \begin{cases} w_i, & \text{for all places } i \in P; \\ \mu, & i = structure. \end{cases}, \quad \text{and}$$
$$\psi(R) = \bigcup_{r_i \in R} \psi(r_i) \text{ with } \psi(r_i) = t_i.$$

Proof. The function ϕ represents a bijection between the multisets of objects of Π and the markings of CPN_Π based on the corresponding links between objects and tokens, and between membranes and places, respectively. Let $(w_1, \ldots, w_k, \mu)$ be the multisets of objects from the membrane configuration M, together with its structure μ. Similarly, for a set of rules $R' = \{r_1, \ldots, r_i\}$ of Π, the function ψ is a bijection constructing the set $\psi(R') = \{t_1, \ldots, t_i\}$ of transitions of CPN_Π from the set R of rules.

A membrane configuration M_1 can evolve to a membrane configuration M_2 by applying an evolution rule r from R' if and only if, given the marking $\phi(M_1)$, one obtains the marking $\phi(M_2)$ by firing a transition t in CPN_Π, where $\psi(R')(t) = r$. Overall, this is a direct consequence of the fact that ψ and ϕ are bijections. $\square$

From the construction above, it results that the initial configuration of Π corresponds through ϕ to the initial marking of CPN_Π. Moreover, according to Theorem 1, it results that the computation of Π coincides with the computation of the CPN_Π.

6   Simulating LDL Degradation by Using CPN Tools

The mobile membranes description of the LDL degradation pathway can be encoded in colored Petri nets. The encoding allows the use of a complex software tool able to verify automatically some important behavioral properties. Some decidability results for behavioral properties of membrane systems with peripheral proteins are presented in [5], but they cannot be proven automatically. For colored Petri nets is available a complex software called *CPN Tools* in which simulations can be performed, and certain behavioral properties can be checked automatically: reachability, boundedness, deadlock, liveness, fairness. CPN Tools (www/cs/au.dk/CPNTools) is a tool for editing, simulating, state space analysis, and performance analysis of systems described as colored Petri nets.

In what follows the rules of mobile membranes used to model the LDL degradation pathway are simulated using the CPN Tools. To make easier to observe how the evolution takes place using CPN Tools, the system is simplified and only the transitions that eventually occur are used.

A CPN model is always created in CPN Tools as a graphical drawing. Figure 3 describes the LDL degradation pathway model, namely the membrane configuration M_1 from Section 3. The diagram contains eight places, four substitution transitions (drawn as double-rectangular boxes), a number of directed arcs connecting places and transitions, and finally some textual inscriptions next to the places, transitions and arcs. The arc expressions are built from variables, constants, operators, and functions. When all variables in an expression are bounded to values of the correct type, the expression can be evaluated. In general, arc expressions may evaluate to a multiset of token colors. Next to each place is an inscription which determines the set of token colors (data values) that the tokens on that place are allowed to have. The set of possible token colors is specified by means of a type (as known from programming languages) which is called the color set of the place. By convention, the color set is written below the place. The place *structure1* has the color set P, while all the others have the color set U; the color set P is used to model the structure of a membrane

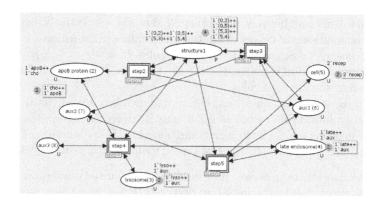

Fig. 3. LDL Degradation Pathway in CPN Tools

configuration (pairs of numbers of the form (i, j)), while the color set U is used to model the set of objects from a mobile membranes.

Color sets are defined using the CPN keyword *colset*:

colset $I = int$;
colset $P = product\ I * I$;
colset $U = with\ cho\ |\ apoB\ |\ lyso\ |\ late\ |\ aux\ |\ aux1\ |\ aux2\ |\ aux3\ |\ aux4\ |$
     $aux5\ |\ recep\ |\ recep1\ |\ recep2\ |\ recep3\ |\ recep4\ |\ recep5$;

The inscription on the upper side of a place specifies the *initial marking* of that place. The inscription of the place *late endosome*(4) is 1'*late* + +1'*aux* specifying that the initial marking of this place consists of two tokens with the values *late* and *aux*. The symbols ' and ++ are operators used to construct a multiset of tokens. The infix operator ' takes a positive integer as its left argument, specifying the number of appearances of the element provided as the right argument. The operator ++ takes two multisets as arguments and returns their union (the sum of their multiplicities). The absence of an inscription specifying the initial marking means that the place initially contains no tokens. The marking of each place is indicated next to the place. The number of tokens on the place is shown in a small circle, and the detailed token colors are indicated in a box positioned next to the small circle.

The four transitions drawn as rectangles represent the events that can take place in the system. The names of the transitions are written inside the rectangles; these names have no formal meaning, but they are important for the readability of the model. In Figure 3 the names of the transitions are *step*2, *step*3, *step*4, and *step*5 indicating that each of these transitions simulates the corresponding steps of the LDL degradation pathway described in Figure 1.

A transition with double-line border is a substitution transition; each of them has a *substitution tag* positioned next to it. The substitution tag contains the name of a submodule which is related to the substitution transition. Intuitively, this means that the submodule presents a more detailed view of the behavior represented by the substitution transition, and it is particularly useful when modeling large systems. The input places of substitution transitions are called *input sockets*, while the output places are called *output sockets*. The socket places of a substitution transition constitute the interface of the substitution transition. To obtain a complete hierarchical model, it must be specified how the interface of each submodule is related to the interface of its substitution transition. This is done by means of a port-socket relation which links the port places of the submodule to the socket places of the substitution transition. Input ports are related to input sockets, output ports to output sockets, and input/output ports to input/output sockets.

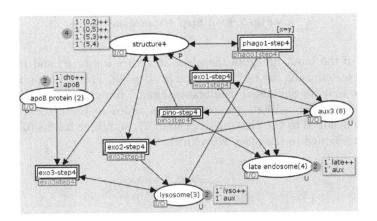

Fig. 4. Step 4 Transition

For instance, behind the substitution transition *step4* is another colored Petri net presented in Figure 4. The substitution transitions are:

- the substitution transition *phago1-step4* simulates the mobile membrane rule 5 from the description of the LDL degradation pathway;
- the substitution transition *exo1-step4* simulates the mobile membrane rule 6 from the description of the LDL degradation pathway;
- the substitution transition *pino-step4* simulates the mobile membrane rule 7 from the description of the LDL degradation pathway;
- the substitution transition *exo2-step4* simulates the mobile membrane rule 8 from the description of the LDL degradation pathway;
- the substitution transition *exo3-step4* simulates the mobile membrane rule 9 from the description of the LDL degradation pathway.

It can be observed that the marking of places appearing in Figure 4 are similar with the one of the corresponding places of Figure 3. The substitution transition *exo1-step4* is replaced by the Petri net presented in Figure 5.

In Figure 6, the enabled transition is *phagostep2* that has a mark in the right corner. It removes a token *apoB* from place *apoB protein*(2), a token *recep* from place *cell*(5), and two tokens $(0,2)$ and $(0,5)$ from place *structure*. The arc

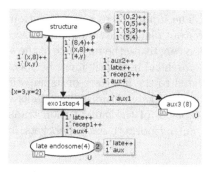

Fig. 5. Exo1 Step 4 Transition

expression of the input arc from the place *structure* are $(x, 2)$ and $(y, 5)$, and so they are tested using the test expression $[x=0, y=0]$. The test is performed in order to see that the simulated membranes 2 and 5 have the same parent 0.

After firing the transition, a token *recep* is added to the place $aux1(6)$, a token *apoB* is added to the place *apoB protein*(2), and three tokens $(0, 5)$, $(6, 2)$ and $(5, 6)$ are added to the place *structure*1.

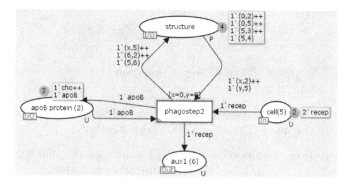

Fig. 6. Phago Step 2 Transition

A state space is a directed graph where there is a node for each reachable marking, and an arc for each occurring transition. The state space of a CPN model can be computed fully automatically, and this makes it possible to automatically analyze and verify several properties concerning the behavior of the model: the minimum and maximum numbers of tokens in a place, reachability, boundedness, etc. When working with Petri nets, some behavioral properties (e.g., reachability, boundedness) are easier to study once a state space is calculated; a good survey for known decidability issues for Petri nets is given in [7].

Similar properties can be defined for mobile membranes with objects on surface. Given a mobile membrane with object on surface Π with initial configuration M_0, a configuration M is *reachable* in Π if there exist the sets of transitions

$U_1, \ldots, U_n$ such that $M_0[U_1\rangle \ldots [U_n\rangle M_n = M$. A *home configuration* is a configuration which can be reached from any reachable configuration. A membrane system is *bounded* if the set of reachable configurations is finite. A membrane system has the *liveness* property if each rule can be applied again in another evolution step, and it is *fair* if no infinite execution sequence contains some configurations which occur only finitely. By considering a colored Petri net CPN_Π obtained from a mobile membrane Π, the following decidability result.

Proposition 1. *If the reachability problem is decidable for CPN_Π, then the reachability problem is also decidable for Π.*

Proof (Sketch). The initial marking of CPN_Π is the same as the initial configuration of Π according to the construction presented in Section 4, and each step of the Petri nets corresponds to an evolution of the mobile membranes with objects on surface (according to Theorem 1). Thus the reachability problem becomes decidable for mobile membranes with objects on surface as soon it is decidable for colored Petri nets.

In a similar way, several properties can be proven, for mobile membranes with objects on surface, as soon they hold for their corresponding colored Petri nets.

Proposition 2.

- *If CPN_Π is bounded, then Π is bounded.*
- *If CPN_Π has the liveness property, then Π has the liveness property.*
- *If CPN_Π is fair, then Π is fair.*

Since the properties of reachability, boundedness, liveness and fairness can be derived automatically by using CPN Tools, these results are of great help when studying similar properties for mobile membranes with objects on surface. For instance, using the CPN Tools and the model for the LDL degradation pathway, it can be checked whether the configuration, in which the membrane marked by *apoB* is inside the membrane marked by *lyso*, can be reached.

Using CPN Tools for the LDL degradation pathway model, the following output file is obtained:

Home Markings: [24]   Dead Markings: [24];
Dead Transition Instances: None   Live Transition Instances: None
Fairness Properties: No infinite occurrence sequences,

meaning that always the configuration M_{24} is reached (home marking), the computation stops here (dead marking), and that there are no infinite occurrence sequences.

The simulation of LDL degradation pathway is not entirely correct from a biological point of view, because a cell is able to process more than one LDL molecule. An arbitrary number of LDL molecules cannot be simulated by using mobile membranes, but it can be simulated in colored Petri nets by adding a new transition *input* and a new place *applied* as in Figure 7.

In Figure 8 the transition *input* is build, namely what are the input arcs and output arcs together with their inscriptions.

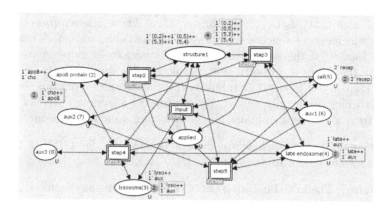

Fig. 7. LDL Degradation Pathway with input transition

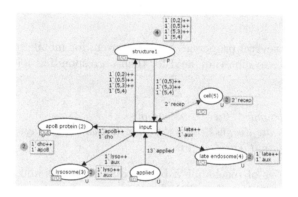

Fig. 8. Input transition

This transition works as follows: if the cell has the initial structure less the initial LDL molecule, then a new LDL molecule is added to the system in order to reiterate the entire process. Applying CPN Tools on this extended system, the following output file is obtained:

Home Markings: All   Dead Markings: None;
Dead Transition Instances: None   Live Transition Instances: All
Fairness Properties: All,

meaning that from any reachable configuration M_i always can reach any configuration M_j (home marking), the computation never stops (dead marking), and so there are infinite occurrence sequences.

7   Conclusion

In this paper we continue the research line started in [4], and present a new connection between the systems of mobile membranes and colored Petri nets.

The novelty of this formal translation, with respect to the one presented in [4], is that the number of membranes in the system could change during evolution. The systems of mobile membranes with objects on surface used in this translation are bounded to a given number of membranes.

The structure of the parallel computations of the mobile membranes is faithfully reflected by the parallel semantics of the corresponding colored Petri nets. In mobile membranes, the parallel way of using the rules means that in each step a maximal set of rules is applied, namely a set of rules such that no further rule can be added to this set. Since mobility is central, each object and each membrane can be used only once in the rules applied in a step.

We have considered the low-density lipoprotein degradation pathway, and described this biological process by using the mobile membranes with objects on membranes. The translation of mobile membranes into colored Petri nets allows to obtain a description of the biological process into colored Petri net, and then use a software called CPN Tools in analyzing several behavioral properties: reachability, boundedness, liveness, fairness. By encoding biological systems in this way, many interesting biological questions can get precise answers. Using CPN Tools, several (potentially infinite) behaviors can be investigated, a fact that is interesting from a biological point of view. Finally, a new link between biology, membrane systems and Petri nets is provided, which is, hopefully, useful for all these areas.

Acknowledgements. The work was supported by a grant of the Romanian National Authority for Scientific Research CNCS-UEFISCDI, project number PN-II-ID-PCE-2011-3-0919.

References

1. Aman, B., Ciobanu, G.: Mobility in Process Calculi and Natural Computing. Springer (2011)
2. Aman, B., Ciobanu, G.: Mutual Mobile Membranes with Objects on Surface. Natural Computing 10, 777–793 (2011)
3. Aman, B., Ciobanu, G.: Simple, Enhanced and Mutual Mobile Membranes. In: Priami, C., Back, R.-J., Petre, I. (eds.) Transa. on Comput. Syst. Biol. XI. LNCS (LNBI), vol. 5750, pp. 26–44. Springer, Heidelberg (2009)
4. Aman, B., Ciobanu, G.: Properties of Enhanced Mobile Membranes via Coloured Petri Nets. Information Processing Letters 112, 243–248 (2012)
5. Cavaliere, M., Sedwards, S.: Decision Problems in Membrane Systems with Peripheral Proteins, Transport and Evolution. Theoretical Computer Science 404, 40–51 (2008)
6. Dal Zilio, S., Formenti, E.: On the Dynamics of PB Systems: A Petri Net View. In: Martín-Vide, C., Mauri, G., Păun, G., Rozenberg, G., Salomaa, A. (eds.) WMC 2003. LNCS, vol. 2933, pp. 153–167. Springer, Heidelberg (2004)
7. Esparza, J., Nielsen, M.: Decibility Issues for Petri Nets - A Survey. Journal of Informatik Processing and Cybernetics 30, 143–160 (1994)
8. Janeway, C.A., Travers, P., Walport, M., Shlomchik, M.J.: Immunobiology - The Immune System in Health and Disease, 5th edn. Garland Publishing (2001)

9. Jensen, K.: Colored Petri Nets; Basic Concepts, Analysis Methods and Practical Use. Monographs in Theoretical Computer Science, vol. 1, 2 and 3. Springer (1992, 1994, 1997)
10. Kleijn, J., Koutny, M.: Petri Nets and Membrane Computing. In: Oxford Handbook of Membrane Computing, pp. 389–412 (2010)
11. Krishna, S.N.: Universality Results for P Systems Based on Brane Calculi Operations. Theoretical Computer Science 371, 83–105 (2007)
12. Levins, R.: The Strategy of Model Building in Population Biology. American Scientist 54, 421–431 (1966)
13. Lodish, H., Berk, A., Matsudaira, P., Kaiser, C., Krieger, M., Scott, M., Zipursky, L., Darnell, J.: Molecular Cell Biology, 5th edn. W.H. Freeman (2003)
14. Păun, G.: Membrane Computing. An Introduction. Springer (2002)
15. Pilegaard, H., Nielson, F., Nielson, H.R.: Static Analysis of a Model of the LDL Degradation Pathway. In: Proceedings Computational Methods in System Biology, pp. 14–26 (2005)
16. Qi, Z., You, J., Mao, H.: P Systems and Petri Nets. In: Martín-Vide, C., Mauri, G., Păun, G., Rozenberg, G., Salomaa, A. (eds.) WMC 2003. LNCS, vol. 2933, pp. 286–303. Springer, Heidelberg (2004)

On Structures and Behaviors of Spiking Neural P Systems and Petri Nets

Francis George C. Cabarle and Henry N. Adorna

Algorithms & Complexity Lab
Department of Computer Science
University of the Philippines Diliman
Diliman 1101 Quezon City, Philippines
fccabarle@up.edu.ph, hnadorna@dcs.upd.edu.ph

Abstract. In this work we investigate further the relationship between Petri nets and Spiking Neural P (SNP) systems: we consider SNP systems that have source (no incoming synapse) and sink (no outgoing synapse) neurons, and the initial configuration of the system is where only the source neuron has only one spike. We then route the initial single spike through the system to the sink neuron, using routing constructs. This type of SNP systems are similar to Petri nets, in particular to Workflow (WF) nets. We observe structural and behavioral properties of these nets for routing a single token can be simulated by SNP systems with source and sink neurons. Certain routing types such as AND-splits and OR-joins are 'natural' in SNP systems, but AND-joins and especially OR-splits seem to be more complex. Our results also suggest the possibility of analysing workflows using SNP systems.

Keywords: Membrane Computing, Spiking Neural P systems, routing, joins, splits, Petri nets, simulations, safe Petri nets, ordinary Petri nets, workflow nets.

1 Introduction

SNP systems, first introduced in 2006 in [8], are inspired by the way biological spiking neurons compute: neurons are abstracted by treating them as *mono-membranar* cells placed on nodes of a directed graph, where synapses or connections between neurons are the directed arcs. *Indistinct* signals in the neurons, called *action potential* or simply spike in biology, are modeled using only the symbol a. Information is encoded not in the symbol or spike itself but in the time interval when spikes are produced or in the spike multiplicity. Time is not just a resource in SNP systems but a way to represent information. Since the introduction of SNP systems they have been used mostly as computing devices with universality results in [8,3], as well as solving **NP**-complete problems as in [16].

Petri nets however, since their introduction in 1962, have enjoyed an extensive theory on Petri net behavior and structure. Petri nets are bipartite directed

E. Csuhaj-Varjú et al. (Eds.): CMC 2012, LNCS 7762, pp. 145–160, 2013.
© Springer-Verlag Berlin Heidelberg 2013

graphs that move tokens using two types of nodes: places and transitions. The theory of Petri nets includes numerous works on the use of Petri nets for modeling, analysis, and verification in business process modeling [20], in industrial control, distributed systems, concurrent processes et al.[1]

Since a possible connection between SNP systems and Petri nets was mentioned in [18], several works have been produced in transforming SNP systems to Petri nets (including extensions of both models).[2] The transformations in works such as [12][13][14] mostly deal with transforming an SNP system to certain Petri net classes in order to check for properties or to "simulate" operations of the SNP system. In [12] methods for transforming SNP systems to Petri nets (and limited types of Petri nets to SNP systems) were introduced. An intuitive simulation of SNP systems and Petri nets was presented, mostly focusing on the correspondence between places and neurons, rules and transitions. In [14], some notes on Petri net behavioral properties such as liveness and boundedness as applied to SNP systems are mentioned. A mapping of the configurations of SNP systems and Petri nets, by using synchronizing places, was also presented in [14]. This mapping is similar to the idea of simulation presented in [6] between the set of configurations of a *simulating* system and the set of configurations of a different, *simulated* system.

The main motivation for this work is the idea of eventually using SNP systems to model certain processes or phenomena. Works on using SNP systems for modeling exist as in [9] and [7], however few compared to the more common computability results in Membrane computing. Before we even begin to use SNP systems for modeling (hopefully in the near future), we start by investigating structural and behavioral properties of SNP systems that will prove useful for modeling processes. Another motivation is more biologically motivated: the human brain can be argued to be one (if not currently) the most complicated and powerful "supercomputer" currently known to us: it performs complex computations from interconnected neurons while consuming about 10 to 20 Watts only [11], and it fits in our skulls. It is therefore desirable to work with as little quantity of "energy" as possible, and we can think of the spike in SNP systems as being such quantity. From these motivations we consider SNP systems that have source (no incoming synapse) and sink (no outgoing synapse) neurons, and the initial configuration of the system is where only the source neuron has only one spike. We then route the initial single spike through the system to the sink neuron, using routing constructs. This type of SNP systems are similar to Petri nets, in particular to Workflow (WF) nets. We then provide structural and behavioral properties of these nets for routing a single token that can be simulated by SNP systems with source and sink neurons. Certain routing types are 'natural' in SNP systems, whereas others seem to be 'unnatural' and are more complex.

This work is organized as follows: Section 2 provides some preliminaries for this work, including definitions and properties of Petri nets, WF nets, and

---

[1] See [15] for a comprehensive list.

[2] Early works connecting membrane systems and Petri nets include [10] and [22]. We also refer to the handbook in [19].

SNP systems. Section 3 provides the main results of this work. Finally, we provide concluding remarks as well as directions for future work in Section 4.

2   Preliminaries

It is assumed that the readers are familiar with the basics of Membrane Computing [3] and formal language theory. We only briefly mention notions and notations which will be useful throughout this work. Let V be an alphabet, V^* is the free monoid over V with respect to concatenation and the identity element λ (the empty string). The set of all non-empty strings over V is denoted as V^+ so $V^+ = V^* - \{\lambda\}$. We call V a *singleton* if $V = \{a\}$ and simply write a^* and a^+ instead of $\{a^*\}$ and $\{a^+\}$. The length of a string $w \in V^*$ is denoted by $|w|$. If a is a symbol in V, $a^0 = \lambda$. A language $L \subseteq V^*$ is regular if there is a regular expression E over V such that $L(E) = L$. A regular expression over an alphabet V is constructed starting from λ and the symbols of V using the operations union, concatenation, and +, using parentheses when necessary to specify the order of operations. Specifically, (i) λ and each $a \in V$ are regular expressions, (ii) if E_1 and E_2 are regular expressions over V then $(E_1 \cup E_2)$, $E_1 E_2$, and E_1^+ are regular expressions over V, and (iii) nothing else is a regular expression over V. With each expression E we associate a language $L(E)$ defined in the following way: (i) $L(\lambda) = \{\lambda\}$ and $L(a) = \{a\}$ for all $a \in V$, (ii) $L(E_1 \cup E_2) = L(E_1) \cup L(E_2)$, $L(E_1 E_2) = L(E_1) L(E_2)$, and $L(E_1^+) = L(E_1)^+$, for all regular expressions E_1, E_2 over V. Unnecessary parentheses are omitted when writing regular expressions, and $E^+ \cup \{\lambda\}$ is written as E^*. Next, we define Petri nets and their mechanisms, slightly modified from [15] and [20].

Definition 1 (Petri nets). *A Petri net is a construct of the form*

$$\mathcal{N} = (P, T, A)$$

where

1. $P = \{p_1, p_2, \ldots, p_m\}$ is a finite set of places,
2. $T = \{t_1, t_2, \ldots, t_n\}$ is a finite set of transitions such that $P \cap T = \emptyset$,
3. $A \subseteq (P \times T) \cup (T \times P)$ is a set of arcs,

A Petri net with a given initial marking is denoted by $(\mathcal{N}, M_0)$. Markings denote the distribution of tokens among places in a Petri net. A marking of a place p is denoted as $M(p)$, and a marking of a place is always a non-negative integer. In this manner, the idea of a marking being defined over a place and as a vector containing every marking of every place in $\mathcal{N}$ are interchangeable, so that $M_0 = \langle M_0(p_1), M_0(p_2), \ldots, M_0(p_m) \rangle$. Places are represented as circles, transitions as rectangles, and tokens as black dots in places. Given two nodes p and t the weight of arc (p, t) is equal to 1. Petri nets where the arc weight is always 1

---

[3] A good introduction is [17], with a handbook in [19] and recent results and information in the P systems webpage at http://http://ppage.psystems.eu/

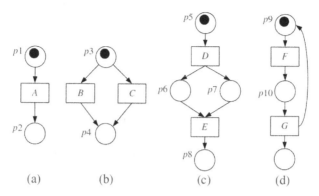

Fig. 1. Routing types: (a) sequential, (b) conditional, (c) parallel, (d) iteration

are known as *ordinary Petri nets.* [4] We use the notation $\bullet p$ to denote the set of input transitions of place p, and the notation $\bullet t$ as the set of input places of transition t. Similarly we use $p\bullet$ and $t\bullet$ to denote the sets of output transitions and places of p and t, respectively. Tokens are indistinct, and a place without an input transition is called a *source place* ($\bullet p = \emptyset$) while a place without an output transition is a *sink place* ($p\bullet = \emptyset$). We assume that there is no place p or transition t such that $\bullet p = p\bullet = \emptyset$ or $\bullet t = t\bullet = \emptyset$.

A transition t is *enabled* iff for every $p \in \bullet t$, p has *at least* one token. An enabled transition t is *fired* when t removes one token from every p, and deposits one token to every place $p' \in t\bullet$. When there exist $t, t' \in p\bullet$, i.e. $|p \bullet| \geq 1$ and $t \neq t'$, then p has to *nondeterministically* choose which among t and t' will be enabled. If $p', p'' \in t\bullet$, then if t fires, t deposits one token each to p' and p''. *Parallelism* in Petri nets comes from the fact that both p' and p'' receive tokens at the same time after t is fired. A marking M_n is *reachable* from a marking M if there is a sequence of enabled transitions $\langle t_1 t_2 \dots t_n \rangle$ that leads from M to M_n. The set of all reachable markings from M_0 given a net $\mathcal{N}$ is denoted as $R(\mathcal{N}, M_0)$ or simply $R(M_0)$ assuming there is no confusion on the referred net. Now we provide some properties of Petri nets.

Definition 2 (Liveness, Boundedness, Safeness (Petri nets) [15,21]). *A Petri net $(\mathcal{N}, M_0)$ is **live** iff for every $M' \in R(M_0)$ and every $t \in T$, there exists a marking M'' reachable from M' which enables t. $(\mathcal{N}, M_0)$ is **bounded** iff for each $p \in P$ there exists a positive integer k, such that for each $M \in R(M_0)$, $M(p) \leq k$ (the net is k-bounded). The net is **safe** iff for each reachable marking $M(p)$ does not exceed 1.*

Definition 2 provides some behavioral properties of Petri nets. A condition known as a *deadlock* occurs when a transition t is unable to fire given a certain marking. If $\mathcal{N}$ is a live net then it is considered deadlock-free.

---

[4] Ordinary and nonordinary Petri nets (i.e. arc weights greater than or equal to 1) have the same modeling power [15].

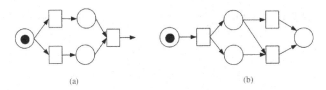

Fig. 2. (a) A net that is not well-handled. (b) A non-free-choice net.

From [21] we can identify four types of routing: sequential, parallel, conditional, and iteration (See Fig. 1). In order to perform these routing types, building blocks in Petri net semantics are used. These building blocks are (again referring to Fig. 1): *AND-split* is the sending of a token by transition D (from $p5$) to two or more output places of t in parallel, in this case $p6$ and $p7$. An *AND-join* is the removal, in parallel, of a token from every input place of E (in this case $p6$ and $p7$) in order to fire E. An *OR-split* is a nondeterministic routing of a token in $p3$ to only one among many output transitions of $p3$ (in this case firing either B or C). An *OR-join* is the sending of a token from B (or C) to $p4$, among several input transitions of $p4$.

From [20] we have the following: For Petri net $\mathcal{N}$, a *path* H from node x_0 to node x_k is a sequence $\langle x_0, x_1, \ldots, x_{k-1}, x_k \rangle$ where $(x_i, x_{i+1}) \in A$, for $1 \leq i \leq k-1$. The *alphabet* of H denoted as $alph(H) = \{x_0, x_1, ..., x_{k-1}, x_k\}$. H is *elementary* if for any nodes x_i and x_k in H, $i \neq k$ implies $x_i \neq x_k$. An elementary path H implies that H must have unique nodes. A net is *strongly connected* iff for every pair of nodes x and y, a path exists from x to y. Using paths and alphabets, we have the following definitions.

Definition 3 (Well-handled, Free-Choice (Petri nets) [20]). *A Petri net $\mathcal{N}$ is* **well-handled** *iff for any pair of nodes x and y such that one of the nodes is a place and the other a transition, and for any pair of elementary paths H_1 and H_2 leading from x to y, $alph(H_1) \cap alph(H_2) = \{x, y\}$ implies $H_1 = H_2$. $\mathcal{N}$ is* **free-choice** *iff for every two transitions t_1 and t_2, $\bullet t_1 \cap \bullet t_2 \neq \emptyset$ implies $\bullet t_1 = \bullet t_2$.*

Definition 3 provides structural properties of Petri nets. The well-handled property makes sure that a token that is split using parallel routing (AND-split) is *synchronized* or *terminated* with an AND-join. The property also assures that a conditionally routed token (OR-split) is synchronized with an OR-join. If an OR-split is synchronized by an AND-join, it is possible to have a *deadlock*. The free-choice property also avoids the possibility of deadlocks (see Fig. 2) and has been studied extensively in literature.[5] A class of Petri nets known as *workflow nets* or WF-nets were introduced in [20] and were used to model workflows. A WF-net is Petri net that has two special places, a source place i ($\bullet i = \emptyset$) and a sink place o ($o\bullet = \emptyset$), and adding a transition t^* from o to i makes the net strongly connected. Next we provide the definition of an SNP system, slightly modified from [18].

---

[5] See for example [5] and [21,20] to name a few. These nets are also known as *extended free-choice* nets in [15] and [4].

Definition 4 (SNP system). *An SNP system without delay of a finite degree* $m \geq 1$, *is a construct of the form*

$$\Pi = (O, \sigma_1, \ldots, \sigma_m, syn, out),$$

where:

1. $O = \{a\}$ is the singleton alphabet (a is called *spike*).
2. $\sigma_1, \ldots, \sigma_m$ are neurons of the form $\sigma_i = (\alpha_i, R_i), 1 \leq i \leq m$, where:

   (a) $\alpha_i \geq 0$ is the number of spikes in σ_i
   (b) R_i is a finite set of rules of the general form

$$E/a^c \rightarrow a^b$$

   where E is a regular expression over O, $c \geq 1$, $b \geq 0$, with $c \geq b$.

3. $syn \subseteq \{1, 2, \ldots, m\} \times \{1, 2, \ldots, m\}$, $(i, i) \notin syn$ for $1 \leq i \leq m$, are synapses between neurons.
4. $out \in \{1, 2, \ldots, m\}$ is the index of the *output* neuron.

A *spiking rule* is a rule $E/a^c \rightarrow a^b$ where $b \geq 1$. A *forgetting rule* is a rule where $b = 0$ is written as $E/a^c \rightarrow \lambda$. If $L(E) = \{a^c\}$ then spiking and forgetting rules are simply written as $a^c \rightarrow a^b$ and $a^c \rightarrow \lambda$, respectively. Applications of rules are as follows: if neuron σ_i contains k spikes, $a^k \in L(E)$ and $k \geq c$, then the rule $E/a^c \rightarrow a^b \in R_i$ is enabled and the rule can be fired or applied. If $b \geq 1$, the application of this rule removes c spikes from σ_i, so that only $k - c$ spikes remain in σ_i. The neuron fires b number of spikes to every σ_j such that $(i, j) \in syn$. If $b = 0$ then no spikes are produced. SNP systems assume a global clock, so the application of rules and the sending of spikes by neurons are all synchronized. The *nondeterminism* in SNP systems occurs when, given two rules $E_1/a^{c_1} \rightarrow a^{b_1}$ and $E_2/a^{c_2} \rightarrow a^{b_2}$, it is possible to have $L(E_1) \cap L(E_2) \neq \emptyset$. In this situation, only one rule will be nondeterministically chosen and applied. The *parallelism* is global for SNP systems, since neurons operate in parallel.

   Given a neuron ordering of $1, \ldots, m$ we can define an initial *system config-uration* as a vector $C_0 = \langle \alpha_{10}, \alpha_{20}, \ldots, \alpha_{m0} \rangle$. A *computation* is a sequence of transitions from an initial configuration. A computation may halt (no more rules can be applied for a given configuration) or not. One way to obtain a result is to take the time difference between the first spike of the output neuron to the environment and the output neuron's second spike e.g. if σ_{out} first spikes at time t and spikes for the second time at time $t + k$ then we say the number $(t + k) - t = k$ is "computed" by the system.[6]

---

[6] Another way to obtain results is to take the time difference between t and every other successive spiking time of σ_{out}.

3   Main Results

We first provide our results in order to simulate routing in Petri nets using SNP systems. The simulation as mentioned earlier is a relation between a set of configurations of a simulated system and a set of configurations of a simulating system as in [6]. The simulated and simulating systems in this work can either be Petri nets or SNP systems i.e. our results allow the simulation of routing (either tokens or spikes) between Petri nets and SNP systems. In constrast to [12], our results include Petri nets with transitions having more than one incoming arc, and without using synchronizing places as was done in [14]. On one hand, simulations of SNP systems to Petri nets seem to be relatively straightforward (e.g. initially in [12] and [13] with some modifications in [14]). On the other hand, simulations of even ordinary Petri nets to SNP systems seem to be straightforward, although we show in this section it is not quite so (at least for certain routing types).

   In this work we focus on ordinary Petri nets (as defined in Definition 1) for the following reasons: (*i*) numerous analysis tools and techniques have been developed for ordinary Petri nets since Petri nets were introduced, including linear algebraic methods, structural and behavioral properties, etc. (*ii*) ordinary Petri nets have been used extensively in literature to model processes and phenomena, (*iii*) ordinary Petri nets are sufficient in order to model (among others) workflows as in [21], [20], [4] for example. For our following results we refer to ordinary Petri nets unless otherwise stated. We introduce similar routing blocks to SNP systems as was done with Petri nets: parallel (AND-joins and splits) and conditional (OR-joins and splits). Sequential and iteration routing also follow. The functioning of the blocks should be the same for Petri nets and SNP systems i.e. if an AND-join Petri net combines tokens from one or more input places in parallel, then an AND-join SNP system should combine spikes from two or more input neurons, and so on. We first perform (easy) sequential routing.

Lemma 1. *Given a Petri net $\mathcal{N}$ that performs sequential routing of a token, there exists an SNP system $\Pi_{\mathcal{N}}$ simulating $\mathcal{N}$ that performs sequential routing of a spike. Conversely, given an SNP system Π with rules of the form $a^c \to a^b$, $b \in \{0,1\}$, that performs sequential routing of a spike, there exists a Petri net $\mathcal{N}_{\Pi}$ simulating Π that performs sequential routing of a token.*

Proof. (An illustration of the proof can be seen in Fig. 3.) Given a Petri net $\mathcal{N}$ with places p, q and a transition t, we have $p \in \bullet t$ and $t \in \bullet q$. Given a marking $M(p)$ over p, $\mathcal{N}$ can be simulated by an SNP system $\Pi_{\mathcal{N}}$ having neurons σ_x, σ_y where $R_x = \{a^+/a \to a\}$, $\alpha_x = M(p)$, and $(x, y) \in syn$ such that t is fired iff σ_x applies rule $a^+/a \to a$. $M(p)$ serves as the number of spikes in σ_x. Rule R_x in σ_x is $a^+/a \to a$ i.e. R_x consumes one spike whenever $\alpha_x \geq 1$, and produces one spike.[7] Transition t is fired if there is at least one token in p. The firing of transition t sends one token to output place q. Similarly, rule R_x is applied if

---

[7] *Variable overloading* is performed because of the use of R_x to mean the set of rules in σ_x and to mean the *only* rule in σ_x.

Fig. 3. The "basic" transformation idea from a Petri net N performing sequential routing and the SNP system Π_N simulating N

neuron σ_t has at least one spike. The neuron sends a spike to its output neuron σ_y after R_x is applied. For N, if $M_0 = (1,0)$ (i.e. only p has a token) and the final configuration is $(0,1)$, Π_N similarly has $C_0 = \langle 1,0 \rangle$ (only σ_x has a spike) and a final configuration of $\langle 0,1 \rangle$ (only σ_y has a spike).

The reverse can be shown in a similar manner: a forgetting rule is a transition with an outgoing arc weight of zero so no token is ever produced, and the environment is a sink place. Every spiking rule of Π has a regular expression E of the restricted form a^c. E is an additional condition before the corresponding transition t in N_Π is fired: if place $p \in \bullet t$, then t is enabled iff $a^{M(p)} \in L(E)$ i.e. when rule R_x is applied then transition t is also fired.   □

Lemma 2. *Given Petri net N that performs AND-split (AND-join) routing of a token, there exists an SNP system Π_N simulating N that performs AND-split (AND-join) routing of a spike.*

Proof. (An illustration of the proof can be seen in Fig. 4.) The proof follows from Lemma 1 and the following constructions: Given an AND-split Petri net N with places i, j, k, transition t, such that $i \in \bullet t$ and $j, k \in t\bullet$, the AND-split SNP system Π_N that simulates N has neurons $\sigma_x, \sigma_y, \sigma_z$ where $R_x = \{a^+/a \rightarrow a\}$, with $(x,y),(x,z) \in syn$. For N we have $M_0 = (1,0,0)$ i.e. only i has a token, with a final marking of $(0,1,1)$ after the firing of t. N performs an AND-split, sending one token each to j and k. For Π_N we have $C_0 = \langle 1,0,0 \rangle$ and the firing of σ_x sends one spike each to σ_y and σ_z. The final configuration is $\langle 0,1,1 \rangle$, thus Π_N performs an AND-split.

If N is an AND-join net such that $i, j \in \bullet t$ and $k \in t\bullet$, then Π_N has neurons $\sigma_x, \sigma_y, \sigma_w, \sigma_z$ with synapses $(x,w),(y,w),(w,z)$ and $R_w = \{(a^+)^v/a^v \rightarrow a\}$ for $v = |\bullet t|$ (in Fig. 4(a), $v = 2$). Given $M_0 = (1,1,0)$ for N i.e. only k has no token, the final marking after the firing of t will be $(0,0,1)$ since N is an AND-join net, combining the tokens from i and j and producing one token to k. Similarly for Π_N there is $C_0 = \langle 1,1,0,0 \rangle$ and the final configuration is $\langle 0,0,0,1 \rangle$. Rule R_w combines the spikes from σ_x and σ_y and produces one spike to σ_z. However, if M_0 is either $(0,1,0)$ or $(1,0,0)$ then t cannot fire. Similarly, σ_w will not spike given that C_0 is either $\langle 0,1,0,0 \rangle$ or $\langle 1,0,0,0 \rangle$ Therefore Π_N also performs an AND-join.   □

Observation 1. *If N is a nonsafe Petri net that performs an AND-join, using the construction for Lemma 2, SNP system Π_N does not perform an AND-join.*

An example of Observation 1 is shown in Fig. 5: the SNP system does not perform an AND-join since the joining neuron σ_t still spikes after accumulating two spikes from its top input neuron σ_j (and from the other spike from σ_i). In the Petri net however, transition t is never fired (a deadlock) since k is never marked, and j is a nonsafe place.

Lemma 3. *Given a Petri net $\mathcal{N}$ that performs an OR-split (OR-join) of a token, there exists an SNP system $\Pi_{\mathcal{N}}$ that performs an OR-split (OR-join) of a spike simulating $\mathcal{N}$.*

Proof. (An illustration of the proof can be seen in Fig. 6 for OR-join and Fig. 7 for OR-split) The proof follows from Lemma 1 and the following construction: Given a Petri net $\mathcal{N}$ that performs an OR-split with places $p1$, $p2$, $p3$, transitions A, B, where $A, B \in p1\bullet$, $A \in p2\bullet$, $B \in p3\bullet$, the OR-split SNP system $\Pi_{\mathcal{N}}$ simulating $\mathcal{N}$ has neurons σ_1, σ_2, σ_3, σ_4, σ_5, σ_6, σ_7, σ_8 with $(1,2), (1,3), (2,4), (3,4), (4,5), (4,6), (5,7), (6,8)$ as synapses, $R_4 = \{r_1, \ldots, r_k\}$ for $k = |p1\bullet|$, σ_1 has k output neurons (σ_2 and σ_3 in Fig. 7, all of which have exactly one rule each and one synapse each to σ_4) and each rule in R_4 is of the form $a^k \to a^j$, $1 \le j \le k$. For some ordering $\mathcal{O} = \langle \sigma_1, \ldots, \sigma_k \rangle$ of every neuron σ_u, $1 \le u \le k$, so that $(4, u) \in syn$ (σ_4 also has k output neurons), r_{uj} is the jth rule of R_u in σ_u, such that r_{uj} is of the form:

$$a^j \to \begin{cases} a, \text{ if } j = u \\ \lambda, \text{ if } j \neq u \end{cases}$$

If only $p1$ has a token, due to nondeterminism a final marking could either be $(0,1,0)$ (only $p2$ has a token) or $(0,0,1)$ (only $p3$ has a token). For $\Pi_{\mathcal{N}}$ we have $C_0 = \langle 1,0,0,0,0,0,0,0 \rangle$ i.e. only σ_1 has a spike initially. An AND-split is first performed by σ_1 which sends one spike each to σ_2 and σ_3, giving $C_1 = \langle 0,1,1,0,0,0,0,0 \rangle$. Both σ_2 and σ_3 fire one spike each to σ_4 (the purpose of the previous step was to create 2 spikes for this step) so σ_4 accumulates 2 spikes giving $C_2 = \langle 0,0,2,0,0,0,0,0 \rangle$. Due to the construction of $\Pi_{\mathcal{N}}$ (and the rules in $\sigma_4, \sigma_5, \sigma_6$) and due to nondeterminism, the final configuration could either be $\langle 0,0,0,0,0,0,1,0 \rangle$ (only σ_5 fires and σ_6 forgets its single spike using its forgetting rule) or $\langle 0,0,0,0,0,0,0,1 \rangle$ (only σ_6 fires and σ_5 forgets its two spikes using its forgetting rule). Therefore $\mathcal{N}$ and $\Pi_{\mathcal{N}}$ both perform an OR-split.

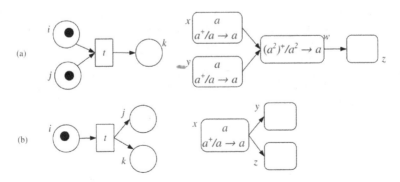

Fig. 4. SNP system (a) AND-join, and (b) AND-split

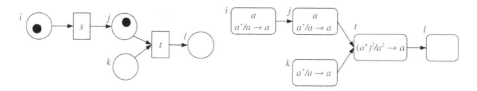

Fig. 5. A nonsafe AND-join Petri net and the "bad" AND-join SNP system from the net, based on Lemma 2

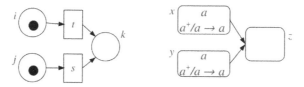

Fig. 6. OR-join Petri net and OR-join SNP system that simulates the net

If N performs an OR-join having places i, j, k, transitions s, t, such that $i \in \bullet t, j \in \bullet s$, and $t, s \in \bullet k$, the OR-join SNP system Π_N that simulates N has neurons $\sigma_x, \sigma_y, \sigma_z$ with synapses $(x, z), (y, z)$. An initial marking of $M_0 = (1, 1, 0)$ for N results in a final marking of $(0, 0, 2)$ after t and s fire. For Π_N we have $C_0 = \langle 1, 1, 0 \rangle$ and a final configuration of $\langle 0, 0, 2 \rangle$ after σ_x and σ_y fire and each send one spike to σ_z. An OR-join is therefore performed by N and Π_N. □

Lemma 2 assumes a safe Petri net so that no place is marked by more than one token. Note that SNP systems by nature split spikes in an AND-split manner. The idea behind Lemma 3 is for Π_N to "multiply" the single starting spike at its source neuron to k spikes, where k is from the k-way OR-split N. The nondeterministic enabling of the k output transitions (in Fig. 7, $k = 2$) of the source place $p1$ is "simulated" when σ_4 has accumulated k spikes and nondeterministically chooses among its k rules. Once σ_4 selects a rule, either σ_5 sends a spike to σ_7 (if σ_4 chose the rule $a^2 \rightarrow a$) or σ_6 sends a spike to σ_8 (if σ_4 chose the rule $a^2 \rightarrow a^2$).

Note that the resulting OR-split SNP system Π_N can be returned to the original OR-split Petri net N, using two reduction techniques (see e.g. in [4]

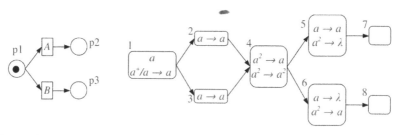

Fig. 7. A 2-way OR-split Petri net N and the 2-way OR-split SNP system Π_N

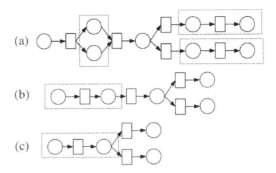

Fig. 8. (a) The direct transformation of Π_N in Fig. 7 back to a Petri net using Lemma 1, (b) Net after parallel and sequential places in (a) were fused, (c) Net after sequential places in (b) are fused. Note that after (c), we obtain the original N in Fig. 7.

and [15], and Fig. 8 for an illustration): (i) The fusion of parallel places, (ii) the reduction of sequential places. Also note that joins in SNP systems are by nature OR-joins. The following observation follows from Lemma 3.

Observation 2. *Given a k-way OR-split net where the deciding (origin) place is p (i.e. $|p \bullet| = k$), then the simulating OR-split SNP system has additional $2k + 1$ neurons.*

Observation 2 is evident from Fig. 7. From the previous definitions and lemmas we have the following theorems.

Theorem 1. *Given a Petri net N that performs one or a combination of the following routing types: sequential, parallel, conditional, and iterative, then there exists an SNP system Π_N that can simulate N.*

Proof. (An illustration of the proof can be seen in Fig. 9) Proof for sequential routing follows from Lemma 1, from Lemma 3 for conditional, and Lemma 2 for parallel routing. For iterative routing, we simply have a sequential routing as in Fig. 9(a) where one or more neurons have synapses going back to previous neurons (Fig. 9(d)). □

Notice that in the SNP system routings of Fig. 9, only conditional routing involves nondeterminism, while the rest are all deterministic systems. Since AND-joins and OR-splits in particular can be quite complex to visualize for SNP systems, we introduce "shorthand" illustrations seen in Fig. 10. An AND-split neuron simply has a thicker border or membrane, meaning it will only spike once enough spikes are sent to the neuron. An OR-split neuron simply has thicker synapses or arcs, indicating that only one of the output neurons will get to fire a spike. Before moving on, we provide definitions of free-choice and well-handled SNP systems as follows.

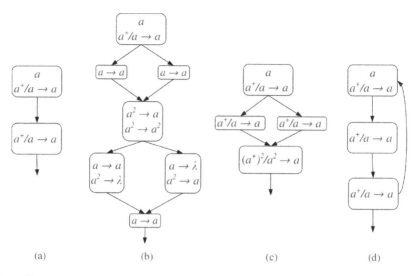

Fig. 9. Routing types using SNP systems: (a) sequential, (b) conditional, (c) parallel, (d) iteration

Definition 5 (Well-handled, free-choice (SNP system)). *Given an SNP system Π, Π is **well-handled** if a spike that is split with an AND-split (OR-split) is synchronized or terminated with an AND-join (OR-join). Π is **free-choice** if given neurons σ_x, σ_y and σ_w in Π and $(w, x), (w, y) \in syn$, then for every neuron σ_z such that $(z, x) \in syn$, we have $(z, y) \in syn$ also. Since a synapse $(i, i) \notin syn$, we include this implicitly in the definition of free-choice property of Π.*

The definition of the well-handled and free-choice properties in Definition 5 follow the idea of the same properties for Petri nets (Definition 3). The proofs for Theorems 2 and 3 below follow from Theorem 1, Lemma 2, and Lemma 3, and can be easily visualized using the shortand illustrations in Fig. 10.

Theorem 2. *If a Petri net N is free-choice (nonfree-choice, respectively) then there exists a free-choice (nonfree-choice, respectively) SNP system Π_N that simulates N.*   □

Theorem 3. *If a Petri net N is well-handled (not well-handled, respectively) then there exists a well-handled (not well-handled, respectively) SNP system Π_N that simulates N.*   □

Observation 3. *Transforming an SNP system Π using the construction for Lemma 1 not necessarily produce an ordinary Petri net N.*

A neuron in Π with a rule $a^2 \to a$ requires and consumes 2 spikes, which in N means an arc for such a rule must have a weight equal to 2. After the structural properties in Definition 5 we present next some behavioral properties of SNP systems from Petri nets.

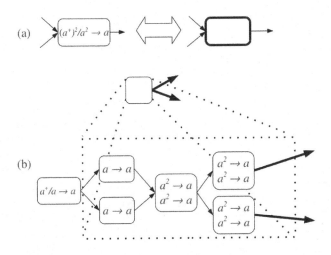

Fig. 10. Shorthand illustrations for an AND-join (a) and an OR-split (b) neuron

Definition 6 (Live, Bounded, Safe (SNP system)). *An SNP system Π is **live** iff for every reachable configuration C_k from C_0 and every rule r in Π there exists a configuration C_j reachable from C_k wherein rule r is applied. Π is **k-bounded** iff for every configuration each neuron has at most k spikes, where k is a positive integer. If $n = 1$ then we say Π is **safe**.*

In [14], properties such as liveness, boundedness, deadlock-free, and terminating properties were introduced. A similar presentation with [14] is an earlier work on P systems and Petri nets in [22]. In our work the definition for liveness and boundedness are similar to those in [14], although our liveness definition is identified by rule application and not by configurations. From the previous results and the properties in Definition 6, we have the following observation.

Observation 4. *If a safe Petri net $\mathcal{N}$ is simulated by an SNP system $\Pi_{\mathcal{N}}$, the bound k for $\Pi_{\mathcal{N}}$ is given by the AND-join transition t in $\mathcal{N}$ such that $k = |\bullet t|$ is maximum in $\mathcal{N}$.*

As seen in Fig. 12 and using the shorthand illustrations from Fig. 10, $\Pi_{\mathcal{N}}$ is 2-bounded, even though $\mathcal{N}$ is a safe net, since transitions $|\bullet t3| = |\bullet t4| = 2$ (the cardinality of sets $\bullet t3$ and $\bullet t4$ are maximum in $\mathcal{N}$).

4 Final Remarks

In this work we have added additional relationships between certain classes of Petri nets (e.g. safe nets, ordinary nets, WF nets) to SNP systems having one initial spike only in the source neuron, which is eventually routed to a sink neuron. In particular we focused on some structural properties of Petri nets that are fundamental to routing tokens: the AND- and OR-splits and joins. As it

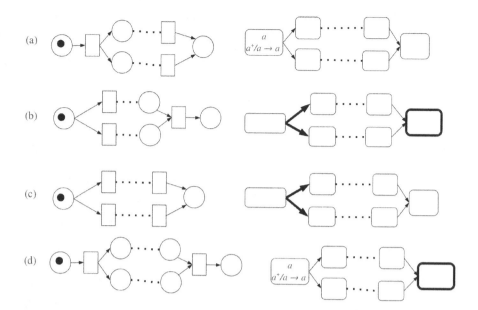

Fig. 11. Not well-handled (a) and (b), and well-handled (c) and (d) Petri nets and SNP systems

turns out, even the relatively simple mechanism of conditional routing in Petri nets, the OR-split, can be quite complex in terms of SNP systems (an additional $2k+1$ neurons to route a spike among k output neurons). It seems that, at least for "standard" SNP systems (as defined in this work) without delays, the routing of spikes to specific or targeted neurons is quite "unnatural" (again recall that splits in SNP systems are by nature AND-splits). Perhaps a similarly complex structure is required in order to peform AND-joins for nonsafe and nonordinary (i.e. generalized) Petri nets.

If SNP systems are to be used for modeling processes, then results on structural and behavioral properties are certainly desirable. Since Petri nets enjoy a rich theory on both kinds of properties, it seems reasonable to further link Petri

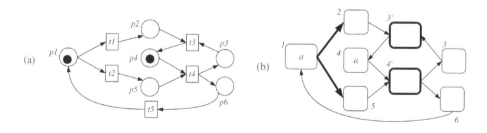

Fig. 12. (a) A safe, nonlive Petri net $\mathcal{N}$ (from [15]), (b) A nonlive, $k = 2$ bounded (nonsafe) SNP system $\Pi_{\mathcal{N}}$

nets (among other formal models) to SNP systems, as several previous works have already done. For our part, this present work can be seen as a precursor to using SNP systems to be used in modeling processes. [8] Some of these processes or phenomena might include multi or distributed processors and workflow processes just to name a few.

Additionally, other classes of Petri nets such as colored and stochastic nets (see for example [15]) just to name a few, could be simulated by SNP systems. Other variants of SNP systems such as those with neuron budding and division as in [16] can also be transformed and simulated by Petri nets. Such investigations will most likely yield interesting and useful theoretical and perhaps even applicative results for both models. Some questions that can arise from this work include: How hard is it to detect structural and behavioral properties in SNP systems? How about joins and splits in other variants? Other structures and behaviors useful to modeling?

Petri nets and their behaviors have been represented as matrix equations, and using these equations several tools have been produced for Petri nets (see [15] and [21]). Similarly, the behavior of SNP systems have been represented as matrices in [23] which was used in the creation of a graphics processing unit based SNP system simulator in [1] and [2]. One desirable feature of the various Petri net tools is their utility for analyses and modeling of processes. Lastly, we may yet somehow contribute to an energy efficient, human brain-like (at least in theory) computer.

Acknowledgments. F.G.C. Cabarle is supported by the DOST-ERDT program. H.N. Adorna is funded by a DOST-ERDT research grant and the Alexan professorial chair of the UP Diliman Department of Computer Science. Both authors also appreciate the support of UP ITDC.

References

1. Cabarle, F.G.C., Adorna, H., Martínez-del-Amor, M.A.: A Spiking Neural P System Simulator Based on CUDA. In: Gheorghe, M., Păun, G., Rozenberg, G., Salomaa, A., Verlan, S. (eds.) CMC 2011. LNCS, vol. 7184, pp. 87–103. Springer, Heidelberg (2012)
2. Cabarle, F.G.C., Adorna, H., Martínez-del-Amor, M.A., Pérez-Jiménez, M.J.: Improving GPU Simulations of Spiking Neural P Systems. Romanian Journal of Information Science and Technology 15(1), 5–20 (2012)
3. Chen, H., Ionescu, M., Ishdorj, T.-O., Păun, A., Păun, G., Pérez-Jiménez, M.J.: Spiking neural P systems with extended rules: universality and languages. Natural Computing 7(2), 147–166 (2008)
4. David, R., Alla, H.: Petri nets and Grafcet: Tools for Modelling Discrete Event Systems. Prentice-Hall, NJ (1992)
5. Desel, J., Esparza, J.: Free Choice Petri nets. Cambridge tracts in theoretical computer science, vol. 40. Cambridge University Press (1995)

---

[8] Even biological processes perhaps, after further theoretical developments are pursued, as mentioned by Păun at the beginning of [17].

6. Frisco, P.: P Systems, Petri Nets, and Program Machines. In: Freund, R., Păun, G., Rozenberg, G., Salomaa, A. (eds.) WMC 2005. LNCS, vol. 3850, pp. 209–223. Springer, Heidelberg (2006)

7. Gutiérrez-Naranjo, M.A., Pérez-Jiménez, M.J.: Hebbian Learning from Spiking Neural P Systems View. In: Corne, D.W., Frisco, P., Păun, G., Rozenberg, G., Salomaa, A. (eds.) WMC 2008. LNCS, vol. 5391, pp. 217–230. Springer, Heidelberg (2009)

8. Ionescu, M., Păun, G., Yokomori, T.: Spiking Neural P Systems. Fundamenta Informaticae 71(2,3), 279–308 (2006)

9. Ionescu, M., Tîrnăcă, C.I., Tîrnăcă, C.: Dreams and spiking neural P systems. Romanian Journal of Information Science and Technology 12(2), 209–217 (2009)

10. Kleijn, J.H.C.M., Koutny, M., Rozenberg, G.: Towards a Petri Net Semantics for Membrane Systems. In: Freund, R., Păun, G., Rozenberg, G., Salomaa, A. (eds.) WMC 2005. LNCS, vol. 3850, pp. 292–309. Springer, Heidelberg (2006)

11. Maass, W.: Computing with spikes. Special Issue on Foundations of Information Processing of TELEMATIK 8(1), 32–36 (2002)

12. Metta, V.P., Krithivasan, K., Garg, G.: Spiking Neural P systems and Petri nets. In: Proc. of the Int'l Workshop on Machine Intelligence Research (2009), http://www.mirlabs.org/nagpur/paper02.pdf

13. Metta, V.P., Krithivasan, K., Garg, G.: Modeling spiking neural P systems using timed Petri nets. In: NaBIC IEEE Conference, pp. 25–30 (2009)

14. Metta, V.P., Krithivasan, K., Garg, G.: Simulation of Spiking Neural P Systems Using Pnet Lab. In: Proc. of the 12th CMC, Paris, France (August 2011), http://cmc12.lacl.fr/cmc12proceedings.pdf

15. Murata, T.: Petri Nets: Properties, analysis and application. Proc. of the IEEE 77(4), 541–580 (1989)

16. Pan, L., Păun, G., Pérez-Jiménez, M.J.: Spiking neural P systems with neuron division and budding. Proc. of the 7th Brainstorming Week on Membrane Computing, RGNC, Sevilla, Spain, 151-168 (2009)

17. Păun, G.: Membrane Computing: An Introduction. Springer (2002)

18. Păun, G., Pérez-Jiménez, M.J.: Spiking Neural P Systems. Recent Results, Research Topics. In: Condon, A., et al. (eds.) Algorithmic Bioprocesses. Springer (2009)

19. Păun, G., Rozenberg, G., Salomaa, A. (eds.): The Oxford Handbook of Membrane Computing. Oxford University Press (2010)

20. van der Aalst, W.M.P.: Structural Characterizations of Sound Workflow Nets. Computing Science Reports 96/23, Eindhoven University of Technology (1996)

21. van der Aalst, W.M.P.: The Application of Petri Nets to Workflow Management. Journal of Circuits, Systems and Computers 8(1), 21–66 (1998)

22. Qi, Z., You, J.-y., Mao, H.: P Systems and Petri Nets. In: Martín-Vide, C., Mauri, G., Păun, G., Rozenberg, G., Salomaa, A. (eds.) WMC 2003. LNCS, vol. 2933, pp. 286–303. Springer, Heidelberg (2004)

23. Zeng, X., Adorna, H., Martínez-del-Amor, M.Á., Pan, L., Pérez-Jiménez, M.J.: Matrix Representation of Spiking Neural P Systems. In: Gheorghe, M., Hinze, T., Păun, G., Rozenberg, G., Salomaa, A. (eds.) CMC 2010. LNCS, vol. 6501, pp. 377–391. Springer, Heidelberg (2010)

2D P Colonies

Luděk Cienciala, Lucie Ciencialová, and Michal Perdek

Institute of Computer Science
and
Research Institute of the IT4Innovations Centre of Excellence,
Silesian University in Opava, Czech Republic
{ludek.cienciala,lucie.ciencialova,michal.perdek}@fpf.slu.cz

Abstract. We continue the investigation of P colonies introduced in [4], a class of abstract computing devices composed of independent agents, acting and evolving in a shared environment. We are introducing 2D P colonies with a 2D environment where the agents are located. Agents have limited information about the contents of the environment where they can move in four directions. To present computations of 2D P colonies we construct a simulation environment.

1 Introduction

P colonies were introduced in the paper [4] as formal models of computing devices inspired by membrane systems and formal grammars called colonies. This model is inspired by the structure and the behaviour of communities of living organisms in a shared environment. The independent organisms living in a P colony are called agents. Each agent is represented by a pair of objects embedded in a membrane. The number of objects inside each agent is the same and constant during computation. For agents the environment is their communication channel and storage place for objects. At any moment all agents "know" about all the objects in the environment and they can access any object immediately. More reading about P colonies the reader can find in [3,1]. P colonies are one of types of P systems. They were introduced in 2000 in [5] by Gheorghe Păun as a formal model inspired by the structure and the behaviour of cells.

With each agent a set of programs is associated. The program, which determines the activity of an agent, is very simple and depends on the contents of agents and on a multiset of objects placed in the environment. An agent can change the contents of the environment through programs and it can affect the behavior of other agents through the environment.

This communication between agents is a key factor in the functioning of the P colony. At any moment each object inside every agent is affected by the execution of the program.

For more information about P systems see [7,6] or [8].

In the real world (as well as the cyber-world) the concentration of substances varies from place to place and living organisms do not know what is "over the horizon".

E. Csuhaj-Varjú et al. (Eds.): CMC 2012, LNCS 7762, pp. 161–172, 2013.

These considerations have inspired us to introduce a new model of P colonies that are placed inside a 2D grid of square cells. The agents are located in this grid and their view is limited to the cells that immediately surround them. Based on the contents of these cells, the agents decide their future locations.

In formulating the rules we draw upon the original model of the P colonies. The agents will use the rewriting - evolution - rules and the communication rules. A communication rule will be applied at a place where the agent using it is located.

The new rule we add is a movement rule. The condition for the movement of an agent is finding specific objects in specific locations in the environment. This is specified by a matrix with elements - objects. The agent is looking for at most one object in every surrounding cell. If the condition is fulfilled then the agent moves one cell up, down, left or right.

According to the original model we assemble the rules into programs. Because every agent contains two objects the programs are formed from two rules. The program can contain at most one movement rule. To achieve the greatest simplicity in agent behavior, we set another condition. If the agent will move, it cannot communicate with the environment. So if the program contains a movement rule, then the second rule is the rewriting rule.

2   Definitions

Throughout the paper we assume that the reader is familiar with the basics of the formal language theory.

Let Σ be the alphabet. Let Σ^* be the set of all words over Σ (including the empty word ε). We denote the length of the word $w \in \Sigma^*$ by $|w|$ and the number of occurrences of the symbol $a \in \Sigma$ in w by $|w|_a$.

A multiset of objects M is a pair $M = (V, f)$, where V is an arbitrary (not necessarily finite) set of objects and f is a mapping $f : V \to N$; f assigns to each object in V its multiplicity in M. The set of all multisets with the set of objects V is denoted by V°. The set $V' \subseteq V$ is called the support of M and is denoted by $supp(M)$ if for all $x \in V'$ $f(x) \neq 0$ holds. The cardinality of finite multiset M, denoted by $|M|$, is defined by $|M| = \sum_{a \in V} f(a)$. Each multiset of objects M with the set (support) of objects $V' = \{a_1, \ldots a_n\}$ can be represented as a string w over alphabet V', where $|w|_{a_i} = f(a_i)$; $1 \leq i \leq n$. Obviously, all words obtained from w by permuting the letters represent the same multiset M. The ε represents the empty multiset.

3   2D P Colonies

We briefly summarize the notion of 2D P colonies. A P colony consists of agents and an environment. Both the agents and the environment contain objects. The environment has size $m \times n$, m columns and n rows of cells, $m, n \in N$. With each agent a set of programs is associated. There are two types of rules in the programs.

The first rule type, called the evolution rule, is of the form $a \rightarrow b$. It means that the object a inside the agent is rewritten (evolved) to the object b. The second rule type, called the communication rule, is of the form $c \leftrightarrow d$. When the communication rule is performed, the object c inside the agent and the object d outside the agent swap their places. Thus, after the execution of the rule, the object d appears inside the agent and the object c is placed outside the agent.

The third rule type, called motion rule, is of the form matrix $3 \times 3 \rightarrow$ move direction. The location of the agent corresponds with the middle of the matrix. If the neighboring cells content objects according to objects inside matrix, an agent can move one step following move direction - to the left, right, up or down. If the positon of the agent is $[r, s], 0 \leq r \leq m - 1, 0 \leq s \leq n - 1$, after the execution of the rule agent change the position - to $[r - 1, s], [r + 1, s], [r, s - 1]$ or $[r, s + 1]$.

A program can contain at most one motion rule. When there is a motion rule inside a program, there can be no communication rule inside the same program.

Definition 1. *The 2D P colony is a construct*
$$\Pi = (A, e, Env, B_1, \ldots, B_k, f), k \geq 1, \text{ where}$$

- *A is an alphabet of the colony, its elements are called objects,*
- *$e \in A$ is the basic environmental object of the colony,*
- *Env is a pair $(m \times n, w_E)$, where $m \times n, m, n \in N$ is the size of the environment and w_E is the initial contents of environment, it is a matrix of size $m \times n$ of multisets of objects over $A - \{e\}$.*
- *B_i, $1 \leq i \leq k$, are agents, each agent is a construct $B_i = (O_i, P_i, [r_i, s_i])$, where*
  - *$[r_i, s_i]$ is an initial position of the agent B_i in 2D environment, $0 \leq r_i \leq m - 1$, $0 \leq s_i \leq n - 1$, $1 \leq i \leq k$,*
  - *O_i is a multiset over A, it determines the initial state (contents) of the agent, $|O_i| = 2$,*
  - *$P_i = \{p_{i,1}, \ldots, p_{i,j_i}\}, j \geq 1, 1 \leq i \leq k$ is a finite set of programs, where each program contains exactly 2 rules, which are in one of the following forms each:*
    - *$a \rightarrow b$, called the evolution rule,*
    - *$c \leftrightarrow d$, called the communication rule,*
    - *$[a_{u,v}] \rightarrow t, 0 \leq u, v \leq 2, t \in \{\Leftarrow, \Rightarrow, \Uparrow, \Downarrow\}$, called the motion rule;*
- *$f \in A$ is the final object of the colony.*

A computational step consists of three parts. The first part lies in determining the applicable set of programs according to the actual configuration of the P colony. There are programs belonging to all agents in this set of programs. In the second part we have to choose one program corresponding to each agent from the set of applicable programs. There is no collision between the communication rules belonging to different programs. The third part is the execution of the chosen programs.

A change of the configuration is triggered by the execution of programs and it involves changing the state of the environment, contents and placement of the agents.

A computation is nondeterministic and maximally parallel. The computation ends by halting when no agent has an applicable program.

The result of the computation is the number of copies of the final object placed in the environment at the end of the computation.

Another way to determine the result of the computation is to take into account not only the number of objects but also their location. The result could then be a grayscale image, a character string or a number that is dependent on both the number and placement of the objects (for example, $g = \sum_{j=0}^{n-1} \left(\sum_{i=0}^{m-1} f(i,j) \right) \cdot n^i$, where $f(i,j)$ is the number of copies of object f in the $[i,j]$-cell).

The reason for the introduction of 2D P colonies is not the study of their computational power but monitoring of their behaviour during the computation. We can define some measures to assess the dynamics of the computation:

– the number of moves of agents
– the number of visited cells (or not visited cells)
– the number of copies of a certain object in the home cell or throughout the environment.

These measures can be observed both for the individual steps of the computation and the computation as a whole.

4   Examples

In this section we show some examples of 2D P colonies. The first 2D P colony can be called a runner on bs.

Example 1. Let Π_1 be 2D P colony defined as follows: $\Pi_1 = (A, e, Env, B_1, f)$, where

– $A = \{e, f, a, b\}$,
– $e \in A$ is the basic environmental object of the colony,
– $Env = (5 \times 5, w_E)$,
– $w_E = \begin{bmatrix} a\ a\ a\ a\ a \\ a\ b\ b\ b\ a \\ a\ b\ a\ b\ a \\ a\ b\ b\ b\ a \\ a\ a\ a\ a\ a \end{bmatrix}$,
– $B_1 = (aa, P_1, [1,1])$,
– $P_1 = \{ \left\langle \begin{bmatrix} *\ b\ * \\ *\ b\ * \\ *\ *\ * \end{bmatrix} \to \Uparrow;\ a \to a \right\rangle; \left\langle \begin{bmatrix} *\ *\ * \\ *\ b\ * \\ *\ b\ * \end{bmatrix} \to \Downarrow;\ a \to a \right\rangle; \}$

$\left\langle \begin{bmatrix} *\ *\ * \\ b\ b\ * \\ *\ *\ * \end{bmatrix} \to \Leftarrow;\ a \to a \right\rangle; \left\langle \begin{bmatrix} *\ *\ * \\ *\ b\ b \\ *\ *\ * \end{bmatrix} \to \Rightarrow;\ a \to a \right\rangle$

The star on the matrix means that the agent does not care about the contents of the corresponding cell.

— $f \in A$ is the final object of the colony.

The agent is placed inside the cell in the second row and the second column of the environment. Every motion rule has object b in the middle of the matrix. Thus, all the programs are applicable only if the agent is positioned in the cell which contents at least one copy of object b. Based on these movement rules the agent moves towards a randomly selected b in the surrounding cells. The agent makes a move at every step of the computation. The environment and its contents remain unchanged. The initial configuration is shown in figure 1.

The second example of 2D P colonies is motivated by Conway's Game of Life([2]). It is a cellular automaton devised by the British mathematician John Horton Conway in 1970. It is the best-known example of a cellular automaton. The universe of the Game of Life is an infinite two-dimensional orthogonal grid of square automata, each of which is in one of two possible states, alive or dead. Every automaton interacts with its eight neighbours, which are the automata that are directly horizontally, vertically, or diagonally adjacent. Many different types of initial configurations (patterns) occur in the Game of Life, including still lifes, oscillators, and patterns that translate themselves across the board ("spaceships"). In our example we use one of still lives patterns called "beacon".

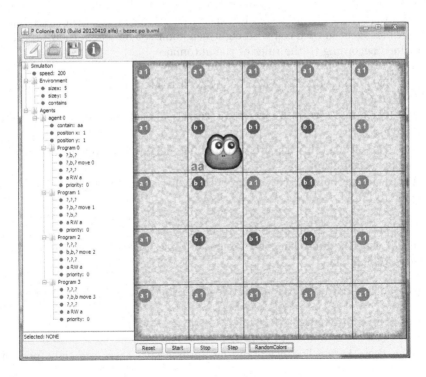

Fig. 1. The initial configuration of Π_1

Example 2. Let Π_2 be 2D P colony defined as follows:

$$\Pi_2 = (A, e, Env, B_1, \ldots, B_{16}, f),$$

where

- $A = \{e, f, D, S, Z, M, O, L, N\}$,
- $e \in A$ is the basic environmental object of the colony,
- $Env = (6 \times 6, w_E)$,
- $w_E = \begin{bmatrix} D\ D\ D\ D\ D\ D \\ D\ S\ S\ D\ D\ D \\ D\ S\ S\ D\ D\ D \\ D\ D\ D\ S\ S\ D \\ D\ D\ D\ S\ S\ D \\ D\ D\ D\ D\ D\ D \end{bmatrix}$,
- $B_1 = (ee, P_1, [1,1])$, $B_2 = (ee, P_2, [1,2])$,..., $B_{16} = (ee, P_{16}, [4,4])$,
- $f \in A$ is the final object of the colony.

The states of the automata are stored inside the cells (D - dead automaton, S - live automaton). There is only one kind of agent in this 2D P colony, so there are sixteen identical agents located in the matrix 4×4 of inner cells (see fig.2). There is one agent in each cell with eight neighbours. The sets of their programs are defined according to the rules of the automata:

- Any live automaton with fewer than two live neighbours dies, due to under-population.
- Any live automaton with more than three live neighbours dies, due to over-crowding.
- Any live automaton with two or three live neighbours lives, unchanged, to the next generation.
- Any dead automaton with exactly three live neighbouring automata will come to life.

The first program is to initialize the agent $\langle e \leftrightarrow e;\ e \to Z \rangle$;

We sort the programs using the number of copies of object S in the condition of the movement rule.

1. when neighbouring automata are dead - a single program for both dead as well as live automaton $\left\langle \begin{bmatrix} D\ D\ D \\ D\ e\ D \\ D\ D\ D \end{bmatrix} \to \Uparrow;\ Z \to M \right\rangle$.

2. when there is one live neighbouring automaton - there are eight possible programs for dead as well as live automata $\left\langle \begin{bmatrix} S\ D\ D \\ D\ e\ D \\ D\ D\ D \end{bmatrix} \to \Uparrow;\ Z \to M \right\rangle$ and seven other combinations.

3. when there are two live neighbouring automata - twenty-eight programs for

live automata $\left\langle \begin{bmatrix} S & S & D \\ D & S & D \\ D & D & D \end{bmatrix} \rightarrow \Uparrow;\ Z \rightarrow O \right\rangle$ and other twenty-seven combi-

nations.

4. when there are two live neighbouring automata - twenty-eight programs for

dead automata $\left\langle \begin{bmatrix} S & S & D \\ D & D & D \\ D & D & D \end{bmatrix} \rightarrow \Uparrow;\ Z \rightarrow M \right\rangle$ and other twenty-seven com-

binations.

5. when there are three live neighbouring automata - fifty-six eight possible

programs for dead as well as live automata $\left\langle \begin{bmatrix} S & S & S \\ D & e & D \\ D & D & D \end{bmatrix} \rightarrow \Uparrow;\ Z \rightarrow O \right\rangle$ and

other fifty-five combinations.

6. when there are four live neighbouring automata - eight possible programs

for dead as well as live automata $\left\langle \begin{bmatrix} S & S & S \\ S & e & D \\ D & D & D \end{bmatrix} \rightarrow \Uparrow;\ Z \rightarrow M \right\rangle$ and other

sixty-nine combinations.

7. when there are at least five live neighbouring automata - fifty- eight possible

programs for dead as well as live automata $\left\langle \begin{bmatrix} S & S & S \\ S & e & S \\ * & * & * \end{bmatrix} \rightarrow \Uparrow;\ Z \rightarrow M \right\rangle$ and

other fifty-five combinations.

After the execution of one of the above programs, all agents move one step
forward and rewrite one of their objects e to object M (automaton will be dead)
or to object O (automaton will be live). The following programs are for downward
movement and for refreshing the state of an automaton - i.e., the replacement
of the object in the cell for an object in the agent to change the state of the
automaton.

$$\left\langle \begin{bmatrix} * & * & * \\ * & e & * \\ * & * & * \end{bmatrix} \rightarrow \Downarrow;\ O \rightarrow S \right\rangle;\ \left\langle \begin{bmatrix} * & * & * \\ * & e & * \\ * & * & * \end{bmatrix} \rightarrow \Downarrow;\ M \rightarrow D \right\rangle;$$

$\langle e \rightarrow\ L;\ S \leftrightarrow S \rangle;\ \langle e \rightarrow\ N;\ D \leftrightarrow S \rangle;\ \langle S \rightarrow\ e;\ L \rightarrow e \rangle;\ \langle S \rightarrow\ e;\ N \rightarrow e \rangle;$
$\langle e \rightarrow\ L;\ S \leftrightarrow D \rangle;\ \langle e \rightarrow\ N;\ D \leftrightarrow D \rangle;\ \langle D \rightarrow\ e;\ L \rightarrow e \rangle;\ \langle D \rightarrow\ e;\ N \rightarrow e \rangle.$

It is easy to see that in such a way we can simulate every classical cellular
automaton.

In the third example we discuss the problem of ants.

Example 3. The aim is to construct a 2D P colony that will simulate the movement of ants searching for food. The agents - ants - are placed in the home cell
from which they start looking for food. Their search is nondeterministic until
they encounter food or a track. If they find food, they take one piece (one object)
and return using the shortest route to the home cell. They mark this route using
a specific object. If they find a track, they follow it.

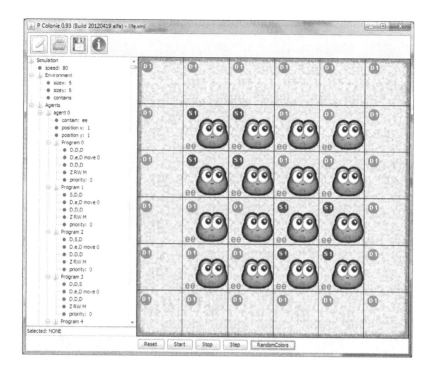

Fig. 2. The initial configuration of Π_2

One agent has forty-seven programs. We can classify them according to their function:

1. An agent explores its environment. $\left\langle \begin{bmatrix} * & * & * \\ * & e & * \\ * & * & * \end{bmatrix} \to \Downarrow;\ S \to S; pri = 0 \right\rangle$

   There are three more similar programs used for other directions. The last parameter of the program is its priority. The priority is the number within the range $\langle 0, 255 \rangle$ and it is used to form the programs into priority levels. In the computational step the applicable program from the highest priority level is executed.

2. If the agent finds the food source, it takes one object F (i.e. the food).

   $\left\langle \begin{bmatrix} * & F & * \\ * & e & * \\ * & * & * \end{bmatrix} \to \Uparrow;\ S \to F; pri = 1 \right\rangle$ and similar three programs used for the other directions,

   $\langle H \to e;\ e \leftrightarrow F; pri = 0 \rangle$ is the program to "eat" the object "food".

3. If the agent finds a path (object P) instead of food, it follows the path:

   $\left\langle \begin{bmatrix} * & P & * \\ * & e & * \\ * & * & * \end{bmatrix} \to \Uparrow;\ S \to Q; pri = 1 \right\rangle$ and similar three programs used for other directions.

$$\left\langle \begin{bmatrix} * & * & * \\ * & P & * \\ * & P & * \end{bmatrix} \rightarrow \Downarrow;\ Q \rightarrow Q; pri = 1 \right\rangle,\ \left\langle \begin{bmatrix} * & * & * \\ P & P & * \\ * & * & * \end{bmatrix} \rightarrow \Leftarrow;\ Q \rightarrow Q; pri = 1 \right\rangle.$$

4. If the agent finds food at the end of the path:

$$\left\langle \begin{bmatrix} * & * & * \\ * & P & * \\ * & Ft & * \end{bmatrix} \rightarrow \Downarrow;\ Q \rightarrow H; pri = 1 \right\rangle,\ \left\langle \begin{bmatrix} * & * & * \\ F & P & * \\ * & * & * \end{bmatrix} \rightarrow \Leftarrow;\ Q \rightarrow H; pri = 1 \right\rangle.$$

5. Then it carries food to the home cell. If there is no path around the food source, the agent will put object P into every cell on the way.

$\langle H \rightarrow\ e;\ e \leftrightarrow F; pri = 0 \rangle,$

$\langle e \rightarrow\ K;\ F \rightarrow E; pri = 0 \rangle,$

$$\left\langle \begin{bmatrix} * & P & * \\ * & e & * \\ * & * & * \end{bmatrix} \rightarrow \Uparrow;\ K \rightarrow G; pri = 1 \right\rangle \text{ and other three programs used for other}$$

directions.

$$\left\langle \begin{bmatrix} * & * & * \\ * & e & * \\ * & * & * \end{bmatrix} \rightarrow \Uparrow;\ K \rightarrow C; pri = 0 \right\rangle,\ \left\langle \begin{bmatrix} * & * & * \\ * & e & * \\ * & * & * \end{bmatrix} \rightarrow \Rightarrow;\ K \rightarrow C; pri = 0 \right\rangle,$$

$\langle E \rightarrow\ E;\ C \rightarrow P; pri = 0 \rangle,$

$\langle E \rightarrow\ E;\ P \leftrightarrow e; pri = 0 \rangle,$

$\langle E \rightarrow\ E;\ e \rightarrow c; pri = 0 \rangle,$

$$\left\langle \begin{bmatrix} * & * & * \\ * & e & * \\ * & * & * \end{bmatrix} \rightarrow \Uparrow;\ c \rightarrow C; pri = 0 \right\rangle,\ \left\langle \begin{bmatrix} * & * & * \\ * & e & * \\ * & * & * \end{bmatrix} \rightarrow \Rightarrow;\ c \rightarrow C; pri = 0 \right\rangle,$$

$$\left\langle \begin{bmatrix} * & H & * \\ * & e & * \\ * & * & * \end{bmatrix} \rightarrow \Uparrow;\ c \rightarrow B; pri = 1 \right\rangle,\ \left\langle \begin{bmatrix} * & * & * \\ * & e & H \\ * & * & * \end{bmatrix} \rightarrow \Rightarrow;\ c \rightarrow B; pri = 1 \right\rangle,$$

$$\left\langle \begin{bmatrix} * & * & * \\ * & e & * \\ * & * & * \end{bmatrix} \rightarrow \Uparrow;\ G \rightarrow G; pri = 0 \right\rangle,\ \left\langle \begin{bmatrix} * & * & * \\ * & e & * \\ * & * & * \end{bmatrix} \rightarrow \Rightarrow;\ G \rightarrow G; pri = 0 \right\rangle,$$

$$\left\langle \begin{bmatrix} * & H & * \\ * & e & * \\ * & * & * \end{bmatrix} \rightarrow \Uparrow;\ G \rightarrow B; pri = 1 \right\rangle,\ \left\langle \begin{bmatrix} * & * & * \\ * & e & H \\ * & * & * \end{bmatrix} \rightarrow \Rightarrow;\ G \rightarrow B; pri = 1 \right\rangle,$$

6. The agent puts object E into the home cell and starts searching again:

$\langle E \leftrightarrow\ e;\ B \rightarrow S; pri = 0 \rangle,$

7. If there is no food at the end of the path, the following program is applicable:

$$\left\langle \begin{bmatrix} * & * & * \\ * & P & * \\ * & * & * \end{bmatrix} \rightarrow \Downarrow;\ Q \rightarrow X; pri = 0 \right\rangle.$$

8. Then the agent starts to delete the path:

$$\left\langle \begin{bmatrix} * & P & * \\ * & e & * \\ * & * & * \end{bmatrix} \rightarrow \Uparrow;\ X \rightarrow x; pri = 0 \right\rangle,\ \left\langle \begin{bmatrix} * & * & * \\ * & e & P \\ * & * & * \end{bmatrix} \rightarrow \Rightarrow;\ X \rightarrow x; pri = 0 \right\rangle,$$

$\langle x \rightarrow\ y;\ e \leftrightarrow P; pri = 0 \rangle,$

$\langle y \rightarrow\ X;\ P \rightarrow e; pri = 0 \rangle.$

9. The agent keeps deleting objects P until it reaches the home cell:

$$\left\langle \begin{bmatrix} * & H & * \\ * & e & * \\ * & * & * \end{bmatrix} \rightarrow \Uparrow;\ X \rightarrow S; pri = 0 \right\rangle, \left\langle \begin{bmatrix} * & * & * \\ * & e & H \\ * & * & * \end{bmatrix} \rightarrow \Rightarrow;\ X \rightarrow S; pri = 0 \right\rangle.$$

When object S appears inside the agent, it starts searching for food again.

The configuration with five agents and three paths is shown on the figure 3.

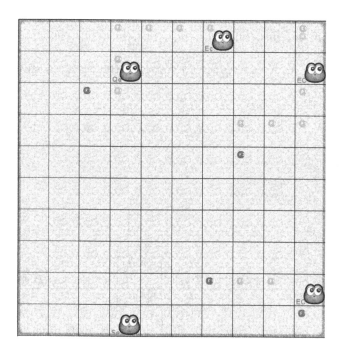

Fig. 3. The configuration of Π_2 with four ants and two paths from food to home cell

5   Implementation of 2D P Colony Simulator

The simulation environment has been written in Java and it allows us to load, save and create simulations using XML markup language. The simulation file is loaded using XML parser and it creates a tree structure of objects using DOM and JAXP. These objects represent parameters of the simulation, which contain a description of the environment and agents in this environment. The information describing the environment includes parameters such as speed of simulation, the size and the contents of the environment. The speed of the simulation determines the time interval between the steps of the simulation. The environment and its contents are represented by a two-dimensional array of objects which is displayed as a 2D grid to the user. The agent is located in this grid and has the ability to move or influence the contents of the environment by using rewriting rules. The environment may contain a special object #, which represents an obstacle or a position that is inaccessible for agents. The agent in the environment activates one of its applicable programs in each simulation step. Each program has an assigned priority and the selection of applicable programs is based on this priority. If there is a state when several programs can be activated with the same priority, we use pseudo-random selection to choose only one of these programs. Multiple agents can be located on different or identical positions in the simulation environment. Collisions may occur in simulations of several agents in a common shared environment which can cause simulation errors. To avoid these problems, agents need to synchronize their access to the environment and again using a pseudo-random selection to decide the order in which the agents will be on the same positions to activate their programs. Environment changes are stored in the stack from which they are projected into the environment. In this way we can avoid the situation when one agent in the simulation step will affect the neighbourhood of another agent or objects in the position where there are more agents. In these cases it could lead to the use of previously unusable agent programs. However, in one simulation step this is not acceptable. Our simulation tool uses the Swing library for creating graphical user interfaces. It is possible to use change the graphics of the environment, the agents and the obstacles and customize the simulation environment and visualization according to user needs. Users now have an interesting tool for the implementation of the simulation of P colonies with the ability to edit the simulation directly from the simulation environment or from any text editor.

6 Conclusion

In this paper we introduce a new kind of P colonies that would be suitable for simulating real-world situations. We created a 2D environment where agents are located. The agents have limited information about the contents of their environment, which better reflects the reality. In order to solve the simulation problems in the example of stigmergy and ants we proposed the introduction of priority of programs. The activities of agents become more natural, because in real-life situations ants prefer to perform certain activities over others. To present and inspect the computation of 2D P colonies we have created a simulation environment. We plan to extend the simulator to use statistical tools and dynamic environment in the future.

Remark 1. This work was supported by the European Regional Development Fund in the IT4Innovations Centre of Excellence project (CZ.1.05/1.1.00/02.0070).

References

1. Csuhaj-Varjú, E., Kelemen, J., Kelemenová, A., Păun, G., Vaszil, G.: Cells in environment: P colonies. Multiple-Valued Logic and Soft Computing 12(3-4), 201–215 (2006)
2. Gardner, M.: Mathematical Games - The fantastic combinations of John Conway's new solitaire game "life". Scientific American 223, 120–123 (1970/2010) ISBN 0-89454-001-7 (Archived from the original on June 03, 2009) (retrieved June 26, 2011)
3. Kelemen, J., Kelemenová, A.: On P colonies, a biochemically inspired model of computation. In: Proc. of the 6th International Symposium of Hungarian Researchers on Computational Intelligence, Budapest TECH, Hungary, pp. 40–56 (2005)
4. Kelemen, J., Kelemenová, A., Păun, G.: Preview of P colonies: A biochemically inspired computing model. In: Bedau, M., et al. (eds.) Workshop and Tutorial Proceedings, Ninth International Conference on the Simulation and Synthesis of Living Systems, ALIFE IX, Boston, Mass, pp. 82–86 (2004)
5. Păun, G.: Computing with membranes. Journal of Computer and System Sciences 61, 108–143 (2000)
6. Păun, G.: Membrane computing: An introduction. Springer, Berlin (2002)
7. Păun, G., Rozenberg, G., Salomaa, A. (eds.): The Oxford Handbook of Membrane Computing. Oxford University Press (2009)
8. P systems web page (May 10, 2012), http://ppage.psystems.eu

Fast Distributed DFS Solutions
for Edge-Disjoint Paths in Digraphs

Hossam ElGindy[1], Radu Nicolescu[2], and Huiling Wu[2]

[1] School of Computer Science and Engineering, University of New South Wales,
Sydney, Australia
elgindyh@cse.unsw.edu.au
[2] Department of Computer Science, University of Auckland,
Private Bag 92019, Auckland, New Zealand
r.nicolescu@auckland.ac.nz, hwu065@aucklanduni.ac.nz

Abstract. We present two new synchronous distributed message-based depth-first search (DFS) based algorithms, Algorithms C and D, to compute a maximum cardinality set of edge-disjoint paths, between a source node and a target node in a digraph. We compare these new algorithms with our previous implementation of the classical algorithm, Algorithm A, and our previous improvement, Algorithm B [10]. Empirical results show that, on a set of random digraphs, our algorithms are faster than the classical Algorithm A, by a factor around 40%. All these improved algorithms have been inspired and guided by a P system modelling exercise, but are suitable for any distributed implementation. To achieve the maximum theoretical performance, our P systems specification uses high-level generic rules applied in matrix grammar mode.

Keywords: edge-disjoint paths, depth-first search, network flow, distributed systems, P systems, generic rules, matrix grammars.

1 Introduction

The edge-disjoint paths problem finds a maximum cardinality set of edge-disjoint paths between a source node and a target node in a *digraph*. The classical algorithm transforms this problem to a maximum flow problem, solved by assigning unit capacity to each arc.

All algorithms discussed in this paper are distributed, totally message-based (no shared memory) and work synchronously: briefly, we call them *distributed*, implicitly assuming their other characteristics. In this paper, Algorithm A is a distributed version of the classical edge-disjoint algorithm, based on Ford-Fulkerson's maximum flow algorithm [5] and the classical distributed DFS [13]. Algorithm A* is its slightly improved version, proposed by Dinneen et al. [3].

Recently, we proposed an improved distributed algorithm [10], here called Algorithm B. Algorithm B improved Algorithms A and A* by (a) using Cidon's distributed DFS [2,13], which avoids revisiting cells in the same round, and (b) a *novel* idea, discarding "dead" cells detected during *failed* rounds, i.e. cells that will never appear in a successful search.

E. Csuhaj-Varjú et al. (Eds.): CMC 2012, LNCS 7762, pp. 173–194, 2013.
© Springer-Verlag Berlin Heidelberg 2013

Here we propose two distributed algorithms: (1) Algorithm C, which, using a *different* idea, discards "dead" cells identified in *successful* and *failed* rounds, and (2) Algorithm D, which *combines* the benefits of Algorithms B and C.

Briefly, in all our algorithms, B, C, and D, search rounds explore *unvisited* cells and arcs. Cells and arcs encountered during the search are tentatively marked as *temporarily visited*. Temporarily visited cells and arcs which are detected "dead" are marked as *permanently visited* and ignored in the next search round. At the end of each search round, remaining *temporarily visited* cells and arcs revert to the *unvisited* status and can be revisited by next search round.

Our algorithms differ (1) in the rules used to detect "dead" cells and (2) in the process used to discard these "dead" cells for the next rounds. Our previous Algorithm B detects "dead" cells at the end of *failed* search rounds (only) and discards them in "real-time", on *shortest paths*. Our new Algorithm C can detect "dead" cells during any kind of search round (regardless if it is *failed* or *successful*) but discards these on the current *search path trace*, which is typically longer than the shortest path possible (especially in digraphs). In contrast, classical algorithms, such as Algorithms A and A*, do not discard any cell, and reset all cells as *unvisited*, at each search round end.

We also consider a *restricted* version of Algorithm C, called Algorithm C*, where we intentionally *omit* to discard "dead" cells found in *failed* rounds: in this sense, Algorithm C* is the opposite of Algorithm B. We can thus better assess the power of the main new idea behind Algorithm C: even its restricted version, C*, still *detects* a superset of all "dead" cells detected by Algorithm B. However, due to digraphs propagation delays, Algorithms C and C* are not always able to *prune* all detected cells in "real-time": they could prune all, if allowed to run longer. Thus, there are scenarios when one of Algorithms B and C is more suitable than the other. Algorithm D achieves maximum performance: it runs fast and detects and prunes all "dead" cells that can be detected by the combination of Algorithms B and C.

All these improved algorithms have been inspired and guided by a P system modelling exercise, but are suitable for any distributed implementation. A P system is a parallel and distributed computational model inspired by the structure and interactions of living cells, introduced by Păun [11]; for a recent overview of the domain, see Păun et al.'s recent monograph [12]. Essentially, a P system is specified by its membrane structure, symbols and rules. The underlying structure is a digraph or a more specialized version, such as a directed acyclic graph (dag) or a tree (which seems the most studied case). Each cell transforms its content symbols and sends messages to its neighbours using formal rules inspired by rewriting systems. Rules of the same cell can be applied in parallel (where possible) and all cells work in parallel, traditionally in the synchronous mode.

In this paper, we also assess P systems as directly executable formal specifications of synchronous distributed algorithms. Thus, we aim to construct P algorithms that compare favourably with high-level non-executable pseudocode: (1) first, in runtime complexity and (2) if possible, in program readability and size (which is independent of the problem size). Toward these goals, we use high-level generic P rules, applied using a new proposed semantics, inspired from *matrix grammars*. Our previous algorithms have used a related, but less powerful, application mode, the so-called weak priority mode. The weak priority mode seems adequate for simple algorithms, but the novel matrix semantics is more suitable for more sophisticated algorithms, such as our new algorithms presented here.

2   Edge-Disjoint Paths in Digraphs

We consider a *digraph*, $G = (V, E)$, where V is a finite set of *nodes*, $V = \{\sigma_1, \sigma_2, \ldots, \sigma_n\}$, and E is a set of *arcs*. For consistency with the P system terminologies, the *nodes* of V are also called *cells*. Digraph arcs define (*parent, child*) relationships, e.g., arc $(\sigma_i, \sigma_j) \in E$ defines σ_j as σ_i's child and σ_i as σ_j's parent; with alternate notations, $\sigma_j \in E(\sigma_i)$, $\sigma_i \in E^{-1}(\sigma_j)$. A *path* is a finite ordered set of nodes successively connected by arcs. A *simple path* is a path with no repeated nodes. Clearly, any path can be "streamlined" to a simple path, by removing repeated nodes. Given a path, π, we define: $\overline{\pi} \subseteq E$, as the set of its arcs and its reversal, $\overline{\pi}^{-1} = \{(\sigma_j, \sigma_i) \mid (\sigma_i, \sigma_j) \in \overline{\pi}\} \subseteq E^{-1}$.

Given a *source* node, $s \in V$, and a *target* node, $t \in V$, the edge-disjoint problem looks for a *maximum cardinality set* of edge-disjoint s-to-t paths. A set of paths are edge-disjoint if they have no common arc. If the edge-disjoint paths are not *simple*, we can always *simplify* them at the end. The edge-disjoint problem can be transformed to a maximum flow problem, by assigning unit capacity to each arc [8].

Given a set of edge-disjoint paths P, we define $\overline{P}$ as the set of their arcs, $\overline{P} = \cup_{\pi \in P} \overline{\pi}$, and the *residual* digraph $G_P = (V, E_P)$, where $E_P = (E \backslash \overline{P}) \cup \overline{P}^{-1}$. Briefly, the residual digraph is constructed by reversing arcs in $\overline{P}$.

Given a set of edge-disjoint paths, P, an *augmenting* path, α, is an s-to-t path in G_P. Augmenting paths are used to extend an already established set of edge-disjoint paths. An augmenting path arc is either (1) an arc in $E \backslash \overline{P}$ or (2) an arc in $\overline{P}^{-1}$, i.e. it reverses an existing arc in $\overline{P}$. Case (2) is known as a *push-back* operation: when it occurs, the arc in $\overline{P}$ and its reversal in $\overline{\alpha}$ "cancel" each other and are discarded. The remaining path fragments are relinked to construct an extended set of edge-disjoint paths, P', where $\overline{P'} = (\overline{P} \backslash \overline{\alpha}^{-1}) \cup (\overline{\alpha} \backslash \overline{P}^{-1})$. This process is repeated, starting with the new and larger set of edge-disjoint paths, P', until no more augmenting paths are found [5].

Figure 1 shows how to find an augmenting path in a residual digraph: (a) shows the initial digraph, G, with two edge-disjoint paths, $P = \{\sigma_0.\sigma_1.\sigma_4.\sigma_7, \sigma_0.\sigma_2.\sigma_5.\sigma_7\}$; (b) shows the residual digraph, G_P, formed by reversing edge-disjoint path arcs; (c) shows an augmenting path, $\alpha = \sigma_0.\sigma_3.\sigma_5.\sigma_2.\sigma_6.\sigma_7$, which uses a reverse arc, (σ_5, σ_2); (d) discards the cancelling arcs, (σ_2, σ_5) and (σ_5, σ_2); (e) relinks the remaining path fragments, $\sigma_0.\sigma_1.\sigma_4.\sigma_7$, $\sigma_0.\sigma_2$, $\sigma_5.\sigma_7$, $\sigma_0.\sigma_3.\sigma_5$ and $\sigma_2.\sigma_6.\sigma_7$, resulting in an incremented set of three edge-disjoint paths, $P' = \{\sigma_0.\sigma_1.\sigma_4.\sigma_7, \sigma_0.\sigma_2.\sigma_6.\sigma_7, \sigma_0.\sigma_3.\sigma_5.\sigma_7\}$; (f) shows the new residual digraph, $G_{P'}$.

Augmenting paths can be repeatedly searched using a DFS algorithm on *residual digraphs* [5], which dynamically builds *DFS trees*. A *search path*, τ, is a path,

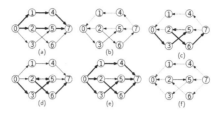

Fig. 1. Finding an augmenting path in a residual digraph. Thin arcs: original arcs; thick arcs: disjoint or augmenting path arcs; dotted arcs: reversed path arcs.

which starts from the source and "tries" to reach the target. A search path explores as far as possible before backtracking. At any given time, a search path is, either (1) a branch in the DFS tree or a prefix of it or (2) a branch in the DFS tree followed by one more arc, which, in a failed attempt, visits another node of the same branch or of another branch.

Our algorithms use a *synchronous* version of Cidon's *distributed* DFS [2,13], which avoids case (2) above. When a node is first visited, it immediately marks all incoming arcs as visited, by sending *visited notifications* to its digraph parents. These notifications run in *parallel* with the main search, without delaying it. All parents are thus timely notified and, if they become visited, will not send the visiting token to this already visited node. For example, in Figure 2 (a), search path $\sigma_0.\sigma_1.\sigma_2.\sigma_3.\sigma_4.\sigma_6$ does not revisit cell σ_3. This is a powerful optimisation, which reduces the DFS complexity from $O(m)$ to $O(n)$; we use it, but this is not intrinsically related to our novel proposal.

When τ cannot explore further, it *backtracks*. The search is *successful* when the search path reaches the target. A successful search path becomes a new *augmenting path* and is used to increase the number of edge-disjoint paths: while conceptually a distinct operation, the new edge-disjoint paths are typically formed while the successful search path returns on its steps, back to the source (this successful return is distinct from the backtrack).

Given a *current* search path arc, (σ_i, σ_j), σ_i is a search path predecessor (*sp-predecessor*) of σ_j, and σ_j is a search path successor (*sp-successor*) of σ_i. Given a *previous* search path arc, (σ_i, σ_j), σ_i is a search tree predecessor (*st-predecessor*) of σ_j, and σ_j is a search tree successor (*st-successor*) of σ_i. Until the end of current search round, these arcs are considered *temporary visited*. At the end of the round, for the next search round, these arcs may become *permanently visited* or revert to *unvisited*.

In this paper, we propose a *novel* procedure to detect "dead" nodes, based on two numerical search-specific attributes: the (known) node *depth* and a new attribute which we call *reach-number*. A node's *depth*, σ_i.depth, is the number of hops from the source to itself in the search tree. A node's *reach-number* is the minimum of its depth and all its st-successors' reach-numbers; more precisely, it is the *greatest fixed point* that satisfies the following recursive equation:

$$\sigma_i.\texttt{reach} = \min(\{\sigma_i.\texttt{depth}\} \cup \{\sigma_j.\texttt{reach} \mid (\sigma_i, \sigma_j) \in E'\})$$

where E' is the current residual arcs set and assuming that *discarded* nodes have *infinite* reach-numbers.

As algorithmically determined, depths and reach-numbers start as *infinite* and are further *iteratively* adjusted during the search process:

1. When the search path first *visits* node σ_i:
   (a) both σ_i's depth and reach-number are set to the current hop count (see 4.7).
2. When the search path *backtracks* from node σ_k to node σ_i:
   (a) σ_i can *decrease* its reach-number, if σ_k.reach $< \sigma_i$.reach (see 4.19);
   (b) σ_k can be *discarded*, if σ_k.reach $> \sigma_i$.depth (see 4.20).
3. When node σ_i is *discarded*:
   (a) σ_i.reach becomes *infinite* (see 5.6);
   (b) σ_i's st-predecessors can *increase* their reach-numbers (see 5.9 and 6.7);
   (c) all σ_i's st-successors can be discarded (this is a recursive procedure, see 5.14).
4. When node σ_j's reach-number is *increased* without being discarded, because its st-successor σ_i has increased its own reach-number:
   (a) σ_j's st-predecessors can also *increase* their reach-numbers (see 6.12);
   (b) σ_i can be *discarded*, if σ_i.reach $> \sigma_j$.depth (see 6.14).

Note that, if finite, a node's reach-number is never greater than its own depth, i.e. σ_i.reach $\leq \sigma_i$.depth. Note also the two cases where a node can be discarded, (2.b) and (4.b), require a similar additional condition: this node's reach-number is changed to a finite number greater than all its parent's depths.

While items (1.a), (2.a) and (3.a) can be easily incorporated in any search, in a message-based distributed algorithm, items (2.b), (3.b), (4.a) and (4.b) must be recursively propagated by *notification messages*, over existing arcs. However, this is a *residual* digraph, where some residual arcs are inverted original arcs, some residual parents are original children and some residual children are original parents. The actual algorithm needs additional housekeeping to properly send such notifications, only to all concerned neighbours. Note that unvisited or discarded cells do not need these notifications.

These notifications travel in *parallel* with the main search activities, without affecting the overall performance. However, these notifications only travel along *search paths traces*, which, in digraphs, are *not* the *shortest* possible paths. Therefore, as we will see in a later example, not all cells can be effectively notified in "real-time", and may be reached by the next search process *before* they get their due discard or update notifications. Briefly, in a digraph based system, we have a *pruning propagation delay*, which may negatively affect its performance.

As we see in Section 3, in Algorithm C, cases (2.b) and (4.b) trigger *discard notifications*, which are propagated by the function Discard and cases (3.b) and (4.a) trigger *update notifications*, propagated by the function Update.

Figure 2 illustrates how the depth and reach-numbers are initially set during forward moves and dynamically adjusted (decreased) during backtrack moves.

In (a), $\sigma_0.\sigma_1.\sigma_2.\sigma_3.\sigma_4.\sigma_5.\sigma_3$ is a search path attempting to visit the already visited node σ_3 (if we use Cidon's optimisation, it will not actually visit σ_3). At this step, the reach-number of each node on the search path is still the same as its depth, $\sigma_i.\texttt{reach} = \sigma_i.\texttt{depth} = i, i \in [0,5]$. A few steps later, in (b), the search path, $\sigma_0.\sigma_1.\sigma_2.\sigma_3$, has backtracked to σ_3. Cells to which we have backtracked, σ_5, σ_4 and σ_3, have updated their reach-numbers: $\sigma_5.\texttt{reach} = \min(\sigma_5.\texttt{depth}, \sigma_3.\texttt{reach}) = 3$; $\sigma_4.\texttt{reach} = \min(\sigma_4.\texttt{depth}, \sigma_6.\texttt{reach}) = 3$ and $\sigma_3.\texttt{reach} = \min(\sigma_3.\texttt{depth}, \sigma_4.\texttt{reach}) = 3$. After one more step, in (c), the search path, $\sigma_0.\sigma_1.\sigma_2.\sigma_3.\sigma_6$, moves forward to σ_6. At this step, $\sigma_6.\texttt{reach} = \sigma_6.\texttt{depth} = 4$. After one more step, in (d), the search path, $\sigma_0.\sigma_1.\sigma_2.\sigma_3$, backtracks again to σ_3 and $\sigma_3.\texttt{reach} = \min(\sigma_3.\texttt{depth}, \sigma_4.\texttt{reach}, \sigma_6.\texttt{reach}) = 3$ (unchanged). At this stage, we *discard* σ_6, because $\sigma_6.\texttt{reach} = 4 > \sigma_3.\texttt{depth} = 3$. One step later, in (e), the search path, $\sigma_0.\sigma_1.\sigma_2$, has backtracked to σ_2, and $\sigma_2.\texttt{reach} = \min(\sigma_2.\texttt{depth}, \sigma_3.\texttt{reach}) = 2$ (unchanged). We can now *discard* σ_3, σ_4 and σ_5, because their reach-numbers are greater than $\sigma_2.\texttt{depth} = 2$.

Another step later, the search will *succeed*, the search path, $\sigma_0.\sigma_1.\sigma_2.\sigma_7$, will reach σ_7 and become an augmenting path. The *discarded* cells, σ_3, σ_4, σ_5 and σ_6, can remain *permanently visited* and need not be further reconsidered. Conceptually, subsequent searches will use a trimmed digraph, which will speed up the algorithm. Our previous Algorithm B [10] does not discard these cells, because it uses a different idea, which only detects "dead" cells in *failed* searches.

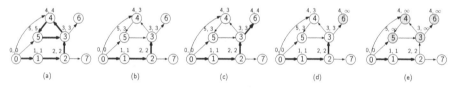

Fig. 2. Thin arcs: original arcs; thick arcs: search path arcs; (`depth`, `reach`) pairs beside each node indicate the node's depth and reach-number; gray cells have been discarded

3   High-Level Pseudocode

Algorithm A is a distributed version of the classical Ford-Fulkerson based edge-disjoint paths algorithm [5]. To find augmenting paths, it uses the classical DFS algorithm [13]. This algorithm uses a **repeat-until** loop, repeatedly probing all unvisited children (both previously unprobed children and previously probed but failed children), resetting all visited nodes and arcs as unvisited after each new augmenting path, until no more augmenting paths are found. Pseudocode 1 shows its high-level description, after unrolling its first DFS call.

To improve the readability, the pseudocode of this distributed algorithm and of all other discussed algorithms are presented in *sequentialized* versions. Each boxed area wraps code which is *essential* in a parallel run, but is *omitted* in the sequential mode. The **fork** keyword indicates the start of a *parallel* execution.

Algorithm A is described by Pseudocodes 1 and 2, which use the following variables: $G = (V, E)$ is the underlying digraph; $\sigma_s \in V$ is the source cell; $\sigma_t \in V$ is the target cell; r is the current round number; P_{r-1} is the set of edge-disjoint paths available at the start of round $\#r$; $G_{r-1} = (V, E_{r-1})$ is the residual digraph available at the start of round $\#r$. Algorithm A starts with an empty set of edge-disjoint paths, $P_0 = \emptyset$ and the trivial residual graph, $G_0 = (V, E_0)$, where $E_0 = E$ (i.e. $G_0 = G$).

Pseudocode 1: Algorithm A

```
1   Input : a digraph G = (V, E), a source cell, σ_s ∈ V,
2            and a target cell, σ_t ∈ V
3   r = 0, P_0 = ∅, G_0 = G
4   repeat
5     α = null
6     β = null
7     while there is an unvisited arc (σ_s, σ_q) ∈ E_{r-1} and β = null
8       r = r + 1
9       set σ_s and (σ_s, σ_q) as visited
10      β = DFS(σ_q, σ_t, G_{r-1})            // see Pseudocode 2
11      if β = null then                       // failed round
12        G_r = G_{r-1}
13      endif
14    endwhile
15    if β ≠ null then                         // successful round
16      α = σ_s.β
17      P̄_r = (P̄_{r-1} \ ᾱ^{-1}) ∪ (ᾱ \ P̄_{r-1}^{-1})
18      G_r = (V, E_r), where E_r = (E \ P̄_r) ∪ P̄_r^{-1}
19      reset all visited cells and arcs to unvisited
20    endif
21  until α = null
22  Output : P_r, which is a maximum cardinality set of edge-disjoint paths
```

Pseudocode 2: Classical DFS, for residual digraph $\mathbf{G_{r-1} = (V, E_{r-1})}$

```
1   DFS(σ_i, σ_t, G_{r-1})
2   Input : the current cell, σ_i ∈ V, the target cell, σ_t ∈ V
3            and the residual digraph, G_{r-1}
4   if σ_i = σ_t then return σ_t
5   if σ_i is visited then return null
6   set σ_i as visited
7   foreach unvisited (σ_i, σ_k) ∈ E_{r-1}
8     set (σ_i, σ_k) as visited
9     β = DFS(σ_k, σ_t, G_{r-1})
10    if β ≠ null return σ_i.β
11  endfor
12  return null
13  Output : a σ_i-to-σ_t path, if any; otherwise, null
```

Our new Algorithm C is described by Pseudocodes 3–6 and uses the same variables as Algorithm A; additionally, this algorithm works in d successive *search rounds*, defined by successive *iterations* of its **for** loop (line 3.8), where d is the outdegree of σ_s. Without loss of generality, we assume that σ_s's children are represented by the set $\{\sigma_{s1}, \sigma_{s2}, \ldots, \sigma_{sd}\}$.

Pseudocode 3: Algorithm C

```
1   Input: a digraph G = (V, E), a source cell, σs ∈ V,
2            and a target cell, σt ∈ V
3   P0 = ∅, G0 = G
4   set  σs as permanently visited
5   foreach  unvisited arc (σj, σs) ∈ E
6      set  (σj, σs) as permanently visited
7   endfor
8   for  r = 1 to  d
9      if  σsr is permanently visited  then  continue
10     set  (σs, σsr) as permanently visited
11     β = NW_DFS(σsr, σt, Gr−1, 1)              // see Pseudocode 4
12     if  β = null  then                        // failed round
13        fork  Discard(σsr, Gr−1)
14        Gr = Gr−1
15        reset  all temporarily visited cells and arcs to unvisited
16     else                                       // successful round
17        α = σs.β
18        P‾r = (P‾r−1 \ α‾−1) ∪ (α‾ \ P‾r−1−1)
19        Gr = (V, Er), where Er = (E \ P‾r) ∪ P‾r−1
20        reset  all temporarily visited cells and arcs to unvisited
21     endif
22   endfor
23   Output: Pr, which is a maximum cardinality set of edge-disjoint paths
```

Pseudocode 4: NW-DFS, adapted for $G_{r-1} = (V, E_{r-1})$

```
1   NW_DFS(σi, σt, Gr−1, depth)
2   Input: the current cell, σi ∈ V, the target cell, σt ∈ V,
3            the residual digraph, Gr−1, and σi's depth, depth
4   if  σi = σt  then  return  σt
5   if σi is permanently visited then return null
6   set  σi as temporarily visited
7   σi.reach = σi.depth = depth
8   foreach  unvisited arc (σj, σi) ∈ Er−1              // see Cidon's DFS
9      set  (σj, σi) as temporarily visited
10  endfor
11  foreach  arc (σi, σk) ∈ Er−1
12     if  (σi, σk) is permanently visited  then  continue
13     elseif  (σi, σk) is temporarily visited  then
14        σi.reach = min(σi.reach, σk.reach)
15     else                                       // unvisited
```

```
16        set  (σ_i, σ_k) as temporarily visited
17        β = NW_DFS(σ_k, σ_t, G_{r-1}, depth + 1)
18        if  β =  null  then
19           σ_i.reach = min(σ_i.reach, σ_k.reach)
20           if  σ_k.reach > σ_i.depth then  fork  Discard(σ_k, G_{r-1}) // see PC 5
21        else
22           return  σ_i.β
23        endif
24     endif
25  endfor
26  return null
27  Output : a σ_i-to-σ_t path, if any; otherwise,  null
```

Pseudocode 5: Discard, adapted for $G_{r-1} = (V, E_{r-1})$

```
1   Discard(σ_i, G_{r-1})
2   Input : a cell to discard, σ_i ∈ V, and the residual digraph, G_{r-1}
3   if  σ_i is permanently visited then  return
4   set  σ_i as permanently visited
5   ioldreach = σ_i.reach
6   σ_i.reach = ∞
7   foreach  arc (σ_j, σ_i) ∈ E_{r-1}
8      if  (σ_j, σ_i) is temporarily visited  then
9         fork  Update(σ_j, G_{r-1}, ioldreach, σ_i)          // see Pseudocode 6
10     endif
11     set  (σ_j, σ_i) as permanently visited
12  endfor
13  foreach  temporarily visited arc (σ_i, σ_k)
14     fork  Discard(σ_k, G_{r-1})
15  endfor
```

Pseudocode 6: Update, adapted for $G_{r-1} = (V, E_{r-1})$

```
1   Update(σ_j, G_{r-1}, ioldreach, σ_i)
2   Input : a cell, σ_j ∈ V, the residual digraph, G_{r-1}, a reach-number, ioldreach,
3           and a cell, σ_i ∈ V
4   if  σ_j.reach = ioldreach  then
5      newreach = σ_j.depth
6      foreach  temporarily visited arc (σ_j, σ_k) ∈ E_{r-1}
7         newreach = min(newreach, σ_k.reach)
8      endfor
9      if  newreach > σ_j.reach  then
10        joldreach = σ_j.reach
11        σ_j.reach = newreach
12        ┌─────────────────────────────────────────────────────┐
          │ foreach  temporarily visited arc (σ_k, σ_j) ∈ E_{r-1} │
          │    fork  Update(σ_k, G_{r-1}, joldreach, σ_j)         │
          │ endfor                                                │
          └─────────────────────────────────────────────────────┘
13     endif
```

14 | if $\sigma_i.\text{reach} > \sigma_j.\text{depth}$ **then**
   | **fork** Discard(σ_i, G_{r-1})
   | **endif**

15   **endif**

Search round #r starts when cell σ_s sends the *forward token*, together with a depth indication of one (lines 3.8–11), to unvisited cell σ_{sr}. A receiving cell marks itself as *temporarily visited* (line 4.6), records its depth and reach-number as the received depth (line 4.7) and sends *visited notification* to all its neighbours (lines 4.8–10), becoming the new frontier cell. A current frontier cell sends the forward token over an arbitrarily selected unvisited arc, together with an incremented depth (lines 4.15–17), then the frontier advances. The visited notification housekeeping is performed in parallel with the main search. A frontier cell, which does not have any (more) unvisited arc, sends back a *backtrack token* to its search path predecessor, to return the frontier.

The search path backtracks to cell σ_i when: (1) σ_i avoids revisiting a temporarily visited child, σ_k (we consider this is a backtrack from σ_k, as in the classical DFS); (2) σ_i receives a backtrack token from σ_k. In both cases, σ_i recomputes its reach-number (lines 4.7, 4.13–15, 4.18–19). If σ_k's reach-number is greater than σ_i's depth, then σ_i sends a *discarding notification* to σ_k (line 4.20).

On receiving a discarding notification, cell σ_i sets itself as *permanently visited* and sets its reach-number as infinite (lines 5.4, 5.6). Also, it sends a *permanently visited notification* and an *update* to its st-predecessors (lines 5.7–5.12), σ_j's. On receiving an update from σ_i, cell σ_j recomputes its reach-number (lines 6.4–11). If σ_j increases its reach-number, it records and sends an update to its st-predecessors, σ_k's (line 6.12). If σ_i's reach-number is greater than σ_j's depth, then σ_j sends a discarding notification to σ_i (line 6.14).

Once cell σ_i is discarded, it sends discarding notifications to its st-successors (lines 5.13–15). This notification travels in parallel with the main search, along search path traces (not the shortest possible path). If a cell is not notified in "real time", it may be visited by the next search process before it gets its due discarding notification. To solve this problem, once discarded, the cell immediately backtracks (line 4.5) and sends an update to its st-predecessors (lines 5.7–12).

If the search path reaches the *target* cell, σ_t (line 4.4), then round #r succeeds and σ_t sends a *path confirmation* back to σ_s. While moving towards σ_s, the confirmation reshapes the existing edge-disjoint paths and the newly found augmenting path, α_r, building a larger set of edge-disjoint paths, and a new residual digraph. Thus, lines 3.17–19 of Pseudocode 3 are actually done within Pseudocode 4, during the return from a successful search. After receiving the path confirmation, σ_s initiates a global *reset*, which changes all temporarily visited cells and arcs to unvisited (line 3.20). This reset runs two steps ahead and in parallel with the next round, without affecting it.

If the search path cannot reach σ_t, the source, σ_s, receives a backtrack token from σ_{sr} and the round fails (line 3.12). Then σ_s sends a discarding notification to σ_{sr} (line 3.13) and initiates a global reset, to change all temporarily visited cells and arcs to unvisited (line 3.15). A failed round does not change the current set of edge-disjoint paths or the current residual digraph (line 3.14).

Although not explicit in the pseudocode, after probing all its children, the source, σ_s, initiates a global finalisation. This is not strictly necessary, but informs all cells that the algorithm has terminated.

Algorithm D combines Algorithms B and C, which discards all "dead" cells that are detected by B and C. Its Pseudocode 7 only changes one line of Pseudocode 3. Algorithm D uses two end-of-round resets, as in Algorithm B: (1) *after-success* reset, which resets all *temporarily visited* cells and arcs to *unvisited*, and (2) *after-failure* reset, which sets all *temporarily visited* cells and arcs as *permanently visited* (to be discarded).

Pseudocode 7: Algorithm D

Same as Pseudocode 3, except line 15 is changed as follows:

15   **set** all *temporarily visited* cells and arcs to *permanently visited*

4 P Systems

We use a refined version of the *simple P module*, as defined in [4], where all cells share the same state and rule sets, extended with generic rules using complex symbols [9] and *matrix* organized rules (proposed here).

Definition 1 (Simple P module). A simple P module with duplex channels is a system $\Pi = (V, E, Q, O, R)$, where V is a finite set of cells; E is a set of structural *parent-child digraph* arcs between cells (functioning as *duplex* channels); Q is a finite set of states; O is a finite non-empty alphabet of symbols; and R is a finite set of multiset rewriting rules (further organized, as described below, in a matrix format).

In this paper, all components of a P module, i.e. V, E, Q, O and R, are immutable. Each cell, $\sigma_i \in V$, has the initial configuration (S_{i0}, w_{i0}), and the current configuration (S_i, w_i), where $S_{i0} \in Q$ is the initial state; $S_i \in Q$ is the current state; $w_{i0} \in O^*$ is the initial multiset of symbols; and $w_i \in O^*$ is the current multiset of symbols. The general form of a rule in R is:

$$S \ x \rightarrow_\alpha S' \ x' \ (y)\beta_\gamma \ldots \ | \ z \ \neg \ z',$$

where: $S, S' \in Q$, $x, x', y, z, z' \in O^*$, $\alpha \in \{\texttt{min}, \texttt{max}\}$, $\beta \in \{\uparrow, \downarrow, \updownarrow\}$, $\gamma \in V \cup \{\forall\}$ and ellipses ($\ldots$) indicate possible repetitions of the last parenthesized item; state S is known as the rule's *starting* state and state S' as its *target* state.

For cell σ_i in configuration (S_i, w_i), a rule $S \ x \rightarrow_\alpha S' \ x' \ (y)\beta_\gamma \ldots \ | \ z \ \neg \ z' \in R$ is applicable if $S = S_i$, $xz \subseteq w_i$, $z' \cap w_i = \emptyset$ and either (a) no other rule was previously applied, in the same step, or (b) all rules previously applied, in the same step, have indicated the same target state, S'. When applied, this rule consumes multiset x and fixes, if not already fixed, the target state to S'. Multiset x', also known as the "here" multiset, remains in the same cell;

in our *matrix* inspired formalism, x' becomes *immediately* available to other rules subsequently applied in the same step. Multiset y is a message *queued* and sent, at the end of the current step, as indicated by the transfer operator β_γ. β's arrow indicates the transfer direction: ↑—to parents; ↓—to children; ↕—in both directions. γ indicates the distribution form: ∀—a broadcast; a *structural neighbour*, $\sigma_j \in V$—a unicast (to this neighbour). Multiset z is a *promoter* and z' is an *inhibitor*, which enables and disables the rule, respectively, without being consumed [12]. Operator α describes the rewriting mode. In the *minimal* mode, an applicable rule is applied once. In the *maximal* mode, an applicable rule is applied as many times as possible.

Matrix Structured Rulesets: We use matrix structured rulesets, which are inspired by matrix grammars with appearance checking [6]. Ruleset R is organized as a *matrix*, i.e. a list of *vectors*: $R = (R_1, \ldots, R_m)$, $1 \leq m$, where vectors are listed from high-to-low priorities; all rules in a vector *share* the same *starting state*. Each vector R_i is a sequence of rules, $R_i = (R_{i,1}, \ldots, R_{i,m_i})$, $1 \leq m_i$, where rules are listed from high-to-low priorities. The matrix semantics combines a *strong priority* for vectors and a version of *weak priority* for rules inside a vector. Pseudocode 8 shows how ruleset R is applied.

A vector is applicable if at least one of its rules is applicable. In a given vector, R_i, rules are considered for application according to their (weak-like) priority order: (a) if applicable, a higher priority rule is applied before considering the next lower priority rule; (b) otherwise (if not applicable), a higher priority rule is silently ignored and the next priority rule is considered.

After a rule is applied, "here" symbols become *immediately available* for the next rule (in the same vector), while outgoing messages are queued until the end of the step (until all rules in the vector are considered). This is the difference with the classical weak priority rule, where "here" symbols do not become available until the end of the step, thus cannot be used by the next priority rule.

Vectors are considered for application in their (strong) priority order: (a) if applicable, a higher priority vector is applied and all lower priority vectors are ignored (for the current step); (b) otherwise (if not applicable), a higher priority vector is silently ignored and the next priority vector is considered. A *step* ends (1) after the application of the highest priority applicable vector, if any (this is an *active* step) or (2) when no vector is applicable (this is an *idle* step).

As a special case, the cell *stops* when it enters a state with no associated vectors, also known as a *final state*. Under this convention, a P system algorithm terminates after all cells enter a final state.

Pseudocode 8: Matrix structured ruleset application

```
1  Input: a P module, Π = (V, E, Q, O, R)
2         R = (R₁, ... Rₘ), 1 ≤ m, and Rᵢ = (R_{i,1}, ..., R_{i,mᵢ}), 1 ≤ mᵢ
3  applied = false
4  for i = 1 to m
5    for j = 1 to mᵢ
6      if R_{i,j} is applicable then
7        apply R_{i,j}: "here" symbols become immediately available
```

```
 8              outgoing messages are queued
 9         applied = true
10       endif
11     endfor
12     if applied then
13       send all queued messages
14       break
15     endif
16   endfor
```

Complex Symbols: While atomic symbols seem sufficient for many theoretical studies (e.g, computational completeness), complex algorithms need adequate complex data structures. We enhance our initial vocabulary, by recursive composition of *elementary symbols* from O into *complex symbols*, which are compound terms of the form: $t(i, \dots)$, where (1) t is an *elementary symbol* representing the functor; (2) i can be (a) an *elementary* symbol, (b) another *complex* symbol, (c) a *free variable* (open to be bound, according to the cell's current configuration), (d) a *multiset* of elementary and complex symbols and free variables.

We often abbreviate complex symbols by using subscripts for term arguments. The following are examples of complex symbols, where a, b, c, d, e, f are elementary symbols and i, j, X are free variables (assuming that these are not listed among elementary symbols): $b(2) = b_2$, $c(i) = c_i$, $d(i, j) = d_{i,j}$, $e(a^2b^3)$, $f(j, c^5) = f_j(c^5)$, $f(j, Xc) = f_j(Xc)$.

Besides modelling complex data structures, such as lists, stacks, trees and dictionaries, or emulating procedure calls, complex symbols are useful for representing and processing any number of cell IDs with a fixed vocabulary. Thus, complex symbols allow the design of *fixed-size* P system algorithms, i.e. algorithms having a fixed number of rules, which does not depend on the number of cells in the underlying P systems.

Here we assume that each cell σ_i is "blessed" with a unique complex *cell ID* symbol, $\iota(i)$, typically abbreviated as ι_i, which is exclusively used as an *immutable promoter*.

Generic Rules: To process complex symbols, we use high-level generic rules, which are *instantiated* using *free variable* matching [1]. A generic rule is identified by an extended version of the classical rewriting mode, in fact, a combined *instantiation.rewriting* mode, where (1) the *instantiation* mode is one of {min, max, dyn} and (2) the *rewriting* mode is one of {min, max}.

The instantiation mode indicates how many instance rules are conceptually generated: (a) the mode min indicates that the generic rules is nondeterministically instantiated only *once*, if possible; (b) the mode max indicates that the generic rule is instantiated as *many* times as possible, without *superfluous* instances (i.e. without duplicates or instances which are not applicable); (c) the newly proposed mode dyn indicates a dynamic instantiation mode, which will be described later. The rewriting mode indicates how each instantiated rule is applied (as in the classical framework).

As an example, consider a system where cell σ_7 contains multiset $f_2 f_3{}^2 v$, and the generic rule ρ_α, where $\alpha \in \{\texttt{min.min, min.max, max.min, max.max}\}$ and i and j are free variables:

$$(\rho_\alpha)\ S_{20}\ f_j\ \rightarrow_\alpha\ S_{20}\ (b_i)\updownarrow_j\ |\ v\ \iota_i$$

1. $\rho_{\texttt{min.min}}$ nondeterministically generates *one* of the following rule instances:

$$S_{20}\ f_2\ \rightarrow_{\texttt{min}}\ S_{20}\ (b_7)\updownarrow_2$$
$$S_{20}\ f_3\ \rightarrow_{\texttt{min}}\ S_{20}\ (b_7)\updownarrow_3$$

2. $\rho_{\texttt{min.max}}$ nondeterministically generates *one* of the following rule instances:

$$S_{20}\ f_2\ \rightarrow_{\texttt{max}}\ S_{20}\ (b_7)\updownarrow_2$$
$$S_{20}\ f_3\ \rightarrow_{\texttt{max}}\ S_{20}\ (b_7)\updownarrow_3$$

3. $\rho_{\texttt{max.min}}$ generates *both* following rule instances:

$$S_{20}\ f_2\ \rightarrow_{\texttt{min}}\ S_{20}\ (b_7)\updownarrow_2$$
$$S_{20}\ f_3\ \rightarrow_{\texttt{min}}\ S_{20}\ (b_7)\updownarrow_3$$

4. $\rho_{\texttt{max.max}}$ generates *both* following rule instances:

$$S_{20}\ f_2\ \rightarrow_{\texttt{max}}\ S_{20}\ (b_7)\updownarrow_2$$
$$S_{20}\ f_3\ \rightarrow_{\texttt{max}}\ S_{20}\ (b_7)\updownarrow_3$$

In a *matrix* organized ruleset, if a generic rule using the **max** instantiation mode generates more than one simple rule, then all generated rules take the generic rule's place in the vector, in some *nondeterministic* order.

Like **max**, **dyn** instantiation mode has the potential to generate any number of rules (depending on the actual cell contents). Like **min**, **dyn** starts by generating one possible instance. However, after the generated rule is applied, **dyn** repeats the generation process, until either no new rules can be generated or a specified bound has been reached (by default, we use the cell's *degree*).

As an example, consider a cell containing the following list of complex symbols: $m(c^{i_0})$, $a_1(c^{i_1})$, $a_2(c^{i_2})$, $\ldots$, $a_n(c^{i_n})$, representing the values i_0, i_1, i_2, $\ldots$, i_n, respectively (where $n \geq 0$). The following generic rule, μ, determines the minimum over this sequence of values, in one single step:

$$(\mu)\ S_0\ m(XY)\ \rightarrow_{\texttt{dyn.min}}\ S_0\ m(X)\ |\ a_j(X)$$

Assume the particular scenario when $n = 3$, $i_0 = 4$, $i_1 = 7$, $i_2 = 2$, $i_3 = 3$, i.e. our cell contains $m(c^4)$, $a_1(c^7)$, $a_2(c^2)$, $a_3(c^3)$. First, μ instantiates *one* of the following rules, μ' or μ'':

$$(\mu')\ S_0\ m(c^2 c^2)\ \rightarrow_{\texttt{min}}\ S_0\ m(c^2)\ |\ a_2(c^2)$$
$$(\mu'')\ S_0\ m(c^3 c)\ \rightarrow_{\texttt{min}}\ S_0\ m(c^3)\ |\ a_3(c^3)$$

If generated, rule μ' transforms $m(c^4)$ into $m(c^2)$, which indicates the required minimum, $2 = \min(4, 7, 2, 3)$. Otherwise, rule μ'' transforms $m(c^4)$ into $m(c^3)$ and then the **dyn** mode instantiates another rule, μ''', which determines the required minimum:

$$(\mu''')\ S_0\ m(c^2c)\ \rightarrow_{\min}\ S_0\ m(c^2)\mid a_2(c^2)$$

The *matrix* organised rulesets and the **dyn** instantiation have been specifically designed to *level the playing field* between P systems and the usual frameworks used in distributed algorithms. Typically, distributed algorithms steps only count messaging rounds, ignoring local computations; therefore, a node in a distributed algorithm can determine the minimum over an arbitrary long local sequence in one single step.

The instantiation of generic rules is only *conceptual*: it explains their high-level semantics by mapping it to a simpler lower-level semantics. Moreover, this instantiation is also *ephemeral*: the generated lower-level rules are not supposed to exist past the end of the step. An actual P system implementation does not need to effectively use rule instantiation, as long as it can support the same high-level semantics by other means.

5 P System Specification

In this section, we present a directly executable P system specification of Algorithm D, having the *same distributed runtime complexity*. We omit Algorithm C, which is contained in its extension, Algorithm D.

The input digraph is given by the P system structure itself and the system is fully distributed, i.e. there is no central node and only local messaging channels (between structural neighbours) are allowed. Moreover, we consider that cells start without any kind of network topology awareness: cells do not know the identities of their children, not even their numbers.

The P specification has a challenging task: to fully formalize the informal description given by the high-level pseudocodes, completing all important details ignored by these, all this without increasing the time complexity. The specification needs to indicate how to build local digraph neighbourhood awareness, how to build and navigate over virtual residual digraphs, how to transform augmenting paths into edge-disjoint paths, how to discard "dead" cells, how to manage concurrent notification processes.

In particular, our pseudocodes use structural and virtual arcs between cells: in the corresponding P system specification, parent and child cells record their corresponding arc end-points, building a simple form of distributed routing tables (such as used in networking).

P Specification 1: Algorithm D

Input: All cells start with the same set of rules and without any topological awareness (they do not even know their local neighbours or even their numbers). All cells start in the same initial state, S_0. Initially, each cell, σ_i, contains an immutable cell ID symbol, ι_i. Additionally, the source cell, σ_s, and the target cell, σ_t, are decorated with symbols, s and t, respectively.

Output: All cells end in the *same final state*, S_{60}. On completion, all cells are *empty*, with exceptions: (1) The source cell, σ_s, and the target cell, σ_t, are still decorated with symbols, s and t, respectively; (2) The cells on edge-disjoint paths contain path link symbols, for predecessors, d'_j, and successors, d''_k.

Table 1 shows the initial and final cells' configurations for the P system based on the digraph illustrated in **Figure 1**.

Table 1. Initial and final configurations of P Specification 1, for Figure 1

Cell	σ_0	σ_1	σ_2	σ_3
Initial	$S_0\ \iota_0\ s$	$S_0\ \iota_1$	$S_0\ \iota_2$	$S_0\ \iota_3$
Final	$S_{60}\ \iota_0\ s\ d''_1\ d''_2\ d''_3$	$S_{60}\ \iota_1\ d'_0\ d''_4$	$S_{60}\ \iota_2\ d'_0\ d''_6$	$S_{60}\ \iota_3\ d'_0\ d''_5$
Cell	σ_4	σ_5	σ_6	σ_7
Initial	$S_0\ \iota_4$	$S_0\ \iota_5$	$S_0\ \iota_6$	$S_0\ \iota_7\ t$
Final	$S_{60}\ \iota_4\ d'_1\ d''_7$	$S_{60}\ \iota_5\ d'_3\ d''_7$	$S_{60}\ \iota_6\ d'_2\ d''_7$	$S_{60}\ \iota_7\ t\ d'_4\ d'_5\ d'_6$

The matrix R of P Specification 1 consists of fifteen vectors, informally presented in five groups, according to their functionality and applicability. Each vector implements an independent function, performed in one step. Symbols i, j and k are free variables related to cell IDs, symbols X and Y are free variables which match multisets; conventionally, we use i, j and k as subscripts and X and Y as arguments.

0. Shared start (S_0–S_2)

0.1.

1. $S_0\ n\ \rightarrow_{\text{min.min}}\ S_1\ (n)\updownarrow_\forall\ (n''_i)\uparrow_\forall\ (n'_i)\downarrow_\forall\ |\ \iota_i$
2. $S_0\ \rightarrow_{\text{min}}\ S_0\ n\ |\ s$

0.2.

1. $S_1\ \rightarrow_{\text{min}}\ S_2$

0.3.

1. $S_2\ n\ \rightarrow_{\text{max}}\ S_3$
2. $S_2\ \rightarrow_{\text{min}}\ S_3$

1. Initial differentiation (S_3): cf. Lines 3.4-7
1.1.

1. $S_3\ \rightarrow_{\text{min}}\ S_{10}\ f\ r_i(c)\ (w_i\ v_i)\updownarrow_\forall\ |\ \iota_i\ s$
2. $S_3\ \rightarrow_{\text{min}}\ S_{30}\ |\ t$
3. $S_3\ \rightarrow_{\text{min}}\ S_{20}$

2. Source cell (S_{10}): cf. Lines 3.8-14, 7.15, 3.20-22
2.1.

1. $S_{10}\ f\ \rightarrow_{\text{min.min}}$
   $S_{10}\ s''_k\ (f_i\ r_i(Xc))\downarrow_k\ |\ n''_k\ h(X)\ \iota_i\ \neg\ w_k\ v_k$
2. $S_{10}\ a\ s''_k\ n''_k\ \rightarrow_{\text{min.min}}\ S_{40}\ p\ d''_k\ (p)\updownarrow$
3. $S_{10}\ a\ \rightarrow_{\text{max}}\ S_{40}$
4. $S_{10}\ b_k\ s''_k\ n''_k\ \rightarrow_{\text{min.min}}\ S_{40}\ q\ (q)\updownarrow$
5. $S_{10}\ b_k\ \rightarrow_{\text{max.max}}\ S_{40}$
6. $S_{10}\ f\ \rightarrow_{\text{min.min}}\ S_{50}\ (g)\updownarrow$

3. Intermediate cells (S_{20})

3.1. Finalisation: cf. Line 3.22

1. $S_{20}\ g\ \rightarrow_{\text{min.min}}\ S_{50}\ (g)\updownarrow$

3.2. Frontier: cf. Lines 4.5-26

1. $S_{20}\ \rightarrow_{\text{min.min}}\ S_{20}\ r_i(X)(r_i(X))\updownarrow_\forall\ |f_j h(X)\iota_i$
2. $S_{20}\ f_j\ \rightarrow_{\text{min.min}}\ S_{20}\ v\ s'_j\ (v_i)\updownarrow_\forall\ f\ |\ \iota_i$
3. $S_{20}\ r_k(X)\ r'_k(Y)\ \rightarrow_{\text{min.min}}\ S_{20}\ r_k(Y)\ |\ b_k$
4. $S_{20}\ \rightarrow_{\text{min.min}}\ S_{20}(x)\downarrow_k\ |h(X)r'_k(XY)b_k\iota_i\neg w_k$
5. $S_{20}\ b_k\ s'_k\ \rightarrow_{\text{min.min}}\ S_{20}\ f\ z''_k$
6. $S_{20}\ b_k\ \rightarrow_{\text{max.max}}\ S_{20}$
7. $S_{20}\ \rightarrow_{\text{min.min}}\ S_{20}\ n(X)\ |\ h(X)\ f\ \iota_i$
8. $S_{20}\ n(XY)\ \rightarrow_{\text{dyn.min}}\ S_{20}\ n(X)|r_j(X)n''_j\ v_j f\iota_i$
9. $S_{20}\ n(XY)\ \rightarrow_{\text{dyn.min}}\ S_{20}\ n(X)|r_j(X)d'_j v_j f\iota_i$
10. $S_{20}\ n(X)\ r_i(XY)\ \rightarrow_{\text{min.min}}$
    $S_{20}\ r_i(X)\ (r'_i(X))\updownarrow_\forall\ |\ \iota_i$
11. $S_{20}\ f\ \rightarrow_{\text{min.min}}$
    $S_{20}\ v_k\ s''_k (f_i h(Xc))\downarrow_k\ |\iota_i\ n''_k\ h(X)\neg v_k\ d'_k\ d''_k$
12. $S_{20}\ f\ \rightarrow_{\text{min.min}}$
    $S_{20}\ v_k\ s''_k (f_i\ h(Xc))\uparrow_k\ |\iota_i\ d'_k\ h(X)\ \neg\ v_k$
13. $S_{20}\ f\ s'_j\ \rightarrow_{\text{min.min}}\ S_{20}\ (b_i)\updownarrow_j\ |\ \iota_i$
14. $S_{20}\ n(X)\ \rightarrow_{\text{min.min}}\ S_{20}$

3.3. Path confirmation: cf. Lines 3.16-19

1. $S_{20}\ a\ s'_j\ s''_k\ \rightarrow_{\text{min.min}}\ S_{20}\ d'_j\ d''_k\ (a)\updownarrow_j$
2. $S_{20}\ a\ \rightarrow_{\text{max}}\ S_{20}$
3. $S_{20}\ d'_k\ d''_k\ \rightarrow_{\text{min.min}}\ S_{20}$

3.4. End-of-round resets: cf. Lines 7.15, 3.20

1. $S_{20}\ \rightarrow_{\text{min}}\ S_{21}\ (q)\updownarrow_\forall\ |\ q$
2. $S_{20}\ \rightarrow_{\text{min}}\ S_{21}\ w\ |\ q\ v\ \neg\ w$
3. $S_{20}\ \rightarrow_{\text{max.max}}\ S_{21}\ w_k\ |\ q\ v_k\ \neg\ w_k$
4. $S_{20}\ z''_k\ \rightarrow_{\text{min}}\ S_{21}\ |\ q$
5. $S_{20}\ \rightarrow_{\text{min}}\ S_{21}\ (p)\updownarrow_\forall\ |\ p$

6. $S_{20}\ v\ \rightarrow_{\min}\ S_{21}\ |\ p\ \neg\ w$
7. $S_{20}\ v_k\ \rightarrow_{\max.\min}\ S_{21}\ |\ p\ \neg\ w_k$

3.5. Transit to the end of a search round

1. $S_{21}\ \rightarrow_{\min}\ S_{40}$

3.6. Update: cf. Lines 6.4-15

1. $S_{20}\ r_j(X)\ \rightarrow_{\max.\max}\ S_{20}\ |\ r_j(X)$
2. $S_{20}\ r'_j(X)\ \rightarrow_{\max.\max}\ S_{20}\ |\ r'_j(X)$
3. $S_{20}\ r_j(X)\ r'_j(Y)\ \rightarrow_{\min.\min}\ S_{20}\ r_j(Y)$
4. $S_{20}\ \rightarrow_{\min.\min}\ S_{20}\ n(X)\ |\ h(X)\ u_k\ \iota_i$
5. $S_{20}n(XY)\ \rightarrow_{\text{dyn.min}}\ S_{20}n(X)|r_j(X)n''_j v_j u_k \iota_i$
6. $S_{20}n(XY)\ \rightarrow_{\text{dyn.min}}\ S_{20}n(X)|r_j(X)d'_j v_j u_k \iota_i$
7. $S_{20}\ n(XY)\ r_i(X)\ \rightarrow_{\min.\min}$
   $S_{20}\ r_i(XY)\ (r'_i(XY)\ u_i)\updownarrow_\forall\ |u_k\ n''_k\ v_k\ \iota_i\neg w$
8. $S_{20}\ n(XY)\ r_i(X)\ \rightarrow_{\min.\min}$
   $S_{20}\ r_i(XY)\ (r'_i(XY)\ u_i)\updownarrow_\forall\ |u_k\ d'_k\ v_k\ \iota_i\neg w$
9. $S_{20}\ n(X)\ \rightarrow_{\min.\min}\ S_{20}$
10. $S_{20}\ u_k\ \rightarrow_{\min.\min}$
    $S_{20}\ (x)\updownarrow_k\ |\ h(X)\ r_k(XY)\ \iota_i\ \neg\ w_k\ w$
11. $S_{20}\ u_k\ \rightarrow_{\max.\max}\ S_{20}$

3.7. Discard: cf. Lines 5.3-15

1. $S_{20}\ z''_k\ \rightarrow_{\max.\min}\ S_{20}\ (x)\updownarrow_k\ |\ x\ \iota_i\ \neg\ w_k$
2. $S_{20}\ x\ \rightarrow_{\min.\min}$
   $S_{20}\ w\ r_i(\infty)\ (w_i\ r'_i(\infty)\ u_i)\updownarrow_\forall\ |\ \iota_i\ \neg\ w$
3. $S_{20}\ z''_k\ \rightarrow_{\max.\max}\ S_{20}\ |\ w$
4. $S_{20}\ s'_j\ s''_k\ \rightarrow_{\min.\min}\ S_{20}\ (b_i)\updownarrow_j\ |\ r_i(X)\ w\ \iota_i$

4. Target cell (S_{30}): cf. Line 4.4

4.1.

1. $S_{30}\ g\ \rightarrow_{\min.\min}\ S_{40}\ (g)\updownarrow$
2. $S_{30}\ f_j\ \rightarrow_{\min.\min}\ S_{30}\ d'_j\ (a)\downarrow_j$
3. $S_{30}\ \rightarrow_{\min}\ S_{40}\ |\ q$
4. $S_{30}\ \rightarrow_{\min}\ S_{40}\ |\ p$

5. All cells (S_{40}, S_{50})

5.1. End of each search round

1. $S_{40}\ v_k\ \rightarrow_{\max.\max}\ S_{40}\ |\ s$
2. $S_{40}\ v_k\ \rightarrow_{\max.\max}\ S_{40}\ |\ t$
3. $S_{40}\ u_j\ \rightarrow_{\max.\max}\ S_{40}$
4. $S_{40}\ c_l\ \rightarrow_{\max.\max}\ S_{40}$
5. $S_{40}\ r_j(X)\ \rightarrow_{\max.\max}\ S_{40}$
6. $S_{40}\ r'_j(X)\ \rightarrow_{\max.\max}\ S_{40}$
7. $S_{40}\ a\ \rightarrow_{\max}\ S_{40}$
8. $S_{40}\ q\ \rightarrow_{\max}\ S_{40}$
9. $S_{40}\ p\ \rightarrow_{\max}\ S_{40}$
10. $S_{40}\ \rightarrow_{\min}\ S_3$

5.2. End of the algorithm

1. $S_{50}\ g\ \rightarrow_{\max}\ S_{50}$
2. $S_{50}\ n'_j\ \rightarrow_{\max.\min}\ S_{50}$
3. $S_{50}\ n''_k\ \rightarrow_{\max.\min}\ S_{50}$
4. $S_{50}\ w_k\ \rightarrow_{\max.\min}\ S_{50}$
5. $S_{50}\ v_k\ \rightarrow_{\max.\min}\ S_{50}$
6. $S_{50}\ z''_k\ \rightarrow_{\max.\min}\ S_{50}$
7. $S_{50}\ w\ \rightarrow_{\max}\ S_{50}$
8. $S_{50}\ v\ \rightarrow_{\max}\ S_{50}$
9. $S_{50}\ \rightarrow_{\min}\ S_{60}$

Cell σ_i uses the following symbols to record its relationships with its neighbouring cells, σ_j and σ_k: n'_j indicates a structural parent; n''_k indicates a structural child; d'_j indicates an edge-disjoint path predecessor (dp-predecessor); d''_k indicates an edge-disjoint path successor (dp-successor); s'_j indicates a current sp-predecessor; s''_k indicates a current sp-successor; z''_k indicates a st-successor; $r_j(c^m)$ records σ_j's reach-number, m (note that here j may indicate the current cell, i, or one of its neighbours).

Additionally, cell σ_i uses the following symbols to record its state: $h(c^m)$ records its depth, m; $n(c^m)$ is used to evaluate the minimum over its own depth and the reach-numbers of its temporarily visited structural children; v indicates that it is temporarily visited; w indicates that it is permanently visited; f indicates that it is the frontier cell.

Cell σ_i sends out messages consisting of the following symbols: f_i is the forward token; b_i is the backtrack token; v_i is the visited notification; w_i is the permanently visited notification; $r'_i(c^m)$ is its updated reach-number, m; x is the discarding notification; a is the path confirmation; q is the after-success reset; p is the after-failure reset; g is the finalise token.

Here we explain a small snippet, vector 3.2, which contains several critical rules for an intermediate cell, σ_i.

Note that (as indicated above), we use two distinct symbols to represent the *visit token*: a *forward token* and *backtrack token*. Each token carries the sender ID: f_i is the forward token sent by σ_i and b_i is the backtrack token sent by σ_i.

Rules 3.2.1–2 process an incoming *forward token*, f_j, from cell σ_j. If it is unvisited, $\neg v$, then cell σ_i (a) initialises its reach-number, $r_i(X)$, as the received depth, $h(X)$; (b) becomes visited, v; (c) records σ_j as its current sp-predecessor, s'_j; (d) broadcasts its visited notification, v_i, to all its neighbours, $\updownarrow_\forall$; and (e) becomes the *search frontier*, f.

Rules 3.2.4–7 process an incoming *backtrack token*, b_k, from cell σ_k. Cell σ_i (a) updates its record for σ_k's reach-number, $r_k(X)$; (b) sends a discarding no-tification to σ_k, if σ_k's reach-number is greater than σ_i's depth; (c) transforms its current sp-successor, s''_k, into a st-successor, z''_k; and (d) becomes the *search frontier*, f.

Rules 3.2.8–14 specify the behaviour of cell σ_i, after it becomes the *search frontier*, f. Rules 3.2.8–10 compute σ_i's reach-number as the *minimum* of its depth, $h(X)$, and the reach-numbers of its temporarily visited residual digraph children, i.e. temporarily visited structural children (n''_k and v_k) or temporarily visited dp-predecessors (d'_k and v_k). Rule 3.2.11 updates and broadcasts σ_i's reach-number, $r'_i(X)$, if this value decreases.

According to rule 3.2.12, if σ_k is an *unvisited structural child*, $n''_k \neg v_k$, that is not on an existing disjoint path, $\neg d'_k d''_k$, then σ_i (a) records σ_k as visited, v_k; (b) records σ_k as its current sp-successor, s''_k; and (c) sends its *forward token*, f_i, with an incremented depth, $h(Xc)$, to σ_k, over an outgoing structural arc, $\downarrow_k$ (i.e. over a direct arc).

If the conditions of rule 3.2.12 are not met (rules are applied in the weak priority order), then rule 3.2.13 is considered. According to rule 3.2.14, if σ_k is an *unvisited dp-predecessor*, $\neg v_k$ and d'_k, then σ_i (a) records σ_k as visited, v_k; (b) records σ_k as its current sp-successor, s''_k; and (c) sends its *forward token*, f_i, to σ_k, with an incremented depth, $h(Xc)$, over an incoming structural arc, $\uparrow_k$ (over a reverse arc).

If the conditions of rules 3.2.12–13 are not met, then rule 3.2.14 is considered. According to rule 3.2.14, if σ_j is the *current sp-predecessor*, s'_j, then σ_i (a) removes s'_j, i.e. the existing record of σ_j as its current sp-predecessor; and (b) sends its *backtrack token*, b_i, to σ_j, over an outgoing or incoming structural arc, $\updownarrow_j$ (over a direct or reverse arc).

6   Runtime Performance

Consider a digraph with n cells and m arcs, where d is the outdegree of the source cell and f is the maximum number of edge-disjoint paths in a given scenario. In Algorithms B, C, C* and D, the source cell starts d search rounds. In each round, using a Cidon-type DFS, visited cells notify their neighbours, so the search does not revisit cells which were visited in the same round and thus completes in at most n steps. As earlier mentioned, all other housekeeping operations are performed in parallel with the main search, thus Algorithms B, C, C* and D all run in $O(nd)$ steps. In fact, because they discard all cells visited in *failed* rounds (which do not find augmenting paths), Algorithms B and D run in $O(nf)$ steps. We conjecture that a similar upperbound can also be found for C and C*.

Proposition 2. Algorithms C and C* run in $O(nd)$ steps; Algorithms B and D run in $O(nf)$ steps.

Table 2 compares the asymptotic complexity of our new Algorithms C, C* and D against our previous Algorithm B and the two other previous DFS-based algorithms used in this paper.

Table 2. Asymptotic worst-case complexity of distributed DFS-based algorithms

Algorithm	Runtime Complexity
Algorithm A (Ford-Fulkerson/DFS [5])	$O(mf)$ steps
Algorithm A* (Dinneen et al. [3])	$O(mf)$ steps
Algorithm B (our previous improvement [10])	$O(nf)$ steps
Algorithm C (here)	$O(nd)$ steps (?)
Algorithm C* (here)	$O(nd)$ steps (?)
Algorithm D (here)	$O(nf)$ steps

However, this theoretical estimation does not fully account for the detection and discarding of "dead" (permanently visited) cells. Therefore, using their executable P specifications, we experimentally compare Algorithms A, B, C, C* and D, on thirty digraphs with 100 cells and 300 arcs, generated using NetworkX [7]. Algorithm C* is a restricted version of Algorithm C, which, using our novel idea, only discards "dead" cells detected during *successful* rounds, intentionally refraining from discarding any "dead" cells detected during *failed* rounds. This way, Algorithm C* is the opposite of our previous Algorithm B, which, using a different idea, only discards "dead" cells detected during *failed* rounds.

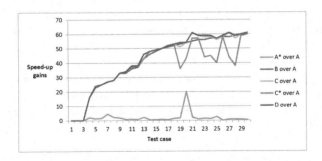

Fig. 3. Speed-up gains of Algorithms A*, B, C, C* and D over A for thirty test cases

Figure 3 shows the speed-up gains of Algorithms B, C, C* and D over A for our thirty test cases. On average, (1) Algorithm B is 41.0% faster than Algorithm A; (2) Algorithm C is 41.8% faster than Algorithm A; (3) Algorithm C* is 38.0% faster than Algorithm A; (4) Algorithm D is 42.1% faster than Algorithm A.

Analysing results (1–3), we found that the "dead" cells *detected* by Algorithms C and C* do cover all "dead" cells detected by Algorithm B, and even a few more. However, not all detected "dead" cells can be effectively *discarded* in "real-time", unless we allow these two algorithms to run longer (which we do not want). Thus, we can find (1) scenarios, such as shown in **Figure 2**, where Algorithms C and C* (and, of course, Algorithm D) outperform Algorithm B, and (2) scenarios, such as shown in **Figure 4**, where Algorithm B runs faster than Algorithms C and C* (but not than D).

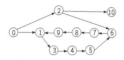

Fig. 4. An example, in which Algorithm B performs better than Algorithm C

In **Figure 4**, Algorithm C does detect all "dead" cells detected by Algorithm B, but, because of pruning propagating delays, does not effectively discard them in "real-time"; briefly, it does not show the same runtime performance.

For Algorithm C, when round #1 search path $\tau = \sigma_0.\sigma_1.\sigma_3.\sigma_4.\sigma_5.\sigma_6.\sigma_7.\sigma_8.\sigma_9$, backtracks to the source cell, σ_0, cells $\sigma_i, i \in \{1\} \cup [3, 9]$ can be discarded, because their reach-numbers are greater than $\sigma_0.\mathtt{depth} = 0$. Cell σ_0 triggers a discarding notification, which follows the *same path* as the backtracked search τ. In round #2, the *new* search path τ', $\tau' = \sigma_0.\sigma_2$ visits σ_6 *before* this cell receives its due discarding notification and then continues to σ_7 and further. Later, cell σ_6 receives its due discarding notification (started in round #1), discards itself and sends an overdue backtrack token to σ_2, which starts looking for other directions to continue path τ'. However, several steps have been lost exploring "dead" nodes (which were not aware of this). Finally, after this mentioned delay, the search path τ' reaches σ_{10}, $\tau' = \sigma_0.\sigma_2.\sigma_{10}$, and becomes a new augmenting path.

For Algorithm B, the round #1 search path, τ, follows the same route as in Algorithm C. When τ backtracks to σ_0, Algorithm B initiates an after-failure reset, which is propagated as a *broadcast*, travelling on *shortest paths*, reaching σ_6 on path $\sigma_0.\sigma_2.\sigma_6$. When the immediately following round #2 search path τ' reaches σ_2, $\tau' = \sigma_0.\sigma_2$, it avoids σ_6, which is already discarded. In the next step, the search path τ' reaches σ_{10}, $\tau' = \sigma_0.\sigma_2.\sigma_{10}$, and becomes a new augmenting path, faster than in Algorithm C.

In this example, due to its pruning propagating delay, Algorithm C shows worse performance than Algorithm B: in their executable P specification, Algorithm C requires 46 steps, while Algorithm B takes only 41 steps.

In **Figure 2**, Algorithm C outperforms Algorithm B. For Algorithm C, when the round #1 search path, τ, backtracks to σ_3 (see (d)), σ_6 can be discarded and is sent a discarding notification. Later, when τ backtracks to σ_2 (see (e)), σ_3, σ_4 and σ_5 can be discarded and are sent discarding notifications. All these discarding notifications reach their targets before the start of the next round. Thus, a round #2 search path, τ', will not (needlessly) probe σ_4 and its descendants.

In contrast, Algorithm B, which uses a different idea, cannot detect "dead" cells during successful rounds. Its round #1 search path, τ, follows the same route as in Algorithm C; however, without triggering any discarding notification. Therefore, a round #2 search path, τ', will needlessly visit again cells σ_4, σ_5, σ_3 and σ_6. In their executable P specification, Algorithm C takes 30 steps, while Algorithm B takes 43 steps.

7   Conclusions

We presented two new distributed DFS-based algorithms, Algorithms C and D, for solving the edge-disjoint path problem in digraphs. Using a novel idea, Algorithm C discards "dead" cells detected during both successful and failed search branches. By combining Algorithm C and our previous Algorithm B [10], which discards "dead" cells detected during failed rounds, Algorithm D discards all "dead" cells that are detected by both B and C.

We first described our distributed algorithms using informal high-level pseudocodes and then we provided an equivalent directly executable formal P specification. Our P systems use high-level generic rules organised in a newly proposed matrix-like structure and with a new **dyn** instantiation mode. The resulting P systems have a reasonably fixed-sized ruleset, i.e. the number of rules does not depend on the number of cells, and achieve the same runtime complexity as the corresponding distributed algorithms.

Experimentally, on a series of random digraphs, all our algorithms seem to show very significant speed-up over the classical Algorithm A and its improved version, Algorithm A*. Interestingly, despite using a different idea, our new algorithms seem to have a similar performance with our previous Algorithm B; in fact, on purely *random* digraphs, Algorithms C and D seem to be marginally faster than Algorithm B.

On the other side, one can construct many sample scenarios where Algorithms C and D vastly outperform Algorithm B and also many sample scenarios where Algorithm B outperforms Algorithm C (but not Algorithm D).

Several interesting questions remain open. Can these results be extrapolated to digraphs with different characteristics, such as size, average node degree, node degree distribution? Will these results remain valid for symmetric digraphs, i.e., undirected graphs? Can we find improved versions of these algorithms for solving the undirected graph problem? How relevant are these algorithms and results for real-life networks, such as transportation networks or other networks which show some kind of clustering? Are there well defined practical (non-random) scenarios where one could recommend one of the algorithm over another? Can we apply similar optimisations to BFS-based algorithms for solving the edge-disjoint paths problem? What are practical strengths and limits of P systems based on our matrix structured generic rules?

Acknowledgment. Two of the authors (R. Nicolescu and H. Wu) wish to thank the assistance received via the University of Auckland FRDF grant 9843/3626216.

References

1. Bălănescu, T., Nicolescu, R., Wu, H.: Asynchronous P systems. International Journal of Natural Computing Research 2(2), 1–18 (2011)
2. Cidon, I.: Yet another distributed depth-first-search algorithm. Inf. Process. Lett. 26, 301–305 (1988)
3. Dinneen, M.J., Kim, Y.B., Nicolescu, R.: Edge- and vertex-disjoint paths in P modules. In: Ciobanu, G., Koutny, M. (eds.) Workshop on Membrane Computing and Biologically Inspired Process Calculi, pp. 117–136 (2010)
4. Dinneen, M.J., Kim, Y.-B., Nicolescu, R.: A Faster P Solution for the Byzantine Agreement Problem. In: Gheorghe, M., Hinze, T., Păun, G., Rozenberg, G., Salomaa, A. (eds.) CMC 2010. LNCS, vol. 6501, pp. 175–197. Springer, Heidelberg (2010)
5. Ford Jr., L.R., Fulkerson, D.R.: Maximal flow through a network. Canadian Journal of Mathematics 8, 399–404 (1956)
6. Freund, R., Păun, G.: A variant of team cooperation in grammar systems. Journal of Universal Computer Science 1(2), 105–130 (1995)
7. Hagberg, A.A., Schult, D.A., Swart, P.J.: Exploring Network Structure, Dynamics, and Function using NetworkX. In: Varoquaux, G., Vaught, T., Millman, J. (eds.) 7th Python in Science Conference (SciPy), pp. 11–15 (2008)
8. Karp, R.M.: Reducibility Among Combinatorial Problems. In: Miller, R.E., Thatcher, J.W. (eds.) Complexity of Computer Computations, pp. 85–103. Plenum Press (1972)
9. Nicolescu, R.: Parallel and Distributed Algorithms in P Systems. In: Gheorghe, M., Păun, G., Rozenberg, G., Salomaa, A., Verlan, S. (eds.) CMC 2011. LNCS, vol. 7184, pp. 35–50. Springer, Heidelberg (2012)
10. Nicolescu, R., Wu, H.: New solutions for disjoint paths in P systems. Natural Computing, 1–15 (2012), doi:10.1007/s11047-012-9342-9
11. Păun, G.: Computing with membranes. Journal of Computer and System Sciences 61(1), 108–143 (2000)
12. Păun, G., Rozenberg, G., Salomaa, A.: The Oxford Handbook of Membrane Computing. Oxford University Press, Inc., New York (2010)
13. Tel, G.: Introduction to Distributed Algorithms. Cambridge University Press (2000)

A New Approach for Solving SAT by P Systems with Active Membranes*

Zsolt Gazdag and Gábor Kolonits

Department of Algorithms and Their Applications
Faculty of Informatics
Eötvös Loránd University
{gazdagzs,kolomax}@inf.elte.hu

Abstract. In this paper we give two families of P systems with active membranes that can solve the satisfiability problem of propositional formulas in linear time in the number of propositional variables occurring in the input formula. These solutions do not use polarizations of the membranes or non-elementary membrane division but use separation rules with relabeling. The first solution is a uniform one, but it is not polynomially uniform. The second solution, which is based on the first one, is a polynomially semi-uniform solution.

Keywords: Membrane computing; P systems; SAT problem.

1 Introduction

P systems are biologically inspired computational models introduced in [8] (for a comprehensive guide see e.g. [10]). A widely investigated variant of these systems are P systems with active membranes [9]. Here the P systems have the possibility of dividing elementary membranes which, combined with the maximal parallelism presented in these models, can yield exponential workspace in linear time. This feature is commonly used in efficient solutions of NP complete problems, e.g. in the solution of the satisfiability problem of propositional formulas (SAT). SAT is probably the best known NP-complete decision problem; the question is whether a given propositional formula in conjunctive normal form (CNF) is satisfiable.

Solving SAT efficiently by P systems with active membranes is a widely investigated area of membrane computing (see e.g. [1], [2], [4], [7], [9], and [12]). These solutions differ, for example, in the types of the rules employed, the number of possible polarizations of the membranes, and the derivation strategy (maximal or minimal parallelism - this latter concept was introduced in [3]). On the other hand, these solutions commonly work in a way where all possible truth valuations of the input formula are created and then a satisfying one (if it exists) is chosen.

---

* This research was supported by the project TÁMOP-4.2.1/B-09/1/KMR-2010-003 of Eötvös Loránd University.

E. Csuhaj-Varjú et al. (Eds.): CMC 2012, LNCS 7762, pp. 195–207, 2013.

In these works the used families of P systems are constructed in a polynomially (semi-)uniform way. This means that the P systems in these families can be constructed in polynomial time by a deterministic Turing machine from the size of the input formula (in the uniform case) or from the formula itself (in the semi-uniform case). The size of the input formula is usually described by the number n of distinct variables and the number m of clauses of the formula. (For more details on polynomially (semi-)uniform families of P systems please refer to [11] or [12].)

The P systems introduced in the above works can solve SAT in polynomial time in $n + m$. In particular, in [4] SAT is solved in linear time in n (i.e., the number of steps of the system is independent from m), but there division of non-elementary membranes is allowed, and the derivation strategy is minimally parallel instead of the commonly used maximal parallel one.

In this paper we give two families of P systems that can solve SAT in linear time in n. Our motivation was to give solutions where the number of the computation steps is independent from the number of the clauses in the input formula and the systems do not use non-elementary membrane division. Our first solution is a uniform one, but the constructed P systems have exponential number of objects and rules in n, i.e., this solution is not polynomially uniform. On the other hand, our second solution, which is based on the first one, is a polynomially semi-uniform solution.

Clearly, it is desirable that a solution of SAT by a P system be polynomially (semi-)uniform. Indeed, in a non-polynomially (semi-)uniform solution there is a possibility of computing the satisfiability of the input formula already during the construction of the P system. If this is the case, then SAT is in fact solved during the construction of the P systems, and not by the P systems itself. To demonstrate that we do not use such a "misleading" construction, we briefly describe the method that we use in our uniform solution.

Let φ be a formula in CNF over n variables. Then there is an equivalent formula φ' in CNF such that every clause of φ' contains every variable of φ negated or without negation. Such clauses are called complete clauses. It can be seen that φ' is satisfiable if and only if it does not contain every possible complete clause over n variables. We will show that our P systems can create φ' from φ and decide if φ' contains every complete clauses over n variables in linear number of steps. Clearly, the cardinality of the set of all complete clauses over n variables is exponential in n. This implies that the cardinality of the object alphabet of our P systems in our uniform solution is also exponential in n. Thus these P systems can not be constructed in polynomial time in n, even if the number m of the clauses in the input formula is polynomial in n (notice that, in general, m can be exponential in n as well).

Despite the fact that the above described systems cannot be constructed in a polynomially uniform way, we think that they are still interesting since, as we have seen above, the construction of these systems does not compute the satisfiability of the input and the solution is uniform. This latter property yields that once we have constructed our P system for a given number n, then we can use it for deciding the satisfiability of every formula having n distinct variables. Moreover, the decision is done in linear number of steps in n and to achieve this efficiency we did not have to use non-elementary membrane division.

Our other solution is a polynomially semi-uniform one based on the uniform solution described above. Here we implemented a method that does not create every possible complete clause but uses several copies of the original clauses of the input formula. The price of this improvement is that we could not make this solution to be uniform.

This paper is an improved version of the paper [5]. The present paper is organised as follows. In Sect. 2 we give the necessary definitions and preliminary results. Sections 3 contains our families of P systems, and Sect. 4 presents some conclusions and remarks.

2 Definitions

Alphabets, Words, Multisets. An *alphabet* Σ is a nonempty and finite set of symbols. The elements of Σ are called *letters*. Σ^* denotes the set of all finite *words* (or *strings*) over Σ, including the *empty word* ε. We will use *multisets* of objects in the membranes of a P system. As usual, these multisets will be represented by strings over the object alphabet of the P system.

The SAT Problem. Let $X = \{x_1, x_2, x_3, \ldots\}$ be a recursively enumerable set of *propositional variables* (*variables*, to be short), and, for every $n \in \mathbb{N}$, where $\mathbb{N}$ denotes the set of natural numbers, let $X_n := \{x_1, \ldots, x_n\}$. An *interpretation of the variables in X_n* (or just an *interpretation* if X_n is clear from the context) is a function $\mathcal{I} : X_n \to \{true, false\}$.

The variables and their negations are called *literals*. A *clause* C is a disjunction of finitely many pairwise different literals satisfying the condition that there is no $x \in X$ such that both x and $\bar{x}$ occur in C, where $\bar{x}$ denotes the negation of x. The set of all clauses over the variables in X_n is denoted by $\mathcal{C}_n$. A *formula in conjunctive normal form* (CNF) is a conjunction of finitely many clauses. We will often treat formulas in CNF as finite sets of clauses, where the clauses are finite sets of literals. A clause $C \in \mathcal{C}_n$ is called a *complete clause* if, for every $x \in X_n$, $x \in C$ or $\bar{x} \in C$. Let $Form$ be the set of all formulas in CNF over the variables in X and, for every $n \in \mathbb{N}$, let $Form_n$ be the set of those formulas in $Form$ that have variables in X_n. It is easy to see that $Form$ is a recursively enumerable set (notice that, for a given $n \in \mathbb{N}$, $Form_n$ is a finite set).

Let $\varphi \in Form_n$ ($n \in \mathbb{N}$) and let $\mathcal{I}$ be an interpretation for φ. We say that $\mathcal{I}$ *satisfies* φ, denoted by $\mathcal{I} \models \varphi$, if φ evaluates to *true* under the truth assignment defined by $\mathcal{I}$. Note that $\mathcal{I} \models \varphi$ if and only if, for every $C \in \varphi$, $\mathcal{I} \models C$. We say that φ is satisfiable if there is an interpretation $\mathcal{I}$ such that $\mathcal{I} \models \varphi$. The SAT *problem* (boolean satisfiability problem of propositional formulas in CNF) can be defined as follows. Given a formula φ in CNF, decide whether or not there is an interpretation $\mathcal{I}$ such that $\mathcal{I} \models \varphi$.

Let $\varphi_1, \varphi_2 \in Form_n$ $(n \in \mathbb{N})$. We say that φ_1 and φ_2 are equivalent, denoted by $\varphi_1 \sim \varphi_2$, if, for every interpretation $\mathcal{I}$, $\mathcal{I} \models \varphi_1$ if and only if $\mathcal{I} \models \varphi_2$. Let $\varphi \in Form$. The set of variables occurring in φ, denoted by $var(\varphi)$, is defined by $var(\varphi) := \{x \in X \mid \exists C \in \varphi : x \in C \text{ or } \bar{x} \in C\}$. For a clause $C \in \mathcal{C}_n$ and a set $Y \subseteq X_n$ $(n \in \mathbb{N})$ such that $var(C) \cap Y = \emptyset$, let C_Y be the following set of clauses. Assume that $Y = \{x_{i_1}, \ldots, x_{i_k}\}$ $(k \leq n, 1 \leq i_1 < \ldots < i_k \leq n)$. Then let $C_Y := \{C \cup \{l_1, \ldots, l_k\} \mid 1 \leq j \leq k : l_j \in \{x_{i_j}, \bar{x}_{i_j}\}\}$. For a formula $\varphi = \{C_1, \ldots, C_m\} \in Form_n$ $(m, n \in \mathbb{N})$, let $\varphi' := \bigcup_{C \in \varphi} C_Y$, where $Y := X_n - var(C)$.

The correctness of the P systems that we are going to construct to solve SAT is based on the following statement which can be easily proved by standard arguments of propositional logic (see also e.g. [6] for deciding SAT by means of complete clauses).

Proposition 1. *For a formula $\varphi = \{C_1, \ldots, C_m\} \in Form_n$ $(m, n \in \mathbb{N})$, φ' contains every complete clause in $\mathcal{C}_n$ if and only if φ is unsatisfiable.*

Proof. Let $\varphi := \{C_1, \ldots, C_m\} \in Form_n$ $(m, n \in \mathbb{N})$. We prove the above statement in two steps. First, we show that $\varphi \sim \varphi'$, then we show that φ' is unsatisfiable if and only if it contains every complete clause in $\mathcal{C}_n$.

To see that $\varphi \sim \varphi'$ we show that, for every interpretation $\mathcal{I}$, $\mathcal{I} \models \varphi$ if and only if $\mathcal{I} \models \varphi'$. Let $\mathcal{I}$ be an interpretation and assume first that $\mathcal{I} \models \varphi$. Let $C \in \varphi$. Then $\mathcal{I} \models C$ and, moreover, for every $C' \in C_Y$, where $Y = X_n - var(C)$, $var(C) \subseteq var(C')$. This clearly implies that, for every $C' \in C_Y$, $\mathcal{I} \models C'$. It follows then that $\mathcal{I} \models \varphi'$ as well.

Now assume that $\mathcal{I} \models \varphi'$. We show that $\mathcal{I} \models C$, for every $C \in \varphi$, which clearly implies that $\mathcal{I} \models \varphi$. Let $C \in \varphi$ and $Y := X_n - var(C)$. Assume that $Y = \{x_{i_1}, \ldots, x_{i_k}\}$ $(k \leq n, 1 \leq i_1 < \ldots < i_k \leq n)$. Let $C' := C \cup \{l_{i_1}, \ldots, l_{i_k}\}$ be that clause in C_Y which satisfies the following property. For every $1 \leq j \leq k$, $l_{i_j} = \bar{x}_{i_j}$ if $\mathcal{I}(x_{i_j}) = true$, and $l_{i_j} = x_{i_j}$ otherwise. Clearly, $\mathcal{I} \models C'$, but $\mathcal{I} \not\models \{l_{i_1}, \ldots, l_{i_k}\}$. This implies that $\mathcal{I}$ should satisfy C.

Next, we show that φ' is unsatisfiable if and only if it contains every complete clauses in $\mathcal{C}_n$. Assume first that φ' contains every complete clauses in $\mathcal{C}_n$ and let $\mathcal{I}$ be an arbitrary interpretation of the variables in X_n. Let $C' = \{l_1, \ldots, l_n\}$ be that clause in $\mathcal{C}_n$ which satisfies the following property. For every $1 \leq i \leq n$, $l_i = \bar{x}_i$ if $\mathcal{I}(x_i) = true$, and $l_i = x_i$ otherwise. Clearly $\mathcal{I} \not\models C'$ which, since $C' \in \varphi'$, means that $\mathcal{I} \not\models \varphi'$. Thus φ' is unsatisfiable.

Assume now that φ' does not contain every complete clauses and let $C' := \{l_1, \ldots, l_n\}$ be a clause that does not occur in φ'. Let $\mathcal{I}$ be the interpretation defined as follows. For every $1 \leq i \leq n$, let $\mathcal{I}(x_i) := true$ if $l_i = \bar{x}_i$, and let $\mathcal{I}(x_i) := false$ otherwise. It can be seen that, for every $C \in \varphi'$, there is a literal $l \in C$ such that $\mathcal{I}(l) = true$. It follows then that $\mathcal{I}$ satisfies every clause in φ'. Thus φ' is satisfiable which completes the proof.

P Systems with Active Membranes. We will use P systems with active membranes to solve SAT. In particular, we will use a model where a certain kind of separation rules is allowed. These separation rules have the possibility of changing the labels of the membranes involved. On the other hand, we will not use the polarizations of the membranes, thus we leave out this feature from the definition of these systems. The following is the formal definition of the P systems we will use (see also [10]).

A *(polarizationless) P system with active membranes* is a construct $\Pi = (O, H, \mu, w_1, \ldots, w_m, R)$, where:

- $m \geq 1$ (the *initial degree* of the system);
- O is the *alphabet of objects*;
- H is a finite set of *labels* for membranes;
- μ is a *membrane structure*, consisting of m membranes, labelled (not necessarily in a one-to-one manner) with elements of H;
- $w_1, \ldots, w_m$ are strings over O, describing the *multisets of objects* (every symbol in a string representing one copy of the corresponding object) placed in the m regions of μ;
- R is a finite set of *developmental rules*, of the following forms:
  (a) $[a \rightarrow v]_h$, for $h \in H, a \in O, v \in O^*$
      (object evolution rules, associated with membranes and depending on the label of the membranes, but not directly involving the membranes, in the sense that the membranes are neither taking part in the application of these rules nor are they modified by them);
  (b) $a[\ ]_h \rightarrow [b]_h$, for $h \in H, a, b \in O$
      (communication rules, sending an object into a membrane; the label cannot be modified);
  (c) $[a]_h \rightarrow [\ ]_h b$, for $h \in H, a, b \in O$
      (communication rules; an object is sent out of the membrane, possibly modified during this process; the label cannot be modified);
  (d) $[a]_h \rightarrow b$, for $h \in H, a, b \in O$
      (dissolving rules; in reaction with an object, a membrane can be dissolved, while the object specified in the rule can be modified);
  (e) $[a]_h \rightarrow [b]_h[c]_h$, for $h \in H, a, b, c \in O$
      (division rules for elementary membranes; in reaction with an object, the membrane is divided into two membranes with the same label; the object a specified in the rule is replaced in the two new membranes by (possibly new) objects b and c respectively, and the remaining objects are duplicated);
  (f) $[\ ]_{h_1} \rightarrow [K]_{h_2}[O - K]_{h_3}$, for $h_1, h_2, h_3 \in H, K \subset O$
      (2-separation rules for elementary membranes, with respect to a given set of objects; the membrane is separated into two new membranes with possibly different labels; the objects from each set of the partition of the set O are placed in the corresponding membrane).

As usual, Π works in a *maximal parallel* manner:

- In one step, any object of a membrane that can evolve must evolve, but one object can be used by only one rule of types (a)-(e);

- when some rules of type (b)-(f) can be applied to a certain membrane, then one of them must be applied, but a membrane can be the subject of only one rule of these rules during each step.

We say that Π is a *recognizing P system* if O has two designated objects *yes* and *no*, and every computation of Π halts and sends out to the environment either *yes* or *no*. We say that Π is a *recognizing P system with input* if (1) Π is a recognizing P system, (2) it has a designated input membrane i_0, and (3) a string w, called the *input of Π*, can be added to the system by placing it into the region i_0 in the initial configuration. A recognizing P system Π (with input) is called *deterministic* if it has only a single computation from its initial configuration to its unique halting configuration.

We say that *SAT can be solved in linear time by a uniform family $\Pi := (\Pi(i))_{i \in \mathbb{N}}$ of recognizing P systems with input*, if the following holds:

(1) for every $n \in \mathbb{N}$, $\Pi(n)$ can be constructed from n by a deterministic Turing machine in polynomial time in n;
(2) for a given formula $\varphi \in Form$ with size n ($n \in \mathbb{N}$), starting $\Pi(n)$ with a polynomial time encoding of φ in its input membrane, $\Pi(n)$ sends out to the environment *yes* if and only if φ is satisfiable;
(3) for every $n \in \mathbb{N}$, the computation of $\Pi(n)$ always halts in linear number of steps in n.

If in the above definition in condition (1) we do not require the Turing machine to be a polynomial time one, then we say that *SAT can be solved in weak linear time by Π*.

Now we give a similar definition corresponding semi-uniform families of recognizing P systems. We say that *SAT can be solved in linear time by a semi-uniform family $\Pi := (\Pi(\varphi))_{\varphi \in Form}$ of recognizing P systems* if, for every $\varphi \in Form$, the following holds:

(1) $\Pi(\varphi)$ can be constructed from φ by a deterministic Turing machine in polynomial time in the size of φ;
(2) $\Pi(\varphi)$ sends out to the environment *yes* if and only if φ is satisfiable;
(3) the computation of $\Pi(\varphi)$ always halts in linear number of steps in the size of φ.

For more details on complexity classes defined by (semi-)uniform families of P systems see e.g. [11] or [12].

3   The Main Results

Here we give our solutions for deciding SAT by P systems with active membranes. The first solution is a uniform but non-polynomial one; the second solution is a polynomially semi-uniform one. First, we discuss how we will encode the formulas in our P systems.

Encoding SAT Instances. Usually, when SAT is solved by a computation device, the formulas are encoded appropriately so that the model can process the formula. Clearly, the used encoding should be carried out efficiently, otherwise it is not ensured that the encoding phase does not compute also the satisfiability of the formulas. According to this, the encoding we use is rather trivial: we use symbols that are in one-to-one correspondence with the clauses in C_n ($n \in \mathbb{N}$). For every $n \in \mathbb{N}$, let O_n be an alphabet with a bijection between C_n and O_n. For a symbol $c \in O_n$, we denote the corresponding clause in C_n by $\hat{c}$. Thus, a formula $\varphi = \{C_1, \ldots, C_m\}$ ($m \in \mathbb{N}$) will be encoded in our membrane systems by the set of objects $cod(\varphi) := \{c_1, \ldots, c_m\} \subseteq O_n$, where, for every $1 \leq i \leq m$, $\hat{c}_i = C_i$. We will need a copy of the symbols in $cod(\varphi)$ thus we will also use the set $cod'(\varphi) := \{c' \mid c \in cod(\varphi)\}$.

The Uniform Solution. Here we define a uniform family $\Pi := (\Pi(i))_{i \in \mathbb{N}}$ of recognizer P systems with input that solves SAT in weak linear time.

Definition 1. *For every $n \in \mathbb{N}$, let $\Pi(n) := (O, H, \mu, w_1, w_2, w_3, R)$, where:*

- $O := O_n \cup \{d_1, \ldots, d_{n+3}, yes, no\}$;
- $H := \{1, \ldots, n+3\}$;
- $\mu := [[[\ ]_3]_2]_1$, *where the input membrane is* $[\ ]_3$;
- $w_1 := \varepsilon, w_2 := d_1$ *and* $w_3 := \varepsilon$;
- R *is the set of the following rules (in some cases we also give explanations of the presented rules):*

(a) $[c \rightarrow c_1 c_2]_{i+2}$, *for every* $1 \leq i \leq n$ *and* $c, c_1, c_2 \in O_n$ *with* $x_i, \bar{x}_i \notin \hat{c}$, $\hat{c}_1 = \hat{c} \cup \{x_i\}$ *and* $\hat{c}_2 = \hat{c} \cup \{\bar{x}_i\}$
(for every $1 \leq i \leq n$, these rules will replace those clauses in membrane $i+2$ that do not contain x_i or $\bar{x}_i$ by two other clauses, a clause that additionally contains x_i, and another one that contains $\bar{x}_i$);

(b) $[\ ]_{i+2} \rightarrow [K_i]_{i+3}[O - K_i]_{i+3}$, *for every* $1 \leq i \leq n$ *and* $K_i = \{c \in O_n \mid x_i \in \hat{c}\}$
(for every $1 \leq i \leq n$, these rules will separate the objects in membranes with label $i+2$ according to that whether the clauses represented by the objects contain x_i or not; the new membranes will have label $i+3$);

(c) $[d_i \rightarrow d_{i+1}]_2$, *for every* $1 \leq i \leq n+2$;

(d) $[c]_{n+3} \rightarrow \varepsilon$, *for every* $c \in O_n$ *such that $\hat{c}$ is a complete clause in C_n;*

(e) $d_{n+2}[\ ]_{n+3} \rightarrow [yes]_{n+3}$,
$[yes]_{n+3} \rightarrow [\ ]_{n+3} yes$,
$[yes]_2 \rightarrow [\ ]_2 yes$,
$[yes]_1 \rightarrow [\ ]_1 yes$;

(f) $[d_{n+2}]_2 \rightarrow [d_{n+3}]_2[no]_2$,
$[no]_2 \rightarrow [\ ]_2 no$,
$[no]_1 \rightarrow [\ ]_1 no$.

Next we give an example to demonstrate how the P systems defined above create new clauses from the input and separate them into new membranes.

Example 1. We show the working of $\Pi(3)$ on a formula in $Form_3$. For the better readability, we denote the variables x_1, x_2, x_3 by x, y and z, respectively. Moreover, the objects in O_3 are denoted by sequences of literals occurring in the corresponding clauses of the formula, i.e., the symbols in O_3 are now strings over the set of literals.

Let the input formula be $\varphi := \{\{x, y, z\}, \{\bar{x}\}, \{\bar{y}\}, \{\bar{z}\}\}$. Then $\Pi(3)$ is started with symbols $xyz, \bar{x}, \bar{y}, \bar{z}$ in the input membrane, thus at the beginning the initial configuration looks as follows:

$$[_{d_1} [[xyz, \bar{x}, \bar{y}, \bar{z}]_3]_2]_1.$$

In the first step, the system creates $x\bar{y}$ and $\bar{x}\bar{y}$ from $\bar{y}$, and $x\bar{z}$ and $\bar{x}\bar{z}$ from $\bar{z}$. Moreover, two new membranes with label 4 are created and the system puts $xyz, x\bar{y}$ and $x\bar{z}$ into the first new membrane and $\bar{x}, \bar{x}\bar{y}$ and $\bar{x}\bar{z}$ into the second one. Thus, after the first step the configuration of the system looks as follows:

$$[_{d_2} [[xyz, x\bar{y}, x\bar{z}]_4, [\bar{x}, \bar{x}\bar{y}, \bar{x}\bar{z}]_4]_2]_1.$$

Then, in the next step, the system creates the clauses $xy\bar{z}, x\bar{y}\bar{z}$ from $x\bar{z}, \bar{x}y, \bar{x}\bar{y}$ from $\bar{x}$, and $\bar{x}y\bar{z}, \bar{x}\bar{y}\bar{z}$ from $\bar{x}\bar{z}$. Moreover, two new membranes with label 5 are created from each membranes with label 4, and the symbols are separated into these new membranes. Thus, after the second step, the system has the following configuration:

$$[_{d_3} [[xyz, xy\bar{z}]_5, [x\bar{y}, x\bar{y}\bar{z}]_5, [\bar{x}y, \bar{x}y\bar{z}]_5, [\bar{x}\bar{y}, \bar{x}\bar{y}, \bar{x}\bar{y}\bar{z}]_5]_2]_1.$$

Finally, after the third step, the configuration of the system is:

$$[_{d_4} [[xyz]_6, [xy\bar{z}]_6, [x\bar{y}z]_6, [x\bar{y}\bar{z}, x\bar{y}\bar{z}]_6,$$
$$[\bar{x}yz]_6, [\bar{x}y\bar{z}, \bar{x}y\bar{z}]_6, [\bar{x}\bar{y}z, \bar{x}\bar{y}z]_6, [\bar{x}\bar{y}\bar{z}, \bar{x}\bar{y}\bar{z}, \bar{x}\bar{y}\bar{z}]_6]_2]_1.$$

In general, the computation of $\Pi(n)$ for some $n \in \mathbb{N}$, when the membrane with label 3 contains the string $c_1 \ldots c_m$ encoding a formula $\varphi = \{\hat{c}_1, \ldots, \hat{c}_m\} \in Form_n$ ($m \in \mathbb{N}$) can be described as follows:

- During the first step, rules in (a) replace in the membrane with label 3 every object c with the property that $\hat{c}$ does not contain x_1 or $\bar{x}_1$ with two objects representing the clauses $\hat{c} \cup \{x_1\}$ and $\hat{c} \cup \{\bar{x}_1\}$. In parallel to this step, a rule in (b) separates the resulting objects into new membranes with label 4, depending on whether the clauses represented by the objects contain x_1 or not. Moreover, in membrane with the label 2, the object d_1 evolves to d_2 by the corresponding rule in (c).
- After n steps, the membrane system contains 2^n membranes with label $n+3$. Each such membrane can contain an object in O_n corresponding to a complete clause in $\mathcal{C}_n$. At this point the computation can continue in two different cases.

Case 1:

- If each of the membranes with label $n + 3$ contains at least one object $c \in O_n$ such that $\hat{c}$ is a complete clause, then the system dissolves these membranes in one step by using the rules in (d). In parallel, d_{n+1} evolves to d_{n+2}.
- In the next step, using the first rule in (f), the system divides the membrane with label 2, and introduces the symbol *no*.
- In the last two steps, the symbol *no* goes out to the environment, and the computation halts.

Case 2:

- If there is at least one membrane with label $n + 3$ that does not contain an object $c \in O_n$ such that $\hat{c}$ is a complete clause, then only the first rule in (e) can be applied, introducing the symbol *yes* (notice that the division rule in (f) cannot be applied as the membrane with label 2 is not elementary in this case).
- In the last three steps of the system, the symbol *yes* goes out to the environment, and the computation halts.

Notice that the membranes with label $n + 3$ can contain objects representing complete clauses only.

It is not difficult to see that $\Pi(n)$ works correctly. Indeed, $\Pi(n)$ sends in every computation to the environment either the symbol *no* or the symbol *yes*. The symbol *no* can be introduced only in *Case 1* above, but in this case φ' must contain every complete clause in C_n, and it follows from Proposition 1 that φ is not satisfiable. On the other hand, *yes* can be introduced only in *Case 2*, but in this case there is a complete clause in C_n that does not occur in φ', which, again by Proposition 1 means that φ is satisfiable. Moreover, it is easy to see that, for every formula $\varphi \in Form_n$, $\Pi(n)$ halts in $n + 5$ steps. Thus we have the following theorem.

Theorem 1. *The SAT problem can be solved in weak linear time by a uniform family $\mathbf{\Pi} := (\Pi(i))_{i \in \mathbb{N}}$ of polarizationless recognizing P systems with input with the following properties: the elements of $\mathbf{\Pi}$ are deterministic, do not use non-elementary membrane division, and the size of an input formula is described by the number of variables occurring in the formula.*

The Semi-Uniform Solution. Here we give a polynomially semi-uniform family of recognizer P systems that solves SAT in linear time. This solution is strongly based on the family of P systems defined in Definition 1. Clearly, the main issue with a P system $\Pi(n)$ $(n \in \mathbb{N})$ of that family is that it can not be constructed in polynomial time in n. As we have mentioned, the reason is that $\Pi(n)$ creates complete clauses from the clauses of the input formula, and the number of these complete clauses can be exponential in n. On the other hand, one can note that the answer of $\Pi(n)$ depends only on whether or not every membrane with label $n + 3$ contains at least one object regardless of whether the set of these objects contains every complete clause or not. Thus, one way to turn

$\Pi(n)$ into a polynomially semi-uniform solution of SAT is to modify $\Pi(n)$ such that it does not create new objects representing clauses but reuses appropriately the original clauses of the input formula in every step of the computation. The following is the formal definition of a family of P systems where we implemented the above described idea.

Definition 2. *Let* $\Pi := (\Pi(\varphi))_{\varphi \in Form}$, *where* $\Pi(\varphi)$ *for some* $\varphi \in Form$ *is defined as follows.* $\Pi(\varphi) := (O, H, \mu, w_1, w_2, w_3, R)$, *where:*

- $O := cod(\varphi) \cup cod'(\varphi) \cup \{d_1, \ldots, d_{n+3}, yes, no\}$;
- $H := \{1, \ldots, n+3\}$;
- $\mu := [[[\ ]_3]_2]_1$;
- $w_1 := \varepsilon, w_2 := d_1$ *and* $w_3 := cod(\varphi)$;
- R *is the set of the following rules:*
    - (a1) $[c \to c']_{i+2}$, *for every* $1 \le i \le n$ *and* $c \in cod(\varphi)$ *with* $\bar{x}_i \in \hat{c}$
      (for every $1 \le i \le n$, *these rules replace in membrane* $i+2$ *every symbol* c *representing a clause which contains* $\bar{x}_i$ *by its primed version* c';
    - (a2) $[c' \to c]_{i+2}$, *for every* $1 \le i \le n$ *and* $c' \in cod'(\varphi)$ *with* $x_i \in \hat{c}$
      (for every $1 \le i \le n$, *these rules replace in membrane* $i+2$ *every symbol* c' *representing a clause which contains* x_i *by the symbol* c;
    - (a3) $[c \to cc']_{i+2}$ *and* $[c' \to cc']_{i+2}$ *for every* $1 \le i \le n$ *and* $c \in cod(\varphi)$ *with* $x_i, \bar{x}_i \notin \hat{c}$
      (for every $1 \le i \le n$, *these rules duplicate those symbols in membrane* $i+2$ *that represent such clauses which do not contain* x_i *or* $\bar{x}_i$;
    - (b) $[\ ]_{i+2} \to [K]_{i+3}[O - K]_{i+3}$, *for every* $1 \le i \le n$, *where* $K = cod(\varphi)$
      (for every $1 \le i \le n$, *these rules will separate the objects in membranes with label* $i+2$ *according to that whether they are primed or not;*
    - (c) $[d_i \to d_{i+1}]_2$, *for every* $1 \le i \le n+2$;
    - (d) $[c]_{n+3} \to \varepsilon$, *for every* $c \in cod(\varphi) \cup cod'(\varphi)$;
    - (e) $d_{n+2}[\ ]_{n+3} \to [yes]_{n+3}$,
      $[yes]_{n+3} \to [\ ]_{n+3}yes$,
      $[yes]_2 \to [\ ]_2 yes$,
      $[yes]_1 \to [\ ]_1 yes$;
    - (f) $[d_{n+2}]_2 \to [d_{n+3}]_2[no]_2$,
      $[no]_2 \to [\ ]_2 no$,
      $[no]_1 \to [\ ]_1 no$.

Now we give an example to make easier to follow the computations of the P systems defined above.

Example 2. Let us consider again Example 1 and the formula $\varphi = \{\{x, y, z\}, \{\bar{x}\}, \{\bar{y}\}, \{\bar{z}\}\}$ in it. Let $\Pi(\varphi)$ be the P system constructed in Definition 2 from φ. The initial configuration of $\Pi(\varphi)$ looks as follows:

$$[d_1 [[xyz, \bar{x}, \bar{y}, \bar{z}]_3]_2]_1.$$

In the first step xyz remains unchanged, $\bar{x}$ is marked with a prime, and from $\bar{y}$ and $\bar{z}$ the symbols, $\bar{y}, \bar{y}'$ and $\bar{z}, \bar{z}'$ are created, respectively. Then, in the same step, $\Pi(\varphi)$ separates the symbols in membrane 3 into the two new membranes according to that whether they are marked with a prime or not. Thus, after the first step the configuration of the system looks as follows:

$$[d_2\,[[xyz,\bar{y},\bar{z}]_4,[\bar{x}',\bar{y}',\bar{z}']_4]_2]_1.$$

In the second step, xyz and $\bar{y}'$ remain unchanged, $\bar{y}$ is marked with a prime, and $\bar{x}'$, $\bar{z}$ and $\bar{z}'$ are each rewritten to $\bar{x}\bar{x}'$, $\bar{z}\bar{z}'$, and $\bar{z}\bar{z}'$, respectively, by the corresponding rules in (a3). Then the symbols are separated into the new membranes as follows:

$$[d_3\,[[xyz,\bar{z}]_5,[\bar{y}',\bar{z}']_5,[\bar{x},\bar{z}]_5,[\bar{x}',\bar{y}',\bar{z}']_5]_2]_1.$$

Finally, after the third step of $\Pi(\varphi)$, its configuration looks as follows:

$$[d_4\,[[xyz]_6,[\bar{z}']_6,[\bar{y}]_6,[\bar{y}',\bar{z}']_6,[\bar{x}]_6,[\bar{x}',\bar{z}']_6,[\bar{x},\bar{y}]_6,[\bar{x}',\bar{y}',\bar{z}']_6]_2]_1.$$

Now, since every membrane with label 6 contains at least one object, $\Pi(\varphi)$ can continue the computation and send out to the environment the symbol no in the same way as $\Pi(3)$ does it.

The correctness of the P system $\Pi(\varphi)$ constructed in Definition 2 from a formula $\varphi \in Form_n$ $(n \in \mathbb{N})$ is based on the following lemma.

Lemma 1. *Let $\varphi \in Form_n$ $(n \in \mathbb{N})$ and $\Pi(n)$, $\Pi(\varphi)$ be the P systems constructed in Definition 1 and Definition 2, respectively. Consider the configurations of $\Pi(\varphi)$ and $\Pi(n)$ started with φ after n steps. Then $\Pi(\varphi)$ has an empty membrane with label $n + 3$ if and only if there is an empty membrane of $\Pi(n)$ with the same label.*

Proof. Clearly these P systems have the same membrane structure after every step of the systems. Consider the configurations of them after the ith step for some $(0 \le i \le n)$ and let m_1 and m_2 be two corresponding membranes with label $i + 3$ in $\Pi(n)$ and $\Pi(\varphi)$, respectively. We show that m_1 and m_2 have the same cardinality which clearly implies the statement of the lemma. It can be seen that, for every object c in m_1, the following holds. There is an object d in the membrane with label 3 of $\Pi(n)$ and there are distinct literals $l_{i_1}, \ldots, l_{i_k}$ $(k \le i)$ over the variables in X_n not occurring in $\hat{d}$ such that c represents the clause that is yielded by adding the above literals to $\hat{d}$. But then d or d' is in m_2 which means that $|m_1| \le |m_2|$. Using similar arguments, one can show that $|m_2| \le |m_1|$ also holds which concludes the proof of the lemma.

Since we know that the configuration of $\Pi(n)$ (started with φ) after n steps has an empty membrane with label $n + 3$ if and only if φ is satisfiable (cf. the discussion after Example 1), we have the following theorem.

Theorem 2. *The SAT can be solved in linear time by a polynomially semi-uniform family $\mathbf{\Pi} : (\Pi(\varphi))_{\varphi \in Form}$ of polarizationless recognizing P systems with the following properties: the elements of $\mathbf{\Pi}$ are deterministic, do not use non-elementary membrane division, and the size of a formula $\varphi \in Form$ is described by the number of variables occurring in the formula.*

4   Conclusions

We proposed a new approach for solving SAT by P systems with active membranes. This approach is based on a method that creates complete clauses from the clauses of a formula in CNF.

We defined a uniform and a semi-uniform family of P systems with active membranes where we implemented the above method. Both systems can decide the satisfiability of a formula in CNF in linear time in the number of variables occurring in the formula. To achieve this efficiency we did not use non-elementary membrane division or polarizations. On the other hand we used separation rules with membrane label changing. The number of computation steps in existing solutions without non-elementary membrane division depends also on the number of clauses in the input formula. However, we cannot say that our results are improvements of the existing ones because of the following reasons. Our uniform solution is not polynomially uniform, while our other solution is not uniform. To improve our results, we are planning to create a polynomially uniform solution based on our method using a formula encoding technique similar to the commonly used one in many existing solutions.

Concerning our existing solutions, it should be mentioned that in Definition 1, the rules in (a) and (c)-(f) have constant size, i.e., they involve a constant number of objects. Moreover, it is not difficult to see that during the evolution of $\Pi(n)$, membranes with label i ($3 \leq i \leq n+3$) have no more objects than the number m of the clauses in the input formula. Thus the separation rules in (b) always should act on membranes with no more than m objects (similar properties also hold in the case of the P systems defined in Definition 2).

It seems that our solutions may be improved by elaborating and implementing the following observations. First, consider again Example 1 and the P system $\Pi(3)$ with input φ in this example. One can observe that since $\bar{x}$ occurs in a membrane with label 4, every membrane with label 6 that is created from this membrane contains a complete clause. Thus, the system could have dissolved this membrane with label 4, without creating those four membranes with label 6 and changing the output of the system. In general this means that if the P system $\Pi(n)$ created in Definition 1 for some $n \in \mathbb{N}$ has a membrane with label $i+3$ ($1 \leq i \leq n-1$) containing a clause that do not contain variables $x_{i+1}, \ldots, x_n$, then $\Pi(n)$ could dissolve this membrane without changing the output of the system and saving the creation of $\mathcal{O}(2^{n-i})$ membranes.

It is also clear that if $\Pi(n)$ has an empty membrane with label $i+3$ for some ($1 \leq i \leq n-1$), then it has an empty membrane with label $n+3$ as well. Thus, the satisfiability of the input formula can turn out earlier than the nth step of the system and this also could save some superfluous membrane creations.

Implementing the above observations we could reduce the number of membranes created during the computation of the system. However, we should note that in general our P systems with the above improvements still would use exponential workspace (in the number of the variables of the input formula).

Since our P system $\Pi(n)$ given in Definition 1 has exponential size in n, it is a reasonable question whether a constant time solution of SAT exists based on $\Pi(n)$. One can see that slightly modifying $\Pi(n)$, a P system $\Pi'(n)$ could be given such that, for a formula $\varphi \in Form_n$, $\Pi'(n)$ can create the complete clauses of φ' only in one step (although in this case some of the rules of $\Pi'(n)$ should introduce an exponential number of objects). On the other hand, it is not clear how could we ensure $\Pi'(n)$ to send out to the environment the correct symbol *yes* or *no* using only constant number of steps.

We are planning to implement our P systems on certain systems using parallel hardware since we would like to see whether our new approach can be utilized in practice as well.

Acknowledgements. The authors are grateful to the reviewer for the many valuable comments and suggestions that improved the manuscript.

References

1. Alhazov, A.: Minimal parallelism and number of membrane polarizations. The Computer Science Journal of Moldova 18(2), 149–170 (2010)
2. Alhazov, A., Pan, L., Paun, G.: Trading polarizations for labels in P systems with active membranes. Acta Inf. 41(2-3), 111–144 (2004)
3. Ciobanu, G., Pan, L., Paun, G., Pérez-Jiménez, M.J.: P systems with minimal parallelism. Theor. Comput. Sci. 378(1), 117–130 (2007)
4. Freund, R., Păun, G., Pérez-Jiménez, M.J.: Polarizationless P Systems with Active Membranes Working in the Minimally Parallel Mode. In: Akl, S.G., Calude, C.S., Dinneen, M.J., Rozenberg, G., Wareham, H.T. (eds.) UC 2007. LNCS, vol. 4618, pp. 62–76. Springer, Heidelberg (2007)
5. Gazdag, Z., Kolonits, G.: A New Approach for Solving SAT by P Systems with Active Membranes. In: Csuhaj-Varjú, E., Gheorghe, M., Rozenberg, G., Salomaa, A., Vaszil, G. (eds.) CMC 2012. LNCS, vol. 7762, pp. 195–207. Springer, Heidelberg (2013)
6. Kusper, G.: Solving and Simplifying the Propositional Satisfiability Problem by Sub-Model Propagation. Ph.D. thesis, RISC, Johannes Kepler University, Linz, Austria (2005)
7. Pan, L., Alhazov, A.: Solving HPP and SAT by P Systems with Active Membranes and Separation Rules. Acta Inf. 43(2), 131–145 (2006)
8. Paun, G.: Computing with membranes. J. Comput. Syst. Sci. 61(1), 108–143 (2000)
9. Paun, G.: P Systems with Active Membranes: Attacking NP-Complete Problems. Journal of Automata, Languages and Combinatorics 6(1), 75–90 (2001)
10. Paun, G.: Introduction to membrane computing. In: Applications of Membrane Computing, pp. 1–42 (2006)
11. Paun, G., Rozenberg, G., Salomaa, A.: The Oxford Handbook of Membrane Computing. Oxford University Press, Inc., New York (2010), http://portal.acm.org/citation.cfm?id=1738939
12. Pérez-Jiménez, M.J., Jiménez, Á.R., Sancho-Caparrini, F.: Complexity classes in models of cellular computing with membranes. Natural Computing 2(3), 265–285 (2003)

Maintenance of Chronobiological Information by P System Mediated Assembly of Control Units for Oscillatory Waveforms and Frequency

Thomas Hinze[1,2], Benjamin Schell[2],
Mathias Schumann[2], and Christian Bodenstein[2]

[1] Brandenburg University of Technology
Institute of Computer Science and Information and Media Technology
Postfach 10 13 44, D-03013 Cottbus, Germany
[2] Friedrich Schiller University Jena
School of Biology and Pharmacy, Department of Bioinformatics
Ernst-Abbe-Platz 1–4, D-07743 Jena, Germany
thomas.hinze@tu-cottbus.de,
{benjamin.schell,mathias.schumann,christian.bodenstein}@uni-jena.de

Abstract. Oscillatory signals turn out to be reliable carriers for efficient processing and propagation of information in both spheres, life sciences and engineering. Each living organism typically comprises a variety of inherent biological rhythms whose periodicities cover a widespread range of scales like split seconds, minutes, or hours, and sometimes even months or years. Due to different molecular principles of generation, those rhythms seem to persist independently from each other. Their combination and assembly in conjunction with recurrent environmental changes can lead to astonishing capabilities and evolutionary advantages. Motivated by the question on how populations of cicadas, an insect species living in the soil, sustain a synchronous life cycle of 17 years away from any known external stimulus of this duration, we aim at exploring potential underlying mechanisms by P system mediated assembly of a set of chemical control units. To this end, we identify a collection of core oscillators responsible for sinusoidal, spiking, and plated waveforms along with pass filters, switches, and modulators. Considering these units as genotypic elementary components, we utilise P system control for selection and (re-)assembly of units towards complex phenotypic systems. Two simulation case studies demonstrate the potential of this approach following the idea of artificial evolution. Our first study inspired by the cicadas converts a chemical frequency divider model 1:17 into counterparts of 1:3, 1:5, and 1:6 just by exchange of single units. In the second study adopted from the mammalian circadian clock system residing within the suprachiasmatic nucleus, we illustrate the stabilisation of the overall clock signal by addition of auxiliary core oscillators.

1 Introduction

When spectating at macroscopic as well as microscopic phenomena of life, it becomes obvious that periodically recurrent behavioural patterns are essential for

E. Csuhaj-Varjú et al. (Eds.): CMC 2012, LNCS 7762, pp. 208–227, 2013.

all life forms known up to now. Molecular mechanisms responsible for creation and maintenance of a phenotype based on genotypic information imply an iterative nature of underlying translational and transcriptional processes. This is due to compensate or counteract the degradation of chemical substances making an organism to be alive. Resulting gene expressions typically oscillate over time, for example consecutive activation peaks repeat within few hours for replacement of rapidly dissociating substances and up to several days for robust proteins [22]. Even procaryotes, the simplest long-term surviving life forms on earth, regularly reproduce themselves by intrinsically cycling processes, mostly by binary fission or budding [18]. Regarding eucaryotic cells, the cell cycle as a more complex mechanism assures periodical cell division by passing through a number of dedicated phases [26]. Subject to distinct species, individual properties, and environmental conditions, the periods of cell cycling range from approximately six hours in some fungi up to about 24 hours in some mammals [21]. For humans, the duration of cell cycles typically varies between 19 and 20 hours according to the specific cell type [17]. Most notably, the time span between two cell divisions much more deviates in different tissues. While cells forming the inner surface of the stomach renew in average every three days [7], more than ten years seem to be enough for the osteocytic cellular skeleton of bones [7].

Beyond phenomena directly related with gene expression, we find a plethora of oscillating processes spanning a much larger diversity of periodicities within each individual organism. Let us consider humans for example. Firing neurons are able to send spikes every 10 milliseconds with a peak time of 2 milliseconds [11]. Several hundred spikes passing a neural axon in a sequence induce a high frequential oscillatory signal by mutual regulation of ion channels [11]. The molecular oscillator residing in the sinu-atrial node commonly generates between 40 and almost 210 heart beats per minute [23]. The suprachiasmatic nucleus as a part of the brain consistently provides the circadian rhythm with a period of approximately one day [3]. Infradian rhythms include monthly cycles like the menstruation. There is also some evidence for saisonally altering hormone concentrations indicating winter and summer [24]. Among other effects, this annual cycle leads to a slight reduction of the average human body temperature within a magnitude of $0.1°C$ during winter [6].

All together, we are aware of a broad spectrum of frequencies caused by biological rhythms. It appears that several molecular oscillators exist independently from each other. They operate simultaneously by individual generation of oscillatory signals, which in turn can act as periodical triggers for regulation of subsequent processes or behavioural patterns. The coexistence of a large number of molecular oscillators in living organisms is no surprise since a simple cyclic reaction scheme comprising at least one feedback loop suffices for obtaining a persistent oscillation. Probably, there are many evolutionary origins and resulting mechanisms of molecular oscillators.

Envisioning a more holistic view, the question arises how those oscillators interact in a way that their signal courses can interfere with each other. Downstream reaction systems can benefit from this richness by utilising a majority of those signals in parallel which enables astonishing capabilities and complex response towards an evolutionary advantage.

A fascinating example in this context is given by cicadas, insects of the species *Magicicada*. Populations in northern America share a synchronous life cycle of 17 years while those in central America prefer 13 years [20]. Most of its existence is spent underground in a dormant state. Shortly before the end of the life cycle, all the adults of a brood emerge at roughly the same time to reproduce for several weeks. After laying their eggs, the adults die off and the cycle begins again. What stands out is that 17 and 13 are prime numbers, which ensures that the reproduction period does not coincide with the life cycles of potential predators. The simultaneous mass awakening of a brood also ensures that predators are overwhelmed by the number of cicadas so that a large number can survive. In order to guarantee a concerted awakening of all members of a brood, the species needs a precise molecular mechanism to measure the passage of the appropriate amount of time. Since it seems that there is no external stimulus with a natural period of 13 or 17 years, its exact estimation exclusively based on annual or even shorter cycles becomes a complicated task [27]. Furthermore, it is worthwhile to know whether or not a *low* number of *slight* evolutionary changes within the molecular mechanism is sufficient to toggle the life cycle between a variety of years. Having this feature at hand, it becomes plausible how a widespread range of life times could emerge where those forming prime numbers resist the evolutionary selection driven by predators.

Complementary to the frequency, also the *waveform* of oscillatory signals can contain crucial information that might help organisms to optimise their response or adaptation regarding relevant environmental stimuli. Most of the biological rhythms studied so far are characterised by one out of three types of oscillatory waveforms. *Sinusoidal* or almost sinusoidal signal courses enable a gradual and smooth alteration such that the transfer between minimal and maximal signal levels consumes a notable amount of time. Commonly, a sinusoidal oscillation passes a stable limit cycle which acts as an attractor. This makes the oscillator quite robust against perturbations affecting the signal course. In contrast, *spiking* signals are a good choice to exhibit triggers. They can be outlined by an intensive signal peak active for a short moment followed by a quiet course close to zero for a much longer duration. The fast raise or fall of the signal value might be easy to detect for subsequent processing units. Remarkably, the average signal value can be kept low which might imply a reduced amount of energy necessary to sustain the oscillation. Contrary to sinusoidal signals, addition of phase-shifted isofrequential spiking oscillations can induce higher frequential overall oscillations in terms of an effective signal amplification. Furthermore, *plated* signal courses reflect a more or less bistable oscillatory behaviour. Here, the waveform over time resembles an almost rectangular shape similar to a binary clock signal. Plated oscillations combine the advantage of fast toggling with the ability for a balanced or weightable ratio between high-level and low-level signal values. To each of all three waveform types, corresponding oscillators can be assigned just by consideration of small or medium-sized chemical reaction networks together with appropriate reaction kinetics. From now on, we call them *core oscillators*. They have in common that the chemical concentration course of one or more dedicated species over time symbolises the oscillation. The reactions and kinetic parameterisation forming a core oscillator are assumed to be fixed. This comes along with the observation that the genetic template composing a core oscillator is often highly conserved against mutations to keep its oscillatory function.

In addition to core oscillators, a collection of reaction network motifs has been identified which allows a dedicated conversion, modification, and combination of oscillatory signals for postprocessing purposes. In this context, a simple linear reaction cascade can act as a low-pass filter. At the same time, it is able to convert spiking or plated oscillations into an almost sinusoidal shape. Vice versa, a mutually entwined scheme of catalysed reactions whose products catalyse the reactions of the next stage embodies a *binary signal separator*. This unit succeeds in conversion of sinusoidal or spiking signals into a plated oscillation. A chemical differentiator employed on plated oscillations generates spikes while an exponentiation of sinusoidal signals has the same effect. Finally, catalysts operating in concert can emulate *switches* and *logic gates* [14].

Our recent studies on generators and processing units for oscillatory signals in terms of biological computations led to a comprehensive collection of reaction networks, each of them individually formalised using appropriate P systems or ordinary differential equations, and analysed by means of simulation studies. What we intend to explore next is the interplay of those units towards new or improved phenomena. Hence, we aim at an assembly of reaction units on the fly. This objective has been flanked by the idea of an higher-level evolution which "plays" with different compositions of reaction units leaving intact the units themselves. Individual units interact via shared species as described in [13] using non-probabilistic P modules. The general concept of P systems provides an excellent formalism to capture *dynamical structures* especially concerning reaction networks. Thus, we are going to employ this framework to trace the recombination as well as the exchange of reaction units towards more complex behavioural patterns. To this end, we introduce a corresponding P meta framework that compiles an *evolutionary program* by assembly and subsequent exchange of reaction units taken from an initial pool.

In Section 2, we familiarise the reader with all denotational and formal prerequisites of our P meta framework for P system mediated assembly of non-probabilistic P modules which in turn define core oscillators and selected postprocessing units. Section 3 is dedicated to our first application study inspired by the synchronous life cycle of cicadas. It is based on a chemical reaction model of a binary counter modulo 17. This initial model comprises three units: a spiking core oscillator (Brusselator, [1,28]), a binary signal separator, and a logical unit. In its original form, the entire model acts as a frequency divider 1:17. In a first scenario, we remove the binary signal separator. Afterwards, we just exchange the Brusselator by the Goodwin oscillator (configurable to be plated or almost sinusoidal, [12]) and by the Repressilator (configurable to be almost sinusoidal or plated, [9]). Please note that we do *not* modify the logical unit.

Interestingly, these slight modifications are sufficient to obtain frequency dividers 1:3, 1:5, and 1:6. Section 4 deals with a second application study. Here, we focus on the almost sinusoidal core oscillator found in the suprachiasmatic nucleus. We arrange an initial setting of 12 core oscillator instances within four layers. Core oscillators placed in adjacent layers are unidirectionally coupled releasing their signals downstream. In this scenario, we estimate the quality of synchronisation taken in the final layer subject to the top level oscillator's phase differences. Then, we add two auxiliary core oscillators. It turns out that this action – just managed by replication of two core oscillators and their connectivity – stabilizes the entire system and contributes to an improved signal quality.

2   A P Meta Framework Capturing Assembly of Non-probabilistic P Modules

In [13], we introduced the term of *non-probabilistic P modules* complementary to other forms [25] and in accordance with the notion of modules in systems biology. Each non-probabilistic P module represents a *container* encapsulating an explicit specification of the dynamical behaviour of a reaction unit based on a *deterministic* scheme like discretised reaction kinetics or event-driven methods. In addition to the inherent dynamical behaviour, a non-probabilistic P module defines its *interface* by dedicated input and output species whose temporal concentration or abundance courses reflect the data managed by the reaction unit. Interacting non-probabilistic P modules communicate via shared molecular species. We define a non-probabilistic P module by a triple

$$\pi = (\pi_\downarrow, \pi_\uparrow, \pi_\square)$$

where $\pi_\downarrow = \{I_1, \ldots, I_i\}$ indicates a finite set of input signal identifiers, $\pi_\uparrow = \{O_1, \ldots, O_o\}$ a finite set of output signal identifiers, and $\pi_\square$ the underlying system specification processing the input signals and producing the output signals (either based on ordinary differential equations [8], or given in discrete manner [4,10,15,16,19], or by transfer functions [2]). Each signal is assumed to represent a real-valued temporal course, hence a specific function $\sigma : \mathbb{R}_{\geq 0} \longrightarrow \mathbb{R}$ ($\mathbb{R}_{\geq 0}$: non-negative real numbers). Chemical reaction kinetics in its standard form (mass-action, Michaelis-Menten, and Hill [8]) constitutes the molecular basis of each non-probabilistic P module expressed by the deterministically defined temporal course of species concentrations. We also refer the reader to [13,14] for detailed prerequisite information about modelling chemical kinetics.

Now, we define our P meta framework able to describe a dynamical assembly of non-probabilistic P modules towards more complex systems following the idea of a controlled evolutionary program. Our P meta framework is a construct

$$\Pi_{\pi\uparrow\downarrow} = (M, P)$$

where M denotes a finite *multiset* of non-probabilistic P modules with finite cardinality while the finite set P keeps the evolutionary program composed by a number of *instructions* affecting the interplay of underlying modules in M. The entirety of non-probabilistic P modules expressed by the support of M can be interpreted as the *genetic potential* of highly conserved reaction units. The multiplicities of modules reflect the limitation of resources available for module composition. Having in mind that the gene expression capacity is restricted, the number of modules maintained simultaneously should also be delimited. Nevertheless, the individual multiplicities might vary among different modules.

When initiating $\Pi_{\pi\uparrow\downarrow}$, a corresponding directed graph $G = (V, E)$ is created that formalises the current *connectivity structure* of interacting non-probabilistic P modules. All available modules on their own instantiate the nodes of G. There are no connections between them before executing the program P:

$$V := \{m[i] \mid m \in \mathrm{supp}(M) \ \wedge \ i \in \{1, \ldots, M(m)\}\}$$
$$E := \emptyset$$

The indexing of all instances (copies) $m[i]$ constituted from a module m allows a unique identification necessary for an appropriate matching of nodes addressed by program instructions.

Directed edges between nodes of G symbolise the connectivity of module instances. Let $a = (a_\downarrow, a_\uparrow, a_\square) \in \mathrm{supp}(M)$ and $b = (b_\downarrow, b_\uparrow, b_\square) \in \mathrm{supp}(M)$ be two module instances derived from M. An edge $(a, b, R_{a \to b}) \in E$ denotes a connection from a to b where dedicated output species of a act as input species of b. To this end, each edge comes with a binary relation $R_{a \to b} \subseteq a_\uparrow \times b_\downarrow$ in which the mapping of a's output species onto b's input is given. $R_{a \to b}$ is handled in an injective manner since one output species is allowed to cover several downstream input species, but each input species must be supplied by at most one upstream output species. Formally, we require: $\forall x, z \in X$ and $\forall y \in Y \ : \ (x, y) \in R \wedge (z, y) \in R \Rightarrow x = z$ where $R \subseteq X \times Y$ stands for $R_{a \to b}$.

Attention must be paid to the composition of non-probabilistic P modules to keep signal semantics and quantitative signal values along with signal identifiers consistent when migrating from one module to another.

The instructions of the evolutionary program P capture the dynamics of our P meta framework $\Pi_{\pi\uparrow\downarrow}$ in (re-)assembly of its module instances. The underlying graph G becomes updated whenever an instruction from P is executed. To bring the individual instructions into a temporal order, we assume a global clock whose progression is expressed by a non-negative real-valued variable t marking points in time. We arrange two types of instructions called `ModuleConnect` and `ModuleDisconnect`. A time stamp t opens each instruction. Let $a = (a_\downarrow, a_\uparrow, a_\square) \in \mathrm{supp}(M)$ and $b = (b_\downarrow, b_\uparrow, b_\square) \in \mathrm{supp}(M)$ be two module instances derived from M:

$t \ : \ \texttt{ModuleConnect}(a \to b, R_{a \to b})$ connects some or all of module a's output species to represent b's input species by sharing species identifiers according to the injective binary relation $R_{a \to b} \subseteq a_\uparrow \times b_\downarrow$. Edge update scheme: $E := E \cup \{(a, b, R_{a \to b})\}$

t : ModuleDisconnect$(a \leftrightarrow b)$ completely disconnects modules a and b by annihilating all cross-modular species sharings. This comes along with removing $R_{a \to b}$ as well as $R_{b \to a}$, respectively. Edge update scheme:
$$E := E \setminus \{(a, b, R_{a \to b})\} \setminus \{(b, a, R_{b \to a})\}$$

Several instructions in P might occur simultaneously if they are *effectively independent* from each other. This is the case if and only if all resulting permutations of sequences, in which instructions marked by the same time stamp t can be executed, lead to equivalent graphs G. Two application case studies demonstrate the practicability of our P meta framework $\Pi_{\pi \uparrow \downarrow} = (M, P)$.

3   Exploration of Chemical Frequency Dividers Inspired by Periodical Cicada's Life Cycles

In a first application study inspired by periodical cicada's life cycles, we demonstrate the practicability of our P meta framework $\Pi_{\pi \uparrow \downarrow} = (M, P)$ for tracing and experimental exploration of controlled module assembly towards new (i.e. more or less unexpected) behavioural patterns of the resulting entire system. First, we introduce in brief a pool of non-probabilistic P modules sufficient to interact as a chemical frequency divider 1:17. To this end, we place a selection of different core oscillators interpreted to be employed for generation of periodical trigger signals. A binary signal separator complements the pool of modules by its capability of binarisation which converts gradually or smoothly altering signal courses into a toggling manner whereas signal values ≥ 1 and those close to 1 converge to 1 while signal values of ≈ 0.6 and smaller become forced down against 0. In addition, we construct a logical unit whose function is a binary chemical counter modulo 17 based on a cycle of five-bit states. Please note that the logical unit remains unchanged during the whole study. After providing the pool of modules, we explore the effect of different core oscillators on the behavioural pattern of the entire frequency divider system in the presence or absence of the binary signal separator. Although leaving intact the logical unit, we observe new frequency division ratios of 1:3, 1:5, and 1:6 just by the effect of module assembly.

3.1   Sketching the Pool of Individual Modules

Taking into account a Brusselator, a Repressilator, and a Goodwin oscillator, we allow for a pool of core oscillators assumed to be formerly emerged independently from each other and based on different molecular mechanisms. Each individual module is considered to be fixed including its previously chosen setting of kinetic parameters. For all simulation studies carried out in this section, we utilise a consistent time unit.

The Brusselator Module

The Brusselator derived from the Belousov-Zhabotinsky reaction is a tool approved for the generation of spiking oscillations forming a limit cycle [1,28]. Here, the oscillatory persistence is exclusively reached by a positive feedback effect of an autocatalytic loop. The non-probabilistic P module brusselator $= (\emptyset, \{S\}, F)$ is completely based on mass-action kinetics captured by five ODEs in F: $\dot{P} = -k_1 PT$; $\dot{Q} = -k_3 Q$; $\dot{S} = k_1 PT - k_2 ST^2$; $\dot{T} = -k_1 PT + k_2 ST^2 + k_3 Q - k_4 T$; $\dot{W} = k_4 T$. Figure 1 depicts the underlying topology of the reaction network in conjunction with the selected parameter setting. Reaction velocities, particularly those of decay $T \xrightarrow{k_4} W$ producing waste W, mainly determine the oscillation frequency. Our parameter setting avoids a transient phase and enables a lower frequency oscillation with distinctive spikes.

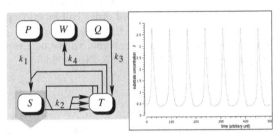

Fig. 1. Brusselator reaction network (left) composed of four reactions: (1) $P+T \xrightarrow{k_1} S$; (2) $S + 2T \xrightarrow{k_2} 3T$; (3) $Q \xrightarrow{k_3} T$; (4) $T \xrightarrow{k_4} W$ for generation of persistently *spiking* oscillations. The concentration course of species S over time (right) acts as module output. Mass-action parameter setting: $k_1 = k_2 = k_3 = k_4 = 0.1$; initial concentrations: $P(0) = 3, Q(0) = 1, W(0) = 0, S(0) = 0.5, T(0) = 0.5$.

The Repressilator Module

The Repressilator is represented by a cyclic gene regulatory network where a progressional inhibition on its own causes an almost sinusoidal oscillation due to a negative feedback. We formalise the dynamical behaviour of the repressilator $= (\emptyset, \{Z\}, F)$ using second-order Hill kinetics by three ODEs [9] in F:

$$\dot{X} = \frac{k_3 H_3^2}{Z^2 + H_3^2} - k_4 X \qquad \dot{Y} = \frac{k_1 H_1^2}{X^2 + H_1^2} - k_5 Y \qquad \dot{Z} = \frac{k_2 H_2^2}{Y^2 + H_2^2} - k_6 Z$$

We parameterise the Repressilator in a way to exhibit a medium frequency limit cycle oscillation emphasising a comparatively small amplitude in concert with small signal values not exceeding a threshold of approximately 0.6, see Figure 2. This threshold is meant to coincide with the ambiguous "forbidden range" in terms of a clear distinction between 0 and 1 of binarily interpreted signals.

The Goodwin Module

The Goodwin oscillator follows the scheme of a three-staged cyclic gene regu-latory network consisting of two subsequent activating transitions along with

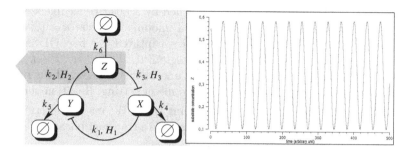

Fig. 2. Repressilator reaction network (left) composed of three inhibiting cycling reactions along with degradation of each species. The concentration course of species Z over time (right) acts as module output. Second order Hill kinetic's parameter setting $H_1 = H_2 = H_3 = 0.6, k_i = 1$ for $i \in \{1, \ldots, 6\}$ chosen to exhibit persistent almost *sinusoidal* oscillations whose amplitude enables signal values between approx. 0.1 and 0.6; initial concentrations: $X(0) = 0.3, Y(0) = 0.15, Z(0) = 0.55$.

a single inhibition completing the loop by a negative feedback [12]. According to the internal balance of reaction velocities, the resulting oscillatory waveform might vary from an almost sinusoidal behaviour towards an asymmetric λ-like shape. Here, a fast growing edge is combined with a slightly sigmoidal diminishment of the signal. This makes the Goodwin oscillator a promising candidate for naturally plated limit cycle oscillations. The non-probabilistic P module goodwin $= (\emptyset, \{X\}, F)$ containing three ODEs

$$\dot{X} = \frac{H}{1 + Z^9} - k_4 X \qquad \dot{Y} = k_1 X - k_5 Y \qquad \dot{Z} = k_2 Y - k_6 Z$$

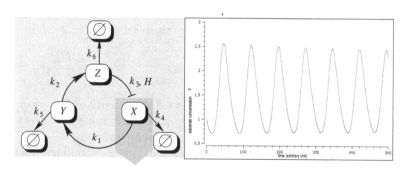

Fig. 3. Goodwin oscillator reaction network (left) in its original form. We assume the concentration course of species X over time (right) to act as module output. Higher-order Hill kinetic's parameter setting $H = 1.5, k_i = 0.05$ for $i \in \{1, \ldots, 6\}$ chosen to maintain slightly *plated* oscillations whose amplitude enables signal values between approx. 0.6 and 2.5; initial concentrations: $X(0) = 1.0, Y(0) = 1.6, Z(0) = 1.7$.

defines the Goodwin oscillator in its original form [12]. The degradation velocities most significantly determine its oscillatory frequency. Our configuration shown in Figure 3 is focused on a lower frequency oscillation of a high amplitude spanned by signal values altering between approx. 0.6 and 2.5. In contrast to the Repressilator's parameterisation, we intend to face the binarily operating signal postprocessing units with intense signals revealing high values for a comparatively longer amount of time.

The Binary Signal Separator Module

Figure 4 illustrates a three-stage signalling cascade whose function consists in binarisation of species concentration courses captured by O_0^F.

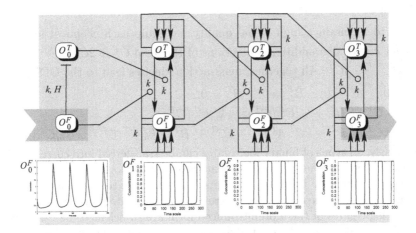

Fig. 4. Signalling cascade for binarisation of input species concentration course O_0^F. Concentrations ≥ 1 and those close to 1 converge to 1 while values smaller than a threshold H are forced down against 0. Michaelis-Menten kinetics and mass-action kinetics describe the dynamical behaviour of the module. Chosen parameter setting: $H = 0.6, k = 0.1$.

The corresponding module separator $= (\{O_0^F\}, \{O_3^F\}, F)$ employs ODEs:

$$\dot{O}_0^T = \frac{kH}{O_0^F + H}$$
$$\dot{O}_i^T = k \cdot O_i^F \cdot O_{i-1}^T - k \cdot O_i^T \cdot O_{i-1}^F - k \cdot O_i^T \cdot (O_i^F)^2 + k \cdot O_i^F \cdot (O_i^T)^2 \quad i = 1, 2, 3$$
$$\dot{O}_i^F = k \cdot O_i^T \cdot O_{i-1}^F - k \cdot O_i^F \cdot O_{i-1}^T - k \cdot O_i^F \cdot (O_i^T)^2 + k \cdot O_i^T \cdot (O_i^F)^2$$

The Logical Unit Forming a Binary Counter Modulo 17

Our construction of a chemical binary counter model modulo 17 is based on a chemical representation of each boolean variable $b \in \{0, 1\}$ by two correlated species B^T and B^F with complementary concentrations such that $B^F + B^T = 1$.

The inequality $B^T \ll B^F$ indicates "false" ($b = 0$) and $B^F \ll B^T$ "true" ($b = 1$), respectively. Following a commonly used requirement in circuit design, we intend by denoting $\ll$ a deviation of at least one order of magnitude.

A chemical counterpart of a logic gate can be obtained if each line of the transition table refers to a dedicated chemical reaction where the boolean input variable values identify corresponding catalysts. These catalysts manage the output variable setting. In case of a NOR gate, the transition table results in the following set of reactions:

a	b	c	corresponding reactions
0	0	1	$C^F + A^F + B^F \xrightarrow{k} C^T + A^F + B^F$
0	1	0	$C^T + A^F + B^T \xrightarrow{k} C^F + A^F + B^T$
1	0	0	$C^T + A^T + B^F \xrightarrow{k} C^F + A^T + B^F$
1	1	0	$C^T + A^T + B^T \xrightarrow{k} C^F + A^T + B^T$

In order to maintain a high signal quality, we equip each chemical logic gate of output c with two additional reactions of the form $C^T + 2C^F \xrightarrow{k_m} 3C^F$ and $C^F + 2C^T \xrightarrow{k_m} 3C^T$. All together, mass-action kinetics lead to the ODEs:

$$\dot{A}^F = 0; \quad \dot{A}^T = 0; \quad \dot{B}^F = 0; \quad \dot{B}^T = 0;$$
$$\dot{C}^T = kC^F A^F B^F + k_m C^F (C^T)^2 - k_m C^T (C^F)^2$$
$$\dot{C}^F = kC^T A^F B^T + kC^T A^T B^F + kC^T A^T B^T + k_m C^T (C^F)^2 - k_m C^F (C^T)^2$$

Analogously, all types of binary logic gates can be transferred into corresponding chemical representations. Please note that each chemical logic gate owns a certain latency determined by the rate constants k and k_m due to the amount of time necessary to switch the output concentrations. Taking into account this latency, chemical logic gates of the aforeintroduced form are sufficient to be cascaded in a way that a gate's output might serve as input for a subsequent gate.

For setting up a binary counter modulo 17, we need to distinguish 17 states, which requires five bits per state. The counting is organised in a way that a periodical clock signal serves as a trigger initiating a state transition $(b_1, \ldots, b_5) \mapsto (b'_1, \ldots b'_5)$. To this end, we utilise a five-bit Gray code, which keeps the total number of logic gates low since almost all state transitions proceed by changing one out of five bits:

count	b_1 b_2 b_3 b_4 b_5	b'_1 b'_2 b'_3 b'_4 b'_5	count	b_1 b_2 b_3 b_4 b_5	b'_1 b'_2 b'_3 b'_4 b'_5
1	0 0 0 0 0	0 0 0 0 1	10	0 1 1 0 1	0 1 1 1 1
2	0 0 0 0 1	0 0 0 1 1	11	0 1 1 1 1	0 1 1 1 0
3	0 0 0 1 1	0 0 0 1 0	12	0 1 1 1 0	0 1 0 1 0
4	0 0 0 1 0	0 0 1 1 0	13	0 1 0 1 0	0 1 0 1 1
5	0 0 1 1 0	0 0 1 1 1	14	0 1 0 1 1	0 1 0 0 1
6	0 0 1 1 1	0 0 1 0 1	15	0 1 0 0 1	0 1 0 0 0
7	0 0 1 0 1	0 0 1 0 0	16	0 1 0 0 0	1 1 0 0 0
8	0 0 1 0 0	0 1 1 0 0	17	1 1 0 0 0	0 0 0 0 0
9	0 1 1 0 0	0 1 1 0 1			

Bit b_1 indicates the accumulation of 17 counts constituting the counter's output. In addition, intermediate states need to be temporarily stored in order to bridge

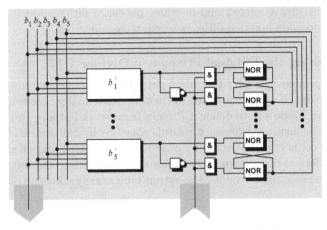

Fig. 5. Sketch of the logical unit representing a chemical model of a binary counter modulo 17. A periodical trigger acts as input providing the counts. Bit b_1 accomplishs the output. For all reactions within the logical unit, we utilise mass-action kinetics along with rate constants consistently set to $k = 1$. This allows a fast toggling which results in a short latency of approx. 10 time units per individual gate.

the time span between successive counts. To this end, we incorporate five RS flip flops into the counter automaton, each of which is composed of two regeneratively coupled NOR gates, see Figure 5. For bitwise state transition, we utilise five boolean functions resulting from the transition table above and syntactically simplified using standard Karnaugh optimisation. We denote these functions in disjunctive normal form:

$$b'_1 = \bar{b}_1 b_2 \bar{b}_3 \bar{b}_4 \bar{b}_5$$
$$b'_2 = \bar{b}_1 b_2 \vee \bar{b}_1 b_2 \bar{b}_3 \bar{b}_4 \bar{b}_5$$
$$b'_3 = \bar{b}_1 \bar{b}_2 b_3 \vee \bar{b}_1 b_3 \bar{b}_4 \vee \bar{b}_1 b_2 b_3 b_5 \vee \bar{b}_1 \bar{b}_2 b_4 \bar{b}_5$$
$$b'_4 = \bar{b}_1 b_4 \bar{b}_5 \vee \bar{b}_1 b_2 b_3 b_5 \vee \bar{b}_1 \bar{b}_2 \bar{b}_3 b_5 \vee \bar{b}_1 \bar{b}_2 \bar{b}_3 b_4 \vee \bar{b}_1 b_2 b_3 b_4$$
$$b'_5 = \bar{b}_1 \bar{b}_2 \bar{b}_3 \bar{b}_4 \vee \bar{b}_1 \bar{b}_2 b_3 b_4 \vee \bar{b}_1 b_2 b_3 \bar{b}_4 \vee \bar{b}_1 b_2 \bar{b}_3 b_4$$

For implementation of these functions, we exclusively use logic AND and OR gates with two input variables and one output variable in a cascaded manner in order to avoid an exponential growth of reactions whose number doubles with any additional input variable. The corresponding cascade lengths (number of subsequent gates to be passed by a binary signal) vary between 4 and 7. As a consequence, the latencies of the cascades also deviate, which might imply an evolutionary potential towards modified functionalities.

Figure 5 sketches the structure of the entire binary counter modulo 17. In the chemical representation, the resulting module $\text{mod}17 = (\{C\}, \{B_1^T\}, F)$ consists of 145 species and subsumes 416 individual reactions. The logical unit was constructed by using standard techniques of circuit design known from engineering.

We consider this unit as a fixed module whose potential with respect to additional, originally unintended functionalities is worth to be found out.

3.2   Composing the Original Frequency Divider 1:17

The original frequency divider 1:17 can be obtained by sequential coupling of the Brusselator with the separator which in turn becomes finally connected with the mod17 module. To do so, we define a P meta framework initially creating a pool consisting of one instance from each module specified by multiset M. Program P generates the connective structure by producing graph G. Figure 6 sketches the coupling and depicts the dynamical behaviour of the resulting reaction system. Periodically after receiving 17 counts, the output temporarily releases a plated pulse.

$$\Pi_{\text{FD17}} = (M, P) \quad \text{with}$$
$$M = \{(\text{brusselator}, 1), (\text{repressilator}, 1), (\text{goodwin}, 1), (\text{separator}, 1), (\text{mod17}, 1)\}$$
$$P = \{0 : \text{ModuleConnect}(\text{brusselator}[1] \rightarrow \text{separator}[1], \{(S, O_0^F)\}),$$
$$0 : \text{ModuleConnect}(\text{separator}[1] \rightarrow \text{mod17}[1], \{(O_3^F, C)\})\}$$

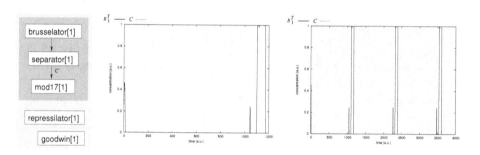

Fig. 6. Dynamical behaviour of the frequency divider 1:17 (center: divider output B_1^T during a period of 17 counts, right: B_1^T for a longer amount of time, C: counts)

3.3   Frequency Divider 1:5 by Removal of Binary Signal Separator

The binary signal separator is responsible for normalisation and binarisation of the core oscillator's output. Primarily, we were going to figure out whether or not this module is essential for the function of the entire frequency divider. Interestingly, the corresponding knockout P meta framework

$$\Pi_{\text{FD5}} = (M, P) \quad \text{with}$$
$$M = \{(\text{brusselator}, 1), (\text{repressilator}, 1), (\text{goodwin}, 1), (\text{separator}, 1), (\text{mod17}, 1)\}$$
$$P = \{0 : \text{ModuleConnect}(\text{brusselator}[1] \rightarrow \text{separator}[1], \{(S, O_0^F)\}),$$
$$0 : \text{ModuleConnect}(\text{separator}[1] \rightarrow \text{mod17}[1], \{(O_3^F, C)\}),$$
$$200 : \text{ModuleDisconnect}(\text{brusselator}[1] \leftrightarrow \text{separator}[1]),$$
$$200 : \text{ModuleConnect}(\text{brusselator}[1] \rightarrow \text{mod17}[1], \{(S, C)\})\}$$

reveals a frequency divider 1:5 although no changes within the logical unit were made. The same effect can be observed if the Brusselator is directly connected with the logical unit from the beginning while avoiding any temporary connection with the binary separator module. Figure 7 shows the behavioural pattern. It appears that a majority of state transitions skip by leaving a reduced scheme with identical signal courses of b_4 and b_5 persistently cycling through five states (after a short transient phase). A most likely reason for that can be found in the waveform in concert with the quantitatively high-valued oscillatory signal released by the Brusselator. Most of the time, its course indicates the logical value "1" solely interrupted by extremely short drops at the 0-level. Since the flip flops had been designed to be set or reset at the 1-level, the circuit loses its synchronicity due to the variable cascade lengths in computing the boolean functions. This in turn might entail a scenario where intermediate stages in the computation of a bit b'_i interfere with the computation of another bit b'_j.

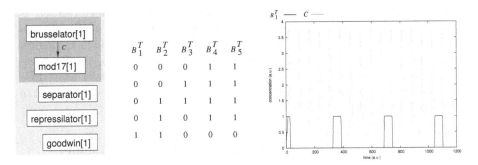

Fig. 7. Dynamical behaviour of the frequency divider 1:5 obtained by skipping the binary signal separator (center: cycle of state transitions, right: counts together with divider output)

3.4   Frequency Divider 1:6 by Repressilator instead of Brusselator

Due to its nature to induce almost sinusoidal and hence more symmetric signal courses, the question arises whether or not the Repressilator module in its function as core oscillator could be able to restore the original qualitative behaviour of the entire system on its own when renouncing the binary signal separator again. Checking out this scenario by the P meta framework

$$\Pi_{FD6} = (M, P) \quad \text{with}$$
$$M = \{(\text{brusselator}, 1), (\text{repressilator}, 1), (\text{goodwin}, 1), (\text{separator}, 1), (\text{mod17}, 1)\}$$
$$P = \{0 : \texttt{ModuleConnect}(\text{repressilator}[1] \rightarrow \text{mod17}[1], \{(Z, C)\})\}$$

leads to the observation that now a frequency divider 1:6 with reliable operation occurred, see Figure 8. After a short transient phase, a stable cycle consisting

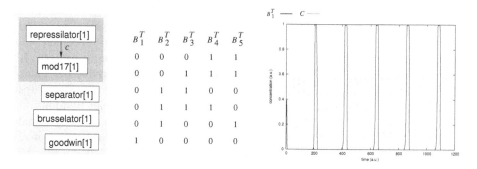

Fig. 8. Dynamical behaviour of the frequency divider 1:6 obtained by replacing the Brusselator with the Repressilator module and skipping the binary signal separator again (center: cycle of state transitions, right: counts together with divider output)

of six state transitions emerged when the Repressilator's parameterisation as introduced before is applied. We assume the reason for that is a deterministically maintained perturbance of the binary function's computation in the logical unit. Contrary to the previously discussed frequency divider 1:5, the Repressilator implies an undersupply of the counting signal with its logical 1-level. This prevents the system from completing the computation and forces the release of an intermediate computational state taken as output.

3.5   Frequency Divider 1:3 by Usage of the Goodwin Module

The Goodwin module along with its capability of rudimentary plated oscillatory signal generation appears to be another interesting candidate to drive our frequency divider. By means of the P meta framework

$$\Pi_{FD3} = (M, P) \quad \text{with}$$
$$M = \{(\text{brusselator}, 1), (\text{repressilator}, 1), (\text{goodwin}, 1), (\text{separator}, 1), (\text{mod17}, 1)\}$$
$$P = \{0 : \texttt{ModuleConnect}(\text{goodwin}[1] \rightarrow \text{mod17}[1], \{(X, C)\})\}$$

we achieve once more a modified qualitative behavioural pattern, this time a frequency division 1:3, see Figure 9. After a short transient phase, the system persistently cycles through three states out of 17 from the original model. It seems that the resulting toggling process runs slightly more fragile than in the Repressilator study. This becomes visible by a pronounced signal tuning, which exhibits damped high frequential micro oscillations in conjunction with output switch. Even several modifications of the experimental setup confirm this behaviour, for instance a more distinctive transient oscillation of the Goodwin module (shown in Figure 9) as well as doubling the rate constants from $k = 0.05$ to $k = 0.1$ within the Goodwin module. Again, the core oscillator continuably disturbes the computation of the bits b'_1 up to b'_5.

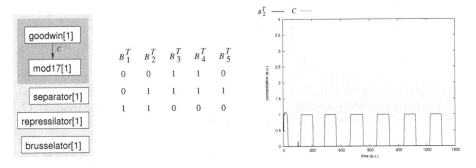

Fig. 9. Dynamical behaviour of the frequency divider 1:3 obtained by replacing the Brusselator with the Goodwin module in absence of the binary signal separator (center: cycle of state transitions, right: counts together with divider output). Instead of B_1^T, we depict B_2^T as divider output due to its more precisely toggling nature.

3.6 Discussion

The experimental results indicate that an originally designed frequency divider 1:17 might change its behaviour revealing division ratios of 1:3, 1:5, and 1:6 just by slight rewiring of few interacting modules. By using a binary counter approach modulo 17, we intentionally employed a pure synthetic reaction system derived from standard concepts in engineering. Although, those systems tend to be quite resistent against evolutionary optimisation, there is some evidence for achievement of new or extended functionalities. A detailed plausibilisation of the observed behavioural pattern directly

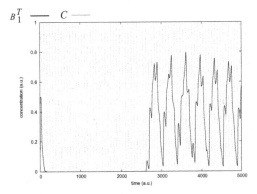

Fig. 10. Dynamical behaviour of the original frequency divider model 1:17 after slowing down all reactions within the logical unit for one order of magnitude

arises from the entirety of concentration courses involved in carrying out the state transitions. In order to emphasise this line of evidence, we conducted an additional simulation study by consistent variation of the rate constants within the logical unit. Slowing down its reactions by setting $k = 0.1$ instead of $k = 1$ leads to complete loss of frequency division by forwarding the core oscillator's period instead. Here, the entire system exhibits a fragile "cycle" at the edge of chaotic behaviour after a longer transient phase, see Figure 10. Obviously, the reaction network attempts to calculate the next step but is unable to do so in time for the next count. This effect preserves for any rate constant $k < 0.15$, which marks the maximum latency of logic gates required to guarantee their function.

For $0.15 \leq k \leq 0.9$, the frequency divider 1:17 operates correctly after a long transient phase of 18 counts necessary to reconstruct minimal concentration levels of auxiliary species. For $k > 0.9$, there is no restriction in the frequency divider's functionality.

Finally, let us return to the life cycle of periodical cicadas which gave the crucial inspiration for our studies. We are aware that the mechanisms evolved in this life form are most probably far away from a binary counter modulo 17. Up to now, we failed in retrieving any scientific publication on potential or even verified mechanisms. A more or less speculative hypothesis aims at a combination of two processes, a slow growth on the one hand and a threshold on the other. Growth means a successive accumulation of a dedicated species. As soon as its concentration exceeds an inherently set threshold, the life cycle becomes finalised indicating the elapsed amount of 17 years. A successive accumulation organised for instance in annual cycles is useful for a high precision. To this end, a core oscillator could provide an annually altering signal of the form $a + \sin(bt)$ subject to time t. A simple signal integration then produces a temporal course of the form $at + c \cdot \sin(bt + d)$ with a successive, staircase-shaped growth. Nevertheless, this strategy is more prone to premature or late alert than an n-ary counter.

4   Core Oscillator's Interplay in Suprachiasmatic Nucleus

A second application study is intended to demonstrate in brief the descriptional capacity of our P meta framework. Let us consider the *suprachiasmatic nucleus*, a region of the human brain, in which each neuron comprises a core oscillator for generation of a circadian rhythm characterised by a controllable period close to 24 hours. A cyclic gene regulatory network consisting of 10 molecular species and 18 reactions including an inhibitory negative feedback forms this core oscillator whose dynamical behaviour had been formalised via specific ODEs based on mass-action and second-order Hill kinetics. For a full description, we refer to [3]. The neuronal core oscillators within the suprachiasmatic nucleus appear to be hierarchically organised in several layers. A small group of independently oscillating neurons constitutes the so-called master-clock layer. Neurons in downstream layers synchronise their oscillation via unidirectional molecular coupling in which the oscillatory outputs of superior layers directly affect oscillations in adjacent subsequent layers. Neurons residing in the deepest layer release their widely synchronised oscillatory signals to peripheral oscillators in other parts of the organism. Figure 11 illustrates a small network composed of 14 core oscillators called n[1] up to n[14] organised within four layers.

We are going to conduct two experimental studies: In a first scenario, we wish to consider a pre-synchronised network with a single neuron in the master-clock layer, see part **A** of Figure 11. This neuron propagates its oscillatory rhythm to all downstream neurons causing a slight signal delay from layer to layer. After a short transient phase, all 12 neurons incorporated in this scenario oscillate synchronously. Although sufficient so far, a single master clock makes the system error-prone and fragile, especially if the master-clock oscillation deviates from

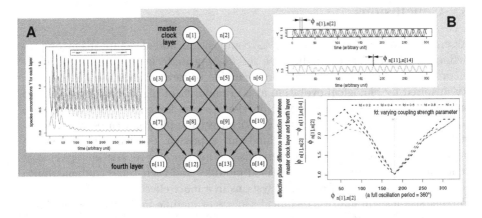

Fig. 11. Hierarchical scheme of unidirectionally coupled neuronal core oscillators organised in four layers. Individual oscillations synchronise by passing through these layers. See text for detailed explanation.

its expected behaviour which can easily happen along with cell ageing. In this case, an incorrect or insufficient oscillatory signal runs through all layers without any correction or control. Additional master-clock neurons with full connectivity to downstream layers can help to stabilise the function of the whole network. Our second scenario depicted in part **B** reflects this aspect. Here, we add a master clock neuron and a second-layer neuron completing the network of 14 neurons. Temporal signal offsets (so-called phase differences) among individual master-clock oscillations are diminished while passing the downstream layers. Finally, a robust "average" oscillatory signal derived from all master clocks is released as global output. Our simulation shows that initial phase differences within the master-clock layer can be reduced up to $\approx$ 2.6-fold by running through three subsequent layers, widely independent of the coupling strength. Antiphasic master-clock oscillations (half-periodic offset, phase difference 180°) turn out to be resistent against synchronisation by passing the layers almost unaffected.

The corresponding experimental setup can be captured by the P meta framework assuming the non-probabilistic P module $n = (X, Y, F)$ from [3] to act as unique neuronal core oscillator from which up to 14 instances are employed:

$$\Pi_{\text{SCN}} = (M, P) \quad \text{with}$$
$$M = \{(n, 14)\}$$
$$P = \{0 : \texttt{ModuleConnect}(n[1] \rightarrow n[3], \{(Y, X)\}),$$
$$\quad 0 : \texttt{ModuleConnect}(n[1] \rightarrow n[4], \{(Y, X)\}), \dots,$$
$$\quad 0 : \texttt{ModuleConnect}(n[10] \rightarrow n[14], \{(Y, X)\})$$
$$\quad 300 : \texttt{ModuleConnect}(n[2] \rightarrow n[4], \{(Y, X)\}), \dots,$$
$$\quad 300 : \texttt{ModuleConnect}(n[6] \rightarrow n[10], \{(Y, X)\})\}$$

5   Conclusions

Assembly and reassembly as well as composition and decomposition of pre-
defined reaction network modules *on the fly* appears to be a promising strategy
in order to achieve complex systems capable of new or extended functionality. Inspired by biological evolution at a granularity of highly conserved genetic
ensembles, our P meta framework provides a tool for control and systematic
conduction of corresponding studies. Within two application cases, we demonstrated the descriptive capacity behind this approach. Particularly at the edge
of straight-forward lines for complex network inference in reverse engineering, a
strict utilisation of previously identified modules and their reuse can contribute
to explore the abilities of resulting systems in a more effective and efficient way.
Further studies will address technical aspects of module integration from different specification platforms. It seems that modules based on ODEs on the one
hand and discrete forms along with rewriting rules on the other, needs to interact with each other via appropriate interfaces. To this end, the Infobiotics
workbench offers an extensive functionality [5]. A fruitful combination of the
universe of P systems featured by their ability to manage dynamical structures
with the universe of ODEs featured by a profound toolbox for analytical exami-
nation could be an innovative clue. In all simulation studies carried out for this
paper, we consistently utilised the Complex Pathway Simulator software CoPaSi
(version 4.7) along with the Gepasi Model Extractor for generation of several
instances from a common module specification. Corresponding source files are
available from the authors upon request.

References

1. Belousov, B.P.: A periodic reaction and its mechanism. Compilation of Abstracts
   in Radiation Medicine 147, 145 (1959)
2. Bequette, B.W.: Process control: modeling, design, and simulation. Prentice Hall
   (2003)
3. Bernard, S., Gonze, D., Cajavec, B., Herzel, H., Kramer, A.: Synchronization-
   induced rhythmicity of circadian oscillators in the suprachiasmatic nucleus. PLoS
   Comput. Biol. 3(4), e68 (2007)
4. Bianco, L., Fontana, F., Manca, V.: P systems with reaction maps. International
   Journal of Foundations of Computer Science 17(1), 27–48 (2006)
5. Blakes, J., Twycross, J., Romero-Campero, F.J., Krasnogor, N.: The Infobiotics
   Workbench: An Integrated in silico Modelling Platform for Systems and Synthetic
   Biology. Bioinformatics 27(23), 3323–3324 (2011)
6. Cagnacci, A.: Melatonin in Relation to Physiology in Adult Humans. Journal of
   Pineal Research 21(4), 200–213 (1996)
7. Carlson, B.M.: Principles of Regenerative Biology. Elsevier Academic Press (2007)
8. Connors, K.A.: Chemical Kinetics. VCH Publishers (1990)
9. Elowitz, M.B., Leibler, S.: A synthetic oscillatory network of transcriptional regulators. Nature 403, 335–338 (2000)
10. Fontana, F., Manca, V.: Discrete solutions to differential equations by metabolic
   P systems. Theoretical Computer Science 372, 165–182 (2007)

11. Gerstner, W., Kistler, W.: Spiking Neuron Models – Single Neurons, Populations, Plasticity. Cambridge University Press (2002)

12. Goodwin, B.C.: Oscillatory behaviour in enzymatic control processes. Advanced Enzyme Regulation 3, 425–438 (1965)

13. Hinze, T., Bodenstein, C., Schau, B., Heiland, I., Schuster, S.: Chemical Analog Computers for Clock Frequency Control Based on P Modules. In: Gheorghe, M., Păun, G., Rozenberg, G., Salomaa, A., Verlan, S. (eds.) CMC 2011. LNCS, vol. 7184, pp. 182–202. Springer, Heidelberg (2012)

14. Hinze, T., Fassler, R., Lenser, T., Dittrich, P.: Register Machine Computations on Binary Numbers by Oscillating and Catalytic Chemical Reactions Modelled using Mass-Action Kinetics. International Journal of Foundations of Computer Science 20(3), 411–426 (2009)

15. Hinze, T., Lenser, T., Dittrich, P.: A Protein Substructure Based P System for Description and Analysis of Cell Signalling Networks. In: Hoogeboom, H.J., Păun, G., Rozenberg, G., Salomaa, A. (eds.) WMC 2006. LNCS, vol. 4361, pp. 409–423. Springer, Heidelberg (2006)

16. Hinze, T., Lenser, T., Escuela, G., Heiland, I., Schuster, S.: Modelling Signalling Networks with Incomplete Information about Protein Activation States: A P System Framework of the KaiABC Oscillator. In: Păun, G., Pérez-Jiménez, M.J., Riscos-Núñez, A., Rozenberg, G., Salomaa, A. (eds.) WMC 2009. LNCS, vol. 5957, pp. 316–334. Springer, Heidelberg (2010)

17. Klevecz, R.R.: Quantized generation time in mammalian cells as an expression of the cellular clock. Proc. Natl. Acad. Sci. USA 73, 4012–4016 (1976)

18. Lengeler, J.W., Drews, G., Schlegel, H.G.: Biology of the Prokaryotes. Thieme (1999)

19. Manca, V.: Metabolic P Systems for Biochemical Dynamics. Progress in Natural Sciences 17(4), 384–391 (2007)

20. Marlatt, C.L.: The periodical cicada. Bull. U.S. Dept. Agri., Div. Entomol. Bull. 18, 52 (1907)

21. Mitchison, J.M.: The Biology of the Cell Cycle. Cambridge University Press (1971)

22. Nath, K., Koch, A.L.: Protein Degradation in Escherichia coli: Measurement of Rapidly and Slowly Decaying Components. The Journal of Biological Chemistry 245(11), 2889–2900 (1970)

23. Panfilov, A.V., Holden, A.V.: Computational Biology of the Heart. John Wiley & Sons (1997)

24. Reiter, R.J.: The Melatonin Rhythm: Both a Clock and a Calendar. Cellular and Molecular Life Sciences 49(8), 654–664 (1993)

25. Romero-Campero, F.J., Twycross, J., Camara, M., Bennett, M., Gheorghe, M., Krasnogor, N.: Modular Assembly of Cell Systems Biology Models using P Systems. International Journal of Foundations of Computer Science 20(3), 427–442 (2009)

26. Tyson, J.J., Novak, B.: Temporal Organization of the Cell Cycle. Current Biology 18, 759–768 (2008)

27. Williams, K.S., Simon, C.: The ecology, behavior and evolution of periodical cicadas. Annual Review of Entomology 40, 269–295 (1995)

28. Zhabotinsky, A.M.: Periodic processes of malonic acid oxidation in a liquid phase. Biofizika 9, 306–311 (1964)

Spiking Neural P Systems with Functional Astrocytes

Luis F. Macías-Ramos and Mario J. Pérez-Jiménez

Research Group on Natural Computing
Department of Computer Science and Artificial Intelligence
University of Sevilla, Spain
Avda. Reina Mercedes s/n. 41012 Sevilla, Spain
{lfmaciasr,marper}@us.es

Abstract. Spiking Neural P Systems (SN P Systems, for short) is a developing field within the universe of P Systems. New variants arise constantly as the study of their properties, such as computational completeness and computational efficiency, grows. Variants frequently incorporate new ingredients into the original model inspired by real neurophysiological structure of the brain. Astrocytes are one of the elements existing in that structure. Also known collectively as astroglia, astrocytes are characteristic star-shaped glial cells in the brain and spinal cord. In this paper, a new variant of Spiking Neural P Systems incorporating astrocytes is introduced. These astrocytes are modelled as computing devices capable of performing function computation in a single computation step. In order to experimentally study the action of Spiking Neural P Systems with astrocytes, it is necessary to develop software providing the required simulation tools. Within this trend, P–Lingua offers a standard language for the definition of P Systems. Part of the same software project, *pLinguaCore* library provides particular implementations of parsers and simulators for the models specified in P–Lingua. Along with the new SN P System variant with astrocytes, an extension of the P–Lingua language allowing definition of these systems is presented in this paper, as well as an upgrade of *pLinguaCore*, including a parser and a simulator that supports the aforementioned variant.

1 Introduction

Spiking Neural P Systems were introduced in [10] in the framework of membrane computing [16] as a new class of computing devices which are inspired by the neurophysiological behaviour of neurons sending electrical impulses (spikes) along axons to other neurons.

A SN P System consists of a set of neurons placed as nodes of a directed graph (called the *synapse graph*). Each neuron contains a number of copies of a single object type, the *spike*. Rules are assigned to neurons to control the way information flows between connected neurons, i.e. rules assigned to a neuron allow it to send spikes to its neighbouring neurons. SN P Systems usually work in a synchronous mode, where a global clock is assumed. In each time unit, for

E. Csuhaj-Varjú et al. (Eds.): CMC 2012, LNCS 7762, pp. 228–242, 2013.

each neuron, only one of the applicable rules is non-deterministically selected to be executed. Execution of rules takes place in parallel amongst all neurons of the system.

Since the introduction of this model, many computational properties of SN P Systems have been studied. It has been proved that they are **Turing**-complete when considered as number computing devices [10], used as language generators [5,3], or computing functions [15]. Also, many variants have come into scene bringing new ingredients into the model (or sometimes dropping some of them), while others modify its behaviour, that is, its semantics. Motivation of this "research boom" can be found in a quest for both enhancing expressivity and efficiency of the model, as well as exploring its computational power.

As a direct result of all of this, there is an extensive (and growing) bibliography related to SN P Systems. For instance, it has been shown [4] how usage of pre-computed resources makes them able to solve computationally hard problems in constant time. Also, study of different kinds of asynchronous "working modes" has been conducted [18]. In what concerns to the addition of new ingredients into the model, this involves (naming only some examples) weights [20], *antispikes* [12], extended rules [18] or budding and division rules [13].

A SN P Systems variant with astrocytes was first introduced in [2]. Astrocytes are glial cells connected to one or more synapses that can sense the whole spike traffic passing along their neighbouring synapses and, eventually, modify it. Their functionalities include biochemical support of endothelial cells that form the blood-brain barrier, provision of nutrients to the nervous tissue, maintenance of extracellular ion balance, and a role in the repair and scarring process of the brain and spinal cord following traumatic injuries. It has been shown that astrocytes propagate intercellular Ca_2^+ waves over long distances in response to stimulation, and, similarly to neurons, release transmitters (called gliotransmitters) in a Ca_2^+-dependent manner.

Moreover, within the dorsal horn of the spinal cord, activated astrocytes have the ability to respond to almost all neurotransmitters [9] and, upon activation, release a multitude of neuroactive molecules that influences neuronal excitability. Synaptic modulation by astrocytes takes place because of the 3-part association between astrocytes and presynaptic and postsynaptic terminals forming the so-called "tripartite synapse" [1].

Such discoveries have made astrocytes an important area of research within the field of neuroscience, thus also an interesting element to consider bringing into Natural Computing disciplines like Membrane Computing.

The model presented in [2], pretty complex, was then simplified in [17], in which only inhibitory astrocytes were considered. This simplification was recently revised again in [14], where "hybrid" astrocytes were introduced. Behaviour of an astrocyte of this kind, inhibitory or excitatory, relied on the amount of spikes passing on its neighbouring synapses, in relation to a given threshold associated to it. Thus, for a given astrocyte ast with associated threshold t with k spikes passing along its neighbouring synapses syn_{ast} at a certain instant, a) if $k > t$, the astrocyte ast has an inhibitory influence on the neighbouring synapses, and the k spikes are simultaneously suppressed (that is, the spikes are removed from the system); b) if $k < t$, the astrocyte ast has an excitatory influence on the neighbouring synapses, all spikes survive and pass to their destination neurons, reaching them simultaneously; c) if $k = t$, the astrocyte ast non-deterministically chooses an inhibitory or excitatory influence on the neighbouring synapses. It is possible for two or more astrocytes to control the same synapse. In this case, only if every astrocyte has an excitatory influence on the synapse the spikes passing along that synapse survive.

In this paper, again, a new variant is introduced. Based upon the original model defined in [2], new ingredients are introduced in order to turn astrocytes into *function computation devices*. Briefly, a set of pairs (threshold, function) is associated with each astrocyte. Existing spike traffic measured on distinguished neighbouring *control synapses* attached to the astrocyte is matched against the thresholds until one of them is selected. Subsequently, the associated function to the matched threshold is selected. At this point, that function is computed taking as arguments the amounts of spikes measured on distinguished neighbouring *operand synapses* attached to the astrocyte. Finally, the result of the function computation is sent through a distinguished operand synapse.

So, by introducing this new kind of astrocytes, not only covering of functionality of the astrocytes defined in [2] is achieved, also any computable partial function between natural numbers can be computed in a single computation step. Moreover, this new ingredient eases the design of machines that calculate functions, as astrocytes can be viewed as "macros".

In addition, a P–Lingua based simulator for the proposed model has been developed, which also simulates the model defined in [14]. The aforementioned simulator is an extension of the one presented in [11]. P–Lingua is a programming language intended to define P Systems [7,8,19], that comes together with a Java library providing several services (e.g., parsers for input files and built-in simulators).

This paper is structured as follows. Section 2 is devoted to introduce the formal specification of SN P Systems with Functional Astrocytes (*SNPSFA* for short). Section 3, is devoted to show applications of the presented model. Section 4 is devoted to simulation: A P–Lingua syntax for defining SNPSFA is introduced, along with several examples. Finally, the simulation algorithm is shown. Section 5 covers conclusions and future work.

2   Spiking Neural P Systems with Functional Astrocytes

In this section, we introduce SN P Systems with Functional Astrocytes.

2.1   Syntax

A *Spiking Neural P System with Functional Astrocytes* (SNPSFA for short) of degree $(m, l), m \geq 1, l \geq 1$, is a construct of the form

$$\Pi = (O, \sigma, syn, ast, out), \text{ where:}$$

- $O = \{a\}$ is the singleton alphabet (a is called *spike*);
- $\sigma = \{\sigma_1, \ldots, \sigma_m\}$ is the finite set of neurons, of the form $\sigma_i = (n_i, R_i), 1 \leq i \leq m$, where:
  - $n_i \geq 0$ is the initial number of spikes contained in σ_i;
  - R_i is a finite set of extended rules of the following form:

$$E/a^c \rightarrow a^p$$

where E is a regular expression over a, and $c \geq 1$, $p \geq 1$ with $c \geq p$;
- $syn = \{s_1, \ldots, s_\theta\} \subseteq \{1, \ldots, m\} \times \{1, \ldots, m\}$ with $(i,i) \notin syn$ is the *set of synapses*;
- $ast = \{ast_1, \ldots, ast_l\}$ is the finite set of astrocytes, with $ast_j, (1 \leq j \leq l)$ of the form

$$ast_j = (syn_j^o, syn_j^c, \omega_j, T_j, F_j, p_j(0), \gamma_j), \text{ where:}$$

  - $syn_j^o = \{s_{j,1}^o, \ldots, s_{j,r_j}^o\} \subseteq syn, r_j \geq 1$, is the astrocyte finite set of *operand synapses*, ordered by a lexicographical order imposed on syn_j^o;
  - $syn_j^c = \{s_{j,1}^c, \ldots, s_{j,q_j}^c\} \subseteq syn, q_j \geq 0$, is the astrocyte finite set of *control synapses*;
  - $\omega_j \in \{true, false\}$ is the astrocyte control-as-operand flag;
  - $T_j = \{T_{j,1}, \ldots, T_{j,k_j}\}, k_j \geq 1$, is the astrocyte finite set of thresholds, such that, $T_{j,\alpha} \in \mathbb{N}, (1 \leq \alpha \leq k_j)$ and $T_{j,1} < \ldots < T_{j,k_j}$;
  - $F_j = \{f_{j,1}, \ldots, f_{j,k_j}\}$ is the astrocyte finite *multiset* (some elements in F_j can be the same) of natural functions such that for each α $(1 \leq \alpha \leq k_j)$:
    * $f_{j,\alpha}$ is a computable function between natural numbers;
    * if $\omega_j = true$ then $f_{j,\alpha}$ is a unary function;
    * if $\omega_j = false$ and $r_j = 1$ then $f_{j,\alpha}$ is a unary constant function;
    * if $\omega_j = false$ and $r_j > 1$ then $f_{j,\alpha}$ has arity $r_j - 1$;
  - $p_j(0) \in \mathbb{N}$ is the astrocyte initial potential;
  - $\gamma_j \in \{true, false\}$ is the astrocyte potential update flag;
- $out \in \sigma$ is the output neuron.

2.2 Semantics

In order to set semantics of a SNPSFA, let us informally introduce some topological aspects of the model and the nature of the firing process. Given a synapse $s_g = (\sigma_{g,1}, \sigma_{g,2}) \in syn$, if an astrocyte is linked to s_g, it can be viewed as that it "makes contact" with s_g in the "space between" s_g^1 and s_g^2 (it can be said that the astrocyte is "attached" to the synapse as well). If there exists several astrocytes attached to s_g, all of them make contact at the same intermediate point. These astrocytes can simultaneously read the spike traffic going from $\sigma_{g,1}$ to $\sigma_{g,2}$ at an instant t and eventually modify it.

Keeping in mind the intuitive ideas expressed above, we proceed now to formally specify the semantics of *SN P Systems with Functional Astrocytes* as an extension of the one defined for the well-known SN P Systems model. A global clock is assumed and in every computation step one and only one rule can be selected for a given neuron. Let us introduce the following notation as a matter of convenience: given a synapse $s_y = (\sigma_y^1, \sigma_y^2)$, we denote by σ_y^1 the input neuron of s_y and by σ_y^2 the output neuron of s_y.

An astrocyte can sense the spike traffic passing along its neighbouring synapses, both control and operand ones. For an astrocyte ast_j, if there are k spikes passing along the control synapses in an instant t and the current potential of ast_j at t is p, then the value $s = k + p$ is computed. At this point, the number h satisfying that $s \in [T_{j,h}, T_{j,h+1})$ is computed out of s. Let us notice that if $s < T_{j,1}$ then $h = 1$, and if $s > T_{j,k_j}$ then $h = k_j$. Following this, by using both h and the boolean value ω_j, a number s' is computed as follows. If $\omega_j = true$ then $s' = f_{j,h}(s)$ directly. Otherwise, two cases are considered: a) if the number of operand synapses r_j is one, then $s' = f_{j,h}(0)$; and b) if the number of operand synapses is greater than one and assuming that $x_1, x_2, \ldots, x_{r_j-1}$ spikes are passing along the respective operand synapses associated to ast_j, then $s' = f_{j,h}(x_1, x_2, \ldots, x_{r_j-1})$. Finally, the multisets of the input and output neurons associated to the operand and control synapses are updated. For the output neurons: a) if they are associated to control synapses, then their corresponding multisets are added the spikes passing along the synapses at instant t; and b) if they are associated to operand synapses, then no change is applied to their multisets, except for neuron s_{j,r_j}^o, which is added s' spikes. Similarly, multisets corresponding to input neurons associated to both operand and control synapses are subtracted the spikes passing along the aforementioned synapses at instant t.

As a last remark, if the astrocyte potential update flag $\gamma_j = true$ then the astrocyte potential in $t + 1$ will be incremented in s units. Otherwise, the astrocyte potential does not change.

3   Applications of Spiking Neural P Systems with Functional Astrocytes

As mentioned before, by introducing SNPSFA covering of functionality of astrocytes defined in [2] is achieved. Also, astrocytes within SNPSFA are able to compute any computable natural partial function $f : \mathbb{N}^m - \to \mathbb{N}$ in a single computation step. Let us illustrate this fact by showing how to re-implement the examples covered in [2] within the scope of our proposed model. Moreover, the corresponding P–Lingua files for the aforementioned examples are covered in Section 4, thus by running the introduced simulator against these files, its working process can be checked in relation to the semantics presented above.

3.1   Excitatory and Inhibitory Astrocytes

First couple of examples shows how to implement excitatory and inhibitory astrocytes respectively, with a given threshold k. Implementation involves defining two functions: $f(x)$, which is the identically zero function of arity one, and $g(x)$.

Excitatory astrocyte, ast_{exc}, is depicted in the Fig. 1 with its formal specification being:

$$ast_{exc} = (\{(p',q)\}, \{(p,q')\}, true, \{0,k\}, \{f(x),g(x)\}, 0, false)$$

and its working equation, assuming that α spikes pass through synapse (p,q') at a given instant t, being:

$$ast_{exc}(\alpha,t) = \begin{cases} f(\alpha) = 0 & \text{if } 0 \leq \alpha < k \\ g(\alpha) & \text{if } \alpha \geq k \end{cases}$$

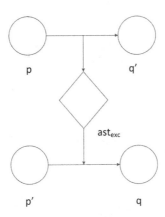

Fig. 1. Excitatory astrocyte

Inhibitory astrocyte, ast_{inh}, is structurally identical to ast_{exc}, with its formal specification being:

$$ast_{inh} = (\{(p',q)\}, \{(p,q')\}, true, \{0,k+1\}, \{g(x),f(x)\}, 0, false)$$

and its working equation, assuming that α spikes pass through synapse (p,q') at a given instant t, being:

$$ast_{inh}(\alpha,t) = \begin{cases} g(\alpha) & \text{if } 0 \leq \alpha \leq k \\ f(\alpha) = 0 & \text{if } \alpha \geq k+1 \end{cases}$$

3.2   Logic Gates

Second couple of examples shows how to implement logical gates, concretely AND-gates and NAND-gates respectively. Implementation involves defining two functions, $f(x)$ and $g(x)$, both of them unary constant functions, which associates the 0 and 1 natural values respectively for every $x \in \mathbb{N}$.

AND-gate astrocyte, ast_{and}, is depicted in the Fig. 2 with its formal specification being:

$$ast_{and} = (\{(p, q)\}, \{(A, A'), (B, B')\}, false, \{1, 2\}, \{f(x), g(x)\}, 0, false)$$

and its working equation, assuming that $\alpha, 0 \le \alpha \le 2$ spikes in total pass through synapses (A, A') and (B, B') at a given instant t, being:

$$ast_{and}(\alpha, t) = \begin{cases} f(0) = 0 & \text{if } 0 \le \alpha \le 1 \\ g(0) = 1 & \text{if } \alpha = 2 \end{cases}$$

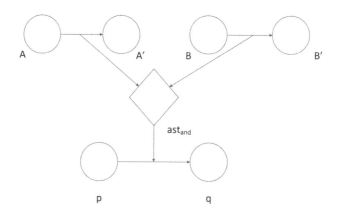

Fig. 2. AND-gate astrocyte

NAND-gate astrocyte, ast_{nand}, is structurally identical to ast_{and}, with its formal specification being:

$$ast_{nand} = (\{(p, q)\}, \{(A, A'), (B, B')\}, false, \{1, 2\}, \{g(x), f(x)\}, 0, false)$$

and its working equation, assuming that $\alpha, 0 \le \alpha \le 2$ spikes in total pass through synapses (A, A') and (B, B') at a given instant t, being:

$$ast_{nand}(\alpha, t) = \begin{cases} g(0) = 1 & \text{if } 0 \le \alpha \le 1 \\ f(0) = 0 & \text{if } \alpha = 2 \end{cases}$$

3.3   Discrete Amplifier

Last example shows how to implement a discrete amplifier which, as soon as the spike amount passing through control synapse (B, B') goes beyond a given threshold k, computes the amplification function $f_{*,n}(x) = n * x$ from the input given at E, otherwise no amplification is performed. Rules $a^l \rightarrow a^l$ belonging to neuron p are interpreted in the same way as in [2]. Implementation involves defining two functions: $g(x) = f_{*,n}(x)$ and $f(x)$, which associates x for every $x \in \mathbb{N}$.

Discrete amplifier astrocyte, ast_{amp}, is depicted in the Fig. 3 with its formal specification being:

$$ast_{amp} = (\{(p, p'), (q', q)\}, \{(B, B')\}, false, \{0, k\}, \{f(x), g(x)\}, 0, false)$$

and its working equation, assuming that at a given instant t α spikes pass through synapse (B, B') and β spikes pass through synapse (p, p'), being:

$$ast_{amp}(\alpha, \beta, t) = \begin{cases} f(\beta) = \beta & \text{if } 0 \leq \alpha < k \\ g(\beta) = n * \beta & \text{if } \alpha \geq k \end{cases}$$

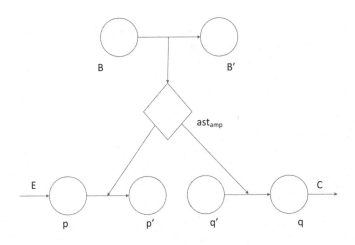

Fig. 3. Discrete amplifier astrocyte

4 A P–Lingua Based Simulator for SNPSFA

This section introduces a P–Lingua simulator for SNPSFA, extending the one presented in [11]. *SNPSFA are only partially simulated because only certain functions can be defined within P–Lingua framework.* Also, let us notice that an extension of the simulator presented here intended to simulate SNPSA as introduced in [14] is being developed.

P–Lingua syntax for specifying aforementioned SNPSFA is introduced, along with several examples. To conclude, the simulation algorithm is shown.

4.1   P–Lingua Syntax

A set of new features has been incorporated into P–Lingua in order to support
SNPSFA. New instructions have been included to define both astrocytes and
functions, extending the P–Lingua model specification framework for Spiking
Neural P Systems. Thus, these instructions can be used only when the source
P–Lingua files defining the models begin with the following sentence:

```
@model<spiking_psystems>
```

In what follows, P–Lingua syntax for defining SNPSFA is introduced.

– *Astrocytes.*

The following sentence can be used to define a SNPSFA astrocyte ast_j^b, with b
standing for *binder*, as the astrocytes presented in [2] inspired the functional
astrocytes presented in this paper:

```
@mastb =
(
    label-j,
    operand-synapses-j,control-synapses-j,control-operand-flag-j,
    set-thresholds-j,set-functions-j,
    potential-j,update-potential-j
);
```

where:
- *label-j* is the label of the astrocyte;
- *operand-synapses-j* is the set of operand synapses associated to the
  astrocyte, with *operand-synapses-j* $= \{s_{j,1}^o, \ldots, s_{j,r_j}^o\}$ and $s_{j,v}^o =$
  $(\sigma_{j,v}^{o,1}, \sigma_{j,v}^{o,2})$, a pair of neuron labels defining the synapse;
- *control-synapses-j* is the set of control synapses associated to the
  astrocyte, with *control-synapses-j* $= \{s_{j,1}^c, \ldots, s_{j,q_j}^c\}$ and $s_{j,u}^c =$
  $(\sigma_{j,u}^{c,1}, \sigma_{j,u}^{c,2})$, a pair of neuron labels defining the synapse;
- *control-operand-flag-j* is the astrocyte control-as-operand flag, with
  control-operand-flag-j $\in \{true, false\}$;
- *set-thresholds-j* is the astrocyte natural set of thresholds, defined as
  set-thresholds-j $= \{T_{j,1}, \ldots, T_{j,k_j}\}$ with $T_{j,1} < \ldots < T_{j,k_j}$;
- *set-functions-j* is the astrocyte set of natural computable functions,
  defined as *set-functions-j* $= \{f_{j,1}, \ldots, f_{j,k_j}\}$, all of them having the
  same arity;
- *potential-j* is the astrocyte initial potential, with *potential-j* $\in \mathbb{N}$;
- *update-potential-j* is the astrocyte potential update flag, verifying that
  update-potential-j $\in \{true, false\}$;

– *Functions.*

The following sentence can be used to define a function of name *f-name*:

```
@mastfunc =
(
    f-name(x1,...,xN),
    f-name(x1,...,xN) = "expr(x1,...,xN)"
);
```

where:
- *f-name* is the function name, a P–Lingua identifier;
- $x1, \ldots, xN$ is the list of arguments; notation for naming arguments must follow the convention of starting with x and immediately being followed by a integer literal, starting with 1 and being incremented in one unit each time;
- $exp(x1, ..., xN)$ is the function defining expression; this expression must yield a natural number; because of the underlying coding library, *exp4j* [6], definition of functions is restricted (see http://projects.congrace.de/exp4j/ for more details about the syntax on defining functions);

Let us notice that, as we are restricted when defining functions, SNPSFA are only partially simulated. The following functions are pre-defined, thus can be used directly, without having to be explicitly defined in the P–Lingua source file:

- $zero(x1)$ is the identically zero function of arity one;
- $identity(x1)$ is the identity function of arity one;
- $pol()$ is a *function template* allowing the definition of a polynomial astrocyte function $pol(x_0, x_1, \ldots, x_n, x)$ of any arity $n + 2, n \geq 0$, defined as follows:

$$pol(x_0, x_1, \ldots, x_n, x) = x_0 + \sum_{i=1}^{n} x_i * x^i$$

with $x_i \in \mathbb{N}, 0 \leq i \leq n, x \in \mathbb{N}$;

$x_0, \ldots, x_n, x$ arguments take value from the spikes passing through the operand synapses associated to a given astrocyte ast_j at a instant t in the following way:

$$\begin{cases} x_0 \leftarrow s^o_{j,1}(t) \\ x_1 \leftarrow s^o_{j,2}(t) \\ \cdots \\ x_n \leftarrow s^o_{j,r_{j-2}}(t) \\ x \leftarrow s^o_{j,r_{j-1}}(t) \end{cases}$$

- $sub()$ is a *function template* allowing the definition of a natural substraction function $sub(x_1, \ldots, x_n)$ of any arity n greater or equal than one, defined as follows:

$$sub(x_1, \ldots, x_n) = \begin{cases} x_1 - x_2 - \cdots - x_n & \text{when} \quad x_1 - x_2 - \cdots - x_n \geq 0 \\ 0 & \text{otherwise} \end{cases}$$

with $x_i \in \mathbb{N}, 1 \leq i \leq n$;

$x_1, \ldots, x_n$ arguments take value from the spikes passing through the operand synapses of a given astrocyte ast_j at an instant t in the following way:

$$\begin{cases} x_1 \leftarrow s_{j,1}^o(t) \\ \cdots \\ x_n \leftarrow s_{j,r_{j-1}}^o(t) \end{cases}$$

Let us notice that if $n = 1$ and the astrocyte control-as-operand-flag is set, then it is trivial to show that $sub(x_1, \ldots, x_n) = potential(j, t) + spikes(j, t)$.

4.2 Examples

In what follows, a set of on-line examples are listed. Each of them corresponds to a P–Lingua file that shows one of the SNPSFA applications presented through Section 3.

- Excitatory astrocyte:
  http://www.p-lingua.org/examples/SNPSFA_excitatory.pli.

- Inhibitory astrocyte:
  http://www.p-lingua.org/examples/SNPSFA_inbitory.pli.

- AND-gate:
  http://www.p-lingua.org/examples/SNPSFA_AND_gate.pli.

For this example, forgetting rules have been used assuming a natural extension of the proposed model. This allows generating "random" boolean signals coming from neurons A and B.

- Discrete amplifier:
  http://www.p-lingua.org/examples/SNPSFA_amplifier.pli.

4.3   Simulation Algorithm

In [8], a Java library called *pLinguaCore* was presented, with this package being released under GPL license. The library provides parsers to handle input files, built–in simulators to generate P System computations and is able to export several output file formats that represent P Systems. *pLinguaCore* is not a closed product because developers with knowledge of Java can add new components to the library, thus extending it. In this paper, an upgrade of the library is presented. Support for SNPSFA has been included, as an extension of the works presented in [11]. As a result of this, *pLinguaCore* is now able to handle input P–Lingua files defining SNPSFA. In addition, a new built–in simulator capable of simulating computations of these systems has been included into the library. For downloading the latest version of *pLinguaCore*, please refer to http://www.p-lingua.org. Also, a simulator for astrocytes as introduced in [14] is in development.

Required Additional Notation. Before presenting the simulation algorithm corresponding to the SNPSFA implementation in pLingaCore, let us introduce some required notation, which follows from Section 2.

- Given an astrocyte ast_j, $(1 \leq j \leq l)$, we denote the synapses attached to ast_j as $s_{j,w}^{\lambda} = (\sigma_{j,w}^{\lambda,1}, \sigma_{j,w}^{\lambda,2})$, $\lambda \in \{o,c\}$, $w \in \{u,v\}$, and:
  - we denote the operand synapses of ast_j as

$$s_{j,v}^{o} = (\sigma_{j,v}^{o,1}, \sigma_{j,v}^{o,2}), 1 \leq v \leq r_j, (r_j \geq 1);$$

  - we denote the control synapses of ast_j as

$$s_{j,u}^{c} = (\sigma_{j,u}^{c,1}, \sigma_{j,u}^{c,2}), 1 \leq u \leq q_j, (q_j \geq 0).$$

- Given an astrocyte ast_j, $(1 \leq j \leq l)$ attached to a synapse $s_{j,w}^{\lambda} = (\sigma_{j,w}^{\lambda,1}, \sigma_{j,w}^{\lambda,2})$ as defined above, we denote $s_{j,w}^{\lambda}(t)$ as the number of spikes fired by $\sigma_{j,w}^{\lambda,1}$ at an instant t of a computation.
- Given a neuron $\sigma_i, 1 \leq i \leq m$, we denote
  - $\sigma_i(t)$ = number of spikes contained in σ_i at instant t by a computation
  - $l_i(t)$ = number of spikes corresponding to the left hand side of the selected rule in neuron σ_i at instant t by a computation
  - $r_i(t)$ = number of spikes corresponding to the right hand side of the selected rule in neuron σ_i at instant t by a computation

Simulation Algorithm in Pseudo-Code Form. The following pseudo-code shows a computation step from instant t to $t + 1$ for a SNPSFA, illustrating the way in which the simulator operates. The pseudo-code is structured in two algorithms, following the semantics of SNPSFA introduced in Section 2. The first one deals with the input neurons of the systems, while the second one deals with astrocytes and output neurons.

Algorithm 1. Neurons loop

1: let $\sigma = \{\sigma_1, \ldots, \sigma_m\}$ be the set of all the neurons in the system
2: **for** $i = 1$ **to** m **do**
3:     $\sigma_i(t+1) \leftarrow \sigma_i(t) - l_i(t)$
4: **end for**

Algorithm 2. Astrocytes loop

1: let $ast = \{ast_1, \ldots, ast_l\}$ be the set of all the astrocytes in the system
2: **for** $j = 1$ **to** l **do**
3:     $spikes(j,t) \leftarrow \sum\limits_{u=1}^{q_j} s_{j,u}^c(t)$
4:     $selector(j,t) \leftarrow spikes(j,t) + p_j(t)$
5:     $h \leftarrow \begin{cases} 1 & \text{if } selector(j,t) < T_{j,1} \\ k_j & \text{if } selector(j,t) > T_{j,k_j} \\ e & \text{if } e = \max\{x \mid 1 \le x \le k_j \wedge T_{j,x} \le selector(j,t)\} \end{cases}$
6:     $f_j^* \leftarrow f_{j,h}$
7:     **if** $\omega_j = true$ **then**
8:         $output(j,t) \leftarrow f_j^*(selector(j,t))$
9:     **end if**
10:    **if** $\omega_j = false$ and $r_j = 1$ **then**
11:        $output(j,t) \leftarrow f_j^*(0)$
12:    **end if**
13:    **if** $\omega_j = false$ and $r_j > 1$ **then**
14:        $output(j,t) \leftarrow f_j^*(s_{j,1}^o(t), \ldots, s_{j,r_j-1}^o(t))$
15:    **end if**
16:    **for** $u = 1$ **to** q_j **do**
17:        $\sigma_{j,u}^{c,2}(t+1) \leftarrow \sigma_{j,u}^{c,2}(t) + s_{j,u}^c(t)$
18:    **end for**
19:    **for** $v = 1$ **to** $r_j - 1$ **do**
20:        $\sigma_{j,v}^{o,2}(t+1) \leftarrow \sigma_{j,v}^{o,2}(t)$
21:    **end for**
22:    $\sigma_{j,r_j}^{o,2}(t+1) \leftarrow \sigma_{j,r_j}^{o,2}(t) + output(j,t)$
23:    **if** $\gamma_j = true$ **then**
24:        $p_j(t+1) \leftarrow spikes(j,t)$
25:    **end if**
26: **end for**

---

5 Conclusions and Future Work

In this paper we present a new variant of Spiking Neural P Systems, wich includes astrocytes capable of calculating computable functions in a simple computation step. Applications of this variant are vast, as exemplified in the study cases shown, but yet to explore. In this sense, a new release of P–Lingua, that extends the previous SN P System simulator has been developed, incorporating the ability to work with astrocytes. This new simulator has been included into the library *pLinguaCore* and tested by simulating examples taken from the literature, concretely the ones existing in [14] and [2] (these ones adapted to the introduced SNPSFA variant).

At the moment, an extension of the implemented simulator supporting Spiking Neural P System with "hybrid" Astrocytes as defined in [14] is in development. Once this work is done, a desirable feature would be to provide a mechanism for defining arbitrary computable functions, thus fully simulating SNPSFA. Additional elements such as weights and antispikes might also be incorporated.

Also, restricted versions of SNPSFAs might be considered. For instance, in nature only a few astrocytes can be "attached" to a synapse. Thus, it would be interesting to define a model in which there exists an upper limit on the number of astrocytes that can be "attached" to a given synapse, say 3.

Acknowledgements. The authors acknowledge the support of the project TIN2009–13192 of the Ministerio de Ciencia e Innovación of Spain, cofinanced by FEDER funds, and the support of the Project of Excellence with *Investigador de Reconocida Valía* of the Junta de Andalucía, grant P08-TIC-04200.

References

1. Araque, A., Parpura, V., Sanzgiri, R.P., Haydon, P.G.: Tripartite synapses: glia, the unacknowledged partner. Trends in Neuroscience 22(5), 208–215 (1999)
2. Binder, A., Freund, R., Oswald, M., Vock, L.: Extended spiking neural P Systems with excitatory and inhibitory astrocytes. In: Proceedings of the 8th Conference on 8th WSEAS International Conference on Evolutionary Computing, EC 2007, vol. 8, pp. 320–325. World Scientific and Engineering Academy and Society (WSEAS), Stevens Point (2007)
3. Chen, H., Freund, R., Ionescu, M., Păun, G., Pérez-Jiménez, M.J.: On string languages generated by spiking neural P Systems. Fundam. Inform. 75(1-4), 141–162 (2007)
4. Chen, H., Ionescu, M., Isdorj, T.O.: On the efficiency of spiking neural P Systems. In: Proceedings of the 8th International Conference on Electronics, Information, and Communication, Ulanbator, Mongolia, pp. 49–52 (06 2006)
5. Chen, H., Ionescu, M., Ishdorj, T.O., Păun, A., Păun, G., Pérez-Jiménez, M.J.: Spiking neural P Systems with extended rules: universality and languages. Natural Computing 7(2), 147–166 (2008)
6. Congrace Developer Team: The exp4j website, http://projects.congrace.de/exp4j/
7. Díaz-Pernil, D., Pérez-Hurtado, I., Pérez-Jiménez, M.J., Riscos-Núñez, A.: A P-Lingua Programming Environment for Membrane Computing. In: Corne, D.W., Frisco, P., Păun, G., Rozenberg, G., Salomaa, A. (eds.) WMC 2008. LNCS, vol. 5391, pp. 187–203. Springer, Heidelberg (2009)
8. García-Quismondo, M., Gutiérrez-Escudero, R., Pérez-Hurtado, I., Pérez-Jiménez, M.J., Riscos-Núñez, A.: An Overview of P-Lingua 2.0. In: Păun, G., Pérez-Jiménez, M.J., Riscos-Núñez, A., Rozenberg, G., Salomaa, A. (eds.) WMC 2009. LNCS, vol. 5957, pp. 264–288. Springer, Heidelberg (2010)

9. Haydon, P.G.: Glia: listening and talking to the synapse. Nature Reviews Neuroscience 2(3), 185–193 (2001)
10. Ionescu, M., Păun, G., Yokomori, T.: Spiking neural P Systems. Fundam. Inform. 71(2-3), 279–308 (2006)
11. Macías–Ramos, L.F., Pérez–Hurtado, I., García–Quismondo, M., Valencia–Cabrera, L., Pérez–Jiménez, M.J., Riscos–Núñez, A.: A P–Lingua Based Simulator for Spiking Neural P Systems. In: Gheorghe, M., Păun, G., Rozenberg, G., Salomaa, A., Verlan, S. (eds.) CMC 2011. LNCS, vol. 7184, pp. 257–281. Springer, Heidelberg (2012)
12. Pan, L., Păun, G.: Spiking neural P Systems with anti-spikes. International Journal of Computers, Communications and Control IV, 273–282 (09 2009)
13. Pan, L., Păun, G., Pérez-Jiménez, M.J.: Spiking neural P Systems with neuron division and budding. Science China Information Sciences 54(8), 1596–1607 (2011)
14. Pan, L., Wang, J., Hoogeboom, H.J.: Asynchronous Extended Spiking Neural P Systems with Astrocytes. In: Gheorghe, M., Păun, G., Rozenberg, G., Salomaa, A., Verlan, S. (eds.) CMC 2011. LNCS, vol. 7184, pp. 243–256. Springer, Heidelberg (2012)
15. Păun, A., Păun, G.: Small universal spiking neural P Systems. Biosystems 90(1), 48–60 (2007)
16. Păun, G.: Computing with membranes (P Systems): An introduction. In: Current Trends in Theoretical Computer Science, pp. 845–866 (2001)
17. Păun, G.: Spiking neural P Systems with astrocyte-like control. J. UCS 13(11), 1707–1721 (2007)
18. Păun, G., Rozenberg, G., Salomaa, A.: The Oxford Handbook of Membrane Computing. Oxford University Press, Inc., New York (2010)
19. Research Group on Natural Computing, University of Seville: The p–lingua website, http://www.p-lingua.org
20. Wang, J., Hoogeboom, H.J., Pan, L., Păun, G., Pérez-Jiménez, M.J.: Spiking neural P Systems with weights. Neural Comput. 22(10), 2615–2646

The Efficiency of Tissue P Systems with Cell Separation Relies on the Environment

Luis F. Macías-Ramos[1], Mario J. Pérez-Jiménez[1], Agustín Riscos-Núñez[1], Miquel Rius-Font[2], and Luis Valencia-Cabrera[1]

[1] Research Group on Natural Computing
Department of Computer Science and Artificial Intelligence
University of Sevilla, Spain
{lfmaciasr,marper,ariscosn,lvalencia}@us.es
[2] Department of Applied Mathematics IV
Universitat Politècnica de Catalunya, Spain
mrius@ma4.upc.edu

Abstract. The classical definition of tissue P systems includes a distinguished alphabet with the special assumption that its elements are available in an arbitrarily large amount of copies. These objects are shared in a distinguished place of the system, called the *environment*. This ability of having infinitely many copies of some objects has been widely exploited in the design of efficient solutions to computationally hard problems by means of tissue P systems.

This paper deals with computational aspects of tissue P systems with cell separation where there is no such environment as described above. The main result is that only tractable problems can be efficiently solved by using this kind of P systems. Bearing in mind that **NP**–complete problems can be efficiently solved by using tissue P systems without environment and with cell division, we deduce that in the framework of tissue P systems without environment, the kind of rules (separation versus division) provides a new frontier of the tractability of decision problems.

Keywords: Membrane Computing, Tissue P System, Cell Separation, Environment of a Tissue, Computational Complexity, Borderline of Tractability.

1 Introduction

Membrane Computing is a young branch of *Natural Computing* initiated by Gh. Păun in the end of 1998 [15]. The computational devices of this paradigm, called *P systems*, operate in a distributed, parallel and non-deterministic manner, getting inspiration from living cells (their structure and functioning), as well as from the way cells are organized in tissues, organs, etc..

Several different models of cell-like P systems have been successfully used to solve computationally hard problems efficiently, by trading space for time, usually following a brute force approach: an exponential workspace is created

E. Csuhaj-Varjú et al. (Eds.): CMC 2012, LNCS 7762, pp. 243–256, 2013.

in polynomial time by using some kind of rules, and then massive parallelism is used to simultaneously check all the candidate solutions. Inspired by living cells, several ways for obtaining exponential workspace in polynomial time were proposed: membrane division (*mitosis*) [16], membrane creation (*autopoiesis*) [7], and membrane separation (*membrane fission*) [12]. These three ways have given rise to the following models: *P systems with active membranes*, *P systems with membrane creation*, and *P systems with membrane separation*.

A new type of P systems, the so-called *tissue P systems*, was considered in [10]. Instead of considering a hierarchical arrangement, membranes/cells are placed in the nodes of a virtual graph. This variant has two biological justifications (see [11]): intercellular communication and cooperation between neurons. The common mathematical model of these two mechanisms is a net of processors dealing with symbols and communicating these symbols along channels specified in advance. The communication among cells is based on symport/antiport rules, which were introduced to P systems in [18]. These models have a special alphabet associated with the environment of the system and it is assumed that the symbols of that alphabet appear in an arbitrary large amount of copies at the initial configuration of the system.

From the seminal definitions of tissue P systems [10,11], several research lines have been developed and other variants have arisen (see, for example, [1,2,4,8,9,14]). One of the most interesting variants of tissue P systems was presented in [19], where the definition of tissue P systems is combined with the one of P systems with active membranes, yielding *tissue P systems with cell division*.

In the biological phenomenon of fission, the contents of the two new cells evolved from a cell can be significantly different, and membrane separation inspired by this biological phenomenon in the framework of cell-like P systems was proved to be an efficient way to obtain exponential workspace in polynomial time [12]. In [13], a new class of tissue P systems based on cell fission, called *tissue P systems with cell separation*, was presented. Its computational efficiency was investigated, and two important results were obtained: (a) only tractable problems can be efficiently solved by using cell separation and communication rules with length at most 1, and (b) an efficient (uniform) solution to the SAT problem by using cell separation and communication rules with length at most 8 was presented. Since then, other results have been presented in this framework (see e.g. [26]), always making use of communication rules to bring the necessary elements from the environment.

In this paper we study the efficiency of tissue P systems with communication rules and cell separation where the alphabet associated with the environment is empty. These systems are called tissue P systems *without environment* and, specifically, we prove that only tractable problems can be solved in polynomial time by families of tissue P systems with communication rules, with cell separation and without environment.

The paper is organized as follows: first, we recall some preliminaries, and then, the definition of tissue P systems with cell separation, recognizer tissue P systems and computational complexity classes in this framework, are briefly described. Section 4 is devoted to the main result of the paper: the polynomial complexity class associated with $\widehat{\mathbf{TSC}}^1$ is the class $\mathbf{P}$. Finally, conclusions and further works are presented.

2   Preliminaries

An *alphabet*, Σ, is a non–empty set whose elements are called *symbols*. A finite sequence of symbols is a *string* over Σ. If u and v are strings over Σ, then so is their *concatenation* uv, obtained by juxtaposition, that is, writing u and v one after the other. The number of symbols in a string u is the *length* of the string, and it is denoted by $|u|$. As usual, the empty string (with length 0) will be denoted by λ. The set of all strings over an alphabet Σ is denoted by Σ^*. In algebraic terms, Σ^* is the free monoid generated by Σ under the operation of concatenation. Subsets of Σ^*, finite or infinite, are referred to as *languages* over Σ.

The *Parikh vector* associated with a string $u \in \Sigma^*$ with respect to the alphabet $\Sigma = \{a_1, \ldots, a_r\}$ is $\Psi_\Sigma(u) = (|u|_{a_1}, \ldots, |u|_{a_r})$, where $|u|_{a_i}$ denotes the number of ocurrences of the symbol a_i in the string u. This is called the *Parikh mapping* associated with Σ. Notice that in this definition the ordering of the symbols from Σ is relevant. If $\Sigma_1 = \{a_{i_1}, \ldots, a_{i_s}\} \subseteq \Sigma$ then we define $\Psi_{\Sigma_1}(u) = (|u|_{a_{i_1}}, \ldots, |u|_{a_{i_s}})$, for each $u \in \Sigma^*$.

A *multiset* m over a set A is a pair (A, f) where $f : A \to \mathbb{N}$ is a mapping. If $m = (A, f)$ is a multiset then its *support* is defined as $supp(m) = \{x \in A \,|\, f(x) > 0\}$. A multiset is empty (resp. finite) if its support is the empty set (resp. a finite set). If $m = (A, f)$ is a finite multiset over A, and $supp(m) = \{a_1, \ldots, a_k\}$ then it will be denoted as $m = \{a_1^{f(a_1)}, \ldots, a_k^{f(a_k)}\}$. That is, superscripts indicate the multiplicity of each element, and if $f(x) = 0$ for $x \in A$, then the element x is omitted. A finite multiset $m = \{a_1^{f(a_1)}, \ldots, a_k^{f(a_k)}\}$ can also be represented by the string $a_1^{f(a_1)} \ldots a_k^{f(a_k)}$ over the alphabet $\{a_1, \ldots, a_k\}$. Nevertheless, all permutations of this string identify the same multiset m precisely. Throughout this paper, whenever we refer to "the finite multiset m" where m is a string, this should be understood as "the finite multiset represented by the string m".

If $m_1 = (A, f_1)$, $m_2 = (A, f_2)$ are multisets over A, then we define the union of m_1 and m_2 as $m_1 + m_2 = (A, g)$, where $g = f_1 + f_2$, that is, $g(a) = f_1(a) + f_2(a)$, for each $a \in A$. We also define the difference $m_1 \setminus m_2$ as the multiset (A, h), where $h(a) = f_1(a) - f_2(a)$, in the case $f_1(a) \geq f_2(a)$, and $h(a) = 0$, otherwise. In particular, given two sets A and B, $A \setminus B$ is the set $\{x \in A \,|\, x \notin B\}$.

In what follows, we assume the reader is already familiar with the basic notions and the terminology of P systems. For details, see [17].

---

[1] $\widehat{\mathbf{TSC}}$ denotes the class of recognizer tissue P systems with cell communication, cell separation and without environment, as it will be explained in Sect. 3.

2.1   Tissue P Systems with Communication Rules and with Cell Separation

A *tissue P system with communication rules and with cell separation* of degree q $(q \geq 1)$ is a tuple $\Pi = (\Gamma, \mathcal{E}, \Gamma_0, \Gamma_1, \mathcal{M}_1, \ldots, \mathcal{M}_q, \mathcal{R}, i_{out})$, where:

1. Γ is a finite *alphabet*.
2. $\mathcal{E} \subseteq \Gamma$.
3. $\{\Gamma_0, \Gamma_1\}$ is a partition of Γ, that is, $\Gamma = \Gamma_0 \cup \Gamma_1$, $\Gamma_0, \Gamma_1 \neq \emptyset$, $\Gamma_0 \cap \Gamma_1 = \emptyset$;
4. $\mathcal{M}_1, \ldots, \mathcal{M}_q$ are strings over Γ.
5. $\mathcal{R}$ is a finite set of rules of the following forms:
   Communication rules: $(i, u/v, j)$, for $i, j \in \{0, \ldots, q\}, i \neq j$, $u, v \in \Gamma^*$, $|u| + |v| > 0$;
   Separation rules: $[a]_i \rightarrow [\Gamma_0]_i [\Gamma_1]_i$, where $i \in \{1, \ldots, q\}$, $a \in \Gamma$ and $i \neq i_{out}$.
6. $i_{out} \in \{0, \ldots, q\}$.

A *tissue P system with communication rules and with cell separation* $\Pi = (\Gamma, \mathcal{E}, \Gamma_0, \Gamma_1, \mathcal{M}_1, \ldots, \mathcal{M}_q, \mathcal{R}, i_{out})$, of degree q can be viewed as a set of q cells, labelled by $1, \ldots, q$ such that: (a) $\mathcal{M}_1, \ldots, \mathcal{M}_q$ represent the finite multisets of objects initially placed in the q cells of the system; (b) $\mathcal{E}$ is the set of objects initially located in the environment of the system, all of them available in an arbitrary number of copies; and (c) i_{out} represents a distinguished *region* which will encode the output of the system. We use the term *region* i $(0 \leq i \leq q)$ to refer to cell i in the case $1 \leq i \leq q$ and to refer to the environment in the case $i = 0$.

A communication rule $(i, u/v, j)$ is called a *symport rule* if $u = \lambda$ or $v = \lambda$. A symport rule $(i, u/\lambda, j)$, with $i \neq 0, j \neq 0$, provides a virtual arc from cell i to cell j. A communication rule $(i, u/v, j)$ is called an *antiport rule* if $u \neq \lambda$ and $v \neq \lambda$. An antiport rule $(i, u/v, j)$, with $i \neq 0, j \neq 0$, provides two arcs: one from cell i to cell j and the other from cell j to cell i. Thus, every tissue P system has an underlying directed graph whose nodes are the cells of the system and the arcs are obtained from communication rules. In this context, the environment can be considered as a virtual node of the graph such that its connections are defined by communication rules of the form $(i, u/v, j)$, with $i = 0$ or $j = 0$.

When applying a rule $(i, u/v, j)$, the objects of the multiset represented by u are sent from region i to region j and, simultaneously, the objects of multiset v are sent from region j to region i. The length of communication rule $(i, u/v, j)$ is defined as $|u| + |v|$.

When applying a separation rule $[a]_i \rightarrow [\Gamma_0]_i [\Gamma_1]_i$, in reaction with an object a, the cell i is separated into two cells with the same label; at the same time, object a is consumed; the objects from Γ_0 are placed in the first cell, those from Γ_1 are placed in the second cell; the output cell i_{out} cannot be separated.

The rules of a system like the above one are used in a non-deterministic maximally parallel manner as customary in membrane computing. At each step, all cells which can evolve must evolve in a maximally parallel way (at each step we apply a multiset of rules which is maximal, no further applicable rule can be added). This way of applying rules has only one restriction: when a cell is separated, the separation rule is the only one which is applied for that cell at that step; thus, the objects inside that cell do not evolve by means of communication rules. The new cells resulting from separation could participate in the interaction with other cells or the environment by means of communication rules at the next step – providing that they are not separated once again. The label of a cell precisely identifies the rules which can be applied to it.

An *instantaneous description* or a *configuration* at any instant of a tissue P system with cell separation is described by all multisets of objects over Γ associated with all the cells present in the system, and the multiset of objects over $\Gamma - \mathcal{E}$ associated with the environment at that moment. Recall that there are infinitely many copies of objects from $\mathcal{E}$ in the environment, and hence this set is not properly changed along the computation. The *initial configuration* is $(\mathcal{M}_1, \cdots, \mathcal{M}_q; \emptyset)$. A configuration is a *halting configuration* if no rule of the system is applicable to it.

Let us fix a tissue P system with cell separation Π. We say that configuration $\mathcal{C}_1$ yields configuration $\mathcal{C}_2$ in one *transition step*, denoted by $\mathcal{C}_1 \Rightarrow_\Pi \mathcal{C}_2$, if we can pass from $\mathcal{C}_1$ to $\mathcal{C}_2$ by applying the rules from $\mathcal{R}$ following the previous remarks. A *computation* of Π is a (finite or infinite) sequence of configurations such that:

1. the first term of the sequence is the initial configuration of the system;
2. each non-initial configuration of the sequence is obtained from the previous configuration by applying rules of the system in a maximally parallel manner with the restrictions previously mentioned; and
3. if the sequence is finite (called *halting computation*) then the last term of the sequence is a halting configuration.

All computations start from an initial configuration and proceed as stated above; only halting computations give a result, which is encoded by the objects present in the output cell i_{out} in the halting configuration.

If $\mathcal{C} = \{\mathcal{C}_t\}_{t<r+1}$ of Π ($r \in \mathbb{N}$) is a halting computation, then the *length of* $\mathcal{C}$, denoted by $|\mathcal{C}|$, is r. That is, the length of the computation corresponds to the number of steps performed, or equivalently to the number of non-initial configurations which appear in the finite sequence $\mathcal{C}$ ($\mathcal{C}_0$ is the *initial configuration*). We also denote by $\mathcal{C}_t(i)$ the contents of region i ($0 \leq i \leq q$) at the configuration $\mathcal{C}_t$.

2.2   Recognizer Tissue P Systems

In order to study the computing efficiency, the notions from classical *computational complexity theory* are adapted for membrane computing, and a special class of cell-like P systems is introduced in [22]: *recognizer P systems* (called *accepting P systems* in a previous paper [21]). For tissue P systems, with the same idea as recognizer cell-like P systems, *recognizer tissue P systems* is introduced in [19].

A *recognizer tissue P system* with communication rules and with cell separation of degree q ($q \geq 1$) is a tuple $\Pi = (\Gamma, \mathcal{E}, \Sigma, \Gamma_0, \Gamma_1, \mathcal{M}_1, \ldots, \mathcal{M}_q, \mathcal{R}, i_{in}, i_{out})$, where:

– $(\Gamma, \mathcal{E}, \Gamma_0, \Gamma_1, \mathcal{M}_1, \ldots, \mathcal{M}_q, \mathcal{R}, i_{out})$ is a tissue P system with communication rules and with cell separation of degree q, as defined in the previous subsection.

– The working alphabet Γ has two distinguished objects yes and no, at least one copy of them present in some initial multisets $\mathcal{M}_1, \ldots, \mathcal{M}_q$.

– Σ is an (input) alphabet strictly contained in Γ such that $\Sigma \cap \mathcal{E} = \emptyset$.

– $\mathcal{M}_1, \ldots, \mathcal{M}_q$ are strings over $\Gamma \setminus \Sigma$.

– $i_{in} \in \{1, \ldots, q\}$ is the input cell.

– $i_{out} = 0$ is the output region, that is, the output of the system is encoded in the environment.

– All computations halt.

– If $\mathcal{C}$ is a computation of Π, then either object yes or object no (but not both) must have been released into the output region, and only at the last step of the computation.

For each $w \in \Sigma^*$, the *computation of the system Π with input* $w \in \Sigma^*$ starts from the configuration of the form $(\mathcal{M}_1, \ldots, \mathcal{M}_{i_{in}} + w, \ldots, \mathcal{M}_q; \emptyset)$, that is, the input multiset w has been added to the contents of the input cell i_{in}, and we denote it by $\Pi + w$. Therefore, we have an initial configuration associated with each input multiset w (over the input alphabet Σ) in this kind of systems.

Given such a recognizer tissue P system and a halting computation $\mathcal{C} = \{\mathcal{C}_t\}_{t < r+1}$ of Π ($r \in \mathbb{N}$), we define the result of $\mathcal{C}$ as follows:

$$
Output(\mathcal{C}) = \begin{cases} \text{yes}, & \text{if } \Psi_{\{\text{yes,no}\}}(M_{r,0}) = (1,0) \wedge \\ & \quad \Psi_{\{\text{yes,no}\}}(M_{t,0}) = (0,0) \text{ for } t = 0, \ldots, r-1 \\ \text{no}, & \text{if } \Psi_{\{\text{yes,no}\}}(M_{r,0}) = (0,1) \wedge \\ & \quad \Psi_{\{\text{yes,no}\}}(M_{t,0}) = (0,0) \text{ for } t = 0, \ldots, r-1 \end{cases}
$$

where Ψ is the Parikh mapping, and $M_{t,0}$ is the multiset over $\Gamma \setminus \mathcal{E}$ associated with region 0 at the configuration $\mathcal{C}_t$, in particular, $M_{r,0}$ is the multiset over $\Gamma \setminus \mathcal{E}$ associated with region 0 at the halting configuration $\mathcal{C}_r$.

We say that a computation $\mathcal{C}$ is an *accepting computation* (respectively, *rejecting computation*) if $Output(\mathcal{C}) = $ yes (respectively, $Output(\mathcal{C}) = $ no), that is, if object yes (respectively, object no) appears in the output region of the corresponding halting configuration of $\mathcal{C}$, and neither object yes nor no appears in the output region of any non–halting configuration of $\mathcal{C}$.

We denote by **TSC** the class of recognizer tissue P systems with cell communication and with cell separation. For each natural number $k \geq 1$, we denote by **TSC**(k) the class of recognizer tissue P systems with cell separation and with communication rules of length at most k.

3   Tissue P Systems with Communication Rules, with Cell Separation and without Environment

Definition 1. *A tissue P system with communication rules, with cell separation and without environment of degree $q + 1$ is a tuple*

$$\Pi = (\Gamma, \Gamma_0, \Gamma_1, \mathcal{M}_0, \mathcal{M}_1, \ldots, \mathcal{M}_q, \mathcal{R}, i_{out}),$$

where:

1. Γ *is a finite* alphabet.
2. $\{\Gamma_0, \Gamma_1\}$ *is a partition of* Γ, *that is,* $\Gamma = \Gamma_0 \cup \Gamma_1$, $\Gamma_0, \Gamma_1 \neq \emptyset$, $\Gamma_0 \cap \Gamma_1 = \emptyset$;
3. $\mathcal{M}_0, \mathcal{M}_1, \ldots, \mathcal{M}_q$ *are strings over* Γ.
4. $\mathcal{R}$ *is a finite set of rules of the following forms:*
   Communication rules: $(i, u/v, j)$, *for* $i, j \in \{0, \ldots, q\}, i \neq j$, $u, v \in \Gamma^*$, $|u| + |v| > 0$;
   Separation rules: $[a]_i \rightarrow [\Gamma_0]_i [\Gamma_1]_i$, *where* $i \in \{0, \ldots, q\}$, $a \in \Gamma$ *and* $i \neq i_{out}$.
5. $i_{out} \in \{0, \ldots, q\}$.

A *tissue P system with communication rules, with cell separation and without environment* is a tissue P system with communication rules and with cell separation such that the alphabet $\mathcal{E}$ of the environment is empty.

Definition 2. *A* recognizer tissue P system *with communication rules, with cell separation and without environment of degree* $q + 1$ *is a tuple*

$$\Pi = (\Gamma, \Sigma, \Gamma_0, \Gamma_1, \mathcal{M}_0, \mathcal{M}_1, \ldots, \mathcal{M}_q, \mathcal{R}, i_{in}, i_{out})$$

where:

- $(\Gamma, \Gamma_0, \Gamma_1, \mathcal{M}_0, \mathcal{M}_1, \ldots, \mathcal{M}_q, \mathcal{R}, i_{out})$ *is a tissue P system with communication rules, with cell separation and without environment of degree* $q + 1$, *as defined previously.*
- *The working alphabet* Γ *has two distinguished objects* **yes** *and* **no**, *at least one copy of them present in some initial multisets* $\mathcal{M}_0, \mathcal{M}_1, \ldots, \mathcal{M}_q$.
- Σ *is an (input) alphabet strictly contained in* Γ.
- $\mathcal{M}_0, \mathcal{M}_1, \ldots, \mathcal{M}_q$ *are strings over* $\Gamma \setminus \Sigma$.
- $i_{in} \in \{1, \ldots, q\}$ *is the input cell.*
- $i_{out} = 0$ *is the output cell.*
- *All computations halt.*
- *If* $\mathcal{C}$ *is a computation of* Π, *then either object* **yes** *or object* **no** *(but not both) must have been released into cell 0, and only at the last step of the computation.*

For each $w \in \Sigma^*$, the *computation of the system* Π *with input* $w \in \Sigma^*$ starts from the configuration of the form $(\mathcal{M}_0, \mathcal{M}_1, \ldots, \mathcal{M}_{i_{in}} + w, \ldots, \mathcal{M}_q; \emptyset)$, that is, the input multiset w has been added to the contents of the input cell i_{in}, and we denote it by $\Pi + w$. Therefore, we have an initial configuration associated with each input multiset w (over the input alphabet Σ) in this kind of systems.

Given a recognizer tissue P system with cell separation, and a halting computation $\mathcal{C}$ of Π, the result of $\mathcal{C}$ is defined as in the previous section.

We denote by $\widehat{\mathbf{TSC}}$ the class of recognizer tissue P systems with cell communication, cell separation and without environment. For each natural number $k \geq 1$, we denote by $\widehat{\mathbf{TSC}}(k)$ the class of recognizer tissue P systems with cell separation, without environment, and with communication rules of length at most k.

3.1 Polynomial Complexity Classes

Next, we define what solving a decision problem in a uniform and efficient way means in the framework of tissue P systems. Since we define each tissue P system to work on a finite number of inputs, to solve a decision problem we define a numerable family of tissue P systems.

Definition 3. *We say that a decision problem* $X = (I_X, \theta_X)$ *is solvable in a uniform way and polynomial time by a family* $\mathbf{\Pi} = \{\Pi(n) \mid n \in \mathbb{N}\}$ *of recognizer tissue P systems with communication rules, with cell separation and without environment if the following holds:*

- *The family* $\mathbf{\Pi}$ *is polynomially uniform by Turing machines, that is, there exists a deterministic Turing machine working in polynomial time which constructs the system* $\Pi(n)$ *from* $n \in \mathbb{N}$.
- *There exists a pair* (cod, s) *of polynomial-time computable functions over* I_X *such that:*
  - *for each instance* $u \in I_X$, $s(u)$ *is a natural number, and* $cod(u)$ *is an input multiset of the system* $\Pi(s(u))$;
  - *for each* $n \in \mathbb{N}$, $s^{-1}(n)$ *is a finite set;*
  - *the family* $\mathbf{\Pi}$ *is polynomially bounded with regard to* (X, cod, s), *that is, there exists a polynomial function* p, *such that for each* $u \in I_X$ *every computation of* $\Pi(s(u))$ *with input* $cod(u)$ *is halting and it performs at most* $p(|u|)$ *steps;*
  - *the family* $\mathbf{\Pi}$ *is sound with regard to* (X, cod, s), *that is, for each* $u \in I_X$, *if* <u>*there exists*</u> *an accepting computation of* $\Pi(s(u))$ *with input* $cod(u)$, *then* $\theta_X(u) = 1$;
  - *the family* $\mathbf{\Pi}$ *is complete with regard to* (X, cod, s), *that is, for each* $u \in I_X$, *if* $\theta_X(u) = 1$, *then* <u>*every*</u> *computation of* $\Pi(s(u))$ *with input* $cod(u)$ *is an accepting one.*

From the soundness and completeness conditions above, we deduce that every P system $\Pi(n)$ is *confluent*, in the following sense: every computation of a system with the *same* input multiset must always give the *same* answer.

Let $\mathbf{R}$ be a class of recognizer tissue P systems. We denote by $\mathbf{PMC_R}$ the set of all decision problems which can be solved in a uniform way and polynomial time by means of families of systems from $\mathbf{R}$. The class $\mathbf{PMC_R}$ is closed under complement and polynomial–time reductions [21].

4 Efficiency of Tissue P Systems with Cell Communication, with Cell Separation and without Environment

4.1 Representation of Tissue P Systems from $\widehat{\mathbf{TSC}}$

Let $\Pi = (\Gamma, \Sigma, \Gamma_0, \Gamma_1, \mathcal{M}_0, \mathcal{M}_1, \ldots, \mathcal{M}_q, \mathcal{R}, i_{in}, i_{out})$ be a recognizer tissue P system of degree $q+1$ with communication rules, with cell separation and without environment.

1. We denote by R_C (R_S respectively) the set of communication rules (separation rules respectively) of Π. We will fix total orders in R_C and R_S.

2. Let $\mathcal{C}$ be a computation of Π, and $\mathcal{C}_t$ a configuration of $\mathcal{C}$. The application of a communication rule keeps the multiset of objects of the whole system unchanged because only movement of objects between the cells of the system is produced. On the other hand, the application of a separation rule causes that an object is removed from the system, and since there is no objects replication, the rest remain unchanged. Thus, the multiset of objects of the system in any configuration $\mathcal{C}_t$ is contained in $\mathcal{M}_0 + \cdots + \mathcal{M}_q$. Moreover, if $M = |\mathcal{M}_0 + \cdots + \mathcal{M}_q|$ then $(q+1)+M$ is an upper bound of the number of cells at any configuration of the system, since each application of a separation rule increases the total number of cells by 1 and decreases the number of objects by 1.

3. In order to identify the cells created by the application of a separation rule, we modify the labels of the new membranes in the following manner:

   - The label of a cell will be a pair (i, σ) where $0 \leq i \leq q$ and $\sigma \in \{0,1\}^*$. At the initial configuration, the labels of the cells are $(0, \lambda), \ldots, (q, \lambda)$.
   - If a separation rule is applied to a cell labelled by (i, σ), then the new created cells will be labelled by $(i, \sigma 0)$ and $(i, \sigma 1)$, respectively. Cell $(i, \sigma 0)$ will contain the objects of cell (i, σ) which belong to Γ_0, and cell $(i, \sigma 1)$ will contain the objects of cell (i, σ) which belong to Γ_1.
   - Note that we can consider a lexicographical order over the set of labels (i, σ) in a natural way.

4. If cells labelled by (i, σ_i) and (j, σ_j) are engaged by a communication rule, then, after the application of the rule, both cells keep their labels.

5. A configuration of Π can be described by a multiset of labelled objects from $\{(a, i, \sigma)|\ a \in \Gamma \cup \{\lambda\}, 0 \leq i \leq q, \sigma \in \{0,1\}^*\}$.

6. Let $r \equiv (i, a_1 \cdots a_s / b_1 \cdots b_{s'}, j)$ be a communication rule of Π. If n is a natural number, then denote by $n \cdot LHS(r, (i, \sigma_i), (j, \sigma_j))$ the multiset of labelled objects "consumed" by applying n times rule r over cells (i, σ_i) and (j, σ_j). That is, $n \cdot LHS(r, (i, \sigma_i), (j, \sigma_j))$ is the following multiset

$$(a_1, i, \sigma_i)^n \cdots (a_s, i, \sigma_i)^n (b_1, j, \sigma_j)^n \cdots (b_{s'}, j, \sigma_j)^n$$

Similarly, $n \cdot RHS(r, (i, \sigma_i), (j, \sigma_j))$ denotes the multiset of labelled objects produced by applying n times rule r over cells (i, σ_i) and (j, σ_j). That is, $n \cdot RHS(r, (i, \sigma_i), (j, \sigma_j))$ is the following multiset

$$(a_1, j, \sigma_j)^n \cdots (a_s, j, \sigma_j)^n (b_1, i, \sigma_i)^n \cdots (b_{s'}, i, \sigma_i)^n$$

7. If $\mathcal{C}_t$ is a configuration of Π we denote by $\mathcal{C}_t + \{(x, i, \sigma)/\sigma'\}$ the multiset obtained by replacing in $\mathcal{C}_t$ every occurrence of (x, i, σ) by (x, i, σ'). Besides, $\mathcal{C}_t + m$ ($\mathcal{C}_t \setminus m$, respectively) is used to denote that a multiset m of labelled objects is added (removed, respectively) to the configuration.

4.2 Efficiency of Tissue P Systems from $\widehat{\text{TSC}}$

The goal of this section is to show that only tractable problems can be solved efficiently by using tissue P systems with communication rules, separation rules and without environment. That is, we will prove that $\mathbf{P} = \mathbf{PMC}_{\widehat{\text{TSC}}}$.

For this purpose, given a family of recognizer tissue P system, we provide a deterministic algorithm $\mathcal{A}$ working in polynomial time that receives as input a recognizer tissue P system from $\widehat{\text{TSC}}$ together with an input multiset, and reproduces the behaviour of a computation of such system. In particular, if the given tissue P system is confluent, then algorithm will provide the same answer of the system, that is, the answer of the algorithm is affirmative if and only if the input tissue P system has an accepting computation.

The pseudocode of the algorithm $\mathcal{A}$ is described as follows:

Input: A recognizer tissue P system Π from $\widehat{\text{TSC}}$ and an input multiset m
    Initialization stage: the initial configuration $\mathcal{C}_0$ of $\Pi + m$
    $t \leftarrow 0$
    while $\mathcal{C}_t$ is a non halting configuration **do**
        Selection stage: Input $\mathcal{C}_t$, Output $(\mathcal{C}_t', A)$
        Execution stage: Input $(\mathcal{C}_t', A)$, Output $\mathcal{C}_{t+1}$
        $t \leftarrow t+1$
    end while
Output: Yes if $\mathcal{C}_t$ is an accepting configuration, No otherwise

The selection stage and the execution stage implement a transition step of a recognizer tissue P system Π. Specifically, the selection stage receives as input a configuration $\mathcal{C}_t$ of Π at an instant t. The output of this stage is a pair $(\mathcal{C}_t', A)$, where A encodes a multiset of rules selected to be applied to $\mathcal{C}_t$, and $\mathcal{C}_t'$ is the configuration obtained from $\mathcal{C}_t$ once the labelled objects corresponding to the application of rules from A have been consumed. The execution stage receives as input the output $(\mathcal{C}_t', A)$ of the selection stage. The output of this stage is the next configuration $\mathcal{C}_{t+1}$ of $\mathcal{C}_t$. Specifically, at this stage, the configuration $\mathcal{C}_{t+1}$ is obtained from $\mathcal{C}_t'$ by adding the labelled objects produced by the application of rules from A.

Next, selection stage and execution stage are described in detail.

Selection Stage.

Input: A configuration $\mathcal{C}_t$ of Π at instant t
    $\mathcal{C}_t' \leftarrow \mathcal{C}_t$; $A \leftarrow \emptyset$; $B \leftarrow \emptyset$
    for $r \equiv (i, u/v, j) \in R_C$ according to the order chosen **do**
        for each pair of cells $(i, \sigma_i), (j, \sigma_j)$ of $\mathcal{C}_t'$ according to the
        lexicographical order **do**
            $n_r \leftarrow$ maximum number of times that r is applicable to $(i, \sigma_i), (j, \sigma_j)$
            if $n_r > 0$ **then**
                $\mathcal{C}_t' \leftarrow \mathcal{C}_t' \setminus n_r \cdot LHS(r, (i, \sigma_i), (j, \sigma_j))$
                $A \leftarrow A \cup \{(r, n_r, (i, \sigma_i), (j, \sigma_j))\}$
                $B \leftarrow B \cup \{(i, \sigma_i), (j, \sigma_j)\}$

```
        end if
      end for
    end for
    for r ≡ [a]_i → [Γ_0]_i[Γ_1]_i ∈ R_S according to the order chosen do
      for each (a, i, σ_i) ∈ C'_t, according to the lexicographical order, and
        such that (i, σ_i) ∉ B do
        C'_t ← C'_t \ {(a, i, σ_i)}
        A ← A ∪ {(r, 1, (i, σ_i))}
        B ← B ∪ {(i, σ_i)}
      end for
    end for
```

This algorithm is deterministic and works in polynomial time. Indeed, the cost in time of the previous algorithm is polynomial in the size of Π because the number of cycles of the first main loop **for** is of order $O(|R| \cdot \frac{(2M+q)(2M+q-1)}{2})$, and the number of cycles of the second main loop **for** is of order $O(|R| \cdot |\Gamma| \cdot (2M + q))$. Besides, the last loop includes a membership test of order $O(2M + q)$.

In order to complete the simulation of a computation step of the system Π, the execution stage takes care of the effects of applying the rules selected in the previous stage: updating the objects according to the RHS of the rules.

Execution Stage.

```
Input: The output C'_t and A of the selection stage
    for each (r, n_r, (i, σ_i), (j, σ_j)) ∈ A do
      C'_t ← C'_t + n_r · RHS(r, (i, σ_i), (j, σ_j))
    end for
    for each (r, 1, (i, σ_i)) ∈ A do
      C'_t ← C'_t + {(λ, i, σ_i)/σ_i0}
      C'_t ← C'_t + {(λ, i, σ_i1)}
      for each (x, i, σ_i) ∈ C'_t according to the lexicographical order do
        if x ∈ Γ_0 then
          C'_t ← C'_t + {(x, i, σ_i)/σ_i0}
        else
          C'_t ← C'_t + {(x, i, σ_i)/σ_i1}
        end if
      end for
    end for
    C_{t+1} ← C'_t
```

This algorithm is deterministic and works in polynomial time. Indeed, the cost in time of the previous algorithm is polynomial in the size of Π because the number of cycles of the first main loop **for** is of order $O(|R|)$, and the number of cycles of the second main loop **for** is of order $O(|R| \cdot |\Gamma| \cdot (2M + q))$. Besides, inside the body of the last loop there is a membership test of order $O(|\Gamma|)$.

Throughout this algorithm we have deterministically simulated a computation of Π in such manner that the answer of the algorithm is affirmative if and only if the simulated computation is accepting.

Theorem 1. $\mathbf{P} = \mathbf{PMC}_{\widehat{\mathbf{TSC}}}$.

Proof. It suffices to prove that $\mathbf{PMC}_{\widehat{\mathbf{TSC}}} \subseteq \mathbf{P}$. Let $k \in \mathbb{N}$ such that $X \in \mathbf{PMC}_{\widehat{\mathbf{TSC}}(k)}$ and let $\{\Pi(n) : n \in \mathbb{N}\}$ be a family of tissue P systems from $\widehat{\mathbf{TSC}}(k)$ solving X according to Definition 3. Let (cod, s) be a polinomial encoding associated with that solution. If $u \in I_X$ is an instance of the problem X, then u will be processed by the system $\Pi(s(u)) + cod(u)$.

Let us consider the following algorithm $\mathcal{A}'$:

Input: an instance u of the problem X.
    Construct the system $\Pi(s(u)) + cod(u)$.
    Run algorithm $\mathcal{A}$ with input $\Pi(s(u)) + cod(u)$.
Output: Yes if $\Pi(s(u)) + cod(u)$ has an accepting computation, No otherwise

The algorithm $\mathcal{A}'$ receives as input an instance u of the decision problem $X = (I_X, \theta_X)$ and works in polynomial time. The following assertions are equivalent:

1. $\theta_X(u) = 1$, that is, the answer of problem X to instance u is affirmative.
2. Every computation of $\Pi(s(u)) + cod(u)$ is an accepting computation.
3. The output of the algorithm with input u is Yes.

Hence, $X \in \mathbf{P}$. □

Remark 1. From the previous theorem we deduce that $\mathbf{P} = \mathbf{PMC}_{\widehat{\mathbf{TSC}}(3)}$. In [23], a polynomial time solution of the SAT problem was given by a family of tissue P systems from $\mathbf{TSC}(3)$ according to Definition 3. Thus, $\mathbf{NP} \cup \mathbf{co\text{-}NP} \subseteq \mathbf{PMC}_{\mathbf{TSC}(3)}$. Hence, in the framework of tissue P systems with cell separation and communication rules of length at most 3, the <u>environment</u> provides a new <u>borderline</u> between efficiency and non-efficiency, assuming $\mathbf{P} \neq \mathbf{NP}$.

Remark 2. From the previous theorem we deduce that $\mathbf{P} = \mathbf{PMC}_{\widehat{\mathbf{TSC}}(2)}$. In [24], it was shown that $\mathbf{PMC}_{\mathbf{TDC}(k+1)} = \mathbf{PMC}_{\widehat{\mathbf{TDC}}(k+1)}$, for each $k \in \mathbb{N}$. In [25], a polynomial time solution of the HAM-CYCLE problem was given by a family of tissue P systems from $\mathbf{TDC}(2)$ according to Definition 3. Thus, $\mathbf{NP} \cup \mathbf{co\text{-}NP} \subseteq \mathbf{PMC}_{\mathbf{TDC}(2)} = \mathbf{PMC}_{\widehat{\mathbf{TDC}}(2)}$. Hence, in the framework of tissue P systems with communication rules of length at most 2 and without environment, the <u>kind of rules</u> (separation versus division) provides a new <u>borderline</u> between the efficiency and non-efficiency, assuming $\mathbf{P} \neq \mathbf{NP}$.

5 Conclusions and Further Works

The efficiency of cell-like P systems for solving **NP**-complete problems has been widely studied. The usual approach is to perform a space-time tradeoff that allows "efficient" (in terms of the number of steps of the computations) solutions to **NP**-complete problems in the framework of *Membrane Computing*. For instance, membrane division, membrane creation, and membrane separation are three efficient ways of obtaining exponential workspace in polynomial time that have been used in the literature. Such tools have been adapted to tissue–like P systems, and linear-time solutions to the SAT problem have been designed both in the model with cell division rules [19], as well as in the case of cell separation [13].

In this paper, the computational efficiency of tissue P systems with cell separation and *without environment* has been studied. We highlight the relevant role played by the environment in this framework from the point of view of efficiency.

Finally, two new borderlines between efficiency and non-efficiency are presented, assuming **P** $\neq$ **NP**. The first of them is related with the environment and the second one is related to the kind of rules (separation versus division).

Acknowledgements. The work was supported by TIN2009-13192 Project of the Ministerio de Economía y Competitividad of Spain and Project of Excellence with *Investigador de Reconocida Valía*, from Junta de Andalucía, grant P08 – TIC 04200, both co-financed by FEDER funds.

References

1. Alhazov, A., Freund, R., Oswald, M.: Tissue P Systems with Antiport Rules and Small Numbers of Symbols and Cells. In: De Felice, C., Restivo, A. (eds.) DLT 2005. LNCS, vol. 3572, pp. 100–111. Springer, Heidelberg (2005)
2. Bernardini, F., Gheorghe, M.: Cell Communication in Tissue P Systems and Cell Division in Population P Systems. Soft Comput. 9(9), 640–649 (2005)
3. Ciobanu, G., Păun, G., Pérez-Jiménez, M.J.: Applications of Membrane Computing. Natural Computing Series. Springer (2006)
4. Freund, R., Păun, G., Pérez-Jiménez, M.J.: Tissue P Systems with channel states. Theor. Comput. Sci. 330, 101–116 (2005)
5. Díaz-Pernil, D., Gutiérrez-Naranjo, M.A., Pérez-Jiménez, M.J., Riscos-Núñez, A.: A uniform family of tissue P systems with cell division solving 3-COL in a linear time. Theor. Comput. Sci. 404(1-2), 76–87 (2008)
6. Gutiérrez-Naranjo, M.A., Pérez-Jímenez, M.J., Romero-Campero, F.J.: A Linear Solution for QSAT with Membrane Creation. In: Freund, R., Păun, G., Rozenberg, G., Salomaa, A. (eds.) WMC 2005. LNCS, vol. 3850, pp. 241–252. Springer, Heidelberg (2006)
7. Ito, M., Martín Vide, C., Păun, G.: A characterization of Parikh sets of ET0L laguages in terms of P systems. In: Ito, M., Păun, G., Yu, S. (eds.) Words, Semigroups and Transducers, pp. 239–254. World Scientific, Singapore (2001)
8. Krishna, S.N., Lakshmanan, K., Rama, R.: Tissue P Systems with Contextual and Rewriting Rules. In: Păun, G., Rozenberg, G., Salomaa, A., Zandron, C. (eds.) WMC 2002. LNCS, vol. 2597, pp. 339–351. Springer, Heidelberg (2003)
9. Lakshmanan, K., Rama, R.: On the Power of Tissue P Systems with Insertion and Deletion Rules. In: Alhazov, A., Martín-Vide, C., Păun, G. (eds.) Preproceedings of the Workshop on Membrane Computing, Tarragona, Report RGML 28/03, pp. 304–318 (2003)

10. Martín-Vide, C., Pazos, J., Păun, G., Rodríguez-Patón, A.: A New Class of Symbolic Abstract Neural Nets: Tissue P Systems. In: Ibarra, O.H., Zhang, L. (eds.) COCOON 2002. LNCS, vol. 2387, pp. 290–299. Springer, Heidelberg (2002)
11. Martín Vide, C., Pazos, J., Păun, G., Rodríguez Patón, A.: Tissue P systems. Theor. Comput. Sci. 296, 295–326 (2003)
12. Pan, L., Ishdorj, T.-O.: P systems with active membranes and separation rules. J. Univers. Comput. Sci. 10(5), 630–649 (2004)
13. Pan, L., Pérez-Jiménez, M.J.: Computational complexity of tissue–like P systems. J. Complexity 26(3), 296–315 (2010)
14. Prakash, V.J.: On the Power of Tissue P Systems Working in the Maximal-One Mode. In: Alhazov, A., Martín-Vide, C., Păun, G. (eds.) Preproceedings of the Workshop on Membrane Computing, Tarragona, Report RGML 28/03, pp. 356–364 (2003)
15. Păun, G.: Computing with membranes. J. Comput. Syst. Sci. 61(1), 108–143 (2000)
16. Păun, G.: Attacking **NP**-complete problems. In: Antoniou, I., Calude, C., Dinneen, M.J. (eds.) Unconventional Models of Computation, UMC 2K, pp. 94–115. Springer (2000)
17. Păun, G.: Membrane Computing. An Introduction. Springer, Berlin (2002)
18. Păun, A., Păun, G.: The power of communication: P systems with symport/antiport. New Generat. Comput. 20(3), 295–305 (2002)
19. Păun, G., Pérez-Jiménez, M.J., Riscos-Núñez, A.: Tissue P Systems with cell division. Int. J. Comput. Commun. 3(3), 295–303 (2008)
20. Păun, G., Rozenberg, G., Salomaa, A.: The Oxford Handbook of Membrane Computing. Oxford University Press (2009)
21. Pérez-Jiménez, M.J., Romero-Jiménez, A., Sancho-Caparrini, F.: Complexity classes in models of cellular computing with membranes. Natural Computing 2(3), 265–285 (2003)
22. Pérez-Jiménez, M.J., Romero-Jiménez, A., Sancho-Caparrini, F.: A polynomial complexity class in P systems using membrane division. J. Autom. Lang. Combin. 11(4), 423–434 (2006)
23. Pérez-Jiménez, M.J., Sosík, P.: Improving the efficiency of tissue P systems with cell separation. In: García-Quismondo, M., et al. (eds.) Proceedings of the Tenth Brainstorming Week on Membrane Computing, Fénix Editora, Sevilla, vol. II, pp. 105–140
24. Pérez-Jiménez, M.J., Riscos-Núñez, A., Rius-Font, M., Romero-Campero, F.J.: The role of the environment in tissue P systems with cell division. In: García-Quismondo, M., et al. (eds.) Proceedings of the Tenth Brainstorming Week on Membrane Computing, Fénix Editora, Sevilla, vol. II, pp. 89–104
25. Porreca, A.E., Murphy, N., Pérez-Jiménez, M.J.: An optimal frontier of the efficiency of tissue P systems with cell division. In: García-Quismondo, M., et al. (eds.) Proceedings of the Tenth Brainstorming Week on Membrane Computing, Fénix Editora, Sevilla, vol. II, pp. 141–166
26. Zhang, X., Wang, S., Niu, Y., Pan, L.: Tissue P systems with cell separation: attacking the partition problem. Science China Information Sciences 54(2), 293–304 (2011)

DCBA: Simulating Population Dynamics P Systems with Proportional Object Distribution

Miguel A. Martínez-del-Amor[1], Ignacio Pérez-Hurtado[1],
Manuel García-Quismondo[1], Luis F. Macías-Ramos[1], Luis Valencia-Cabrera[1],
Álvaro Romero-Jiménez[1], Carmen Graciani[1], Agustín Riscos-Núñez[1],
Mari A. Colomer[2], and Mario J. Pérez-Jiménez[1]

[1] Research Group on Natural Computing
Department of Computer Science and Artificial Intelligence
University of Seville
Avda. Reina Mercedes s/n, 41012 Sevilla, Spain
{mdelamor,perezh,mgarciaquismondo,lfmaciasr,lvalencia,
romero.alvaro,cgdiaz,ariscosn,marper}@us.es
[2] Department of Mathematics
University of Lleida
Avda. Alcalde Rovira Roure, 191, 25198 Lleida, Spain
colomer@matematica.udl.es

Abstract. *Population Dynamics P systems* provide a formal framework for ecological modelling having a probabilistic (while keeping the maximal parallelism). Several simulation algorithms have been developed always trying to reach higher reliability in the way they reproduce the behaviour of the ecosystems being modelled.

It is natural for those algorithms to classify the rules into blocks, comprising rules that share identical left-hand side. Previous algorithms, such as the Binomial Block Based (BBB) or the Direct Non Deterministic distribution with Probabilities (DNDP), do not define a deterministic behaviour for blocks of rules competing for the same resources. In this paper we introduce the Direct distribution based on Consistent Blocks Algorithm (DCBA), a simulation algorithm which addresses that inherent non-determinism of the model by distributing proportionally the resources.

Keywords: Membrane Computing, Population Dynamics P systems, Simulation Algorithm, Probabilistic P systems, DCBA, P-Lingua, pLinguaCore.

1 Introduction

Since the devising of the field of *Membrane Computing* [13,15], it has established as a feasible background for the modelling of biochemical phenomena. Within *Computational Systems Biology*, for example, it is complementary and an alternative [1,5,14,16] to more classical approaches (ODEs, Petri Nets, etc). Taking into account the particularities of ecosystem dynamics, P systems

E. Csuhaj-Varjú et al. (Eds.): CMC 2012, LNCS 7762, pp. 257–276, 2013.

also suit as the base for their computational modelling. In this regard, the success attained with the models of several phenomena (population dynamics of *Gypaetus barbatus* [3] and *Rupicapra p. pyrenaica* [6] in the Catalan Pyrenees; population density of *Dreissena polymorpha* in Ribarroja reservoir [2]) has led to the development of a P systems based computing framework for the modelling of *Population Dynamics* [2].

One of the assets of this framework is the ability to conduct the simultaneous evolution of a high number of species, as well as the management of a large number of auxiliary objects (that could represent, for instance, grass, biomass or animal bones). Moreover, the compartmentalized structure, both as a directed graph (environments) and as a rooted tree (membranes), allows to differentiate multiple geographical areas. The framework also facilitates the elaboration of models for which a straightforward interpretation of the simulations can be easily obtained.

The development of efficient algorithms capable of capturing the semantics described by the framework is a challenging task. These algorithms should select rules in the models according to their associated probabilities, while keeping the maximal parallelism semantics of P systems. In this scenario, the concept of *rule blocks* arises. A rule block is a set of rules sharing the same left-hand side (more precisely, the necessary and sufficient conditions for them to be applicable are exactly the same). That is, given a particular P system configuration, either all or none of the rules in the block can be applied. On each step of computation one or more blocks are selected, according to the semantics associated with the modelling framework. For every selected block, its rules are applied a number of times in a probabilistic manner according to their associated probabilities, also known as *local probabilities*.

The way in which the blocks and rules in the model are selected depends on the specific simulation algorithm employed. These algorithms should be able to deal with issues such as the possible competition of blocks and rules for objects. So far, several algorithms have been developed in order to capture the semantics defined by the modelling framework. Some of these algorithms are the Binomial Block Based algorithm, BBB, and the Direct Non Deterministic algorithm with Probabilities, DNDP. A comparison on the performance of these algorithms can be found on [7].

The algorithms mentioned above share a common drawback, regarding a distorted selection of blocks and rules. Indeed, instead of blocks and rules being selected according to their probabilities in a uniform manner, the selection process is biased towards those with the highest probabilities. This paper introduces a new algorithm, known as Direct distribution based on Consistent Blocks Algorithm, *DCBA*, that overcomes the aforementioned distortion, thus not biasing the selection process towards the most likely blocks and rules.

The rest of the paper is structured as follows: Section 2 introduces the formal modelling framework. Section 3 describes the DCBA algorithm. The behaviour of DCBA when simulating a real ecosystem model is shown in Section 4. The simulated model has been adapted and improved from the original version. The paper ends with some conclusions and ideas for future work.

2   The P Systems Based Framework

Let us present the formal definition of Population Dynamics P systems, which have been specifically tailored for modelling the evolution of ecosystems. The intuition behind this framework is that the ecosystem being modelled is splitted into small geographical areas (environments) that are connected, and then the dynamics of each environment is simulated by a dedicated P system using cooperative and probabilistic rules.

Definition 1. *A Population Dynamics P system of degree (q, m) with $q \geq 1$, $m \geq 1$, and taking T time steps, is a tuple*

$$\Pi = (G, \Gamma, \Sigma, T, R_E, \mu, R, \{f_{r,j} : r \in R, 1 \leq j \leq m\}, \{\mathcal{M}_{ij} : 1 \leq i \leq q, 1 \leq j \leq m\})$$

where:

- $G = (V, S)$ *is a directed graph. Let* $V = \{e_1, \ldots, e_m\}$;
- Γ *is the working alphabet and* $\Sigma \subsetneq \Gamma$;
- T *is a natural number greater or equal to 1;*
- R_E *is a finite set of communication rules of the form*

$$(x)_{e_j} \xrightarrow{\ p\ } (y_1)_{e_{j_1}} \cdots (y_h)_{e_{j_h}}$$

  where $x, y_1, \ldots, y_h \in \Sigma$, $(e_j, e_{j_l}) \in S$ $(1 \leq l \leq h)$ *and p is a computable function from* $\{1, \ldots, T\}$ *to* $[0, 1]$. *If for any rule p is the constant function 1, then we can omit it. These functions verify the following:*
  - *For each $e_j \in V$ and $x \in \Sigma$, the sum of functions associated with the rules whose left-hand side is $(x)_{e_j}$, is the constant function 1.*
- μ *is a membrane structure consisting of q membranes injectively labelled by* $1, \ldots, q$. *The skin membrane is labelled by 1. We also associate electrical charges from the set* $EC = \{0, +, -\}$ *with membranes.*
- R *is a finite set of evolution rules of the form*

$$u[\,v\,]_i^{\alpha} \rightarrow u'[\,v'\,]_i^{\alpha'}$$

  where $u, v, u', v' \in \Gamma^*$, i $(1 \leq i \leq q)$, $u + v \neq \lambda$ *and* $\alpha, \alpha' \in \{0, +, -\}$.
  - *If $(x)_{e_j}$ is the left-hand side of a rule from R_E, then none of the rules of R has a left-hand side of the form $u[v]_1^{\alpha}$, for any $u, v \in \Gamma^*$ and $\alpha \in \{0, +, -\}$, having $x \in u$.*
- *For each $r \in R$ and for each j $(1 \leq j \leq m)$, $f_{r,j} : \{1, \ldots, T\} \longrightarrow [0, 1]$ is computable. These functions verify the following:*
  - *For each $u, v \in \Gamma^*$, i $(1 \leq i \leq q)$, $\alpha, \alpha' \in \{0, +, -\}$ and j $(1 \leq j \leq m)$ the sum of functions associated with j and the rules whose left-hand side is $u[v]_i^{\alpha}$ and whose right-hand side has polarization α', is the constant function 1.*
- *For each j $(1 \leq j \leq m)$, $\mathcal{M}_{1j}, \ldots, \mathcal{M}_{qj}$ are strings over Γ.*

In other words, a system as described in the previous definition can be viewed as a set of m environments $e_1, \ldots, e_m$ linked between them such that they form a directed graph G.

Each environment e_j contains a P system, $\Pi_j = (\Gamma, \mu, R_{\Pi_j}, \mathcal{M}_{1j}, \ldots \mathcal{M}_{q,j})$, of degree q, where every rule $r \in R$ has a computable function $f_{r,j}$ (specific for environment j) associated with it. The set of rules $r \in R$ of Π having included the functions $f_{r,j}$ is denoted by R_{Π_j}, for each environment e_j. All environments include an almost identical P system, sharing the same membrane structure and set of rules. The only differences between them reside in the functions associated with the rules, and in the initial multisets. As customary in Membrane Computing, the q strings $\mathcal{M}_{1j}, \ldots, \mathcal{M}_{qj}$ represent the initial multisets associated with the q regions of μ, within the environment e_j.

Communications between environments are allowed, restricted to a subset of the alphabet $\Sigma \subsetneq \Gamma$. Note that objects from Σ located in an environment cannot participate on any evolution rule.

A *configuration* of the system at any instant t is a tuple of multisets of objects present in the m environments and at each of the regions of each Π_j, together with the polarizations of the membranes in each P system. At the initial configuration of the system we assume that all environments are empty and all membranes have a neutral polarization. The evolution of the system is restricted to T transitions. That is, even if the system could keep evolving, we impose a bound on the number of steps to be simulated.

We assume that a global clock exists, marking the time for the whole system, that is, all membranes and the application of all rules (from R_E and all R_{Π_j}) are synchronized in all environments.

The P system can pass from one configuration to another by using the rules from $\bigcup_{j=1}^{m} R_{\Pi_j} \cup R_E$ as follows: at each transition step, the rules to be applied are selected according to the probabilities assigned to them, and all applicable rules are simultaneously applied in a maximal way – that is, no rule can be further applied.

If an evolution rule of the form $u[v]_i^{\alpha} \rightarrow u'[v']_i^{\alpha'}$ is selected to be applied on membrane i of Π_j (for some $1 \leq j \leq m$), then multisets v and u will be deleted from region i and the parent region of i, respectively, and for the next step new multisets v' and u' will be generated in region i and the parent region of i, respectively. Besides, the charge of membrane i in Π_j will be set to α'. Notice that if two rules defined over membrane i have different charges on their right-hand side, then they cannot be selected to be applied in the same step in the same environment.

When a communication rule $(x)_{e_j} \xrightarrow{p} (y_1)_{e_{j_1}} \cdots (y_h)_{e_{j_h}}$ between environments is applied, object x passes from e_j to $e_{j_1}, \ldots, e_{j_h}$ possibly modified into objects $y_1, \ldots, y_h$ respectively. At any moment t ($1 \leq t \leq T$) for each object x in environment e_j, if there exist communication rules whose left-hand side is $(x)_{e_j}$, then one of these rules will be applied. If more than one communication rule can be applied to an object, the system randomly selects one, according to their probability which is given by $p(t)$.

3 Direct Distribution Based on Consistent Blocks Algorithm (DCBA)

In this section we describe the Direct distribution based on Consistent Blocks Algorithm (DCBA), together with some auxiliary definitions and properties necessary for it. The DCBA is introduced in order to solve some distortions generated by the previous algorithm, DNDP, concerning the number of applications for competing rules (with overlapping left-hand sides). The DNDP algorithm assigns randomly the number of applications, by shuffling the list of rules, while the DCBA introduces a mechanism to distribute the number of applications proportionally. Moreover, the management of consistency in application of rules has been improved by introducing the new concept of consistent block. More details can be obtained from the following definitions and the description of the DNDP algorithm [11,12].

3.1 Definitions for Blocks and Mutual Consistency

The selection mechanism starts from the assumption that rules in R and R_E can be classified into blocks of rules having the same left-hand side, following the Definitions 2, 3 and 4 given below.

Definition 2. *The left and right-hand sides of the rules are defined as follows:*

(a) *Given a rule $r \in R_E$ of the form $(x)_{e_j} \xrightarrow{\ p\ } (y_1)_{e_{j_1}} \cdots (y_h)_{e_{j_h}}$ where $e_j \in V$ and $x, y_1, \ldots, y_h \in \Sigma$:*
  - *The left-hand side of r is $LHS(r) = (e_j, x)$.*
  - *The right-hand side of r is $RHS(r) = (e_{j_1}, y_1) \cdots (e_{j_h}, y_h)$.*

(b) *Given a rule $r \in R$ of the form $u[v]_i^{\alpha} \to u'[v']_i^{\alpha'}$ where $1 \leq i \leq q$, $\alpha, \alpha' \in \{0, +, -\}$ and $u, v, u', v' \in \Gamma^*$:*
  - *The left-hand side of r is $LHS(r) = (i, \alpha, u, v)$.*
  - *The right-hand side of r is $RHS(r) = (i, \alpha', u', v')$.*

  The charge of $LHS(r)$ is the second component of the tuple (idem for $RHS(r)$).

Definition 3. *For each $e_j \in V$, $x \in \Gamma$, we denote by $B_{e_j,x}$ the block of communication rules having $(x)_{e_j}$ as left-hand side.*

Definition 4. *For each $1 \leq i \leq q$, $\alpha, \alpha' \in EC$, $u, v \in \Gamma^*$, we denote by $B_{i,\alpha,\alpha',u,v}$ the block of evolution rules having $u[v]_i^{\alpha}$ as left-hand side, and having α' in the right-hand side.*

Recall that, according to the semantics of the model, the sum of probabilities of all the rules belonging to the same block is always equal to 1 – in particular, rules with probability equal to 1 form individual blocks. Note that rules with overlapping (but different) left-hand sides are classified into different blocks.

Remark 1. Note that **all** the rules $r \in B_{i,\alpha,\alpha',u,v}$ can be consistently applied, in the sense that each membrane i with charge α goes to the **same** charge α' by any rule of $B_{i,\alpha,\alpha',u,v}$.

Definition 5. *Two blocks $B_{i_1,\alpha_1,\alpha'_1,u_1,v_1}$ and $B_{i_2,\alpha_2,\alpha'_2,u_2,v_2}$ are mutually consistent with each other, if and only if $(i_1 = i_2 \wedge \alpha_1 = \alpha_2) \Rightarrow (\alpha'_1 = \alpha'_2)$.*

Definition 6. *A set of blocks $\mathcal{B} = \{B^1, B^2, \ldots, B^s\}$ is self consistent (or mutually consistent) if and only if $\mathcal{B}$ is a pairwise mutually consistent family.*

Remark 2. In such a context, a set of blocks $\mathcal{B}$ has a relation from $H \times EC$ into EC, associated with it, as follows: $((i, \alpha), \alpha')$ belongs to the relation if and only if there exists two strings $u, v \in \Gamma^*$ such that $B_{i,\alpha,\alpha',u,v} \in \mathcal{B}$. Then, a set of blocks is mutually consistent if and only if the associated relation is functional.

3.2   DCBA Pseudocode

This new simulation algorithm for PDP systems has the same general scheme than its predecessor, DNDP [11,12]. The main loop (Algorithm 1) is divided into two stages: selection and execution of rules, similarly to the DNDP and BBB algorithms.

Algorithm 1. DCBA MAIN PROCEDURE

Require: A Population Dynamics P system of degree (q, m), $T \geq 1$ (time units), and $A \geq 1$ (*Accuracy*). The initial configuration is called C_0.

1: *INITIALIZATION*   ▷ (Algorithm 2)
2: **for** $t \leftarrow 1$ to T **do**
3:     Calculate probability functions $f_{r,j}(t)$ and $p(t)$.
4:     $C'_t \leftarrow C_{t-1}$
5:     *SELECTION* of rules.
       • *PHASE 1*: distribution   ▷ (Algorithm 3)
       • *PHASE 2*: maximality   ▷ (Algorithm 4)
       • *PHASE 3*: probabilities   ▷ (Algorithm 5)
6:     *EXECUTION* of rules.   ▷ (Algorithm 6)
7:     $C_t \leftarrow C'_t$
8: **end for**

Note that the algorithm selects and executes rules, but not blocks of rules. Blocks are used by DCBA in order to select rules, and this is made in three micro-stages as seen in Algorithm 1. Phase 1 distributes objects to the blocks in a certain proportional way. Phase 2 assures the *maximality* by checking the maximal applications of each block. Finally, Phase 3 passes from block applications to rule applications by computing random numbers following the multinomial distribution with the corresponding *probabilities*. Recall that the DNDP algorithm uses only two micro-stages within phase 1, since it directly select rules without using blocks.

Before starting to select and execute rules in the system, some data initialization is required (Algorithm 2). For instance, the selection stage uses a table in order to distribute the objects among the blocks. This table $\mathcal{T}$,

---

Algorithm 2. INITIALIZATION

1: Construction of the *static distribution* table $\mathcal{T}$:
   - Column labels: consistent blocks $B_{i,\alpha,\alpha',u,v}$ of rules from R.
   - Row labels: pairs (x, i), for all objects $x \in \Gamma$, and $0 \leq i \leq q$.
   - For each row, for each cell of the row: place $\frac{1}{k}$ if the object in the row label appears in its associated compartment with multiplicity k in the LHS of the block of the column label.
2: **for** $j = 1$ **to** m **do**   ▷ (Construct the *expanded static tables* $\mathcal{T}_j$)
3:     $\mathcal{T}_j \leftarrow \mathcal{T}$.   ▷ (Initialize the table with the original $\mathcal{T}$)
4:     For each rule block $B_{e_j,x}$ from R_E, add a column labelled by $B_{e_j,x}$ to $\mathcal{T}_j$;
       place the value 1 at row $(x, 0)$ for that column.
5:     Initialize the multisets $BLOCKS_j \leftarrow \emptyset$ and $RULES_j \leftarrow \emptyset$
6: **end for**

---

also called *static table*, is used in each time step, so it is initialized only once, at the beginning of the algorithm. The *static table* has one column per each consistent block of rules, and one row per each pair of object and compartment (i.e., each membrane and the environment). An expanded static table $\mathcal{T}_j$ is also constructed for each environment, to consider also blocks from environment e_j communication rules. Finally, two multisets $BLOCKS_j$ and $RULES_j$, are initialized for each environment. They are used by the algorithm in order to store the selected blocks and the selected rules in the environment e_j, respectively.

The distribution of objects among the blocks is performed in Selection Phase 1 (Algorithm 3), taking into account overlapping LHS, if any. The expanded static table $\mathcal{T}_j$ is used for this purpose in each environment. Three filters are defined in order to adapt $\mathcal{T}_j$ to the configuration C_t of the system; that is, to select which blocks are going to receive objects. FILTER 1 discards the columns of the table corresponding to non-applicable blocks due to mismatch charges (i.e. charges on the LHS of each block are compared with the current charges of the corresponding membranes in C_t). FILTER 2 discards the columns corresponding to non-applicable blocks due to the objects from the LHS. The goal of FILTER 3 is to save space in the table, by discarding irrelevant rows (associated with objects not present in the configuration). These three filters are applied at the beginning of phase 1, yielding a *dynamic table* $\mathcal{T}_j'$ for each environment j.

Filter Procedures for Selection Phase 1

   procedure FILTER 1(table $\mathcal{T}$, configuration C)   ▷ (Columns by charges)
       Discard columns from table $\mathcal{T}$, whenever the charge of the membrane in the LHS of the corresponding block differs from the configuration C.
   end procedure

procedure FILTER 2(table $\mathcal{T}$, configuration C)   ▷ (Columns by multiplicities)
    Discard columns from table $\mathcal{T}$, such that for any row (o, i) or $(x, 0)$, the multiplicity of that object in C multiplied by $1/k$ (the value in the table), returns a number $\kappa, 0 \leq \kappa < 1$. If all the values for that column are null, it is also filtered.
end procedure

procedure FILTER 3(table $\mathcal{T}$, configuration C)   ▷ (Rows by multiplicities)
    Discard rows from $\mathcal{T}$ labelled by (o, i) and $(x, 0)$ when the corresponding objects are not present in the multisets of C.
end procedure

Recall that the *static table* $\mathcal{T}$ collects all consistent blocks within the columns. The set of all consistent blocks is unlikely to be mutually consistent. However, two non-mutually consistent blocks, $B_{i,\alpha,\alpha'_1,u_1,v_1}$ and $B_{i,\alpha,\alpha'_2,u_2,v_2}$ (assigning a different charge to the same membrane), will not cause major troubles provided that they have different LHS (either $u_1 \neq u_2$ or $v_1 \neq v_2$) and that they are not applicable simultaneously. At each step, the non-applicable block will be discarded by FILTER 2. This situation is commonly handled by the model designers, in order to avoid losing control of the model evolution.

It is very important to have a set of mutually consistent blocks before distributing objects to the blocks. For this reason, after applying FILTERS 1 and 2, the mutual consistency is checked. If it fails, meaning that an inconsistency was encountered, the simulation process is halted, providing a warning message to the user. Nevertheless, it can be interesting to find a way to continue the execution by non-deterministically constructing a subset of mutually consistent blocks. Since this method can be exponentially expensive in time, it is optional for the user whether to activate it or not.

Once the columns of the *dynamic table* represent a set of mutually consistent blocks, the distribution process starts. This is carried out by updating the values in the table by the following products:

- The corresponding multiplicity of the object in the current configuration C'_t.
- The value in the original dynamic table (i.e. $\frac{1}{k}$). This indicates the number of possible applications of the block with the corresponding object.
- The normalized value with respect to the row; that is, the value divided by the total sum of the row.

This calculates a way to *proportionally* distribute the corresponding object along the blocks. Since it depends on the multiplicities in the LHS of the blocks, the distribution, in fact, penalize the blocks requiring more copies of the same object, which is inspired in the amount of energy required to join individuals from the same species. In fact, this is the major difference with the DNDP algorithm, which performed a non-deterministic distribution.

After the object distribution process, the number of applications for each block is computed by selecting the minimum value in each column. This number is then used for consuming the LHS from the configuration. However, this application could be not maximal. The distribution process can eventually deliver objects to blocks that are restricted by other objects. As this situation may occur

Algorithm 3. SELECTION PHASE 1: DISTRIBUTION

1: **for** $j = 1$ **to** m **do**   ▷ (For each environment e_j)
2:     Apply filters to $\mathcal{T}_j$ using C'_t, obtaining the dynamic table $\mathcal{T}'_j$, as follows:
   a. $\mathcal{T}'_j \leftarrow \mathcal{T}_j$
   b. FILTER 1 $(\mathcal{T}'_j, C'_t)$.
   c. FILTER 2 $(\mathcal{T}'_j, C'_t)$.
   d. Check *mutual consistency* for the blocks remaining in $\mathcal{T}'_j$. If there is at least one inconsistency **then** report the information about the error, and optionally halt the execution (in case of not activating step *3.*)
   e. FILTER 3 $(\mathcal{T}'_j, C'_t)$.
3:     *(OPTIONAL)* Generate a set S_j of sub-tables from $\mathcal{T}'_j$, formed by sets of *mutually consistent* blocks, in a maximal way in $\mathcal{T}'_j$ (by the inclusion relationship). Replace $\mathcal{T}'_j$ with a randomly selected table from S_j.
4:     $a \leftarrow 1$
5:     **repeat**
6:         **for all** rows X in $\mathcal{T}'_j$ **do**
7:             $RowSum_X \leftarrow$ total sum of the non-null values in the row X.
8:         **end for**
9:         $\mathcal{TV}_j \leftarrow \mathcal{T}'_j$ ▷ (A temporary copy of the dynamic table)
10:        **for all** non-null positions (X, Y) in $\mathcal{T}'_j$ **do**
11:            $mult_X \leftarrow$ multiplicity in C'_t at e_j of the object at row X.
12:            $\mathcal{TV}_j(X, Y) \leftarrow \lfloor mult_X \cdot \frac{(\mathcal{T}'_j(X,Y))^2}{RowSum_X} \rfloor$
13:        **end for**
14:        **for all** not filtered column, labelled by block B, in $\mathcal{T}'_j$ **do**
15:            $N_B \leftarrow \min_{X \in rows(\mathcal{T}'_j)} (\mathcal{TV}_j(X, B))$ ▷ (The minimum of the column)
16:            $BLOCKS_j \leftarrow BLOCKS_j + \{B^{N_B}\}$ ▷ (Accumulate the value)
17:            $C'_t \leftarrow C'_t - LHS(B) \cdot N_B$ ▷ (Delete the LHS of the block.)
18:        **end for**
19:        FILTER 2 $(\mathcal{T}'_j, C'_t)$
20:        FILTER 3 $(\mathcal{T}'_j, C'_t)$
21:        $a \leftarrow a + 1$
22:     **until** $(a > A) \vee$ *(all the selected minimums at step 15 are 0)*
23: **end for**

frequently, the distribution and the configuration update process is performed A times, where A is an input parameter referring to *accuracy*. The more the process is repeated, the more accurate is the distribution, but the less could be the performance of the simulation. We have experimentally checked that $A = 2$ gives the best accuracy/performance ratio.

In order to repeat efficiently the loop for A, and also before going to the next phase (maximality), FILTERS 2 and 3 are applied again. This way, once the configuration is updated by consuming the objects on the LHS of the selected blocks, the blocks that are not applicable any more are discarded from the table.

After phase 1, some objects may be left without being consumed. This can be caused by a low A value or by rounding artefacts when calculating sums and minimums of inverse numbers in the distribution process. Due to

Algorithm 4. SELECTION PHASE 2: MAXIMALITY

1: **for** $j = 1$ **to** m **do**   ▷ (For each environment e_j)
2:     Set a random order to the blocks remaining in the last updated table $\mathcal{T}_j'$.
3:     **for all** block B, following the previous random order **do**
4:         $N_B \leftarrow$ number of possible applications of B in C_t'.
5:         $BLOCKS_j \leftarrow BLOCKS_j + \{B^{N_B}\}$ ▷ (Accumulate the value)
6:         $C_t' \leftarrow C_t' - LHS(B) \cdot N_B$ ▷ (Delete the LHS of block B, N_B times.)
7:     **end for**
8: **end for**

the requirements of P systems semantics, a maximality phase is now applied (Algorithm 4). Following a random order, a maximal number of applications is calculated for each block still applicable. As a consequence, no object that can be consumed is left in the current configuration. In order to minimize the distortion towards the most probable blocks, this phase is performed after phase 1, as a residual number of objects is expected to be consumed in this phase.

Algorithm 5. SELECTION PHASE 3: PROBABILITY

1: **for** $j = 1$ **to** m **do**   ▷ (For each environment e_j)
2:     **for all** block $B^{N_B} \in BLOCKS_j$ **do**
3:         Calculate $\{n_1, \ldots, n_l\}$, a random multinomial $M(N_B, g_1, \ldots, g_l)$ with
            respect to the probabilities of the rules $r_1, \ldots, r_l$ within the block.
4:         **for** $k = 1$ **to** l **do**
5:             $RULES_j \leftarrow RULES_j + \{r_k^{n_k}\}$.
6:         **end for**
7:     **end for**
8:     Delete the multiset of selected blocks $BLOCKS_j \leftarrow \emptyset$.
9: **end for**

After the application of phases 1 and 2, a maximal multiset of selected (mutually consistent) blocks has been computed. The output of the selection stage has to be, however, a maximal multiset of selected rules. Hence, phase 3 (Algorithm 5) passes from blocks to rules, by applying the corresponding probabilities (at the local level of blocks). The rules belonging to a block are selected according to a multinomial distribution $M(N, g_1, \ldots, g_l)$, where N is the number of applications of the block, and $g_1, \ldots, g_l$ are the probabilities associated with the rules $r_1, \ldots, r_l$ within the block, respectively.

Once the rules to be applied on the current simulation step are selected, the execution stage (Algorithm 6) is applied. This stage consists on executing the previously selected multiset of rules. As the objects present on the left hand side of these rules have already been consumed, the only operation left is the application of the RHS of the selected rules. Therefore, for each selected rule, the objects present on the RHS are added to the corresponding membranes and the indicated membrane charge is set.

Algorithm 6. EXECUTION

1: **for** $j = 1$ **to** m **do**   ▷ (For each environment e_j)
2:     **for all** rule $r^n \in RULES_j$ **do**   ▷ (Apply the RHS of selected rules)
3:         $C'_t \leftarrow C'_t + n \cdot RHS(r)$
4:             Update the electrical charges of C'_t from $RHS(r)$.
5:     **end for**
6:     Delete the multiset of selected rules $RULES_j \leftarrow \emptyset$.
7: **end for**

4 Validation

4.1 Improved Model for the Scavenger Bird Ecosystem

In this section, it is presented a novel model for an ecosystem related to the Bearded Vulture in the Pyrenees (NE Spain), by using PDP systems. This model is an improved model from the one provided in [4]. The Bearded Vulture (*Gypaetus barbatus*) is an endangered species in Europe that feeds almost exclusively on bone remains of wild and domestic ungulates. In this model, the evolution of six species is studied: the Bearded Vulture and five subfamilies of domestic and wild ungulates upon which the vulture feeds.

The model consists of a PDP system of degree $(2, 1)$,

$$\Pi = (G, \Gamma, \Sigma, T, R_E, \mu, R, \{f_{r,1} : r \in R\}, \mathcal{M}_1, \mathcal{M}_2)$$

where:

- $G = (V, S)$ with $V = \{e_1\}$ and $S = \emptyset$.
- In the alphabet Γ, we represent the seven species of the ecosystem (index i is associated with the species and index j is associated with their age, and the symbols X, Y and Z represent the same animal but in different states); it also contains the auxiliary symbol B, which represents 0.5 kg of bones, and C, which allows a change in the polarization of the membrane labeled by 2 at a specific stage.

$$\Gamma = \{X_{i,j}, Y_{i,j}, Z_{i,j} : 1 \leq i \leq 7, 0 \leq j \leq k_{i,4}\} \cup \{B, C\}$$

The species are the following:

- Bearded Vulture ($i = 1$)
- Pyrenean Chamois ($i = 2$)
- Female Red Deer ($i = 3$)
- Male Red Deer ($i = 4$)
- Fallow Deer ($i = 5$)
- Roe Deer ($i = 6$)
- Sheep ($i = 7$)

Note that although the male red deer and female red deer are the same species, we consider them as different species. This is because mortality of male deer is different from the female deer by reason of hunting.

- $\Sigma = \emptyset$.
- Each year in the real ecosystem is simulated by 3 computational steps, so $T = 3 \cdot Years$, where $Years$ is the number of years to simulate.
- $R_E = \emptyset$.
- $\mu = [\,[\,]_2\,]_1$ is the membrane structure and the corresponding initial multisets are:
  - $\mathcal{M}_1 = \{\, X_{i,j}^{q_{i,j}} : 1 \leq i \leq 7, 0 \leq j \leq k_{i,4}\}$
  - $\mathcal{M}_2 = \{\, C, B^{\alpha}\}$ where $\alpha = \lceil \sum\limits_{j=1}^{k_{1,4}} q_{1,j} \cdot 1.10 \cdot 682 \rceil$

    Value α represents an external contribution of food which is added during the first year of study so that the Bearded Vulture survives. In the formula, $q_{1,j}$ represents the number of bearded vultures that are j years old, the goal of the constant factor 1.10 is to guarantee enough food for 10% population growth. At present, the population growth is estimated an average 4%, but this figure can reach higher values. Thus, to avoid problems related with the underestimation of this value the first year we have overestimated the population growth at 10%. The constant value 682 represents the amount of food needed per year for a Bearded Vulture pair to survive.
- The set R is defined as follows:
  - Reproduction rules for ungulates

    Adult males
    $$r_{0,i,j} \equiv [X_{i,j}]_1 \xrightarrow{1-k_{i,13}} [Y_{i,j}]_1 : k_{i,2} \leq j \leq k_{i,4}, 2 \leq i \leq 7$$
    Adult females that reproduce
    $$r_{1,i,j} \equiv [X_{i,j}]_1 \xrightarrow{k_{i,5}k_{i,13}} [Y_{i,j}, Y_{i,0}]_1 : k_{i,2} \leq j < k_{i,3}, 2 \leq i \leq 7, i \neq 3$$
    Red Deer females produce 50% of female and 50% of male springs
    $$r_{2,j} \equiv [X_{3,j}]_1 \xrightarrow{k_{3,5}k_{3,13}0.5} [Y_{3,j}Y_{3,0}]_1 : k_{3,2} \leq j < k_{3,3}$$
    $$r_{3,j} \equiv [X_{3,j}]_1 \xrightarrow{k_{3,5}k_{3,13}0.5} [Y_{3,j}Y_{4,0}]_1 : k_{3,2} \leq j < k_{3,3}$$
    Fertile adult females that do not reproduce
    $$r_{4,i,j} \equiv [X_{i,j}]_1 \xrightarrow{(1-k_{i,5})k_{i,13}} [Y_{i,j}]_1 : k_{i,2} \leq j < k_{i,3}, 2 \leq i \leq 7$$
    Not fertile adult females
    $$r_{5,i,j} \equiv [X_{i,j}]_1 \xrightarrow{k_{i,13}} [Y_{i,j}]_1 : k_{i,3} \leq j \leq k_{i,4}, 2 \leq i \leq 7$$
    Young ungulates that do not reproduce
    $$r_{6,i,j} \equiv [X_{i,j}]_1 \xrightarrow{1} [Y_{i,j}]_1 : 0 \leq j < k_{i,2}, 2 \leq i \leq 7$$
  - Growth rules for the Bearded Vulture
    $$r_{7,j} \equiv [X_{1,j}]_1 \xrightarrow{k_{1,6}+k_{1,10}} [Y_{1,k_{1,2}-1}Y_{1,j}]_1 : k_{1,2} \leq j < k_{1,4}$$
    $$r_{8,j} \equiv [X_{1,j}]_1 \xrightarrow{1-k_{1,6}-k_{1,10}} [Y_{1,j}]_1 : k_{1,2} \leq j < k_{1,4}$$
    $$r_9 \equiv [X_{1,k_{1,4}}]_1 \xrightarrow{k_{1,6}} [Y_{1,k_{1,2}-1}Y_{1,k_{1,4}}]_1$$
    $$r_{10} \equiv [X_{1,k_{1,4}}]_1 \xrightarrow{1-k_{1,6}} [Y_{1,k_{1,4}}]_1$$

- Mortality rules for ungulates
  Young ungulates which survive
  $$r_{11,i,j} \equiv Y_{i,j}[\,]_2 \xrightarrow{1-k_{i,7}-k_{i,8}} [Z_{i,j}]_2 : 0 \le j < k_{i,1}, 2 \le i \le 7$$
  Young ungulates which die
  $$r_{12,i,j} \equiv Y_{i,j}[\,]_2 \xrightarrow{k_{i,8}} [B^{k_{i,11}}]_2 : 0 \le j < k_{i,1}, 2 \le i \le 7$$
  Young ungulates which are retired from the ecosystem
  $$r_{13,i,j} \equiv Y_{i,j}[\,]_2 \xrightarrow{k_{i,7}} [\,]_2 : 0 \le j < k_{i,1}, 2 \le i \le 7$$
  Adult ungulates that do not reach the average life expectancy
    Those which survive
  $$r_{14,i,j} \equiv Y_{i,j}[\,]_2 \xrightarrow{1-k_{i,10}} [Z_{i,j}]_2 : k_{i,1} \le j < k_{i,4}, 2 \le i \le 7$$
    Those which die
  $$r_{15,i,j} \equiv Y_{i,j}[\,]_2 \xrightarrow{k_{i,10}} [B^{k_{i,12}}]_2 : k_{i,1} \le j < k_{i,4}, 2 \le i \le 7$$
  Ungulates that reach the average life expectancy
    Those which die in the ecosystem
  $$r_{16,i} \equiv Y_{i,k_{i,4}}[\,]_2 \xrightarrow{k_{i,9}+(1-k_{i,9})k_{i,10}} [B^{k_{i,12}}]_2 : 2 \le i \le 7$$
    Those which die and are retired from the ecosystem
  $$r_{17,i} \equiv Y_{i,k_{i,4}}[\,]_2 \xrightarrow{(1-k_{i,9})(1-k_{i,10})} [\,]_2 : 2 \le i \le 7$$
- Mortality rules for the Bearded Vulture
  $$r_{18,j} \equiv Y_{1,j}[\,]_2 \xrightarrow{1-k_{1,10}} [Z_{1,j}]_2 : k_{1,2} \le j < k_{1,4}$$
  $$r_{19,j} \equiv Y_{1,j}[\,]_2 \xrightarrow{k_{1,10}} [\,]_2 : k_{1,2} \le j < k_{1,4}$$
  $$r_{20} \equiv Y_{1,k_{1,4}}[\,]_2 \xrightarrow{1} [Z_{1,k_{1,2}-1}]_2$$
  $$r_{21} \equiv Y_{1,k_{1,2}-1}[\,]_2 \xrightarrow{1} [Z_{1,k_{1,2}-1}]_2$$
- Feeding rules
  $$r_{22,i,j} \equiv [Z_{i,j}B^{k_{i,14}}]_2 \xrightarrow{1} X_{i,j+1}[\,]_2^+ : 0 \le j \le k_{i,4}, 1 \le i \le 7$$
- Balance rules
  Elimination of remaining bones
  $$r_{23} \equiv [B]_2^+ \xrightarrow{1} [\,]_2$$
  Adult animals that die because they have not enough food
  $$r_{24,i,j} \equiv [Z_{i,j}]_2^+ \xrightarrow{1} [B^{k_{i,12}}]_2 : k_{i,1} \le j \le k_{i,4}, 1 \le i \le 7$$
  Young animals that die because the have not enough food
  $$r_{25,i,j} \equiv [Z_{i,j}]_2^+ \xrightarrow{1} [B^{k_{i,11}}]_2 : 0 \le j < k_{i,1}, 1 \le i \le 7$$
  Change the polarization
  $$r_{26} \equiv [C]_2^+ \xrightarrow{1} [C]_2$$

The constants associated with the rules have the following meaning:

- $k_{i,1}$: Age at which adult size is reached. This is the age at which the animal consumes food as an adult does, and at which, if the animal dies, the amount of biomass it leaves behind is similar to the total left by an adult. Moreover, at this age it will have surpassed the critical early phase during which the mortality rate is high.
- $k_{i,2}$: Age at which it begins to be fertile.
- $k_{i,3}$: Age at which it stops being fertile.
- $k_{i,4}$: Average life expectancy in the ecosystem.
- $k_{i,5}$: Fertility ratio (number of descendants by fertile females).
- $k_{i,6}$: Population growth (this quantity is expressed in terms of 1).
- $k_{i,7}$: Animals retired from the ecosystem in the first year, age $< k_{i,1}$ (this quantity is expressed in terms of 1).
- $k_{i,8}$: Natural mortality ratio in first years, age $< k_{i,1}$ (this quantity is expressed in terms of 1).
- $k_{i,9}$: 0 if the live animals are retired at age $k_{i,4}$, in other cases, the value is 1.
- $k_{i,10}$: Mortality ratio in adult animals, age $\geq k_{i,1}$ (this quantity is expressed in terms of 1).
- $k_{i,11}$: Amount of bones from young animals, age $< k_{i,1}$.
- $k_{i,12}$: Amount of bones from adult animals, age $\geq k_{i,1}$.
- $k_{i,13}$: Proportion of females in the population (this quantity is expressed in terms of 1).
- $k_{i,14}$: Amount of food necessary per year and breeding pair (1 unit is equal to 0.5 kg of bones).

In [4] can be found actual values for the constants associated with the rules as well as actual values for the initial populations $q_{i,j}$ for each species i with age j. There are two sets of initial populations values, one beginning on year 1994 and another one beginning on year 2008.

4.2   Simulation Results

PLinguaCore is a software library for simulation that accepts an input written in P-Lingua [8] and provides simulations of the defined P systems. For each supported type of P system, there are one or more simulation algorithms implemented in pLinguaCore. It is a software framework, so it can be expanded with new simulation algorithms.

Thus, we have extended the pLinguaCore library to include the DCBA simulation algorithm for PDP systems. The current version of pLinguaCore is 3.0 and can be downloaded from [18].

In this section, we use the model of the Bearded Vulture described above to compare the simulation results produced by the pLinguaCore library using two different simulation algorithms: DNDP [12] and DCBA. We also compare the results of the implemented simulation algorithms with the results provided by the C++ *ad hoc* simulator and with the actual ecosystem data, both obtained from [4]. In [19] it can be found the P-Lingua file which defines the model and instructions to reproduce the comparisons.

We have set the initial population values with the actual ecosystem values for the year 1994. For each simulation algorithm we have made 100 simulations of 14 years, that is, 42 computational steps. The simulation workflow has been implemented on a Java program that runs over the pLinguaCore library (this Java program can be downloaded from [19]). For each simulated year (3 computational steps), the Java program counts the number of animals for each species i, that is: $X_i = \sum_{j=0}^{k_{i,4}} X_{i,j}$. After 100 simulations, the Java program calculates average values for each year and species and writes the output to a text file. Finally, we have used the GnuPlot software [17] to produce the population graphics.

The population graphics for each species and simulation algorithm are represented in Figures 1 to 7.

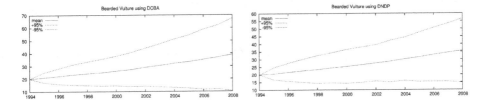

Fig. 1. Evolution of the Bearded Vulture birds

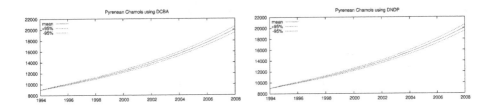

Fig. 2. Evolution of the Pyrenean Chamois

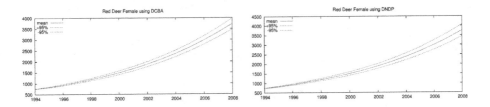

Fig. 3. Evolution of the female Red Deer

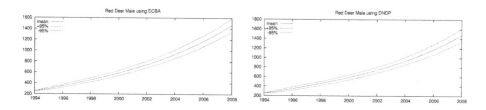

Fig. 4. Evolution of the male Red Deer

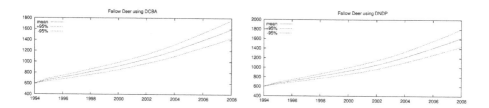

Fig. 5. Evolution of the Fallow Deer

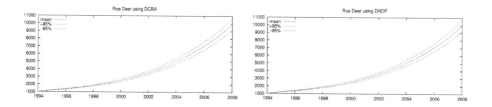

Fig. 6. Evolution of the Roe Deer

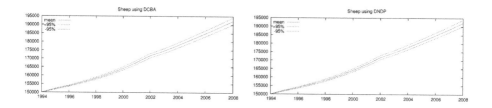

Fig. 7. Evolution of the Sheep

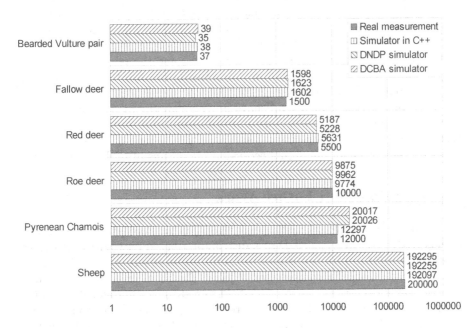

Fig. 8. Data of the year 2008 from: real measurements of the ecosystem, original simulator in C++, simulator using DNDP and simulator using DCBA.

The main difference between the DNDP and the DCBA algorithms is the way they distribute the objects between different rule blocks that compete for the same objects. In the model, the dynamics of the ungulates are modelled by using rule blocks that do not compete for objects. Therefore, similar results are obtained by the simulator for both DCBA and DNDP algorithms. However, in the case of the Bearded Vulture, there is a set of rules $r_{22,i,j}$ that compete for B objects because $k_{1,14}$ is not 0 (the Bearded Vulture needs to feed on bones to survive). The initial amount of bones and the amount of bones generated during the simulation is enough to support the Bearded Vulture population regardless the way the simulation algorithm distributes the bones among vultures of different ages (rules $r_{22,1,j}$). Since there is a small initial population of bearded vultures (20 pairs), some small differences, motivated by the probabilistic component of the simulators, can be noticed between the results from DCBA, DNDP, C++ simulator and the actual ecosystem data for the Bearded Vulture (39 bearded vultures with DCBA for year 2008, 36 with DNDP, 38 with the C++ simulator and 37 on the actual ecosystem). Although the total number of vultures evolves in a similar way for all simulators, the distribution of bones among vultures of different ages is performed in a more natural way by DCBA, according to the ecologists opinion.

In Figure 8 it is shown the comparison between the actual data for the year 2008 and the simulation results obtained by using the C++ *ad hoc* simulator, the DNDP algorithm and the DCBA algorithm implemented in pLinguaCore. In the case of the Pyrenean Chamois, there is a difference between the actual population data on the ecosystem (12000 animals) and the results provided by the other simulators (above 20000 animals), this is because the population of Pyrenean Chamois was restarted on year 2004 [4]. Taking this into account, one can notice that all the simulators behave in a similar way for the above model and they can reproduce the actual data after 14 simulated years. So, the DCBA algorithm is able to reproduce the semantics of PDP systems and it can be used to simulate the behaviour of actual ecosystems by means of PDP systems.

5   Conclusions and Future Work

In this paper we have introduced a novel algorithm for Population Dynamics P systems (PDP systems), called Direct distribution based on Consistent Blocks Algorithm (DCBA). This new algorithm performs an object distribution along the rules that eventually compete for objects. The main procedure is divided into two stages: selection and execution. Selection stage is also divided into three micro-phases: phase 1 (distribution), where by using a table and the construction of rule blocks, the distribution process takes place; phase 2 (maximality), where a random order is applied to the remaining rule blocks in order to assure the maximality condition; and phase 3 (probability), where the number of application of rule blocks is translated to application of rules by using random numbers respecting the probabilities. The algorithm is validated towards a real ecosystem model, showing that they reproduce similar results as the original simulator written in C++.

The accelerators in High Performance Computing offer new approaches to accelerate the simulation of P systems and Population Dynamics. An initial parallelization work of the DCBA by using multi-core processors is described in [9]. The analysis of the two parallel levels (simulations and environments), and the speedup achieved by using the different cores, make interesting the search for more parallel architectures. In this respect, the massively parallel processors of graphics cards (GPUs) have been recently used to achieve higher accelerations [10]. In future work, we will improve those parallel simulators, and reconnect them to the pLinguaCore framework through efficient and robust communication protocols.

Acknowledgements. The authors acknowledge the support of "Proyecto de Excelencia con Investigador de Reconocida Valía" of the "Junta de Andalucía" under grant P08-TIC04200, and the support of the project TIN2009-13192 of the "Ministerio de Economía y Competitividad" of Spain, both co-financed by FEDER funds.

References

1. Bianco, L., Manca, V., Marchetti, L., Petterlini, M.: Psim: a simulator for biomolecular dynamics based on P systems. In: IEEE Congress on Evolutionary Computation, pp. 883–887 (2007)
2. Cardona, M., Colomer, M.A., Margalida, A., Palau, A., Pérez-Hurtado, I., Pérez-Jiménez, M.J., Sanuy, D.: A computational modeling for real ecosystems based on P systems. Natural Computing 10(1), 39–53 (2011)
3. Cardona, M., Colomer, M.A., Margalida, A., Pérez-Hurtado, I., Pérez-Jiménez, M.J., Sanuy, D.: A P System Based Model of an Ecosystem of Some Scavenger Birds. In: Păun, G., Pérez-Jiménez, M.J., Riscos-Núñez, A., Rozenberg, G., Salomaa, A. (eds.) WMC 2009. LNCS, vol. 5957, pp. 182–195. Springer, Heidelberg (2010)
4. Cardona, M., Colomer, M.A., Pérez-Jiménez, M.J., Sanuy, D., Margalida, A.: Modeling Ecosystems Using P Systems: The Bearded Vulture, a Case Study. In: Corne, D.W., Frisco, P., Păun, G., Rozenberg, G., Salomaa, A. (eds.) WMC 2008. LNCS, vol. 5391, pp. 137–156. Springer, Heidelberg (2009)
5. Cheruku, S., Păun, A., Romero-Campero, F.J., Pérez-Jiménez, M.J., Ibarra, O.H.: Simulating FAS-induced apoptosis by using P systems. Progress in Natural Science 17(4), 424–431 (2007)
6. Colomer, M.A., Lavín, S., Marco, I., Margalida, A., Pérez-Hurtado, I., Pérez-Jiménez, M.J., Sanuy, D., Serrano, E., Valencia-Cabrera, L.: Modeling Population Growth of Pyrenean Chamois (Rupicapra p. pyrenaica) by Using P-Systems. In: Gheorghe, M., Hinze, T., Păun, G., Rozenberg, G., Salomaa, A. (eds.) CMC 2010. LNCS, vol. 6501, pp. 144–159. Springer, Heidelberg (2010)
7. Colomer, M.A., Pérez-Hurtado, I., Pérez-Jiménez, M.J., Riscos-Núñez, A.: Comparing simulation algorithms for multienvironment probabilistic P system over a standard virtual ecosystem. Natural Computing 11(3), 369–379 (2012)
8. García-Quismondo, M., Gutiérrez-Escudero, R., Pérez-Hurtado, I., Pérez-Jiménez, M.J., Riscos-Núñez, A.: An Overview of P-Lingua 2.0. In: Păun, G., Pérez-Jiménez, M.J., Riscos-Núñez, A., Rozenberg, G., Salomaa, A. (eds.) WMC 2009. LNCS, vol. 5957, pp. 264–288. Springer, Heidelberg (2010)
9. Martínez-del-Amor, M.A., Karlin, I., Jensen, R.E., Pérez-Jiménez, M.J., Elster, A.C.: Parallel Simulation of Probabilistic P Systems on Multicore Platforms. In: Proceedings of the Tenth Brainstorming Week on Membrane Computing, vol. II, pp. 17–26 (2012)
10. Martínez-del-Amor, M.A., Pérez-Hurtado, I., Gastalver-Rubio, A., Elster, A.C., Pérez-Jiménez, M.J.: Population Dynamics P Systems on CUDA. In: Gilbert, D., Heiner, M. (eds.) CMSB 2012. LNCS, vol. 7605, pp. 247–266. Springer, Heidelberg (2012)
11. Martínez-del-Amor, M.A., Pérez-Hurtado, I., Pérez-Jiménez, M.J., Riscos-Núñez, A., Sancho-Caparrini, F.: A simulation algorithm for multienvironment probabilistic P systems: A formal verification. International Journal of Foundations of Computer Science 22(1), 107–118 (2011)
12. Martínez-del-Amor, M.A., Pérez-Hurtado, I., Pérez-Jiménez, M.J., Riscos-Núñez, A., Colomer, M.A.: A new simulation algorithm for multienvironment probabilistic P systems. In: Proceedings of the 5th IEEE International Conference on Bio-Inspired Computing: Theories and Applications, vol. 1, pp. 59–68 (2010)

13. Păun, G.: Computing with membranes. Journal of Computer and System Sciences 61(1), 108–143 (2000); Turku Center for Computer Science-TUCS Report No 208
14. Păun, G., Romero-Campero, F.J.: Membrane Computing as a Modeling Framework. Cellular Systems Case Studies. In: Bernardo, M., Degano, P., Zavattaro, G. (eds.) SFM 2008. LNCS, vol. 5016, pp. 168–214. Springer, Heidelberg (2008)
15. Păun, G., Rozenberg, G., Salomaa, A. (eds.): The Oxford Handbook of Membrane Computing (2010)
16. Terrazas, G., Krasnogor, N., Gheorghe, M., Bernardini, F., Diggle, S., Cámara, M.: An Environment Aware P-System Model of Quorum Sensing. In: Cooper, S.B., Löwe, B., Torenvliet, L. (eds.) CiE 2005. LNCS, vol. 3526, pp. 479–485. Springer, Heidelberg (2005)
17. The GNUplot web page, http://www.gnuplot.info
18. The P-Lingua web page, http://www.p-lingua.org
19. The Bearded Vulture ecosystem model in P-Lingua, http://www.p-lingua.org/wiki/index.php/bvBWMC12

Membranes with Boundaries

Tamás Mihálydeák[1] and Zoltán Ernő Csajbók[2]

[1] Department of Computer Science, Faculty of Informatics, University of Debrecen
Egyetem tér 1, H-4010 Debrecen, Hungary
mihalydeak.tamas@inf.unideb.hu
[2] Department of Health Informatics, Faculty of Health, University of Debrecen,
Sóstói út 2-4, H-4400 Nyíregyháza, Hungary
csajbok.zoltan@foh.unideb.hu

Abstract. Active cell components involved in real biological processes have to be close enough to a membrane in order to be able to pass through it. Rough set theory gives a plausible opportunity to model boundary zones around cell-like formations. However, this theory works within conventional set theory, and so to apply its ideas to membrane computing, first, we have worked out an adequate approximation framework for multisets. Next, we propose a two–component structure consisting of a P system and an approximation space for multisets. Using the approximation technique, we specify the closeness around membranes, even from inside and outside, via boundaries in the sense of multiset approximations. Then, we define communication rules within the P system in such a way that they operate in the boundary zones solely. The two components mutually cooperate.

Keywords: Approximation of sets, rough multisets, membrane computing.

1 Introduction

As it is well known, P systems (membrane systems) were introduced by Păun [21–23]. P systems can be considered as distributed computing devices which were motivated by the structure and functioning of living cells. Membranes delimit compartments (regions), which are arranged in a cell–like (hence hierarchical) structure. A set of rules is given for every region. These rules can model reactions inside a region (like chemical reactions work), or processes of passing objects through membranes (like biological processes work). In the general model, regions are represented by multisets and two types of rules are given: rewriting rules for the first type and communication rules (either symport or antiport fashion) for the second type. There are some generalizations of P systems in which nonhierarchical arrangements of compartments are also considered.

In the case of communication rules objects pass through membranes. If we pay our attention to biological processes we can say that an object has to be

E. Csuhaj-Varjú et al. (Eds.): CMC 2012, LNCS 7762, pp. 277–294, 2013.

close enough to a membrane in order to be able to pass through it. In different versions of P systems one can find some variants which embody the concept of space and position inside a region (see for example [1, 6]), and so these systems are able to give a special meaning of 'to be close enough to a membrane'. But we have no precise information about the nature of the space of objects or their positions in general.[1] If we look at the regions of a P system as multisets, then a very general theory, the theory of approximation for multisets can help us to introduce a correct concept of 'closeness to a membrane' (or 'to be close enough to a membrane').

Different ways of set approximations go back (at least) to rough set theory which was originated by Pawlak in the early 1980's [18, 19]. In his theory and its different generalizations lower and upper approximations of a given set appear which are based on different kinds of indiscernibility relations. An indiscernibility relation on a given set of objects provides the set of base sets by which any set can be approximated from lower and upper sides. Its generalization, the so–called partial approximation of sets (see [7–9, 16]) gives a possibility to embed available knowledge into an approximation space. The lower and upper approximations of a given set rely on base sets which represent available knowledge. If we have concepts of lower and upper approximations, the concept of boundary can be introduced.

From the set–theoretical point of view, regions in membrane computing can be represented by multisets, msets for short, therefore at first we have to generalize the theory of set approximations for multisets. With the membrane structure as a background, an underlying mset approximation space can be formed in its own right. It is called the general mset approximation space. The nature of this space is basically determined by its constituents, to a certain extent, independently of the membrane structure (cf., Definition 2).

Mset approximations rely on a beforehand given set of msets called base msets. Using the common approximation technique, the lower and upper approximations, the boundaries of msets can be given by means of base msets. Since the set–theoretic representations of regions are msets, boundaries of regions delimited by membranes can be formed, too. In short, they are also called boundaries of membranes or simply membrane boundaries. Then, we can say that an object is close enough to a membrane if it is a member of its boundary. What is more we can specify inside and outside boundaries of membranes, thus the closeness to membranes from inside and outside. Last, it is assumed that the communication rules in the P system execute only in base msets of membrane boundaries. Thus, a living cell can be represented more precisely.

Communication rules modify the regions by changing the inside and outside boundaries of membranes. However, these changes take place within the base msets. Consequently, the changes do not modify the general mset approximation space. It can only be modified when there is no any communication rule which

---

[1] This problem has been also addressed in the recent paper [10] by E. Csuhaj–Varjú, M. Georghe and M. Stannett.

can be executed in the boundaries, i.e. the membrane computation has halted. Just then, triggers are activated.[2]

Triggers are rules which are associated with the base msets. Their forms are similar to communication rules, more precisely to symport rules of the form $\langle u, in \rangle$. However, we strictly have to differentiate base msets from regions and also triggers from rules in the membrane computing sense.

The membrane computation may cause a shortage of objects in the inside and/or outside parts of the base msets in the membrane boundaries. In order to supplement the missing objects by the objects of the same type, a suction effect is started up against the neighbor base msets being inside and/or outside regions, respectively. The suction effect is achieved through the triggers as far as possible. Each time, when the membrane computation has halted, the triggers associated with the base msets within membrane boundaries are activated. So, in this phase, the general mset approximation space changes into a new one, therefore new boundaries (from inside and outside) can be defined for regions as msets. Hence, the membrane computation can start again. The whole computation process stops when there is no any trigger activity.

The rest of the paper is organized as follows. In Section 2, we define the general mset approximation space and discuss its fundamental properties. Section 3 connects general mset approximation spaces with membrane systems. Using the approximation technique, we specify the closeness to membranes, even from inside and outside, via boundary zones. The executions of communication rules are restricted to the base msets in membrane boundaries. Last, we explain the overall computational process in detail.

2 Multiset Approximations

The section deals with a general theory of multiset approximations. There are (at least) two readings of different versions of rough set theory. The first one is about vagueness based on indiscernibility, whereas the second one is about possible approximations of sets. In the present paper we focus on the second reading, and we ask how to treat multisets in a very general approximation framework. The answer to this question is a minimal condition for applying multiset approximations in membrane computing.

---

[2] In [17], we used the term daemon instead of trigger. Daemon-like constructions are known e.g. as daemons in Unix, services in Windows, also daemons in artificial intelligence, and trigger in database management systems (DBMS's). In operating systems, daemon-like processes are used to provide services that can well be done in background without any user interaction, i.e. *without any outside interference*. On the other hand, triggers in DBMS's are activated by just user interactions. In our approach, mset approximation spaces and P systems cooperate mutually. Thus in our framework, the concept of database triggers has served for us as a more realistic pattern in order to model operations of such type.

2.1 Fundamental Notions of Multiset Theory

Multisets are well–known generalizations of sets [2, 3, 5, 14, 25]. We can say that an object can have more than one occurrences in a multiset or some copies of an object (one or more than one) can belong to a multiset. The use of multisets in mathematics has a long history. For instance, Richard Dedekind used the term multiset in a paper published in 1888 [4, 12]. Nowadays multisets are used not only in mathematics but informatics [13, 20, 24, 26].

Definition 1. *Let U be a finite nonempty set. A multiset M, or mset M for short, over U is a mapping $M : U \to \mathbb{N} \cup \{\infty\}$, where $\mathbb{N}$ is the set of natural numbers.*

1. *Multiplicity relation for an mset M over U is:*
   $a \in M$ $(a \in U)$, if $M(a) \geq 1$;
2. *n–times multiplicity relation for an mset M over U is:*
   $a \in^n M$ $(a \in U)$, if $M(a) = n$;
3. *an mset M is said to be an empty mset (in notation $M = \emptyset$) if $M(a) = 0$ for all $a \in U$;*
4. *$\mathcal{MS}(U)$ is the set of msets over U;*
5. *$\mathcal{MS}^n(U)$ $(n \in \mathbb{N})$ is the set of msets over U such that if $M \in \mathcal{MS}^n(U)$, then $M(a) \leq n$ for all $a \in U$;*
6. *$\mathcal{MS}^{<\infty}(U) = \bigcup_{n=0}^{\infty} \mathcal{MS}^n(U)$.*

Remark 1. In the general theory of msets, the set U may be infinite. There is no need to deal with this case in our investigation.

Remark 2. $\mathcal{MS}(U)$ is also called the macroset [15].

Remark 3. If $a \in U$, then $M(a)$ gives the number of occurrences of the element a in the mset M. If $U = \{a_1, a_2, \ldots, a_n\}$, then

- an mset M over U can be given in the form
  $\{\langle a_1, M(a_1)\rangle, \langle a_2, M(a_2)\rangle, \ldots, \langle a_n, M(a_n)\rangle\}$;
- in membrane computing if $M(a) < \infty$ for all $a \in U$, the mset M over U can be represented by all permutations of the string w:
  $$w = \begin{cases} a_{k_1}^{M(a_{k_1})} a_{k_2}^{M(a_{k_2})} \cdots a_{k_l}^{M(a_{k_l})}, & \text{if } M \text{ is not an empty mset;} \\ \lambda, & \text{otherwise;} \end{cases}$$
  where λ is the empty string.

Remark 4. If all $a \in U$ have (countable) infinite occurrences in the mset M over U i.e. $M(a) = \infty$ for all $a \in U$, then M is denoted by M^∞.

Set–theoretical operations and relations can be generalized for msets. Let M_1 and M_2 be two msets over U.

1. $M_1 = M_2$, if $M_1(a) = M_2(a)$ for all $a \in U$;
2. $M_1 \sqsubseteq M_2$, if $M_1(a) \leq M_2(a)$ for all $a \in U$;

3. $M_1 \sqsubseteq^n M_2$, if $nM_1(a) \leq M_2(a)$ for all $a \in U$ and there is an $a' \in U$ such that $(n+1)M_1(a') > M_2(a')$;

4. $(M_1 \sqcap M_2)(a) = \min\{M_1(a), M_2(a)\}$ for all $a \in U$;

5. if $\mathcal{M} \subseteq \mathcal{MS}(U)$, then $(\sqcap\mathcal{M})(a) = \min\{M(a) \mid M \in \mathcal{M}\}$ for all $a \in U$;

6. set–type ($\sqcup$) and mset–type ($\oplus$) union can be defined:
   (a) $(M_1 \sqcup M_2)(a) = \max\{M_1(a), M_2(a)\}$ for all $a \in U$;
   (b) if $\mathcal{M} \subseteq \mathcal{MS}^{<\infty}(U)$, then $(\bigsqcup\mathcal{M})(a) = \max\{M(a) \mid M \in \mathcal{M}\}$ for all $a \in U$. By definition, $\bigsqcup \emptyset = \emptyset$.
   (c) $(M_1 \oplus M_2)(a) = M_1(a) + M_2(a)$ for all $a \in U$ (mset–type union is often called mset addition);
   (d) $\oplus_n M$ can be given by the following inductive definition:
      i. $\oplus_0 M = \emptyset$,
      ii. $\oplus_1 M = M$,
      iii. $\oplus_{n+1}M = M \oplus \oplus_n M$;

7. $(M_1 \ominus M_2)(a) = \max\{M_1(a) - M_2(a), 0\}$ for all $a \in U$ (mset subtraction);

8. if $M \in \mathcal{MS}^n(U)$ for an $n \in \mathbb{N}$, then $\overline{M}^n(a) = n - M(a)$ for all $a \in U$. $\overline{M}^n$ is the complement of mset M with respect to n.

Remark 5. $M_1 \sqsubseteq^n M_2$ iff $\oplus_n M_1 \sqsubseteq M_2$ and $\oplus_{n+1}M_1 \not\sqsubseteq M_2$.

2.2 General Multiset Approximation Space

A general approximation space for msets or for short mset approximation space depends on four different components:

– At first, we have to give the *domain* of the approximation space whose members are approximated. In our case the domain is a set of msets.

– The next step is to determine on which the approximations rely. Some distinguished members of the domain are chosen in order to use them as the bases of approximations. They are called *base msets*. The most fundamental aspect of available knowledge can be represented by base msets. In membrane computing they can be taken, for instance, as the representation of coexistence in chemical processes or symbiosis in living nature.

– The third component is called the set of *definable msets*. Here 'definable' means that these msets can be given by using only base msets. Of course, the base msets and the empty mset are definable. The way of getting a definable mset shows how base msets are used in a whole approximation process. There are many different ways of giving definable msets. Definable msets are considered as possible approximations of members of the domain.

– The last step is to give the *approximation pair* of the space. These functions determine the lower and upper approximations of any mset of the domain.

Definition 2. *Let U be a nonempty set.*
The ordered 5-tuple $\mathsf{MAS}(U) = \langle \mathcal{MS}^{<\infty}(U), \mathfrak{B}, \mathfrak{D}_{\mathfrak{B}}, \mathsf{l}, \mathsf{u} \rangle$ *is a general mset approximation space over U with the domain* $\mathcal{MS}^{<\infty}(U)$, *if*

1. $\mathfrak{B} \subseteq \mathcal{MS}^{<\infty}(U)$ *and if* $B \in \mathfrak{B}$, *then* $B \neq \emptyset$ *(in notation* $\mathfrak{B} = \{B_\gamma \mid \gamma \in \Gamma\}$*); members of* $\mathfrak{B}$ *are called base msets, or* $\mathfrak{B}$*-msets for short;*

2. $\mathfrak{D}_{\mathfrak{B}} \subseteq \mathcal{MS}^{<\infty}(U)$ *is an extension of* $\mathfrak{B}$ *satisfying the following minimal requirements:*
   - $\emptyset \in \mathfrak{D}_{\mathfrak{B}}$,
   - *if* $B \in \mathfrak{B}$, *then* $\oplus_n B \in \mathfrak{D}_{\mathfrak{B}}$ *for all* n $(n = 1, 2, \dots)$;
   members of $\mathfrak{D}_{\mathfrak{B}}$ *are called* $\mathfrak{B}$-*definable msets, or simply definable;*

3. *the functions* $\mathsf{l}, \mathsf{u} : \mathcal{MS}^{<\infty}(U) \to \mathcal{MS}^{<\infty}(U)$ *form an approximation pair* $\langle \mathsf{l}, \mathsf{u} \rangle$ *(functions* l, u *give the lower and upper approximation respectively), if the following conditions hold:*
   (a) $\mathsf{l}(\mathcal{MS}^{<\infty}(U)), \mathsf{u}(\mathcal{MS}^{<\infty}(U)) \subseteq \mathfrak{D}_{\mathfrak{B}}$ *(definability of* l, u*);*[3]
   (b) *the functions* l *and* u *are monotone, i.e. for all* $M_1, M_2 \in \mathcal{MS}^{<\infty}(U)$ *if* $M_1 \sqsubseteq M_2$ *then* $\mathsf{l}(M_1) \sqsubseteq \mathsf{l}(M_2)$ *and* $\mathsf{u}(M_1) \sqsubseteq \mathsf{u}(M_2)$ *(monotonicity of* l *and* u*);*
   (c) $\mathsf{u}(\emptyset) = \emptyset$ *(normality of* u*);*
   (d) *if* $M \in \mathfrak{D}_{\mathfrak{B}}$, *then* $\mathsf{l}(M) = M$ *(granularity of* $\mathfrak{D}_{\mathfrak{B}}$*, i.e.* l *is standard);*
   (e) *if* $M \in \mathcal{MS}^{<\infty}(U)$, *then* $\mathsf{l}(M) \sqsubseteq \mathsf{u}(M)$ *(weak approximation property).*

Remark 6. In Definition 2 each condition in *3 (a)–(e)* is independent of the other four.

Of course, there may be more than one msets with the same lower and upper approximations. If $M \in \mathcal{MS}^{<\infty}(U)$, the set

$$\mathcal{RM}(M) = \{M' \in \mathcal{MS}^{<\infty}(U) \mid \mathsf{l}(M) = \mathsf{l}(M') \text{ and } \mathsf{u}(M) = \mathsf{u}(M')\}$$

is called a rough mset connected to M.

2.3   Some Fundamental Properties of Multiset Approximation Spaces

The following propositions show that general mset approximation spaces fulfill the most fundamental requirements of approximations.

Proposition 1. *Let* $\mathsf{MAS}(U) = \langle \mathcal{MS}^{<\infty}(U), \mathfrak{B}, \mathfrak{D}_{\mathfrak{B}}, \mathsf{l}, \mathsf{u} \rangle$ *be a general mset approximation space over* U.

1. $\mathsf{l}(\emptyset) = \emptyset$ *(normality of* l*).*
2. $\forall M \in \mathcal{MS}^{<\infty}(U) (\mathsf{l}(\mathsf{l}(M)) = \mathsf{l}(M))$ *(idempotency of* l*).*
3. $M \in \mathfrak{D}_{\mathfrak{B}}$ *if and only if* $\mathsf{l}(M) = M$.
4. $\mathsf{u}(\mathcal{MS}^{<\infty}(U)) \subseteq \mathsf{l}(\mathcal{MS}^{<\infty}(U)) = \mathfrak{D}_{\mathfrak{B}}$.

Proposition 2. *Let* $\mathsf{MAS}(U) = \langle \mathcal{MS}^{<\infty}(U), \mathfrak{B}, \mathfrak{D}_{\mathfrak{B}}, \mathsf{l}, \mathsf{u} \rangle$ *be a general mset approximation space over* U.

1. *For any* $M_1, M_2 \in \mathcal{MS}^{<\infty}(U)$
   (a) $\mathsf{l}(M_1) \sqcup \mathsf{l}(M_2) \sqsubseteq \mathsf{l}(M_1 \sqcup M_2)$, $\mathsf{l}(M_1 \sqcap M_2) \sqsubseteq \mathsf{l}(M_1) \sqcap \mathsf{l}(M_2)$,
   (b) $\mathsf{u}(M_1) \sqcup \mathsf{u}(M_2) \sqsubseteq \mathsf{u}(M_1 \sqcup M_2)$, $\mathsf{u}(M_1 \sqcap M_2) \sqsubseteq \mathsf{u}(M_1) \sqcap \mathsf{u}(M_2)$.

---

[3] As usual, $\mathsf{l}(\mathcal{MS}^{<\infty}(U))$ and $\mathsf{u}(\mathcal{MS}^{<\infty}(U))$ denote the range of l and u.

In other words, both lower and upper approximations are superadditive and submultiplicative.

2. *In the case of $M_1 \sqsubseteq M_2$, all inclusions in Point 1 can be replaced by equalities:*

   (a) $\mathsf{l}(M_1) \sqcup \mathsf{l}(M_2) = \mathsf{l}(M_1 \sqcup M_2)$, $\mathsf{l}(M_1 \sqcap M_2) = \mathsf{l}(M_1) \sqcap \mathsf{l}(M_2)$,

   (b) $\mathsf{u}(M_1) \sqcup \mathsf{u}(M_2) = \mathsf{u}(M_1 \sqcup M_2)$, $\mathsf{u}(M_1 \sqcap M_2) = \mathsf{u}(M_1) \sqcap \mathsf{u}(M_2)$.

The following proposition gives a simple property of lower and upper approximations.

Proposition 3. *Let $\mathsf{MAS}(U) = \langle \mathcal{MS}^{<\infty}(U), \mathfrak{B}, \mathfrak{D}_\mathfrak{B}, \mathsf{l}, \mathsf{u} \rangle$ be a general mset approximation space over U.*

For any $M \in \mathcal{MS}^{<\infty}(U)$

1. *$\mathsf{l}(M) = \bigsqcup \mathsf{L}(M)$, where $\mathsf{L}(M) = \{D \in \mathfrak{D}_\mathfrak{B} \mid D \sqsubseteq \mathsf{l}(M)\}$;*
2. *$\mathsf{u}(M) = \bigsqcup \mathsf{U}(M)$, where $\mathsf{U}(M) = \{D \in \mathfrak{D}_\mathfrak{B} \mid D \sqsubseteq \mathsf{u}(M)\}$.*

The definitions of definable and crisp msets can be given as usual in rough set theory.

Definition 3. *Let $\mathsf{MAS}(U) = \langle \mathcal{MS}^{<\infty}(U), \mathfrak{B}, \mathfrak{D}_\mathfrak{B}, \mathsf{l}, \mathsf{u} \rangle$ be a general mset approximation space over U.*

An mset M over U is crisp in the general mset approximation space $\mathsf{MAS}(U)$, if $\mathsf{l}(M) = \mathsf{u}(M)$.

Remark 7. Definable msets are not crisp in general.

2.4 Types of General Multiset Approximation Spaces

As it was mentioned base msets together with definable msets represent available knowledge, therefore we need a huge flexibility in giving mset approximation spaces. From the theoretical point of view a general mset approximation space can be specified in the following different ways:

– giving some requirements for the base msets;
– giving a special way how to get the set of definable msets;
– specifying the approximation pair.

Definition 4. *Let $\mathsf{MAS}(U) = \langle \mathcal{MS}^{<\infty}(U), \mathfrak{B}, \mathfrak{D}_\mathfrak{B}, \mathsf{l}, \mathsf{u} \rangle$ be a general mset approximation space over U.*

– *The requirements from the base set point of view are:*
   - *$\mathsf{MAS}(U)$ is bounded in occurrences by n ($n \in \mathbb{N}$), if for all $M \in \mathfrak{B}$ $M(a) \leq n$ for all $a \in U$;*
   - *$\mathsf{MAS}(U)$ is single layered, if $B \in \mathfrak{B}$, then $B \not\sqsubseteq \sqcup\{B' \mid B' \in \mathfrak{B} \setminus \{B\}\}$;*
   - *$\mathsf{MAS}(U)$ is one–layered, if $B_1 \sqcap B_2 = \emptyset$ for all $B_1, B_2 \in \mathfrak{B}$, $B_1 \neq B_2$.*
– *The requirements from the set $\mathfrak{D}_\mathfrak{B}$ point of view are:*
   - *$\mathsf{MAS}(U)$ is a set–type union mset approximation space, if $\oplus_n B_1 \sqcup \oplus_k B_2 \in \mathfrak{D}_\mathfrak{B}$ for all $B_1, B_2 \in \mathfrak{B}$ and n, k ($n, k = 1, 2, \dots$);*

- MAS(U) *is a minimal set–type union mset approximation space, if* $\mathfrak{D}_{\mathfrak{B}}$
  is given by the following inductive definition:
  1. $\emptyset \in \mathfrak{D}_{\mathfrak{B}}$;
  2. $\mathfrak{B} \subseteq \mathfrak{D}_{\mathfrak{B}}$;
  3. *if* $B_1, B_2 \in \mathfrak{B}$, *then* $\oplus_n B_1 \sqcup \oplus_k B_2 \in \mathfrak{D}_{\mathfrak{B}}$ $(n, k = 1, 2, \dots)$.
- MAS(U) *is a strict set–type union mset approximation space, if* $\mathfrak{D}_{\mathfrak{B}}$ *is
  given by the following inductive definition:*
  1. $\emptyset \in \mathfrak{D}_{\mathfrak{B}}$;
  2. $\mathfrak{B} \subseteq \mathfrak{D}_{\mathfrak{B}}$;
  3. *if* $\mathfrak{B}^{\oplus} = \{\oplus_n B \mid B \in \mathfrak{B}\ n = 1, 2, \dots\}$ *and* $\mathfrak{B}' \subseteq \mathfrak{B}^{\oplus}$, *then* $\bigsqcup \mathfrak{B}' \in$
     $\mathfrak{D}_{\mathfrak{B}}$;
- MAS(U) *is a mset–type union mset approximation space, if*
  $\oplus_n B_1 \oplus \oplus_k B_2 \in \mathfrak{D}_{\mathfrak{B}}$ *for all* $B_1, B_2 \in \mathfrak{B}$ *and* n, k $(n, k = 1, 2, \dots)$;
- MAS(U) *is an intersection type general mset approximation space, if*
  $B_1 \sqcap B_2 \in \mathfrak{D}_{\mathfrak{B}}$ *for all* $B_1, B_2 \in \mathfrak{B}$;
- MAS(U) *is total, if for all* $M \in \mathcal{MS}^{<\infty}(U)$ *there is a definable mset* D
  $(D \in \mathfrak{D}_{\mathfrak{B}})$ *such that* $M \sqsubseteq D$;
- MAS(U) *is partial, if it is not total;*
- MAS(U) *relies on Pawlakian definable msets, if it is one–layered and
  total.*

- *The requirements from the approximation pair point of view are:*
  - MAS(U) *is lower semi–strong, if* $\mathsf{l}(M) \sqsubseteq M$ *for all* $M \in \mathcal{MS}^{<\infty}(U)$;
  - MAS(U) *is upper semi–strong, if* $M \sqsubseteq \mathsf{u}(M)$ *for all* $M \in \mathcal{MS}^{<\infty}(U)$;
  - MAS(U) *is strong, if lower and upper semi–strong, i.e.*
    $\mathsf{l}(M) \sqsubseteq M \sqsubseteq \mathsf{u}(M)$ *for all* $M \in \mathcal{MS}^{<\infty}(U)$;
  - MAS(U) *is an approximation space with generalized Pawlakian approxi-
    mation pair, if for any mset* $M \in \mathcal{MS}^{<\infty}(U)$
    1. $\mathsf{l}(M) = \bigsqcup\{\oplus_n B \mid B \in \mathfrak{B}\ and\ B \sqsubseteq^n M\}$;
    2. $\mathsf{b}(M) = \bigsqcup\{\oplus_n B \mid B \in \mathfrak{B}, B \sqcap M \neq \emptyset, B \not\sqsubseteq M\ and\ B \sqcap M \sqsubseteq^n M\}$
       (the function b *gives the boundary of mset* M);
    3. $\mathsf{u}(M) = (\mathsf{l}(M) \oplus \mathsf{b}(M)) \ominus (\mathsf{l}(M) \sqcap \mathsf{b}(M))$.

Proposition 4. *If* MAS(U) *is a strict set–type union general mset approximation space, then for any* $M \in \mathcal{MS}^{<\infty}(U)$

1. $\mathsf{l}(M) = \bigsqcup\{B \in \mathfrak{B} \mid B \sqsubseteq \mathsf{l}(M)\}$,
2. $\mathsf{u}(M) = \bigsqcup\{B \in \mathfrak{B} \mid B \sqsubseteq \mathsf{u}(M)\}$.

3   *P* Systems with Membrane Boundaries

The main questions of the section are the following:

- How can general mset approximation spaces be used in membrane computing
  in order to give membrane boundaries representing the notion of 'to be close
  enough to a membrane'?

- How can the computational process with communication rules constrained for the base msets in membrane boundaries be given?

In this section we focus on hierarchical P systems with communication rules.

Definition 5. *A membrane structure μ of degree m ($m \geq 1$) is a rooted tree with m nodes identified with the integers $1, \ldots, m$.*

Remark 8. If μ is a membrane structure of degree m, then μ can be represented by the set R_μ, $R_\mu \subseteq \{1, \ldots, m\} \times \{1, \ldots, m\}$. $\langle i, j \rangle \in R_\mu$ means, that there is an edge from i (parent) to j (child) of tree μ ($\mathsf{parent}(j) = i$).

Definition 6. *Let μ be a membrane structure with m nodes and V be a finite alphabet. The tuple*

$$\Pi = \langle V, \mu, w_1^0, w_2^0, \ldots, w_m^0, R_1, R_2, \ldots, R_m \rangle$$

is a P system if

1. $w_i^0 \in \mathcal{MS}^{<\infty}(V)$ *for $i = 1, 2, \ldots, m$;*
2. R_i *is a finite set of rules for $i = 1, 2, \ldots, m$ such that if $r \in R_i$, then the form of the rule r is one of the following:*
    (a) *symport rules: $\langle u, in \rangle$, $\langle u, out \rangle$, where $u \neq \lambda$ and there is an mset $M \in \mathcal{MS}^{<\infty}(V)$ such that u represents M;*
    (b) *antiport rule: $\langle u, in; v, out \rangle$, where $u \neq \lambda, v \neq \lambda$ and there are msets $M_1, M_2 \in \mathcal{MS}^{<\infty}(V)$ such that u, v represent M_1, M_2, respectively.*

3.1   Membrane Boundaries Given by General Multiset Approximation Spaces

Section 2 shows there are many different versions of mset approximation spaces. If a P system Π is given, then we have to specify an mset approximation space ($\mathsf{MAS}(\Pi)$) which is convenient for our purpose, i.e. which can add available (background) knowledge to the membrane system in order that membrane boundaries could be treated.

There is only one requirement for the domain of approximations: all regions delimited by membranes have to appear as msets which can be approximated. Therefore if the finite alphabet of the membrane system Π is V, then the set $\mathcal{MS}^{<\infty}(V)$ is a good choice. Base msets represent the most important part of available knowledge in general approximation theory. Here we want to use them in order to define membrane boundaries, in order to represent the notion of 'to be close enough to a membrane'. For example coexistence in chemical processes or symbiosis in living nature can serve as the patterns of the base msets, but there is no any theoretical requirement form the general point of view. We focus on membrane boundaries, therefore the mset approximation space can be a strict set–type union one, and the approximation pair can be a generalized Pawlakian one because it gives and uses the boundary of an mset directly.

In the following let $\Pi = \langle V, \mu, w_1^0, w_2^0, \ldots, w_m^0, R_1, R_2, \ldots, R_m \rangle$ be a P system and $\mathsf{MAS}(\Pi) = \langle \mathcal{MS}^{<\infty}(V), \mathfrak{B}, \mathfrak{D}_{\mathfrak{B}}, \mathsf{l}, \mathsf{u} \rangle$ be a strict set–union type general mset approximation space with generalized Pawlakian approximation pair (see in Definition 4).

Remark 9. All members of $\mathfrak{B}$ are msets, but they are not regions in general. More precisely, $\mathfrak{B}$-msets are not necessarily compartments delimited by membranes from above and below (if any exists). The crucial difference between them is that the $\mathfrak{B}$-msets do not generally form a hierarchical structure, i.e. it may happen that if $B_1 \sqcap B_2 \neq \emptyset$ $(B_1, B_2 \in \mathfrak{B})$, then $B_1 \not\sqsubseteq B_2$ and $B_2 \not\sqsubseteq B_1$.

Proposition 5. $\mathsf{MAS}(\Pi)$ *is lower semi–strong, i.e.* $\mathsf{l}(M) \sqsubseteq M$ *for all* $M \in \mathcal{MS}^{<\infty}(V)$.

According to Proposition 5, the lower approximation of a membrane determines an mset inside it which can be a candidate to be a new region, i.e. a new member in the membrane structure.

If we have a membrane system Π, and a joint membrane approximation space $\mathsf{MAS}(\Pi)$, then we can define the boundary of a region (a membrane boundary) as an mset. To introduce constrains on symport/antiport rules we need not only the boundary of a region but 'inside' and 'outside' boundaries as well.

Definition 7. *Let* $\Pi = \langle V, \mu, w_1^0, w_2^0, \ldots, w_m^0, R_1, R_2, \ldots, R_m \rangle$ *be a* P *system and* $\mathsf{MAS}(\Pi) = \langle \mathcal{MS}^{<\infty}(V), \mathfrak{B}, \mathfrak{D}_{\mathfrak{B}}, \mathsf{l}, \mathsf{u} \rangle$ *be a strict set–union type general mset approximation space with generalized Pawlakian approximation pair (see in Definition 4). If* $B \in \mathfrak{B}$ *and* $i = 1, 2, \ldots, m$, *then let*

$$N(B, i) = \begin{cases} 0, & \text{if } B \sqcap w_i^0 = \emptyset \text{ or } B \sqsubseteq w_i^0; \\ n, & \text{if } i = 1 \text{ and } B \sqcap w_1^0 \sqsubseteq^n w_1^0; \\ \min\{k, n \mid B \sqcap w_i^0 \sqsubseteq^k w_i^0, \text{ and } B \ominus w_i^0 \sqsubseteq^n w_{\mathsf{parent}(i)}^0\}, & \text{otherwise.} \end{cases}$$

Then

1. $\mathsf{bnd}(w_i^0) = \bigsqcup\{\oplus_{N(B,i)} B \mid B \in \mathfrak{B}, B \sqcap w_i^0 \neq \emptyset, B \not\sqsubseteq w_i^0\};$
2. $\mathsf{bnd}^{\mathsf{out}}(w_i^0) = \mathsf{bnd}(w_i^0) \ominus w_i^0;$
3. $\mathsf{bnd}^{\mathsf{in}}(w_i^0) = \mathsf{bnd}(w_i^0) \ominus \mathsf{bnd}^{\mathsf{out}}(w_i^0)$

Remark 10. $N(B, i)$ gives the maximum multiplicity of base mset B in the boundary of membrane w_i^0 appearing in $w_{\mathsf{parent}(i)}^0$.

Remark 11. The mset $\mathsf{bnd}(w_i^0)$ is definable in the joint membrane approximation space $\mathsf{MAS}(\Pi)$ for all i.

Remark 12. Approximative functions $\mathsf{l}, \mathsf{u}, \mathsf{b}$ given in Definition 4 of generalized Pawlakian approximation pair can be used to approximate any region (as an mset), but they do not obey the membrane structure: in general case if $i \neq 1$, then $\mathsf{b}(w_i^0) \neq \mathsf{bnd}(w_i^0)$.

Remark 13. Membrane boundaries given by function bnd obey the membrane structure:

- if $i \neq 1$, then $\mathsf{bnd}^{\mathsf{out}}(w_i^0) \sqsubseteq w_{\mathsf{parent}(i)}^0$;
- $\mathsf{bnd}^{\mathsf{in}}(w_i^0) \sqsubseteq w_i^0$.

Remark 14. If there is only one membrane (w_1^0) in the membrane system (i.e. there is no specific membrane structure), then $\mathsf{b}(w_1^0) = \mathsf{bnd}(w_1^0)$ and not only the lower but the upper approximation of w_1^0 can be used to describe the behavior of w_1^0.

Using the boundaries of regions, the following constraint for rule executions can be prescribed: a given rule $r \in R_i$ of a membrane i has to work only in the boundaries of its region. In order to be so, let the execution of a rule $r \in R_i$ $(i = 1, 2, \dots, m)$ define in the following forms:

- if a symport rule has the form $\langle u, in \rangle$, it is executed only in that case when $u \sqsubseteq \mathsf{bnd}^{\mathsf{out}}(w_i^0)$;
- if a symport rule has the form $\langle u, out \rangle$, it is executed only in that case when $u \sqsubseteq \mathsf{bnd}^{\mathsf{in}}(w_i^0)$;
- if an antiport rule has the form $\langle u, in; v, out \rangle$, it is executed only in that case when $u \sqsubseteq \mathsf{bnd}^{\mathsf{out}}(w_i^0)$ and $v \sqsubseteq \mathsf{bnd}^{\mathsf{in}}(w_i^0)$.

The next theorem shows that the membrane computation actually works in the membrane boundaries.

Theorem 1. *Let* $\Pi = \langle V, \mu, w_1^0, w_2^0, \dots, w_m^0, R_1, R_2, \dots, R_m \rangle$ *be a* P *system where the communication rules in* R_i *(i = 1, 2, \dots, m) are constrained as above, and* $\mathsf{MAS}(\Pi) = \langle \mathcal{MS}^{<\infty}(V), \mathfrak{B}, \mathfrak{D}_{\mathfrak{B}}, \mathsf{l}, \mathsf{u} \rangle$ *be a joint membrane approximation space. After the membrane computation, let the* P *system* Π' *be of the form* $\Pi' = \langle V, \mu, w_1, w_2, \dots, w_m, R_1, R_2, \dots, R_m \rangle$.
Then for all i *(i = 1, 2, \dots, m)*

1. *if* $a \in^k \mathsf{bnd}^{\mathsf{out}}(w_i^0)$, $a \in^n w_i^0$ *and* $a \in^j w_i$, *then* $j \leq n + k$;
2. *if* $a \notin \mathsf{bnd}^{\mathsf{out}}(w_i^0)$, $a \in^n w_i^0$ *and* $a \in^j w_i$, *then* $j \leq n$;
3. *if* $a \in^k \mathsf{bnd}^{\mathsf{in}}(w_i^0)$, $a \in^n w_i^0$ *and* $a \in^j w_i$, *then* $j \geq n - k$;
4. *if* $a \notin \mathsf{bnd}^{\mathsf{in}}(w_i^0)$, $a \in^n w_i^0$ *and* $a \in^j w_i$, *then* $j \geq n$;
5. $w_i \sqsubseteq \mathsf{u}(w_i^0)$;
6. *if* $\mathsf{MAS}(\Pi)$ *one-layered, then* $\mathsf{l}(w_i^0) \sqsubseteq w_i \sqsubseteq \mathsf{u}(w_i^0)$

3.2   The Computational Process

The whole computational process has two inputs (see Fig. 1):

- a P system Π with an initial configuration;
- an initial general mset approximation space $\mathsf{MAS}(\Pi)$.

The computation process itself consists of consecutive iterations of membrane computations in the P system Π and trigger activities in the mset approximation space $\mathsf{MAS}(\Pi)$.

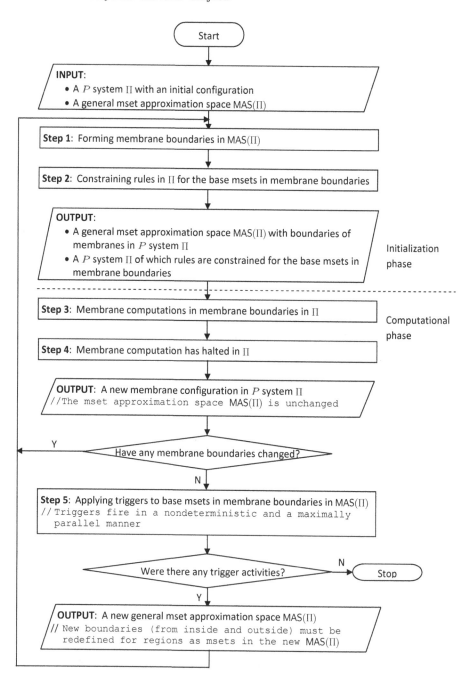

Fig. 1. The overall computational process

Each iteration is composed of two phases which, in turn, are made up of some consecutive steps:

1. **The initialization phase**

   Step 1. Forming the membrane boundaries of the P system Π within the mset approximation space $\mathsf{MAS}(\Pi)$.

   Step 2. Constraining the scope of the executions of communication (symport/antiport) rules of the P system Π for the base msets which belong to membrane boundaries.

2. **The computation phase**

   Step 3. The P system Π works, i.e. the communication rules constrained for the base msets belonging to membrane boundaries are executed.

   `// During Step 3, the mset approximation space MAS(`Π`) does`
   `not change.`

   Step 4. The membrane computation halts.

   `// A new membrane configuration emerges.`
   `// The mset approximation space MAS(`Π`) is unchanged.`

   If some membrane boundaries have changed

       then go to **Step 1**

       `// During the membrane computation, e.g. a base mset can`
       `entirely become a part of or get out of a region.`
       In such cases, membrane boundaries must be redefined.
       After that, the membrane computation can start again.

   Step 5. Applying triggers associated with the base msets in $\mathsf{MAS}(\Pi)$ to the base msets which belong to membrane boundaries.

   Triggers fire in a nondeterministic and a maximally parallel manner.

   If there were some trigger activities

       then go to **Step 1**

       `// A new mset approximation space MAS(`Π`) emerges in which`
       `the membrane boundaries must be redefined.`
       Thus, the membrane computation can start again.

       else Stop

       `// If there were no any trigger activities, the whole com-`
       `putational process stops.`

The P system Π and the mset approximation space $\mathsf{MAS}(\Pi)$ alter iteration by iteration. If the whole computational process stops, it has two outputs:

- a P system Π which has been changed due to the membrane computations;
- a general mset approximation space $\mathsf{MAS}(\Pi)$ which has been changed due to the trigger activities.

In our framework, the concept of database triggers — in particular, triggers in Oracle database system, see e.g. in [11] — has served as a pattern to model operations in mset approximation spaces which just start each time when a sort of event occurs in P systems.

Triggers are associated with the base msets of the general mset approximation space MAS(Π). They have three parts (see Algorithm 1):

- a triggering event: an event that causes a trigger to fire;
- a trigger restriction: a Boolean expression which must be true for the trigger to fire, otherwise the trigger action is not executed;
- a trigger action: a rule of the form $\langle u, in \rangle$ (it looks like as a symport rule in membrane computing).

Triggering Event. Triggering events are bound to the membrane computation in the P system Π. We have only one triggering event. Just having halted the membrane computation in the P system Π, a maintain-natured process in the general mset approximation space MAS(Π) starts up.

Trigger Restriction. A trigger actually begins to work in the base mset with which it is associated, when the two following conditions simultaneously fulfill after the halting of the membrane computation:

- the base mset belongs to a membrane boundary;
- a shortage of objects attends in the inside and/or outside part of the base mset.

Trigger Action. The shortage of objects in the base mset enforces a suction effect that the trigger tries to fulfill as far as possible. They make an attempt to supplement the missing objects by the objects of the same type from the neighbor base msets. Two msets are neighbor when their intersection is nonempty.

If the shortage of objects occurs in the inside (outside) part of the base mset, the supplementation must come from inside (outside) the considered region solely.

When the supplementation of missing objects has happened from one or more neighbor base msets, in them additional suction effects also be generated which are tried to meet by the trigger as far as possible, too. This successive supplementation process finishes when

1. either all neighbor base msets do not have any other neighbor base msets;
2. or all base msets have other neighbor base msets but they do not contain any object of the required type.

In the end, when all the trigger executions stop, the membrane approximation space MAS(Π) is changed and new boundaries (from inside and outside) must be redefined for regions as multisets. Hence, the membrane computation can start again in the P system Π. This successive computation process stops definitively when there is no any trigger activity after a membrane computation.

Algorithm 1. A trigger which is associated with base msets

TRIGGER NAME: TriggerAssociatedWithBaseMsets

TRIGGERING EVENT
COMPUTATION HALTS in the P system Π

TRIGGER RESTRICTION
$\exists i \in \{1, \ldots, m\}$ (*the current base mset* $\in \mathsf{bnd}(w_i)$) $\to$
    (*there is a shortage of objects in* $\mathsf{bnd}^{in}(w_i)$ **or**
     there is a shortage of objects in $\mathsf{bnd}^{out}(w_i)$))
// The current base mset is that to which the trigger is
   just applied.

TRIGGERED ACTION
$CUR \leftarrow$ current base mset
$ACT^{in}, ACT^{out} \leftarrow CUR$ // ACT^{in}, ACT^{out} are auxiliary variables
if *there is a shortage of objects in* $\mathsf{bnd}^{in}(w_i)$ then
   forall the $\langle u, out \rangle \in R_i$ *which are applied to* CUR
    and *neighbor base msets* N *of* ACT^{in} *inside* w_i *such that* $u \sqsubseteq N$
   in a nondeterministic and a maximally parallel manner do
   begin
     remove u from N
     put u in ACT^{in}
     $ACT^{in} \leftarrow$ another neighbor base mset N of ACT^{in} such that
       $u \sqsubseteq N$, if any

if *there is a shortage of objects in* $\mathsf{bnd}^{out}(w_i)$ then
   forall the $\langle v, in \rangle \in R_i$ *which are applied to* CUR
    and *neighbor base msets* N *of* ACT^{out} *outside* w_i *such that* $v \sqsubseteq N$
   in a nondeterministic and a maximally parallel manner do
   begin
     remove v from N
     put v in ACT^{out}
     $ACT^{out} \leftarrow$ another neighbor base mset N of ACT^{out} such that
       $v \sqsubseteq N$, if any

3.3 An Illustrative Example

Let V be a finite alphabet, μ be a membrane structure with 1 node, and $\Pi = \langle V, \mu, w_1^0, R_1 \rangle$ be the sample P system.

Let the base system $\mathfrak{B}$ of the sample mset approximation space $\mathsf{MAS}(\Pi)$ consist of three $\mathfrak{B}$-msets: $\mathfrak{B} = \{B_1, B_2, B_3\}$. In the figures below, the $\mathfrak{B}$-msets B_1, B_2 and B_3 are represented by circle, triangle and square, respectively. For the sake of clarity, we depict only a fragment of the whole mset approximation space focusing on the only membrane boundary solely.

Fig. 2 shows a special case when the base system $\mathfrak{B}$ is one–layered, whereas Fig. 3 represents the general case.

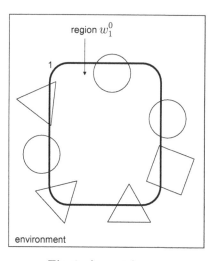

Fig. 2. A special case:
the base system $\mathfrak{B}$ is one–layered

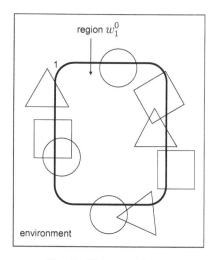

Fig. 3. The general case

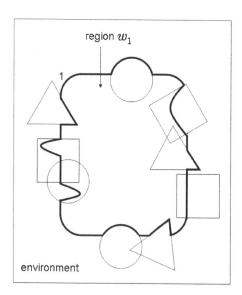

Fig. 4. Membrane just after the membrane computation has halted

Let us suppose that Fig. 3 depicts a membrane system with a membrane boundary just before the membrane computation starts. Execution of rules in R_1 are constrained in the 𝔅-msets of the membrane boundary. Then, Fig. 4 shows how these executions changed the membrane within them: 3 𝔅-msets entirely got out of the region; 2 𝔅-msets entirely became a part of the region; in addition inside 3 𝔅-msets the membrane moved away; and inside 1 𝔅-mset the membrane was not changed. Meanwhile, as the Fig. 4 also shows, all 𝔅-msets were not changed.

After just the membrane computation has halted, the triggers are activated. They, in general, change the 𝔅-msets, therefore the mset approximation space and the membrane boundary as well. Thus, when the trigger activity stops, the membrane computation can start again.

Acknowledgements. The publication was supported by the TÁMOP–4.2.2.C–11/1/KONV–2012–0001 project. The project has been supported by the European Union, co-financed by the European Social Fund.
The authors are thankful to György Vaszil for valuable suggestions.

References

1. Barbuti, R., Maggiolo-Schettini, A., Milazzo, P., Pardini, G., Tesei, L.: Spatial P systems. Natural Computing 10(1), 3–16 (2011)
2. Blizard, W.D.: Multiset theory. Notre Dame Journal of Formal Logic 30(1), 36–66 (1989)
3. Blizard, W.D.: The development of multiset theory. Modern Logic 1, 319–352 (1991)
4. Blizard, W.D.: Dedekind multiset and function shells. Theoretical Computer Science 110(1), 79–98 (1993)
5. Calude, C.S., Pun, G., Rozenberg, G., Salomaa, A. (eds.): Multiset Processing. LNCS, vol. 2235. Springer, Heidelberg (2001)
6. Cardelli, L., Gardner, P.: Processes in Space. In: Ferreira, F., Löwe, B., Mayordomo, E., Mendes Gomes, L. (eds.) CiE 2010. LNCS, vol. 6158, pp. 78–87. Springer, Heidelberg (2010)
7. Csajbók, Z.: Partial approximative set theory: A generalization of the rough set theory. In: Martin, T., Muda, A.K., Abraham, A., Prade, H., Laurent, A., Laurent, D., Sans, V. (eds.) Proceedings of SoCPaR 2010, Cergy Pontoise / Paris, December 7-10, pp. 51–56. IEEE (2010)
8. Csajbók, Z.: Approximation of sets based on partial covering. Theoretical Computer Science 412(42), 5820–5833 (2011); rough Sets and Fuzzy Sets in Natural Computing
9. Csajbók, Z., Mihálydeák, T.: Partial approximative set theory: A generalization of the rough set theory. International Journal of Computer Information Systems and Industrial Management Applications 4, 437–444 (2012)
10. Csuhaj-Varjú, E., Gheorghe, M., Stannett, M.: P Systems Controlled by General Topologies. In: Durand-Lose, J., Jonoska, N. (eds.) UCNC 2012. LNCS, vol. 7445, pp. 70–81. Springer, Heidelberg (2012)
11. Cyran, M., et al.: Oracle Database Concepts, 10g Release 2 (10.2). Oracle (2005), http://docs.oracle.com/cd/B19306_01/server.102/b14220.pdf
12. Dedekind, R.: Essays on the Theory of Numbers. Dover, New York (1963); translated by Beman, W.W

13. Girish, P., John, S.J.: Rough multisets and information multisystems. Advances in Decision Sciences 2011, 17 pages (2011)
14. Knuth, D.E.: The Art of Computer Programming. Seminumerical Algorithms, 2nd edn., vol. 2. Addison-Wesley, Reading (1981)
15. Kudlek, M., Martín-Vide, C., Păun, G.: Toward a formal macroset theory. In: Calude, et al. (ed.) [5], pp. 123–134
16. Mihálydeák, T.: Partial First-order Logic with Approximative Functors Based on Properties. In: Li, T., Nguyen, H.S., Wang, G., Grzymala-Busse, J., Janicki, R., Hassanien, A.E., Yu, H. (eds.) RSKT 2012. LNCS(LNAI), vol. 7414, pp. 514–523. Springer, Heidelberg (2012)
17. Mihálydeák, T., Csajbók, Z.: Membranes with Boundaries. In: Csuhaj-Varjú, E., Gheorghe, M., Rozenberg, G., Salomaa, A., Vaszi, G. (eds.) CMC 2012. LNCS, vol. 7762, pp. 277–294. Springer, Heidelberg (2013)
18. Pawlak, Z.: Rough sets. International Journal of Computer and Information Sciences 11(5), 341–356 (1982)
19. Pawlak, Z.: Rough Sets: Theoretical Aspects of Reasoning about Data. Kluwer Academic Publishers, Dordrecht (1991)
20. Pawlak, Z.: Hard and soft sets. In: Ziarko, W. (ed.) Rough Sets, Fuzzy Sets and Knowledge Discovery, Proceedings of the International Workshop on Rough Sets and Knowledge Discovery (RSKD 1993), October 12-15, pp. 130–135. Springer, Banff (1994)
21. Păun, G.: Computing with membranes. Journal of Computer and System Sciences 61(1), 108–143 (2000)
22. Păun, G.: Membrane Computing. An Introduction. Springer, Berlin (2002)
23. Păun, G., Rozenberg, G., Salomaa, A. (eds.): The Oxford Handbook of Membrane Computing. Oxford Handbooks. Oxford University Press, Inc., New York (2010)
24. Singh, D., Ibrahim, A.M., Yohanna, T., Singh, J.N.: An overview of the applications of multisets. Novi Sad J. Math. 37(2), 73–92 (2007)
25. Syropoulos, A.: Mathematics of multisets. In: Calude, et al. (ed.) [5], pp. 347–358
26. Yager, R.R.: O, the theory of bags. International Journal of General Systems 13(1), 23–37 (1986)

On Efficient Algorithms for SAT

Benedek Nagy

Department of Computer Science, Faculty of Informatics
University of Debrecen, Egyetem tér 1., 4032 Debrecen, Hungary
nbenedek@inf.unideb.hu

Abstract. There are several papers in which SAT is solved in linear time by various new computing paradigms, and specially by various membrane computing systems. In these approaches the used alphabet depends on the number of variables. That gives different classes of the problem by the number of the variables. In this paper we show that the set of valid SAT-formulae and n-SAT-formulae over finite sets of variables are regular languages. We show a construction of deterministic finite automata which accept the SAT and n-SAT languages in conjunctive normal form checking both their syntax and satisfiable evaluations. Thus, theoretically the words of the SAT languages can be accepted in linear time with respect to their lengths by a traditional computer.

Keywords: SAT-problem, membrane computing, efficiency, new computing paradigms, P-NP, regular languages, finite automata, uniform solution.

1 Introduction

Computer science deals with problems that can be solved by algorithms. Some problems can be solved by very effective algorithms, some of them seem not to be. In complexity theory there are several classes of problems depending on the complexity of the possible solving algorithms. A problem is in P if there exists a polynomial deterministic algorithm that solves it (on a Turing machine). A problem is in NP if there exists a non-deterministic polynomial algorithm that solves it (on a Turing machine). One of the most challenging problems is to prove or disprove that the classes P and NP are the same. Most scientists think that NP strictly includes P.

The SAT problem is the most basic NP-complete problem [16,33]. It has several forms. The first is the satisfiability of arbitrary Boolean formulae. A restricted, and widely used version uses only formulae in conjunctive normal forms (in this paper we also use this restriction on the used formulae). The most restricted version we deal with is the so-called 3-SAT. It is still NP-complete; and it has a huge literature. It is a very interesting fact, that SAT connects some of the most important fields of theoretical computer science, such as logic, formal languages, theory of algorithms and complexity theory. A deterministic polynomial time solution of an NP-complete problem (on a Turing machine)

E. Csuhaj-Varjú et al. (Eds.): CMC 2012, LNCS 7762, pp. 295–310, 2013.

infers P=NP. Therefore one of the aims of many people in computer science is to solve the SAT (or the 3-SAT) problem in an efficient way. There are several attempts by usual algorithms on traditional computers for both the original and some more restricted versions [5,9,19]. There is also an annual conference series: International Conference on Theory and Applications of Satisfiability Testing, where scientists present their newly developed algorithms/approaches. There is also a competition where the practical efficiency of various computer programs are tested [45].

When one introduces a new computing paradigm the first two general questions are the following. Is the new model universal, i.e., can all the Turing machine solvable problems be solved in this paradigm? The other question is about the efficiency of the new model: how effectively a known intractable problem can be solved in the new model? Hence, one of the main motivations of new computational paradigms is to solve hard problems, as SAT and n-SAT, by fast methods. Membrane computing offers various ways for polynomial solutions to SAT, by trading exponential space for time [37]. For a small collection of these methods, see [24]. In these new computing paradigms the preparation of the solution depends on the formula as we recall in Section 2. In this paper we assume that the reader is familiar with most of the terms of membrane computing and therefore we do not spend a large number of pages for full descriptions of the recalled systems. We list several approaches and give references where the formal descriptions of the mentioned models can be found. It is important to note that all the feasible solutions to hard problems can be found in the literature do not use a single P system, but a family of systems. These solutions can be divided in two groups: the semi-uniform solutions, which associate with each instance of the problem one P system solving it; and the uniform solutions, which associate with each possible size of the instances of the problem one P system that can solve all instances of that size [41]. Independently of the group, we underlie the fact that the size of the used alphabet depends on the problem instance (or some of its parameters).

In Section 3, using alphabet that depends on the number of used Boolean variables, first we check the syntactical part of the logical formulae in conjunctive normal form by regular expressions. After this we show how we can recognize the satisfiable formulae by a deterministic finite automaton (that is appropriate for the number of used variables). It is well-known that regular languages can be recognized in linear time, moreover deciding if a word belongs to the language or not can be done in "real time" by the deterministic finite automaton for the given language. Therefore the fact that the languages of (n-)SAT are regular can help us to solve these problems in a very fast way, even if they are NP-complete problems (unfortunately, in practice our automata do not work, as we will discuss). Finally we see the original problem (coding unbounded number of variables with a finite alphabet) and discuss its hardness.

Due to the numerous number of published solutions one may think that to solve the SAT by membrane computing is not a challenging task any more. With this paper we want to reopen this research field asking for new solution algorithms that requires only a fixed number of object types independently of the input. These new algorithms could play the same role as the traditional algorithms play in classical computing defining a "general uniform" approach in membrane computing. We have a small discussion on these ideas in Section 5.

1.1   Basic Definitions and Preliminaries

We recall some basic definitions, such as normal forms, CNF and SAT expressions and regular expressions. We will deal with SAT only containing formulae in conjunctive normal form.

The Boolean variables and their negations are positive and negative literals, respectively. A logical formula is called an elementary conjunction (clause), if it is a conjunction of literals. The disjunction of elementary conjunctions is a disjunctive normal form (DNF). If all clauses contain the same number (let us say, n) of literals, then we call the form n-ary disjunctive form. Similarly, an elementary disjunction is a disjunction of literals. A conjunction of elementary disjunctions is a conjunctive normal form (CNF, we are using also the terms CNF expression/CNF formula). (For sake of simplicity we use brackets for all elementary disjunctions.) The SAT problem is the following: given a propositional formula in conjunctive normal form, decide whether it is satisfiable (or not). If the formula is unsatisfiable, then it is equivalent to logical falsity. If the given formulae are in n-ary conjunctive normal form, then the problem is known as the n-SAT problem.

It is well-known that the SAT and n-SAT problems (for $n \geq 3$) are NP-complete (see [14,33]). Let us fix an alphabet. Let F be a formula in CNF over the alphabet. If there is a satisfying assignment to the variables such that F evaluates to true, then F is in the SAT language (and vice-versa, if a word is in the language, then it is a satisfiable formula in CNF form). We will also say that F is SAT expression/formula. Similarly we define languages n-SAT, which contain only those formulae of the SAT language in which each elementary disjunction contains exactly n literals ($n \in \mathbb{N}$). In this case F is also an n-SAT expression (or formula).

Note that there is a dual problem for the SAT problem. In the dual problem the DNF is used. The problem to solve is to decide whether the given formula is a tautology, (or not). We will refer to this form as the dual SAT-problem. The dual of the SAT and n-SAT problems are also NP-complete problems (for $n \geq 3$). Actually, an NP-complete problem is to decide if a formula in CNF is satisfiable. To decide if a formula in CNF is not satisfiable is co-NP-complete. Similarly, to decide if a formula in DNF is a tautology (logical law) is NP-complete. To decide whether a formula in DNF is not a tautology is co-NP-complete. The relation of NP and co-NP is usually shown by these examples, the power of non-deterministic computation is to have at least one computation that gives the result. However to prove the opposite, i.e., the non-existence of such computation can have a different complexity from the complexity of the original problem. (The class co-NP also contains the class P. However, if P=NP, then NP=co-NP.) Here we just want to mention one interesting fact: The problem to decide if a formula in DNF is satisfiable or not, is almost trivial: one needs only read the formula clause by clause, if there is no such a Boolean variable that occurs both in positive and negative form in the actual clause (we say that a literal is contradictory in a clause if both of its forms occur in the clause), then the formula is satisfiable. If every clause contains a contradictory literal, then the formula is unsatisfiable. In a similar way, to decide if a Boolean formula in CNF is a tautology or not is trivial. The problem is that the straightforward translations of the formulae from DNF to CNF and vice-versa based on distributive laws enlarge the size of the formula exponentially.

In the next parts we will use the concept of regular expressions (see any text books on the topic of formal languages, e.g., [14,22]). In regular expressions we use the letters of the alphabet and symbols of union $+$, concatenation $\cdot$ (it is omitted several times) and Kleene-star $*$. Brackets may also be used to show the order of the operations. The empty word is denoted by λ. We will use the abbreviation r^n, denoting the regular expression in which the regular expression r is concatenated by itself with (a fixed) n (non-overlapping) occurrences.

The ordered quintuple $A = (K, T, M, \sigma_0, H)$ is called a deterministic finite automaton (DFA), where K is the finite, non-empty set of states, T is the finite alphabet of input symbols, M is the transition function, mapping from $K \times T$ to K, $\sigma_0 \in K$ is the initial state, and $H \subseteq K$ is the set of accepting states.

A language is regular if there is a regular expression which describes it. The same class of languages are accepted by DFA's due to the well-known Kleene's theorem.

2   Solving SAT by Membrane Computing

In this section we recall a very important class of unconventional computing techniques and analyse the proposed solutions to SAT in that frameworks. Over the last decade, molecular computing has been a very active field of research. The great promise of performing computations at a molecular level is that the small size of the computational units potentially allows for massive parallelism in the computations. Thus, computations that seem to be intractable in sequential modes of computation can be performed (at least in theory) in polynomial or even linear time.

In this section we are dealing with Membrane Computing. It is a branch of biocomputing, and developing very rapidly. New algorithmic ways are used to solve hard (intractable) problems. This field was born by the paper [35]. An early textbook presenting several variations of these systems is [37]. There are various ways for trading space for time, i.e., by parallelism exponential space can be obtained in linear time, for instance, by active membranes. The SAT is solved by various models in effective ways. In the next subsections we recall some of these methods (dealing only with some aspects that are important for our point of view, without further details due to the page limit; for further details we recommend to check the literature at [43]; we assume that the reader is familiar with the various concepts of these systems or she/he can look for them in the cited literature). Since SAT is one of the most known and most important NP-complete problems there are several attempts by older and newer methods.

We use the terms uniform and semi-uniform by the definition of [41,42]: in a semi-uniform algorithm a specific membrane system is created for a given instance of the problem, while a uniform algorithm can solve all instances having same instance size (e.g., number of clauses, number of variables). We use the parameters: m clauses and k variables of the solvable CNF formula. Note that in [25] it is pointed out that at problems connected to complexity classes P, NP and PSPACE the choice of uniformity or semi-uniformity leads to the characterizations of the same complexity classes.

2.1   Membrane Creation

Using membrane creation one can use an exponential growth (exponential space can be easily obtained) during the computation.

We briefly describe how membrane creation can be used to solve SAT in linear time. First we have an initial membrane with only one object. Applying the only applicable rule for this object we introduce two new objects corresponding to the possible values of the first variable, and a technical object to continue the process. Then the new objects of the logical variable create new membranes (and copy some symbols to the new membranes). Now for each new membrane two new objects are introduced corresponding to the next variable, these new objects create new ones again, etc. Finally the membrane structure forms a complete k-level binary tree. Each path from the initial to a leaf-membrane represents a possible truth-assignment. Now, each membrane in the k-th level computes objects corresponding to satisfied clauses of the analysed formula. (It can be done easily by a comparison among the literals of the clauses and the given truth-assignment of the membrane.) Using a cooperative rule a special symbol is sent out if all clauses are satisfied in a membrane. In the next step the membranes at the previous level forward this symbol. Therefore this special symbol moves up all k levels, and finally leaves the system and terminates the process with answer 'satisfiable'. More technical details about such a method can be found in [37].

In this process the power of parallelism builds up a complete tree by levels in linear time. In each membrane in the deepest level there are rules for each clause, therefore the evaluation of clauses can go in a parallel way.

This semi-uniform approach, using membrane creation to solve SAT uses an alphabet with cardinality approximately $3k + 2^m$ in [37] where the number of rules and therefore, the description of the system is not polynomial size of the problem instance (however the initial configuration contains only one membrane and one symbol in it). The algorithm has a linear time complexity: it solves the problem in $3k+1$ steps. Another proposed semi-uniform system uses $4k+5m+6$ object types and solves the SAT instance in $4k + m + 5$ steps.

Finally, the SAT is solved in uniform way by membrane creation in [12]. The proposed system with input uses input alphabet of size $2km$, while the full working alphabet consists of $6km + 5k + 4m + 32$ elements.

2.2   Membrane Division

Membrane division is another usual option for active membranes to increase the number of membranes exponentially in the starting phase of the computation.

Membrane division generally allows to obtain finitely many membranes from the initial one having the same contents but the object specified at the rule which is replaced in the new membranes by possibly new objects. It is turned out that divisions producing only two membranes have enough power.

The SAT problem can be solved by a P system with division of non-elementary membranes in a time which is linear on the number of variables and the number of clauses. The algorithm also uses polarization of membranes. In the algorithm found in [36] the size of the alphabet is $5k + m$.

In another algorithm ([37]) using membrane division and polarizations the alphabet (the set of object-symbols) has cardinality about $4k + 2m$. This algorithm solves SAT in linear time with respect to $k + 2m$. In the same book and also in [39] a parallel computer model is also shown in which the 'parallel core' performs a massive parallel computation (brute-force) and then a 'checker' checks the result and a 'messenger' sends out the answer. This framework is used to solve the SAT with alphabet of size $4k + m + 2$. This model uses only division of elementary membranes but uses cooperative rules. In [47] about $4k + 2m$ kinds of object are used in a linear algorithm using polarities of membranes to solve SAT using only division of elementary membranes without cooperation.

In [3] SAT can be deterministically decided in linear time (linear with respect to $k + m$) by a uniform family of P systems with active membranes with two polarizations and global evolution rules, move out and membrane division (only for elementary membranes) rules. The size of the alphabet is approximately mk^2 using global rules. It is also proved that SAT can be deterministically decided in linear time with respect to km by a uniform family of P systems with active membranes with two polarizations and special rules: global split rules, exit only with switching polarization, yes out rule (for ejecting the result) and global polarizationless division rules. These systems use an alphabet of size approximately mk^2.

In [38] membrane division without polarizations is used by the help of tables of rules. In this way SAT is solved in linear time (approx. $k + m$ steps) using obligatory rules (at most one in each table) with $2mk + 5k + 4m + 8$ different types of objects.

Symport/Antiport Systems. The SAT is also solved by symport/antiport systems using membrane division by an alphabet of size approximately $11k + 2km + (9k + m + k \log m) \log(9k + m + k \log m)$. The details of this algorithm can be seen in [1].

Minimal Parallelism and Asynchronous P Systems. The SAT is also solved effectively by membrane systems with minimal parallelism, now we list a wide range of papers that use membrane division and minimal parallelism. P systems constructed in a uniform manner and working in the minimally parallel mode using non-cooperative rules, non-elementary membrane divisions, move in and out rules and label changing can solve SAT in linear time. The size of the used alphabet is $4mk + 13k + 3m + 15$. Similar models are used to solve SAT in linear time with respect to the number of the variables and the number of clauses: P systems constructed in a uniform manner, working in the minimally parallel mode using cooperative rules, non-elementary membrane divisions, and move in and out rules solve SAT in linear time. Similarly, P systems working in the minimally parallel mode with cooperative rules, elementary membrane divisions and move out rules solve SAT in linear time; moreover they are constructed in a semi-uniform manner in [15].

The satisfiability of any propositional formula in CNF can be decided in a linear time with respect to k by a P system with active membranes using object evolution, move in and out rules, membrane dissolution and division; and working in the minimally parallel mode. Moreover, the system is constructed in a linear time with respect to k and m in a semi-uniform way [7]. This method uses an alphabet of size $7k + m + 11$.

The n-SAT can be solved by recognizing P systems with active membranes operating under minimal parallelism without polarities, and using evolution rules, move in and out rules, membrane division and membrane creation(!). The P system requires exponential space and linear time [11]. Here the size of the used alphabet is $5k + 4m + 8$.

In [2] polarity is also used. Here the parameter ℓ refers to the number of occurrences of literals in the formula (with multiplicities). A uniform family of P systems with evolution rules, move out rules and membrane divisions; working in minimally parallel way can solve SAT with four polarizations in a quadratic number (i.e., $(\ell(m + n))$) of steps. The size of the alphabet is approximately $4km(k + m) + 2\ell(m + k) + 2k\ell + m + k + k(4\ell + 3) + m(4\ell + 1)$.

Asynchronous systems allows to use the rules in various ways. In [46] fully asynchronous parallelism in membrane computing and an asynchronous P systems for the SAT problem is considered. The proposed P system computes SAT in approximately $mk2^k$ sequential steps or in approximately mk parallel steps using approximately mk kinds of objects using membrane division.

2.3 Membrane Separation

Another way is to grow the number of the used membranes exponentially is the membrane separation. In this way the content of the given membrane is divided in two parts by a separation rule for elementary membranes, with respect to a given set of objects. In [32] evolution rules, move out rules and separation rules are used; the most significant part of the alphabet contains approximately mk^2 symbols. A uniform way is presented in [31] where the input is coded by multisets over an alphabet of size $2mk$ and the system uses alphabet with approximately mk^2 elements also. In [4] evolution, communication, membrane merging, membrane separation, membrane release are used to solve the SAT problem in linear time. The size of the used alphabet is approximately $k^2 + k + m$.

2.4   Membrane Systems with String Objects

There is another way to deal with exponential information in the system without active membranes and it goes by complex objects, namely string-, or so-called worm-, objects.

The solution of the SAT can be done by generating all truth-assignment in the form of strings. In all the three algorithms of this subsection the depth of the initial membrane structure depends (i.e., linear) on m. The evaluation goes layer by layer from inside to outside.

In [37] there is a method for SAT that uses string replication (replicated rewriting). The process uses $4k + 2$ kinds of objects in the alphabet and solves the problem in $k + m + 1$ steps. In [18] the SAT is solved in linear time by one-sided contextual rules using an alphabet of size $3k + m + 2$. Worms are used in [6] with alphabet of size $2k$ with string replications. The time to get the solution is linear with $k + m$.

Neural-Like Membrane Systems. Neural-like membrane systems (or tissue P systems) are nets of cells working with multisets. One of the main difference between this model and the previous ones is that the structure of membranes is not necessarily a tree in tissue P systems. Each cell has a finite state memory, processes multisets of symbol-impulses, and can send impulses (excitations) to the connected cells. The maximal mode of rules application and the replicative mode of communication between cells are at the core of the efficiency of these systems [40]. Neural-like membrane systems can solve SAT in linear time by using an alphabet of chemical objects (or excitations/impulses) with cardinality $2^{k+1} - 1$, since the system first generates all the truth-assignments in the form of strings of length k using letters t_i and f_i with $1 \leq i \leq n$. Then filtering similarly as Lipton's DNA algorithm [23] for SAT.

2.5   Quantum P-Systems

In this subsection we recall a mixed paradigm, the quantum UREM P-systems [21]. Quantum computing is also counted as a new computing paradigm based on some 'unconventional' features of quantum mechanics. There is no space here to recall all details, there are various textbooks for this topic also (see, e.g., [13]). The main features of this paradigm are the following. A quantum bit (qubit) can have infinitely many values, technically any unit vector of a four dimensional space (complex coefficients for both of the possible values $|0\rangle$ and $|1\rangle$), the quantum superposition of the two possible states. The used unitary operations (rotations) can be written by 2×2 (complex valued) matrices. However by measurement only the 'projection' of the superposition is obtained, the system reaches one of the states $|0\rangle$ and $|1\rangle$ with the probability based on their coefficients. Having a system with n qubits the dimension of its state (i.e., the stored information) grows exponentially: the state can be described by a 2^n dimensional vector. The corresponding operators are described by matrices of size $2^n \times 2^n$ (which can be obtained by tensor product). By a special quantum effect, called entanglement, a state in superposition of some qubits together may not be constructible by the tensor product of the qubits. In this way exponential 'space' can be used. (Theoretically it is nice, technologically it is very hard task to produce systems that can use larger (e.g., 30) number of qubits in a system.)

In UREM P-systems there are unit rules and energy assigned to membranes. The rules in these systems are applied in a sequential way: at each computation step, one rule is selected from the pool of currently active rules, and it is applied. The system further developed by mixing it with quantum computing. Quantum UREM P-systems are proved to be universal without priority relation among the rules [20]. In this way, a quantum computing solution to SAT by the quantum register machine is simulated. The given semi-uniform algorithm uses the alphabet to describe the possible quantum states, and as the number of possible states of the system is exponential on the number of used qubits, the size of the alphabet is exponential on the input formula.

2.6   Solving SAT by Pre-computed Resources

Last but not least, we recall a method where we do not need active membranes that could create exponential space in linear time. This method is introduced in [8]. In the initial configuration of these P systems there is an arbitrarily large number of unactivated base-membranes, which, in a polynomial time, are activated in an exponential number. Using these types of systems the SAT problem is solved in a linear time, with respect to the number of variables and clauses using alphabet of size $9k + 2m + 13$.

Similarly, in [37] one of the fastest algorithms for SAT uses a pre-computation technique. It is assumed that the initial membrane structure is given "for free"; the pre-computation (without any costs) gives a system that is large enough for the input formula. (If a larger formula is given, then we need to shift to a larger pre-computed system.) In this way a membrane structure that one can obtain, for instance, by membrane divisions, is assumed to be ready to use at the beginning of the process. However the size of the used alphabet is exponential on k.

In some models the cardinality of the alphabet is cubic or exponential with the number of the variables. Common fact of these P systems that the alphabet depends on the problem, i.e., it has at least linear size on the number of variables.

3   Solving SAT in Linear Time by Traditional Computing

In the next part of this paper we analyse the SAT in a similar form as the new computing paradigms solve it (theoretically) in effective ways allowing a linear size alphabet with respect to the number of variables (see also the previous section). We will prove an interesting and surprising (at least for first sight) result in a constructive way (recalling the results of [26]). The construction goes in two steps. In the next subsection, the first step, the syntactically correct (CNF) formulae will be described.

3.1   The Syntactic Forms of the SAT Languages

In this part we present the syntax of valid instances of the considered versions of the SAT problem. Let us answer what is the form of w if the question "Is w satisfiable?" has sense.

We describe the syntactically correct CNF formulae over $k \in \mathbb{N}$ variables. Let the alphabet be $\{a_1, ..., a_k, [,], \neg, \wedge, \vee\}$ to allow to use the curly brackets '(' and ')' to show the order of the regular operations of the expression.

For the $(n\text{-})$SAT languages we need the CNF forms: Let A abbreviate the expression $(a_1 + a_2 + ... + a_k)$ to make our formula more readable. Every CNF formula is of the following regular form:

$$[(A + \neg A)(\vee(A + \neg A))^*] (\wedge [(A + \neg A)(\vee(A + \neg A))^*])^*.$$

Every n-ary CNF formula (for the n-SAT languages) is of the form:

$$[(A + \neg A)(\vee(A + \neg A))^{n-1}] (\wedge [(A + \neg A)(\vee(A + \neg A))^{n-1}])^*.$$

3.2   Deterministic Finite Automata for the SAT Languages

In this section, we construct the following automata: an automaton which accepts exactly the SAT-language and automata accepting the n-SAT languages (for any fixed n) with fixed k.

Let C be the set of subsets of powerset 2^k. We will interpret the elements of C as the sets of the values of the variables when the given logical expression is false. We use this part in this construction to know when the longest prefix of the formula which is a syntactically correct CNF expression is not satisfied.

Let Y be the set of the possible states of a DFA $A = (Y, T, M_A, y_0, \{y_f\})$ which accepts the syntactically correct CNF expressions.

Let D be the set of $k + 1$ dimensional vectors over $\{0, 1, 2\}$. This vector will count which variables are in the new clause. 0 on the i-th place of a vector $d \in D$ means that the i-th variable is not (yet) in the clause currently being read. 1 and 2 on the i-th place mean the occurrence of the i-th variable without negation and with negation, respectively. The value 1 on the $(k + 1)$-th element denotes that there is a variable in the actual clause with both types of occurrences (positive and negative).

The states of the automaton are given by the Cartesian product of the sets C, Y and D, where Y refers to the CNF syntax; and the sets C and D hold the semantical content, i.e., for which values of the variables the formula is false.

Let the initial state $\sigma_0 = (\{\}, y_0, \underline{0})$, where $\{\}$ is a value from C, y_0 is the initial state of A, and $\underline{0}$ is the $k + 1$ dimensional null vector containing only 0's.

For the input alphabet T of the automaton, we use the same alphabet as at the CNF expressions: $\{a_1, a_2, ..., a_k, [,], \neg, \wedge, \vee\}$.

Let the transition function be defined in the following way: $((c, y, d), t) \rightarrow (c', y', d')$

- if $t \in \{\wedge, \vee, \neg, [\}$, then only the syntactical part will change: $c' = c, d' = d$ and y' is the corresponding state of A, i.e., $y' = M_A(y, t)$.
- if t is a variable, then $c' = c$, $y' = M_A(y, t)$ and we have the following cases for calculating the value of d':
  - if the previous symbol was $\neg$ (we know it from part y of the given state), then there are two possibilities: if the corresponding value of the given variable in d is 1, then let the $k + 1$-st value of d' be 1 (and the other items can be the same as they were in d); if the corresponding value is not 1, then let it be 2 in d' and all other values are the same as they are in d.
  - if the previous symbol is not $\neg$, then: if the corresponding value of the given state is 2 in d, then let the $k + 1$-st item of d' be 1 and all other values of d' can be copied from the corresponding values of d. And if the corresponding value of d is not 2, then let it be 1 in d' and each of the other values will be the same as the corresponding value of d.
- if $t =]$, then let $c' = c$ if the $k + 1$-st value of d is 1. In other cases let $c' = c \cup N$, where N is the set containing all k-tuples in which the value of those variables which have corresponding values of 1 in d is 0 and the value of those variables which have corresponding values of 2 in d is 1. And let $y' = M_A(y,])$, finally $d' = \underline{0}$.

Let W be the maximal element of C, i.e., it contains all the 2^k possibilities. For our automaton let the set of final states be the following: all states $(c, y_f, \underline{0})$ for which $c \neq W$, i.e., c does not contain all the possibilities and y_f is the final state of A.

Since the form of the accepted expressions is correct, and the part c does not contain all possible evaluations of the variables in the final state, the automaton defined above can recognize exactly the SAT languages, i.e., the satisfiable Boolean formulae in CNF.

Using a language n-SAT instead of SAT, one needs to modify the above construction only by replacing automaton A with the automaton that accepts the syntactically correct n-ary CNF expressions.

The formula evaluates to true for those vectors that are not in c of the accepting state. Note here that the SAT languages are infinite even if the set of variables is finite. We allow repetitions of a Boolean variable in a clause, moreover the repetitions of the clauses are also allowed. (Without allowing these repetitions the SAT language is finite for any finite set of variables.) We have constructed finite automata accepting the languages of SAT and n-SAT. Therefore it is proved that:

Theorem 1. *The languages of satisfiable Boolean formulae in conjunctive normal form over any (fixed) finite sets of variables are regular languages. Similarly, the languages of n-SAT formulae ($n \in \mathbb{N}$) over any finite sets of variables are also regular.*

Due to the deterministic finite automata accepting these languages, one can decide if a word is in the language in at most as many steps as the length of the word. So, as an immediate consequence of the previous theorem we state about the classical computing paradigm the following.

Corollary 1. *The SAT and n-SAT problems (over any finite sets of variables) can be solved by deterministic linear time sequential algorithms.*

We note here that our solution is a uniform solution. However the size of our DFA is not necessarily polynomial on the size of the input. Actually, if it was polynomial, then it would prove that P=NP since the structure of the DFA cannot change during the computation. Opposite to this fact the structure of the membrane system can grow (exponentially) during the computation, and therefore in uniform solution it is usually required that the initial size of the membrane structure is polynomial on the length of the input (it can be since with active membranes the structure can grow during the computation). Our automata are related to the way as pre-computation is used in the previous section.

Now we are going to make some short notes on complexity. Looking the part C of the states, which is the most complex part of our automata one can see that the state-complexity of our automaton (depending on k) is $EXP(EXP(k))$. Even, in practice, there are automata with high number (over some millions) of states are used, our construction cannot be used in practice. (In contrast, for small values of k there are some efficient programs which can decide the SAT-problem in reasonable time [5,44].) It is possible that a minimal DFAs accepting the SAT languages has smaller number of states, but it has also at least $EXP(k)$ state complexity unless P=NP. Thus, our result is more theoretical than practical.

4   The SAT over Unbounded Set of Variables

In [10] seven circumstances are given when the power of context-free languages is not enough to describe some phenomena of the world. One of them is a logical example: the language of tautologies is not context free, as it is shown in [34]. The complexity of the decision whether a Boolean formula is tautology is closely connected to the complexity of SAT as we already described: A Boolean formula is a tautology if and only if its negation is unsatisfiable; and it is satisfiable if and only if its negation is not a tautology. In [10,34] the authors use the tautologies over arbitrarily many variables (coding their names by finite sets of letters) and using the connectives negation, conjunction, disjunction and implication.

In [26] it is proved that the language of Boolean tautologies over an infinite alphabet (using coding to a finite alphabet) is not regular and not context-free, but it is a context-sensitive language, even if only formulae in DNF are used. It is not a surprising fact, since the membership problem of context-sensitive languages is a PSPACE complete problem ([14,17]), while the word problem for context-free languages is in P. Therefore, this language can be accepted by a linear bounded Turing-machine. The dual problems of the SAT and n-SAT are hard with unbounded number of variables. Knowing that the dual problems have similarly large complexities, we can say that over arbitrary many variables the SAT and n-SAT languages are not regular; they are much more complex languages/problems.

5   Conclusions, Further Remarks

The most of new computational paradigms, such as membrane computing systems, solve the SAT in effective ways. Usually the alphabet depends on the particular problem, i.e., on the number of the variables. The number of rules is also growing with the growing alphabet when larger problem instances are solved. Due to page limitations we could not recall all the details of the mentioned solutions to SAT (it could give a nice survey). We have shown that the SAT and n-SAT languages are regular over any (fixed) finite set of variables, and therefore it seems that a set of (much) easier problems is solved (even in uniform way). Actually, our finite automata check all Boolean combinations and, therefore, they need an exponential number of states. In membrane systems the evaluation process goes in a parallel manner in an exponential space that can be obtained in a linear time, hence the initial system does not need to be exponential on any parameter of the input. Our automata check also the syntax of the input expressions (words), while in membrane systems it is usually assumed that the input is in a correct form and therefore the computation checks only the satisfiability of the input formulae. The regular languages can be recognized in linear time. If there is a correct upper limit to the number of variables for a given formula, then using the DFA respecting this limit, it is linear time decidable whether the formula is satisfiable. Unfortunately, as we discussed, our result is more theoretical and mathematical than practical. Our result shows that in SAT the length of the formulae are not so important factor. It is interesting, because in complexity theory the measure uses the input-length as a parameter. In the complexity of SAT the number of variables of the formula plays a more essential role.

We leave open the problem to build a more efficient DFA that accepts one of the SAT languages. (Do we really need $EXP(EXP(k))$ states?) The minimization of our automata may suffice. Other option is based on clauses without any repetitions of a variable or with a similar constraint...

There are several algorithms to solve SAT by various P-systems. With this paper we wanted to reopen this particular field. We are looking for new ideas, collaborations to solve SAT by a method with fixed alphabet independently of the number of variables. Note here that there is another new computational paradigm, the so-called interval-valued computation (introduced in [27,28] and further developed in [29,30]). It offers also a linear solution to SAT (moreover to q-SAT, the PSPACE-complete quantified version of SAT, also). This 'general uniform' algorithm gives the answer for every Boolean formula, independently of its length and of the number of variables. This method also uses exponential space of the number of used variables. The space complexity is measured by the used number of subintervals of the basic interval $[0, 1)$. The algorithm consists of a linear number of steps (operations) on the length of the input formula, so that the interval-values of a linear number of subformulae are computed and stored. It could be an interesting and challenging task to mix the features of interval-valued computing and P-systems. This mixture could help to develop further highly parallel algorithms that can solve SAT and other intractable problems in their original form (as it is discussed in Section 4).

The advised solution could be:

(1) the SAT problem is hard enough in the present form. It is regular, but in practice hard to solve it, therefore it is still a challenge and great result if one could give polynomial (or linear deterministic) solution for classes with a fixed number of variables. This would be the easy solution, but maybe it is not satisfying...

(2) we need to encode the (potentially infinite set of variables of the) input with a fixed sized alphabet. This could be done by complex objects. The first step is already done, by strings/worms. The next step should be the coding similarly as it is done by Turing machine solutions (strings are used that case also). Other such option could be to use interval-values in membranes.

(3) as a consequence of our result we may need more types of 'uniformity' for membrane systems. The semi-uniform solution defines a new P system for every instance. The uniform solution can solve all the instances of the same size, as we did also by our DFA family. The 'general uniform' solution could be a solution similar to Turing machine solutions in the fact that it works for all (correctly) coded input formula. Actually, and our result underlines this fact, the coding is the essential problem with the classical solutions. This general uniform approach may also help to establish a new connection between traditional complexity classes and membrane computing. It is also interesting to address the question 'how can we produce the solving P systems' instead the usual Turing machine construction. To find a new reasonable method (maybe a preconstruction by another membrane system with input) to this question could also help to produce general uniform solutions.

We believe that this task could also be fruitful for the problem P=NP...

Acknowledgements. The author is grateful to Gy. Vaszil and the reviewers for their valuable advices. The work is partly supported by the TÁMOP 4.2.1/B-09/1/KONV-2010-0007 and TÁMOP 4.2.2/C-11/1/KONV-2012-0001 projects. The projects are implemented through the New Hungary Development Plan, co-financed by the European Social Fund and the European Regional Development Fund.

References

1. Alhazov, A.: Solving SAT by Symport/Antiport P Systems with Membrane Division. In: ESF PESC Exploratory Workshop, Sevilla, pp. 1–6 (2005)
2. Alhazov, A.: Minimal Parallelism and Number of Membrane Polarizations. Computer Science Journal of Moldova 18, 149–170 (2010)

3. Alhazov, A., Freund, R.: On the Efficiency of P Systems with Active Membranes and Two Polarizations. In: Mauri, G., Păun, G., Jesús Pérez-Jímenez, M., Rozenberg, G., Salomaa, A. (eds.) WMC 2004. LNCS, vol. 3365, pp. 146–160. Springer, Heidelberg (2005)
4. Alhazov, A., Ishdorj, T.-O.: Membrane Operations in P Systems with Active Membranes. RGNC report 01/2004, Second BWMC, Sevilla, 37–44 (2004)
5. Brueggeman, T., Kern, W.: An improved deterministic local search algorithm for 3-SAT. Theoretical Computer Science 329, 303–313 (2004)
6. Castellanos, J., Păun, G., Rodríguez-Patón, A.: Computing with Membranes: P Systems with Worm-Objects. In: SPIRE 2000, pp. 65–74 (2000)
7. Ciobanu, G., Pan, L., Păun, G., Pérez-Jiménez, M.J.: P systems with minimal parallelism. Theoretical Computer Science 378, 117–130 (2007)
8. Czeizler, E.: Self-Activating P Systems. In: Păun, G., Rozenberg, G., Salomaa, A., Zandron, C. (eds.) WMC-CdeA 2002. LNCS, vol. 2597, pp. 234–246. Springer, Heidelberg (2003)
9. Dantsin, E., Goerdt, A., Hirsch, E.A., Kannan, R., Kleinberg, J., Papadimitriou, C.H., Raghavan, P., Schöning, U.: A deterministic $(2 - 2/(k + 1))n$ algorithm for k-SAT based on local search. Theoretical Computer Science 289, 69–83 (2002)
10. Dassow, J., Păun, G.: Regulated rewriting in Formal Language Theory. Akademie-Verlag, Berlin (1989)
11. Frisco, P., Govan, G.: P Systems with Active Membranes Operating under Minimal Parallelism. In: Gheorghe, M., Păun, G., Rozenberg, G., Salomaa, A., Verlan, S. (eds.) CMC 2011. LNCS, vol. 7184, pp. 165–181. Springer, Heidelberg (2012)
12. Gutiérrez-Naranjo, M.A., Pérez-Jiménez, M.J., Romero-Campero, F.J.: A uniform solution to SAT using membrane creation. Theoretical Computer Science 371, 54–61 (2007)
13. Hirversalo, M.: Quantum Computing. Springer (2003)
14. Hopcroft, J.E., Ullman, J.D.: Introduction to Automata Theory, Languages and Computation. Addison-Wesley, Reading (1979)
15. Ishdorj, T.-O.: Minimal Parallelism for Polarizationless P Systems. In: Mao, C., Yokomori, T. (eds.) DNA12. LNCS, vol. 4287, pp. 17–32. Springer, Heidelberg (2006)
16. Johnson, D.S.: A Catalog of Complexity Classes. In: Handbook of Theoretical Computer Science, vol. A, Algorithms and Complexity. Elsevier (1990)
17. Karp, R.: Reducibility Among Combinatorial Problems. In: Symposium on the Complexity of Computer Computations, pp. 85–103. Plenum Press, New York (1972)
18. Krishna, S.N., Lakshmanan, K., Rama, R.: On the power of P systems with contextual rules. Fundamenta Informaticae 49, 167–178 (2002)
19. Kusper, G.: Solving the resolution-free SAT problem by submodel propagation in linear time. Ann. Math. Artif. Intell. 43, 129–136 (2005)
20. Leporati, A., Mauri, G., Zandron, C.: Quantum Sequential P Systems with Unit Rules and Energy Assigned to Membranes. In: Freund, R., Păun, G., Rozenberg, G., Salomaa, A. (eds.) WMC 2005. LNCS, vol. 3850, pp. 310–325. Springer, Heidelberg (2006)
21. Leporati, A., Felloni, S.: Three "quantum" algorithms to solve 3-SAT. Theoretical Computer Science 372, 218–241 (2007)
22. Linz, P.: An Introduction to Formal Languages and Automata. D.C. Heath and Co. (1990)
23. Lipton, R.J.: DNA solution of HARD computational problems. Science 268, 542–545 (1995)

24. Manca, V.: DNA and Membrane Algorithms for SAT. Fundamenta Informaticae 49, 205–221 (2002)
25. Murphy, N., Woods, D.: The computational complexity of uniformity and semi-uniformity in membrane systems. In: BWMC7, vol. 2, pp. 73–84 (2009)
26. Nagy, B.: The languages of SAT and n-SAT over finitely many variables are regular. Bulletin of the EATCS 82, 286–297 (2004)
27. Nagy, B.: An interval-valued computing device. In: CiE 2005, Computability in Europe: New Computational Paradigms (X-2005-01), pp. 166–177 (2005)
28. Nagy, B., Vályi, S.: Interval-valued computations and their connection with PSPACE. Theoretical Computer Science 394, 208–222 (2008)
29. Nagy, B.: Effective Computing by Interval-values. In: 14th IEEE International Conference on Intelligent Engineering Systems, pp. 91–96 (2010)
30. Nagy, B., Vályi, S.: Prime factorization by interval-valued computing. Publicationes Mathematicae Debrecen 79, 539–551 (2011)
31. Pan, L., Alhazov, A., Ishdorj, T.-O.: Further remarks on P systems with active membranes, separation, merging, and release rules. Soft Computing 9, 686–690 (2005)
32. Pan, L., Alhazov, A.: Solving HPP and SAT by P Systems with Active Membranes and Separation Rules. Acta Informatica 43, 131–145 (2006)
33. Papadimitriou, C.H.: Computational complexity. Addison-Wesley (1994)
34. Păun, G.: The propositional calculus languages versus the Chomsky hierarchy. Stud. Cerc. Mat. 33, 299–310 (1981) (in Romanian)
35. Păun, G.: Computing with Membranes. Journal of Computer and System Sciences 61, 108–143 (2000); TUCS Report No. 208 (1998)
36. Păun, G.: P-systems with active membranes: attacking NP complete problems. In: UMC, pp. 94–115 (2000)
37. Păun, G.: Membrane Computing: An introduction. Springer, Berlin (2002)
38. Păun, G., Pérez-Jímenez, M.J., Riscos-Núñez, A.: P Systems with Tables of Rules. In: Karhumäki, J., Maurer, H., Păun, G., Rozenberg, G. (eds.) Theory Is Forever. LNCS, vol. 3113, pp. 235–249. Springer, Heidelberg (2004)
39. Păun, G., Suzuki, Y., Tanaka, H., Yokomori, T.: On the power of membrane division in P systems. Theoretical Computer Science 324, 61–85 (2004)
40. Pazos, J., Rodríguez-Patón, A., Silva, A.: Solving SAT in Linear Time with a Neural-Like Membrane System. In: Mira, J., Álvarez, J.R. (eds.) IWANN 2003. LNCS, vol. 2686, pp. 662–669. Springer, Heidelberg (2003)
41. Pérez-Jiménez, M.J., Romero-Jiménez, A., Sancho-Caparrini, F.: Computationally hard problems addressed through P systems. In: Applications of Membrane Computing, pp. 315–346. Springer, Berlin (2006)
42. Pérez-Jiménez, M.J., Riscos-Núñez, A., Romero-Jiménez, A., Woods, D.: Complexity – Membrane Division, Membrane Creation, ch. 12, pp. 302–336 (2009)
43. P-system home page, old, http://psystems.disco.unimib.it/, and new http://ppage.psystems.eu
44. Schöning, U.: A Probabilistic Algorithm for k-SAT Based on Limited Local Search and Restart. Algorithmica 32, 615–623 (2002)
45. The international SAT Competitions web page, http://www.satcompetition.org/
46. Tagawa, H., Fujiwara, A.: Solving SAT and Hamiltonian Cycle Problem Using Asynchronous P Systems. IEICE Transactions on Information and Systems E95-D(3), 746–754 (2012)
47. Zandron, C., Ferretti, C., Mauri, G.: Solving NP-complete problems using P systems with active membranes. In: Unconventional Models of Computation (UMC), pp. 289–301 (2000)

Multigraphical Membrane Systems Revisited

Adam Obtułowicz

Institute of Mathematics, Polish Academy of Sciences
Śniadeckich 8, P.O.B. 21, 00-956 Warsaw, Poland
A.Obtulowicz@impan.gov.pl

Abstract. A concept of a (directed) multigraphical membrane system [21], akin to membrane systems in [23] and [20], for modeling complex systems in biology, evolving neural networks, perception, and brain function is recalled and its new inspiring examples are presented for linking it with object recognition in cortex, an idea of neocognitron for multidimensional geometry, fractals, and hierarchical networks.

1 Introduction

Statecharts described in [17] and their wide applications, including applications in system biology, cf. [11], and the formal foundations for natural reasoning in a visual mode presented in [27] challenge a prejudice against visualizations in exact sciences that they are heuristic tools and not valid elements of mathematical proofs.

We recall from [21] a concept of a (directed) multigraphical membrane system to be applied for modelling complex systems in biology, evolving neural networks, perception, and brain function. A precise mathematical definition of this concept and its topological representation by Venn diagrams and the usual graph drawings constitute a kind of visual formalism related to that discussed in [17]. The concept of a multigraphical membrane system is some new variant of the notion of a membrane system in [23] and [20].

We extend [21] by presenting the new inspiring examples of the concept of multigraphical membrane system for linking it with multidimensional object recognition in cortex, an idea of neocognitron for multidimensional geometry, hierarchical networks, and even fractals. These new examples are based on the idea of drawing multidimensional hypercubes (Boolean n-cubes) due to Tamiko Thiel (cf. [28]) and the figures Fig. 3–6 recalling this idea in the present paper are also due to her.

2 Multigraphical Membrane System

Membrane system in [23] and [20] are simply finite trees with nodes labelled by multisets, where the finite trees have a natural visual presentation by Venn diagrams.

We introduce (*directed*) *multigraphical membrane systems* to be finite trees with nodes labelled by (directed) multigraphs.

E. Csuhaj-Varjú et al. (Eds.): CMC 2012, LNCS 7762, pp. 311–322, 2013.

We consider directed multigraphical membrane systems of a special feature described formally in the following way.

A *sketch-like membrane system* $\mathcal{S}$ is given by:

- its *underlying tree* $\mathbb{T}_\mathcal{S}$ which is a finite graph given by the set $V(\mathbb{T}_\mathcal{S})$ of *vertices*, the set $E(\mathbb{T}_\mathcal{S}) \subseteq V(\mathbb{T}_\mathcal{S}) \times V(\mathbb{T}_\mathcal{S})$ of *edges*, and the *root* r which is a distinguished vertex such that for every vertex v different from r there exists a unique path from v into r in $\mathbb{T}_\mathcal{S}$, where for every vertex v we define $\mathrm{rel}(v) = \{v' \,|\, (v', v) \in E(\mathbb{T}_\mathcal{S})\}$ which is the set of vertices *immediately related to* v;
- its family $(G_v \,|\, v \in V(\mathbb{T}_\mathcal{S}))$ of finite directed multigraphs for G_v given by the set $V(G_v)$ of *vertices*, the set $E(G_v)$ of *edges*, the *source function* $s_v : E(G_v) \to V(G_v)$, and the *target function* $t_v : E(G_v) \to V(G_v)$ such that the following conditions hold:
  1) $V(G_v) = \{v\} \cup \mathrm{rel}(v)$,
  2) $E(G_v)$ is empty for every *elementary* vertex v, i.e. such that $\mathrm{rel}(v)$ is empty,
  3) for every *non-elementary* vertex v, i.e. such that $\mathrm{rel}(v)$ is a non-empty set, we have
     (i) $G_v(v, v')$ is empty for every $v' \in V(G_v)$,
     (ii) $G_v(v', v)$ is a one-element set for every $v' \in \mathrm{rel}(v)$,
     where $G_v(v_1, v_2) = \{e \in E(G_v) \,|\, s_v(e) = v_1 \text{ and } t_v(e) = v_2\}$.

For every non-elementary vertex v of $\mathbb{T}_\mathcal{S}$ we define:

- the *v-diagram* $\mathrm{Dg}(v)$ to be that directed multigraph which is the *restriction* of G_v to $\mathrm{rel}(v)$, i.e. $E(\mathrm{Dg}(v)) = \{e \in E(G_v) \,|\, \{s_v(e), t_v(e)\} \subseteq \mathrm{rel}(v)\}$, $V(\mathrm{Dg}(v)) = \mathrm{rel}(v)$, and the source and target functions of $\mathrm{Dg}(v)$ are the obvious restrictions of s_v, t_v to $E(\mathrm{Dg}(v))$, respectively,
- the *v-cocone* to be a family $(e_{v'} \,|\, v' \in \mathrm{rel}(v))$ of edges of G_v such that $s_v(e_{v'}) = v'$ and $t_v(e_{v'}) = v$ for every $v' \in \mathrm{rel}(v)$.

By a *model* of a sketch-like membrane system $\mathcal{S}$ in a category $\mathbb{C}$ with finite colimits we mean a family of graph homomorphisms $h_v : G_v \to \mathbb{C}$ (v is a non-elementary vertex of $\mathbb{T}_\mathcal{S}$) such that $h_v(v)$ is a colimit of the diagram $h_v \upharpoonright \mathrm{Dg}(v) : \mathrm{Dg}(v) \to \mathbb{C}$ and $(h_v(e_{v'}) \,|\, v' \in \mathrm{rel}(v))$ is a colimiting cocone for the v-cocone $(e_{v'} \,|\, v' \in \mathrm{rel}(v))$, where $h_v \upharpoonright \mathrm{Dg}(v)$ is the restriction of h_v to $\mathrm{Dg}(v)$. For all categorical and sketch theoretical notions like graph homomorphism, colimit of the diagram, and colimiting cocone we refer the reader to [4].

The idea of a sketch-like membrane system and its categorical model is a special case of the concept of a sketch and its model described in [4] and [19], where one finds that sketches can serve as a visual presentation of some data structure and data type algebraic specifications. On the other hand the idea of a sketch-like membrane system is a generalization of the notion of ramification used in [8], [9], [10] to investigate hierarchical categories with hierarchies determined by iterated colimits understood as in [8]. Hierarchical categories with hierarchies determined by iterated colimits are applied in [2] and [9] to describe various emergence phenomena in biology and general system theory. The iterated colimits identified with binding of patterns in neural net systems are expected in [9] and [10] to be applied in the investigations of binding problems in vision systems (associated with perception and brain function) in [30] and [31], hence the notion of sketch-like membrane system is aimed to be a tool for these investigations.

More precisely, sketch-like membrane systems are aimed to be presentations of objects of state categories of Memory Evolutive Systems in [8] and [9], where these state categories are hierarchical categories with hierarchies determined by iterated colimits. Hierarchical feature of sketch-like membrane systems and their categorical semantics reflect iterated colimit feature of objects of state categories of Memory Evolutive Systems [10].

If we drop condition 3) in the definition of a sketch-like membrane system, we obtain those directed multigraphical membrane systems which appear useful to describe alternating organization of living systems discussed in [3] with regard to nesting (represented by the underlying tree $\mathbb{T}_S$) and interaction of levels of organization (represented by family of directed multigraphs G_v ($v \in V(\mathbb{T}_S)$)). According to [3] the edges in $G_v(v', v)$ describe integration, the edges in $G_v(v, v')$ describe regulation, and the edges of v-diagram $\mathrm{Dg}(v)$ describe interaction.

A directed multigraphical (a sketch-like) membrane system is illustrated in Fig. 1, whose semantics (model) in a hierarchical category is illustrated in Fig. 2.

Concerning the underlying trees of multigraphical membrane systems we recommend to read [1] containing a discussion of advantages and disadvantages of using trees for visual presentation and an analysis of complex systems.

Multigraphical membrane system corresponding to 2-ramification:

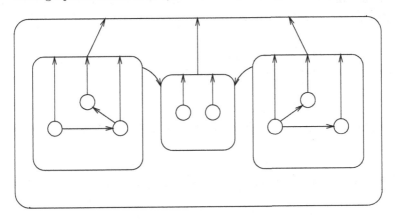

nodes—membranes, edges—objects,
neurons—membranes, synapses—objects.

Fig. 1.

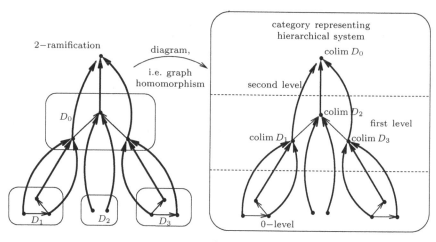

the fat arrows are colimiting injections,
i.e. the elements of colimiting cocones,
respectively

Fig. 2.

3 Inspiring Examples

Following the idea of drawing hypercubes[1] from [28] recalled in Fig. 3–6 we show
the examples of sketch-like multigraphical membrane systems which approach
this idea in some formal way.

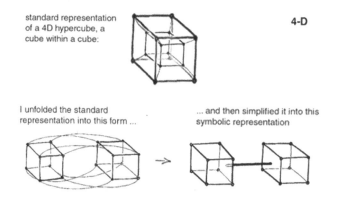

Fig. 3. 4th dimension of a hypercube

---

[1] For a notion of a hypercube see [22], [6], [26].

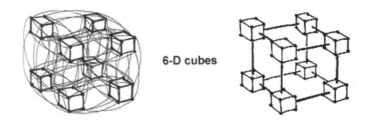

Fig. 4. 6th dimension of a hypercube

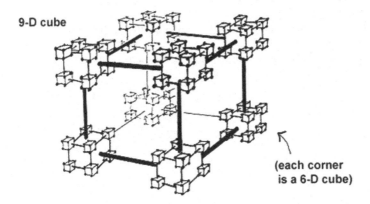

Fig. 5. 9th dimension of a hypercube

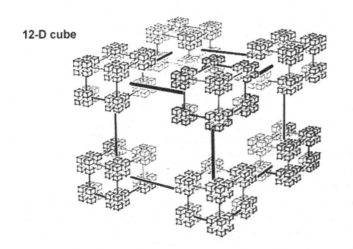

A large cube whose corners are smaller cubes can be treated as a large virtual membrane, where smaller cubes are treated as smaller virtual membranes contained in this large virtual membrane.

Fig. 6. 12th dimension of a hypercube

For natural numbers $n > 0$ and $i \in \{1, 2, 3\}$ we define sketch-like multigraphical membrane systems $\mathcal{S}_n^i$, the claimed examples, in the following way:

– the underlying tree $\mathbb{T}_n^i$ of $\mathcal{S}_n^i$ is such that
  • the set $V(\mathbb{T}_n^i)$ of vertices is the set of all strings (sequences) of length not greater than n of digits in $D^1 = \{0, 1\}$ for $i = 1$, in $D^2 = \{0, 1, 2, 3\}$ for $i = 2$, and in $D^3 = \{0, 1, 2, 3, 4, 5, 6, 7\}$ for $i = 3$,
  • the set $E(\mathbb{T}_n^i)$ of edges of $\mathbb{T}_n^i$ is such that $E(\mathbb{T}_n^i) = \{(\Gamma j, \Gamma) \,|\, \{\Gamma j, \Gamma\} \subset V(\mathbb{T}_n^i) \text{ and } j \in D^i\}$ with source and target functions being the projections on the first and the second component, respectively, where Γj is the string obtained by juxtaposition a new digit j on the right end of Γ,
– the family $(G_\Gamma \,|\, \Gamma \in V(\mathbb{T}_n^i))$ of directed graphs of $\mathcal{S}_n^i$ is such that for every non-elementary vertex $\Gamma \in V(\mathbb{T}_n^i)$ the Γ-diagram $\mathrm{Dg}(\Gamma)$ is determined in the following way:
  • for $i = 1$ the diagram $\mathrm{Dg}(\Gamma)$ is a graph consisting of a single edge $\Gamma 0 \to \Gamma 1$,
  • for $i = 2$ the diagram $\mathrm{Dg}(\Gamma)$ is the following square:

  • for $i = 3$ the diagram $\mathrm{Dg}(\Gamma)$ is the following cube:

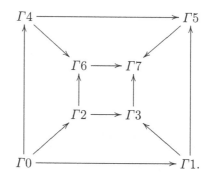

The above sketch-like multigraphical membrane systems drawn by using Venn diagrams (with discs d_Γ corresponding to vertices Γ of $\mathbb{T}_n^i$ such that $d_{\Gamma j}$ is an immediate subset of d_Γ) coincide with the drawings shown in [28].

The following *interpretation* of $\mathcal{S}_n^i$ by an $i \cdot n$-dimensional hypercube $[\![\mathcal{S}_n^i]\!]$ ($n > 0$ and $i \in \{1, 2, 3\}$) completes the proposed formal approach to the idea of drawing hypercubes in [28].

We introduce the following notion to define hypercubes $[\![\mathcal{S}_n^i]\!]$. For a natural number $n \geq 0$ and a finite directed graph G whose vertices are natural numbers and the set $E(G)$ of edges of G is such that $E(G) \subseteq V(G) \times V(G)$ we define a new graph $G \uparrow n$, called the *translation of G to n*, by

$$V(G \uparrow n) = \{i + n \,|\, i \in V(G)\},$$
$$E(G \uparrow n) = \{(i + n, j + n) \,|\, (i, j) \in E(G)\}.$$

The hypercubes $[[\mathcal{S}_n^i]]$ ($n > 0$, $i \in \{1, 2, 3\}$) are defined by induction on n in the following way:

- for every $i \in \{1, 2, 3\}$ the hypercube $[[\mathcal{S}_1^i]]$ is the diagram $\mathrm{Dg}(\Lambda)$ of $\mathcal{S}_1^i$, where Λ is the empty string and the digits in $V(\mathrm{Dg}(\Lambda))$ are identified with corresponding natural numbers,
- for all $n > 0$ and $i \in \{1, 2, 3\}$ the hypercube $[[\mathcal{S}_{n+1}^i]]$ is such that

$$V([[\mathcal{S}_{n+1}^i]]) = \bigcup_{0 \le j < 2^i} V([[\mathcal{S}_n^i]] \uparrow (j \cdot 2^{i \cdot n})),$$

$$E([[\mathcal{S}_{n+1}^i]]) = \bigcup_{0 \le j < 2^i} E([[\mathcal{S}_n^i]] \uparrow (j \cdot 2^{i \cdot n}))$$

$$\cup \bigcup_{(k,m) \in E([[\mathcal{S}_1^i]])} \{(j + k \cdot 2^{i \cdot n}, j + m \cdot 2^{i \cdot n}) \mid j \in V([[\mathcal{S}_n^i]])\}.$$

We introduce the following constructs to prove the main theorems of the paper and to show the links of $\mathcal{S}_n^i$ ($i \in \{1, 2, 3\}$, $n > 0$) to Cantor set which is a known fractal, cf. [12].

For natural numbers k, n with $n > 0$ and $0 \le k < 2^n$ we define a binary vector $\mathrm{bin}^n(k)$ by induction on n:

$$\mathrm{bin}^1(k) = k,$$

$$\mathrm{bin}^{n+1}(k) = \begin{cases} [0, x_1, \ldots, x_n] & \text{if } k < 2^n \text{ and } [x_1, \ldots, x_n] = \mathrm{bin}^n(k), \\ [1, y_1, \ldots, y_n] & \text{if } k \ge 2^n \text{ and } [y_1, \ldots, y_n] = \mathrm{bin}^n(k - 2^n). \end{cases}$$

We propose some spatial *realization* of $\mathcal{S}_n^i$ itself in the space $\mathbb{R}^i$, where $\mathbb{R}^i$ is a Cartesian product of i copies of the set $\mathbb{R}$ of real numbers. This spatial realization is determined by a graph space$(\mathcal{S}_n^i)$ defined by induction on n. For $\Delta \in \{V, E\}$ we define

$$\Delta(\mathrm{space}(\mathcal{S}_1^i)) = \Delta([[\mathcal{S}_1^i]])$$

$$\Delta(\mathrm{space}(\mathcal{S}_{n+1}^i)) = \Delta(\tfrac{1}{3} \cdot \mathrm{space}(\mathcal{S}_n^i))$$

$$\cup \bigcup_{(k,m) \in E([[\mathcal{S}_1^i]])} \Delta(\tfrac{1}{3} \cdot \mathrm{space}(\mathcal{S}_n^i) \uparrow (\tfrac{2}{3} \cdot \mathrm{bin}^i(m))),$$

where for a graph G with $E(G) \subseteq V(G) \times V(G)$ and $V(G) \subseteq \mathbb{R}^i$, for a real number α with $0 \le \alpha \le 1$, and a vector $[x_1, \ldots, x_i] \in \mathbb{R}^i$ we define *contraction* $\alpha \cdot G$ and *translation* $G \uparrow [x_1, \ldots, x_i]$ to be graphs given by

$$V(\alpha \cdot G) = \{\alpha \cdot v \mid v \in V(G)\}, \quad E(\alpha \cdot G) = \{(\alpha \cdot v, \alpha \cdot v') \mid (v, v') \in E(G)\},$$

$$V(G \uparrow [x_1, \ldots, x_i]) = \{v + [x_1, \ldots, x_i] \mid v \in V(G)\},$$

$$E(G \uparrow [x_1, \ldots, x_i]) = \{(v + [x_1, \ldots, x_i], v' + [x_1, \ldots, x_i]) \mid (v, v') \in E(G)\},$$

where $\cdot$ denotes scalar multiplication of a vector and $+$ denotes vector sum.

The correctness of the proposed formal approach to the drawing of hypercubes in [28] is provided by the following theorem.

Theorem 1. *For all natural numbers $n > 0$ and $i \in \{2,3\}$*

- *$[[\mathcal{S}_n^1]]$ is an n-dimensional hypercube,*
- *$[[\mathcal{S}_n^i]] = [[\mathcal{S}_{i \cdot n}^1]]$.*

Proof. The proof of the theorem is by induction on n. The graphs $[[\mathcal{S}_n^1]]$ are identified with n-dimensional hypercubes (Boolean n-cubes) by identifying the numbers k in $V([[\mathcal{S}_n^1]])$ with binary vectors $\mathrm{bin}^n(k) \in \mathbb{R}^n$, respectively.

One sees that the edges of Γ-diagrams $\mathrm{Dg}(\Gamma)$ of $\mathcal{S}_n^i$ are the results of compression or binding the edges linking appropriate disjoint subhypercubes of $[[\mathcal{S}_n^i]]$, where the idea of this compression or binding is fundamental for the drawing of hypercubes in [28]. The elements of cocones for $\mathcal{S}_n^i$ correspond to the embeddings between appropriate subhypercubes of $[[\mathcal{S}_n^i]]$.

The following theorem shows the links between hypercubes, the sketch-like multigraphical membrane systems $\mathcal{S}_n^i$ ($i \in \{1,2,3\}$, $n > 0$) and Cantor set $\mathbb{C}$.

Theorem 2. *For all natural numbers $i \in \{1,2,3\}$ and $n > 0$ the following conditions hold:*

- *there exists an embedding, i.e. a graph homomorphism which is an injection of $\mathrm{space}(\mathcal{S}_n^i)$ into $[[\mathcal{S}_n^i]]$ such that the image of this embedding is $[[\mathcal{S}_n^i]]$ excluding all compressed edges, i.e. those belonging for $n > 1$ to*

$$\bigcup_{0 < q < n} \bigcup_{0 \leq p < 2^{i \cdot (n-q-1)}} \bigcup_{(k,m) \in E([[\mathcal{S}_1^i]])} \{(j + k \cdot 2^{i \cdot q}, j + m \cdot 2^{i \cdot q}) \mid j \in V_{p,q}^i\},$$

$$\text{where } V_{p,q}^i = V\big([[\mathcal{S}_q^i]] \uparrow (p \cdot 2^{i \cdot (q+1)})\big),$$

- *the undirected connectedness components of $\mathrm{space}(\mathcal{S}_n^i)$ coincide in a one to one correspondence with connectedness components of the Cartesian product $\mathbb{C}_n^i$ of i copies of the n-th iteration $\mathbb{C}_n = \frac{\mathbb{C}_{n-1}}{3} \cup (\frac{2}{3}, \frac{\mathbb{C}_{n-1}}{3})$ of the Cantor set.*

Proof. The proof of the theorem is by induction on n. The connectedness components of $\mathbb{C}_n^i$ are intervals of $\mathbb{R}$ for $i = 1$, the squares with their interiors in $\mathbb{R}^2$ for $i = 2$, the cubes with their interiors in $\mathbb{R}^3$ for $i = 3$. For $i > 1$ the edges of these squares and cubes are the intervals laying on the straight lines connecting the vertices $\boldsymbol{v}, \boldsymbol{v}'$ of the pair $(\boldsymbol{v}, \boldsymbol{v}') \in E(\mathrm{space}(\mathcal{S}_i^n))$ and these vertices are the ends of the intervals, respectively. Thus one obtains a one to one correspondence between connectedness components of $\mathrm{space}(\mathcal{S}_n^i)$ and $\mathbb{C}_n^i$. The small cubes in Fig. 5, 6 illustrate both the connectedness components of $\mathrm{space}(\mathcal{S}_n^3)$ and $\mathbb{C}_n^3$. The connectedness components of some iteration of 3D Cantor set $\mathbb{C}^3$ are shown also as small cubes in [32].

Remark 1. Thus the sketch-like multigraphical membrane systems $\mathcal{S}_n^i$ represent some internal *fractal-like structure* of hypercubes $[[\mathcal{S}_n^i]]$ which was not visible at first glance, e.g. in the drawing of 6-dimensional hypercube in Figure 1 in [26], shown in Fig. 7 of the present paper.

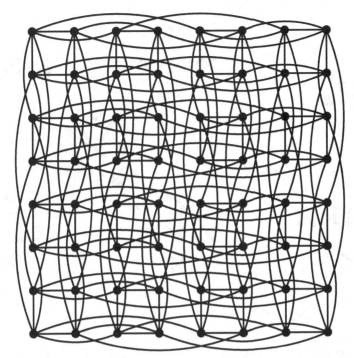

Fig. 7. Shown here is a two-dimensional projection of a six-dimensional hyper-cube, or binary 6-cube, which corresponds to a 64-node machine

The internal fractal-like structure represented by $\mathcal{S}_n^i$ can be described and explained by the following two representations.

The underlying tree $\mathbb{T}_n^i$ of $\mathcal{S}_n^i$ represents that *hierarchical organization* of both space($\mathcal{S}_n^i$) and $\mathbb{C}_n^i$ which is determined by inclusion relation and the scales corresponding to the fractions $(\frac{1}{3})^k$ $(0 \le k \le n)$. Moreover, the trees $\mathbb{T}_n^i$ have some common features with the trees generated by some iteration function systems, cf. [7], for fractals $\mathbb{C}^i$ being iD Cantor sets, where $\mathbb{C}_n^i$ are the iterations of $\mathbb{C}^i$ ($i \in \{1,2,3\}$).

For $n > 2$ and $i \in \{2,3\}$ the Γ-diagrams $\widehat{G}_\Gamma = \mathrm{Dg}(\Gamma)$ of $\mathcal{S}_n^i$ with $V(\widehat{G}_\Gamma)$ being a set of non-elementary vertices in $\mathcal{S}_n^i$, called *spatial arrangement diagrams* of $\mathcal{S}_n^i$, represent some uniform spatial arrangement of subgraphs of space($\mathcal{S}_n^i$) in $\mathbb{R}^i$. Namely, for every spatial arrangement diagram $\widehat{G}_\Gamma$ of $\mathcal{S}_n^i$ the virtual membrane Γ of space($\mathcal{S}_n^i$) (illustrated in Fig. 6 and corresponding to the real membrane Γ of $\mathcal{S}_n^i$) contains those 2^i different translations of the contraction $(\frac{1}{3})^{l(\Gamma)+1} \cdot$ space($\mathcal{S}_{n-l(\Gamma)-1}^i$) which are mutually related (arranged) according to the edges of $E(\widehat{G}_\Gamma)$, where $l(\Gamma)$ denotes the length of a string Γ. For instance, for $i = 2$ if Γ is empty word Λ, then $(\frac{1}{3}) \cdot$ space($\mathcal{S}_{n-1}^2$) $\uparrow \frac{2}{3} \cdot (\mathrm{bin}^2(3))$ is located above $(\frac{1}{3}) \cdot$ space($\mathcal{S}_{n-1}^2$) $\uparrow \frac{2}{3} \cdot (\mathrm{bin}^2(1))$ with distance $\frac{1}{3}$ according to $(1,3) \in E(\widehat{G}_\Lambda)$. The iterations $\mathbb{C}_n^i$ have an analogous spatial arrangement represented by the spatial arrangement diagrams of $\mathcal{S}_n^i$.

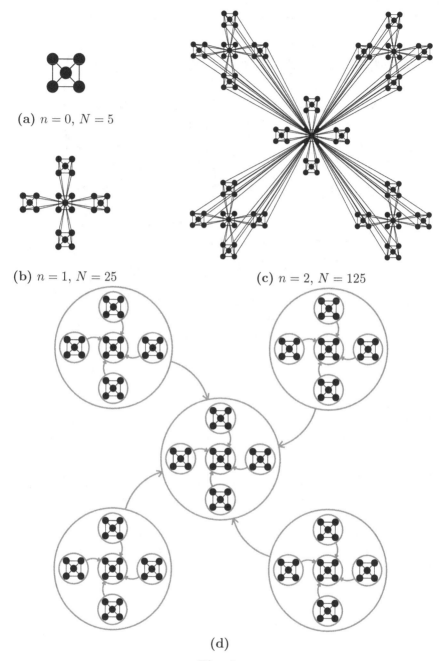

(a) $n = 0$, $N = 5$

(b) $n = 1$, $N = 25$

(c) $n = 2$, $N = 125$

(d)

Fig. 8.

Remark 2. The presentation of multidimensional hypercubes by sketch-like multigraphical membrane systems $\mathcal{S}_n^i$ with their interpretations $[[\mathcal{S}_n^i]]$, respectively, suggest a similar presentation of hierarchical networks in [24] (see Fig. 1 in [24]) and [5] by applying sketch-like multigraphical membrane systems, which is outlined in Fig. 8 of the present paper, where Fig. 8(a)–(c) is Fig. 1 in [24].

The arcs (links) from the peripheral nodes of each cluster to the central node of the original cluster (in Fig. 8(c)) are compressed to the arcs between non-elementary membranes (in Fig. 8(d)) corresponding to the clusters. The skin membrane (root) is omitted in Fig. 8(d).

4 Conclusion

The sketch-like multigraphical membrane systems play a dual role in object recognition and visual processing realized in brain neural networks and by artificial neural network of neocognitron [14]. Namely, they present the "objective" multilevel features[2] to be represented neuronally (at best by embedding) in "subjective" multilayer brain neural networks[3], cf. e.g. [13], [29], and in artificial neural networks of neocognitron.

The idea of drawing multidimensional hypercubes outlined in [28] together with its formal treatment by sketch-like multigraphical membrane systems shown in Section 3 propose a new approach to feature recognition and visual processing of multidimensional objects by information compression[4], may be different from that proposed in [18]. Thus one can ask for reliability of processes of feature recognition of multidimensional objects by neocognitron in the manner of [15] and according to this new approach.

Remarks 1 and 2 suggest the new applications of sketch-like multigraphical membrane systems for representation of fractal iterations (respecting the discussion in [16]) and for presentation of hierarchical networks.

References

1. Alexander, C.: A city is not a tree. Reprint from the Magazine Design No. 206, Council of Industrial Design (1966)
2. Baas, N.B., Emmeche, C.: On Emergence and Explanation. Intellectica 2(25), 67–83 (1997)
3. Bailly, F., Longo, G.: Objective and Epistemic Complexity in Biology, invited lecture. In: International Conference on Theoretical Neurobiology, New Delhi (February 2003), http://www.di.ens.fr/users/longo

---

[2] With respect to e.g. natural abstraction levels: pixel level, local feature level, structure-level, object-level, object-set-level, and scene characteriztion, or with respect to the levels of subhypercubes (faces) of a multidimensional hypercube.

[3] Like in a classical model of visual processing in cortex which is hierarchy of increasingly sophisticated representations extending in natural way the model of simple to complex cells (neurons) of Hubel and Wisel, cf. [25].

[4] Realized e.g. by binding some links between subhypercubes of a given multidimensional hypercube.

4. Barr, F., Welles, C.: Category Theory for Computing Science, 2nd edn. Prentice–Hall, New York (1990, 1993)
5. Barrière, L., et al.: Deterministic hierarchical networks. Networks (2006) (submitted)
6. Domshlak, C.: On recursively directed hypercubes. Electron. J. Combin. 9, #R23 (2002)
7. Edalat, A.: Domains for computation in mathematics, physics and exact real arithmetic. The Bulletin of Symbolic Logic 3, 401–452 (1997)
8. Ehresmann, A.C., Vanbremeersch, J.-P.: Multiplicity Principle and Emergence in Memory Evolutive Systems. SAMS 26, 81–117 (1996)
9. Ehresmann, A.C., Vanbremeersch, J.-P.: Consciousness as Structural and Temporal Integration of the Context, http://perso.orange.fr/vbm-ehr/Ang/W24A7.htm
10. Ehresmann, A.C., Vanbremeersch, J.-P.: Memory Evolutive Systems. Studies in Multidisciplinarity, vol. 4. Elsevier, Amsterdam (2007)
11. Eroni, S., Harel, D., Cohen, I.R.: Toward Rigorous Comprehension of Biological Complexity: Modeling, Execution, and Visualization of Thymic T-Cell Maturation. Genome Research 13, 2485–2497 (2003)
12. Falconer, K.: Fractal Geometry. Mathematical Foundations and Applications. Wiley, Hoboken (2003)
13. Felleman, D.J., Van Essen, D.C.: Distributed hierarchical processing in the primate cerebral cortex. Cerebral Cortex 1(1), 1–47 (1991)
14. Fukushima, K.: Neocognitron: A hierarchical neural network capable of visual pattern recognition. Neural Networks 1(2), 119–130 (1988)
15. Fukushima, K.: Neocognitron trained with winner-kill-loser rule. Neural Networks 23, 926–938 (2010)
16. Gutierrez-Naranjo, M.A., Perez-Jimenez, M.J.: Fractals and P systems. In: Proc. of 4th BWMC, vol. II, pp. 65–86. Sevilla Univ. (2006)
17. Harel, D.: On Visual Formalisms. Comm. ACM 31, 514–530 (1988)
18. Inseberg, A.: Parallel Coordinates: Visual Multidimensional Geometry and its Applications. Springer, Berlin (2008)
19. Lair, C.: Elements de la theorie des Patchworks. Diagrammes 29 (1993)
20. Membrane computing web page, http://ppage.psystems.eu
21. Obtułowicz, A.: Multigraphical membrane systems: a visual formalism for modeling complex systems in biology and evolving neural networks. In: Preproceedings of Workshop of Membrane Computing, Thessaloniki, pp. 509–512 (2007)
22. Ovchinnikov, S.: Partial cubes: characterizations and constructions. Discrete Mathematics 308, 5597–5621 (2008)
23. Păun, G.: Membrane Computing. An Introduction. Springer, Berlin (2002)
24. Ravasz, E., Barabási, A.-L.: Hierarchical organization in complex networks. Physical Review 67, 026112 (2003)
25. Reisenhuber, M., Poggio, T.: Hierarchical models of object recognition in cortex. Nature Neuroscience 11, 1019–1025 (1999)
26. Seitz, C.L.: The cosmic cube. Comm. ACM 28, 22–33 (1985)
27. Shin, S.-J.: The Logical Status of Diagrams, Cambridge (1994)
28. Thiel, T.: The design of the connection machine, DesignIssues, vol. 10(1), pp. 5–18. MIT Press, Cambridge (1994), see also http://www.mission-base.com/tamiko/theory/cm_txts/di-frames.html
29. Van Essen, D.C., Maunsell, J.H.R.: Hierarchical organization and functional streams in the visual cortex. Trends in NeuroScience, 370–375 (September 1983)
30. von der Malsburg, C.: Binding in Models of Perception and Brain Function. Current Opinions in Neurobiology 5, 520–526 (1995)
31. von der Malsburg, C.: The What and Why of Binding: The Modeler's Perspective. Neuron, 95–104, 94–125 (1999)
32. http://commons.wikimedia.org/wiki/File:3D_Cantor_set.jpg

An Analysis of Correlative and Static Causality in P Systems

Roberto Pagliarini[1], Oana Agrigoroaiei[2], Gabriel Ciobanu[2], and Vincenzo Manca[3]

[1] Telethon Institute of Genetics and Medicine, Via P. Castellino 111, Naples, Italy
r.pagliarini@tigem.it
[2] Romanian Academy, Institute of Computer Science
oanaag@iit.tuiasi.ro, gabriel@info.uaic.ro
[3] Verona University, Computer Science Dept., Strada Le Grazie 15, Verona, Italy
vincenzo.manca@univr.it

Abstract. In this paper we present two approaches, namely correlative and static causality, to study cause-effect relationships in reaction models and we propose a framework which integrates them in order to study causality by means of transition P systems. The proposed framework is based on the fact that statistical analysis can be used to building up a membrane model which can be used to analyze causality relationships in terms of multisets of objects and rules in presence of non-determinism and parallelism. We prove that the P system which is defined by means of correlation analysis provides a correspondence between the static and correlative notions of causality.

1 Introduction

Since their first introduction, membrane systems [15], also known as P systems, have been widely investigated in the framework of formal language theory as innovative compartmentalized parallel multiset rewriting systems, and different variants have been analyzed along with their computational power (for a complete list of references, see http://ppage.psystems.eu). Although they were originally introduced as computational models, their biologically inspired structure and functioning, together with their feasibility as models of cellular and biomolecular processes, turned out to be a widely applicable modeling technique in several domains.

If we see P systems as biochemical reaction models[1], then it is possible to apply them to study causality in living cells, that is, the ways that entities of a reaction system influence each other. In particular, cause-effect relationships can be analyzed by following two ways: *i)* a *statistical approach*, and *ii)* a *static approach*.

---

[1] These models are a formal representation of interactions between biochemical reactions.

E. Csuhaj-Varjú et al. (Eds.): CMC 2012, LNCS 7762, pp. 323–341, 2013.

From a statistical point of view, causality is the relationship between an event, the cause, and a second event, the effect, where the second event is understood as a consequence of the first. Causality can also be seen as the relationship between a set of factors and a phenomenon. The statistical notion can be estimated directly by observational studies and experimental data, for which causal direction can be inferred if information about time is available. This is due to the fact that causes must precede their effects in the time line. Then the use of temporal data can permit to discover causal direction.

Differently, from a static point of view, causality is studied in terms of multisets of objects and of multisets of rules in presence of non-determinism and parallelism. To this goal, several approaches have been proposed to translate them into different formalisms to study cause-effect relationships, as for example [3,5,11]. These approaches do not consider the quantities involved in multisets of objects but rather the objects themselves. For this reason, a different approach to causality was started in [1] and has been extended in [2], where it was called *quantitative causality* since it emphasised the causal analysis of various quantities of objects. Here we refer to the concepts introduced in [2] as *static causality* to better contrast it to correlative (statistical) causality and to emphasise the fact that the causal analysis is performed without direct reference to the evolution of a system. This approach requires a reaction model representing the membrane system under consideration. Along this research line, if a set of rules is not known, a question arises: *"is it possible to study causality starting from a set of experimental data"*?

The aim of this work is twofold. Firstly, it introduces the two approaches that we developed to study cause-effect relationships. Secondly, it proposes a framework which integrates the two approaches in order to study static causality by means of membrane systems, from temporal series of data collected on the concentration of different reactants. It integrates two different methods. In a first step, interrelations between elements are interpreted by means of correlation analysis and measures of similarity based on time-lagged time series. In this way, a set of rules modelling statistical causalities is inferred. This set can give us indication about the network topology of the reactions and the regulative mechanisms in the phenomena under study. In a second step, this set of rules is used to building up a reaction model useful to study static causality by means of membrane systems.

The paper is organized as follows. Section 2 recalls the concepts of membrane systems and multisets, and introduces static causality over multisets of objects. In Section 3, a theoretical network analysis which can be used to distinguish statistical causal interactions in biological pathways starting from pure observations of species dynamics is described. Section 4 proposes a procedure to integrate the two approaches, while Section 5 considers two case studies. Finally, Section 6 ends the paper by some discussions on the proposed approach and some possible future theoretical studies useful to analyze the relationships between static and correlative causality.

2   Static Causality in Membrane Systems

Membrane computing is a branch of natural computing, the area of research concerned with computation taking place in nature and with human-designed computing inspired by nature. Membrane computing abstracts computing models from the architecture and the functioning of living cells, as well as from the organization of cells in tissues, organs and, brain.

A transition P system is the simplest form of membrane system consisting of a hierarchy of nested membranes, each membrane containing objects, rules and possibly other membranes. The hierarchy of membranes models the compartments of the biological pathway, the objects represent the species in each compartments, and the rules correspond to the biochemical reactions forming the pathways. The rules are considered to be applied in a maximally parallel manner. The simplest form of transition P system is the one with only one membrane, which basically consists of a set of rules and possibly an initial multiset of objects.

A multiset w over a set A is a function $w : A \rightarrow \mathbb{N}$ from A to the set of natural numbers $\mathbb{N}$; the multiplicity of an element $a \in A$ is $w(a)$. We denote the empty multiset having multiplicity 0 for all $a \in A$ by 0_A, or simply by 0 if the set A is clear from the context. When describing a multiset characterized by, for example, $w(a) = 4$, $w(b) = 2$ and $w(c) = 0$ for $c \in A \backslash \{a, b\}$, we use the representation $4a + 2b$. For two multisets v, w over A we say that v is contained in w if $v(a) \leq w(a)$ for all $a \in A$, and we denote this by $v \leq w$. If $v \leq w$, we can define $w - v$ by $(w - v)(a) = w(a) - v(a)$. For two multisets v and w we use the notation $v \cap w$ for the largest multiset contained in both v and w. In other words, $v \cap w$ is defined by $(v \cap w)(a) = \min\{v(a), w(a)\}$, for all $a \in A$. We denote by $v \backslash w$ the multiset $v - v \cap w$. We sometimes use the notation $a \in w$ to denote the fact that $w(a) > 0$, i.e., the multiset w contains at least one a.

Formally, a transition P system with only one membrane is a tuple $\Pi = (O, R, u_0)$, where O is an alphabet of objects, R is a set of rules, while u_0 is a multiset of objects which is initially in the membrane. Each rule r has the form $r : u \rightarrow v$, where u and v are multisets of objects and u is non-empty.

We use multisets of objects over O to represent resources available or being produced inside the membrane. Then, u_0 evolves by applying the rules in R. We use the notation $lhs(r)$ for the left hand side u of a rule of form $r : u \rightarrow v$ and similarly $rhs(r)$ for the right hand side v. Therefore, by the application of the rule r the $lhs(r)$ is being subtracted from u_0, if possible, and the $rhs(r)$ is added. In this way, the rules application models biological reactions. These notations are extended naturally to multisets of rules.

We define causality directly, for a multiset of objects v. Note that this definition differs from the presentation found in [2], where it has been obtained as a theorem describing (global) causality. Here we present it directly as a definition, in the interest of brevity.

Definition 1 (Static Causality). *A multiset of rules G is called a cause for a multiset of objects v whenever the following hold:*

- *there is no rule* r *such that* $lhs(r) \leq v \backslash rhs(G)$;
- $rhs(G) \cap v > rhs(G - r) \cap v$ *for any rule* $r \in G$.

The underlining idea for this definition is that when some (multiset of) objects v appear during the course of an evolution of a P system, we look for some (multiset of) rules G which have produced them. By producing we understand that we have an evolution step $u \overset{F}{\Longrightarrow} u'$ in which $u' \geq v$ and $F \geq G$ such that exactly the rules in G are those responsible for the apparition of v. Note that v can be written as the sum of $v \cap rhs(G)$ and $v \backslash rhs(G)$. The $v \cap rhs(G)$ part is the one produced by G since it is included in $rhs(G)$; for the remainder $v \backslash rhs(G)$ we require that it is composed only of objects which do not evolve in the considered evolution step (this is what the first condition amounts to). In other words, all the objects of v are either produced by rules of G or are not interacting with any rule. The second condition is equivalent to saying that no rule r can be subtracted from G such that the part of v produced by G remains the same - there are no "useless" rules in G with respect to producing elements of v.

To view the notions above introduced, let us consider the following example of a transition P system with only one membrane, with rules

$$r_1 : x \to a + b, r_2 : y \to b, r_3 : a + b \to y$$

and an initial multiset of objects $u_0 = x + y + 2a$. The only possible evolution is

$$x + y + 2a \overset{r_1 + r_2}{\Longrightarrow} 3a + 2b \overset{2r_3}{\Longrightarrow} a + 2y \overset{2r_2}{\Longrightarrow} a + 2b \overset{r_3}{\Longrightarrow} b + y \overset{r_2}{\Longrightarrow} 2b$$

In [2], a general inductive procedure for finding the causes of a multiset has been introduced. Here we reason directly over the example considered, loosely following the inductive procedure.

Let $v = a + b$ be the multiset for which we intend to find its causes. We start by considering the empty multiset 0 as a potential cause for v. The empty multiset is discarded because $lhs(r_3) \leq v \backslash rhs(0) = v \backslash 0$ (they are actually equal) which contradicts the first part of Definition 1. The next possible candidates for causes of v are either r_1 or r_2 or r_3. Clearly r_3 suffers from the same problem as 0, it does not fulfill the first condition of Definition 1. However, both r_1 and r_2 verify the conditions to be causes of v. The next step is to add rule r_3 to either multiset r_1 or r_2, i.e., we consider as potential causes $r_1 + r_3$ and $r_2 + r_3$. We find that rule r_3 is actually "useless" as it does not produce any object of v. In other words, r_3 has the problem that $rhs(G) \cap v = rhs(G - r_3) \cap v$ for $G = r_1 + r_3$ or $G = r_2 + r_3$. Moreover, this happens for any $G \geq r_1 + r_3$ or $G \geq r_2 + r_3$. This means that no cause of v can contain r_3. If we try $G = r_1 + r_2$, then r_2 becomes the "useless" rule: $rhs(G) \cap v = rhs(G - r_2) \cap v$. This also happens for $G \geq r_1 + r_2$. All we have left to check are either $G = k \cdot r_1$ or $G = k \cdot r_2$, for $k \geq 2$. When $G = k \cdot r_1$ we have that an instance of r_1 is a "useless" rule: $rhs(G) \cap v = rhs(G - r_1) \cap v$; in other words, any additional r_1 besides a single r_1 are "useless". The case of $G = k \cdot r_2$ for $k \geq 2$ is similar. Thus the only possible causes for $v = a + b$ are either r_1 or r_2.

3   Correlative Causality

Associations among time-series of biological entities represent at least the strength of relation between two species x_i and x_j. They can be measured by several coefficient types, which can be classified into *similarity* and *dissimilarity* measures. The first ones reflect the extent of similarity between species. The larger the similarity between x_i and x_j, the more they are similar. In contrast, dissimilarity measures reflect dissimilarities between x_i and x_j.

Correlation coefficients belong to the group of similarity measures and describe at least the magnitude of the relation between two species. As a corollary of the Cauchy-Schwarz inequality, the absolute value of each correlation coefficient cannot exceed 1. However, these coefficients can be extended in order to describe both magnitude and direction. Magnitude of a correlation represents the strength of the relation: the strength of the tendency of variables to move in the same or the opposite direction or how strong they covary across the set of observations. The larger the absolute correlation, the stronger the variables are associated. The direction of a correlation coefficient describes how two variables are associated. If such a coefficient is positive, then the two variables move in the same direction. Differently, if it is negative, then they move in opposite directions.

Consider m to be the length of time-series available for each species of a set $X = \{x_1, x_2, \ldots, x_n\}$. The time-series of x_i and x_j can be correlated directly to compute the pairwise *Pearson correlation coefficient* given by:

$$\rho(x_i, x_j) = \frac{\sum_{t=0}^{m} ((x_i[t] - \bar{x}_i)(x_j[t] - \bar{x}_j))}{\sqrt{(\sum_{t=0}^{m} (x_i[t] - \bar{x}_i)^2)(\sum_{t=0}^{m} (x_j[t] - \bar{x}_j)^2)}} \tag{1}$$

where $\bar{x}_i$ and $\bar{x}_j$ are the averages of $x_i[t]$ and $x_j[t]$, respectively. However, let us suppose that at least one between x_i and x_j is in a stable-state, and then $\rho(x_i, x_j)$ can not be defined. In this case, we assume that $\rho(x_i, x_j) = 0$ because no interesting relationships can be found between the two species.

A high Pearson correlation is an indication of coordinate and concurrent behaviours, and can be used to gain knowledge about the regulative mechanisms and then regarding cause-effect relationships. Pearson correlation values close to 1 indicate positive linear relationships between x_i and x_j, correlations equal to 0 indicate no linear associations, while correlations near to -1 indicate negative linear relationships. Namely, the closer the coefficient is to either -1 or 1, the stronger is the correlation between the variables (Fig. 1).

In particular, a high correlation between two time-series may indicate a direct interaction, an indirect interaction, or a joint regulation by a common unknown regulator (Fig. 2). However, only the direct interactions are of interest to infer the regulatory mechanisms of a biological network.

For a better illustration, let us consider a simple example consisting of three species: x_1, x_2 and x_3. Let us assume that, as represented in Fig. 3 (a), the reactions $x_1 \rightarrow x_2$ and $x_1 \rightarrow x_3$ exist, and that these reactions induce strong correlations for the pairs (x_1, x_2) and (x_1, x_3). Therefore, we also observe a strong

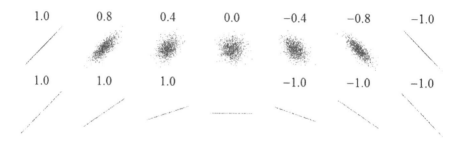

Fig. 1. Several sets of (x_i, x_j) points, with the Pearson correlation of x_i and x_j for each set. Note that the correlation reflects the noisiness and direction of a linear relationship (top row), but not the slope of that relationship (bottom row).

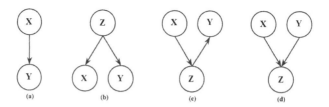

Fig. 2. Elementary interaction patterns. *(a)*: direct interaction between two species; *(b)*: regulation of two species by a common regulator; *(c)* regulative chain via an intermediate regulator; *(d)*: co-regulation of a species by two regulators.

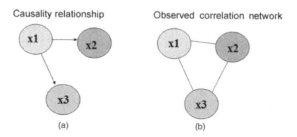

Fig. 3. (a) Illustration of causal relationships between variables (x_1, x_2) and (x_1, x_3), and (b) the resulting network derived by correlation analysis

correlation of the pair (x_2, x_3), which might jeopardize downstream network analysis by putting an (non oriented) edge between x_2 and x_3, Fig. 3 (b), because there will be more weight placed to the nodes x_2 and x_3 than there actually is.

Since Pearson correlation alone cannot distinguish between direct and indirect interactions, the use of *partial correlation* can be useful to analyze if a direct interaction between two time-series exists [10]. The *minimum first order partial correlation* between x_i and x_j is defined as:

$$\rho_{C_1}(x_i, x_j) = \min_{k \neq i,j} |\rho(x_i, x_j \mid x_k)| \tag{2}$$

where

$$\rho(x_i, x_j \mid x_k) = \frac{\rho(x_i, x_j) - \rho(x_i, x_k)\rho(x_j, x_k)}{\sqrt{(1 - \rho(x_i, x_k)^2)(1 - \rho(x_j, x_k)^2))}}. \tag{3}$$

If there is $x_k \neq x_i, x_j$ which explains all the correlation between x_i and x_j, then $\rho_{C_1}(x_i, x_j) \cong 0$ and the pair (x_i, x_j) is conditionally independent given x_k. In this case, we say that on an undirected graph x_i and x_j are not adjacent but separated by x_k. Therefore, if $\rho_{C_1}(x_i, x_j)$ is smaller than a given threshold, then we consider that there isn't a significant interaction between x_i and x_j. From the definition, we have that if $x_i[t] = x_k[t]$ or $x_j[t] = x_k[t]$, for all t, then (3) is not defined. In this case, we set $\rho(x_i, x_j \mid x_k) = 0$.

The first order partial correlation allows us to remove many false positives computed by Pearson correlation alone. However, low values of the coefficients (1) and (2) guarantee that an interaction between two time-series is missing, while high values of (2) do not guarantee that two time-series interact. Therefore, we consider $\rho_{C_{all}}(x_i, x_j)$, which describes the partial correlation between x_i and x_j conditioned on all the other $n - 2$ species. We follow this strategy because it is possible that the correlation conditioned to a single species is high, but the correlation conditioned to all the other species is low. Let Ω be the correlation matrix of the n species of X, that is the $n \times n$ matrix whose (i, j)-th entry is $\rho(x_i, x_j)$. A very powerful result allows us to compute $\rho_{C_{all}}(x_i, x_j)$ by using Ω^{-1} [13]. In fact, we have

$$\rho_{C_{all}}(x_i, x_j) = -\frac{\omega_{i,j}}{\sqrt{\omega_{i,i}\omega_{j,j}}} \tag{4}$$

where $\omega_{i,j}$ is the (i, j)-th entry of Ω^{-1}. The critical step in the application of (4) is the reliable estimation of the inverse of the correlation matrix when Ω is either singular or else numerically very close to singularity. We apply the *spectral decomposition*, which is based on the use of eigenvalues and eigenvectors, to compute Ω^{-1}. According to the spectral decomposition, a rank-deficient matrix can be decomposed into a smaller number of factors than the original matrix and still preserve all of the information in the matrix.

The following definition provides the rules to infer direct interactions among species and represents the first step in order to study correlative cause-effect relationships among them.

Definition 2 (Directed Correlation). *We say that two time-series x_i and x_j are directly correlated if indexes $|\rho(x_i, x_j)|$ and $|\rho_{C_{all}}(x_i, x_j)|$ are above two fixed thresholds.*

Although a combination in the use of Pearson and partial correlation can be viewed as a technique to develop new hypothesis of interactions among biochemical components [7], we point out that the study of time-shifts in biological data-sets can be useful to infer causality interactions. With the term causality, we intend that the analysis of interactions establishes a directional pattern in which species action may trigger or suppress and be triggered or suppressed by the actions of other species in the network. Although this causal connectivity alone is not sufficient to fully describe the dynamics of a network, it reveals the logic of the systems which constraints its potential behaviour. In more detail, a direct causal relationship $x_1 \to x_2$ implies that the time-series of x_1 "influences" the time-series of x_2. An indirect causal relationship $x_1 \to x_{i_1} \to x_{i_2} \to \ldots \to x_{i_k} \to x_2$ is a link from x_1 to x_2 through a sequence of direct casual relationships involving a set of one or more intermediates species $x_{i_1}, x_{i_2}, \ldots x_{i_k}$.

Usually, cell biologists use perturbations to prove the existence of cause-effect relationships in biological pathways. An interesting hypothesis is that biological networks constitute dynamical systems which are continuously subjects to fluctuations and oscillations due to changes in the environment as well as to patterns of regulations [17,18]. Dynamics changes induce variability in species concentrations, propagate through the networks and generate emergent patterns of *time-lagged correlations*. Therefore time-lags are ubiquitous in biological systems. As a simple example, Fig. 4 shows an experimental result in which a time delay τ_1 between two genes is present. This implies that biological network topologies, and then causality, involve many interlocked network motifs which have inherent delays.

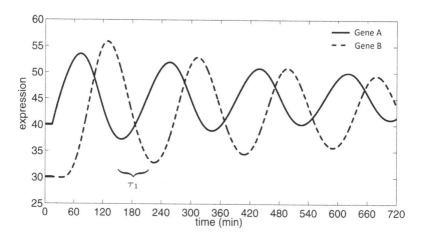

Fig. 4. A gene expression experimental result where time lag τ_1 could be an indication of an underlying cascade of biochemical reactions

Then, if we conduce computational experiments which allow the comparison of shifted behaviours, it could be possible to identify directed causal-effect relationships between time-series. This is rooted on the fact that time indicates directionality: what happens first ought to be upstream of what happens next [20].

Cross-correlation can be applied to infer causal-effect relationships among time-series. It extends Pearson correlation [6] by determining the best correlations among variables shifted in time. For time-series x_i and x_j of length m, the cross-correlation at lag τ is defined as:

$$\phi(x_i, x_j, \tau) = \frac{\sum_{t=0}^{m-\tau} ((x_i[t] - \bar{x}_i)(x_j[t + \tau] - \bar{x}_j))}{\sqrt{(\sum_{t=0}^{m} (x_i[t] - \bar{x}_i)^2)(\sum_{t=0}^{m} (x_j[t] - \bar{x}_j)^2)}}. \tag{5}$$

In particular, if at least one between x_i and x_j is in a stable-state, then we set $\phi(x_i, x_j, \tau) = 0$ because stable-state is an indication that a species is not involved in a cause-effect relationships.

By using the cross-correlation we introduce a definition of cause-effect between time-series which extends that of directed correlation. This concept of causality rests on the fact that predictability can be tested by determining if one time-series is related to past or current values of another time-series.

Definition 3 (Cross-Correlation Causality). *We say that a time-series x_i causes another time-series x_j with lag τ if*

$$\max_{\theta} \{|\phi(x_i, x_j, \theta)|\} = |\phi(x_i, x_j, \tau)|. \tag{6}$$

Let us assume that x_i causes x_j with a lag τ_1, $x_i \overset{\tau_1}{\to} x_j$, but that there is x_z such that an indirect causal relationship $x_i \to x_z \to x_j$ exists. Given τ_1, we consider the *first order partial cross-correlation* to correct for the delayed effect of x_z on the cross-correlation between x_i and x_j:

$$\phi_{C_1}(x_i, x_j) = \min_{0 \leq \tau_2 < \tau_1} |\psi(x_i, x_j, \tau_1 \mid x_z, \tau_2)| \tag{7}$$

where

$$\psi(x_i, x_j, \tau_1 \mid x_z, \tau_2) = \frac{\phi(x_i, x_j, \tau_1) - \phi(x_i, x_z, \tau_2)\rho(x_j^{\tau_1}, x_z^{\tau_2})}{\sqrt{(1 - \phi(x_i, x_z, \tau_2)^2)(1 - \rho(x_j^{\tau_1}, x_z^{\tau_2})^2)}} \tag{8}$$

with

$$(x_k[t] \mid t = 0, 1, \ldots, m - \tau_1, k = i, j, z),$$

$$(x_j^{\tau_1}[t] \mid t = \tau_1, \tau_1 + 1, \ldots, m),$$

$$(x_z^{\tau_2}[t] \mid t = \tau_2, \tau_2 + 1, \ldots, m - \tau_1 + \tau_2).$$

Extending the observation introduced for partial-correlation, we have that if x_i and x_j are correlated with a certain lag τ_1, and if there is $x_z \neq x_i, x_j$ which explains all the correlation between x_i and x_j by considering a lag $\tau_2 < \tau_1$, then $\phi_{C_1}(x_i, x_j) \cong 0$ and the pair (x_i, x_j) is conditionally independent given x_k. In this case, we say that x_i does not directly cause x_j, $x_i \overset{\tau_1}{\to} x_j$, but that an indirect causal relationship between them exists, that is, $x_i \overset{\tau_2}{\to} x_z \overset{\tau_1 - \tau_2}{\to} x_j$. Therefore, if $\rho_{C_1}(x_i, x_j)$ is smaller than a given threshold, then we consider that there isn't a significant direct cause-effect relationship between x_i and x_j. From the definition, we have that if $x_i[t] = x_z[t + \tau_2]$ or $x_j[t] = x_z[t + \tau_2]$, for $t = 0, 1, m - \tau_1$, then (8) is not defined. In this case, we set $\psi(x_i, x_j, \tau_1 \mid x_z, \tau_2) = 0$.

As in the case of partial correlation, we can start from (7) and (8) to obtain the *partial cross-correlation* between x_i and x_j conditioned on all the other $n - 2$ species in the set $Z = X - \{x_i, x_j\}$:

$$\phi_{C_{all}}(x_i, x_j) = \min_{0 \leq \tau_2 < \tau_1} |\psi(x_i, x_j, \tau_1 \mid Z, \tau_2)|. \tag{9}$$

Also in this case, we apply the spectral decomposition to compute $\phi_{C_{all}}(x_i, x_j)$, where Ω is the correlation matrix of the n columns of the matrix $\Psi \in \mathbb{R}^{(1+m-\tau_1+1) \times n}$ obtained in this way. The first column represents the time-series of x_i, that is, $(x_i[t] \mid t = 0, 1, \ldots, m - \tau_1)$, the second one the time-series of x_j, namely, $(x_j[t] \mid t = \tau_1, \tau_1 + 1, \ldots, m)$, while the last $n - 2$ columns are related to the time-series of the species in Z, that is, $(x_z[t] \mid t = \tau_2, \tau_2+1, \ldots, m-\tau_1+\tau_2)$ for each $z \in Z$.

Starting from the introduced analysis, we can give the definition of directed cross-correlation causality. It provides us with an intuitive way to express causal knowledge by extending the definition of directed correlation.

Definition 4 (Directed Cross-Correlation Causality). *We say that a time-series x_i directly causes another time-series x_j with lag τ_1 if: i) x_i causes x_j with lag τ_1 as in Definition 3; ii) $\phi_{C_{all}}(x_i, x_j)$ is above a fixed threshold.*

The directed cross-correlation causality relies on two piece of information to infer a cause-effect relationship. The first one is the time, which indicates directionality. The second one is the partial cross-correlation, which gives us knowledge about the existence of a directed relation of cause-effect.

4   From Correlative to Static Causality

In this section, we integrate the two approaches introduced in Section 2 and 3 to study causalities in membrane systems.

Let us suppose to have a set $X = \{x_1, x_2, \ldots, x_n\}$ of species for which time-series of length m are available. In a first phase, correlative causality is used to infer a set R of rules for a transition P system as follows. For each $x_i \in X$, a set C_{x_i}, that we call *direct correlation set*, is obtained by using Definition 2. Namely, C_{x_i} contains all the species in the set $X - \{x_i\}$ which are directly correlated with x_i. Moreover, a set D_{x_i}, named *direct causality set*, is obtained by applying Definition 4. That is, $x_j \in X - \{x_i\}$ is in D_{x_i} if x_i directly causes x_j for some lag τ_1. Then the set R contains exactly the following rules:

1. $\{r_i : x_i \rightarrow \alpha_i\}$, for each $x_i \in X$ such that $C_{x_i} \neq \emptyset$, where α_i is the multiset corresponding to the set C_{x_i}, with multiplicity one for each element;
2. $\{r^i : \alpha_i \rightarrow x_i\}$, for each $x_i \in X$ such that $C_{x_i} \neq \emptyset$, where α_i is equal to the one introduced in the previous point;

3. $\{r_{ij} : x_i \to \beta_j\}$, for each $x_i \in X$ and each $x_j \in D_{x_i}$ such that $D_{x_i} \neq \emptyset$, where β_j is the multiset corresponding to the set $\{x_j\} \cup C_{x_j}$, with multiplicity one for each element.

Note that there can be rules which have different labels but are identical, for example if $C_x = \{y\}$ then $r^x = r_y$ and $r_x = r^y$.

By applying the above procedure to preliminary case studies, we inferred the network topology of the reactions and the regulative mechanisms from time-series of reaction models modelling synthetic metabolic phenomena. In particular, since experiments conducted under identical conditions do not necessarily lead to identical results, we also focused on different factors causing this variability, such as, enzymatic variability, intrinsic variability, and environmental variability[2]. This is due to the fact that the rules that constitute the set R reflect the meanings of the statistical indexes that we introduced in Section 3. The rules introduced at the first two points represent the fact that correlation and cross-correlation do not give information about the direction of cause-effect interactions, and then we have to consider both the verses of the possible relationships. From a biological point of view, these types of cause-effects interactions can be the result of regulative mechanisms governing the behaviours of the system under investigation. Differently, the rules introduced at the third point model the causality relationships due both to the biological network topology and regulative mechanisms. This combination induces dynamic changes and variability in species concentrations which have inherent delays, giving us knowledge about the existence of directed relations of cause-effect.

In a second phase, the sets X and R are used for building up a model useful to associate correlative causality and static causality by means of membrane systems, namely a transition P system $\Pi = (X, R, u_0)$ with one membrane. Using it we can analyze the situations which lead to at least one x_i to appear and compare them to their correlative counterpart.

Proposition 1. *Consider $x_i \in X$. Then any possible cause for x_i is either 0_R (the empty multiset of rules) or it is a multiset r with just one element.*

Proof. We show that any cause G for the multiset x_i in Π has at most one element. Suppose that G has at least two elements. From Definition 1 we have that $rhs(G) \cap x_i > rhs(G - r) \cap x_i$ for any $r \in G$. By the definition of $\cap$, $rhs(G) \cap x_i$ is either x_i or 0. From the previous inequality, $rhs(G)$ cannot be 0; thus $rhs(G) = x_i$. Hence x_i is an element of the right hand side of some rule $s \in G$. Since G has at least two elements there exists some $s' \in R$, not necessarily

---

[2] To mimic enzymatic variability a random variation of approximately $\pm 10\%$ has been introduced by multiplying each metabolic flux values with a random number from a normal distribution with unit mean and 0.05 standard deviation. To induce intrinsic variability we add a stochastic term to each substance of the system. This term is a random number from unit Normal distribution. In order to generate data subject to environmental variability, we add a stochastic term only to the flux associated with the reactions which introduce matter in the system.

different from s, such that $G \geq s+s'$, which is equivalent to $G-s' \geq s$. Therefore $rhs(G) \cap x_i = x_i = rhs(G - s') \cap x_i$ which contradicts G being a cause for x_i.

We show that each possible cause of x_i corresponds to a certain correlation of x_i as a time-series with the other time-series in X. In Proposition 2 we show that for a time-series x_i not to be cross-correlated with any other time-series nor to cause any other time-series is equivalent to the object x_i having the empty multiset of rules as cause in Π.

Proposition 2. *The empty multiset of rules 0_R is a cause for x_i in Π if and only if both C_{x_i} and D_{x_i} are empty.*

Proof. If 0_R is a cause for x_i then it follows that there is no rule $r \in R$ such that $lhs(r) \leq x_i$, which is equivalent to saying that x_i cannot be the left hand side of any rule, therefore both C_{x_i} and D_{x_i} are empty.

If both C_{x_i} and D_{x_i} are empty then there is no rule $r \in R$ such that $lhs(r) \leq x_i \backslash rhs(0_R) = x_i$ therefore the first condition of Definition 1 is fulfilled. The second condition follows immediately since there is no rule r such that $r \in 0_R$.

In the next proposition we show that having certain rules which correspond to a time-series x_j as causes for x_i is equivalent to x_i *i)* being directly correlated with x_j, *ii)* being directly caused by x_j or *iii)* being directly correlated with a time-series directly caused by x_j.

Proposition 3. *Consider $x_i \in X$. Then the following hold:*

1. *r_j is a cause for $x_i \Leftrightarrow x_i \in C_{x_j} \Leftrightarrow r_i$ is a cause for x_j;*
2. *r^j is a cause for $x_i \Leftrightarrow i = j$ and $C_{x_i} \neq \emptyset$;*
3. *r_{jk} is a cause for $x_i \Leftrightarrow x_i \in C_{x_k}$, or $i = k$ and $x_i \in D_{x_j}$.*

Proof. We start by showing that for any rule s, the multiset $G = s$ is a cause for x_i in Π if and only if $x_i \in rhs(s)$.

If $x_i \in rhs(s)$ then the first condition of Definition 1 is always fulfilled, since $x_i \backslash rhs(G) = 0$ and therefore there exists no rule r such that $lhs(r) \leq x_i \backslash rhs(G)$. The second condition follows from $r \in G$ implies $r = s$, thus $rhs(G - r) \cap x_i = 0 < rhs(G) \cap x_i = x_i$.

If $G = s$ is a cause for x_i then $rhs(s) \cap x_i > 0$ (supposing otherwise would contradict the second condition of Definition 1), i.e., $x_i \in rhs(s)$.

Therefore r_j is a cause for x_i iff $x_i \in \alpha_j$, which is equivalent to $x_i \in C_{x_j}$. However direct correlation is symmetrical therefore it is equivalent to $x_j \in C_{x_i}$. The latter is equivalent to $x_j \in \alpha_i = rhs(r_i)$, which is equivalent to r_i is a cause for x_j.

We have that r^j is a cause for x_i iff $x_i = x_j$ and $C_{x_j} = C_{x_i} \neq \emptyset$. We have that r_{jk} is a cause for x_i iff $x_i \in \{x_k\} \cap C_{x_k}$, which amounts to $x_i \in C_{x_k}$, or $i = k$ and $x_i \in D_{x_j}$.

When we consider just one time-series, static causality corresponds to both direct correlation and to direct causality in the correlative causality framework.

For the case of several time-series considered together with multiplicities, we need more data regarding the sets C_{x_i} and D_{x_i} to advance the correspondences between correlative and static causalities. A start towards establishing such correspondences is made in the following section by analyzing two case studies.

5   Case Studies

In this section we consider two examples which indicate how we can study in a more general manner static causality starting from correlative causality. For the second one, we set 0.7 (a value indicating high correlation) as threshold for correlations and cross-correlations, and 0.2 as threshold for partial correlations.

5.1   The Yeast Glycolytic Network

Glycolysis is at the heart of classical biochemistry and, as such, it has been thoroughly studied. Glycolysis is the metabolic pathway that converts glucose into pyruvate. The free energy released in this process is used to form the high-energy compounds, ATP (adenosine triphosphate) and NADH (reduced nicotinamide adenine dinucleotide). It is a definite sequence of ten reactions involving several intermediate compounds. The intermediates provide entry points to glycolysis. For example, most monosaccharides, such as fructose, glucose, and galactose, can be converted to one of these intermediates. The intermediates may also be directly useful. For instance, the intermediate dihydroxyacetone phosphate is a source of the glycerol that combines with fatty acids to form fat.

We applied our framework on the first reactions from the upper part of glycolysis pathway of Saccharomyces cerevisiae. These reactions represent the pathway which leads to the degradation of glucose in order to yield energy and building blocks for cellular processes. In [14], this pathway, as well as the reactions balancing the energy currency ATP and ADP, have been translated into a Metabolic P system[3]. This formulation provided us dynamics in accordance with experimental values observed in [19] and differential models developed in [9]. Starting from these dynamics, we applied the correlative framework to infer a set R of rules modelling statistical causality associated with the glycolisis pathway. Entering into the details, we have a set of species $X = \{Fruc6P, Gluc6P, Fruc16P2, AMP, ATP, ADP\}$ having the following directed correlation sets: $C_{Fruc6P} = \{Gluc6P, Fruc16P2\}$, $C_{Gluc6P} = \{Fruc6P\}$, $C_{Fruc16P2} = \{Fruc6P\}$, $C_{ATP} = \{AMP\}$, $C_{AMP} = \{ATP\}$, $C_{ADP} = \emptyset$. Moreover, we inferred the following sets expressing cause-effect relationships: $D_{Fruc6P} = \{ATP, AMP\}$, $D_{Gluc6P} = \{ATP, AMP\}$, $D_{Fruc16P2} = \{ADP\}$, $D_{ATP} = \emptyset$, $D_{AMP} = \emptyset$, $D_{ADP} = \emptyset$.

After that, the set R composed by the rules reported in Table 1 has been obtained by applying the procedure introduced in Section 4, and the transition P system $\Pi = (X, R)$ has been used as starting point to analyze static causality according with the approach described in Section 2.

---

[3] Metabolic P systems [12] are a class of deterministic P systems introduced for expressing biological phenomena.

Table 1. The set of rules modelling correlative causality of the yeast glycolytic network

r_{Fruc6P} :	$Fruc6P$	$\to Fruc16P2 + Gluc6P$
r^{Fruc6P} :	$Fruc16P2 + Gluc6P$	$\to Fruc6P$
r_{Gluc6P} :	$Gluc6P$	$\to Fruc6P$
r^{Gluc6P} :	$Fruc6P$	$\to Gluc6P$
$r_{Fruc16P2}$:	$Fruc16P2$	$\to Fruc6P$
$r^{Fruc16P2}$:	$Fruc6P$	$\to Fruc16P2$
$r_{ATP} = r^{AMP}$:	ATP	$\to AMP$
$r^{ATP} = r_{AMP}$:	AMP	$\to ATP$
$r_{Fruc6P,ATP} = r_{Fruc6P,AMP}$:	$Fruc6P$	$\to ATP + AMP$
$r_{Gluc6P,ATP} = r_{Gluc6P,AMP}$:	$Gluc6P$	$\to ATP + AMP$
$r_{Fruc16P2,ADP}$:	$Fruc16P2$	$\to ADP$

Let us consider $v = ATP + AMP$. We look for the possible causes for this multiset, which corresponds to considering two time-series together. To find its causes, we start by considering $G = 0_R$ as a potential cause. Then we proceed by adding rules to 0_R, one by one, until no more are needed to make v appear. More details regarding this inductive procedure for finding the cause of a multiset can be found in [2].

For $G = 0_R$ the condition $lhs(r) \leq v \backslash rhs(G)$ does not take place for $r = r_{ATP}$; from the point of view of correlative causality, this corresponds to saying that ATP is directly correlated with another time-series therefore it cannot have an empty cause. We continue by adding to the (now discarded) potential cause 0_R rules r which have in the right hand side $rhs(r)$ at least one common element with v. The set of these rules is $S = \{r_{ATP}, r_{AMP}, r_{Fruc6P,ATP}\}$. For $G_1 = G + s$, $s \in S \backslash \{r_{Fruc6P,ATP}\}$ the condition $lhs(r) \leq v \backslash rhs(G_1)$ remains unfulfilled, since either ATP or AMP will appear in $v \backslash rhs(G_1)$ and both of them are left hand sides of rules. So we choose $G_1 = r_{Fruc6P,ATP}$ and it verifies that it is a cause for v. To find the other causes, we look at the discarded causes with one element (i.e., to the rules from S) and add one element from S to each of them, namely we consider all the multisets with two elements of S. By checking all of them we find that $r_{ATP} + r_{AMP}$ is a cause for v. Note that $r_{Fruc6P,ATP}$ cannot be a part of a cause with two elements since that rule alone is sufficient in producing v. Moreover, there is no cause with more than two elements since having three or more rules in G would mean that one of them does not contribute to the appearance of the two elements of v. In the end, we have obtained that the causes of v are $r_{Fruc6P,ATP}$ and $r_{ATP} + r_{AMP}$. This corresponds to the time-series $Gluc6P$ and $Fruc6P$ being direct causes for ATP and AMP (recall that $r_{Fruc6P,ATP} = r_{Gluc6P,ATP}$) and to ATP being directly correlated with AMP.

5.2   The Signal Transduction Cascades

Cyclic motifs are extremely common in biochemical networks. They can be found in metabolic, genetic, and particularly signaling pathways. These motifs are often composed in order to form a vertical signaling cascade, which have been used in [8] to model the mitotic oscillator in early amphibian embryos involving cyclin and cdc2 kinase, Fig. 5. Cyclin is synthesized at a constant rate, v_i, and triggers, in a first cycle, the transformation of inactive (i.e., phosphorylated), m^+, into active, m (i.e., dephosphorylated), cdcd2 kinase by enhancing the rate of a phosphatase. A kinase reverts this modification by allowing the transformation from m to m^+. In the second cascade cycle, cdc2 kinase drives the transformation from the inactive, x^+, into the active, x, form of a protease which degrades the cyclin. This second cycle is closed by a reaction regulated by a protease, which elicits the transition from x to x^+. The constants V_i, $1 \le i \le 4$, represent the kinetics of the enzyme involved in the two cycles of post-translation modification. The dynamics of this model, obtained by a numerical solution of the set of differential equations proposed in [8], considering the initial conditions $c = 0.01 \mu M$ and $m = x = 0.01$, shows an oscillatory behaviour in the activation of the three model's substances, that repeatedly go through a state in which cells enter in a mitotic cycle. We sampled the dynamics with $\tau = 1$ minute to obtain 100 macro observation of the substances' dynamics. After that, we studied correlative causality among the substances. As it was expected, since in a cyclic motif the concentration of species activated by a stimulus have a constant amount, we obtained that both $\rho(m^+, m)$ and $\rho(m^+, m)$ are approximately equal to -1, and both $|\rho_{C_{all}}(m^+, m)|$ and $|\rho_{C_{all}}(m^+, m)|$ are above 0.2. Moreover, we found a statistical significant cross-correlation, with $\tau = 3$ minutes between c and m, and between m and x. These results are in accordance with the cascade model for mitotic oscillation in early amphibian embryos, and allowed us to obtain the set R of rules modelling statistical cause-effect relationships reported in Table 2.

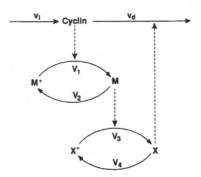

Fig. 5. The Goldbeter's cascade model for mitotic oscillation in early amphibian embryos [8]

We consider the multiset $v = 2x + x^+$ which corresponds to considering the time-series x with doubled values together with the time-series x^+. Since x and x^+ are left hand sides for some of the rules in R it follows that for any cause

Table 2. The set of rules modelling correlative causality in the mitotic oscillation in early amphibian embryos

$$
\begin{array}{lll}
r_x = r^{x^+} : & x & \to x^+ \\
r_{x^+} = r^x : & x^+ & \to x \\
r_m = r^{m^+} : & m & \to m^+ \\
r_{m^+} = r^m : & m^+ & \to m \\
r_{c,m} = r_{c,m^+} : & c & \to m + m^+ \\
r_{m,x} = r_{m,x^+} : & m & \to x + x^+ \\
r_{m^+,x} = r_{m^+,x^+} : & m^+ & \to x + x^+
\end{array}
$$

G we must have $v\backslash rhs(G) = 0$ which implies $v \leq rhs(G)$. As reasoned before, G can have at most three elements since a fourth element would not contribute anything to the appearance of v. These elements must belong to the set $S = \{r_x, r_{x^+}, r_{m,x}, r_{m^+,x}\}$ since their right hand side must have at least one object in common with v. By analyzing all possibilities we obtain that the causes of v are $r_{x^+} + r_{m,x}$; $r_{x^+} + r_{m^+,x}$; $r_{m,x} + r_{m^+,x}$; $2r_{m,x}$; $2r_{m^+,x}$ and $2r_{x^+} + r_x$. This corresponds, according with the biological point of view of the mitotic cascade, to the time-series m and m^+ being direct causes for x and x^+ (which indicates that x^+ is directly correlated with x).

6 Conclusions and Discussions

In this paper we introduced two approaches to analyze cause-effect relationships in reaction models and we proposed a way to integrate them in order to study causality in terms of multisets of objects and multisets of rules in presence of non-determinism and parallelism. Our approach is based on the fact that statistical analysis can be used to build up a transition P system in a polynomial complexity time. In fact, the computation of the different correlation indexes that we use has polynomial order on the number n of species. From a computational point of view, this means that it can become time expensive for n of the order of thousands. However, this problem can be circumvented by using a parallel implementation of the procedure, but it is not the aim of the paper to analyse this point.

An important point is that the inferred transition P systems can be analyzed by means of static causality. The statistical approach that we proposed starts from the fact that dynamics changes induce variability in species concentrations, propagate through the networks and generate emergent patterns of correlations. It combines several correlation coefficients to develop similarity indexes which can be interpreted as fingerprint of underlying cause-effect events in biological pathways. In particular, since experiments conducted under identical conditions do not necessarily lead to identical results, we also focused, in Section 4, on different factors causing this variability. In fact, the computation of correlation indexes from experimental data is necessarily complicate by uncertainty due to measurements errors, natural fluctuations, noise, artifacts, unexpected external variations effecting the experiment and missing data. As a consequence, noise can affect the correlative signals, by making it weak. Therefore, the correlative analysis that we described should take these uncertainties into account as it could influence the correlation estimates and the predictive accuracy of the resulting P system model.

As an ulterior step, to fix this problem, an initial phase of data preparation and preprocessing could be applied [4]. It has to involve the elimination of both noise and artifacts from experimental data. Let us consider a set of experimental data obtained by sampling, possibly at a constant rate τ, substance concentrations and chemo-physical parameter values of a certain biochemical system. To remove artifacts from substance and parameter time-series, we can consider *curve fitting methods*[4] which are often employed to find a smooth curve which fits noisy data by reducing their random component while preserving the main trend of the dynamics under investigation. Of course, if data are affected by other kinds of errors regarding, for instance, consistency, integrity, or outliers, then ad hoc techniques must be used [16], but it is out of the scope of this paper to consider particular methods to process raw data. After such a preprocessing of experimental data, we assume that fluctuations and measurement errors are normally distributed around the average trend of the system dynamics, therefore each observed substance and parameter time-series is fitted by a smooth function using least-squares theory.

The transition P system Π which is defined based on the correlative causality relations provides a correspondence between the static and the correlative notions of causality. When considering a time-series as an object of the transition P system, its causes can either be nonexistent, which shows that the time-series is not correlated to any other or it can be a single rule, which serves to pinpoint the set of directly correlated or directly caused time-series. It remains to be seen how these results presented in Section 4 can be extended to a more varied combination of time-series (which corresponds to a generic multiset in Π). The case studies in Section 5 present the static-correlative correspondence for more general cases.

Finally, we would like to point out that when causality is extracted by means of correlative relations between time-series, then it has to be present between variables generating the observed data. This does not imply that all the cases of causality can be discovered in this way. Of course, other more complex relations can remain hidden or misunderstood. However, when observed phenomena are produced by big population dynamics, the methods is statistically reliable. This is the case of a lot of important biological processes due to the molecule

---

[4] Curve fitting is the process of constructing a curve which has the best fit to a series of data points. Curve fitting can involve either interpolation, where an exact fit to the data is required, or smoothing, in which a "smooth" function is constructed that approximately fits the data.

population interactions. When causes depend on the actions of single or few molecules, of course, statistics is out of order.

Acknowledgements. We thank the anonymous reviewers for their helpful comments. The work of the authors from Iaşi was supported by a grant of the Romanian National Authority for Scientific Research, CNCS-UEFISCDI, project number PN-II-ID-PCE-2011-3-0919.

References

1. Agrigoroaiei, O., Ciobanu, G.: Rule-based and Object-based Event Structures for Membrane Systems. Journal of Logic and Algebraic Programming 79(6), 295–303 (2010)
2. Agrigoroaiei, O., Ciobanu, G.: Quantitative Causality in Membrane Systems. In: Gheorghe, M., Păun, G., Rozenberg, G., Salomaa, A., Verlan, S. (eds.) CMC 2011. LNCS, vol. 7184, pp. 62–72. Springer, Heidelberg (2012)
3. Busi, N.: Causality in Membrane Systems. In: Eleftherakis, G., Kefalas, P., Păun, G., Rozenberg, G., Salomaa, A. (eds.) WMC 2007. LNCS, vol. 4860, pp. 160–171. Springer, Heidelberg (2007)
4. Castellini, A., Franco, G., Pagliarini, R.: Data analysis pipeline from laboratory to MP models. Natural Computing 10(1), 55–76 (2011)
5. Ciobanu, G., Lucanu, D.: Events, Causality, and Concurrency in Membrane Systems. In: Eleftherakis, G., Kefalas, P., Păun, G., Rozenberg, G., Salomaa, A. (eds.) WMC 2007. LNCS, vol. 4860, pp. 209–227. Springer, Heidelberg (2007)
6. Fisher, R.A.: On the Mathematical Foundations of Theoretical Statistics. Philosophical Transactions of the Royal Society of London. Series A, Containing Papers of a Mathematical or Physical Character 222, 309–368 (1922)
7. Fuente, A., Bing, N., Hoeschele, I., Mendes, P.: Discovery of meaningful associations in genomic data using partial correlation coefficients. Bioinformatics 20(18), 3565–3574 (2004)
8. Goldbeter, A.: A Minimal cascade model for the mitotic oscillator involving cyclin and cdc2 Kinase. PNAS 88(20), 9107–9111 (1991)
9. Hynne, F., Danø, S., Sørensen, P.G.: Full-scale model of glycolysis in saccharomyces cerevisiae. Biophysical Chemistry 94(1-2), 121–163 (2001)
10. Junker, B.H., Schreiber, F.: Analysis of Biological Networks (Wiley Series in Bioinformatics). Wiley-Interscience (2008)
11. Kleijn, J.H.C.M., Koutny, M., Rozenberg, G.: Towards a Petri Net Semantics for Membrane Systems. In: Freund, R., Păun, G., Rozenberg, G., Salomaa, A. (eds.) WMC 2005. LNCS, vol. 3850, pp. 292–309. Springer, Heidelberg (2006)
12. Manca, V.: Fundamentals of Metabolic P Systems. In: Păun, G., Rozenberg, G., Salomaa, A. (eds.) Handbook of Membrane Computing. Oxford University Press (2009)
13. Muirhead, R.J.: Aspects of Multivariate Statistical Theory. Wiley-Interscience (2005)
14. Pagliarini, R.: Modelling and Reverse-Engineering of Biological Phenomena by means of Metabolic P Systems. PhD thesis, University of Verona, Italy (2011)
15. Păun, G.: Membrane Computing. An Introduction. Springer, Berlin (2002)
16. Pyle, D.: Data Preparation for Data Mining (The Morgan Kaufmann Series in Data Management Systems). Morgan Kaufmann (1999)

17. Steuer, R., Kurths, J., Fiehn, O., Weckwerth, W.: Interpreting correlations in metabolomic networks. Biochem. Soc. Trans. 31(Pt. 6), 1476–1478 (2003)
18. Steuer, R., Kurths, J., Fiehn, O., Weckwerth, W.: Observing and interpreting correlations in metabolomic networks. Bioinformatics 19(8), 1019–1026 (2003)
19. Theobald, U., Mailinger, W., Baltes, M., Rizzi, M., Reuss, M.: In vivo analysis of metabolic dynamics in Saccharomyces cerevisiae: I. Experimental observations. Biotechnology and Bioengineering 55(2), 305–316 (1997)
20. Vilela, M., Danuser, G.: What's wrong with correlative experiments? Nature Cell Biology 13(9), 1011 (2011)

Sublinear-Space P Systems with Active Membranes

Antonio E. Porreca, Alberto Leporati, Giancarlo Mauri, and Claudio Zandron

Dipartimento di Informatica, Sistemistica e Comunicazione
Università degli Studi di Milano-Bicocca
Viale Sarca 336/14, 20126 Milano, Italy
{porreca,leporati,mauri,zandron}@disco.unimib.it

Abstract. We introduce a weak uniformity condition for families of
P systems, **DLOGTIME** uniformity, inspired by Boolean circuit complexity. We then prove that **DLOGTIME**-uniform families of P systems
with active membranes working in logarithmic space (not counting their
input) can simulate logarithmic-space deterministic Turing machines.

1 Introduction

Research on the space complexity of P systems with active membranes [4] has
shown that these devices, when working in polynomial and exponential space,
have the same computing power of Turing machines subject to the same restrictions [7,1]. In this paper we investigate the behaviour of P systems working in
sublinear space.

This requires us, first of all, to define a meaningful notion of sublinear space
in the framework of P systems, inspired by sublinear space Turing machines,
where the size of the input is not counted as work space.

Since sublinear-space Turing machines are weaker (possibly strictly weaker)
than those working in polynomial time, we also define a uniformity condition
for the families of P systems that is weaker than the usual **P** uniformity, i.e.,
DLOGTIME uniformity, as usually employed for families of Boolean circuits [2].

Using these restrictions, we show that logarithmic-space P systems with active membranes are able to simulate logarithmic-space deterministic Turing machines, and thus to solve all problems in **L**.

2 Definitions

Here we recall the basic definition of P systems with active membranes, while
at the same time introducing an input alphabet with specific restrictions.

Definition 1. *A P system with (elementary) active membranes of initial degree*
$d \geq 1$ *is a tuple* $\Pi = (\Gamma, \Delta, \Lambda, \mu, w_1, \ldots, w_d, R)$, *where:*

- *Γ is an alphabet, i.e., a finite non-empty set of symbols, usually called*
  objects;

E. Csuhaj-Varjú et al. (Eds.): CMC 2012, LNCS 7762, pp. 342–357, 2013.
© Springer-Verlag Berlin Heidelberg 2013

- Δ is another alphabet, disjoint from Γ, called the input alphabet;
- Λ is a finite set of labels for the membranes;
- μ is a membrane structure (i.e., a rooted unordered tree, usually represented by nested brackets) consisting of d membranes enumerated by $1, \ldots, d$; furthermore, each membrane is labeled by an element of Λ in a one-to-one way;
- $w_1, \ldots, w_d$ are strings over Γ, describing the initial multisets of objects placed in the d regions of μ;
- R is a finite set of rules over $\Gamma \cup \Delta$.

Each membrane possesses, besides its label and position in μ, another attribute called *electrical charge* (or polarization), which can be either neutral (0), positive (+) or negative (−) and is always neutral before the beginning of the computation.

A description of the available kinds of rule follows. This description differs from the original definition [4] only in that new input objects may not be created during the computation.

- *Object evolution rules*, of the form $[a \to w]_h^\alpha$
  They can be applied inside a membrane labeled by h, having charge α and containing an occurrence of the object a; the object a is rewritten into the multiset w (i.e., a is removed from the multiset in h and replaced by every object in w). At most one input object $b \in \Delta$ may appear in w, and only if it also appears on the left-hand side of the rule (i.e., if $b = a$).
- *Send-in communication rules*, of the form $a \, [\,]_h^\alpha \to [b]_h^\beta$
  They can be applied to a membrane labeled by h, having charge α and such that the external region contains an occurrence of the object a; the object a is sent into h becoming b and, simultaneously, the charge of h is changed to β. If $b \in \Delta$ then $a = b$ must hold.
- *Send-out communication rules*, of the form $[a]_h^\alpha \to [\,]_h^\beta \, b$
  They can be applied to a membrane labeled by h, having charge α and containing an occurrence of the object a; the object a is sent out from h to the outside region becoming b and, simultaneously, the charge of h is changed to β. If $b \in \Delta$ then $a = b$ must hold.
- *Dissolution rules*, of the form $[a]_h^\alpha \to b$
  They can be applied to a membrane labeled by h, having charge α and containing an occurrence of the object a; the membrane h is dissolved and its contents are left in the surrounding region unaltered, except that an occurrence of a becomes b. If $b \in \Delta$ then $a = b$ must hold.
- *Elementary division rules*, of the form $[a]_h^\alpha \to [b]_h^\beta \, [c]_h^\gamma$
  They can be applied to a membrane labeled by h, having charge α, containing an occurrence of the object a but having no other membrane inside (an *elementary membrane*); the membrane is divided into two membranes having label h and charges β and γ; the object a is replaced, respectively, by b and c while the other objects in the initial multiset are copied to both membranes. If $b \in \Delta$ (resp., $c \in \Delta$) then $a = b$ and $c \notin \Delta$ (resp., $a = c$ and $b \notin \Delta$) must hold.

Each instantaneous configuration of a P system with active membranes is described by the current membrane structure, including the electrical charges, together with the multisets located in the corresponding regions. A computation step changes the current configuration according to the following set of principles:

- Each object and membrane can be subject to at most one rule per step, except for object evolution rules (inside each membrane several evolution rules can be applied simultaneously).
- The application of rules is *maximally parallel*: each object appearing on the left-hand side of evolution, communication, dissolution or elementary division rules must be subject to exactly one of them (unless the current charge of the membrane prohibits it). The same principle applies to each membrane that can be involved to communication, dissolution, or elementary division rules. In other words, the only objects and membranes that do not evolve are those associated with no rule, or only to rules that are not applicable due to the electrical charges.
- When several conflicting rules can be applied at the same time, a nondeterministic choice is performed; this implies that, in general, multiple possible configurations can be reached after a computation step.
- In each computation step, all the chosen rules are applied simultaneously (in an atomic way). However, in order to clarify the operational semantics, each computation step is conventionally described as a sequence of microsteps as follows. First, all evolution rules are applied inside the elementary membranes, followed by all communication, dissolution and division rules involving the membranes themselves; this process is then repeated to the membranes containing them, and so on towards the root (outermost membrane). In other words, the membranes evolve only after their internal configuration has been updated. For instance, before a membrane division occurs, all chosen object evolution rules must be applied inside it; this way, the objects that are duplicated during the division are already the final ones.
- The outermost membrane cannot be divided or dissolved, and any object sent out from it cannot re-enter the system again.

A *halting computation* of the P system Π is a finite sequence of configurations $\mathcal{C} = (\mathcal{C}_0, \ldots, \mathcal{C}_k)$, where $\mathcal{C}_0$ is the initial configuration, every $\mathcal{C}_{i+1}$ is reachable by $\mathcal{C}_i$ via a single computation step, and no rules can be applied anymore in $\mathcal{C}_k$. A *non-halting* computation $\mathcal{C} = (\mathcal{C}_i : i \in \mathbb{N})$ consists of infinitely many configurations, again starting from the initial one and generated by successive computation steps, where the applicable rules are never exhausted.

P systems can be used as *recognisers* by employing two distinguished objects yes and no; exactly one of these must be sent out from the outermost membrane during each computation, in order to signal acceptance or rejection respectively; we also assume that all computations are halting. If all computations starting from the same initial configuration are accepting, or all are rejecting, the P system is said to be *confluent*. If this is not necessarily the case, then we have a *non-confluent* P system, and the overall result is established as for nondeterministic Turing machines: it is acceptance iff an accepting computation exists. All P systems we will consider in this paper are confluent.

In order to solve decision problems (i.e., decide languages over an alphabet Σ), we use *families* of recogniser P systems $\Pi = \{\Pi_x : x \in \Sigma^\star\}$. Each input x is associated with a P system Π_x that decides the membership of x in the language $L \subseteq \Sigma^\star$ by accepting or rejecting. The mapping $x \mapsto \Pi_x$ must be efficiently computable for each input length [3].

Definition 2. *Let E and F be classes of functions. A family of P systems $\Pi = \{\Pi_x : x \in \Sigma^\star\}$ is said to be (E, F)-uniform if and only if*

- *There exists a function $f \in F$ such that $f(1^n) = \Pi_n$, i.e., mapping the unary representation of each natural number to an encoding of the P system processing all inputs of length n.*
- *There exists a function $e \in E$ mapping each string $x \in \Sigma^\star$ to a multiset $e(x) = w_x$ (represented as a string) over the input alphabet of Π_n, where $n = |x|$.*
- *For each $x \in \Sigma^\star$ we have $\Pi_x = \Pi_n(w_x)$, i.e., Π_x is Π_n with the multiset encoding x placed inside the input membrane.*

Generally, the above mentioned classes of functions E and F are complexity classes; in the most common uniformity condition E and F denote polynomial-time computable functions.

Any explicit encoding of Π_x is allowed as output of the construction, as long as the number of membranes and objects represented by it does not exceed the length of the whole description, and the rules are listed one by one. This restriction is enforced in order to mimic a (hypothetical) realistic process of construction of the P systems, where membranes and objects are presumably placed in a constant amount during each construction step, and require actual physical space proportional to their number; see also [3] for further details on the encoding of P systems.

Finally, we describe how space complexity for families of recogniser P systems is measured, and the related complexity classes. The following definition differs from the standard one [6] in one aspect: the input objects do not contribute to the size of the configuration of a P system. This way, only the actual working space of the P system is measured, and P systems working in sublinear space may be analysed. To the best knowledge of the authors, no previously published space complexity result is invalidated by assuming that the input multiset is not counted (the two space measures differ only by a polynomial amount).

Definition 3. *Let $\mathcal{C}$ be a configuration of a P system Π. The size $|\mathcal{C}|$ of $\mathcal{C}$ is defined as the sum of the number of membranes in the current membrane structure and the total number of objects in Γ (i.e., the non-input objects) they contain. If $\mathcal{C} = (\mathcal{C}_0, \dots, \mathcal{C}_k)$ is a halting computation of Π, then the space required by $\mathcal{C}$ is defined as*

$$|\mathcal{C}| = \max\{|\mathcal{C}_0|, \dots, |\mathcal{C}_k|\}$$

or, in the case of a non-halting computation $\boldsymbol{C} = (\mathcal{C}_i : i \in \mathbb{N})$,

$$|\boldsymbol{C}| = \sup\{|\mathcal{C}_i| : i \in \mathbb{N}\}.$$

Non-halting computations might require an infinite amount of space (in symbols $|\boldsymbol{C}| = \infty$*): for example, if the number of objects strictly increases at each computation step.*

The space required by Π *itself is then*

$$|\Pi| = \sup\{|\boldsymbol{C}| : \boldsymbol{C} \text{ is a computation of } \Pi\}.$$

Notice that $|\Pi| = \infty$ *might occur if either* Π *has a non-halting computation requiring infinite space (as described above), or* Π *has an infinite set of halting computations requiring unbounded space.*

Finally, let $\boldsymbol{\Pi} = \{\Pi_x : x \in \Sigma^\star\}$ *be a family of recogniser P systems, and let* $f \colon \mathbb{N} \to \mathbb{N}$. *We say that* $\boldsymbol{\Pi}$ *operates within space bound* f *iff* $|\Pi_x| \leq f(|x|)$ *for each* $x \in \Sigma^\star$.

By (E, F)-**MCSPACE**$_{\mathcal{D}}(f(n))$ we denote the class of languages which can be decided by (E, F)-uniform families of confluent P systems of type $\mathcal{D}$ where each $\Pi_x \in \boldsymbol{\Pi}$ operates within space bound $f(|x|)$. The class of problems solvable in (E, F)-logarithmic space is denoted by (E, F)-**LMCSPACE**$_{\mathcal{D}}$.

3   DLOGTIME-Uniform Families of P Systems

When using uniformity conditions for a family of devices, one should ensure that the chosen uniformity condition is less powerful than the devices themselves if the results deriving from the existence of such family are to be meaningful. For instance, polynomial-time uniformity [5] is acceptable when the resulting family of P systems is able to solve **NP** or **PSPACE**-complete problems (which are conjectured to be outside **P**) in polynomial time. Indeed, in this case the constructed P systems are stronger than the Turing machine constructing them (assuming **P** $\neq$ **NP** or **P** $\neq$ **PSPACE**, respectively). On the other hand, a polynomial-time uniformity condition is not appropriate when solving a problem in **P**, as the entire computation can be carried out during the construction of the family (by encoding the input instance as a **yes** or as a **no** object, which can be done in polynomial time by hypothesis), and the P systems themselves can accept or reject immediately by sending out the aforementioned object during their first computation step.

Choosing an appropriate uniformity condition is thus very important when the family of devices is, in some sense, "weak". The question has already been investigated in the setting of membrane computing by Murphy and Woods [3], where $\mathbf{AC}^0$ circuits (or, equivalently, a variant of constant-time concurrent random access machines) are used. Here we propose deterministic log-time Turing machines (the usual uniformity condition for $\mathbf{AC}^0$ circuits) themselves as a uniformity condition for P systems. In a later section we shall argue that this particularly weak construction is probably sufficient to replicate most solutions in the literature without requiring major changes.

Definition 4 (Mix Barrington, Immerman [2]). *A deterministic log-time* (**DLOGTIME**) *Turing machine is a Turing machine having a read-only input tape of length* n, *a constant number of read-write work tapes of length* $O(\log n)$, *and a read-write address tape, also of length* $O(\log n)$. *The input tape is not accessed by using a sequential tape head (as the other tapes are); instead, during each step the machine has access to the* i-*th symbol on the input tape, where* i *is the number written in binary on the address tape (if* $i \geq |n|$ *the machine reads an appropriate end-of-input symbol, such as a blank symbol). The machine is required to operate in time* $O(\log n)$.

Notice how only $O(\log n)$ bits of information of the input may be read during a **DLOGTIME** computation. These machines are able to compute the length of their input, compute sums, differences and logarithms of numbers of $O(\log n)$ bits, decode simple pairing functions on strings of length $O(\log n)$ and extract portions of the input of size $O(\log n)$ [2]. Due to their time restrictions, **DLOGTIME** machines are not used to compute the whole representation of a circuit, but rather to describe the "local" connections between the gates (by deciding the immediate predecessors and the type of a single gate [8]).

As P systems are more complicated devices than Boolean circuits, we define a *series* of predicates describing the various features. These predicates will define a function $1^n \mapsto \Pi_n$ for $n \in \mathbb{N}$.

Let $\Pi_n = (\Gamma, \Delta, \Lambda, \mu, w_1, \ldots, w_d, R)$.[1]

Alphabet. The predicate ALPHABET$(1^n, m)$ holds for a single integer m such that $\Gamma \cup \Delta \subseteq \{0,1\}^m$, i.e., each symbol of the alphabets of Π_n (whose index is provided in unary notation) can be represented as a binary number of m bits. Here m is not necessarily the *minimum* number of bits needed; we can choose a larger number of bits for simplicity, but the number must be $O(\log n)$ as the alphabet is at most polynomial in size with respect to n.

Labels. Analogously, the predicate LABELS$(1^n, m)$ is true for a single integer m such that $\Lambda \subseteq \{0,1\}^m$, with the same restrictions as the ALPHABET predicate.

Membrane Structure. The predicate OUTERMOST$(1^n, h)$ holds iff the membrane labelled by h is the outermost membrane of the P system Π_n. The predicate INSIDE$(1^n, h_1, h_2)$ holds iff the membrane labelled by h_1 is immediately contained in h_2 in the initial configuration of Π_n. The resulting graph $\mu = (V, E)$, where

$$V = \{h : \text{OUTERMOST}(1^n, h)\} \cup \{h_1 : \text{INSIDE}(1^n, h_1, h_2)\}$$

$$E = \big\{\{h_1, h_2\} : \text{INSIDE}(1^n, h_1, h_2)\big\},$$

must be a tree, where the root is identified by the predicate OUTERMOST. Furthermore, μ must be polynomial in size with respect to n. Here the labels h, h_1, h_2 are provided as strings of bits of appropriate length, as described above. The predicate INPUT$(1^n, h)$ holds iff the input membrane of Π_n is h.

---

[1] We use this simplified form for the P system instead of the more formally correct $\Pi_n = (\Gamma_n, \Delta_n, \Lambda_n, \mu_n, w_1, \ldots, w_{d_n}, R_n)$ in order to ease the notation.

Initial Multisets. For each multiset in the initial configuration of Π_n choose a fixed string $w \in \Gamma^*$ representing it. The predicate MULTISET$(1^n, h, i, a)$ holds iff the i-th symbol of the string representing the multiset contained in membrane h is a, where the symbol a is provided as a string of bits as described above. The predicate is always false for $i \geq |w|$. The length of w must be at most polynomial with respect to n.

Evolution Rules. The predicate #EVOLUTION$(1^n, h, \alpha, a, m)$ holds iff Π_n has m object evolution rules of the form $[a \to w]_h^\alpha$, where m is polynomial in n.

The right-hand side of each rule can be recovered by evaluating the predicate EVOLUTION$(1^n, h, \alpha, a, i, j, b)$, which is true when the i-th rule of the form $[a \to w]_h^\alpha$ (under any chosen, fixed total order of the rules) has $w_j = b$ (and is false for $j \geq |w|$). Once again, $|w|$ must be polynomial in n.

Other Kinds of Rules. The following predicates describe the communication, dissolution and elementary division rules of Π_n:

$$\text{SEND-IN}(1^n, h, \alpha, a, \beta, b) \quad \Longleftrightarrow \quad a\,[\,]_h^\alpha \to [b]_h^\beta \in R;$$

$$\text{SEND-OUT}(1^n, h, \alpha, a, \beta, b) \quad \Longleftrightarrow \quad [a]_h^\alpha \to [\,]_h^\beta\, b \in R;$$

$$\text{DISSOLVE}(1^n, h, \alpha, a, b) \quad \Longleftrightarrow \quad [a]_h^\alpha \to b \in R;$$

$$\text{ELEM-DIVIDE}(1^n, h, \alpha, a, \beta, b, \gamma, c) \quad \Longleftrightarrow \quad [a]_h^\alpha \to [b]_h^\beta\,[c]_h^\gamma \in R$$
$$\text{and } h \text{ is elementary.}$$

These predicates completely describe a mapping $1^n \mapsto \Pi_n$ for every $n \in \mathbb{N}$.

Definition 5. *The mapping* $1^n \mapsto \Pi_n$ *is said to be* **DLOGTIME**-*computable if all the predicates* LABELS, ALPHABET, OUTERMOST, INSIDE, INPUT, MULTISET, #EVOLUTION, EVOLUTION, SEND-IN, SEND-OUT, DISSOLVE, *and* ELEM-DIVIDE *are* **DLOGTIME**-*computable.*

Each P system Π_n will be used to process all inputs $x \in \Sigma^n$, once they have been suitably encoded as a multiset w_x over the input alphabet of Π_n.

Input Multiset. The predicate ENCODING(x, i, a) holds when the i-th object of the input multiset encoding x is a (the predicate is false if there is no i-th object). The multiset size must be polynomial with respect to $n = |x|$.

Definition 6. *The mapping* $x \mapsto w_x$ *is said to be* **DLOGTIME**-*computable iff the predicate* ENCODING *is* **DLOGTIME**-*computable.*

We are now finally able to define (**DLOGTIME, DLOGTIME**)-uniform (or (**DLT, DLT**)-uniform for brevity) families of P systems according to Definition 2.

4   Simulating Logspace Turing Machines

In this section we prove that logarithmic-space Turing machines can be simulated by logarithmic-space families of P systems with active membranes even if we use a (**DLT, DLT**) uniformity condition.

Theorem 1. *Let M be a deterministic Turing machine with an input tape (of length n) and a work tape of length $O(\log n)$. Then, there exists a $(\mathbf{DLT}, \mathbf{DLT})$-uniform family Π of confluent recogniser P systems with active membranes working in logarithmic space such that $L(M) = L(\Pi)$.*

Proof. Let $s(n) = k \log n$ be an upper bound on the length of the work tape of the Turing machine M, let Σ be the alphabet of M (including the blank symbol $\sqcup$) and Q its set of non-final states. Also, for all $n \in \mathbb{N}$, let $\ell(n)$ be the minimum number of bits required in order to represent the integers $\{0, \ldots, n-1\}$, that is, $\ell(n) = \lfloor \log(n-1) \rfloor + 1$.

The initial configuration of Π_n, the P system simulating M on inputs of length n, consists of:

- An outermost membrane labelled by $\mathbf{h}$. This membrane contains the object $q_{0,0}$, whose subscripts are written using $\ell(n)$ and $\ell(s(n))$ bits respectively. This is called the *state object*. In general, the existence of the object $q_{i,w}$ for some $q \in Q$ and $i, w \in \mathbb{N}$ indicates that the simulated Turing machine M is currently in state q and its tape heads are located on the i-th symbol on the input tape and on the w-th symbol of the work tape.
- $\ell(n)$ nested membranes labelled by $\mathbf{i}_0, \ldots, \mathbf{i}_{\ell(n)-1}$ (where the subscripts are all represented in binary with exactly $\ell(\ell(n))$ bits), called the *input tape membranes*. The innermost membrane $\mathbf{i}_0$ is the input membrane of Π_n.
- $s(n)$ membranes placed inside $\mathbf{h}$ and labelled by $\mathbf{w}_0, \ldots, \mathbf{w}_{s(n)-1}$ (using $\ell(s(n))$ bits for the subscripts), called the *work tape membranes*. Each membrane $\mathbf{w}_w$ initially contains the object $\sqcup$, indicating that the w-th cell of the work tape of M is blank.
- Two sets of membranes $\{a_{\mathbf{i}} : a \in \Sigma\}$ and $\{a_{\mathbf{w}} : a \in \Sigma\}$, placed inside $\mathbf{h}$ and respectively called *input tape symbol membranes* and *work tape symbol membranes*.

The input $x \in \Sigma^*$ of Π_n is encoded as a multiset by subscripting each symbol with its position inside x, counting from 0 and using $\ell(n)$ bits. This multiset is then placed inside membrane $\mathbf{i}_0$. (See Fig. 1.)

Now assume that a few steps of M have been simulated by Π_x. The current configuration of the P system will be similar to the initial one, except that the initial state object $q_{0,0}$ is replaced by some $q_{i,w}$ (with $q \in Q$, $0 \le i < n$, $0 \le w < s(n)$) and the membranes $\mathbf{w}_0, \ldots, \mathbf{w}_{s(n)-1}$ contain objects corresponding to the symbols on the work tape of M. (See Fig. 2.)

The state object now enters the membranes $\mathbf{i}_{\ell(n)-1}, \ldots, \mathbf{i}_0$ in that order; at the same time, it sets the charge of membrane $\mathbf{i}_j$ to negative, if the j-th least significant bit (counting from 0) of its subscript i is 0, and to positive if that bit is 1. The following rules are used in order to perform this process:

$$q_{i,w} \, [\;]_{\mathbf{i}_j}^0 \to [q_{i,w}]_{\mathbf{i}_j}^- \qquad \text{if the } j\text{-th least significant bit of } i \text{ is 0} \qquad (1)$$

$$q_{i,w} \, [\;]_{\mathbf{i}_j}^0 \to [q_{i,w}]_{\mathbf{i}_j}^+ \qquad \text{if the } j\text{-th least significant bit of } i \text{ is 1.} \qquad (2)$$

These rules are replicated for all $q \in Q$, $0 \le i < n$, $0 \le w < s(n)$, $0 < j < \ell(n)$.

For the innermost membrane i_0 instead we use the following rules, which add a binary counter of $\ell(n)$ bits (starting from 0) as a superscript to the state object:

$$q_{i,w} \; [\;]^0_{i_0} \to [q^0_{i,w}]^-_{i_0} \qquad \text{if the least significant bit of } i \text{ is 0} \qquad (3)$$

$$q_{i,w} \; [\;]^0_{i_0} \to [q^0_{i,w}]^+_{i_0} \qquad \text{if the least significant bit of } i \text{ is 1.} \qquad (4)$$

These rules are replicated for all $q \in Q$, $0 \le i < n$, $0 \le w < s(n)$.

When membrane i_0 becomes non-neutral, the input objects a_i (for $0 \le i < n$) are sent out. Membranes $i_0, \ldots, i_{\ell(n)-1}$ behave as "filters" in the following sense: object a_i may pass through i_j only if the charge of the membrane corresponds to the j-th bit of i (where positive denotes a 1, and negative a 0). Exactly one input object will traverse all of them and reach the outermost membrane, namely, the object corresponding to the symbol under the tape head in the current configuration of M, whose position on the input tape is represented by the subscript i of the object $q_{i,w}$. Indeed, it is never the case that two or more input objects reach the outermost membrane, since the subscripts of the input symbols are unique (i.e., no two input objects a_{i_1}, a_{i_2} have identical bits in all $\ell(n)$ positions of their subscripts); moreover, one of them always does, since the simulated Turing machine, being a legitimate one, has a symbol under its input tape head at all times. The time required for the correct input object to reach the outermost membrane depends on the nondeterministic order in which the objects are sent out from the membranes $i_0, \ldots, i_{\ell(n)-1}$; in the following discussion we use a worst-case upper bound of $\frac{n}{2} + \ell(n) + 1$.

Formally, the required rules are:

$$[a_i]^-_{i_j} \to [\;]^-_{i_j} \; a_i \qquad \text{if the } j\text{-th bit of } i \text{ is 0} \qquad (5)$$

$$[a_i]^+_{i_j} \to [\;]^+_{i_j} \; a_i \qquad \text{if the } j\text{-th bit of } i \text{ is 1.} \qquad (6)$$

These rules are replicated for all $a \in \Sigma$, $0 \le i < n$, $0 \le j < \ell(n)$.

The single object that reaches the outermost membrane h is then used in order to set to positive the charge of the corresponding membrane a_i (thus signalling that the symbol under the input tape head is a):

$$a_i \; [\;]^0_{a_i} \to [a_i]^0_{a_i} \qquad (7)$$

$$[a_i]^0_{a_i} \to [\;]^+_{a_i} \; a_i \qquad (8)$$

These rules are replicated for all $a \in \Sigma$, $0 \le i < n$.

The number of steps required for these operations to be carried out (starting from the moment membrane i_0 becomes non-neutral) is bounded by $\frac{n}{2} + \ell(n) + 1$. During this time, the head object waits inside i_0 by using the following rules:

$$[q^t_{i,w} \to q^{t+1}_{i,w}]^\alpha_{i_0} \qquad \text{for } 0 \le t < \frac{n}{2} + \ell(n) + 1 \qquad (9)$$

These rules are replicated for all $q \in Q$, $0 \le i < n$, $0 \le w < s(n)$, $\alpha \in \{+, -\}$. (See Fig. 3.)

When the superscript t reaches $\frac{n}{2} + \ell(n) + 1$, the state object travels back to membrane h while resetting the charges of $i_0, \ldots, i_{\ell(n)-1}$ to neutral:

$$[q_{i,w}^{\frac{n}{2}+\ell(n)+1}]_{i_0}^{\alpha} \to [\ ]_{i_0}^{0}\ q'_{i,w} \tag{10}$$

$$[q'_{i,w}]_{i_j}^{\alpha} \to [\ ]_{i_j}^{0}\ q'_{i,w} \tag{11}$$

$$[q'_{i,w}]_{i_{\ell(n)-1}}^{\alpha} \to [\ ]_{i_{\ell(n)-1}}^{0}\ q^{0}_{i,w} \tag{12}$$

These rules are replicated for all $q \in Q, 0 \leq i < n, 0 \leq w < s(n), 0 < j < \ell(n)-1$, $\alpha \in \{+, -\}$.

When membranes i_j revert to neutral, the input objects a_i are sent back in, all the way to the input membrane h_0:

$$a_i\ [\ ]_{i_j}^{0} \to [a_i]_{i_j}^{0} \tag{13}$$

These rules are replicated for all $0 \leq i < n$, $0 \leq j < \ell(n)$, $a \in \Sigma$.

Once again, the state object waits $\frac{n}{2} + \ell(n) + 1$ steps (this time, inside membrane h) for this process to complete:

$$[q_{i,w}^{t} \to q_{i,w}^{t+1}]_{h}^{0} \qquad \text{for } 0 \leq t < \frac{n}{2} + \ell(n) + 1 \tag{14}$$

These rules are replicated for all $q \in Q$, $0 \leq i < n$, $0 \leq w < s(n)$.

The time required up to now is $O\left(\frac{n}{2} + \ell(n)\right) = O(n)$ steps. The remainder of the simulation of the current step of M will only require a constant number of steps. First, the state object $q_{i,w}^{\frac{n}{2}+\ell(n)+1}$ enters membrane w_w and changes its charge, thus causing the object a inside it to be sent out.

$$q_{i,w}^{\frac{n}{2}+\ell(n)+1}\ [\ ]_{w_w}^{0} \to [q''_{i,w}]_{w_w}^{+} \tag{15}$$

$$[a]_{w_w}^{+} \to [\ ]_{w_w}^{-}\ a \tag{16}$$

These rules are replicated for all $q \in Q$, $0 \leq i < n$, $0 \leq w < s(n)$, $a \in \Sigma$.

When the charge of w_w becomes negative, the state object is sent out to h, while object a enters the corresponding membrane a_w and sets its charge to positive.

$$[q''_{i,w}]_{w_w}^{-} \to [\ ]_{w_w}^{-}\ q''_{i,w} \tag{17}$$

$$a\ [\ ]_{a_w}^{0} \to [a]_{a_w}^{+} \tag{18}$$

These rules are replicated for all $q \in Q$, $0 \leq i < n$, $0 \leq w < s(n)$, $a \in \Sigma$.

Now the configuration of Π_x (see Fig. 4) has the following properties:

- Exactly one membrane among $w_0, \ldots, w_{s(n)-1}$ is negatively charged (this is the membrane corresponding to the work tape cell currently scanned by M) while the others are neutral.

- Exactly one membrane a_i is positively charged (the one corresponding to the input tape symbol currently read by M), while b_i is neutral for all $b \in \Sigma - \{a\}$.
- Exactly one membrane a_w is positively charged (the one corresponding to the work tape symbol currently read by M), while b_w is neutral for all $b \in \Sigma - \{a\}$.

While the object a inside membrane a_w is deleted by the following rule, replicated for all $a \in \Sigma$:

$$[a \to \lambda]_{a_w}^+ \tag{19}$$

the state object can identify the symbols currently read by M by checking the charges of the corresponding membranes (resetting them to neutral), and store those symbols as superscripts:

$$q_{i,w}'' \ [\ ]_{a_i}^+ \to [q_{i,w}'']_{a_i}^+ \tag{20}$$

$$[q_{i,w}'']_{a_i}^+ \to [\ ]_{a_i}^0 \ q_{i,w}^a \tag{21}$$

$$q_{i,w}^a \ [\ ]_{b_w}^+ \to [q_{i,w}^a]_{b_w}^+ \tag{22}$$

$$[q_{i,w}^a]_{b_w}^+ \to [\ ]_{b_w}^0 \ q_{i,w}^{a,b} \tag{23}$$

These rules are replicated for all $q \in Q$, $0 \le i < n$, $0 \le w < s(n)$, $a, b \in \Sigma$.

Now the state object possesses all the information needed in order to simulate the transition of M, namely, the state itself and the two symbols currently scanned by the Turing machine. Let

$$\delta \colon Q \times \Sigma^2 \to Q \times \Sigma \times \{+1, -1\}^2$$

be the transition function of M; here we assume δ is only defined for non-final states, and that the head movements are represented by ± 1. Assume that

$$\delta(q, a, b) = (r, c, d_1, d_2).$$

Then, the following rules produce the object representing the new work tape symbol that replaces a:

$$[q_{i,w}^{a,b} \to \hat{q}_{i,w}^{a,b} \ c']_h^0 \tag{24}$$

These rules are replicated for all $q \in Q$, $0 \le i < n$, $0 \le w < s(n)$, $a, b \in \Sigma$.

The object c' is sent to the membrane simulating the tape cell it is written on, i.e., the only negatively charged membrane w_w, and it resets its charge to neutral (while losing the prime):

$$c' \ [\ ]_{w_w}^- \to [c]_{w_w}^0 \tag{25}$$

This rule is replicated for all $0 \le w < s(n)$, $c \in \Sigma$.

Simultaneously, the state object has to update three pieces of information (state and positions on the tapes) in order to complete the simulation of the current step of M:

$$[\hat{q}_{i,w}^{a,b} \to r_{i',w'}]_h^0 \qquad \text{where } i' = i + d_1, \ w' = w + d_2 \tag{26}$$

These rules are replicated for all $q \in Q$, $0 \leq i < n$, $0 \leq w < s(n)$, $a, b \in \Sigma$.

The configuration of Π_x now encodes the configuration of M after having simulated the step performed by the Turing machine in $O(n)$ time. The simulation may now proceed with the next step of M.

If M reaches an accepting state q, then the following rule is applied:

$$[q_{i,w}]_h^0 \rightarrow [\ ]_h^0 \text{ yes} \tag{27}$$

while the following one is applied for a rejecting state:

$$[q_{i,w}]_h^0 \rightarrow [\ ]_h^0 \text{ no} \tag{28}$$

These rules are replicated for all $0 \leq i < n$, $0 \leq w < s(n)$.

This completes the description of the family of P systems $\boldsymbol{\Pi} = \{\Pi_x : x \in \Sigma^\star\}$ simulating M. Each P system Π_x only requires $O(\log |x|)$ membranes and objects besides the input objects (and these are not modified nor created during the computation). The time required by the simulation is $O(n \cdot t(n))$, where $t(n)$ is the maximum number of steps performed by M on inputs of length n.

In order to prove Theorem 1 we still need to show that the family $\boldsymbol{\Pi}$ is indeed $(\mathbf{DLT}, \mathbf{DLT})$-uniform. Here we provide a proof sketch for this result.

Consider the mapping $x \mapsto w_x$, encoding each input string of M as a multiset over the alphabet of Π_n (with $n = |x|$): each symbol of x has to be subscripted with an index of $\ell(n)$ bits representing its position in x. The corresponding ENCODING predicate is

$$\text{ENCODING}(x, i, a_j) \iff j = i \wedge x_i = a.$$

It is easy to check in **DLOGTIME** if the predicate holds for each (x, i, a_j). First, we copy the portions of the input representing i and a_j (of length $O(\log n)$) on auxiliary work tapes and we check if the third argument is indeed of the form a_j for some $a \in \Sigma$ by simulating a finite state automaton. By scanning i and j we can ensure that $i = j$. Then, we extract the i-th symbol of x by copying i on the address tape of the machine, and we check if that symbol is a. Since symbol-by-symbol comparisons require linear time with respect to the length of the strings, the evaluation of ENCODING can be carried out in logarithmic time.

The alphabet of Π_n can be represented by using $O(\ell(n))$ bits, where the hidden constants also depend on the size of the alphabet Σ of M. For simplicity, we can use $k \cdot \ell(n)$ for some appropriate k as an upper bound, and set

$$\text{ALPHABET}(1^n, m) \iff m = k \cdot \ell(n).$$

This predicate can be checked in **DLOGTIME**, as multiplication by a constant can be implemented by repeated additions. The reasoning for the predicate LABELS is similar.

The membrane structure of Π_n (see Fig. 1 for an example with $n = 5$) is described as follows:

$$\text{OUTERMOST}(1^n, h) \iff h = \mathbf{h}$$

$$\text{INSIDE}(1^n, h_1, h_2) \iff (h_1 = \mathbf{i}_{\ell(n)-1} \wedge h_2 = \mathbf{h}) \vee$$
$$(h_1 = \mathbf{i}_j \wedge h_2 = \mathbf{i}_{j+1} \wedge 0 \le j < \ell(n) - 1) \vee$$
$$(h_1 = \mathbf{w}_j \wedge h_2 = \mathbf{h} \wedge 0 \le j < s(n)) \vee$$
$$(h_1 = a_{\mathbf{i}} \wedge h_2 = \mathbf{h} \wedge a \in \Sigma) \vee$$
$$(h_1 = a_{\mathbf{w}} \wedge h_2 = \mathbf{h} \wedge a \in \Sigma)$$

that is, by a disjunction of a constant number of conjuncts, each one consisting of a constant number of terms whose truth can be verified in **DLOGTIME** by executing comparisons or simple computations on numbers of $O(\log n)$ bits. The input membrane is identified by

$$\text{INPUT}(1^n, h) \iff h = \mathbf{i}_0.$$

The initial multisets are described by

$$\text{MULTISET}(1^n, h, i, a) \iff (h = \mathbf{h} \wedge i = 0 \wedge a = \mathbf{q}_{0,0}) \vee$$
$$(h = \mathbf{w}_j \wedge i = 0 \wedge a = \sqcup \wedge 0 \le j < s(n))$$

which is also decidable in **DLOGTIME**.

We shall not describe in detail the predicates for the rules of Π_x. As an example, consider the rules of kind (14) on page 351:

$$[q_{i,w}^t \to q_{i,w}^{t+1}]_{\mathbf{h}}^0 \qquad \text{for } 0 \le t < \frac{n}{2} + \ell(n) + 1$$

It is easy to see that

$$\#\text{EVOLUTION}(1^n, \mathbf{h}, 0, a, 1)$$

holds for $a = q_{i,w}^t$, $q \in Q$, $0 \le i < n$, $0 \le w < s(n)$, $0 \le t < \frac{n}{2} + \ell(n) + 1$; this is one of the conjuncts of the full definition of $\#\text{EVOLUTION}$. The value $\frac{n}{2} + \ell(n) + 1$ can be computed from 1^n in **DLOGTIME**. The part of the predicate EVOLUTION dealing with rules of kind (14)

$$\text{EVOLUTION}(1^n, \mathbf{h}, 0, q_{i,w}^t, 0, j, b)$$

then holds when $j = 0$ and $b = q_{i,w}^{t+1}$, and this can be checked in **DLOGTIME** as described before.

The full definition of EVOLUTION (and of all the other predicates for the rules of Π_n) is a disjunction of a constant number of conjuncts (each one dealing with a different kind of evolution rules, depending on the elements on the left-hand side of the rule) where each conjunct can be checked in **DLOGTIME**.   □

An immediate corollary of Theorem 1 is that the class of problems solved by logarithmic-space Turing machines is contained in the class of problems solved by $(\mathbf{DLT}, \mathbf{DLT})$-uniform, logarithmic-space P systems with active membranes.

Corollary 1. $\mathbf{L} \subseteq (\mathbf{DLT}, \mathbf{DLT})\text{-}\mathbf{LMCSPACE}_{\mathcal{AM}}.$ □

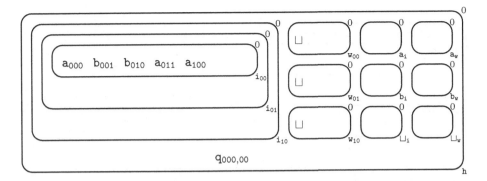

Fig. 1. The initial configuration of Π_x, that is Π_n with $n = 5$ and input $x = \mathbf{abbaa}$, assuming M uses $\log n$ space, has $\Sigma = \{\mathbf{a}, \mathbf{b}, \sqcup\}$ as its alphabet and $\mathbf{q}$ as its initial state

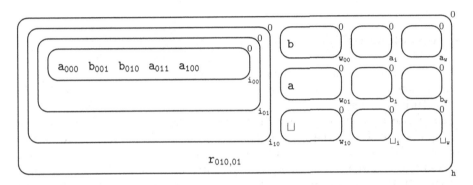

Fig. 2. A possible configuration of the P system Π_x (see Fig. 1) simulating the Turing machine M after a few computation steps have been simulated. Here the current state of M is $\mathbf{r}$, the work tape contains the string $\mathbf{ba}$, the input tape head is on cell 2 (binary 010), and the work tape head is on cell 1 (binary 01).

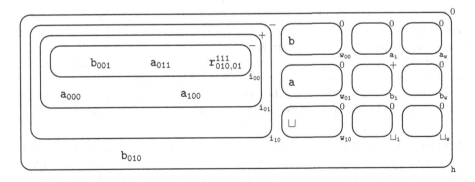

Fig. 3. Configuration of Π_x (from Fig. 1) after the object $\mathbf{b}_{010}$ (corresponding to the symbol under the input tape head) has set the charge of membrane $\mathbf{b}_i$ to positive, allowing the state-object to identify it

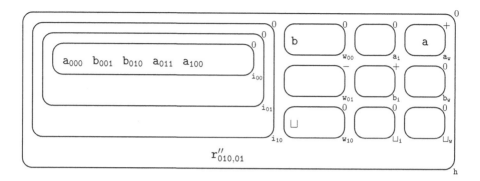

Fig. 4. Configuration of Π_x after the object a has set the charge of membrane $\mathbf{a}_\mathbf{w}$ to positive, thus identifying the symbol under the work tape head

5   Conclusions

In this paper we extended the definition of space complexity for P systems [6] in order to consider sublinear-space computations and compare them to logarithmic-space Turing machines.

To ensure that the P systems themselves perform the actual computation (as opposed to letting the uniformity machine solve the problem), we needed to weaken the usual polynomial-time uniformity condition (as $\mathbf{L} \subseteq \mathbf{P}$). We showed how a variant of a common uniformity condition for Boolean circuits, **DLOGTIME** uniformity, may also be used to define families of P systems with active membranes.

We were then able to define **DLOGTIME**-uniform families of P systems working in logarithmic space and simulating logarithmic-space Turing machines, thus showing that the former devices are at least as computationally powerful as the latter ones, in symbols $\mathbf{L} \subseteq (\mathbf{DLT}, \mathbf{DLT})\text{-}\mathbf{LMCSPACE}_{\mathcal{AM}}$.

Although the **DLOGTIME** uniformity condition we proposed, like the $\mathbf{AC}^0$ uniformity already considered in the literature [3], is weaker than the usual **P** uniformity, it nevertheless seems powerful enough to be applied to many already published results. Indeed, we conjecture that most previously defined **P**-uniform families of P systems can be adapted to **DLOGTIME** uniformity.

It remains to be established whether $(\mathbf{DLT}, \mathbf{DLT})\text{-}\mathbf{LMCSPACE}_{\mathcal{AM}} = \mathbf{L}$, or if that class includes harder problems like, for instance, those in **NL**.

Acknowledgements. The authors would like to thank Artiom Alhazov, Luca Manzoni, Niall Murphy, and Marco S. Nobile for the suggestions they provided. This work was partially supported by Università degli Studi di Milano-Bicocca, Fondo di Ateneo per la Ricerca (FAR) 2011.

References

1. Alhazov, A., Leporati, A., Mauri, G., Porreca, A.E., Zandron, C.: The computational power of exponential-space P systems with active membranes. In: Martínez-del-Amor, M.A., Păun, G., Pérez-Hurtado, I., Romero-Campero, F.J. (eds.) Proceedings of the Tenth Brainstorming Week on Membrane Computing, vol. I, pp. 35–60. Fénix Editora (2012)

2. Mix Barrington, D.A., Immerman, N., Straubing, H.: On uniformity within NC^1. Journal of Computer and System Sciences 41(3), 274–306 (1990)

3. Murphy, N., Woods, D.: The computational power of membrane systems under tight uniformity conditions. Natural Computing 10(1), 613–632 (2011)

4. Păun, G.: P systems with active membranes: Attacking NP-complete problems. Journal of Automata, Languages and Combinatorics 6(1), 75–90 (2001)

5. Pérez-Jiménez, M.J., Romero-Jiménez, A., Sancho-Caparrini, F.: Complexity classes in models of cellular computing with membranes. Natural Computing 2(3), 265–284 (2003)

6. Porreca, A.E., Leporati, A., Mauri, G., Zandron, C.: Introducing a space complexity measure for P systems. International Journal of Computers, Communications & Control 4(3), 301–310 (2009)

7. Porreca, A.E., Leporati, A., Mauri, G., Zandron, C.: P systems with active membranes working in polynomial space. International Journal of Foundations of Computer Science 22(1), 65–73 (2011)

8. Ruzzo, W.L.: On uniform circuit complexity. Journal of Computer and System Sciences 22(3), 365–383 (1981)

Modelling Ecological Systems with the Calculus of Wrapped Compartments

Pablo Ramón[1] and Angelo Troina[2]

[1] Departamento de Ciencias Naturales, Sección Ecología
Universidad Tecnica Particular de Loja
[2] Dipartimento di Informatica
Università di Torino

Abstract. The Calculus of Wrapped Compartments is a framework based on stochastic multiset rewriting in a compartmentalised setting originally developed for the modelling and analysis of biological interactions. In this paper, we propose to use this calculus for the description of ecological systems and we provide the modelling guidelines to encode within the calculus some of the main interactions leading ecosystems evolution. As a case study, we model the distribution of height of *Croton wagneri*, a shrub constituting the endemic predominant species of the dry ecosystem in southern Ecuador. In particular, we consider the plant at different altitude gradients (i.e. at different temperature conditions), to study how it adapts under the effects of global climate change.

1 Introduction

Answers to ecological questions could rarely be formulated as general laws: ecologists deal with *in situ* methods and experiments which cannot be controlled in a precise way since the phenomena observed operate on much larger scales (in time and space) than man can effectively study. Actually, to carry on ecological analyses, there is the need of a "macroscope"!

Theoretical and Computational Ecology, the scientific disciplines devoted to the study of ecological systems using theoretical methodologies together with empirical data, could be considered as a fundamental component of such a macroscope. Within these disciplines, quantitative analysis, conceptual description techniques, mathematical models, and computational simulations are used to understand the fundamental biological conditions and processes that affect populations dynamics (given the underlying assumption that phenomena observable across species and ecological environments are generated by common, mechanistic processes) [39].

Ecological models can be deterministic or stochastic [18]. Given an initial system, deterministic simulations always evolve in the same way, producing a unique output [43]. Deterministic methods give a picture of the average, expected behaviour of a system, but do not incorporate random fluctuations. On the other hand, stochastic models allow to describe the random perturbations that may affect natural living systems, in particular when considering small populations

E. Csuhaj-Varjú et al. (Eds.): CMC 2012, LNCS 7762, pp. 358–377, 2013.

evolving at slow interactions. Actually, while deterministic models are approximations of the real systems they describe, stochastic models, at the price of an higher computational cost, can describe exact scenarios.

A model in the Calculus of Wrapped Compartments (CWC for short) consists of a term, representing a (biological or ecological) system and a set of rewrite rules which model the transformations determining the system's evolution [27,24]. Terms are defined from a set of atomic elements via an operator of compartment construction. Each compartment is labelled with a nominal type which identifies the set of rewrite rules that may be applied into it. The CWC framework is based on a stochastic semantics and models an exact scenario able to capture the stochastic fluctuations that can arise in the system.

The calculus has been extensively used to model real biological scenarios, in particular related to the AM-symbiosis [24,19].[1] An hybrid semantics for CWC, combining stochastic transitions with deterministic steps, modelled by Ordinary Differential Equations, has been proposed in [25,26].

While the calculus has been originally developed to deal with biomolecular interactions and cellular communications, it appears to be particularly well suited also to model and analyse interactions in ecology. In particular, we present in this paper some modelling guidelines to describe, within CWC, some of the main common features and models used to represent ecological interactions and population dynamics. A few generalising examples illustrate the abstract effectiveness of the application of CWC to ecological modelling.

As a real case study, we model the distribution of height of *Croton wagneri*, a shrub in the dry ecosystem of southern Ecuador, and investigate how it could adapt to global climate change.

2   The Calculus of Wrapped Compartments

The Calculus of Wrapped Compartments (CWC) (see [27,25,26]) is based on a nested structure of compartments delimited by wraps with specific proprieties.

Term Syntax. Let $\mathcal{A}$ be a set of *atomic elements* (*atoms* for short), ranged over by a, b, ..., and $\mathcal{L}$ a set of *compartment types* represented as *labels* ranged over by $\ell, \ell', \ell_1, \ldots$

Definition 1 (CWC terms). *A CWC term is a multiset $\overline{t}$ of simple terms t defined by the following grammar:*

$$t ::= \quad a \quad | \quad (\overline{a} \rfloor \overline{t'})^{\ell}$$

A simple term is either an atom or a compartment consisting of a *wrap* (represented by the multiset of atoms $\overline{a}$), a *content* (represented by the term $\overline{t'}$) and a

---

[1] Arbuscular Mycorrhiza (AM) is a class of fungi constituting a vital mutualistic interaction for terrestrial ecosystems. More than 48% of land plants actually rely on mycorrhizal relationships to get inorganic compounds, trace elements, and resistance to several kinds of pathogens.

type (represented by the label ℓ). Multisets are identified modulo permutations of their elements. The notation $n * t$ denotes n occurrences of the simple term t. We denote an empty term with •.

In applications to ecology, atoms can be used to describe the individuals of different species and compartments can be used to distinguish different ecosystems, habitats or ecological niches. Compartment wraps can be used to model geographical boundaries or abiotic components (like radiations, climate, atmospheric or soil conditions, etc.). In evolutionary ecology, individuals can also be described as compartments, showing characteristic features of their *phenotype* in the wrap and keeping their *genotype* (or particular *alleles* of interest) in the compartment content.

An example of CWC term is $20 * a\ 12 * b\ (c\ d \rfloor 6 * e\ 4 * f)^{\ell}$ representing a multiset (denoted by listing its elements separated by a space) consisting of 20 occurrences of a, 12 occurrences of b (e.g. 32 individuals of two different species) and an ℓ-type compartment $(c\ d \rfloor 6 * e\ 4 * f)^{\ell}$ which, in turn, consists of a wrap (a boundary) with two atoms c and d (e.g. two abiotic factors) on its surface, and containing 6 occurrences of the atom e and 4 occurrences of the atom f (e.g. 10 individuals of two other species). Compartments can be nested as in the term $(a\ b\ c \rfloor (d\ e \rfloor f)^{\ell'}\ g\ h)^{\ell}$.

Rewrite Rules. System transformations are defined by rewrite rules, defined by resorting to CWC terms that may contain variables.

Definition 2 (Patterns and Open terms). *Simple patterns P and simple open terms O are given by the following grammar:*

$$
\begin{array}{rcl}
P & ::= & a \quad \mid \quad (\overline{a}\ x \rfloor \overline{P}\ X)^{\ell} \\
O & ::= & a \quad \mid \quad (\overline{q} \rfloor \overline{O})^{\ell} \quad \mid \quad X \\
q & ::= & a \quad \mid \quad x
\end{array}
$$

where $\overline{a}$ is a multiset of atoms, $\overline{P}$ is a pattern (i.e., a, possibly empty, multiset of simple patterns), x is a wrap variable (can be instantiated by a multiset of atoms), X is a content variable (can be instantiated by a CWC term), $\overline{q}$ is a multiset of atoms and wrap variables and $\overline{O}$ is an open term (i.e., a, possibly empty, multiset of simple open terms).

We will use patterns as the l.h.s. components of a rewrite rule and open terms as the r.h.s. components of a rewrite rule. Patterns are intended to match, via substitution of variables, with ground terms (containing no variables). Note that we force *exactly* one variable to occur in each compartment content and wrap of our patterns. This prevents ambiguities in the instantiations needed to match a given compartment.[2]

---

[2]   The linearity condition, in biological terms, corresponds to excluding that a transformation can depend on the presence of two (or more) identical (and generic) components in different compartments (see also [36]).

Definition 3 (Rewrite rules). *A rewrite rule is a triple* $(\ell, \overline{P}, \overline{O})$*, denoted by* $\ell : \overline{P} \longmapsto \overline{O}$*, where the pattern* $\overline{P}$ *and the open term* $\overline{O}$ *are such that the variables occurring in* $\overline{O}$ *are a subset of the variables occurring in* $\overline{P}$*.*

The rewrite rule $\ell : \overline{P} \mapsto \overline{O}$ can be applied to any compartment of type ℓ with $\overline{P}$ in its content (that will be rewritten with $\overline{O}$). Namely, the application of $\ell : \overline{P} \mapsto \overline{O}$ to term $\overline{t}$ is performed in the following way:

1. find in $\overline{t}$ (if it exists) a compartment of type ℓ with content $\overline{t'}$ and a substitution σ of variables by ground terms such that $\overline{t'} = \sigma(\overline{P}\ X)$;[3]
2. replace in $\overline{t}$ the subterm $\overline{t'}$ with $\sigma(\overline{O}\ X)$.

For instance, the rewrite rule $\ell : a\ b \mapsto c$ means that in compartments of type ℓ an occurrence of $a\ b$ can be replaced by c. We write $\overline{t} \mapsto \overline{t'}$ to denote a *reduction* obtained by applying a rewrite rule to $\overline{t}$ resulting to $\overline{t'}$.

While a rewrite rule does not change the label ℓ of the compartment where it is applied, it may change the labels of the compartments occurring in its content. For instance, the rewrite rule $\ell : (a\ x \rfloor X)^{\ell_1} \mapsto (a\ x \rfloor X)^{\ell_2}$ means that, if contained in a compartment of type ℓ, a compartment of type ℓ_1 containing an a on its wrap can be changed to type ℓ_2.

CWC Models. For uniformity reasons we assume that the whole system is always represented by a term consisting of a single (top level) compartment with distinguished label $\top$ and empty wrap, i.e., any system is represented by a term of the shape $(\bullet \rfloor \overline{t})^{\top}$, which, for simplicity, will be written as $\overline{t}$. Note that while an infinite set of terms and rewrite rules can be defined from the syntactic definitions in this section, a *CWC model* consists of an initial system $(\bullet \rfloor \overline{t})^{\top}$ and a finite set of rewrite rules $\mathcal{R}$.

2.1   Stochastic Simulation

A stochastic simulation model for ecological systems can be defined by incorporating a collision-based framework along the lines of the one presented by Gillespie in [32], which is, *de facto*, the standard way to model quantitative aspects of biological systems. The basic idea of Gillespie's algorithm is that a rate is associated with each considered reaction which is used as the parameter of an exponential probability distribution modelling the time needed for the reaction to take place. In the standard approach the reaction *propensity* is obtained by multiplying the rate of the reaction by the number of possible combinations of reactants in the compartment in which the reaction takes place, modelling the law of mass action.

Stochastic rewrite rules are thus enriched with a rate k (notation $\ell : \overline{P} \xrightarrow{k} \overline{O}$). Evaluating the propensity of the stochastic rewrite rule $R = \ell : a\ b \xrightarrow{k} c$ within the term $\overline{t} = a\ a\ a\ b\ b$, contained in the compartment $u = (\bullet \rfloor \overline{t})^{\ell}$, we must

---

[3] The implicit (distinguished) variable X matches with all the remaining part of the compartment content.

consider the number of the possible combinations of reactants of the form a b in $\bar{t}$. Since each occurrence of a can react with each occurrence of b, this number is $3 \cdot 2$, and the propensity of R within u is $k \cdot 6$. A detailed method to compute the number of combinations of reactants can be found in [27].

The stochastic simulation algorithm produces essentially a *Continuous Time Markov Chain* (CTMC). Given a term $\bar{t}$, a set $\mathcal{R}$ of rewrite rules, a global time δ and all the reductions $e_1, \ldots, e_M$ applicable in all the different compartments of $\bar{t}$ with propensities $r_1, \ldots, r_M$, Gillespie's "direct method" determines:

- The exponential probability distribution (with parameter $r = \sum_{i=1}^{M} r_i$) of the time τ after which the next reduction will occur;
- The probability r_i/r that the reduction occurring at time $\delta + \tau$ will be e_i.

The CWC simulator [2] is a tool under development at the Computer Science Department of the Turin University, based on Gillespie's direct method algorithm [32]. It treats CWC models with different rating semantics (law of mass action, Michaelis-Menten kinetics, Hill equation) and it can run independent stochastic simulations over CWC models, featuring deep parallel optimizations for multi-core platforms on the top of FastFlow [5]. It also performs online analysis by a modular statistical framework [4,3].

3 Modelling Ecological Systems in CWC

We present some of the characteristic features leading the evolution of ecological systems, and we show how to encode it within CWC.

3.1 Population Dynamics

Models of population dynamics describe the changes in the size and composition of populations.

The *exponential growth model* is a common mathematical model for population dynamics, where, using r to represent the pro-capita growth rate of a population of size N, the change of the population is proportional to the size of the already existing population:

$$\frac{dN}{dt} = r \cdot N$$

CWC Modelling 1 (Exponential Growth Model). *We can encode within CWC the exponential growth model with rate r using a stochastic rewrite rule describing a reproduction event for a single individual at the given rate. Namely, given a population of species a living in an environment modelled by a compartment with label ℓ, the following CWC rule encodes the exponential growth model:*

$$\ell : a \xmapsto{r} a\ a$$

Counting the number of possible reactants, the growth rate of the overall population is automatically obtained by the stochastic semantics underlying CWC.

A *metapopulation*[4] is a group of populations of the same species distributed in different patches[5] and interacting at some level. Thus, a metapopulation consists of several distinct populations and areas of suitable habitat.

Individual populations may tend to reach extinction as a consequence of demographic stochasticity (fluctuations in population size due to random demographic events); the smaller the population, the more prone it is to extinction. A metapopulation, as a whole, is often more stable: immigrants from one population (experiencing, e.g., a population boom) are likely to re-colonize the patches left open by the extinction of other populations. Also, by the *rescue effect*, individuals of more dense populations may emigrate towards small populations, rescuing them from extinction.

Populations are affected by births, deaths, immigrations and emigrations (BIDE model [23]). The number of individuals at time $t + 1$ is given by:

$$N_{t+1} = N_t + B + I - D - E$$

where N_t is the number of individuals at time t and, between time t and $t + 1$, B is the number of births, I is the number of immigrations, D is the number of deaths and E is the number of emigrations.

CWC Modelling 2 (BIDE model). *We can encode within CWC the BIDE model for a compartment of type ℓ using stochastic rewrite rules describing the given events with their respective rates r, i, d, e:*

$$\ell : a \xmapsto{r} a\ a \qquad\qquad (birth)$$
$$\top : a\ (x \rfloor X)^\ell \xmapsto{i} (x \rfloor a\ X)^\ell \quad (immigration)$$
$$\ell : a \xmapsto{d} \bullet \qquad\qquad (death)$$
$$\top : (x \rfloor a\ X)^\ell \xmapsto{e} a\ (x \rfloor X)^\ell \quad (emigration)$$

Starting from a population of N_t individuals at time t, the number N_{t+1} of individuals at time $t + 1$ is computed by successive simulation steps of the stochastic algorithm. The race conditions computed according to the propensities of the given rules assure that all of the BIDE events are correctly taken into account.

Example 1. Immigration and extinction are key components of island biogeography. We model a metapopulation of species a in a context of 5 different patches: 4 of which are relatively close, e.g. different ecological regions within a small continent, the last one is far away and difficult to reach, e.g. an island. The continental patches are modelled as CWC compartments of type ℓ_c, the island is modelled as a compartment of type ℓ_i. Births, deaths and migrations in the continental patches are modelled by the following CWC rules:

$$\ell_c : a \xmapsto{0.005} a\ a \qquad \ell_c : a \xmapsto{0.005} \bullet$$
$$\top : (x \rfloor a\ X)^{\ell_c} \xmapsto{0.01} a\ (x \rfloor X)^{\ell_c} \qquad \top : a\ (x \rfloor X)^{\ell_c} \xmapsto{0.5} (x \rfloor a\ X)^{\ell_c}$$

---

[4] The term metapopulation was coined by Richard Levins in 1970. In Levins' own words, it consists of "a population of populations" [34].

[5] A patch is a relatively homogeneous area differing from its surroundings.

These rates are drawn considering days as time unites and an average of life expectancy and reproduction time for the individuals of the species a of 200 days ($\frac{1}{0.005}$). For the modelling of real case studies, these rates could be estimated from data collected *in situ* by tagging individuals.[6] In this model, when an individual emigrates from its previous patch it moves to the top-level compartment from where it may reach one of the close continental patches (might also be the old one) or start a journey through the sea (modelled as a rewrite rule putting the individual on the wrapping of the island compartment):

$$\top : a \ (x \rfloor X)^{\ell_i} \stackrel{0.2}{\longmapsto} (x \ a \rfloor X)^{\ell_i}$$

Crossing the ocean is a long and difficult task and individuals trying it will probably die during the cruise; the luckiest ones, however, might actually reach the island, where they could eventually benefit of a better life expectancy for them and their descendants:

$$\top : (x \ a \rfloor X)^{\ell_i} \stackrel{0.333}{\longmapsto} (x \rfloor X)^{\ell_i} \qquad \top : (x \ a \rfloor X)^{\ell_i} \stackrel{0.0005}{\longmapsto} (x \rfloor a \ X)^{\ell_i}$$
$$\ell_i : a \stackrel{0.007}{\longmapsto} a \ a \qquad \ell_i : a \stackrel{0.003}{\longmapsto} \bullet$$

Considering the initial system modelled by the CWC term:

$$\bar{t} = (\bullet \rfloor 30 * a)^{\ell_c} \ (\bullet \rfloor 30 * a)^{\ell_c} \ (\bullet \rfloor 30 * a)^{\ell_c} \ (\bullet \rfloor 30 * a)^{\ell_c} \ (\bullet \rfloor \bullet)^{\ell_i}$$

we can simulate the possible evolutions of the overall diffusion of individuals of species a in the different patches. Notice that, on average, one over $\frac{0.333}{0.0005}$ individuals that try the ocean journey, actually reach the island. In Figure 1 we show the result of a simulation plotting the number of individuals in the different patches in a time range of approximatively 10 years. Note how, in the final part of the simulation, empty patches get recolonised. In this particular simulation, also, an exponential growth begins after the colonisation of the island. The full CWC model describing this example can be found at: http://www.di.unito.it/~troina/cmc13/metapopulation.cwc.

In ecology, using r to represent the pro-capita growth rate of a population and K the *carrying capacity* of the hosting environment,[7] r/K selection theory [38] describes a selective pressure driving populations evolution through the *logistic model* [47]:

$$\frac{dN}{dt} = r \cdot N \cdot \left(1 - \frac{N}{K}\right)$$

where N represents the number of individuals in the population.

CWC Modelling 3 (Logistic Model). *The logistic model with growth rate r and carrying capacity K, for an environment modelled by a compartment with label ℓ, can be encoded within CWC using two stochastic rewrite rules describing (i) a reproduction event for a single individual at the given rate and (ii) a*

---

[6] In the remaining examples we will omit a detailed time description.

[7] I.e., the population size at equilibrium.

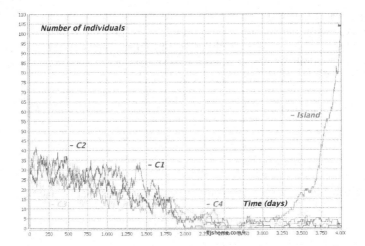

Fig. 1. Metapopulation dynamics

death event modelled by a fight between two individuals at a rate that is inversely proportional to the carrying capacity:

$$\ell : a \overset{r}{\longmapsto} a\ a$$
$$\ell : a\ a \overset{\frac{2 \cdot r}{K-1}}{\longmapsto} a$$

If N is the number of individuals of species a, the number of possible reactants for the first rule is N and the number of possible reactants for the second rule is, in the exact stochastic model, $\binom{N}{2} = \frac{N \cdot (N-1)}{2}$, i.e. the number of distinct pairs of individuals of species a. Multiplying this values by the respective rates we get the propensities of the two rules and can compute the value of N when the equilibrium is reached (i.e., when the propensities of the two rules are equal): $r \cdot N = \frac{2 \cdot r}{K-1} \cdot \frac{N \cdot (N-1)}{2}$, that is when $N = 0$ or $N = K$.

For a given species, this model allows to describe different growth rates and carrying capacities in different ecological regions. Identifying a CWC compartment type (through its label) with an ecological region, we can define rules describing the growth rate and carrying capacity for each region of interest.

Species showing a high growth rate are selected by the r factor, they usually exploit low-crowded environments and produce many offspring, each of which has a relatively low probability of surviving to adulthood. By contrast, K-selected species adapt to densities close to the carrying capacity, tend to strongly compete in high-crowded environments and produce fewer offspring, each of which has a relatively high probability of surviving to adulthood.

Example 2. There is little, or no advantage at all, in evolving traits that permit successful competition with other organisms in an environment that is very likely to change rapidly, often in disruptive ways. Unstable environments thus favour species that reproduce quickly (r-selected species). Stable environments, by contrast, favour the ability to compete successfully for limited resources (K-selected species). We consider individuals of two species, a and b. Individuals of species a are modelled with an higher growth rate with respect to individuals of species b ($r_a > r_b$). Carrying capacity for species a is, instead, lower than the carrying capacity for species b ($K_a < K_b$). The following CWC rules describe the r/K selection model for $r_a = 5$, $r_b = 0.00125$, $K_a = 100$ and $K_b = 1000$:

$$\ell : a \xmapsto{5} a\ a \qquad \ell : b \xmapsto{0.00125} b\ b$$
$$\ell : a\ a \xmapsto{0.1} a \qquad \ell : b\ b \xmapsto{0.0000025} b$$

We might consider a disruptive event occurring on average every 4000 years with the rule:

$$\top : (x \rfloor X)^\ell \xmapsto{0.00025} (x \rfloor a\ b)^\ell$$

devastating the whole content of the compartment (modelled with the variable X) and just leaving one individual of each species. In Figure 2 we show a 10000 years simulation for an initial system containing just one individual for each species. Notice how individuals of species b are disadvantaged with respect to individuals of species a who reach the carrying capacity very soon. A curve showing the growth of individuals of species b in a stable (non disruptive) environment is also shown. The full CWC model describing this example can be found at: `http://www.di.unito.it/~troina/cmc13/rK.cwc`.

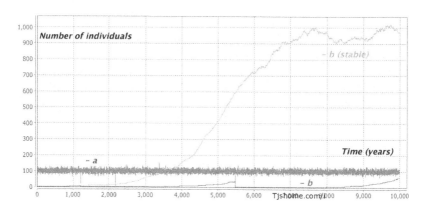

Fig. 2. r/K selection in a disruptive environment

3.2   Competition and Mutualism

In ecology, *competition* is a contest for resources between organisms: animals, e.g., compete for water supplies, food, mates, and other biological resources. In the long term period, competition among individuals of the same species (*intraspecific competition*) and among individuals of different species (*interspecific competition*) operates as a driving force of adaptation, and, eventually, by natural selection, of evolution. Competition, reducing the fitness of the individuals involved,[8] has a great potential in altering the structure of populations, communities and the evolution of interacting species. It results in the ultimate survival, and dominance, of the best suited variants of species: species less suited to compete for resources either adapt or die out. We already depicted a form of competition in the context of the logistic model, where individuals of the same species compete for vital space (limited by the carrying capacity K).

Quite an apposite force is *mutualism*, contest in which organisms of different species biologically interact in a relationship where each of the individuals involved obtain a fitness benefit. Similar interactions between individuals of the same species are known as *co-operation*. Mutualism belongs to the category of symbiotic relationships, including also *commensalism* (in which one species benefits and the other is neutral, i.e. has no harm nor benefits) and *parasitism* (in which one species benefits at the expense of the other).

The general model for competition and mutualism between two species a and b is defined by the following equations [44]:

$$\frac{dN_a}{dt} = \frac{r_a \cdot N_a}{K_a} \cdot (K_a - N_a + \alpha_{ab} \cdot N_b)$$
$$\frac{dN_b}{dt} = \frac{r_b \cdot N_b}{K_b} \cdot (K_b - N_b + \alpha_{ba} \cdot N_a)$$

where the r and K factors model the growth rates and the carrying capacities for the two species, and the α coefficients describe the nature of the relationship between the two species: if α_{ij} is negative, species N_j has negative effects on species N_i (i.e., by competing or preying it), if α_{ij} is positive, species N_j has positive effects on species N_i (i.e., through some kind of mutualistic interaction).

The logistic model, already discussed, is included in the differential equations above. Here we abstract away from it and just focus on the components which describe the effects of competition and mutualism we are now interested in.

CWC Modelling 4 (Competition and Mutualism). *For a compartment of type ℓ, we can encode within CWC the model about competition and mutualism for individuals of two species a and b using the following stochastic rewrite rules:*

$$\ell : a\ b \xmapsto{f_a \cdot |\alpha_{ab}|} \begin{cases} a\ a\ b & \text{if } \alpha_{ab} > 0 \\ b & \text{if } \alpha_{ab} < 0 \end{cases} \qquad \ell : a\ b \xmapsto{f_b \cdot |\alpha_{ba}|} \begin{cases} a\ b\ b & \text{if } \alpha_{ba} > 0 \\ a & \text{if } \alpha_{ba} < 0 \end{cases}$$

where $f_i = \frac{r_i}{K_i}$ is obtained from the usual growth rate and carrying capacity. The α coefficients are put in absolute value to compute the rate of the rule, their signs affect the right hand part of the rewrite rule.

Example 3. Mutualism has driven the evolution of much of the biological diversity we see today, such as flower forms (important to attract mutualistic

---

[8] By fitness it is intended the ability of surviving and reproducing. A reduction in the fitness of an individual implies a reduction in the reproductive output. On the opposite side, a fitness benefit implies an improvement in the reproductive output.

pollinators) and co-evolution between groups of species [45]. We consider two different species of pollinators, a and b, and two different species of angiosperms (flowering plants), c and d. The two pollinators compete between each other, and so do the angiosperms. Both species of pollinators have a mutualistic relation with both angiosperms, even if a slightly prefers c and b slightly prefers d. For each of the species involved we consider the rules for the logistic model and for each pair of species we consider the rules for competition and mutualism. The parameters used for this model are in Table 1. So, for example, the mutualistic relations between a and c are expressed by the following CWC rules

$$\mathsf{T} : a\ c \xmapsto{\frac{r_a}{K_a} \cdot \alpha_{ac}} a\ a\ c \qquad\qquad \mathsf{T} : a\ c \xmapsto{\frac{r_c}{K_c} \cdot \alpha_{ca}} a\ c\ c$$

Figure 3 shows a simulation obtained starting from a system with 100 individuals of species a and b and 20 individuals of species c and d. Note the initially balanced competition between pollinators a and b. This random fluctuations are resolved by the "long run" competition between the angiosperms c and d: when d predominates over c it starts favouring the pollinator b that now can win its own competition with pollinator a. The model is completely symmetrical: in other runs, a faster casual predominance of a pollinator may lead the evolution of its preferred angiosperm. The CWC model describing this example can be found at: http://www.di.unito.it/~troina/cmc13/compmutu.cwc.

Table 1. Parameters for the model of competition and mutualism

Species (i)	r_i	K_i	α_{ai}	α_{bi}	α_{ci}	α_{di}
a	0.2	1000	●	-1	+0.03	+0.01
b	0.2	1000	-1	●	+0.01	+0.03
c	0.0002	200	+0.25	+0.1	●	-6
d	0.0002	200	+0.1	+0.25	-6	●

3.3   Trophic Networks

A *food web* is a network mapping different species according to their alimentary habits. The edges of the network, called *trophic links*, depict the feeding pathways ("who eats who") in an ecological community [30]. At the base of the food web there are autotroph species[9], also called basal species. A *food chain* is a linear feeding pathway that links monophagous consumers (with only one exiting trophic link) from a top consumer, usually a larger predator, to a basal species. The length of a chain is given by the number of links between the top consumer and the base of the web. The influence that the elements of a food web have on each other determine important features of an ecosystem like the presence

---

[9] Self-feeding: able to produce complex organic compounds (e.g by *photosynthesis* or *chemosynthesis*).

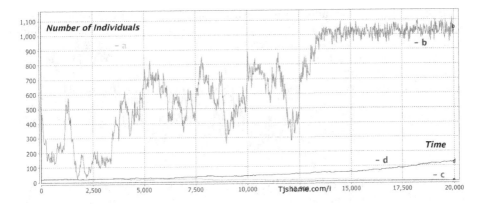

Fig. 3. Competition and Mutualism

of strong interactors (or *keystone species*), the total number of species, and the structure, functionality and stability of the ecological community.

To model quantitatively a trophic link between species a and b (i.e., a particular kind of competition) we might use Lotka-Volterra equations [48]:

$$\frac{dN_b}{dt} = N_b \cdot (r_b - \alpha \cdot N_a)$$
$$\frac{dN_a}{dt} = N_a \cdot (\beta \cdot N_b - d)$$

where N_a and N_b are the numbers of predators and preys, respectively, r_b is the rate for prey growth, α is the prey mortality rate for per-capita predation, β models the efficiency of conversion from prey to predator and d is the mortality rate for predators.

CWC Modelling 5 (Trophic Links). *Within a compartment of type ℓ, given a predation mortality α and conversion from prey to predator β, we can encode in CWC a trophic link between individuals of species a (predator) and b (prey) by the following rules:*

$$\ell : a\ b \xmapsto{\alpha} a$$
$$\ell : a\ b \xmapsto{\beta} a\ a\ b$$

Here we omitted the rules for the prey exponential growth (absent predators) and predators exponential death (absent preys). These factors are present in the Lotka-Volterra model between two species, but could be substituted by the effects of other trophic links within the food web. In a more general scenario, a trophic link between species a and b could be expressed condensing the two rules within the single rule:

$$\ell : a\ b \xmapsto{\gamma} a\ a$$

with a rate γ modelling both the prey mortality rate and the predator conversion factor.

Example 4. Trophic cascades occur when predators in a food web suppress the abundance of their prey, thus limiting the predation of the next lower trophic level. For example, an herbivore species could be considered in an intermediate trophic level between a basal species and an higher predator. Trophic cascades are important for understanding the effects of removing top predators from food webs, as humans have done in many ecosystems through hunting or fishing activities. We consider a three-level food chain between species a, b and c. The basal species a reproduces with the logistic model, the intermediate species b feeds on a, species c predates species b:

$$\ell : a \overset{0.4}{\longmapsto} a\, a \qquad \ell : a\, a \overset{0.0002}{\longmapsto} a \qquad \ell : a\, b \overset{0.0004}{\longmapsto} b\, b \qquad \ell : b\, c \overset{0.0008}{\longmapsto} c\, c$$

Individuals of species c die naturally, until an hunting species enters the ecosystem. At a rate lower than predation, b may also die naturally (absent predator). An atom h may enter the ecosystem and start hunting individuals of species c:

$$\ell : c \overset{0.52}{\longmapsto} \bullet \qquad \ell : b \overset{0.03}{\longmapsto} \bullet \qquad \top : h\, (x \rfloor X)^{\ell} \overset{0.003}{\longmapsto} (x \rfloor X\, h)^{\ell} \qquad \ell : h\, c \overset{0.5}{\longmapsto} h$$

Figure 4 shows a simulation for the initial term $h\ (\bullet \rfloor 1000 * a\ 100 * b\ 10 * c)^{\ell}$. When the hunting activity starts, by removing the top predator, a top-down cascade destroys the whole community. The CWC model describing this example can be found at: http://www.di.unito.it/~troina/cmc13/trophic.cwc.

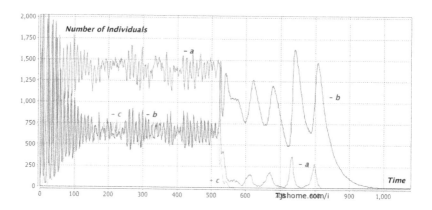

Fig. 4. A Throphic Cascade

4   An Application: *Croton wagneri* and Climate Change

Dry ecosystems are characterised by the presence of discontinuous vegetation that may reflect less than 60% of the available landscape. The main pattern in arid ecosystems is a vegetation mosaic composed of patches and clear sites. In [31] about 1300 different species belonging to the dry ecosystems in Northwest South America have been identified.

For this study we focused on the species *Croton wagneri Müll. Arg.*, belonging to the Euphorbiaceae family. This species, particularly widespread in tropical regions, can be identified by the combination of latex, alternate simple leaves, a pair of glands at the apex of the petiole, and the presence of stipules. *C. wagneri* is the dominant endemic shrub in the dry scrub of Ecuador and has been listed as Near Threatened (NT) in the Red Book of Endemic Plants of Ecuador [46]. This kind of shrub could be considered as a nurse species[10] and is particularly important for its ability to maintain the physical structure of the landscape and for its contribution to the functioning of the ecosystem (observing a marked mosaic pattern of patches having a relatively high biomass dispersed in a matrix of poor soil vegetation) [33].

The study site is located in a dry scrub in the south of Ecuador (03°58′29″ S, 01°25′22″ W) near the Catamayo Valley, with altitude ranging from 1400m to 1900m over the sea level. Floristically, in this site we can find typical species of xerophytic areas (about 107 different species and 41 botanical families). The seasonality of the area directly affects the species richness: about the 50% of the species reported in the study site emerge only in the rainy season. Most species are shrubs (including *C. wagneri*) although there are at least 12 species of trees with widely scattered individuals, at least 50% of the species are herbs. The average temperature is 20° C with an annual rainfall around 600 mm, the most of the precipitation occurs between December and March. Generally, this area is composed by clay, rocky and sandy soils [1].

In the area, 16 plots have been installed along four levels of altitude gradients (1400m, 1550m, 1700m and 1900m): two 30mx30m plots per gradient in plane terrain and two 30mx30m plots per gradient in a slope surface (with slope greater than 10°). The data collection survey consisted in enumerating all of the *C. wagneri* shrubs in the 16 plots: the spatial location of each individual was registered using a digital laser hypsometer. Additionally, plant heights were measured directly for each individual and the crown areas were calculated according to the method in [42]. Weather stations collect data about temperatures and rainfall for each altitude gradient. An extract of data collected from the field can be found at: `http://www.di.unito.it/~troina/cmc13/croton_data_extract.xlsx`. This data show a morphological response of the shrub to two factors: temperature and terrain slope. A decrease of the plant height is observed at lower temperatures (corresponding to higher altitude gradients), or at higher slopes.

4.1   The CWC Model

A simulation plot is modelled by a compartment with label P. Atoms g, representing the plot gradient (one g for each metre of altitude over the level of the sea), describe an abiotic factor put in the compartment wrap.

According to the temperature data collected by the weather stations we correlate the mean temperatures in the different plots with their respective gradients.

---

[10] A nurse plant is one with an established canopy, beneath which germination and survival are more likely due to increased shade, soil moisture, and nutrients.

In the content of a simulation plot, atoms t, representing $1°C$ each, model its temperature. Remember that, in this case, the higher the gradient, the lower the temperature. Thus, we model a constant increase of temperature within the simulation plot compartment, controlled by the gradient elements g on its wrap:

$$\top : (x \rfloor X)^P \overset{1}{\longmapsto} (x \rfloor t\ X)^P \qquad \top : (g\ x \rfloor t\ X)^P \overset{0.000024}{\longmapsto} (g\ x \rfloor X)^P$$

Atoms i are also contained within compartments of type P, representing the complementary angle of the plot's slope (e.g., $90 * i$ for a plane plot or $66 * i$ for a $24°$ slope).

We model $C.$ $wagneri$ as a CWC compartment with label c. Its observed trait, namely the plant height, is specified by atomic elements h (representing one mm each) on the compartment wrap.

To model the shrub heights distribution within a parcel, we consider the plant in two different states: a "young" and an "adult" state. Atomic elements y and a are exclusively, and uniquely, present within the plant compartment in such a way that the shrub height increases only when the shrub is in the young state (y in its content). The following rules describe (i) the passage of the plant from y to a state with a rate corresponding to a 1 year average value, and (ii) the growth of the plant, affected by temperature and slope, with a rate estimated to fit the field collected data:

$$c : y \overset{0.00274}{\longmapsto} a \qquad P : t\ i\ (x \rfloor y\ X)^c \overset{0.000718}{\longmapsto} t\ i\ (x\ h \rfloor y\ X)^c$$

4.2   Simulation Results

Now we have a model to describe the distribution of $C.$ $wagneri$ height using as parameters the plot's gradient ($n * g$) and slope ($m * i$). Since we do not model explicitly interactions that might occur between $C.$ $wagneri$ individuals, we consider plots containing a single shrub. Carrying on multiple simulations, through the two phase model of the plant growth, after 1500 time units (here represented as days), we get a snapshot of the distribution of the shrubs heights within a parcel. The CWC model describing this application can be found at: http://www.di.unito.it/~troina/cmc13/croton.cwc.

Each of the graphs in Figure 5 is obtained by plotting the height deviation of 100 simulations with initial term $(n * g \rfloor m * i\ (\bullet \rfloor y)^c)^P$. The simulations in Figures 5 (a) and (c) reflect the conditions of real plots and the results give a good approximation of the real distribution of plant heights. Figures 5 (b) and (d) are produced considering an higher slope than the ones on the real plots from were the data has been collected. These simulation results can be used for further validation of the model by collecting data on new plots corresponding to the parameters of the simulation.

If we already trust the validity of our model, we can remove the correlation between the gradient and the temperature, and directly express the latter. Predictions can thus be made about the shrub height at different temperatures, and how it could adapt to global climate change. Figure 6 shows two possible distributions of the shrub height at lower temperatures (given it will actually survive these more extreme conditions and follow the same trend).

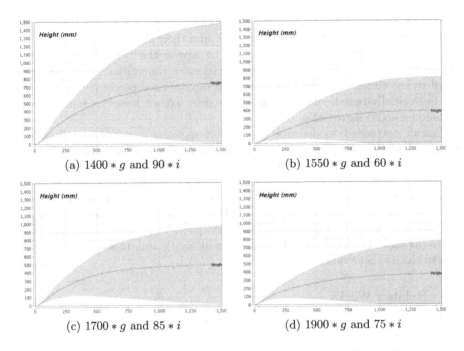

(a) $1400 * g$ and $90 * i$ (b) $1550 * g$ and $60 * i$

(c) $1700 * g$ and $85 * i$ (d) $1900 * g$ and $75 * i$

Fig. 5. Deviation of the height of *Croton wagneri* for 100 simulations

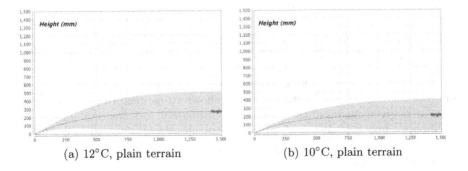

(a) $12°$C, plain terrain   (b) $10°$C, plain terrain

Fig. 6. Deviation of the height of *Croton wagneri* for 100 simulations

5   Conclusions and Related Works

The long-term goal of Computational Ecology is the development of methods to predict the response of ecosystems to changes in their physical, chemical and biological components. Computational models, and their ability to understand and predict the biological world, could be used to express the mechanisms governing the structure and function of natural populations, communities, and ecosystems. Until recent times, there was insufficient computational power to run stochastic, individually-based, spatially explicit models. Today, however, some of these techniques could be investigated [37].

Calculi developed to describe process interactions in a compartmentalised setting are well suited for the description and analysis of the evolution of ecological systems. The topology of the ecosystem can be directly encoded within the nested structure of the compartments. These calculi can be used to represent structured natural processes in a greater detail, when compared to purely numerical analysis. As an example, food webs can give rise to combinatorial interactions resulting in the formation of complex systems with emergent properties (as signalling pathways do in cellular biology), and, in some cases, giving rise to chaotic behaviour.

5.1   Related Works

As P-Systems [40,41] and the Calculus of Looping Sequences (CLS, for short) [11], the Calculus of Wrapped Compartments is a framework modelling topological compartmentalisation inspired by biological membranes, and with a semantics given in terms of rewrite rules.

CWC has been developed as a simplification of CLS, focusing on stochastic multiset rewriting. The main difference between CWC and CLS consists in the exclusion of the sequence operator, that constructs ordered strings out of the atomic elements of the calculus. While the two calculi keep the same expressiveness, some differences arise on the way systems are described. On the one hand, the Calculus of Looping Sequences allows to define ordered sequences in a more succinct way (for examples when describing sequences of genes in DNA or sequences of amino acids in proteins).[11] On the other hand, CWC reflects in a more realistic way the fluid mosaic model of the lipid bilayer (for example in the case of cellular membrane description, where proteins are free to float), and, the addition of compartment labels allows to characterise the properties peculiar to given classes of compartments. Ultimately, focusing on multisets and avoiding to deal explicitly with ordered sequences (and, thus, variables for sequences) strongly simplifies the pattern matching procedure in the development of a simulation tool.

The Calculus of Looping Sequences has been extended with type systems in [6,28,29,8,16]. As an application to ecology, stochastic CLS (see [7]) is used in [12] to model population dynamics.

---

[11] An ordered sequence can be expressed in CWC as a series of nested compartments, ordered from the outermost compartment to the innermost one.

P-Systems have been proposed as a computational model inspired by biological structures. They are defined as a nesting of membranes in which multisets of objects can react according to pre defined rewrite rules. Maximal-parallelism is the key feature of P-Systems: at each evolution step all rewrite rules, in all membranes, are applied as many times as possible. Such a feature makes P-Systems a very powerful computational model and a versatile instrument to evaluate expressiveness of languages. However, it is not practical to describe stochastic systems with a maximally-parallel evolution: exact stochastic simulations based on race conditions model systems evolutions as a sequence of successive steps, each of which with a particular duration modelled by an exponential probability distribution.

There is a large body of literature about applications of P-Systems to ecological modelling. In [20,21,22], P-Systems are enriched with a probabilistic semantics to model different ecological systems in the Catalan Pyrenees. Rules could still be applied in a parallel fashion since reduction durations are not explicitly taken into account. In [13,14,15], P-Systems are enriched with a stochastic semantics and used to model metapopulation dynamics. The addition of *mute rules* allows to keep a form of parallelism reducing the maximal consumption of objects.

While all these calculi allow to manage systems topology through nesting and compartmentalisation, explicit spatial models are able to depict more precise localities and *ecological niches*, describing how organisms or populations respond to the distribution of resources and competitors [35]. The spatial extensions of CWC [17], CLS [9] and P-Systems [10] could be used to express this kind of analysis allowing to deal with spatial coordinates.

References

1. Aguirre, Z., Kvist, P., Sánchez, O.: Floristic composition and conservation status of the dry forests in ecuador. Lyonia 8(2) (2005)
2. Aldinucci, M., Coppo, M., Damiani, F., Drocco, M., Giovannetti, E., Grassi, E., Sciacca, E., Spinella, S., Troina, A.: CWC Simulator. Dipartimento di Informatica, Università di Torino (2010), http://cwcsimulator.sourceforge.net/
3. Aldinucci, M., Coppo, M., Damiani, F., Drocco, M., Sciacca, E., Spinella, S., Torquati, M., Troina, A.: On Parallelizing On-Line Statistics for Stochastic Biological Simulations. In: Alexander, M., D'Ambra, P., Belloum, A., Bosilca, G., Cannataro, M., Danelutto, M., Di Martino, B., Gerndt, M., Jeannot, E., Namyst, R., Roman, J., Scott, S.L., Traff, J.L., Vallée, G., Weidendorfer, J. (eds.) Euro-Par 2011, Part II. LNCS, vol. 7156, pp. 3–12. Springer, Heidelberg (2012)
4. Aldinucci, M., Coppo, M., Damiani, F., Drocco, M., Torquati, M., Troina, A.: On designing multicore-aware simulators for biological systems. In: Proc. of Intl. Euromicro PDP 2011: Parallel Distributed and Network-Based Processing, pp. 318–325. IEEE Computer Society Press (2011)
5. Aldinucci, M., Torquati, M.: FastFlow website. FastFlow (Octber 2009), http://mc-fastflow.sourceforge.net/
6. Aman, B., Dezani-Ciancaglini, M., Troina, A.: Type disciplines for analysing biologically relevant properties. Electr. Notes Theor. Comput. Sci. 227, 97–111 (2009)

7. Barbuti, R., Maggiolo-Schettini, A., Milazzo, P., Tiberi, P., Troina, A.: Stochastic calculus of looping sequences for the modelling and simulation of cellular pathways. Transactions on Computational Systems Biology IX, 86–113 (2008)
8. Barbuti, R., Dezani-Ciancaglini, M., Maggiolo-Schettini, A., Milazzo, P., Troina, A.: A formalism for the description of protein interaction. Fundam. Inform. 103(1-4), 1–29 (2010)
9. Barbuti, R., Maggiolo-Schettini, A., Milazzo, P., Pardini, G.: Spatial calculus of looping sequences. Theoretical Computer Science 412(43), 5976–6001 (2011)
10. Barbuti, R., Maggiolo-Schettini, A., Milazzo, P., Pardini, G., Tesei, L.: Spatial p systems. Natural Computing 10(1), 3–16 (2011)
11. Barbuti, R., Maggiolo–Schettini, A., Milazzo, P., Troina, A.: The Calculus of Looping Sequences for Modeling Biological Membranes. In: Eleftherakis, G., Kefalas, P., Păun, G., Rozenberg, G., Salomaa, A. (eds.) WMC 2007. LNCS, vol. 4860, pp. 54–76. Springer, Heidelberg (2007)
12. Basuki, T.A., Cerone, A., Barbuti, R., Maggiolo-Schettini, A., Milazzo, P., Rossi, E.: Modelling the dynamics of an aedes albopictus population. In: AMCA-POP, vol. 33, pp. 18–36. EPTCS (2010)
13. Besozzi, D., Cazzaniga, P., Pescini, D., Mauri, G.: Seasonal variance in p system models for metapopulations. Progress in Natural Science 17(4), 392–400 (2007)
14. Besozzi, D., Cazzaniga, P., Pescini, D., Mauri, G.: Modelling metapopulations with stochastic membrane systems. Biosystems 91(3), 499–514 (2008)
15. Besozzi, D., Cazzaniga, P., Pescini, D., Mauri, G.: An analysis on the influence of network topologies on local and global dynamics of metapopulation systems. In: AMCA-POP, vol. 33, pp. 1–17. EPTCS (2010)
16. Bioglio, L., Dezani-Ciancaglini, M., Giannini, P., Troina, A.: Typed stochastic semantics for the calculus of looping sequences. Theor. Comp. Sci. 431, 165–180 (2012)
17. Bioglio, L., Calcagno, C., Coppo, M., Damiani, F., Sciacca, E., Spinella, S., Troina, A.: A spatial calculus of wrapped compartments. In: MeCBIC, vol. abs/1108.3426. CoRR (2011)
18. Bolker, B.: Ecological models and data in R. Princeton University Press (2008)
19. Calcagno, C., Coppo, M., Damiani, F., Drocco, M., Sciacca, E., Spinella, S., Troina, A.: Modelling spatial interactions in the arbuscular mycorrhizal symbiosis using the calculus of wrapped compartments. In: CompMod 2011, vol. 67, pp. 3–18. EPTCS (2011)
20. Cardona, M., Colomer, M.A., Margalida, A., Palau, A., Pérez-Hurtado, I., Pérez-Jiménez, M.J., Sanuy, D.: A computational modeling for real ecosystems based on p systems. Natural Computing 10(1), 39–53 (2011)
21. Cardona, M., Colomer, M.A., Margalida, A., Pérez-Hurtado, I., Pérez-Jiménez, M.J., Sanuy, D.: A P System Based Model of an Ecosystem of Some Scavenger Birds. In: Păun, G., Pérez-Jiménez, M.J., Riscos-Núñez, A., Rozenberg, G., Salomaa, A. (eds.) WMC 2009. LNCS, vol. 5957, pp. 182–195. Springer, Heidelberg (2010)
22. Cardona, M., Colomer, M.A., Pérez-Jiménez, M.J., Sanuy, D., Margalida, A.: Modeling Ecosystems Using P Systems: The Bearded Vulture, a Case Study. In: Corne, D.W., Frisco, P., Păun, G., Rozenberg, G., Salomaa, A. (eds.) WMC9 2008. LNCS, vol. 5391, pp. 137–156. Springer, Heidelberg (2009)
23. Caswell, H.: Matrix population models: Construction, analysis and interpretation, 2nd edn. Sinauer Associates, Sunderland (2001)
24. Coppo, M., Damiani, F., Drocco, M., Grassi, E., Guether, M., Troina, A.: Modelling ammonium transporters in arbuscular mycorrhiza symbiosis. Transactions on Computational Systems Biology XIII, 85–109 (2011)

25. Coppo, M., Damiani, F., Drocco, M., Grassi, E., Sciacca, E., Spinella, S., Troina, A.: Hybrid calculus of wrapped compartments. In: MeCBIC, vol. 40, pp. 103–121. EPTCS (2010)
26. Coppo, M., Damiani, F., Drocco, M., Grassi, E., Sciacca, E., Spinella, S., Troina, A.: Simulation techniques for the calculus of wrapped compartments. Theor. Comp. Sci. 431, 75–95 (2012)
27. Coppo, M., Damiani, F., Drocco, M., Grassi, E., Troina, A.: Stochastic Calculus of Wrapped Compartments. In: QAPL, vol. 28, pp. 82–98. EPTCS (2010)
28. Dezani-Ciancaglini, M., Giannini, P., Troina, A.: A type system for required/excluded elements in CLS. In: DCM 2009, vol. 9, pp. 38–48. EPTCS (2009)
29. Dezani-Ciancaglini, M., Giannini, P., Troina, A.: A type system for a stochastic cls. In: MeCBIC 2009, vol. 11, pp. 91–105. EPTCS (2009)
30. Elton, C.: Animal Ecology. Sidgwick and Jackson (1927)
31. Gentry, A.: A Field Guide to the Families and Genera of Woody Plants of Northwest South America (Colombia, Ecuador, Peru): with supplementary notes on herbaceous taxa, Washington DC, Conservation International (1993)
32. Gillespie, D.: Exact stochastic simulation of coupled chemical reactions. J. Phys. Chem. 81, 2340–2361 (1977)
33. Gutiérrez, J.: Importancia de los Arbustos Leñosos en los Ecosistemas de la IV Región, Libro Rojo de la Flora Nativa y de los Sitios Prioritarios para su Conservación: Región de Coquimbo, vol. 16. Ediciones Universidad de La Serena, Chile (2001)
34. Levins, R.: Some demographic and genetic consequences of environmental heterogeneity for biological control. Bulletin of the Entomological Society of America 15, 237–240 (1969)
35. Lomolino, M.V., Brown, J.W.: Biogeography. Sinauer Associates, Sunderland (1998)
36. Oury, N., Plotkin, G.: Multi-level modelling via stochastic multi-level multiset rewriting. Mathematical Structures in Computer Science (2012)
37. Petrovskii, S., Petrovskaya, N.: Computational ecology as an emerging science. Interface Focus 2(2), 241–254 (2012)
38. Pianka, E.: On r and k selection. American Naturalist 104(940), 592–597 (1970)
39. Pielou, E.: Mathematical ecology. Wiley (1977)
40. Păun, G.: Computing with membranes. Journal of Computer and System Sciences 61(1), 108–143 (2000)
41. Păun, G.: Membrane Computing. An Introduction. Springer (2002)
42. Shiponeni, N., Allsopp, N., Carrick, P., Hoffman, M.: Competitive interactions between grass and succulent shrubs at the ecotone between an arid grassland and succulent shrubland in the karoo. Plant. Ecol. 212(5), 795–808 (2011)
43. Sugihara, G., May, R.: Nonlinear forecasting as a way of distinguishing chaos from measurement error in time series. Nature 344(6268), 734–741 (1990)
44. Takeuchi, Y.: Cooperative systems theory and global stability of diffusion models. Acta Applicandae Mathematicae 14, 49–57 (1989)
45. Thompson, J.: The geographic mosaic of coevolution. University of Chicago Press (2005)
46. Valencia, R., Pitman, N., León-Yánez, S., Jorgensen, P.: Libro Rojo de las Plantas Endémicas del Ecuador. Herbario QCA, Pontificia Universidad Católica del Ecuador, Quito (2000)
47. Verhulst, P.: Notice sur la loi que la population pursuit dans son accroissement. Corresp. Math. Phys. 10, 113–121 (1838)
48. Volterra, V.: Variazioni e fluttuazioni del numero dindividui in specie animali conviventi. Mem. Acad. Lincei Roma 2, 31–113 (1926)

Observer/Interpreter P Systems

Dragoş Sburlan

Ovidius University of Constanta
Faculty of Mathematics and Informatics
Constanta, Mamaia 124, Romania

Abstract. In this paper we discuss Observer/Interpreter P systems, i.e., a model of computation inspired by the possibility of tracking and detecting fluorescent proteins in living cells and interpreting the results by visualizing molecular events in real time. In this regard, we define Observer/Interpreter P systems as a couple of two independent systems: a P system with symbol objects and multiset rewriting rules and a finite state machine able to perform an operation (addition/subtraction) on a register. We investigate the computational power of the model when different features are taken into account.

1   Introduction

One important breakthrough in the study of living cells was the possibility to label proteins for imaging use. This was achieved by using some genetically encoded fluorescent fusion tags (for instance, the Nobel Prize in Chemistry in 2008 was awarded to Osamu Shimomura, Martin Chalfie and Roger Tsien for the discovery and development of green fluorescent protein – GFP, that was used by researchers to study the development of nerve cells in the brain or how cancer cells spread). The gene for GFP was originally isolated from the jellyfish, *Aequorea victoria*, and since then, a lot of scientific effort has been focused on the discovery of processes occurring inside cells. By visualizing molecular events happening within the living cells one can trace the molecules function and regulation. In general, the common methods for labeling molecules in biological systems are based on the genetic fusion of fluorescent tags. Using these tags one can watch at nanometer scale the behavior of molecules (the movement, positions, and interactions), hence one can unravel the regulatory mechanisms of biological systems.

Nowadays, the code for GFP can be inserted at any given position in the genome and once there, it will act as a label for the other genes around it. Accordingly, one can place a GFP gene next to a given gene of interest and then study how the corresponding protein behaves by watching the green fluorescence. Moreover, the sequence of aminoacids in the GFP can be genetically engineered such that it will produce fluorescent proteins glowed in many different colors. In this way, several distinct types of proteins can be marked by different colors, hence one can gather useful data regarding the proteins interactions in one single experiment. For example, by shining UV light on the sample, one can visualize the fine detail of the interior of cells, reflecting the position and the amount of particular tagged proteins.

E. Csuhaj-Varjú et al. (Eds.): CMC 2012, LNCS 7762, pp. 378–389, 2013.
© Springer-Verlag Berlin Heidelberg 2013

Having as inspiration the way by which the behavior of glowing proteins in a living cell can be externally watched, here we propose a computational model composed by two independent systems: a standard P system with symbol objects and multiset rewriting rules (which corresponds to a mathematical model for the living cell) and a finite state machine with output that *observes* (changes its state) and *interprets* (produces an output action) the computation of the P system. A related model was introduced in [2] and since then a similar idea was applied for many types of abstract machines (see [4], [1], and [3]). However, here the observation is performed from a different perspective. Firstly, we assume that given a nano-computing bio-device, which operates at the level of bio-reactions, it will be very difficult to count the number of objects in a given configuration. Consequently, the original method for collecting the results of a successful computation will be hard to be implemented. Instead, we believe that it will be much easier to detect the increasing/decreasing of the number of objects in consecutive configurations. More precisely, we are interested by the changes that appear between consecutive configurations (and not by the apparition of certain symbols as in the cases studied in the existing literature).

2 Background

We presume the reader to be aware of the basic knowledge from formal language theory, theory of computation, and membrane computing (see [6], [7] for the classical theory of formal languages; see [5], [9], and [10] for the theory of membrane computing). Here we will only recall several concepts and results which are related strictly to what will be further presented.

We denote by FIN, REG, CF, CS, and RE the families of finite, regular, context-free, context-sensitive, and recursively enumerable languages, respectively. The Chomsky hierarchy states that $FIN \subset REG \subset CF \subset CS \subset RE$. If FL is a family of languages then we denote by NFL the family of length sets of languages in FL. In terms of length sets, the Chomsky hierarchy is $NFIN \subset NREG = NCF \subset NCS \subset NRE$.

Generalized Sequential Machines
The family of regular languages REG is equal with the family of languages accepted by finite state machines.

Generalized sequential machines (GSM) are finite state machines with output. More formally, a GSM is a tuple $M = (Q, \Sigma, \Delta, \delta, q_0, F)$ where Q is the state set, Σ is the input alphabet, Δ is the output alphabet, $\delta : Q \times \Sigma \to \mathscr{P}(Q \times \Delta^*)$ is the transition function, $q_0 \in Q$ is the initial state, and $F \subseteq Q$ is the set of final states. In order to describe the functioning of M, the transition function δ can be extended to a function on $Q \times \Sigma^*$ as follows:

- $\delta(q, \lambda) = \{(q, \lambda)\}$
- if $x \in \Sigma^*$ and $a \in \Sigma$ then

$$\delta(q, xa) = \{(p, w) \mid w = w_1 w_2 \text{ and } (\exists)\, p' \in Q, \text{ such that}$$
$$(p', w_1) \in \delta(q, x) \text{ and } (p, w_2) \in \delta(p', a)\}.$$

If M is a GSM defined as above and $x \in \Sigma^*$ then $M(x)$ denotes the set

$$\{y \mid (\exists)p \in F \text{ such that } (p, y) \in \delta(q_0, x)\}.$$

If $L \subseteq \Sigma^*$ is a language, then $M(L) = \bigcup_{w \in L} M(w)$.

A GSM always maps a regular language to a regular language.

Register Machines

A *register machine* is a tuple $M = (n, \mathcal{P}, l_0, l_h)$, where $n \geq 1$ is the number of registers (each register stores a natural number), $\mathcal{P}$ is a finite set of uniquely labeled instructions ($\mathcal{P}$ is called the program and the labels of the instructions are from a set $lab(\mathcal{P})$), l_0 is the initial label, and l_h is the halting label.

The instructions can be of the following forms:

- $l_1 : (add(r), l_2, l_3)$ – where $l_1, l_2, l_3 \in lab(\mathcal{P})$, adds 1 to register r and non-deterministically proceeds to one of the instructions l_2 or l_3.
- $l_1 : (sub(r), l_2, l_3)$ – where $l_1, l_2, l_3 \in lab(\mathcal{P})$, subtracts 1 from register r if the number stored by register r is greater than zero and goes to the instruction with the label l_2, otherwise goes to the instruction with the label l_3.
- $l_h : halt$ – where $l_h \in lab(\mathcal{P})$, halts the machine.

M starts with all registers being empty and runs the program $\mathcal{P}$, starting from the instruction with the label l_0. Considering the content of register 1 for all possible computations of M which are ended by the execution of the instruction labeled l_h, one gets the set $N(M) \subseteq \mathbb{N}$ – the set generated by M.

The following result concerns the computational power of register machines.

Theorem 1. *For any recursively enumerable set $Q \subseteq \mathbb{N}$ there exists a non-deterministic register machine with 3-registers generating Q such that when starting with all registers being empty, M non-deterministically computes and halts with n in register 1, and registers 2 and 3 being empty iff $n \in Q$.*

Lindenmayer Systems

Lindenmayer systems are parallel computing devices representing a development model inspired by multicellular organisms growth. A 0L system is a tuple $G = (V, \omega, P)$ where V is an alphabet, $\omega \in V^*$ is the axiom, and $P \subseteq V \times V^*$ is a complete finite set of rules. For $w_1, w_2 \in V^*$ we write $w_1 \Rightarrow w_2$ if $w_1 = a_1 \ldots a_n$, $w_1 = x_1 \ldots x_n$, for $a_i \to x_i \in P$, $1 \leq i \leq n$. The language generated by G is $L(G) = \{x \in V^* \mid \omega \Rightarrow^* x\}$ where $\Rightarrow^*$ denotes the reflexive and transitive closure of $\Rightarrow$.

An extended tabled interactionless Lindenmayer system (ET0L system, for short) is a tuple $H = (V, T, \omega, \Delta)$ where $\Delta \subseteq V$ is the terminal alphabet, $T = \{P_1, \ldots, P_k\}$ is a finite nonempty set of tables and such that each triple $G_i = (V, \omega, P_i)$, $1 \leq i \leq k$, represents a 0L system. The language generated by H is

$$L(H) = \{x \in \Delta^* \mid \omega \Longrightarrow_{P_{j_1}} w_1 \Longrightarrow_{P_{j_2}} \cdots \Longrightarrow_{P_{j_m}} w_m = x,$$
$$m \geq 0, 1 \leq j_i \leq k, 1 \leq i \leq m\}.$$

It is known that $CF \subset ET0L \subset CS$ and that $NCF \subset NET0L \subset NCS$. The set $\{2^n \mid n \geq 0\} \in NET0L \setminus NCF$.

The following result represents a normal form for the ET0L systems ([7]).

Lemma 1. *For each $L \in ET0L$ there is an extended tabled interactionless Lindenmayer system $H = (V, T, \omega, \Delta)$ with two tables ($T = \{T_1, T_2\}$) generating L, such that for each $a \in \Delta$ if $a \to \alpha \in T_1 \cup T_2$ then $\alpha = a$.*

P Systems with Symbol Objects and Multiset Rewriting Rules

A P system with symbol objects and multiset rewriting rules of degree $m \geq 1$ is a tuple

$$\Pi = (O, C, \mu, w_1, \ldots, w_m, R_1, \ldots, R_m, i_0) \text{ where}$$

- O is a finite set of objects;
- $C \subseteq O$ is the set of catalysts;
- μ is a tree structure of m uniquely labeled membranes which delimit the regions of Π; the set of labels is $\{1, \ldots, m\}$;
- w_i, $1 \leq i \leq m$, is the multiset of objects, initially present in the region i of Π;
- R_i, $1 \leq i \leq m$, is a finite set of multiset rewriting rules associated with the region i; the rules are of type $ca \to cv$ or $a \to v$, where $c \in C$, $a \in O \setminus C$, and $v \in ((O \setminus C) \times \{here, out, in\})^*$.

The initial configuration of Π is $C_0 = (\mu, w_1, \ldots, w_m)$. A transition between configurations means to apply in parallel a maximal multiset of evolution rules (the rules are nondeterministically chosen and they compete for the available objects), in all the regions of Π. The application of a rule $u \to v$ in a region containing the multiset w consists of subtracting from w the multiset u and then adding the objects composing v in the regions indicated by the targets *in*, *out*, and *here* (we usually omit the target *here*). The P system iteratively takes parallel steps until there remain no applicable rules in any region Π; then, the system halts. The number of objects in the region i_0 of Π in the *halting configuration* represents the result of the underlying computation of Π. By collecting the results of all possible computations of Π one gets the set of natural numbers $N(\Pi)$ generated by Π. The families of all sets of numbers generated by P systems with symbol objects, multiset rewriting rules, with at most m membranes, and with at most k catalysts (i.e., $card(C) = k$) is denoted by $NOP_m(cat_k)$.

The following results regard the computational power of the P system model defined above ([10]).

Proposition 1. $NOP_m(cat_k) = NOP_1(cat_k)$, *for any $k \geq 0$*

Theorem 2. $NREG = NOP_1(cat_0) \subset NOP_1(cat_2) = NRE$.

The exact characterization of the computational power of catalytic P systems with only one catalyst remains an open problem.

3 Observation / Interpretation

Based on the motivation exposed in the Introduction, one can imagine a computational device $\Phi = (\Pi, \mathcal{M})$ (called Observer/Interpreter P system) composed by a pair of systems: a P system Π (called the *core system*) and a finite state machine with output $\mathcal{M}$ which is able to detect in any configuration a change in the multiset of a region of the core system and which can perform a certain operation based on the observation.

Without any loss of generality and for the simplicity of exposition, we may assume that the core system Π is a P system with symbol objects and multiset rewriting rules and which has only one membrane, that is $\Pi = (O, C, \mu = [\,]_1, R_1, w_1, i_0 = 1)$ having the components defined as the P system model presented in Section 2 (this can be assumed true because one can encode the presence of an object a in a given region l as an index of a, e.g., a_l; next, rewriting the rules from all the regions accordingly, one can obtain an equivalent P system with only one region). Because Π has only one membrane we can define a configuration of Π as a multiset $w \in O^*$. The initial configuration is $C_0 = w_1$. Given two configurations C_1 and C_2 of Π, we say that C_2 is obtained from C_1 in one transition step (denoted by $C_1 \vdash C_2$) by applying the rules from R_1 in a nondeterministic maximal parallel manner and with the competition on objects. The reflexive and transitive closure of $\vdash$ is denoted by $\vdash^*$. The system continues performing parallel steps until there remain no applicable rules; then the system halts (the underlying computation is a halting one). The number of objects from O contained in the output region $i_0 = 1$ is the result of the underlying computation of Π.

Given a multiset $M : O \to \mathbb{N}$ then $M(a)$, $a \in O$, represents the multiplicity of a in M. For an ordered pair (M_1, M_2) of multisets $M_1, M_2 : O \to \mathbb{N}$, we denote by $a \uparrow$ the case when $M_1(a) < M_2(a)$ (which indicates the increasing of the number of objects a from M_1 to M_2), by $a \downarrow$ the case when $M_1(a) > M_2(a)$ (which indicates the decreasing of the number of objects a from M_1 to M_2), and finally by $a-$ the case when $M_1(a) = M_2(a)$. A (partial) observation of the pair (M_1, M_2) is a subset of $\{a \uparrow \mid a \in O, M_1(a) < M_2(a)\} \cup \{a \downarrow \mid a \in O, M_1(a) > M_2(a)\} \cup \{a- \mid a \in O, M_1(a) = M_2(a)\}$. Considering that $O = \{a_1, \dots, a_k\}$, then the set of all possible observations is denoted by

$$\mathcal{O} = \{\{x_1, \dots, x_k\} \mid (\exists)\, \{y_1, \dots, y_k\} \subseteq O \text{ and} \\ x_i \in \{y_i \uparrow, y_i \downarrow, y_i-\}, \text{ for } 1 \le i \le k\}.$$

The Observer/Interpreter P system is a finite state machine with output

$$\mathcal{M} = (Q, \mathcal{O}, \Delta, \delta, \lambda, q_0, F, r)$$

where Q is a finite set of states, $\mathcal{O}$ is the set of all possible observations, $q_0 \in Q$ is the initial state, $F \subseteq Q$ is the set of final states, and r is a data register able to store an integer (r is initially set to 0). The transition function $\delta : Q \times \mathcal{O} \to Q$ defines the functioning of the machine: if M is in a state $q \in Q$ and given an observation $o \in \mathcal{O}$, then M moves to the state $\delta(q, o)$. The interpretation function $\lambda : Q \times \mathcal{O} \to \{inc, dec, skip\}$ describes the output actions performed by M: assuming that M is in a state $q \in Q$ and given an observation $o \in \mathcal{O}$, then M will perform the action $\lambda(q, o)$ (it increments register r if $\lambda(q, o) = inc$, it decrements register r if $\lambda(q, o) = dec$, and it does not modify the content of r if $\lambda(q, o) = skip$). The output of $\mathcal{M}$ in response to a sequence of observations $o_1, o_2, \ldots, o_k$ consists in the applications of the actions given by $\lambda(q_0, o_1), \ldots, \lambda(q_{k-1}, o_k)$ on register r, where $q_0, \ldots, q_n$ is the sequence of states such that $\delta(q_{i-1}, o_i) = q_i$, $1 \le i \le n$; the sequence of observations $o_1, o_2, \ldots, o_k$ is called accepted by $\mathcal{M}$ iff $q_n \in F$.

The system $\Phi = (\Pi, \mathcal{M})$ computes as follows. The systems Π and $\mathcal{M}$ run in parallel: at each passing from a configuration C_1 to C_2 in a computation of Π, based on the observation $\{x_1, \ldots, x_k\}$ of the pair (C_1, C_2), the system $\mathcal{M}$ changes its current state q to a new one $p = \delta(q, \{x_1, \ldots, x_k\})$; in addition, $\mathcal{M}$ performs the action defined by $\lambda(q, \{x_1, \ldots, x_k\})$. A computation of Φ is considered successful if the above procedure is applied for each pair of consecutive configurations in a halting computation of Π and the system $\mathcal{M}$ accepts the sequence of observations determined by the computation of Π, providing that the number stored by r never becomes negative; in this case, the result of the computation is the number stored in register r at its end. Collecting all the values stored by r at the end of all possible successful computations of Φ one obtains the set of integers $N(\Phi(\Pi, \mathcal{M}))$.

In case of a non-halting computation of Π, the system Φ does not produce any output. The same outcome is obtained when $\mathcal{M}$ does not accept the sequence of observations determined by the underlying computation of Π or when during the computation the number stored by r becomes negative.

The families of all sets of numbers generated by Observer/Interpreter P systems, having as core systems P systems with symbol objects, multiset rewriting rules, at most k catalysts and one membrane is denoted by $NOI(cat_k)$.

Because the system $\mathcal{M}$ recalls the definition of a GSM, in what follows we will use a similar notation for the transition graph.

Example 1. *Let* $\Phi = (\Pi, \mathcal{M})$ *such that* $\Pi = (O, C, \mu, R_1, w_1, i_0)$ *where* $O = \{a, \bar{a}, \bar{\bar{a}}, c\}$, $C = \{c\}$, $\mu = [\ ]_1$, $w_1 = a$, $i_0 = 1$, *and* R_1 *is defined as follows:*

$$R_1 = \{a \to aa,$$
$$a \to \bar{a},$$
$$\bar{a} \to \bar{\bar{a}},$$
$$c\bar{\bar{a}} \to c\}.$$

The system $\mathcal{M}$ is defined by the transition graph depicted in Figure 1.

The computation of Φ proceeds as follows. If the rule $a \to aa$ is the only rule applied in the first k consecutive configurations of Π, then 2^{k-1} objects a are produced. During this exponential generation of objects a, the system $\mathcal{M}$ remains in state q_0 (this is because $\mathcal{M}$ detects that the number of objects $\bar{a}$ does not change). Assuming that in the k-th configuration both the rules $a \to aa$ and $a \to \bar{a}$ are applied, then $\mathcal{M}$, being in state q_0, can either remain in the same state q_0 and the computation stops (an unsuccessful computation; the case $a-$ or $a \uparrow, \bar{a} \uparrow$) or it can pass to state q_1 (the case $a \downarrow, \bar{a} \uparrow$). However, there is no guarantee that all the objects a were rewritten by $a \to \bar{a}$; $\mathcal{M}$ will arrive in state

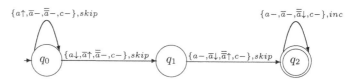

Fig. 1. The system $\mathcal{M}$ "observes" the couples of consecutive configurations of Π and "interprets" them

q_2 iff all the objects a were rewritten firstly into $\bar{a}$ and then into $\bar{\bar{a}}$. Finally, by applying the loop transition from state q_2 one gets as output 2^{k-1}.

In what follows, we are interested by the computational power of these systems and their relations with the classical families of sets of numbers.

Theorem 3. *For any language L generated by an ET0L system $H = (V, T, \omega, \Delta)$ and any word $w \in \Delta^*$ there exists an Observer/Interpreter P system $\Phi = (\Pi, \mathcal{M})$ such that Π is a P system with symbol objects and non-cooperative multiset rewriting rules and that halts generating 0 iff $|w| \in length(L)$.*

Proof. Without any loss of generality assume that $card(T) = 2$.
  Let $\overline{V_{-\Delta}} = \{\bar{a} \mid a \in V \setminus \Delta\}$ and $h : V^* \to (\overline{V_{-\Delta}} \cup \Delta)^*$ such that
• $h(a) = \bar{a}$ if $a \in V \setminus \Delta$
• $h(a) = a$ if $a \in \Delta$
• $h(\lambda) = \lambda$
• $h(x_1 x_2) = h(x_1)h(x_2)$, for $x_1, x_2 \in V^*$.
Then we can construct an Observer/Interpreter P system $\Phi(\Pi, \mathcal{M})$ that simulates the computation of H as follows.
  $\Pi = (O, C, \mu = [\,]_1, R_1, w_1, i_0 = 1)$ where

$$O = V \cup \overline{V_{-\Delta}} \cup \{t, e, T_1, T_2\},$$
$$C = \emptyset,$$
$$w_1 = wt.$$

The set of rules is defined below:

$$R_1 = \{t \to t,\ t \to \lambda,\ T_1 \to \lambda,\ T_2 \to \lambda\}$$
$$\cup \{A \to h(\alpha)T_1 \mid A \to \alpha \in T_1, A \in V \setminus \Delta\}$$
$$\cup \{A \to h(\alpha)T_2 \mid A \to \alpha \in T_2, A \in V \setminus \Delta\}$$
$$\cup \{\overline{A} \to A \mid A \in V \setminus \Delta\}.$$

The finite state machine $\mathcal{M}$ is defined in Figure 2.
  Assuming that $\mathcal{M}$ is in state q_0 and Π is in a configuration wt where $w \in V^*$ (w corresponds to a string derived by H), then $\mathcal{M}$ passes from state q_0 to state

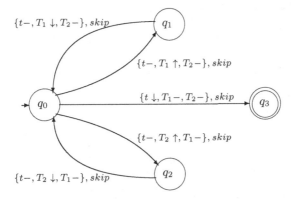

Fig. 2. The system $\mathcal{M}$ that is used to regulate the computation of Π

q_1 if Π executes the rules $t \to t$, the rules corresponding to the Table 1 of system H (i.e., rules from the set $\{A \to h(\alpha)T_1 \mid A \to \alpha \in T_1, A \in V \setminus \Delta\}$, and no rules corresponding to the Table 2 (recall that the observation set is $\{t-, T_1 \uparrow, T_2-\}$). Next, if $\mathcal{M}$ is in state q_1, then the only way for $\mathcal{M}$ to comeback to the state q_0 is that Π executes the rules $t \to t$, $T_1 \to \lambda$, and the rules from the set $\{\overline{A} \to A \mid A \in V \setminus \Delta\}$.

The applications of rules of Π in these two steps ("regulated" in a certain sense by the actions of $\mathcal{M}$) correspond to an application of Table 1 of H. Moreover, if $\mathcal{M}$ is in the state q_0 and Π executes the rule $t \to \lambda$ and at least one rule from the set $\{A \to h(\alpha)T_1 \mid A \to \alpha \in T_1, A \in V \setminus \Delta\} \cup \{A \to h(\alpha)T_2 \mid A \to \alpha \in T_2, A \in V \setminus \Delta\}$ then $\mathcal{M}$ will halt in state q_0 by rejecting; if instead Π executes $t \to \lambda$ and no rule that produces object(s) T_1 or T_2 (that is, the number of objects T_1 and T_2 does not grow between consecutive configurations) then $\mathcal{M}$ passes from the state q_0 to q_3 and accepts (actually, Π halts by having in its region a multiset composed only by terminals and which correspond to a string generated by H). However, $N(\Phi(\Pi, \mathcal{M})) = \{0\}$ and $\Phi(\Pi, \mathcal{M})$ halts by having 0 in its register iff $w \in L(H)$.

The following result shows the computational power of the Observer/ Interpreter systems when P systems with symbol objects and multiset rewriting rules (with one catalyst) are used as core systems.

Theorem 4. $NOI(cat_1) = NRE$.

Proof. The inclusion $NOI(cat_1) \subseteq NRE$ is supposed to be true by invoking the Turing-Church thesis. The opposite inclusion $NOI(cat_1) \supseteq NRE$ can be shown by simulating an arbitrary register machine $M = (n, \mathcal{P}, l_0, l_h)$ with 3 registers ($n = 3$) with an Observer/Interpreter P system $\Phi(\Pi, \mathcal{M})$; the P system Π uses non-cooperative and/or catalytic rules with one catalyst. The core system $\Pi = (O, C, \mu = [\,]_1, R_1, w_1, i_0 = 1)$ is defined as follows:

$$O = lab(\mathcal{P}) \cup \{\overline{p} \mid p \in lab(\mathcal{P})\} \cup \{a_1, a_2, a_3, \overline{a_1}, \overline{a_2}, \overline{a_3}, \overline{\overline{a_1}}, \overline{\overline{a_2}}, \overline{\overline{a_3}}\}$$

$$\cup \{X_1, X_2, X_3\} \cup \{c\},$$
$$C = \{c\},$$
$$w_1 = l_0,$$

and the set of rules R_1 is defined below:
• the following rules are added to R_1

$$a_i \to \overline{a_i}, \text{ for } 1 \le i \le 3$$
$$\overline{a_i} \to a_i, \text{ for } 1 \le i \le 3$$

• for any instruction $l_1 : (sub(r), l_2, l_3) \in \mathcal{P}$ the following rules are added to R_1

$$c\overline{a_r} \to cX_r$$
$$X_r \to \lambda$$
$$l_1 \to \overline{l_2}$$
$$\overline{l_2} \to l_2$$
$$l_1 \to \overline{l_3}$$
$$\overline{l_3} \to l_3$$

In case of $\mathcal{M}$, the states and the transitions between them are defined as follows.

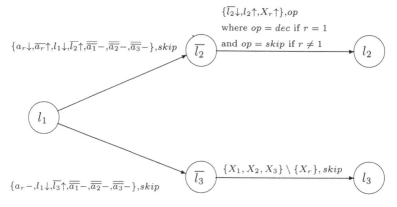

• for any instruction $l_1 : (add(r), l_2, l_3) \in \mathcal{P}$

$$l_1 \to \overline{l_1}$$
$$\overline{l_1} \to l_2 a_r$$
$$\overline{l_1} \to l_3 a_r$$

In case of $\mathcal{M}$, the states and the transitions between them are defined as follows.

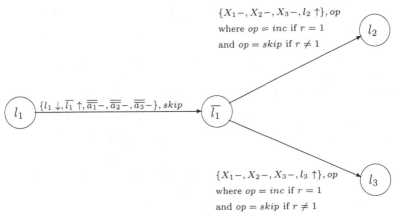

$\{X_1-, X_2-, X_3-, l_2 \uparrow\}, op$
where $op = inc$ if $r = 1$
and $op = skip$ if $r \neq 1$

$\{l_1 \downarrow, \overline{l_1} \uparrow, \overline{a_1}-, \overline{a_2}-, \overline{a_3}-\}, skip$

$\{X_1-, X_2-, X_3-, l_3 \uparrow\}, op$
where $op = inc$ if $r = 1$
and $op = skip$ if $r \neq 1$

- for the instruction $l_h : halt \in \mathcal{P}$

$$l_h \to \lambda$$
$$a_i \to \overline{\overline{a_i}}, 1 \leq i \leq 3$$

In case of $\mathcal{M}$, the states and the transitions between them are defined as follows.

$$l_h \quad \{l_h \downarrow, \overline{a_1}-, \overline{a_2}-, \overline{a_3}-\}, skip \quad l_H$$

Here is shown how $\Phi(\Pi, \mathcal{M})$ works. At the beginning of a computation in the region 1 of Π there exists the multiset composed by just one object l_0 (that corresponds to the label of the first register machine instruction). This object will be iteratively rewritten during the computation (according with the register machine program) into the label of an instruction. In any configuration in a computation of Π, the number of objects a_r corresponds to the number stored in register r, $1 \leq r \leq 3$. Following the register machine definition, in the initial configuration there will be no objects a_r, $1 \leq r \leq 3$, because the register machine M starts with all registers being empty.

Assume now that the current register machine instruction to be simulated is $l_1 : (add(r), l_2, l_3)$; then Π is in a configuration $C = l_1 a_1^{k_1} a_2^{k_2} a_3^{k_3}$ and $\mathcal{M}$ is in the state labeled l_1. In this configuration, Π executes the rules $l_1 \to \overline{l_1}$ and $a_r \to \overline{a_r}$, for $1 \leq r \leq 3$. Consequently, the next configuration is $C' = \overline{l_1} \overline{a_1}^{k_1} \overline{a_2}^{k_2} \overline{a_3}^{k_3}$, hence $\mathcal{M}$ passes from state l_1 to state $\overline{l_1}$. Next, Π non-deterministically executes one of the rules $\overline{l_1} \to l_2 a_r$ and $\overline{l_1} \to l_3 a_r$ (exactly one of them, because there is only one object $\overline{l_1}$), and the rules $\overline{a_r} \to a_r$; in this way the next configuration will be $C'' = l_2 a_1^{k_1} a_2^{k_2} a_3^{k_3} a_r$ or $C'' = l_3 a_1^{k_1} a_2^{k_2} a_3^{k_3} a_r$ where $1 \leq r \leq 3$. It follows that $\mathcal{M}$ passes from state $\overline{l_1}$ to the state l_2 or l_3, therefore the simulation of the addition instruction was correctly performed. However, as we will see later on, there might be the case when Π, being in configuration C', it also executes rules of type $c\overline{a_r} \to cX_r$. In this case, the finite state machine $\mathcal{M}$ cannot pass from state $\overline{l_1}$ to l_2 or l_3 and the input is rejected.

Without any loss of generality, let us consider that the current register machine instruction to be executed is $l_1 : (sub(r_1), l_2, l_3)$ (that is M attempts to decrement register 1) and that Π is in a configuration $C = l_1 a_1^{k_1} a_2^{k_2} a_3^{k_3}$, with $k_1, k_2, k_3 \geq 0$. We have two possible cases:

Case 1: $k_1 \geq 1$. In this case Π executes the rule $a_1 \to \overline{a_1}$ (if in the current multiset there are also the objects a_2 and a_3, then also the rules $a_2 \to \overline{a_2}$ and $a_3 \to \overline{a_3}$ are executed) and one of the rules $l_1 \to \overline{l_2}$ or $l_1 \to \overline{l_3}$. If the rule $l_1 \to \overline{l_2}$ is executed, then M passes from state l_1 to $\overline{l_2}$, otherwise M halts in state l_1 rejecting the computation. Next, if M is in state $\overline{l_2}$ and the system Π is in configuration $\overline{l_2} \overline{a_1}^{k_1} \overline{a_2}^{k_2} \overline{a_3}^{k_3}$ the rules that can be applied are: $\overline{l_2} \to l_2$, $\overline{a_r} \to a_r$, and $c\overline{a_r} \to CX_r$, for $1 \leq r \leq 3$ (from these rules only the rule $\overline{l_2} \to l_2$ will surely be applied, while the others will be applied, depending on the values of k_1, k_2, and k_3, in any combination but such that at least one of the rules $\overline{a_r} \to a_r$ and $c\overline{a_r} \to CX_r$, $1 \leq r \leq 3$, will be selected for application; moreover if a rule involving the catalyst c is applied, then all the other rules involving c are not applied). Consequently M can pass from state $\overline{l_2}$ to state l_2 if and only if $ca_1 \to cX_1$ is applied (that is, $X_1 \uparrow$ appears in the observation set).

Case 2: $k_1 = 0$. In this situation, Π cannot execute the rule $a_1 \to \overline{a_1}$ because there is no object a_1, hence the number of objects a_1 remains unchanged. It follows that M goes from state l_1 to $\overline{l_3}$ if the rule $l_1 \to \overline{l_3}$ is executed (the observation set is $\{a_1-, l_1 \downarrow, \overline{l_3} \uparrow\}$). Next, M will pass from state $\overline{l_3}$ to state l_3 iff the rules $c\overline{a_2} \to cX_2$ and $c\overline{a_3} \to cX_3$ are not applied (that is, if there exist the objects $\overline{a_2}$ and $\overline{a_3}$, then only the rules $\overline{a_2} \to a_2$ and $\overline{a_3} \to a_3$ are applied).

Assuming now that M is in the state labeled l_h and the object with the same name l_h is generated by Π, then M changes its state to l_H iff the rules $l_h \to \lambda$ and $a_i \to \overline{\overline{a_i}}$, $1 \leq i \leq 3$, are applied (the observation set $\{l_h \downarrow, \overline{a_1}-, \overline{a_2}-, \overline{a_3}-\}$ guarantees that the rules $a_i \to \overline{a_i}$ are not applied because the number of objects $\overline{a_i}$ remains constant between the two consecutive configurations). Hence, the computations of Π and M halt and the generated set is the content of register r.

4   Conclusions and Further Work

In this paper we have introduced and studied Observer/Interpreter P systems which were motivated by the possibility of tracking and detecting genetically encoded fluorescent proteins in living cells. Their discovery produced a major development in the live imaging of cells. In this respect, intracellular dynamics was able to be monitored and studied. Moreover, the discovery of these proteins allowed the creation of specific biosensors which were further used to monitor a wide range of intracellular phenomena (like apoptosis, pH and metal-ion concentration, protein kinase activity, membrane voltage, cyclic nucleotide signaling, and so on).

We introduced a formal system composed by a P system with symbol objects and multiset rewriting rules Π and a finite state machine with output M which is able to detect changes in consecutive configurations from a computation of Π;

based on what it detects, $\mathcal{M}$ changes its state and produces an output (it increments, decrements, or performs no action on a register able to store an integer). We were interested in the computational capabilities of the model. In this regard, we showed how one can simulate the computation of an ET0L system using an Observer/Interpreter P system which has as core system a P system with non-cooperative rules; however, in this case we were not able to produce as output the same number as the length of the word generated by the ET0L system (hence we could not give the exact characterization in terms of computational power). We also proved that when catalytic P systems (with one catalyst) are used one can generate any recursively enumerable set of numbers.

Several open problems can be formulated for the proposed model. For example we are interested by the case when purely catalytic P systems are used as core languages. Another interesting topic regards the computational power of the model when the cardinality of any observation cannot exceed k, $1 \leq k \leq card(O)$. In the same line of research one can put a bound on the number of states of $\mathcal{M}$ and study the computational power of the Observer/Interpreter P systems with respect to these constraints. Yet another interesting idea concerns the possibility of defining the moments when observations can be performed.

Acknowledgments. We would like to thank the anonymous reviewers for their valuable comments.

References

1. Alhazov, A., Cavaliere, M.: Computing by Observing Bio-systems: The Case of Sticker Systems. In: Ferretti, C., Mauri, G., Zandron, C. (eds.) DNA10. LNCS, vol. 3384, pp. 1–13. Springer, Heidelberg (2005)
2. Cavaliere, M., Leupold, P.: Evolution and Observation–A Non-standard Way to Generate Formal Languages. Theoretical Computer Science 321(2-3), 233–248 (2004)
3. Cavaliere, M., Frisco, P., Hoogeboom, H.J.: Computing by Only Observing. In: Ibarra, O.H., Dang, Z. (eds.) DLT 2006. LNCS, vol. 4036, pp. 304–314. Springer, Heidelberg (2006)
4. Cavaliere, M., Leupold, P.: Observation of String-Rewriting Systems. Fundamenta Informaticae 74(4), 447–462 (2006)
5. Ciobanu, G., Păun, G., Pérez-Jiménez, M.J.: Applications of Membrane Computing. Springer, Berlin (2006)
6. Dassow, J., Păun, G.: Regulated Rewriting in Formal Language Theory. Springer, Berlin (1989)
7. Rozenberg, G., Salomaa, A. (eds.): Handbook of Formal Languages. Springer, Berlin (2004)
8. Păun, G., Thierrin, G.: Multiset Processing by Means of Systems of Sequential Transducers, CDMTCS Research Reports CDMTCS-101 (1999)
9. Păun, G.: Membrane Computing. An Introduction. Springer, Berlin (2002)
10. Păun, G., Rozenberg, G., Salomaa, A. (eds.): The Oxford Handbook of Membrane Computing. Oxford University Press, New York (2010)

Limits of the Power of Tissue P Systems
with Cell Division

Petr Sosík[1,2]

[1] Departamento de Inteligencia Artificial, Facultad de Informática,
Universidad Politécnica de Madrid, Campus de Montegancedo s/n,
Boadilla del Monte, 28660 Madrid, Spain
[2] Research Institute of the IT4Innovations Centre of Excellence,
Faculty of Philosophy and Science, Silesian University in Opava
74601 Opava, Czech Republic
petr.sosik@fpf.slu.cz

Abstract. Tissue P systems generalize the membrane structure tree usual in original models of P systems to an arbitrary graph. Basic operations in these systems are communication rules, enriched in some variants with cell division or cell separation. Several variants of tissue P systems were recently studied, together with the concept of uniform families of these systems. Their computational power was shown to range between **P** and **NP** ∪ **co-NP**, thus characterizing some interesting borderlines between tractability and intractability. In this paper we show that computational power of these uniform families in polynomial time is limited by the class **PSPACE**. This class characterizes the power of many classical parallel computing models.

1 Introduction

P systems (also membrane systems) can be described as bio-inspired computing models trying to capture information and control aspects of processes in living cells. P systems are focusing, e.g., on molecular synthesis within cells, selective particle recognition by membranes, controlled transport through protein channels, membrane division, membrane dissolution and many others. These processes are modeled in P systems by means of operations on multisets in separate cell-like regions.

Tissue P systems were introduced first in [9] where they were described as a kind of abstract neural nets. Instead of considering a hierarchical arrangement usual in previous models of P systems, membranes/cells are placed in the nodes of a virtual graph. Biological justification of the model (see [10]) is the intercellular communication and cooperation between neurons and, generally, between tissue cells. The communication among cells is based on symport/antiport rules which were introduced to P systems in [14]. Symport rules move objects across a membrane together in one direction, whereas antiport rules move objects across a membrane in opposite directions. In tissue P systems these two variants were unified as a unique type of rule. From the original definitions of tissue P systems

E. Csuhaj-Varjú et al. (Eds.): CMC 2012, LNCS 7762, pp. 390–403, 2013.

[9,10], several research lines have been developed and other variants have arisen (see, for example, [1,2,5,7,8,11,12]).

An interesting variant of tissue P systems was presented in [15] and named *tissue P systems with cell division*. The model is enriched with the operation of cell replication, that is, two new cells are generated from one original cell by a division rule. The new cells have exactly the same objects except for at most a pair of different objects. The following results were obtained: (a) only tractable problems can be efficiently solved when the length of communication rules is restricted to 1, and (b) an efficient (uniform) solution to the SAT problem exists when using communication rules with length at most 3 (and, of course, division rules). Hence, in the framework of recognizer tissue P systems with cell division, the length of the communication rules provides a borderline between efficiency and non-efficiency.

In this paper we impose an upper bound on the power of several types of tissue P systems. Specifically, we show that tissue systems with cell division can be simulated in polynomial space. As a consequence, the class of problems solvable by uniform families of these systems in polynomial time is limited by the class PSPACE.

The paper is organized as follows: first, we recall some preliminaries, and then the definition of tissue P systems with cell division is given. Next, recognizer tissue P systems and computational complexity classes in this framework are briefly described. In Section 3 we demonstrate that any such tissue P system can be simulated by a classical computer (and, hence, also by Turing machine) in polynomial space. The last section contains conclusions and some open problems.

2 Tissue P Systems with Cell Division

We fix some notation first. A *multiset* m with underlying set A is a pair (A, f) where $f : A \to \mathbb{N}$ is a mapping. If $m = (A, f)$ is a multiset then its *support* is defined as $supp(m) = \{x \in A \mid f(x) > 0\}$. The total number of elements in a multiset, including repeated memberships, is the *cardinality* of the multiset. A multiset is empty (resp. finite) if its support is the empty set (resp. a finite set). If $m = (A, f)$ is a finite multiset over A, and $supp(m) = \{a_1, \ldots, a_k\}$ then it can also be represented by the string $a_1^{f(a_1)} \ldots a_k^{f(a_k)}$ over the alphabet $\{a_1, \ldots, a_k\}$. Nevertheless, all permutations of this string precisely identify the same multiset m. Throughout this paper, we speak about "the finite multiset m" where m is a string, and meaning "the finite multiset represented by the string m".

If $m_1 = (A, f_1)$, $m_2 = (A, f_2)$ are multisets over A, then we define the union of m_1 and m_2 as $m_1 + m_2 = (A, g)$, where $g = f_1 + f_2$.

For any sets A and B the *relative complement* $A \setminus B$ of B in A is defined as follows:

$$A \setminus B = \{x \in A \mid x \notin B\}$$

In what follows, we assume the reader is already familiar with the basic notions and the terminology of P systems. For details, see [16].

2.1   Basic Definition

Tissue P Systems with cell division is based on the cell-like model of P systems with active membranes [13]. The biological inspiration is the following: alive tissues are not static network of cells but new cells are produced by membrane division in a natural way. In these models, the cells are not polarized; the two cells obtained by division have the same labels as the original cell, and if a cell is divided, its interaction with other cells or with the environment is blocked during the division process.

Definition 1. *A tissue P system with cell division of degree $q \geq 1$ is a tuple*

$$\Pi = (\Gamma, \mathcal{E}, \mathcal{M}_1, \ldots, \mathcal{M}_q, \mathcal{R}, i_{out}),$$

where:

1. *Γ is a finite alphabet whose elements are called* objects*;*
2. *$\mathcal{E} \subseteq \Gamma$ is a finite alphabet representing the set of objects initially in the environment of the system, and 0 is the label of the environment (the environment is not properly a cell of the system); let us assume that objects in the environment appear in inexhaustibly many copies each;*
3. *$\mathcal{M}_1, \ldots, \mathcal{M}_q$ are strings over Γ, representing the finite multisets of objects placed in the q cells of the system at the beginning of the computation; $1, 2, \cdots, q$ are labels which identify the cells of the system;*
4. *$\mathcal{R}$ is a finite set of rules of the following forms:*
   (a) *Communication rules: $(i, u/v, j)$, for $i, j \in \{0, 1, 2, \ldots, q\}, i \neq j$, $u, v \in \Gamma^*$, $|uv| > 0$. When applying a rule $(i, u/v, j)$, the objects of the multiset represented by u are sent from region i to region j and, simultaneously, the objects of the multiset v are sent from region j to region i;*
   (b) *Division rules: $[a]_i \to [b]_i[c]_i$, where $i \in \{1, 2, \ldots, q\}$ and $a, b, c \in \Gamma$, and $i \neq i_{out}$. In reaction with an object a, the cell i is divided into two cells with the same label; in the first cell the object a is replaced by b; in the second cell the object a is replaced by c; the output cell i_{out} cannot be divided;*
5. *$i_{out} \in \{0, 1, 2, \ldots, q\}$ is the output cell.*

A communication rule $(i, u/v, j)$ is called a *symport rule* if $u = \lambda$ or $v = \lambda$. A symport rule $(i, u/\lambda, j)$, with $i \neq 0, j \neq 0$, provides a virtual arc from cell i to cell j. A communication rule $(i, u/v, j)$ is called an *antiport rule* if $u \neq \lambda$ and $v \neq \lambda$. An antiport rule $(i, u/v, j)$, with $i \neq 0, j \neq 0$, provides two arcs: one from cell i to cell j and another one from cell j to cell i. Thus, every tissue P systems has an underlying directed graph whose nodes are the cells of the system and the arcs are obtained from communication rules. In this context, the environment can be considered as a virtual node of the graph such that their connections are defined by the communication rules of the form $(i, u/v, j)$, with $i = 0$ or $j = 0$. Let us agree that no symport rule is permissible which would send an infinite number of objects from the environment to some cell. The length of the communication rule $(i, u/v, j)$ is defined as $|u| + |v|$.

The rules of a system like the above one are used in the non-deterministic maximally parallel manner as customary in Membrane Computing. At each step, all cells which can evolve must evolve in a maximally parallel way (at each step we apply a multiset of rules which is maximal, no further rule can be added being applicable). There is one important restriction: when a cell is divided, the division rule is the only one which is applied for that cell at that step; thus, the objects inside that cell do not evolve by means of communication rules. The label of a cell precisely identify the rules which can be applied to it.

A *configuration* of a tissue P system with cell division at any instant is described by all multisets of objects over Γ associated with all the cells present in the system, and the multiset of objects over $\Gamma - \mathcal{E}$ associated with the environment at that moment. Bearing in mind the objects from $\mathcal{E}$ have infinite copies in the environment, they are not properly changed along the computation. The *initial configuration* is $C_0 = (\mathcal{M}_1, \cdots, \mathcal{M}_q; \emptyset)$. A configuration is a *halting configuration* if no rule of the system is applicable to it.

We say that configuration C_1 yields configuration C_2 in one *transition step*, denoted $C_1 \Rightarrow_{\Pi} C_2$, if we can pass from C_1 to C_2 by applying the rules from $\mathcal{R}$ as specified above. A *computation* of Π is a (finite or infinite) sequence of configurations such that:

1. the first term of the sequence is the initial configuration of the system;
2. each non-initial configuration of the sequence is obtained from the previous configuration by applying rules of the system in a maximally parallel manner with the restrictions previously mentioned; and
3. if the sequence is finite (called *halting computation*) then the last term of the sequence is a halting configuration.

Halting computations give a result which is encoded by the objects present in the output cell i_{out} in the halting configuration.

2.2   Recognizer Tissue P Systems with Cell Division

Let us denote a *decision problem* as a pair (I_X, θ_X) where I_X is a language over a finite alphabet (whose elements are called *instances*) and θ_X is a total boolean function over I_X. A natural correspondence between decision problems and languages over a finite alphabet can be established as follows. Given a decision problem $X = (I_X, \theta_X)$, its associated language is $L_X = \{w \in I_X : \theta_X(w) = 1\}$. Conversely, given a language L over an alphabet Σ, its associated decision problem is $X_L = (I_{X_L}, \theta_{X_L})$, where $I_{X_L} = \Sigma^*$, and $\theta_{X_L} = \{(x, 1) : x \in L\} \cup \{(x, 0) : x \notin L\}$. The solvability of decision problems is defined through the recognition of the languages associated with them, by using languages recognizer devices.

In order to study the computational efficiency of membrane systems, the notions from classical *computational complexity theory* are adapted for Membrane Computing, and a special class of cell-like P systems is introduced in [18]: *recognizer P systems*. For tissue P systems, with the same idea as recognizer cell-like P systems, *recognizer tissue P systems* is introduced in [15].

Definition 2. *A recognizer tissue P system with cell division of degree $q \geq 1$ is a tuple*

$$\Pi = (\Gamma, \Sigma, \mathcal{E}, \mathcal{M}_1, \ldots, \mathcal{M}_q, \mathcal{R}, i_{in}, i_{out})$$

where:

1. $(\Gamma, \mathcal{E}, \mathcal{M}_1, \ldots, \mathcal{M}_q, \mathcal{R}, i_{out})$ *is a tissue P system with cell division of degree $q \geq 1$ (as defined in the previous section).*
2. *The working alphabet Γ has two distinguished objects* yes *and* no *being, at least, one copy of them present in some initial multisets $\mathcal{M}_1, \ldots, \mathcal{M}_q$, but none of them are present in $\mathcal{E}$.*
3. *Σ is an (input) alphabet strictly contained in Γ, and $\mathcal{E} \subseteq \Gamma \setminus \Sigma$.*
4. *$\mathcal{M}_1, \ldots, \mathcal{M}_q$ are strings over $\Gamma \setminus \Sigma$;*
5. *$i_{in} \in \{1, \ldots, q\}$ is the input cell.*
6. *The output region i_{out} is the environment.*
7. *All computations halt.*
8. *If $\mathcal{C}$ is a computation of Π, then either object* yes *or object* no *(but not both) must have been released into the environment, and only at the last step of the computation.*

For each $w \in \Sigma^*$, the *computation of the system Π with input $w \in \Sigma^*$* starts from the initial configuration of the form $C_0 = (\mathcal{M}_1, \mathcal{M}_2, \ldots, \mathcal{M}_{i_{in}} + w, \ldots, \mathcal{M}_q; \emptyset)$, that is, the input multiset w has been added to the contents of the input cell i_{in}. Therefore, we have an initial configuration associated with each input multiset w (over the input alphabet Σ) in this kind of systems.

Given a recognizer tissue P system with cell division, we say that a computation $\mathcal{C}$ is an *accepting computation* (respectively, *rejecting computation*) if object yes (respectively, object no) appears in the environment associated with the corresponding halting configuration of $\mathcal{C}$.

For each natural number $k \geq 1$, we denote by **TDC**(k) the class of recognizer tissue P systems with cell division and communication rules of length at most k. We denote by **TDC** the class of recognizer tissue P systems with cell division and without restriction on the length of communication rules. Obviously, **TDC**$(k) \subseteq$ **TDC** for all $k \geq 1$.

2.3 Polynomial Complexity Classes of Tissue P Systems

Next, we define what means solving a decision problem in the framework of tissue P systems efficiently and in a uniform way. Bearing in mind that they provide devices with a finite description, a numerable family of tissue P systems will be necessary in order to solve a decision problem.

Definition 3. *We say that a decision problem $X = (I_X, \theta_X)$ is solvable in a uniform way and polynomial time by a family $\mathbf{\Pi} = \{\Pi(n) \mid n \in \mathbb{N}\}$ of recognizer tissue P systems (with cell division) if the following holds:*

1. *The family $\mathbf{\Pi}$ is polynomially uniform by Turing machines, that is, there exists a deterministic Turing machine working in polynomial time which constructs the system $\Pi(n)$ from $n \in \mathbb{N}$.*

2. *There exists a pair* (cod, s) *of polynomial-time computable functions over* I_X *such that:*
   (a) *for each instance* $u \in I_X$, $s(u)$ *is a natural number and* $cod(u)$ *is an input multiset of the system* $\Pi(s(u))$;
   (b) *for each* $n \in \mathbb{N}$, $s^{-1}(n)$ *is a finite set;*
   (c) *the family* **Π** *is polynomially bounded with regard to* (X, cod, s), *that is, there exists a polynomial function* p, *such that for each* $u \in I_X$ *every computation of* $\Pi(s(u))$ *with input* $cod(u)$ *is halting and it performs at most* $p(|u|)$ *steps;*
   (d) *the family* **Π** *is sound with regard to* (X, cod, s), *that is, for each* $u \in I_X$, *if* <u>*there exists*</u> *an accepting computation of* $\Pi(s(u))$ *with input* $cod(u)$, *then* $\theta_X(u) = 1$;
   (e) *the family* **Π** *is complete with regard to* (X, cod, s), *that is, for each* $u \in I_X$, *if* $\theta_X(u) = 1$, *then* <u>*every*</u> *computation of* $\Pi(s(u))$ *with input* $cod(u)$ *is an accepting one.*

From the soundness and completeness conditions above we deduce that every P system $\Pi(n)$ is *confluent*, in the following sense: every computation of a system with the *same* input multiset must always give the *same* answer.

Let **R** be a class of recognizer tissue P systems. We denote by **PMC$_R$** the set of all decision problems which can be solved in a uniform way and polynomial time by means of families of systems from **R**. The following results have been proved:

Theorem 1 ([6]). $\mathbf{P} = \mathbf{PMC}_{TDC(1)}$

Theorem 2 ([15]). $\mathbf{NP} \cup \mathbf{co\text{-}NP} \subseteq \mathbf{PMC}_{TDC(3)}$

As a consequence, both **NP** and **co-NP** are contained in the class $\mathbf{PMC}_{TDC}$. In this paper we impose an upper bound on $\mathbf{PMC}_{TDC}$.

3   Simulation of Tissue P Systems with Cell Division in Polynomial Space

In this section we demonstrate that any computation of a recognizer tissue P system with cell division can be simulated in space polynomial to its initial size and the number of steps. Instead of simulating a computation of a P system from its initial configuration onwards (which would require exponential space for storing configurations), we create a recursive function which computes content of any cell h after a given number of steps. Thus we do not need to store content of cells interacting with h but we calculate it recursively whenever needed.

Simulated P systems are confluent, hence possibly nondeterministic, but the simulation will be performed in a deterministic way: only one possible sequence of configurations of the P system is traced. This corresponds to a weak priority relation between rules:

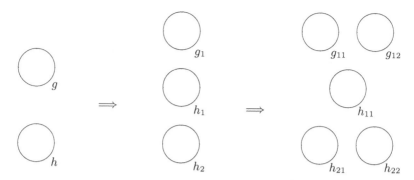

Fig. 1. An example of indexing of cells during first two computational steps

(i)   division rules are always applied prior to communication rules,
(ii) priority between communication rules given by the order they are listed,
(iii) priority between cells to which the rules are applied.

However, the confluency condition ensures that such a simulation is correct as all computations starting from the same initial configuration must lead to the same result.

Each cell of Π is assigned a unique label at initial configuration. But cells may be divided during computation of Π, producing more membranes with the same label. To identify membranes uniquely, we add to each label a *compound index*. Each index is an empty string at initial configuration. If a membrane is not divided at a computational step, digit 1 is attached to its index. If a division rule is applied to it, the first resulting membrane has attached 1 and the second membrane 2 to its index. At a configuration C_n, $n \geq 0$, index of each membrane is an n-tuple of digits from $\{1, 2\}$. Notice that some n-tuples may denote non-existing membranes as membranes need not divide at each step. The situation is illustrated in Fig. 1: membrane h is divided at first step, membranes g_1 and h_2 are divided at second step. Membrane h_{12} does not exist, for instance.

Consider a confluent recognizer tissue P system with cell division of degree $q \geq 1$, described formally as

$$\Pi = (\Gamma, \Sigma, \mathcal{E}, \mathcal{M}_1, \ldots, \mathcal{M}_q, \mathcal{R}, i_{in}, i_{out}).$$

For any cell of Π we denote the multiset of objects contained in it at any instant simply as its *content*. A simplified scheme of the function `content` computing recursively the content of any cell labeled h with index ind of Π at configuration C_n, $n \geq 0$ follows:

1. verify whether the ancestor of cell h existed at previous configuration; if not, the cell does not exist;
2. store empty multiset to a variable `rulesAppliedTo`h;
3. for each rule $r_i = (j, u/v, k)$, $1 \leq i \leq |\mathcal{R}|$ repeat steps 3a and 3b, while keeping the total multiset of already applied rules $r_1, \ldots, r_{i-1}$.

(a) for each pair of cells labeled j and k with various compound indices:
   i. calculate recursively contents of these two cells at previous configuration;
   ii. apply rules $r_1, \ldots, r_{i-1}$ from the stored multiset to this pair of cells, but only removing objects, not adding any, to get the remaining contents of cells unaffected by these rules;
   iii. calculate the maximal multiset of rules r_i applicable to this pair of cells with their remaining contents and store it;
   iv. if one of the two cells is identical to h with index ind, add the multiset of applicable rules r_i to `rulesAppliedTo`h;
(b) Add the total multiset of rules r_i applicable to all cells in step 3(a)iii to the total multiset of already applied rules $r_1, \ldots, r_{i-1}$;
4. calculate recursively the content of cell h with index ind at previous configuration and apply the rules in `rulesAppliedTo`h to get a new content of the cell.

All rules at a particular step n are applied in a maximally parallel way to all cells but we simulate this process sequentially, following a fixed order of rules in $\mathcal{R}$ and a fixed order of pair cells to which these rules are applied.

Observe that the recursion includes only the number of configuration n and not the number of already applied rules, although, obviously, an application of a rule r_i can depend on the contents of many (possibly all) cells which were already affected by rules $r_1, \ldots, r_{i-1}$ at the same step. However, one does not need to store the subsequent contents of all cells during step n nor to simulate the previous effects of rules $r_1, \ldots, r_{i-1}$ one-by-one. Instead, it is enough to keep the *total* multiset of rules $r_1, \ldots, r_{i-1}$ already applied at the same step., without recording . Due to the *maximal parallelism* and *fixed order* of rules and pairs of cells, one can easily re-calculate multisets of rules $r_1, \ldots, r_{i-1}$ already applied to a particular pairs of cells by just applying the maximum possible multiset. Therefore, before application of rule r_i to a particular pair of cells, all what happened already at step n to this pair of cells is re-calculated at paragraphs 3(a)i and 3(a)ii above.

A detailed presentation of the function `content` follows. Assume for simplicity that an input multiset of objects w is already included in the initial multiset $\mathcal{M}_{i_{in}}$.

function content

Input: $h \in \{1, \ldots, q\}$ – label of a cell
   $i_1 i_2 \ldots i_n$ – a compound index
   $n \geq 0$ – a number of configuration

Output: the content of cell labeled h with compound index $i_1 i_2 \ldots i_n$ at configuration C_n, or `null` if such a cell does not exist.

Auxiliary variables:

```
rulesAppliedToh, rulesAppliedTotal, rulesForCell1, rulesForCell2;
```
(Multisets of applicable or applied rules with underlying set $\mathcal{R}$)

```
contentCell1, contentCell2, contentFinal;
```
(Multisets storing contents of cells)

```
if n = 0 then return Mh; (return the initial multiset of cell h)
store empty multiset to rulesAppliedTotal and rulesAppliedToh;
```

```
for each communication rule ri = (j, u/v, k), 1 ≤ i ≤ |R| do begin
```
  (Now we scan all existing copies of cells labeled j and k affected by the rule.)

```
  rulesForCell1 := rulesAppliedTotal;
```

```
  for each possible compound index j1j2...jn−1 do begin
    contentCell1 = content(j, j1j2...jn−1, n − 1);
```
    (Content of cell j with index $j_1 j_2 \ldots j_{n-1}$ at the previous configuration.)

```
    if (contentCell1 = null) or (cell can apply a division rule)
      then skip the rest of the cycle;
```

```
    calculate the maximal multiset of rules in rulesForCell1
      applicable to cell j with objects contentCell1;
    remove these rules from multiset rulesForCell1;
    remove the corresponding objects from contentCell1;
```

```
    rulesForCell2 := rulesAppliedTotal;
```

```
    for each possible compound index k1k2...kn−1 do begin
      contentCell2 = content(k, k1k2...kn−1, n − 1);
```
      (Content of cell k with index $k_1 k_2 \ldots k_{n-1}$ at the previous configuration.)

```
      if contentCell2 = null or cell can apply a division rule
        then skip the rest of the cycle;
```

```
      calculate the maximal multiset of rules in rulesForCell2
        applicable to cell k with contentCell2;
      remove these rules from multiset rulesForCell2;
      remove the corresponding objects from contentCell2;
```

      (Now contentCell1 and ContentCell2 contain objects remaining in cell j with index $j_1 j_2 \ldots j_{n-1}$ and in cell k with index $k_1 k_2 \ldots k_{n-1}$, respectively, after application of rules $r_1, \ldots, r_{i-1}$.)

```
      let x = maximum copies of rule ri = (j, u/v, k) applicable to cells
```

j, k with contentCell1 and contentCell2, respectively;

remove x copies of u from contentCell1;
add x copies of rule r_i to rulesAppliedTotal;

if one of the cells j or k with their respective indices is
    identical to cell h with index $i_1 i_2 \ldots i_{n-1}$ then
        add x copies of rule r_i to rulesAppliedToh;

   end cycle; *(cell k with index $k_1 k_2 \ldots k_{n-1}$)*
  end cycle; *(cell j with index $j_1 j_2 \ldots j_{n-1}$)*
end cycle; *(rule r_i)*

(At this moment, variable rulesAppliedToh*contains the complete multiset
of rules applied in step n to cell h with indices $i_1 i_2 \ldots i_{n-1}$.)*

contentFinal = content(h, $i_1 i_2 \ldots i_{n-1}$, $n-1$);
(Content of cell h with index $i_1 i_2 \ldots i_{n-1}$ at previous configuration $n-1$.)

if contentFinal = null then return null and exit;

if a division rule $[a]_h \to [b]_h [c]_h$ exists such that
contentFinal contains a then
  if $i_n = 1$ then
    remove a from contentFinal and add b;
  else
    remove a from contentFinal and add c;
  (Cell h with index $i_1 i_2 \ldots i_{n-1}$ divides in step n)

else
  if $i_n = 2$ then
    return null and exit;
  *(The last element i_n of compound index corresponds to a copy of cell h
  dividing in step n which is not the case, hence this copy does not exist.)*

  else
    apply all rules in rulesAppliedToh to contentFinal, i.e.,
      add/remove multisets of objects corresponding to cell h
      in rules to/from contentFinal;

return contentFinal;

We defined explicitly internal variables with largest memory demands in function
content in its preamble. Other variables are used implicitly. This is necessary
for the following result.

Theorem 3. *A result of any computation consisting of n steps of a recognizer confluent tissue P system with cell division can be computed with Turing machine in space polynomial to n.*

Proof. Consider a recognizer confluent tissue P system with cell division

$$\Pi = (\Gamma, \Sigma, \mathcal{E}, \mathcal{M}_1, \ldots, \mathcal{M}_q, \mathcal{R}, i_{in}, i_{out}).$$

The function `content` described above evaluates the content of a particular cell after n steps, but simultaneously also an application of all possible rules during n-th step in all cells is also simulated. By Definition 2, the system always halts at a configuration when the object *yes* or *no* is released to the environment. The result of computation of Π with an input w can be therefore obtained as follows:

1. Prepare the initial configuration of Π, add w to $\mathcal{M}_{i_{in}}$.
2. Subsequently compute `content`$(i_{out}, 11 \ldots 1, n)$ for $n = 0, 1, 2, \ldots$ until the presence of objects *yes* or *no* in the environment.
3. Return the corresponding result of computation.

Space complexity of the function `content`$(h, index, n)$ is determined by variables storing multisets of objects and applicable rules. The first type represents a multiset of objects contained in a particular cell. Its cardinality is limited from above by the total number of objects in the system after n steps. Denote this number by o_n. Therefore,

$$o_0 = \sum_{i=1}^{q} card(\mathcal{M}_i) + |w|. \tag{1}$$

At each step each cell can divide (which does not increase the number of its objects) or it can introduce new object to the system from the environment via antiport rules. Denote $\mathcal{R}_a$ the set of antiport rules in $\mathcal{R}$. Hence, we can write that $o_n \leq co_{n-1}$ for $n \geq 1$ and a constant c, where

$$c = \max\{ \max_{(i,u/v,j)\in\mathcal{R}_a} \{|u|/|v|\}, \max_{(i,u/v,j)\in\mathcal{R}_a} \{|v|/|u|\}\}. \tag{2}$$

At configuration C_n we have

$$o_n \leq o_0 c^n \tag{3}$$

which is a value representable by dn bits for a constant

$$d \leq \log o_0 + \log c. \tag{4}$$

Finally, $|\Gamma|dn$ bits are necessary to describe any multiset with cardinality dn and with the underlying set Γ. This is also the maximum size of any variable of this type.

The situation is similar for multisets of applicable rules. The cardinality of each such multiset at n-th computational step is limited by the number o_n of objects in the system. Hence the space required for of each such variable is at most $|\mathcal{R}|dn$.

Finally, let us analyze the space complexity of function content. Function content with parameter n performs recursive calls of itself with parameter $n - 1$. It uses three variables storing multisets of objects and four variables with multisets of rules. For its space complexity $C(n)$ we can therefore write:

$$C(0) = \log o_0 \tag{5}$$

$$C(n) \leq C(n-1) + 3|\Gamma|dn + 4|\mathcal{R}|dn, \qquad n \geq 1. \tag{6}$$

The solution to this recurrence is

$$C(n) = \mathcal{O}((|\Gamma| + |\mathcal{R}|)dn^2 + \log o_0). \tag{7}$$

Hence, with the aid of the function content described above, a conventional computer can simulate n steps of computation of the systems Π in space polynomial to n, and as the space necessary for Turing machine performing the same computation is asymptotically the same, the statement follows.   □

Theorem 4. $\mathbf{PMC}_{TDC} \subseteq \mathbf{PSPACE}$

Proof. Consider a family $\boldsymbol{\Pi} = \{\Pi(n) \mid n \in \mathbb{N}\}$ of recognizer tissue P systems with cell division satisfying conditions of Definition 3, which solves in a uniform way and polynomial time a decision problem $X = (I_X, \theta_X)$. For each instance $u \in I_X$, denote

$$\Pi(s(u)) = (\Gamma, \Sigma, \mathcal{E}, \mathcal{M}_1, \dots, \mathcal{M}_q, \mathcal{R}, i_{in}, i_{out})$$

and let $w = cod(u)$ be the corresponding input multiset. By Definition 3, paragraphs 1 and 2(a), the values of $card(w)$, $card(\mathcal{M}_1), \dots, card(\mathcal{M}_q)$, and lengths of rules in $\mathcal{R}$ are exponential with respect to $|u|$ (they must be constructed by a deterministic Turing machine in polynomial time). Furthermore, values of $|\Gamma|$ and $|\mathcal{R}|$ are polynomial to $|u|$. (Actually, the alphabet Γ could possibly have exponentially many elements but only polynomially many of them could appear in the rules of system $\Pi(s(u))$ and the rest could be ignored.)

By Definition 3, paragraph 2(c), also the number of steps n of any computation of system $\Pi(s(u))$ is polynomial to $|u|$. By Theorem 3, the computation of system $\Pi(s(u))$ can be simulated with Turing machine in space polynomial to n using the function content. Its space complexity is described by the equation (7) containing constants d and o_0. By (1)–(4) the value of both d and $\log o_0$ is polynomial to $|u|$ and, hence, so is the space complexity of function content. Therefore, each instance $u \in I_X$ can be solved with a Turing machine in space polynomial to $|u|$.   □

4   Discussion

The results presented in this paper establish a theoretical upper bound on the power of confluent tissue P systems with cell division. Note that the characterization of power of non-confluent (hence non-deterministic) tissue P systems with cell division remains open. The presented proof cannot be simply adapted to this case by using a non-deterministic Turing (or other) machine for simulation. Observe that in our recursive algorithm the same configuration of a P system is typically re-calculated many times during one simulation run. If the simulation was non-deterministic, we could obtain different results for the same configuration which would make the simulation inconsistent.

If we defined a descriptional complexity (i.e., a size of description) of any tissue P system with cell division, Theorem 3 could be rephrased as follows: any computation of such a P systems can be simulated in space polynomial to the size of description of that P system and to the number of steps of its computation.

Another variant one could consider is the case when a cell can divide using a rule of type $[a]_h \to [b]_h [c]_h$ and it can communicate in the same step. To be consistent, one should perform communication first (preserving the object a) and then divide the resulting cell to two membranes, replacing a with b or c, respectively. The presented proofs can be simply adapted to this variant.

The presented result is related to two other results which also deals with the relation of the class **PSPACE** to the computational power of certain families of P systems. The first of them is the result presented in [20] which deals with P systems with active membranes, equipped with a similar division of membranes as here. The P systems with active membranes, however, use an acyclic communication graph (a tree of membrane structure), while here we work with an arbitrary graph which makes the structure of the proof different. It was shown in [20] that the class **PSPACE** characterizes precisely the computational power of P systems with active membranes. The second related result [19] studies the model very similar to that used here: tissue P systems with cell separation. The upper bound **PSPACE** to their computational power is proven in [19]. It remains open whether this upper bound on the power of polynomially uniform families of tissue P systems with cell division or cell separation can be still improved or not.

Acknowledgements. This work was supported by the European Regional Development Fund in the IT4Innovations Centre of Excellence project (CZ.1.05/1.1.00/02.0070), and by the Silesian University in Opava under the Student Funding Scheme, project no SGS/7/2011.

References

1. Alhazov, A., Freund, R., Oswald, M.: Tissue P Systems with Antiport Rules and Small Numbers of Symbols and Cells. In: De Felice, C., Restivo, A. (eds.) DLT 2005. LNCS, vol. 3572, pp. 100–111. Springer, Heidelberg (2005)
2. Bernardini, F., Gheorghe, M.: Cell Communication in Tissue P Systems and Cell Division in Population P Systems. Soft Computing 9(9), 640–649 (2005)
3. Christinal, H.A., Díaz-Pernil, D., Gutiérrez-Naranjo, M.A., Pérez-Jiménez, M.J.: Tissue-like P systems without environment. In: Martínez-del-Amor, M.A., Păun, G., Pérez-Hurtado, I., Riscos-Núñez, A. (eds.) Proceedings of the Eight Brainstorming Week on Membrane Computing, Sevilla, Spain, February 1-5, pp. 53–64, Fénix Editora, Report RGNC 01/2010 (2010)

4. Díaz-Pernil, D., Gutiérrez-Naranjo, M.A., Pérez-Jiménez, M.J., Riscos-Núñez, A., Romero–Campero, F.J.: Computational efficiency of cellular division in tissue-like P systems. Romanian Journal of Information Science and Technology 11(3), 229–241 (2008)
5. Freund, R., Păun, G., Pérez-Jiménez, M.J.: Tissue P Systems with channel states. Theoretical Computer Science 330, 101–116 (2005)
6. Gutiérrez–Escudero, R., Pérez–Jiménez, M.J., Rius–Font, M.: Characterizing Tractability by Tissue-Like P Systems. In: Păun, G., Pérez-Jiménez, M.J., Riscos-Núñez, A., Rozenberg, G., Salomaa, A. (eds.) WMC 2009. LNCS, vol. 5957, pp. 289–300. Springer, Heidelberg (2010)
7. Krishna, S.N., Lakshmanan, K., Rama, R.: Tissue P Systems with Contextual and Rewriting Rules. In: Păun, G., Rozenberg, G., Salomaa, A., Zandron, C. (eds.) WMC 2002. LNCS, vol. 2597, pp. 339–351. Springer, Heidelberg (2003)
8. Lakshmanan, K., Rama, R.: On the Power of Tissue P Systems with Insertion and Deletion Rules. In: Alhazov, A., Martín-Vide, C., Păun, G. (eds.) Preproceedings of the Workshop on Membrane Computing, pp. 304–318, Tarragona, Report RGML 28/03 (2003)
9. Martín-Vide, C., Pazos, J., Păun, G., Rodríguez-Patón, A.: A New Class of Symbolic Abstract Neural Nets: Tissue P Systems. In: Ibarra, O.H., Zhang, L. (eds.) COCOON 2002. LNCS, vol. 2387, pp. 290–299. Springer, Heidelberg (2002)
10. Martín Vide, C., Pazos, J., Păun, G., Rodríguez Patón, A.: Tissue P systems. Theoretical Computer Science 296, 295–326 (2003)
11. Pan, L., Ishdorj, T.-O.: P systems with active membranes and separation rules. Journal of Universal Computer Science 10(5), 630–649 (2004)
12. Pan, L., Pérez-Jiménez, M.J.: Computational complexity of tissue–like P systems. Journal of Complexity 26(3), 296–315 (2010)
13. Păun, G.: P systems with active membranes: attacking NP complete problems. J. Automata, Languages and Combinatorics 6(1), 75–90 (2001)
14. Păun, A., Păun, G.: The power of communication: P systems with symport/antiport. New Generation Computing 20(3), 295–305 (2002)
15. Păun, G., Pérez-Jiménez, M.J., Riscos-Núñez, A.: Tissue P System with cell division. Int. J. of Computers, Communications and Control 3(3), 295–303 (2008)
16. Păun, G., Rozenberg, G., Salomaa, A.: The Oxford Handbook of Membrane Computing. Oxford University Press (2009)
17. Pérez-Jiménez, M.J., Romero-Jiménez, A., Sancho-Caparrini, F.: Complexity classes in models of cellular computing with membranes. Natural Computing 2(3), 265–285 (2003)
18. Pérez-Jiménez, M.J., Romero-Jiménez, A., Sancho-Caparrini, F.: A polynomial complexity class in P systems using membrane division. Journal of Automata, Languages and Combinatorics 11(4), 423–434 (2006)
19. Sosík, P., Cienciala, L.: Tissue P Systems with Cell Separation: Upper Bound by PSPACE. In: Dediu, A.-H., Martín-Vide, C., Truthe, B. (eds.) TPNC 2012. LNCS, vol. 7505, pp. 201–215. Springer, Heidelberg (2012)
20. Sosík, P., Rodríguez-Patón, A.: Membrane computing and complexity theory: A characterization of PSPACE. J. Comput. System Sci. 73(1), 137–152 (2007)
21. The P Systems Web Page, http://ppage.psystems.eu/ (cit. May 29, 2012)

Fast Hardware Implementations of P Systems

Sergey Verlan[1] and Juan Quiros[2]

[1] LACL, Département Informatique, Université Paris Est,
61, av. Général de Gaulle, 94010 Créteil, France
verlan@univ-paris12.fr
[2] ID2 Group, Department of Electronic Technology, University of Sevilla,
Avda. Reina Mercedes s/n, 41012, Sevilla, Spain
jquiros@dte.us.es

Abstract. In this article we present the design of a fast hardware simulator for P systems using the field-programmable gate array (FPGA) technology. The simulator is non-deterministic and it uses a constant time procedure to choose one of the computational paths. The obtained strategy is fair and it is based on a pre-computation of all possible rule applications. This pre-computation is obtained by using the representation of all possible multisets of rules' applications as context-free languages. Then using a standard technique involving formal power series it is possible to obtain the generating series of corresponding languages that permits to construct the structure representing all possible rule applications for any configuration. We give a hardware design implementing some concrete examples and present the obtained results which feature an important speed-up.

1 Introduction

The problem of computer simulation of different variants of P systems arose at the early beginning of the development of the area. The first software simulators [5,16] were quite inefficient, but they provided an important understanding of the related problems. Since most variants of P systems are by definition inherently parallel and non-deterministic, it is natural to use distributed or parallel architectures in order to achieve better performances [1,17,6].

Another fruitful idea is to use specialized hardware for the simulation and this approach was realized in [14,11] using FPGA reconfigurable hardware technology. The first implementation from [14] has the design based on region processors which have rules as instructions and multiplicity of objects as data. Although it has several limitations, it demonstrates that P systems can be executed on FPGAs. In the other approach [8,10] two possible designs are detailed: rule-oriented and region-oriented systems. In the first one, each rule is considered as a basic processing unit and, in consequence, has a specific hardware core. As a result, the system achieves maximum degree of parallelism, due to all rules are executed in parallel by specific hardware components. In the second case the basic processing units are regions. Thus, communications between regions acquire more relevance: local rules are processed by the region processors and, after

E. Csuhaj-Varjú et al. (Eds.): CMC 2012, LNCS 7762, pp. 404–423, 2013.

that, a communication process between regions takes place in order to update the multiplicity of objects. In both architectures, there is a control logic which synchronizes the operations of processing units and updating of registers which save system's configuration. How registers are grouped and what is considered as a basic processing unit depend on the approach (rules or regions).

An important point for a (parallel) computing platform for membrane computing is to achieve a good balance between performance, flexibility and scalability. This is especially important for hardware simulators because the high performance comes often at an important price of flexibility or scalability. The important drawback of FPGA simulators from [14,11] is that they suppose that the evolution of P system is deterministic, and thus these simulators will yield always the same result for the same initial configuration. However, the non-determinism in P system plays an important role and its absence drastically reduces the classes of P systems that can be used with the above simulators.

In this paper we present basic ideas of the construction of FPGA simulators for non-deterministic P systems with the choice between possibilities being done randomly with a uniform distribution. Such a construction can be done in a rather simple strait manner, however the resulting performance is not very high. We concentrated on more complex designs that permit to achieve a performance close to the maximal theoretical performance for FPGA based simulators. Our approach also implies less flexibility as it cannot be applied to all kinds of P systems. However, the important difference with previous approaches is that in our case its applicability depends not on the class of considered P systems, but on the complexity of rules dependencies, which makes it applicable for a wide range of P systems. To exemplify our approach we present an implementation based on our ideas yielding a simulator performing around 2×10^7 computational steps per second, independently of the number of used rules.

This paper is organized as follows. First, in Section 2 we give a brief introduction to the theory of formal power series and give examples of the computation of generating series for different languages. In Section 3 we explain our method of pre-computation of all possible rules' applications. Section 4 gives an example of an FPGA implementation of a concrete P systems using our ideas: in subsection 4.1 we present the mathematical details concerning the example, subsection 4.2 overviews the hardware design for the simulator and subsection 4.3 presents the obtained results.

2   Preliminaries

We assume that the reader is familiar with the notions of formal language theory. We refer to [15] for more details. We denote by $|w|$ the length of the word w or the cardinality of the multiset or set w.

We also assume that the reader is familiar with the basic notions about P systems and we refer to the books [13,12] for more details.

We will need some notions from the formal power series theory, especially related to the theory of formal languages. We suggest the reading of [15] for more details on this topic.

For our purposes we consider that a formal power series f is a mapping $f : A^* \to \mathbb{N}$, where A is an alphabet and $\mathbb{N}$ is the set of non-negative integers (in the general case a formal power series is a mapping from a free monoid to a semiring). This mapping is usually written as

$$f = \sum_{w \in A^*} f(w)w.$$

It is known that a context-free grammar $G = (N, T, S, P)$ can be seen as a set of equations $x_i = \alpha_1 + \cdots + \alpha_{n_i}$, for each non-terminal x_i of G, where α_j are the right-hand sides of productions $x_i \to \alpha_j$, $1 \le j \le n_i$. A solution of G is a set of formal power series $s_1, \ldots, s_k$, such that the substitution of x_i by s_i in above equations converts them to the identity, $i.e.$ corresponding series are equal term by term. It is well known [2] that $s_i = \sum_{w \in A^*} f_i(w)w$, where $f_i(w)$ is the number of distinct leftmost derivations of w starting from x_i. Under the mapping that sends any symbol from A to the same symbol, say x, we obtain the generating series for a non-terminal x_i:

$$f_i = \sum_{n=0}^{\infty} \sum_{|w|=n} f_i(w)x^n.$$

Let $f_i(n) = \sum_{|w|=n} f_i(w)$. Then the above equation can be rewritten as:

$$f_i = \sum_{n=0}^{\infty} f_i(n)x^n.$$

Suppose that $x_1 = S$, where S is the starting symbol of G. Then f_1 is called the generating series of G. If G is unambiguous, then $f_1(n)$ gives the number of words of length n in G. We denote by $[x^n]f$ the n-th coefficient of f, $i.e.$ $[x^n]f = f(n)$.

Let ϕ be the morphism defined by

$$\phi(\lambda) = 1,$$
$$\phi(a) = x \qquad \forall a \in T,$$
$$\phi(x_i) = f_i \qquad x_i \in N.$$

Let $x_i \to v_{i1} \mid \cdots \mid v_{ik}$ be the set of productions associated to x_i. Then f_i can be obtained as the solution of the following system of equations:

$$f_i = \sum_{j=1}^{k} \phi(v_{ij}). \tag{1}$$

For a regular grammar G the system (1) becomes linear. By considering a finite automaton $\mathcal{A} = (V, \mathbb{Q}, q_0, Q_f, \delta)$ equivalent to G we obtain that system (1) corresponds to the following system (recall that x is considered as a constant)

$$Q = xMQ + F. \tag{2}$$

where

- $Q = [q_1 \ldots q_n]^t$, $q_i \in \mathbb{Q}$, $1 \leq i \leq n$ is the vector containing all states.
- $F = [a_0 \ldots a_n]^t$, is the final state characteristic vector, $i.e.$, $a_i = 1$ if q_i is a final state and 0 otherwise.
- M is the transfer matrix of the automaton $\mathcal{A}$, $i.e.$, the incidence matrix of the graph represented by $\mathcal{A}$ with negative values replaced by zero.

We remark that in the case of a regular language it is also possible to count the number of words of length n by summing the columns corresponding to the final states of the n-th power of the transfer matrix of the corresponding automaton:

$$f_i(n) = \sum_{q_j \in Q_f} (M^n)_{i,j}.$$

It is known that the generating series f for a regular language is rational. That implies that there exists a finite recurrence $f(n) = \sum_{j=1}^{k} a_j f(n - j)$, $k > 0$, $a_j \in \mathbb{Z}$ which holds for large n.

Example 1. Consider the regular language L_I recognized by the following automaton

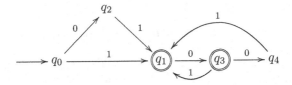

Then the final state characteristic vector F of this automaton is defined by $F = [0, 1, 0, 1, 0]^t$ and the transfer matrix M by

$$M = \begin{pmatrix} 0 & 1 & 1 & 0 & 0 \\ 0 & 0 & 0 & 1 & 0 \\ 0 & 1 & 0 & 0 & 0 \\ 0 & 1 & 0 & 0 & 1 \\ 0 & 1 & 0 & 0 & 0 \end{pmatrix}$$

The corresponding system (2) of linear equations has the following solution

$$q_0 = \frac{x^3 + 2x^2 + x}{1 - x^2 - x^3},$$

$$q_1 = \frac{x + 1}{1 - x^2 - x^3},$$

$$q_2 = \frac{x^2 + x}{1 - x^2 - x^3},$$

$$q_3 = \frac{x^2 + x + 1}{1 - x^2 - x^3},$$

$$q_4 = \frac{x^2 + x}{1 - x^2 - x^3}.$$

We can expand q_0 to obtain $q_0(n)$ ($= [x^n]q_0$)

$$q_0 = x + 2x^2 + 2x^3 + 3x^4 + 4x^5 + 5x^6 + 7x^7 + 9x^8 + \ldots$$

The coefficients of the above series give the number of words of the corresponding length. For example, there are 9 words of length 8 in L_I.

It is not difficult to verify that the coefficients $[x^n]q_k$, $0 \leq k \leq 4$, of the corresponding power series are particular cases of the Padovan sequence $q_k(n) = q_k(n-2) + q_k(n-3)$, $n > 3$, with the following starting values:

k	$q_k(0)$	$q_k(1)$	$q_k(2)$
0	1	1	2
1	1	1	1
2	0	1	1
3	1	1	2
4	0	1	1

3   Formal Part of the Simulator's Design

We will follow the approach given in [3], however we will not enter into deep details concerning the notation and the definition of derivation modes given there. Consider a (static) P system Π of any type evolving in any derivation mode. The key point of the semantics of P systems is that according to the type of the system and the derivation mode δ for any configuration of the system C a set of multisets (over $\mathcal{R}$) of applicable rules, denoted by $Appl(\Pi, C, \delta)$, is computed. After that, one of the elements R from this set is chosen, non-deterministically, for the further evolution of the system.

The main idea for the construction of a fast simulator is to avoid the computation of the set $Appl(\Pi, C, \delta)$ and to compute R, the multiset of rules to be applied directly. In this article we are interested in algorithms that permit to perform this computation on FPGA in *constant* time. We remark that, in a digital FPGA circuit synchronized by a global clock signal, in one cycle of FPGA it is possible to compute any functions whose implementation has a delay which does not exceed the period of the global clock signal. A pipeline using arithmetical operations and, in general, any combinatorial and sequential asynchronous subsystems, are usually included in this group.

In order to simplify the problem we split it into two parts corresponding to the construction of the following *recursive* functions:

$NBVariants(\Pi, C, \delta)$:
   gives the cardinality of the set $Appl(\Pi, C, \delta)$
$Variant(n, \Pi, C, \delta)$, where $1 \le n \le NBVariants(\Pi, C, \delta)$:
   gives the multiset of rules corresponding to the n-th element of some initially fixed enumeration of $Appl(\Pi, C, \delta)$.

It is clear that if each function is computed in constant time, then the multiset of rules to be applied can also be computed in a constant time. In what follows we will discuss methods for the construction of these two functions for different classes of P systems.

In the following we will need the notion of the rules' *dependency graph*. This is a weighted bipartite graph where the first partition U contains a node labeled by a for each object a of Π, while the second partition V contains a node labeled by r for each rule r of Π. There is an edge between a node $r \in V$ and a node $a \in U$ labeled by a weight k if $a^k \in lhs(r)$ (and $a^{k+1} \notin lhs(r)$).

Example 2. Consider a P system Π_1 having two rules $r_1 : ab \to u$ and $r_2 : bc \to v$. These rules have the following dependency graph:

Let N_a, N_b and N_c be the number of objects a, b and c in a configuration C. We define

$$N_1 = \min(N_a, N_b),$$
$$N_2 = \min(N_b, N_c),$$
$$N = \min(N_1, N_2).$$

Suppose that Π evolves in a maximally parallel derivation mode. Then the set $Appl(\Pi, C, max)$ can be computed as follows:

$$Appl(\Pi, C, max) = \bigcup_{p+q=N} \left\{ r_1^{p+k_1} r_2^{q+k_2} \right\},$$

where $k_j = N_j \ominus N$, $1 \le j \le 2$, where $\ominus$ is the positive subtraction operation.

From this representation it is clear that $NBVariants(\Pi, C, max) = N + 1$, which can be computed in constant time on an FPGA.

The $Variant(n, \Pi, C, max)$ function can be defined as the n-th element in the lexicographical ordering of elements of $Appl(\Pi, C, max)$ and it has the following formula

$$Variant(n, \Pi, C, max) = r_1^{N-n-1+k_1} r_2^{n-1+k_2}.$$

We remark that the above formula can also be computed in constant time using an FPGA.

We could obtain the $NBVariants$ formula using formal power series. In order to do this we observe that the language $\cup_{N>0} L_N$, where $L_N = \{r_1^p r_2^q \mid p+q = N\}$ is regular. Moreover, it holds that $L_N = r_1^* r_2^* \cap A^N$, with A being the alphabet $\{r_1, r_2\}$. Below we give the automaton A_1 for the language $r_1^* r_2^*$.

The transfer matrix of this automaton is $\begin{pmatrix} 1 & 1 \\ 0 & 1 \end{pmatrix}$ and the final state characteristic vector is $[1, 1]^t$. Using Equation (2) this yields the generating function for L_N: $q_0 = \frac{1}{(1-x)^2}$. It is easy to verify that $[x^n] q_0 = n+1$.

We modify the previous example by considering weighted rules.

Example 3. Consider a P system Π_1 having two rules $r_1 : a^{k_a} b^{k_{b1}} \to u$ and $r_2 : b^{k_{b2}} c^{k_c} \to v$. These rules have the following dependency graph:

Let N_a, N_b and N_c be the number of objects a, b and c in a configuration C. We define

$$N_1 = \min([N_a/k_a], [N_b/k_{b1}]),$$
$$N_2 = \min([N_b/k_{b2}], [N_c/k_c]),$$
$$N = \min(N_1, N_2),$$
$$\bar{N} = \min(k_{b1} N_1, k_{b2} N_2).$$

Suppose that Π evolves in a maximally parallel derivation mode. Let A_2 be the automaton recognizing the language $(r_1^{k_{b1}})^* (r_2^{k_{b2}})^*$

Let $L'_N = A_2 \cap A^N$ ($A = \{r_1, r_2\}$). Then it is clear that

$$Appl(\Pi, C, max) = \bigcup_{pk_{b1} + qk_{b2} = \bar{N}} \left\{ r_1^{p+k_1} r_2^{q+k_2} \right\},$$

where $k_1 = k_a(N_1 \ominus N)$, $k_2 = k_c(N_2 \ominus N)$.

The transfer matrix of A_2 (considering the weights) is $\begin{pmatrix} k_{b1} & k_{b2} \\ 0 & k_{b2} \end{pmatrix}$ and the vector $F = [1, 1]$. This gives the following generating function for A_2:

$$q_0 = \frac{1}{(1 - x^{k_{b1}})(1 - x^{k_{b2}})}.$$

The coefficients $[x^n]q_0$ can be obtained by the recurrence $a(n) = a(n - k_{b1}) + a(n - k_{b2}) - a(n - k_{b1} - k_{b2})$, $n \geq k_{b1} + k_{b2}$. The initial values are given by the following cases (we suppose that $k_{b1} \geq k_{b2}$):

$$\begin{cases} 1, & n = 0, \\ 0, & 1 \leq n \leq k_{b2} - 1, \\ 1, & k_{b2} \leq n \leq k_{b1} - 1 \text{ and } n = 0 \pmod{k_{b2}}, \\ 0, & k_{b2} \leq n \leq k_{b1} - 1 \text{ and } n \neq 0 \pmod{k_{b2}}, \\ 2, & k_{b1} \leq n \leq k_{b1} + k_{b2} \text{ and } n = 0 \pmod{k_{b2}} \text{ and } n = 0 \pmod{k_{b1}}, \\ 1, & k_{b1} \leq n \leq k_{b1} + k_{b2} \text{ and } n = 0 \pmod{k_{b2}} \text{ or } n = 0 \pmod{k_{b1}}, \\ 0, & k_{b1} \leq n \leq k_{b1} + k_{b2} - 1 \text{ and } n \neq 0 \pmod{k_{b2}} \text{ or } n \neq 0 \pmod{k_{b1}}. \end{cases}$$

Now we concentrate of the function $Variant$. If the set $Appl(\Pi, C, \delta)$ is regular, then we can use the following algorithm to compute $Variant(n, \Pi, C, \delta)$. Let $A(\Pi, C, \delta) = (Q, V, q_0, F)$ be the automaton corresponding to the language defined by rules joint applicability and let s_j, $q_j \in Q$ be the generating series for the state q_j.

Algorithm 1

1. *Start in state q_0, step $= 0$, $nb = s_0(n)$, out $= \lambda$.*
2. *If step $= n$ then stop.*
3. *Otherwise let $\{t : (q_i, a_t, q_{j_t})\}$, $1 \leq t \leq k_i$ be the set outgoing transitions from q_i. Compute $S(k) = \sum_{m=1}^{k} s_{j_m}(n - step)$. We put by definition $S(0) = 0$. Then there exists k such that $S(k) \geq nb$ and there is no $k' < k$ such that $S(k') > nb$.*
4. *Consider $nb = nb - S(k - 1)$ and out $=$ out $\cdot a_k$.*
5. *Go to step 2.*

The main idea of this algorithm is to compute the n-th variant using the lexical ordering of transitions using an algorithm similar to the computation of the number written in the combinatorial number system. Being in a state q and looking for a sequence of applications of k rules we will use the transition t : (q, r, q') (and add r to the multiset of rules) if the transition t is the first in the lexicographical ordering of transitions having the property that the number of words of length $k - 1$ that can be obtained using all outgoing transitions from state q that are less or equal than t is greater than n.

4   Example of Simulator Construction

In this section we will present the design of a hardware simulator using FPGA that implements the ideas and the algorithms discussed in the previous section.

4.1   Tested System

We used the following example to illustrate the FPGA implementation for our ideas. We considered multiset rewriting rules working in set-maximal mode ($smax$). This mode corresponds to the maximally parallel execution of rules, but where the rules cannot be applied more than once. This mode can be formally defined as follows (where $asyn$ is the asynchronous mode [3] and $\mathcal{R}$ is the set of all rules):

$$S_1 = \{R \in Appl(\Pi, C, asyn) \mid |R|_{r_j} \leq 1, 1 \leq j \leq |\mathcal{R}|\},$$
$$Appl(\Pi, C, smax) = \{R \in S_1 \mid \text{there is no } R' \in S_1 \text{ such that } R' \supset R\}.$$

We remark that $smax$ mode corresponds to min_1 mode [3] with a specific partition of rules: the size of the partition is $|\mathcal{R}|$ and each partition p_j contains exactly one rule $r_j \in \mathcal{R}$.

Consider now a multiset rewriting system (corresponding to a P system with one membrane) evolving in $smax$ mode. To simplify the construction we consider rules having a dependency graph in a form of chain without weights.

Let N_{a_i} be the number of objects a_i in configuration C. We denote by $NBV([r_1, \ldots, r_k], C)$, $k > 0$ the number of variants of applications of a chain of rules $r_1, \ldots, r_k$ to the configuration C in $smax$ mode. We remark that for a P system Π having the set of rules $\mathcal{R}$, $NBVariants(\Pi, C, smax) = NBV(\mathcal{R}, C)$.

It is possible to distinguish 3 cases with respect to the number of objects N_{a_i}, $0 \leq i \leq n$ (consider that $0 \leq s \leq i \leq e \leq n$):

$N_{a_i} = 0$. Then the two surrounding rules (r_i and r_{i+1}) are not applicable. In this case the parts of the chain at the left and right of a_i are independent, so the number of variants is a product of corresponding variants:
$NBV(r_s, \ldots, r_e, C) = NBV(r_s, \ldots, r_{i-1}, C) * NBV(r_{i+2}, \ldots, r_e, C)$

$N_{a_i} > 1$. As in the previous case the chain can be split into two parts because both rules r_i and r_{i+1} can be applied:
$$NBV(r_s, \ldots, r_e, C) = NBV(r_s, \ldots, r_i, C) * NBV(r_{i+1}, \ldots, r_e, C)$$
$N_{a_i} = 1$. In this case r_i and r_{i+1} are in conflict.

Now let us concentrate on the last case. Without loss of generality we can suppose that $N_{a_i} = 1$, $0 \le i \le n$. We remark that the language of binary strings of length n corresponding to the joint applicability vector of rules $r_1, \ldots, r_n$ coincides with the language L_I from Example 1. Hence the number of possibilities of application of such a chain of rules of length n is equal to $NBV(r_1, \ldots, r_n, C) = [x^n]q_0$, i.e., $q_0(0) = 1$, $q_0(1) - 1$, $q_0(2) = 2$ and $q_0(n) = q_0(n-2) + q_0(n-3)$, $n > 3$.

Hence in order to compute $NBVariants(\Pi, C, smax)$ we first split the chain into $k > 0$ parts of length n_j according to the multiplicities of objects and compute the NBV function for each part using the decomposition above.

The function $Variant$ for each part can be computed using Algorithm 1.

The next section gives more details on the implementation of the above algorithms on FPGA.

4.2 Implementation Details

FPGAs contain lots of programmable logic blocks and reconfigurable interconnects. When a system is implemented using this kind of devices, finding a path which communicates two logic blocks is usually the task where speed, i.e. performance, is compromised. Thus, modular designs which minimize long paths between logic components are the ones which best fit in this kind of technology. Our design is based on layers with interfaces clearly defined. Each layer is a block which performs a main task of the algorithm, and it only communicates with the previous layer, whose outputs are its inputs, and next layer, which receives its outputs.

Overall Design. In order to design the simulator, the graph of dependencies between rules has been chosen as starting point to model P systems. This approach reduces complexity, due to deleting some elements, like membranes and, in consequence, the hierarchical structure of them. Objects and rules are the only elements which have been having in mind to model the system. Moreover, the implementation is based on mathematical foundations described in the previous section, following a division of tasks, which assures enough encapsulation to achieve a design with a right flexibility. The objects are explicitly represented using registers which is not the case for the rules. Their logic is distributed along most of the components, thus there is no correspondence between a rule and a hardware core.

An execution of a P system consists in running iterations until it reaches a stop condition. At each iteration there is a set of operations to be carried out in order to obtain the next configuration. To implement the simulator, these tasks have been divided in the following stages:

– *Initial stage*: Calculate the maximum number of applications of each rule.
– *Assignment stage*: Choose which rules will be applied (and how many times).
– *Application stage*: Apply the rules, computing new values for multiplicity of objects.
– *Updating stage*: Update the current configuration.

The Algorithms

In order to simplify the explanation, the design is detailed following functional division (Fig. 1) commented on the previous introduction.

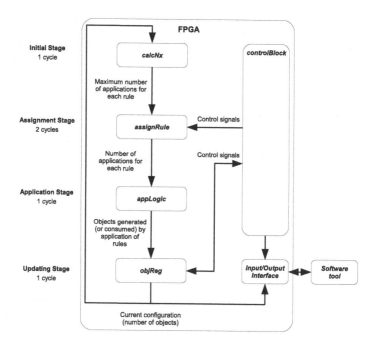

Fig. 1. Overview of the architecture. This illustration shows the main blocks and the flow of information between blocks.

Initial Stage. The first block is called *calcNx*. It receives as input the number of objects of the current configuration from *ObjReg*, which is detailed below. Its functionality is to compute the maximum number that rules can be applied, N_{r_x}. It is, in consequence, an arithmetical component. It is necessary to remark that these outputs depend on the evolving mode. For example, considering a chain of rules evolving in *smax* mode, only three values are interesting for the execution (Section 4.1): $N_{r_x} = 0$ and $N_{r_x} > 1$, which indicates rule execution is independent of others; and $N_{r_x} = 1$ that indicates that its execution is dependent on others (i.e., the system has to choose which rule will be applied).

Assignment Stage. This stage is the most complex and important in the design, and it is implemented by the block called *assignRule*. Its task is to select which rules (and how many times) will be applied. The number of functionalities which are carried out by it and, in consequence, its implementation, depends on the evolving mode selected. We consider a chain of rules evolving in *smax* mode and computation based on algorithms detailed in Section 3. According to these assumptions, the block has to perform following steps:

Algorithm 2

1. *Split the chain into k parts as it is described in section 4.1.*
2. *For each part.*
   (a) *Compute $NBVariants(\Pi, C, smax)$. For this purpose algorithm detailed in 3 and 4.1 is used.*
   (b) *Obtain the value of n indicating which combination will be chosen (n - th element). Hence his domain is from 0 to $NBVariants(\Pi, C, smax) - 1$.*
      i. *Generate a random number rn, where*

$$0 \le rn \le \lceil \lg_2(NBVariants(\Pi, C, smax)) \rceil$$

   ii. *If $rn < NBVariants(\Pi, C, smax)$ then $n = rn$. Otherwise, $n = rn + NBVariants(\Pi, C, smax)$.*
   (c) *Compute $Variant(n, \Pi, smax)$, according to algorithm 1.*

The computation of $NBVariants(\Pi, C, smax)$ uses a subset of operations needed to compute $Variant(n, \Pi, smax)$, moreover these operations can be done in parallel with the generation of the random number n, necessary to compute $Variant(n, \Pi, smax)$. Hence, this stage can be performed in 2 clock cycles by dividing operations in two sets, called *right* and *left propagation* respectively.

This block contains one sub-block per rule, which implements operations required in order to obtain the number of applications of its rule associated. Interconnections between components are based on design keys and propagation concepts: a sub-block is only connected to blocks located on its right and left. As it is showed by Fig. 2, left propagation is the first to be executed. In this sub-stage, steps 2.a and 2.b.i of algorithm 2 are computed from the last rule to the first one. Right propagation, which is compound by steps 2.b.ii and 2.c, is executed in opposite way in the next clock cycle. One advantage of this approach is that it is not necessary to divide, implicitly, the chain of rules in k parts, deleting a step of the algorithm which let us reduce the number of required cycles from three to two. This logic is implemented, explicitly, by signals *prevIsDep* and *chainStateSignal*. After this stage, all rules have a random multiplicity assigned.

Application Stage. Once the system has chosen which rules will be applied (and how many times), the *appLogic* block computes how many objects will be generated and consumed by rules application. Like *calcNx*, it is an arithmetical block.

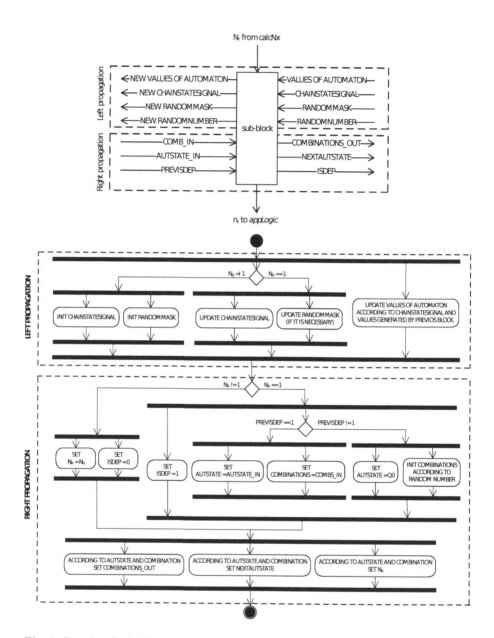

Fig. 2. Details of sub-blocks which compound the *assignRule* block. Flow of information between sub-blocks in left and right propagation is showed at the top of the figure. Below it, the algorithm is detailed using UML notation.

Updating Stage. The block which saves and updates the current configuration is called *ObjReg*. It contains a register per object which saves multiplicity of the associated object for the present configuration. In order to update it, each register adds up its content and values generated by the previous core. Besides that, this core rises a control signal when the current configuration is equal to the previous one, i.e., it indicates that system has reached a stop condition to unit control.

Unit Control and Output Interface. Besides the previous cores, an additional block, called *controlBlock*, is required to provide communication and control logic. Control is implemented using a finite state machine, which requires five states, and it generates all control signals. Although the input/output interface has not been developed yet, some debug cores are used to control execution and to get results.

In conclusion, the proposed hardware design requires only five clock cycles per iteration, which is a good achievement, although the final speed depends on the relation cycles-frequency. Our design takes advantages of FPGA technology and the implementation achieves a high degree of parallelism of objects in the *initial stage*, and of rules in the others. However, the key of system's performance is the implementation of the automaton in the *assignment stage*. All operations required to compute $NBVariants(\Pi, C, smax)$ and $Variant(n, \Pi, smax)$ are defined recursively and can be pipelined. In *assignRule*, each sub-block associated to the n-th rule computes, asynchronously, the value of N (associated to its rule), basing on values obtained by previous block. This permits to execute all operations in only two cycles, one for left propagation and another for right propagation, while a synchronous version requires, at least, n cycles.

4.3 Experimental Results

We tested the design on a series of concrete examples. All of them consider rules whose dependency graph forms a chain, the difference being in the right-hand side. We consider four P systems with the alphabet $O = \{o_0, \ldots, o_N\}$, $N > 0$ and having the following rules (we consider index operations modulo $N + 1$):

- System 1 (circular)

$$r_i : \begin{cases} o_{i-1}o_i \to o_i o_{i+1} & 1 \leq i < N - 1, \\ o_{N-1}o_N \to o_0 o_1 & i = N. \end{cases}$$

- System 2 (2-circular)

$$r_i : o_{i-1}o_i \to o_{i+1}o_{i+2} \qquad 1 \leq i \leq N.$$

- System 3 (linear)

$$r_i : \begin{cases} o_{i-1}o_i \to o_i o_{i+1} & 1 \leq i < N - 1, \\ o_{N-1}o_N \to o_N o_N & i = N. \end{cases}$$

- System 4 (opposite), $1 \leq i \leq N$

$$r_i : \begin{cases} o_{i-1}o_i \rightarrow o_i o_{i+1} & i \bmod 2 = 0, \\ o_i o_{i+1} \rightarrow o_i o_{i-1} & \text{otherwise} . \end{cases}$$

For each of four types a system with N equal to 10, 20 and 50 was considered with the initial multiplicity of all objects equal to one. Then for each obtained system 1024 executions of 8192 transitions have been carried out. Each execution differs from the others by the seed required by the random number generator in the initialization stage. In consequence, different values are obtained during the assignment stage, which results in different executions. As results of experiments the following values are collected: the cardinality of objects in the last configuration, the seed of the random number generator and the number of steps to reach the halting configuration if the system reached it.

The target circuit for executions was the Xilinx Virtex-5 XC5VFX70T, code for different P systems were generated by a Java software and this code was synthesised, placed and routed using Xilinx tools. Since the input/output interface has not been developed yet, CHIPSCOPE, a XILINX debug tool has been used. This tool let us, synchronously, change and capture the above values directly from the FPGA.

Table 1 shows hardware resource consumption and clock rate in MHz of the system without the debug logic. The implementation achieves high performance, with frequencies higher than 100 MHz, i.e., it permits to simulate around 2×10^7 computational steps per second. On the other hand, the hardware resource consumption depends only on the number of rules. This is coherent with the fact that rules of all systems do not change the total number of objects and share the same dependency graph.

Table 1. Hardware resource consumption and clock rate of hardware implementation

Type	Size (Nb. of rules)	Slices	LUTs	BRAMs	Clock rate
	10	2 %	2 %	1 %	120.02 MHz
Circular	20	6 %	10 %	1 %	101.44 MHz
	50	41 %	31 %	1 %	100.68 MHz
	10	2 %	2 %	1 %	120.02 MHz
2-circular	20	7 %	6 %	1 %	110.77 MHz
	50	37 %	31 %	1 %	100.44 MHz
	10	2 %	2 %	1 %	120.02 MHz
Linear	20	10 %	6 %	1 %	100.56 MHz
	50	40 %	31 %	1 %	100.85 MHz
	10	2 %	2 %	1 %	120.02 MHz
Opposite	20	7 %	6 %	1 %	105.73 MHz
	50	37 %	31 %	1 %	100.89 MHz

Table 2 gives some statistics concerning the experiments. As expected, linear and 2-circular systems reach a halting configuration, while in the other two cases it cannot be reached. It can be seen that the simulation of non-determinism is done correctly – in some cases all resulting configurations are different. Figure 3 shows the maximal, minimal and mean value of the number of different objects. We show only the case of 10 rules, the other cases present a similar picture. It can be seen that in the case of linear system there is a high chance to have a big value for the last object and in the case of 2-circular systems the second and before the last objects are never present. In the case of circular systems it is possible to see an equiprobable distribution of objects, while for the opposite systems even values have a higher value. It can be easily seen that the used rules should exhibit exactly this behavior.

Table 2. Statistics concerning the runs of example systems

Type	N	Different final conf.	Halting		
			Y/N	min	max
Circular	10	982	No	-	-
	20	1024	No	-	-
	50	1024	No	-	-
2-circular	10	161	Yes	5	89
	20	818	Yes	11	197
	50	1024	Yes	57	609
Linear	10	204	Yes	7	17
	20	944	Yes	14	29
	50	1024	Yes	50	65
Opposite	10	4	No	-	-
	20	938	No	-	-
	50	1024	No	-	-

5 Discussion

The method discussed in Section 3 allows the construction of simulators having a constant time execution step (in terms of FPGA). While it is possible to design ad-hoc functions that describe the rules' execution strategy, we concentrated on the cases where the multisets of rules that can be applied form a non-ambiguous context-free language. This permits to easily compute the generating function of the corresponding language and gives a simple algorithm for the enumeration strategy.

The class of P systems where the set $Appl(\Pi, C, \delta)$ corresponds to a non-ambiguous context-free language is quite big and it is not restricted to the rules

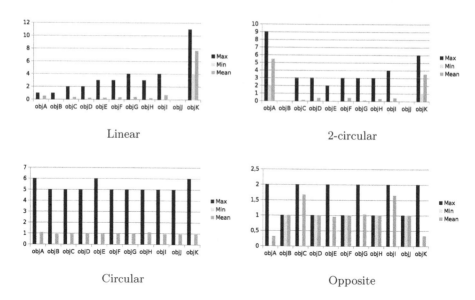

Fig. 3. Objects min/max/mean values for the experiments using 10 rules

whose dependency graph forms a chain. For example, consider a set rules forming a circular dependency graph for a system working in the *smax* mode.

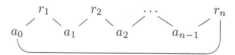

Now let C be a configuration where all these rules are applicable exactly one time (corresponding to the case 3 described in Section 4.1). Then the joint applicability vectors of these rules (i.e. binary strings of length n with value 1 in i-th position corresponding to the choice of rule r_i) can be described by taking the words of length n of the following automaton

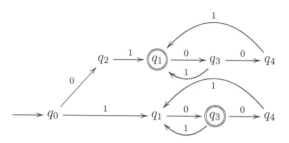

This automaton is obtained from the automaton for the language L_I from Example 1 by adding an additional condition: if rule r_1 is chosen then r_n is not chosen and conversely.

Using similar ideas it is possible to describe with regular languages sequences of rules forming more complicated structures. For example, the following structure

can be represented as regular language over the binary alphabet if the number of symbols a_2 is known. This language can be constructed in a similar way as the language above for circular dependency. This permits to compute the function $NBVariants(\Pi, C, smax)$ by first choosing the appropriate automaton based on the value of N_{a_2} and after that computing its generating function. Clearly, this can be done in constant time on FPGA.

In a similar way it is possible to describe the regular languages for the applicability of rules having the dependency graph that has no intersecting cycles.

We would like to point out another algorithm for the rule application, applicable to any type of rule dependency.

Let Π be a P system evolving in the set-maximal derivation mode. Let $\mathcal{R}$ be the set of rules of Π and $n = |\mathcal{R}|$. Let C be a configuration.

Algorithm 3

1. *Compute a permutation of rules of $\mathcal{R}$: $\sigma = (r_{i_1}, \ldots, r_{i_n})$, $i_k \neq i_m$, $k \neq m$.*
2. *For $j = 1, 2, \ldots, n$ if r_{i_j} is applicable then apply r_{i_j} to C.*

The step 1 of the above algorithm can be optimized using the Fisher-Yates shuffle algorithm [4] (Algorithm P). However, the implementation of Algorithm 3 is slower than the implementation we presented in Section 4.2 because the computation of the rules' permutation needs a register usage, so it cannot be done in one clock cycle and it is dependent on the number of rules.

By extending Algorithm 3 it is possible to construct a similar algorithm for the maximally parallel derivation mode.

Algorithm 4

1. *Compute a permutation of rules of $\mathcal{R}$: $\sigma = (r_{i_1}, \ldots, r_{i_n})$, $i_k \neq i_m$, $k \neq m$.*
2. *Compute the applicability vector of rules $V = (m_1, \ldots, m_n)$, where m_j, $1 \leq j \leq n$ is the number of times rule r_{i_j} can be applied.*
3. *If the vector V is null, then stop.*
4. *Otherwise, repeat step 5 for $j = 1, \ldots, n$.*
5. *Compute a random number t between 0 and $V[j]$. Apply r_{i_j} t times.*
6. *Goto step 2.*

This algorithm has similar drawbacks and the number of clock cycles it uses is at least proportional to the number of rules.

6   Conclusions

In this article we presented a new design for a fast hardware implementation of a simulator for P systems. The obtained circuit permits to simulate a non-deterministic computational step of the system in a constant time (5 clock cycles). Hence, the obtained simulator achieves a high performance that is close to the maximal possible value (one cycle per step). The key point of our approach is the representation of the sequences of all possible rule applications as words of some regular or non-ambiguous context-free language. In this case using the generating series for the corresponding language it is possible to generate functions that precompute all possible rule applications. It is worth to note that the speed of the computation does not depend on the number of rules. However, there is a dependency between this number and the space on the chip. With the used board it is possible to simulate P systems having up to 100 rules.

We exemplified our approach by an FPGA implementation of different P systems working in maximal set mode with rules dependency graph in a form of a chain. We obtained a speed of about 2×10^7 computational steps per second. Our different tests showed that the computation is non-deterministic and that the values of the parameters have expected mean values.

As a future research we plan to develop a software that will allow us to generate the hardware design in an automatical way based on the regular language describing the rules joint applicability.

The design described in this article is quite generic and does not use many features of FPGA. Therefore, it could be interesting to use the presented method for the speed-up of the existing software simulators of P systems.

Acknowledgements. This work has been partially supported by the Ministerio de Ciencia e Innovación of the Spanish Government under project TEC2011-27936 (HIPERSYS), by the European Regional Development Fund (ERDF) and by the Ministry of Education of Spain (FPU grant AP2009-3625). The first author also acknowledges the support of ANR project SynBioTIC.

References

1. Ciobanu, G., Wenyuan, G.: P Systems Running on a Cluster of Computers. In: Martín-Vide, C., Mauri, G., Păun, G., Rozenberg, G., Salomaa, A. (eds.) WMC 2003. LNCS, vol. 2933, pp. 123–139. Springer, Heidelberg (2004)
2. Chomsky, N., Schützenberger, M.-P.: The Algebraic Theory of Context-Free Languages. In: Braffort, P., Hirschberg, D. (eds.) Computer Programming and Formal Systems, pp. 118–161. North Holland (1963)
3. Freund, R., Verlan, S.: A Formal Framework for Static (Tissue) P Systems. In: Eleftherakis, G., Kefalas, P., Păun, G., Rozenberg, G., Salomaa, A. (eds.) WMC 2007. LNCS, vol. 4860, pp. 271–284. Springer, Heidelberg (2007)
4. Knuth, D.E.: The Art of Computer Programming, 3rd edn. Seminumerical Algorithms, vol. 2. Addison-Wesley (1997)

5. Maliţa, M.: Membrane computing in Prolog. In: Calude, C.S., et al. (eds.) Pre-proceedings of the Workshop on Multiset Processing, Curtea de Argeş, Romania, CDMTCS TR 140, Univ. of Auckland, pp. 159–175 (2000)
6. Martinez-del-Amor, M.A., Perez-Hurtado, I., Perez-Jimenez, M.J., Cecilia, J.M., Guerrero, G.D., Garcia, J.M.: Simulation of recognizer P systems by using many-core GPUs. In: Martinez-del-Amor, M.A., et al. (eds.) Seventh Brainstorming Week on Membrane Computing, Fenix Editora, Sevilla, Spain, vol. II, pp. 45–58 (2009)
7. Nguyen, V., Kearney, D.A., Gioiosa, G.: Balancing Performance, Flexibility, and Scalability in a Parallel Computing Platform for Membrane Computing Applications. In: Eleftherakis, G., Kefalas, P., Păun, G., Rozenberg, G., Salomaa, A. (eds.) WMC 2007. LNCS, vol. 4860, pp. 385–413. Springer, Heidelberg (2007)
8. Nguyen, V., Kearney, D., Gioiosa, G.: An Implementation of Membrane Computing Using Reconfigurable Hardware. Computing and Informatics 27(3), 551–569 (2008)
9. Nguyen, V., Kearney, D., Gioiosa, G.: An Algorithm for Non-deterministic Object Distribution in P Systems and Its Implementation in Hardware. In: Corne, D.W., Frisco, P., Păun, G., Rozenberg, G., Salomaa, A. (eds.) WMC 2008. LNCS, vol. 5391, pp. 325–354. Springer, Heidelberg (2009)
10. Nguyen, V., Kearney, D., Gioiosa, G.: A Region-Oriented Hardware Implementation for Membrane Computing Applications. In: Păun, G., Pérez-Jiménez, M.J., Riscos-Núñez, A., Rozenberg, G., Salomaa, A. (eds.) WMC 2009. LNCS, vol. 5957, pp. 385–409. Springer, Heidelberg (2010)
11. Nguyen, V., Kearney, D., Gioiosa, G.: An extensible, maintainable and elegant approach to hardware source code generation in Reconfig-P. J. Log. Algebr. Program. 79(6), 383–396 (2010)
12. Păun, G.: Membrane Computing. An Introduction. Springer (2002)
13. Păun, G., Rozenberg, G., Salomaa, A.: The Oxford Handbook of Membrane Computing. Oxford University Press (2010)
14. Petreska, B., Teuscher, C.: A Reconfigurable Hardware Membrane System. In: Martín-Vide, C., Mauri, G., Păun, G., Rozenberg, G., Salomaa, A. (eds.) WMC 2003. LNCS, vol. 2933, pp. 269–285. Springer, Heidelberg (2004)
15. Rozenberg, G., Salomaa, A. (eds.): Handbook of Formal Languages. Springer, Berlin (1997)
16. Suzuki, Y., Tanaka, H.: On a LISP implementation of a class of P systems. Romanian J. Information Science and Technology 3, 173–186 (2000)
17. Syropoulos, A., Mamatas, E.G., Allilomes, P.C., Sotiriades, K.T.: A Distributed Simulation of Transition P Systems. In: Martín-Vide, C., Mauri, G., Păun, G., Rozenberg, G., Salomaa, A. (eds.) WMC 2003. LNCS, vol. 2933, pp. 357–368. Springer, Heidelberg (2004)